Books by Frank Freidel

FRANKLIN D. ROOSEVELT
The Apprenticeship

FRANKLIN D. ROOSEVELT
The Ordeal

FRANKLIN D. ROOSEVELT
The Triumphs

FRANKLIN D. ROOSEVELT
Launching the New Deal

FRANCIS LIEBER
Nineteenth-Century Liberal

THE SPLENDID LITTLE WAR

THE GOLDEN AGE OF AMERICAN HISTORY
(editor)

AMERICA IN THE TWENTIETH CENTURY

OVER THERE

F.D.R. AND THE SOUTH

THE PRESIDENTS OF THE UNITED STATES

OUR COUNTRY'S PRESIDENTS

UNION PAMPHLETS OF THE CIVIL WAR
(editor)

FRANKLIN D. ROOSEVELT
Launching the New Deal

FRANKLIN D. ROOSEVELT

Launching the New Deal

by FRANK FREIDEL

with Illustrations

LITTLE, BROWN AND COMPANY — BOSTON – TORONTO

FIRST EDITION

T 10/73

Library of Congress Cataloging in Publication Data

Freidel, Frank Burt.
    Franklin D. Roosevelt.

    Includes bibliographical references.
    CONTENTS: 1. The apprenticeship.--2. The ordeal.--
3. The triumph. [etc.]
    1. Roosevelt, Franklin Delano, Pres. U. S., 1882-
1945.
E807.F74   923.173   52-5521
ISBN 0-316-29303-2 (v. 4)

Published simultaneously in Canada
by Little, Brown & Company (Canada) Limited

PRINTED IN THE UNITED STATES OF AMERICA

To
David

Contents

Illustrations

FRANKLIN D. ROOSEVELT

Launching the New Deal

Victory—and Responsibility

America was privileged to show the world in that year
of crisis that democracy can find within itself the elements necessary to its own salvation.

— FDR, *1937*.

It was very late on election night, November 8, 1932. The wild excitement at the Democratic headquarters was tapering toward a bleary end,
and the object of the celebration, the new President-elect, Franklin D.
Roosevelt, had gone home. The victory had become overwhelming as
the mounting returns gave him the electoral votes of all but six states.
Since the 1890s the Democrats had been the minority party, but Roosevelt had won by a landslide surpassed only by those of the Republicans
Harding and Hoover. No previous Democrat, even Jackson, had won
by such a wide margin of the popular vote. Elected with Roosevelt were
13 additional Democratic senators and 90 representatives, providing him
with substantial majorities of his party in both houses of Congress. It
was an exhilarating but also a sobering outcome, to win the presidency
with its enormous responsibilities as the Great Depression entered its
fourth year, a time of acute national and world crisis.

Within the United States suffering and pessimism prevailed; without,
several other nations were trying to solve their problems through resort
to totalitarian methods and threats of armed aggression against weaker
countries. A fearful challenge faced the President-elect. Could he lead
the American people toward workable solutions to their problems without destroying the existing economic system or curtailing traditional
personal liberties? Could recovery be achieved only through resort to
concentration camps, bayonets, and bombers, or could the United States
demonstrate to all mankind that prosperity and security could be attained
through peaceable, democratic means? The answers were by no means
certain that bleak November.

During the election night jubilation, Eleanor Roosevelt made no effort
to disguise the ambiguity of her feelings. "You're always pleased to have

any one you're very devoted to have what he wants," she remarked, then
added, "It is an extremely serious thing to undertake, you know. . . .
It is not something you just . . . say you're pleased about." [1]

As for Roosevelt, if he flinched in the slightest at assuming this
enormous burden, he kept his qualms to himself through the last farewell that he waved as he entered his house on Sixty-fifth Street in New
York City. Only in private, as his son James helped him into his bed —
the same bed where he had lain so helpless for months after his polio
attack in 1921 — did he share with someone his inner thoughts. He
talked a long time about many things, then as James kissed him goodnight, he revealed himself as he seldom did, even within his family.
Previously, he had never admitted to more than a single worry, a paraplegic's fear of fire, but that night he confessed he was afraid of something else.

"Afraid of what, Pa?" James asked. His father answered:

"I'm just afraid that I may not have the strength to do this job. After
you leave me tonight, Jimmy, I am going to pray. I am going to pray
that God will help me, that he will give me the strength and the guidance
to do this job and to do it right. I hope you will pray for me, too,
Jimmy." [2]

It was indeed a solemn commitment which Roosevelt had undertaken.
Neither the advisers with whom he was surrounded nor the unhappy
condition of the nation would permit him to forget it for long. Like
the Secret Service men who had been newly assigned to him earlier
that evening, the needy American people were to be constantly in the
periphery of his vision. At Christmastime that year, his New York State
industrial commissioner, Frances Perkins, out of her own religious devotion and her sympathetic awareness that Roosevelt shared her feelings,
wrote him: "I incline to prayer when I think of all that the humble
and lowly and hurt of this land are expecting of you. . . . Joy in the
humble homes and the laughter of courage, hope and happiness on the
lips of the working millions. . . . [Y]ou dear friend are perhaps the
tool to be used for this lowly purpose." [3]

In commonplace terms — the only sort he seemed capable of using
in a personal interchange of this sort —Roosevelt replied to Miss Perkins
that she was quite right. "My hope is that I can accomplish something
worthwhile for the man at the foot of the ladder." His approach was
so plain that it might seem to those who were not his closest intimates
to speak less of humility than of superficiality. Anne O'Hare McCormick
of the *New York Times* had detected the difference when she interviewed him some months earlier: [4]

When I asked him once, before his nomination, why he wanted to be
President in a time like this, he answered, smiling, that some one

had to be, some one with no more than human capacity, to meet a crisis
that eventually would have to be resolved by human intelligence. The
answer was made lightly. . . . But even then I saw it was not meant
lightly.[5]

It was with a considerable simplicity, and as his intimate adviser Raymond Moley noted, in a "mood of modesty, humility, and generosity,"
that Roosevelt had concluded his campaigning that fall. These feelings
carried over into the days ahead.

He was up rather early the next morning, a bit sleepy-eyed, but ready
to exchange banter as usual with newspapermen. When one of them
addressed him as "Mr. President," he retorted instantly, "Don't call me
President; Governor is good enough." He drove to Poughkeepsie where,
despite the November rain, enthusiastic crowds setting off red flares
and aerial bombs made the streets gala. At his home town, Hyde Park,
which he had failed to carry by 139 votes, a cheering throng gathered
on the broad lawn in front of his home. Hailing them as his neighbors,
and calling various of them by their first names, he exclaimed, "I'll
always be plain Franklin Roosevelt in this part of the country, and don't
forget that." Several days later Josephus Daniels, under whom he had
served for seven years as assistant secretary of the navy in the Wilson
administration, began a letter addressing him as Chief, thus reversing
Roosevelt's habitual salutation of nearly twenty years. Roosevelt replied,
"My dear Chief: That title still stands! and I am still Franklin to you." [6]

Roosevelt never gave up addressing Daniels as Chief, but there was
never the slightest question who had come into command. He was ready
to return to the office of President the strength and moral power that he
had sensed in it during the administrations of Theodore Roosevelt and
Woodrow Wilson. He had won office just at a time when the American
people had lost their faith of the 1920s in an economy and government
combining economic conservatism and technical efficiency. The great
mass producer of cheap automobiles, Henry Ford, with his assembly-
line know-how and bucolic ideology, and the "great engineer" in government, President Herbert Hoover, were no longer the idols they had
been before 1929. Roosevelt, still holding to progressive ideals, believed
the Chief Executive should be a moral leader, personifying government
to the citizen, and within the federal system expressing the popular will.
He explained to Mrs. McCormick:

> The presidency . . . is not merely an administrative office. That's
> the least of it. It is more than an engineering job, efficient or ineffi-
> cient. It is predominantly a place of moral leadership. All our great
> Presidents were leaders of thought at times when certain historic ideas
> in the life of the nation had to be clarified. Washington personified the
> idea of federal union. Jefferson practically originated the party system

as we know it by opposing the democratic theory to the republicanism of Hamilton. This theory was reaffirmed by Jackson. Two great principles of our government were forever put beyond question by Lincoln. Cleveland, coming into office following an era of great political corruption, typified rugged honesty. T.R. and Wilson were both moral leaders, each in his own way and his own time, who used the Presidency as a pulpit.

Isn't that what the office is — a superb opportunity for reapplying, applying in new conditions, the simple rules of human conduct we always go back to? I stress the modern application, because we are always moving on; the technical and economic environment changes, and never so quickly as now. Without leadership alert and sensitive to change, we are bogged up or lose our way, as we have lost it in the past decade.[7]

It never occurred to Roosevelt that he should not be a vigorous, innovative President. Although he might at first regard with caution his sudden great accrual of power and responsibility, it was in keeping with his background and upbringing to plan to use it to the fullest once he was inaugurated. His mother continued to sit at the head of the table in the house at Hyde Park, as she had before, but she had brought up her son to be a man of strength.

In an essay Roosevelt had written in 1900 while he was a Harvard undergraduate, he had extolled the progressiveness, the democratic spirit and the virility of the Roosevelts: "They have never felt that because they were born in a good position they could put their hands in their pockets and succeed. They have felt, rather, that . . . there was no excuse for them if they did not do their duty by the community." These were his life-long views. They had become part of him during his upbringing on the lovely estate at Hyde Park, so like the holdings of some English squire. In the last months of his life he wrote, "In thinking back to my earliest days I am impressed by the peacefulness and regularity of things both in respect to places and people. Up to the age of seven, with the exception of one trip to England, Hyde Park was the center of the world." [8] In the larger tradition of *noblesse oblige* and in innumerable small accustomed ways, Roosevelt drew either strength or comfort from the family history and the familiar surroundings.* The traditions and lore of his relatives and their circle, extending to include

---

* FDR, an inveterate collector, extended this feeling in an almost ludicrous fashion to a strange souvenir. At Christmas, 1932, a resident of Goshen, New York, sent him the tail of a famous trotting horse, Gloster, the first to trot a mile under 2:20, which his father had bred at Hyde Park, "I was particularly pleased to receive this gift because there is a lot of sentiment about Gloster in my family," Roosevelt told reporters. "In 1873, Gloster trotted a mile under 2:29 three times, finally reaching a mark of 2:17¼." He took the tail to the White House with him, and through his presidency kept it draped from a wardrobe in the corner of his bedroom.[9]

the idol of his youth, Theodore Roosevelt, were of continuing importance to him. He felt hurt that few of the Roosevelts supported him in the campaign of 1932, and complained to a cousin,

> What a pity that one or two of the clan are acting in a way which one day they probably will regret. I shall never forget my father telling me in 1898 that although a life-long Democrat he was going to vote for Theodore Roosevelt as Governor. In the same way my first Presidential vote, although I was a Democrat, went to cousin Theodore in 1904.[10]

The sense of obligation growing out of his social position was also instilled in him at Groton School. "It will be a proud day for Groton when an old boy is in the White House," one of his former masters had written him, but the student body did not agree. Though it must have stung him that a student poll went four to one for Hoover, and that the headmaster, Endicott Peabody, regretfully voted the same way, Roosevelt more than once reiterated in years that followed that he was trying not to forget his Groton ideals.[11]

Nor did the only somewhat less overwhelming disapproval among his fellow Harvard graduates dim Roosevelt's affection and loyalty toward his university. A few weeks after the election, he attended a large dinner at the Harvard Club in New York City in honor of the retiring president of Harvard, A. Lawrence Lowell. Roosevelt confided to his one-time law partner, Langdon P. Marvin, that he had not had time to prepare a talk, since his day had been filled with conferences. Between interruptions at the dinner, he managed to pencil a few words on a pad. Quite obviously the President-elect of the United States overshadowed the retiring president of Harvard, and the assembled alumni were in a mood to be easily resentful. When Roosevelt was finally called upon, Marvin recalled: "He spoke about having studied Government I under President Lowell, about the time when he was at Cambridge . . . — a wholly delightful Harvard speech with no touch of politics or any axes to grind. Everybody was delighted with him and he made a great personal hit." Yet into the speech, Roosevelt managed to slip something of his viewpoint. Like all of American society, he pointed out, Harvard had changed through the years so that it stood for "bigger things and at the same time simpler things than it used to." He asserted, "I wouldn't have had it stand still for a minute any more than I'd rather the nation stood still." That, he pointed out, was why he had been called a radical, because he advocated change.[12]

Already, so many of Roosevelt's distant relatives, his classmates, and his youthful social circle were acting as though he were betraying the credo in which they had all been reared. This credo was a rather simple faith in Christian stewardship, a belief that the best people through personal service and private philanthropy should minister to the under-privileged. Social responsibility had been drilled into him at Hyde Park, Groton, and Harvard, and through his participation in socialite charitable activities in the New York of the early 1900s. At Groton, he himself had worked at a charitable camp for poor boys from the slums; when he was courting Eleanor Roosevelt, he once helped her carry home a sick girl from the Rivington Street Settlement house, and exclaimed when he saw the apartment, "My gosh, I didn't know anyone lived like that!" In part it was the desire for excitement, but in part also the feeling that he must aid the less fortunate which caused him as a young lawyer to avoid the more dignified and potentially lucrative avenues of the law and instead throw himself with enthusiasm into the arguing of petty claims cases involving poor people. Once or twice he helped some of these people out of his own pocket. Thus far his Groton and Harvard classmates would have followed his course with approval.[13]

Roosevelt never rejected these philanthropic beliefs. Rather, as was implicit in his remarks at the Harvard Club, he better than many of his contemporaries had accepted the changes during the nearly three decades since the class of '04 had been graduated. These changes had early led him to add to his credo the ideology of progressivism. He was not content like so many of his well-born contemporaries to reserve the solution of national problems (of which the misery of the underprivileged was only one) to private initiative or personal charity, but was willing like the progressives to accept an additional means — government action. Undoubtedly he first acquired these new views from Theodore Roosevelt. As he never ceased reminiscing in private conversation, he had listened deeply to his wife's Uncle Ted during exciting visits to the White House. And T.R. had never tired of telling the young men standing around him in an admiring circle that it was their duty to enter public service — politics. Franklin D. Roosevelt, even while he was a law clerk, dreamed of a political career, and since his name was Roosevelt, even let his dreams carry him to the White House. Meanwhile his legal work with small claims cases was giving him some political grounding. In November 1932, when a former fellow law clerk reminded him of the dream, Roosevelt replied, "I often think that my Municipal Court work laid the foundation for politics better than any other factor in my life." [14]

When Roosevelt entered politics in 1910 he did so as a Democrat only because his branch of the family had been traditionally Democratic, and the Dutchess County Democratic organization urged him to run for state senator. In his campaign and in his lively first career in Albany from 1911 into 1913, he proved that his membership in the Democratic party was less important than his growing commitment to the progressivism that was infiltrating both major parties. He stood increasingly for reform, and when reforms could not be achieved by solely private methods (in keeping with the concept of Christian stewardship), he went further and fought for legislation which would bring the government to the rescue of the weak.

It was logical for Roosevelt to become an early supporter of Woodrow Wilson, who became the Democratic candidate for President in 1912. He followed Wilson to Washington to serve for seven years as assistant secretary of the navy. Both in Albany and Washington, Roosevelt seemed in many respects still closely associated with the background from which he was emerging, still basically conservative, rather frivolous, and overconcerned with social life. He was so dashing and debonair that it was sometimes hard for even those close to him to realize how hard he was working at administration and politics, how firmly he was maturing in his perceptions and actions. He had grown sufficiently to be nominated for the vice presidency on the Democratic ticket in 1920 when he was only thirty-eight years old. He made the most of the hopeless campaign, utilizing his speaking tours crisscrossing the nation to become better acquainted with scores of Democratic leaders. They remembered him with favor after the Harding landslide had buried the ticket.

The following summer, Roosevelt suffered an acute attack of polio. He seemed hopelessly crippled and out of politics. Thomas Wolfe, visiting near Hyde Park, had caught the comment of one of the aristocratic neighbors and later reproduced it in a novel: "Pity this thing had to happen to him just at the start of his career." Everyone assumed Roosevelt was permanently through — everyone except his wife, his secretary, Louis McHenry Howe, and Roosevelt himself. With their aid, drawing upon the splendid personal courage and stoicism which his family background demanded of him, he remained uninterruptedly in politics. He appeared in his early forties as a sort of "elder statesman," rising above faction in the badly split Democratic party, since as he reiterated, until he regained the use of his legs he would not be a candidate for office.[15]

Roosevelt went to Massachusetts and Florida to try various types of treatment, and although his legs improved only slightly, he remained unflagging in his optimism. Then in the warm mineral water of the pool at a run-down resort, Warm Springs, Georgia, he began to feel some improvement. He determined to build it into a curative center for polio victims, and with his characteristic combination of faith and energy risked most of his personal fortune in the enterprise. He fought for national publicity for Warm Springs, and gradually obtained patients, therapists, and new buildings. In late November 1932, when he returned to Warm Springs as President-elect, he could look with satisfaction at what he had achieved there. As he gazed down the long dining hall where 275 persons were eating their Thanksgiving dinner, he recalled that at the first such dinner in 1926 there had been only thirty-five patients. Remarking on the fine buildings, he recalled that the first cottages were so dilapidated that one had to undress for bed in the dark if one were not to risk being seen through the cracks in the walls. "The cottage in which I lived in my early days . . . was white," Roosevelt remembered, and a Georgia newspaperman, Tom Loyless, had immediately begun calling it "The Little White House." "Since then," Roosevelt declared, "there always has been a 'Little White House' at Warm Springs and there is going to be for another four years anyway." [16]

During those trying years, Roosevelt had never relinquished his vision of occupying the White House in Washington. In 1928 he attained a way-station, the governor's mansion in Albany. Although he still could not walk unaided, he succumbed to the insistent pleading of Al Smith, the Democratic nominee for President, that he strengthen the ticket by becoming the party's candidate for governor of New York. In the campaign, Roosevelt demonstrated such political and personal vitality that he won the governorship by a hair's breadth, while Smith lost the state and the nation. Even before he took office, he was being talked of as a likely nominee for the presidency in 1932. Following Smith, who had been a phenomenally popular and successful governor, Roosevelt concentrated upon trying to achieve an effective record in the state. He was a vigorous and hard-working administrator, concentrating upon aid for farmers and reform of public utilities. He mastered devices for squeezing his program through a Republican legislature. There were coaching sessions for the Democratic legislative leaders — Monday noon lunches which because of the nature of the repast, both literally and figuratively, became known as the meetings of the "cold turkey cabinet." There were also intimate talks over the radio to the people of New York State, urging them to bring pressure upon the legislature. Roosevelt obtained his legislation and convinced the voters that credit for it should go to the Democratic governor rather than the Republican majority in the legislature. As soon as he had obtained his measures he pressured his department heads to put them into effective operation. "Thirteen million people in the State don't want so damn many reports," he would tell his cabinet. "We all want a bit more action." And he got action. At a dinner in his honor in December 1932, Roosevelt remarked with good reason, "Being Governor is a mighty good training before going down to Washington." [17]

In 1930, with the state and nation starting to slide into the trough of depression, Roosevelt after two years as governor was reelected by a phenomenal margin of 725,000 votes, double what Smith had ever achieved. In his second administration he was forced to combat the depression even while he was striving for the presidential nomination. At first his concept of the role of the government in the economy was, like that of President Herbert Hoover, mildly progressive — that the government should intervene only to the minimum that was essential. But Roosevelt soon went beyond Hoover in his experimentation, and indeed beyond every other governor. At the Governors' Conference in June 1931, he asserted unequivocally:

> More and more, those who are the victims of dislocations and defects of our social and economic life are beginning to ask respectfully, but insistently, of us who are in positions of public responsibility why government can not and should not act to protect its citizens from disaster. I believe the question demands an answer and that the ultimate answer is that government, both state and national, must accept the responsibility of doing what it can do.[18]

Thus, before he obtained the nomination for the presidency, Roosevelt as governor of New York was accepting in theory as well as in action the challenge to assume greater responsibility for the economic welfare of those in distress.

By the fall of 1932 and winter of 1933, the distress was deeper, and the challenge consequently all the more serious. Business activity was between a third and a quarter below normal. Although it was slowly improving, there were — according to the most optimistic estimate, Hoover's figure in his campaign speeches — ten million unemployed, about one worker out of every five. A more pessimistic figure was thirteen million — one worker in four. Most of those on relief were seriously undernourished. In Chicago, at least one in three was unemployed. In this period of acute deflation, the unemployed and their families could be fed relatively cheaply. Governor Gifford Pinchot of Pennsylvania was able to demonstrate to Mrs. Roosevelt in February 1933 that through buying foodstuffs in large quantities at wholesale, he could provide an adequate relief meal for about 5½ cents, but many states and cities were able to provide only a fraction of that amount.

Some people who were employed and thus not eligible for relief were not much better off, they worked so few hours or for such low pay. In February 1933, employees of the Briggs Manufacturing Company, which produced automobile bodies in Detroit, went on strike against piecework wages averaging as little as 10 cents an hour. Briggs broke the strike by returning to a guaranteed hourly wage of 25 cents.* In

---

* According to the Bureau of Labor Statistics, the highest average wage being paid in December, 1932, was to printers working for newspapers, who received $33.88 per week. In a wide array of industries it was less than $15 per week. For example:

cotton goods	$10.39
shirts and collars	10.67
iron and steel	12.50
agricultural implements	14.75 [19]

the sweatshops of New York City, one woman by lining a slipper every forty-five seconds was able to earn $1.05 in a nine-hour day; a girl sewing aprons was being paid 2½ cents per apron and earned only 20 cents a day. One quarter of the women in Chicago were receiving less than 10 cents an hour.[20]

These were the conditions which drove some people to the lengths Edmund Wilson witnessed:

> There is not a garbage-dump in Chicago which is not diligently haunted by the hungry. Last summer in the hot weather when the smell was sickening and the flies were thick, there were a hundred people a day coming to one of the dumps, falling on the heap of refuse as soon as the truck had pulled out and digging in it with sticks and hands. They would devour all the pulp that was left on the old slices of water-melon and canteloupe till the rinds were thin as paper; and they would take away and wash and cook discarded onions, turnips, potatoes, cab-bage or carrots. Meat is a more difficult matter, but they salvage a good deal of that too. . . . Before [one widow] picked up the meat, she would always take off her glasses so that she couldn't see the maggots.[21]

The irony was that while hunger was leading some city dwellers to such a desperate search for food, stores were full of five-cent bread and five-cent a pound hamburger; surpluses of produce were clogging the grain elevators and deteriorating on farms.* In California, tons of peaches rotted on the ground, or even in great piles in front of can-neries, which had contracted for them but could not profitably pack them. Truckloads of cull oranges were dumped in gullies and covered with quicklime so that they could not be salvaged for food; surplus raisins were sprayed with rancid oil and fed to cattle. Grain created one of the most acute problems. On October 29, 1932, wheat for December delivery dropped to 43⅞ cents per bushel on the Chicago market, the lowest since the reign of Queen Elizabeth I three hundred years earlier. The price continued to fall. In Iowa, a bushel of corn held over from the previous season was worth less than a package of chewing gum. This corn sold for $1.40 a ton, and in the same areas a ton of coal cost $4. Throughout the corn belt acrid blue smoke, smelling rather like roasting coffee, gave indication that farmers were keeping warm by burning corn in their winter stoves.[23]

These were the people Roosevelt was pledging himself to aid. Presi-

---

* An indication of the acuteness of the deflation are these specials that a Los Angeles market advertised on September 6, 1932:

Bread, 1 lb. loaf	5 cents
Lettuce, per head	1 cent
Oranges, 3 doz.	10 cents
Sliced bacon, per lb.	10 cents
Spring lamb chops, per lb.	12½ cents [22]

dent Hoover had not forgotten them, and indeed had attempted much national intervention upon their behalf. By urging upon Congress measures through which the federal government would aid directly in strengthening the faltering economy, he had shattered many old precedents and established new ones. He felt he had gone about far enough. But the depression continued, and to a large part of the electorate, the Hoover measures seemed to be distressingly inadequate. Roosevelt, avoiding specifics, promised a much more vigorous program to bring rapid recovery. Both as governor and as candidate for President, his mail had been full of imploring letters from the needy; he had talked to some of them individually and he had seen their faces in crowds from coast to coast.

President Hoover campaigned as though he felt these people needed only patience to tide them over until his measures righted the economy. His sharp antagonism toward Roosevelt and his contrasting concept of what constituted responsibility in the presidency requires examination, since it carried over into the treacherous months after the election. To some degree Hoover's views shaped the course of American history. To a greater degree they helped fix a myth firmly believed by some people that Hoover had set the nation back onto the path of recovery and that Roosevelt, by the recklessness of his irresponsibility both during the campaign and in the black months between his election in November 1932 and his inauguration in March 1933,* precipitated the nation back into needless extra years of depression.[24]

Again and again, Hoover in his lengthy, sober campaign speeches constructed unbudgeable logical structures, anchored firmly in the bedrock of the earlier economic theories. Step by step he enumerated the measures his administration had undertaken to combat the depression; point by point he denounced the recklessness of Roosevelt for promising to go further. Before the campaign was over, Hoover had erected the framework for most of his future strictures upon the New Deal. "This campaign is more than a contest between two parties," he warned on October 31. "It is a contest between two philosophies of government." † On November 5, he charged that certain unspecified groups

---

* Because the Twentieth Amendment had not yet gone into effect, abolishing lame duck sessions of Congress and the long waiting period before the inauguration of the new President, Roosevelt would not take office until March 4, 1933.
† It is instructive, in view of the way in which the New Deal did in fact develop, that Hoover was warning that Roosevelt and his political supporters, if elected, would introduce the following program, allegedly destructive of American institutions: (1) expansion of government spending; (2) currency inflation; (3) government entrance into banking; (4) reduction of protective tariff to competitive level; (5) government development of power; (6) provision of employment for all surplus labor at all times; (7) destruction of independence of Supreme Court; (8) acceptance of the view that America had reached the height of its development.[25]

were bringing forth an ideology which would destroy the traditional
American system:

> Indeed this is the same philosophy of government which has poisoned
> all Europe. They have been the fumes of the witch's caldron which
> boiled in Russia and in its attenuated flavor spread over the whole of
> Europe, and would by many be introduced into the United States in an
> attempt to secure votes through protest of discontent against emergency
> conditions.[26]

No sober observer, whether Roosevelt's political enemy or friend,
would have agreed in the fall of 1932 that there was this much of a
gulf between the two candidates. Both had been schooled in laissez-faire
economics; both had been admirers of the two progressive Presidents,
Theodore Roosevelt and Woodrow Wilson; both were ready to utilize
the government in an unprecedented fashion as a force to bring recovery. Some of the supposed differences between them which had been
aired during the campaign were not much more than political bombast.
Hoover assumed the role of an internationalist in economic matters,
who through cooperation among nations hoped to alleviate a depression
of world origins and scope.* Yet he had signed an unprecedentedly
high protective tariff bill, and warned that if the Democrats won, they
would so lower the tariff that the "grass will grow in streets of a
hundred cities, a thousand towns." As for Roosevelt, assuming the stance
of a nationalist, he charged that the depression was of strictly American
origins, the outcome of erroneous Republican policies, and remediable
through national measures. On the tariff, he seemed to take the traditional Democratic low-duties stand, but under pressure he so equivo-
cated that Hoover compared his statements to "the dreadful position
of the chameleon on the Scotch plaid." [28]

The campaign had indeed brought out certain contrasts in the policies
of the two men. Roosevelt was ready to go further in direct federal intervention to restore the economy through a new farm program, public
works and conservation projects, and federal development and regulation of water power resources. Hoover was correct in suspecting that
Roosevelt might countenance currency inflation although there was
nothing in his campaign speeches to indicate it.

In addition, the personalities and thought-habits of the two men were
sharply different, as their campaign styles indicated. Hoover's cheerless

---

* Hoover, in his campaign speeches, had referred repeatedly to the moratorium
on payment of external debts which he had negotiated to save the German people
"from a collapse that would have set a prairie afire and possibly have involved all
civilization itself," and his plans for "a world-wide economic conference with view
to relieving pressure upon us from foreign countries, to increase their stability, to
deal with silver, and to prevent recurrence of these calamities for the future." [27]

warnings were a polar opposite to Roosevelt's buoyant optimism; Hoover wove an overall pattern of a certain consistency into his speeches so that they formed the sort of Scotch plaid across which Roosevelt swept his generalities with blithe disregard. Hoover's was the logic of a doctrinaire mind which fitted everything into a single pattern by sheer force of intellect rather than circumstance. Roosevelt's was the logic of a supple politician. He appeared to his detractors as a rank opportunist; his supporters could argue that while Hoover was determined to weave people into his orderly scheme of things, Roosevelt was disposed to let his program evolve out of human needs.

Two of the traits which most alarmed Hoover and his adherents were Roosevelt's readiness to take advantage of his opportunities, and his skill in incorporating the conflicting aspirations of diverse interests into a unified program. The very characteristics that to Hoover were iniquities were assets to one of Roosevelt's admirers, Professor Felix Frankfurter of the Harvard Law School. Frankfurter in adulatory terms set forth the positive worth of these traits. In 1931 he wrote Roosevelt that nothing surprised him more than "the way public men pass up opportunities made to order for them — they are so scared by the so-called prudences. But you are seizing your opportunities." And upon Roosevelt's election in 1932, he commented upon the other characteristic, "You will . . . be the comprehending expression of the diverse interests, feelings, hopes, and thoughts of the multiple forces which are unified into the nation." [29]

It was vital for Roosevelt to cope with the multiple forces, since with the defeat of Hoover all the divergent pressures, from those wishing to preserve the old order and those eager for a "new deal," converged upon Roosevelt: liberals and conservatives in the Democratic party and the Republican, the unemployed and the rich, the farmers, laborers, and white-collar workers, members of the Brain Trust who had advised him during the campaign, and members of Congress determined to protect their own power, even the outgoing President. All of them wanted to commit the President-elect in advance to one or another course of action.

Had economic conditions been relatively stable, Roosevelt could have resisted the pressures fairly easily. His schedule of action during the third of a year ahead would have been simple: close out his affairs as governor with a minimum of effort, obtain a good rest, and while resting decide upon his major appointments and formulate his main policies. And had he followed his pattern of 1928 when he was governor-elect, he would have dribbled the news of appointments and policies to the reporters so as to obtain continuing favorable notice in the press and increasing public support. The mounting crisis of the winter of 1932–1933 threw awry much of this simple scheme, and endowed the plans and actions of the President-elect with a more than usual significance.

During the campaign, Roosevelt had been shrewd in enunciating strongly and clearly the basic objective that he sought — a revitalization of prosperity — and in outlining only enigmatically the course of action by which he hoped to achieve it. In this way he had gathered to himself the support of all those who for one or another reason were dissatisfied with Hoover. They might quarrel seriously among themselves, but each could unite with the others on Roosevelt, hopeful that his own plan for recovery would prevail. Even Republican leaders by no means agreed among themselves what Roosevelt's victory might signify. Some, like Hoover, feared cataclysm, but a prominent Republican senator, Charles L. McNary of Oregon, wrote privately, "The victory was rather larger than I expected, but inasmuch as it had to be, I'm rather glad that it was overwhelming. It may cause an upturn in business." [30]

As for the staunchly Republican middle class, following the initial shock their view seemed to be "wait and see." No one could articulate their visceral reactions more vividly than the famous Kansas editor, William Allen White. In the shock of the morning after the election, he confided to a friend, "The recovery probably may not be in our lifetime. Roosevelt will wreck the Democratic party." But by February 1, White had become cautiously optimistic, writing to Theodore Roosevelt, Jr.:

> Your distant relative is an X in the equation. He may develop his stubbornness into courage, his amiability into wisdom, his sense of superiority into statesmanship. Responsibility is a winepress that brings forth strange juices out of men. I don't know. I can't prophesy. But if he fails seriously, watch out for the fireworks.[31]

Only one factor seemed certain, as Walter Lippmann pointed out in the aftermath of the election, "The people have willed the end without willing the means to that end."

With the election won, it seemed important for Roosevelt to preserve a fluidity of action through not committing himself too soon before he possessed power in his own right. As Lippmann saw, Roosevelt was setting forth with favorable omens which would carry him far if he did not succumb to immediate pressures:

> Luckily for him the public has not been taught to look upon him as a superman. His abilities have, if anything, been underrated. Luckily for him he can remind this party that they have won not on their own charms but because there was a rebellion among the Republicans. Luckily for him he has not made or had to make very many specific pledges to the voters which will rise to plague him. He has ample

power. He is free to draw around himself the ablest and most disinterested men he can find. His good-will no one questions. He has proved that he has the gift of political sagacity. If only he will sail by the stars and not where the winds of opinion will take him, he will bring the ship into port.[32]

To maintain until the right time an independence of course, to refuse serious responsibility and rigid policy pledges before authority had descended to him, this course was difficult. For the time being Roosevelt made few commitments and avoided outward manifestations that he was anyone more than governor of New York. On election night, his last words to the newspapermen were, "I have work to do on the State Budget. That will keep me busy for the next few days. I'm not President yet." Two days after the election, in response to newspaper speculations upon his cabinet and suggestions that he announce its makeup immediately, he formally stated: "No decision has been reached and no decision will be reached in regard to any appointments for at least two months. . . . From now until January 1, 1933, the greater part of my time will be occupied with my duties as Governor of the State of New York." [33]

It could be argued that by keeping relatively enigmatic, Roosevelt could assure himself of unified support when he entered the White House and assumed power. Yet there were frightful perils in prospect if the nation had to wallow for four months more in the trough of the worst depression in its history, with the policies of the defeated President repudiated, and those of the incoming President a mystery. Whatever he did or did not do, circumstances forced upon Roosevelt a fearful responsibility as soon as he became President-elect.

CHAPTER II

A Fresh Challenge from Hoover

> On the subjects to which you refer, as in all matters
> relating to the welfare of the country, I am glad to co-
> operate in every appropriate way, subject, of course, to
> the requirements of my present duties as Governor of
> this State.
> — FDR TO PRESIDENT HERBERT HOOVER,
> *November 14, 1932.*

Since a new President had been elected, it seemed cruel to expect the
American nation in its desperate economic plight to wait four more
months for the promised New Deal. Understandably pleas came from
all directions for Governor Roosevelt not to delay until March 4, 1933,
but to commit his prestige immediately to recovery. Two especially
heavy forces began to operate, like two giant millstones, between which
Roosevelt might find himself ground if he were not wary. One was
from the relatively conservative Democratic leadership in Congress,
seeking endorsement of its own limited nationalistic recovery program,
which it hoped to enact during the lame duck session between December
1932 and March 1933. The other was from President Hoover, who,
having lost at the polls still hoped to save the country by converting
his successor to a program for international economic recovery.

The pressure from Hoover, which continued intermittently through
the interregnum, was one of the strangest struggles in the history of the
presidency. Never before or since has a defeated outgoing chief executive tried to commit a victorious incoming successor to abandon his
new program in advance. By February 1933, Hoover was attempting
just that.

To Roosevelt, the negotiations with Hoover came as a surprise. In a
euphoric mood on the quiet Saturday before the election, he had speculated with one of his Brain Trusters, Adolf A. Berle, Jr., on the possible
outcome of the election. Berle feared the majority might be amazing
(he cited an impossible figure, twenty-five million) and trigger the nation into demanding "economic action far more quickly than any politi-

cal engineering could arrange it." Roosevelt responded that the majority would be about ten million (in fact, it turned out to be seven million). The sort of program he had in mind, he said, would indeed take some time, but if the election results were too lopsided there would be pressure for Hoover to appoint Roosevelt secretary of state, persuade Vice President Curtis to resign, and himself resign, which under legislation at that time would automatically make Roosevelt President. Roosevelt thought this eventuality possible although not probable.[1]

In the aftermath of the election there were indeed scattered suggestions, even occasionally from Republicans, that the depression emergency dictated that Hoover resign in Roosevelt's favor. Hoover's reaction was quite the reverse; his response to the emergency was to try to persuade Roosevelt to accept the Hoover program. The result was controversy. Much of it centered upon the dreary question of war debts, but long after the debts had been permanently repudiated and forgotten, the dramatic clash between the outgoing and incoming Presidents was remembered.

The debate forced Roosevelt into decisions affecting the economic aspects of foreign policy, as, whether he consciously willed it or not, he began immediately to formulate and apply his views. The birth pains of the New Deal did not await Roosevelt's inauguration but began with his victory at the polls.

As for the defeated President, acting from statesmanlike motives but not abandoning in the slightest any of the firm positions he had taken during the campaign, he expressed his eagerness to cooperate with Roosevelt in furthering economic recovery for the good of the country. Yet he considered the election of Roosevelt the cause of the cataclysm; from the summer of 1932 through the rest of his life, Hoover believed that the political success of Roosevelt spelled disaster. In June 1932, just before the Democratic convention, the President, smiling grimly, suggested to Stimson that the nomination of Roosevelt would probably bring on a panic. Gradually the thesis grew until in his *Memoirs* he has written: [2]

> After mid-July the whole world was on the march out of the depression. All nations with a free economy other than our own were rapidly recovering. With the ominous election returns from Maine on September 14th, the country began to realize that Roosevelt would win and there would be an abrupt change in policies. After that date the business world at once began to weigh the consequences of his policies. Whether his policies were justified or unjustified, they immediately caused our business world to stop, wait, and listen. The prices of commodities and securities immediately began to decline, and unemployment increased.

To counteract what he saw as the trend, President Hoover determined to bridge over the four months' interregnum, which he recognized as a time always creating "a particularly difficult period, especially when there was a change of political parties, with all the overcharged campaign emotions." He thought Roosevelt would want Congress to enact various of the recovery measures upon which the two of them agreed — the balancing of the budget, the reform of banking and bankruptcy laws, and reorganization of the administrative branch of the government. "Indeed," writes Hoover, "if these matters were out of the way, such political liabilities as were in them would be on my back, and the new administration would have a propitious beginning." Above all, since questions of foreign policy had not been raised in the campaign, he hoped for cooperation on matters concerning the Japanese invasion of Manchuria, war debts payments, the pending World Economic Conference, and the continuing World Disarmament Conference.[3]

The difficulty was that the animosities of the campaign and its preliminaries had created such a suspicion between the two men as to make amicable cooperation next to impossible. Further, there seemed to Roosevelt to be compelling reasons why he should be wary of commitment to Hoover.

The morning after the election, Roosevelt began to parry the President. Propped in bed after breakfast, he conferred with Moley on a suitable reply to a telegram of congratulations he had received from the President. "In the common purpose of all of us," Hoover had wired in part, "I shall dedicate myself to every possible helpful effort." On the back of it, Roosevelt penciled, "I appreciate your generous telegram. . . . I want to assure you that subject to my necessary executive duties as Governor during the balance of this year, I hold myself in readiness to cooperate with you in our common purpose to help our country." Roosevelt pondered, crossed out the phrase, "in readiness to cooperate with you," and wrote instead that he was "ready to further in every way" their common purpose. Moley jotted another draft on the back of an envelope, and off to Hoover went a noncommittal reply, "I appreciate your generous telegram. For the immediate as well as for the most distant future I join in your gracious expression of a common purpose in helpful effort for our country." [4]

The way in which Roosevelt hesitated over the draft was indicative of his uncertainty how to proceed. He was indeed ready to cooperate, and a few days later said so in another wire to Hoover, but implicit was Roosevelt's unwillingness to compromise his own plans and freedom of action.

For the moment, an attack of influenza, described to the press as mild, forced Roosevelt to rest. He canceled appointments and plans for a weekend at Hyde Park, and stayed secluded in the Executive Mansion in Albany from Friday, November 11, until Wednesday, November 16. He sent word to the newspapermen that he would not hold his customary four o'clock conference with them, and that there would temporarily be a "lid on" news. At leisure in private he began dipping into the enormous stacks of letters and telegrams that had been piling higher and higher since election day. It was a pleasant task riffling through the innumerable letters of congratulations, many of them from old friends and associates. Suddenly, on Sunday, into this quiet weekend intruded a long and urgent telegram President Hoover sent from Yuma, Arizona, en route from California to Washington. The British, reported Hoover, were asking for an immediate review of the existing system of intergovernmental financial obligations, and wished in the meanwhile a suspension of the war debt payments, including the $95 million installment due on December 15. Other debtor nations were about to make similar requests.* "I am loath to proceed with recommendations to the Congress," Hoover wired, "until I can have an opportunity to confer with you personally at some convenient date in the near future." He wished an interchange of views with Roosevelt upon three questions: the suspension of war debt payments, the course of the disarmament conference in which the United States was taking a leading role, and plans for a world economic conference scheduled for the winter. These interrelated matters all had a direct bearing upon the state of international economic conditions. "The building up of world economic stability is, of course," Hoover pointed out, "of the greatest importance in the building up of our recovery." [6]

Here was a serious challenge to Roosevelt. Hoover was reiterating his long-held view that the depression was a worldwide calamity, and that the United States must help find an international road to recovery. The bothersome question of war debts, if properly answered, might take the United States and other nations a few steps along that road. In this context, as a possibly vital factor in the world economy, the long and boringly complex problem of war debts assumed an absorbing importance. The debts represented money which the United States had loaned to the Allies, principally to England, France, and Italy, during and immediately after the First World War. Linked to them almost

---

* The British note had dropped upon Secretary of State Henry L. Stimson like a "bombshell." Acting under President Hoover's instructions, Stimson and Secretary of the Treasury Ogden Mills drafted a telegram to Roosevelt, which Hoover altered to include much historical justification of his own position. "The President still has the aroma of battle on him," Stimson noted, "and it is very hard for him to lift himself up above the plane on which he has been for so many months." Stimson worried for fear Hoover's removal of the "simple and magnanimous tone which we tried to get into the telegram" would have a bad effect on Roosevelt.[5]

immediately in fact, although not in treaty or law, were concomitant reparations for war damages which the Allies assessed against Germany. The United States consistently took the view that there was no connection between debts and reparations. Nonetheless, after two funding programs had been devised in the twenties, German payments of reparations to the Allies balanced, and were a little bit over, the Allies' debt payments to the United States. Even in times of relative prosperity this still left a problem. Although the Allies had incurred the debts by taking goods and services — munitions of war for the most part — the United States was loath to take goods in return since they would compete with the output of American factories. Consequently the United States kept its tariff barriers high, and demanded payment in gold. The problem was not insuperable in the late twenties, since through 1928 American private investors were pouring sufficient capital into Germany to enable Germany to meet its reparations installments, and the former Allies their debt payments.* It was a curious triangular flow of capital. Increasingly in 1928 surplus American capital was diverted into the soaring stock market; after the market crashed in the fall of 1929 there was no more surplus capital.

Economic conditions in Europe, which had never fully recovered from the war, blackened long before the United States felt the brunt of the depression. In the spring of 1931, the failure of the central bank in Austria seemed about to bring down with it the financial structure of Germany; England was forced off the gold standard, and imminent collapse in western Europe threatened serious economic repercussions in the United States. To stop this chain reaction, in June 1931 President Hoover negotiated with the approval of Congress a one-year moratorium in both war debt and reparations payments. It came too late to help stimulate recovery, but it did stay somewhat the financial deterioration in Europe. Before the moratorium expired, European nations began pressuring for cancellation of both reparations and debts, and negotiated at Lausanne, Switzerland, in June 1932, an agreement scaling down German reparations to a token level, but hinging ratification of the agreement upon debt reduction. Secretary of State Henry L. Stimson and numerous well-informed Americans favored canceling the debts, but President Hoover considered them a moral obligation and a bargaining crowbar with which the United States could pry trade and other economic concessions out of the debtors. Now, in an unprecedented fashion, President Hoover wished to share with the President-elect this complex

* The former Allies owed the United States about $10 billion, which seemed a staggering sum in 1932. They had repaid about $2.6 billion, receiving in turn about $2 billion in reparations from Germany. Private American loans to German governmental units or corporations had amounted to about $2.5 billion.

problem he regarded as vital to American and indeed world economic recovery.[7]

Immediately Roosevelt had to decide upon his reply to Hoover's request. He telephoned Moley to come at once to Albany, and after lunch that Sunday, November 13, 1932, began discussing the problem with another of his Brain Trusters, Professor Rexford G. Tugwell of Columbia University, who was there on other matters. Later in the day he conferred with both Tugwell and Moley. "The President's telegram took us completely by surprise," Moley has reminisced:

> We could not remember any other case in which an outgoing President, during the interregnum, had asked for the advice and assistance of his successful opponent. And as we talked over the problems the Hoover proposal raised . . . we concluded that the President could scarcely have chosen a field in which there was less probability of sympathetic co-operation between the two administrations." [8]

The telegram forced Roosevelt immediately to study in detail a complex of foreign policy questions which had not been campaign issues. It was a foregone conclusion that as yet he was not expert upon them. "If Franklin were to come in," Thomas Lamont, a Morgan partner, wrote earlier that fall to Walter Lippmann, "he would have to do an awful lot of educating himself on foreign questions of disarmament, war debts, etc. But I suppose that always holds true of any change in Administration." [9]

The popular view on war debts was unmistakable, and apocryphal words attributed to Calvin Coolidge epitomized it. Coolidge was supposed to have remarked, like the holder of a small personal loan, "They hired the money, didn't they?" It was a Vermont story, but a view particularly attractive in the very areas where Roosevelt was politically strongest, beyond the Appalachians and below the Mason-Dixon line.

Many Eastern sophisticates favored canceling the debts as the British had those of their allies after the defeat of Napoleon. Roosevelt earlier had shared their opinion. In 1926 he scoffed at Coolidge's alleged words and pointed out that aside from questions of moral justice, the ill will the United States would incur would in the end cost more billions than could be gained in interest from strict debt collection.[10]

By 1932 the intellectual and economic elite had come to believe that it was essential to forgive the financial obligations, and if possible to obtain in return for their cancellation a general lowering of tariffs and preservation of the gold standard. These proposals, Moley has written,

> were the twin deities of an unshakable orthodoxy — the international bankers, the majority of our economists, and almost every graduate of every Eastern university who had dipped into the fields of foreign

relations or economics . . . . [I]n academic and presumably "intellectual circles" . . . it was actually unrespectable not to accept them.[11]

During the campaign, voters could only guess which position Roosevelt favored, that which was intellectually respectable, or that which was politically popular. Colonel Edward M. House, once President Wilson's confidential agent, had tried to negotiate between Hoover and Roosevelt to keep reparations and war debts out of the debate. No agreement had been reached, but Roosevelt did not allude to the subjects in his addresses.* The general tenor of his speeches left little doubt, though, that he had accepted a position of economic nationalism, which meant the recovery program must be basically domestic. He was not sympathetic with Hoover's explanation of the international causes of the depression and presumably would not look for international ways out. Key figures of the Brain Trust, including Moley, Tugwell, and Berle, widely diverging in their views on most economic matters, were united in their belief that cancellation of the debts was not wise. Far more important, the Democratic leaders in Congress flatly opposed cancellation, and these were the men upon whom Roosevelt would have to depend for passage of his New Deal legislation. On one side, Roosevelt came under firm pressure from them; on the other, under counterpressure — less from President Hoover, whom he disliked, than from the intellectuals whose respect he sought — quite possibly from his oldest and most trusted adviser, Louis Howe, and most certainly from the Wilsonian internationalist wing of the Democratic party — men like Owen D. Young, and Colonel House. As House asserted in *Foreign Affairs* that winter, "It must not be forgotten that Mr. Roosevelt was a member of Woodrow Wilson's official family and came under the spell of that courageous and idealistic leader." [13]

Colonel House and like-minded Wilsonians thought they had Roosevelt's ear on foreign policy matters and gave this impression to the

---

* FDR did attack the incongruity of making loans to foreign countries, yet through a high protective tariff preventing the goods of these countries from entering the United States. He said in attacking Hoover that by 1931:

1. Those famous loans to "backward and crippled countries," which he said would provide uninterrupted employment and uninterrupted industrial activity by expanding our export trade, no longer could be made.

2. Retaliation against his monstrous . . . tariff . . . had already begun to strangle the world trade of all Nations, including our own.

3. Debtor nations, no longer sustained by our improvident loans and no longer able to export goods, were drained of gold for debts and, one by one, were forced to abandon specie payments.

4. Finally, as a direct result of all these influences, our export markets dried up, our commodity prices slumped and our own domestic business itself declined at a more rapid rate than business in some of the backward and crippled countries.[12]

British Embassy. Sir Ronald Lindsay, the British ambassador, who shared the current view that Roosevelt although a lightweight was an amiable and impressionable one, sent cables to Whitehall that Roosevelt was under the influence of House and predicted that the President-elect would favor deferring the debt payment, but "would only sell further concessions for [the] maximum price obtainable in the way of disarmament and trade agreements." [14]

During the next few weeks, undoubtedly Roosevelt inclined one way when conferring with House and Young and another when talking to Moley and Tugwell. Out of his discussion with his advisers, Roosevelt gradually developed an approach. Tugwell in his diary recorded the crucial process:

> I felt at that time that all the problems before us ought to be included in the discussions of the conference: disarmament, intergovernmental debts, the problem of stabilization of currency, the control of commodity production throughout the world, and tariffs. He was reluctant from the first to involve all these things in one general discussion and began to work out in his mind at that time the distinction which afterwards became so clear. This was that some problems are and remain economic but that some economic problems suddenly become political questions. He was not able at first to state this point of view very clearly and I did not at once grasp the distinction, but afterwards it seemed to me perfectly obvious. . . .
>
> The Governor convinced me that this was a political more than an economic problem and that although we might think it better to forgive the debts, still what was the use if public opinion was dead set against it. Besides, I must confess that in going into it further I came to see . . . that it was unnecessary to cancel the debts entirely.[15]

There might be some doubt as to which side Roosevelt would ultimately favor, but there was no question he did not wish to commit himself to Hoover. Roosevelt had no qualms about adding to some extent to the growing impasse. "If anything was clear to us that Sunday night in Albany," Moley points out, "it was that Roosevelt must not be saddled with that responsibility." Thus it was that on November 14, Roosevelt replied courteously to the President that he would be glad to cooperate "in every appropriate way," and would be delighted to confer in a wholly informal and personal fashion when he passed through Washington on his way to Warm Springs. Then came the crux of the telegram:

> I had already arranged to meet a number of the Democratic leaders of the present Congress late this month at Warm Springs. It will be helpful for me to have your views and all pertinent information when I meet with them.
>
> I hope that you also will see them at the earliest opportunity, because

in the last analysis, the immediate question raised by the British, French and other notes creates a responsibility which rests upon those now vested with executive and legislative authority.[16]

Roosevelt was serving notice that the responsibility remained Hoover's, and that Hoover could not negotiate without taking into account the Democratic leaders in Congress. Stimson considered the telegram a rebuff to Hoover, but seemed pleased enough that Roosevelt had not rejected the invitation.

Hoover seems not to have been as sanguine, since, as Stimson noted, "He had wrapped himself in the belief that the state of the country really depended upon his reelection." When Stimson lunched with the President two days after Roosevelt's reply, he found Hoover free from the terrible strain and pressure of the previous weeks, but still with "some of the spirit of the campaign on him." In consequence, Hoover and Roosevelt prepared for the conference with mutual suspicion as dark as though they were heads of two great rival states near the brink of war. Stimson noted in his diary that Hoover was unhappy over Roosevelt's suggestion that they confer by themselves: "The President doesn't want to see him alone. He has been warned by so many people that Roosevelt will shift his words, that he wants some witnesses. So he is proposing to call some Congressional leaders to meet Roosevelt at that time. Roosevelt doesn't want to meet them." Stimson managed to persuade Hoover that he should see Roosevelt alone briefly, but need not at that time take up the critical matters about which they were meeting.[17]

On November 17, President Hoover telephoned Governor Roosevelt to make detailed arrangements for the meeting, and while they conversed with wary cordiality, Hoover took the unusual precaution of assigning a White House stenographer to take down their every word. This transcript, and one of a subsequent brief telephone conversation in January contain no significant revelations, but are evidence both of Hoover's suspicions and the flavor of actual discourse between the President and the President-elect. They indicate Roosevelt's tendency to give seeming quick agreement to a matter about which he would then have second thoughts:

HH: Good morning.
FDR: Good morning, Mr. President, how are you?
HH: All right.
FDR: They tell me you had a little rest.
HH: I have and I hope you have had too.
FDR: I have been in bed for five days. I had a real case of flu.
HH: That is too bad.

FDR: I got up today, for the first time came downstairs. I want to know if it is all right for you if I come on Tuesday next.

HH: That will be fine.

FDR: I thought if that is all right I would take the ten thirty out of New York and get in at three thirty to Washington and if it is all right come to the White House from the train.

HH: I have a number of things I would like to discuss with you, and I wonder if you could bring someone with you. Because there are a lot of things ought to be looked into which cannot be decided on the minute. A secretary or somebody —

FDR: Yes, I can bring a secretary. I hadn't thought of anybody.

HH: I would like to bring in Ogden Mills because I would like to give you an outline of what is going on abroad, and I wonder if there is someone you could bring along. I would like to have somebody on your side to start studying these questions as a matter of helpfulness to you, as I have a feeling that we have to put up national solidarity.

FDR: That is right.

HH: There is another thing. I had expected to call on either Tuesday or Wednesday a meeting of the ranking members of the two finance committees as I have to make a reply to these foreign countries. I was wondering whether you would like to have me call them an hour after you have come into conference with me and we could go on and have a time with them about it.

FDR: Yes. I was planning to stop over at the Mayflower on Tuesday night and see them Wednesday morning before I go on to Warm Springs.

HH: There is one thing in the whole thing that requires immediate action and that is the reply to those countries.

FDR: Yes, that is right.

HH: There are other things that need ironing out with respect to their commitments, but the one definite thing is a note of reply that we should send to them.

FDR: That is right. Perhaps we could do that on Wednesday morning.

HH: Get the leaders in on Wednesday morning together.

FDR: Fine. I will see you on Tuesday then. Thank you.[18]

Roosevelt was being as cautious as Hoover even though his words seemed to convey only assent. A little later that same day, Hoover wired Roosevelt that he was calling the three Republican and Democratic members of the Senate Finance Committee and the House Ways and Means Committee, which had hitherto dealt with the debt question, to meet with him on Wednesday morning. He hoped Roosevelt would join the meeting, as Roosevelt had suggested in the telephone conversation would be agreeable. By the time Roosevelt received the telegram, he had changed his mind, and wired back: "In pursuance of my thought expressed to you in my first telegram that our conversation should be wholly personal and informal, it seems best that I should determine whether it is proper for me to attend your conference on Wednesday . . . after you and I have talked on Tuesday afternoon." [19]

Roosevelt informed Hoover that he was bringing Moley, and that evening when Moley arrived from New York asked him to come to the conference. Tugwell commented in his diary, "I was naturally very much pleased at this since it meant that the advice of academic people still continued to be valuable to him even though he was now in the position of President-elect and could, of course, command the advice and time of anyone in the country." [20]

As they prepared to meet the President, Roosevelt and Moley were suspicious because the Hoover administration had not brought up the debt question earlier when Great Britain failed to make provision for payment of the installment in its budget. Roosevelt was so influenced by a rumor that Hoover had made some covert promise of debt postponement or forgiveness to the British prime minister, Ramsay Mac-Donald, or the French premier, Pierre Laval, during their visits to Washington that he jotted on one of several cards he was preparing as reminders to use during the conference, the notation, "secret agreements by Pres." [21]

And ominously in the background was Congress as a brake on Roosevelt. Stimson wrote on November 16:

> The President is willing to recommend a revision to Congress. On the other hand, Congress is coming back red hot against any concession whatever. Every Congressman is shooting his mouth off in the newspapers with fulminations against any concession of any installment, or any amount whatever; and the situation is very difficult, because Roosevelt probably will not take any strong hand in the middle of the session, particularly when it is principally not his own. On the other hand an incompetent position on debt relations will probably set back the whole situation of recovery.[22]

The debt question was only one of the pressures of the congressional Democrats upon Roosevelt. Of far more importance, they were trying to negotiate with him an entire recovery program. Even if Roosevelt had favored Hoover's viewpoint, he would scarcely have dared jeopardize these relationships in advance of assuming office. Worried Wall Street financiers doubted if Roosevelt could control Congress if he wished. Lamont, who believed failure to allow debtor nations to postpone their December 15 payments would have "far-reaching adverse consequence," telephoned Stimson that Owen D. Young, who had negotiated the funding of the war debts, had had two talks with Roosevelt. While Roosevelt wanted to be cooperative, he continued to insist that the question of postponement was a problem the Hoover administration must meet. Roosevelt would promise, according to Young, that only if Hoover would boldly propose postponement for six months would he urge his followers in Congress not to object. But Young, who was upset, admitted to Secretary of the Treasury Ogden L. Mills that Roosevelt would not be able to prevent the Democratic wild men in Congress from refusing any concession.[23]

Even as minor a matter as Roosevelt's announcement that he would confer with Hoover in Washington led to some ominous rumblings. Senator Key Pittman of Nevada, who was to become chairman of the Senate Foreign Relations Committee in the new Congress, complained privately:

> I have become very uneasy at the drift of things. The Governor and his advisers seem to have forgotten that Franklin is not yet President. They have also forgotten Franklin's oft-repeated statement that he intends to cooperate and work in complete harmony with Congress. Some recent hasty statements would indicate that this has been forgotten. Moratoriums and war debts are a matter of governmental action, not executive.
>
> A few of us aided in keeping Franklin out of mistakes on the tour and it seems there are some usurpers who are not so much interested in the matter. This beautiful picture can be smashed in a second by the careless handling of an axe. Silence, golden silence, on the part of the victor will be the safest and soundest program.[24]

Governor Roosevelt in Albany did not need to be told to be laconic. On November 15, still weak from influenza, he received a few reporters in his upstairs bedroom. There, in the massive mahogany bed, propped up with three pillows, he puffed on a cigarette and in high spirits parried their queries about the forthcoming meeting with Hoover. To each question he responded only by laughing and putting his finger to his lips.[25]

Two days later, downstairs in the front study at the Executive Mansion, Roosevelt displayed himself to the reporters as being actively the governor of New York; he was busy drafting his Thanksgiving proclamation and earlier had been working on the state budget, which he pledged would embody large economies and be absolutely balanced. The following day he surprised the newspapermen by admitting to his study three leaders of a group of hunger-marchers. For forty-five minutes leaning forward in his chair, he listened while the three men, one of them tieless, sat in a semicircle around him, presenting their demands for greater aid. Repeatedly he broke in, and scarcely raising his voice, firmly challenged their statements. "In the next six weeks," asserted one of the men, "many people will be dying."

"Don't be silly," Roosevelt retorted, "No one is going to starve. We have plenty of money to last until the next Legislature meets."

Several times the men demanded that Roosevelt tell President Hoover he must leave them alone when they set out on a march to Washington later that month. "I am just a private citizen," Roosevelt replied, "and I cannot tell the President to do anything." [26]

In this spirit Roosevelt went to Washington.

CHAPTER III

The Meeting at the White House

I felt . . . my hands should not be tied by preliminary
limitations.
— FDR, *1937.*

On the interlocking questions of war debts, disarmament, and the forthcoming World Economic Conference, Roosevelt in his negotiations
with President Hoover refused to commit himself in advance of assuming authority. He insisted that his visit to the White House on November
22, 1932, would be only one item on a crowded Washington agenda
which would include a visit to the National Press Club and numerous
talks with congressional leaders. He declared that he would go to
President Hoover as a listener, expecting to retain his "objective attitude
as a 'private citizen' " unless, as he did not expect, the President submitted a specific debt revision program. He dramatized his close association with Congress by arranging for Speaker Garner to board his train
at Baltimore. Roosevelt had asked Garner to ride with him before arrangements had been made for the White House meeting, but on the
way to Washington he invited Garner to attend the conference. The
invitation was entirely correct on Roosevelt's part, since Hoover had
asked him to bring any of the Democratic congressional leaders he
wished. But when the rumor reached the President that Garner might
unexpectedly come, he telephoned Secretary Stimson in some agitation
to ready himself to balance the Speaker if need be. Garner declined
Roosevelt's invitation, and equilibrium was restored.[1]

When Roosevelt arrived at the White House at about 3:45, a crowd
of several hundred people at the south gate greeted him with warm
informality shouting, "Hurrah for President Roosevelt!" Roosevelt,
grinning and waving his hat, left these friendly faces to encounter
the grim ones of President Hoover and Secretary Ogden Mills. Since
Hoover had insisted upon Mills' attending, Roosevelt brought along
Raymond Moley. The Chief Usher conducted them into the Red Room,

where President Hoover, looking grave and uneasy, greeted them.*
They seated themselves in red chairs around a small mahogany table. A
crackling wood fire cast highlights on four presidential portraits on the
walls, of Adams, Jefferson, Madison, and Grant, and was reflected in
the large crystal chandelier. Cigars and cigarettes were passed; Hoover
took a cigar and Roosevelt a cigarette. Everyone lit up rather nervously,
and through a growing haze of smoke the discussion began.

President Hoover launched upon a lengthy review of American policy
on the debts, glancing only occasionally at Roosevelt, and instead fixed
his gaze first upon the carpet, and later upon Moley, to Moley's discomfort. "Before he had finished," Moley recalls, "it was clear that we
were in the presence of the best-informed individual in the country on
the question of debts. His story showed a mastery of detail and a clarity
of arrangement that compelled admiration." He pointed out that the
loans had been made in good faith, that negotiations had always been
with each separate nation, that debts had already been scaled down in
relation to the ability of each nation to pay, and that they must be
treated separately from reparations. And yet it might well be that the
British could not, and the French would not, pay their December installments. According to Moley, who wrote out full notes that night:

> And then Mr. Hoover moved to one of those plausible generalizations
> into which he so frequently fell. Either cancellation *or* default, he said
> would shake international credit. And that would cause economic
> shivers to pass through this country.
>
> He did not add what was unquestionably in his mind at that point
> — his complete rejection of the Roosevelt theory of the depression. . . .
> To have said that at the moment, of course, would have brought out
> into the open a fundamental difference of opinion between Roosevelt
> and himself. But the mere fact that the argument remained unspoken
> did not make the moment less awkward.†

* I have followed two contemporary first-hand accounts of the conference, one
by Moley and the other by Hoover. Moley's, based on extensive notes written that
evening, was published in *After Seven Years* in 1939, at a time when he was dis-
illusioned with Roosevelt. Any bias in Moley's account would not be likely to be
in favor of Roosevelt. Hoover wrote a full and illuminating memorandum that
same day, which unfortunately he failed to follow when he wrote his reminiscences. On the conference itself and much that preceded and followed it,
Hoover's memory is faulty. Thus in his *Memoirs* Hoover confuses the conference
of November 22, 1932, with a later conference of January 20, 1933. He declared
that Stimson attended, which was true in January and not in November, and men-
tions several issues which were of focal importance in January, and either not
mentioned or peripheral in November. He does not mention the January conference in his *Memoirs*.[2]
† In the detailed memorandum that he wrote immediately after the conference,
Hoover declared:

> We canvassed the probable attitude of each of the principal governments in
> the matter of the December 15th payments; the possibilities of default and its

There was a pause. Then Hoover cleared his throat and continued. While *both* cancellation and default ought to be avoided at all costs, we could not insist upon payment without extending some hope of revision or re-examination unless we wanted to force the European nations to establish a united front against us on economic questions.[4]

Dire consequences would follow if the United States refused a request from the debtor governments to discuss their obligations, Hoover predicted. He declared (according to the *aide-mémoire* he wrote that same day), "It would mean a breakdown of the Economic Conference, the Arms Conference, and might break down the alignment of Europe in support of our mutual policies in the Far East and leave us isolated in this field."

Roosevelt interrupted to ask Hoover the questions he had jotted in advance on cards. These elicited additional information from the President, and occasionally from the secretary of the treasury. Then Hoover went on with his exposition, detailing how no change in debt arrangements could be made without the approval of Congress, and that he felt Congress would refuse to approve any new arrangement. This was the crux of the matter. The way out of the impasse would be to reconstitute as a negotiating body the Debt Commission (which had produced the Dawes and Young plans of the 1920s), with three members from each house of Congress and three presidential appointees, the latter to be named with Roosevelt's approval. Negotiations with the debtor nations could begin at once and carry into the Roosevelt administration.

Roosevelt, nodding his head, said, "I see no reason why the old legal maxim that a debtor ought to have access to the creditor shouldn't prevail," and turning to Moley sought his adviser's reaction. Moley protested that the commission might create more uncertainty than it would settle, and that the best way might be for the State Department to undertake separate exploratory discussions with each of the nations during the next few months. These would require no approval from Congress. Roosevelt (Moley thought) was ready to accept Hoover's premises, but preferred rather than the Debt Commission that the President directly negotiate revisions. Hoover's impression (as he recorded it later that day) was rather different:

consequences. We pointed out that these consequences would be first, the great difficulty of reviving the debts, the fact that the United States would have to pursue the question instead of being pursued by the debtors as at the present moment, for some basis of agreement. We also pointed out the dangers to the world of having a process of default signified by such a gigantic action. We pointed out the probabilities of consolidated joint action in the different governments against us, and that we would be unable to make those distinctions between governments necessary if we were to realize the largest sum possible out of these obligations, pointing out that France could pay in full without difficulty, whereas perhaps some others would have to have at least some partial temporary postponements.[3]

I finally proposed that I would recommend to Congress the establishment of a properly authorized commission to deal with this whole question. The Governor undertook to express his approval in principle. It was finally agreed that Mr. Mills should meet with him on Wednesday morning, show him the statement which we proposed and submit a draft of the supporting statement which he would issue. He made no reservations on this undertaking except that he would not expect to become responsible for every word of the statement, but would support the principle of creation of a definite body authorized for negotiation.[5]

Considerable pulling and hauling between Roosevelt and Hoover followed. Finally they decided to issue separate statements on the discussion, in the hope that the overlapping areas of agreement in them would be large enough to reassure the nation. With this agreed, Mills and Moley left Hoover and Roosevelt, who had a few minutes of private conversation. Shortly after six the meeting ended.

It ended, shockingly enough, with Roosevelt and Moley firm in their view that they had not accepted Hoover's proposal to reconstitute the Debt Commission, and with Hoover and Mills equally certain that there had indeed been an agreement to reconstitute it.

From Moley's and Hoover's sets of notes, both put on paper within a few hours, it is easy to see how out of the complex discussion misunderstanding developed. Assent to the method of issuing a communiqué may have seemed to Hoover and Mills assent to the idea of a Debt Commission. Part of the trouble, no doubt, was Roosevelt's ready affability. There was, as the transcript of his telephone conversation with Hoover shows, a willingness to say "yes" when he actually meant "I see what you are saying." Further, Roosevelt desired to reach an accommodation, and may well have decided definitely against the idea of a Debt Commission only after he had left the meeting. During the meeting it was Moley more than Roosevelt who opposed creating the commission. An indication of Roosevelt's willingness to act in cooperation with Hoover, if the President-elect could do so on his own terms, is what transpired during the few minutes of private conversation between the two. Roosevelt asked Hoover to help obtain passage of a farm bill permitting the domestic allotment; Hoover refused, since he opposed the scheme. Each man would cooperate, but only in keeping with his principles.

The meeting was pleasant enough, and only in retrospect came to seem an occasion of animus and deceit. Immediately afterward, Hoover jotted down concerning Roosevelt, "The impression he left on my mind was a man amiable, pleasant, anxious to be of service, very badly informed and of comparatively little vision. My impression at the moment is that he will not carry through on his agreement." [6]

Less than an hour after the meeting, when Secretary of State Stimson called the President to ask what had transpired, Hoover, according to Stimson: "told me that they had spent most of their time in educating a very ignorant, and as he expressed it, a well-meaning young man. But they thought they had made some progress. He told me that Roosevelt had promised to come out in favor of the President's and Mills' plan."

Stimson was startled, since he had just heard on a 6:45 news broadcast that Roosevelt had told newspapermen that he did not intend to coerce Congress and that the responsibility for debt negotiations rested with the present administration. "This looks," wrote Stimson, "as if after having told the President at six o'clock that he would go with him, he had by six forty-five said something quite different to the press. This made a very unpleasant impression." At 9:15 the next morning, when Stimson saw the President and Mills at the White House, he found them "both very much excited over Roosevelt's attitude the night before, and both had the same idea that I had gotten, only more accentuated, that he had let them down." [7]

Meanwhile, Roosevelt had spent the previous evening in a meeting of much more significance to him than that with Hoover — a lengthy conference with the Democratic leaders of Congress to settle upon a course of action for the lame duck session, which would run until inauguration day. As was imperative, if he were to retain their confidence, he described to them at some length what had transpired at the White House, and assured them he had made no commitments except to agree with President Hoover that there should be no request to Congress for suspension of the December 15 debt payments. With the debt question cleared away, he went on to matters of domestic legislation which seemed more important.[8]

When Hoover faced the same congressional leaders, sitting around the cabinet table at 10 o'clock on the morning of November 23, he found them unyielding. He explained conditions to them as he had to Roosevelt, but they were, in Stimson's words, "a pretty hard-boiled lot." Speaker Garner and Majority Leader Henry T. Rainey, acting as spokesmen, declared the House would not vote for a debts conference or any suspension of December 15 payments.[9]

As for Roosevelt, he talked sympathetically for about a half-hour to Secretary Mills that morning of November 23 when Mills brought him the President's statement to read before its release.* Roosevelt himself

---

* Hoover in his *Memoirs* asserts that when Mills called the next morning, Moley informed Mills that Roosevelt would not be able to see him. Stimson, on the other hand, recorded in his diary the informal, easy way in which FDR talked to Mills, and Moley reports an interchange between them:

Mills was grave and tense, Roosevelt gay and nonchalant.

After the amenities had been satisfied, Mills sat down, opening a typewritten manuscript. "Well, Ogden," said Roosevelt facetiously, "you must have sat up

issued a statement later in the day en route to Warm Springs, drafted by Moley with the aid of Bernard Baruch, in which, as he had promised, he endorsed Hoover's four historic principles, but suggested that future negotiations could take place through "the constituted channels of diplomatic intercourse." In essence, newspapers declared Roosevelt was saying that debts were not his baby. Some newspapers were critical of Roosevelt's attitude. The *Baltimore Sun* asserted that might legally be so, but "this baby, which is not now his, may soon develop into an unruly stepchild, permanently lodged under his roof, and disposed to play with matches." President Hoover had won the round in newspaper editorial columns; Roosevelt had aligned himself with public opinion and the strong prejudice of the Democratic leaders in Congress.[11]

The colloquy in the White House and the issuance of two rival communiqués to the press did more harm than good. It carried over and intensified in both Hoover and Roosevelt, who fundamentally were both men of good will, an unjustified suspicion that the other was not acting in good faith.

The gulf between Roosevelt's and Hoover's positions would on the surface seem relatively minor; it was the difference between conducting negotiations through a special commission and through regular channels. What made it deep was that President Hoover felt nothing could be accomplished concerning either debtor nations or Congress without Roosevelt's endorsement. Hoover points out in his *Memoirs*, "The suggestion that I should use my powers to negotiate through diplomatic channels was futile because no foreign power would seriously negotiate with a disappearing administration. Further, the Congress would take no action without his approval." [12]

Hoover's compelling feeling that he could make no progress without Roosevelt's active cooperation, and that economic recovery depended upon international action, led to renewed pressure in the days that followed. Secretary of Commerce Roy D. Chapin reported at a cabinet meeting that since the week before the election, when it had become apparent Roosevelt would win, business had been deteriorating to a critical point. The President, Mills, and Stimson felt that the only way to check the deflationary spiral was to get the world back onto a gold standard, and that could be done only by first restoring it in Great Britain. A British return to gold in turn could come only through a prompt settlement of the debt question. Hoover's advisers urged him to recommend to Congress as strongly as possible the necessity of settling the debts. Hoover agreed to do so.*

all night working on that." Mills' face hardened. Without looking at Roosevelt he said, "This is a very important document," and proceeded at once to read the statement.[10]
* Stimson wrote in his diary:

After December 15, when the British paid their debt installment and the French defaulted, Hoover acted. Preliminary to sending a message to Congress on December 17, he tried to enlist the support of Roosevelt in an elaborate scheme. On Saturday evening, December 17, he sent a lengthy telegram inviting Roosevelt to join with him in the selection of a commission which should first negotiate separate agreements with each debtor nation, perhaps coordinately be involved in the arms conference already underway, and then, above all, participate in the forthcoming World Economic Conference. Once again Hoover was trying to obtain Roosevelt's endorsement of a scheme, and this time it was one which would directly tie together the questions of debts, armaments, and international economic recovery.[14]

Already on the previous day Moley and Tugwell had forewarned Roosevelt that Hoover might make another effort to force him into an international program for recovery which would be incompatible with the domestic measures they were planning. They had suspected what was coming because of their conversations with the two delegates President Hoover had sent to the preliminary meeting in Geneva on October 27 to plan the World Economic Conference. These were Dr. Edmund E. Day, of the Rockefeller Foundation, and John H. Williams, professor of political economy at Harvard, both exponents of views attractive to Hoover and Mills. Williams was especially eager to persuade Great Britain to return to the gold standard. Before leaving for Geneva, Day had shown the agenda to Tugwell, although the presidential campaign was not yet over. To Tugwell it had seemed negative; neither war debts nor tariffs were to be discussed. Tugwell, who had consulted with Roosevelt, suggested that since the tariff had been one of the chief issues during the campaign, it should be added to the agenda if Roosevelt's group had anything to say.[15]

After the election, when Day and Williams returned from Geneva, Day reported to Tugwell that the meeting there had been fairly futile. Another organization meeting would be held in January to prepare for the conference itself in April. Moley and Tugwell, meeting with Day at the Harvard Club in New York City, explained to him their view that

He said the people had been quiet for three years, and had shown wonderful patience, but that they are nearing the end of that patience. The election, he actually said, had been a good thing so far as the condition of the people was concerned. It gave them a chance to blow off steam. But now, when they find that this new crowd are not going to settle the question and save them, there is going to be real trouble, and it is coming right off. He pointed out the great number of business orders which had been given before election contingent on the success of Hoover. All of these had been withdrawn and business has slumped again. We all agreed that it was necessary to take some bold step in order to change this psychology. For once I was delighted to hear the President say, as he did, that it would play into the hands of the Democrats but my goodness, the country was more important than anything else.[13]

debts should not be canceled, and could not even be diminished until public opinion in the United States had been prepared. Consequently, they should be kept separate from the conference agenda. They tried with some difficulty to convince Day that there should be three separate questions for international negotiation which ought not be confused: debts, disarmament, and concerns to take up at the Economic Conference. The matters for the conference to consider, they had established in conversations with Roosevelt, should be: "the general regulation of commodity production throughout the world to reduce surpluses, the problem of stability of exchanges which was especially acute because of the recent fall in the pound after Great Britain went off the gold standard, the matter of negotiated tariffs, and other matters which could be said to be much more strictly economic and less involved in controversies of a political nature."

Already by December 10, Tugwell and Moley were aware that Hoover planned to mix debts and disarmament with the other economic questions and expected to communicate with Roosevelt again. Consequently, they arranged for Roosevelt to confer with Day, Williams, and the two of them at Hyde Park on Sunday, December 18. By coincidence it was the previous evening that Hoover had sent his telegram to Roosevelt requesting cooperation in selecting delegates. Moley was absent from the conference because of illness, but Roosevelt explained his position to the two delegates and laid out a tentative time schedule. As Tugwell recorded it:

> We were to have informal conversations with the British in order to come to a tentative arrangement with them which both Day and Williams and we agreed was absolutely necessary to the success of the Conference. However, these conversations were not to begin until about the 25th of February so that they could last until March 4th when Roosevelt had become President. The final agenda meeting was to be held in London on the fifteenth of March and the Conference itself was not to be held until about July 1st.

What complicated Roosevelt's proposed schedule was the firm feeling he shared with his advisers that he must refuse to join with President Hoover in the immediate appointment of delegates, for fear Hoover would pressure them toward his opposing viewpoints. Day and Williams, who were to see Hoover and Mills on December 20, promised to try to delay the January planning meeting, since it was likely to be as fruitless as the October meeting had been. Roosevelt wanted results. According to Tugwell: "We did not want the Conference to fail. In fact, we felt that a great deal depended on it but we wanted time in which to negotiate about the debts and to carry further the disarmament conversations which Mr. Norman Davis had been conducting in Europe." [16]

Consequently, Roosevelt and his advisers encountered some difficulty in answering Hoover's telegram. Its threat that Hoover would lay the matter before Congress if Roosevelt failed to cooperate did not add to its attractiveness. Tugwell found it quite confused. The problem was "to straighten out the questions involved and to make a concise and understandable document of our reply." Roosevelt enlisted almost everyone available. In the morning he discussed the telegram and his approach with an old friend, Adolph Miller of the Federal Reserve Board, who happened to be calling that day. Miller drafted a reply. Roosevelt took Tugwell and Representative Lewis Douglas of Arizona back to Albany with him and spent that evening preparing an answer. Meanwhile, Berle took a copy of Hoover's telegram to Moley who was ill in New York so that Moley could telephone suggestions to Albany.

Roosevelt also must have been under some pressure to cooperate with Hoover. On Monday, December 19, still mulling over his draft reply, he conferred for several hours with Owen D. Young. Afterwards Roosevelt told the press they had engaged in "a general discussion of economics" — and indeed government reorganization had been taken up.

"Did you discuss the war debts situation?" a reporter asked.

"Wouldn't you like to know?" Roosevelt replied smilingly.

"Have you received any word from President Hoover?" another asked.

"I can't tell you." [17]

Obviously the answer to both questions was "yes," and further, Young must have tried to persuade Roosevelt to accept Hoover's view.

The President, just before sending the telegram, had called Colonel House to enlist his support. House promised to telephone Roosevelt at once. Hoover also told House (who presumably informed Roosevelt) that he was planning to send a message to Congress on Monday. Thus the reference to the forthcoming message in Hoover's telegram was intended to be a statement of fact (not an implied threat as some of Roosevelt's advisers had assumed) that Hoover would act unilaterally if Roosevelt would not accept. Then, when Roosevelt's secretary called the White House on Monday to explain that because Hoover's telegram had not reached him until Sunday evening he would not be able to get an answer back until that night, the men in the White House in turn were suspicious. "It seemed that this was rather a fishy story," Stimson noted tartly. "Our inference was that Roosevelt was waiting to see what the message was before he answered." [18]

Hoover's message to Congress on December 19 emphasized that the deflationary deterioration of world price levels had been seriously affected by the abandonment of the gold standard. Restoration of currency "is still the only practicable basis of international settlements and monetary stability so far as the more advanced industrial nations are concerned." Therefore Hoover declared he would immediately appoint a commission to deal with the interrelated questions of debts, armaments, and the world economy — meaning above all, currency stabilization.[19]

The President's emphasis upon the necessity of seeking a return to prosperity by restoring the gold standard among advanced countries drove a still wider gulf between Hoover and Roosevelt than did the interchange of telegrams. That became apparent only later. In drafting a reply, Roosevelt and those who assisted him had concentrated upon Hoover's effort to intertwine the three questions of debts, disarmament and the agenda of the Economic Conference, and his insistence upon a commission for which the two men would be jointly responsible. Roosevelt could see clearly enough why Hoover wanted to interrelate the economic questions, but was puzzled by the President's determination to act through a commission. Tugwell commented at the time:

> I think my solution was the only tenable one in the circumstances. It is that Mr. Hoover is a different kind of man than Mr. Roosevelt; he is a business executive type and feels he must delegate everything, which is why he cannot grasp the notion that the new administration will be run differently. The formal set up of governmental structure will, I imagine, never mean much to Mr. Roosevelt. It means almost everything to Mr. Hoover.[20]

So far as Roosevelt was concerned, Hoover could have his commission but not with Roosevelt's cooperation. In his reply, sent the evening of December 19, Roosevelt declared that for the time being the three international economic questions must be kept separate even though ultimately a relationship between two or all three of them might become clear. He endorsed Hoover's efforts to obtain disarmament, and reiterated his feeling that any debtor nation that wished to approach the United States should have the opportunity to do so. But concerning the impending Economic Conference he insisted that "a permanent economic program for the world should not be submerged in conversations relating to disarmament or debts." He granted there was a relationship, but insisted the questions were not identical. Therefore personnel conducting conversations in these three areas should not be the same. For this reason, and further because he refused to accept responsibility at a time when he was still lacking attendant authority, he firmly and flatly refused to join with President Hoover in the selection of delegates.[21]

Hoover and his advisers in Washington failed to understand and refused to accept the reasoning behind Roosevelt's carefully organized, courteous reply. They were sure of the correctness of their position and treated Roosevelt as if he were willfully ignorant. To them it indicated only a lack of understanding rather than a clear, fixed determination to follow an alternate course of action. Stimson wrote in his diary:

The telegram showed a most laughable, if it were not so lamentable, ignorance of the situation in which Roosevelt is going to find himself when he gets in on March 4th. The President was drawing up a telegram of his own in reply in an attempt to show how terribly off Roosevelt's message was, and it was a little bit combative and offensive. Mills and I, however, got him to tone down one or two sentences somewhat. Roosevelt had put himself terribly in the wrong, and I don't blame the President for wishing to show him up. [Roosevelt's] telegram was drafted for public consumption largely, but I cannot believe that with a little tact we can get him to yield the main point yet, and I was exercising my influence for that.

Williams and Day, reporting on their interchange with Roosevelt at Hyde Park on Sunday, corroborated Stimson's view that Roosevelt simply did not understand what he was facing. Day suggested that Roosevelt might be more cooperative, especially if he could be convinced that Hoover was playing fair and would give him a free hand in the selection of representatives. So Stimson and Mills persuaded Hoover to reframe his telegram in that direction.[22]

Thus it was that Hoover sent a conciliatory but emphatic second message to Roosevelt on the afternoon of December 20. "In the face of foreign conditions which are continually degenerating agricultural prices, increasing unemployment and creating economic difficulties for our people," he asserted, "I am unwilling to admit that cooperation cannot be established between the outgoing and incoming administrations which will give earlier solution and recovery from these difficulties." What he sought was not a solution but a device which could expedite the ultimate solution after March 4. "What I deem of the utmost importance is that when you assume responsibility on March 4 machinery of your approval will be here, fully informed and ready to function according to the policies you may determine." He conceded that debts, disarmament, and the agenda of the Economic Conference might require separate treatment, but insisted that they needed coordination and preparation by the then President or his designees. Therefore, Hoover proposed that Roosevelt send Owen D. Young, Colonel House, or whoever else of his party he trusted, "to sit with the principal officers of this administration in [an] endeavor to see what steps can be taken to avoid delays of precious time and inevitable losses that will ensue from such delays." [23]

To back the telegram, Hoover and his advisers tried to bring additional pressure upon Roosevelt. Stimson was still functioning under the assumption that nothing blocked cooperation "except the temperamental difficulties of the two men." Stimson tried to use Lew Douglas, who had been with Roosevelt on Sunday night, as a go-between to break the deadlock. He took Douglas to lunch and convinced him that the administration viewpoint was sound. Douglas suggested that Roosevelt failed to appreciate that time was running out, and proposed various ways to impress Roosevelt of the danger.* Ultimately, at Hoover's suggestion, Douglas had a long telephone conversation with Roosevelt from Stimson's house, forwarding Hoover's proposal that Roosevelt send someone like Young to Washington to discuss a timetable. Douglas declared afterwards that he was rather disappointed with Roosevelt's position, but thought it better than previously. Roosevelt was still refusing to take any responsibility for appointment of negotiators.

In the evening, Hoover at the White House told Stimson and Mills that he had learned the reason for Roosevelt's reticence. Confidential information had reached him that Roosevelt through Colonel House was preparing for a big dramatic meeting in Washington in March with Prime Minister MacDonald and perhaps the French, to arrange a settlement. A New York banking house was confidentially advising Roosevelt on questions involving exchange and the debts. Stimson regretted that this course would involve a loss of time and probably not bring a solution of the debt problem, but admitted to himself that it "is on the whole such a natural thing for him to do, that I think it is probably the real solution." [24]

Stimson failed to note that Roosevelt's rumored course of action (and there was some truth to the reports) meant that even while he was refusing to cooperate with Hoover, he was himself taking over some conduct of foreign affairs. Other nations wishing to negotiate must look to Albany or Hyde Park as well as Washington.

Roosevelt's reply on the evening of December 21 was very unsatisfactory to the White House. He reiterated his unwillingness to engage in joint action. Press reports from abroad, Roosevelt declared, already indicated that it would be interpreted there as "much more of a policy commitment than either you or I actually contemplate." [25]

This time President Hoover accepted Roosevelt's reiterated "no." He bluntly wired Roosevelt, "There are so many garbled versions and so much speculation as to our recent communications being circulated that I am today releasing them to the press in order that there may be no misunderstandings." And so he did, adding only a terse public statement: "Governor Roosevelt considers that it is undesirable for him to assent to my suggestions for cooperative action on the foreign problems outlined in my recent message to Congress. I will respect his wishes." [26]

---

* The groping for the proper entree to FDR was complicated. Douglas suggested that Mills call FDR, but Stimson felt the men distrusted each other too strongly. Stimson telephoned Mills who telephoned Hoover who suggested that Douglas call FDR.

Roosevelt could not let Hoover's announcement pass unchallenged, and immediately penciled a countercommuniqué to the press:

I am rather surprised at the W[hite] H[ouse] Statement issued this afternoon. It is a pity not only for this country but for the solution of world problems that any statement or intimation should be given that I consider it undesirable to assent to co-operative action on foreign problems.

I have made to the President the definite suggestion that he select his representatives to make preliminary studies. I have asked to be kept advised as to the progress of these preliminaries. I have offered to consult with the President freely between now and March 4th.

I hope that this practical program and definite offer of co-operation will be accepted.[27]

Of course, President Hoover had no intention of accepting these terms. Neither would he go ahead without Roosevelt to appoint a commission, since as Stimson had noted several days previously, if Roosevelt did not take responsibility it would be hard for the President to achieve anything unilaterally. Stimson was sure Hoover would "be very reluctant to hang around his own neck the sole responsibility for starting it." [28]

"There is little I can do now," Hoover confided to the United Press White House correspondent, Henry F. Misselwitz.

It isn't going to be as simple as he seems to think. He is going to find it tough going. . . . Those war debts are a liability to any administration, and the poor devil is going to discover they can't be solved by talking about them. . . .

[Every] new man that comes to this job thinks he can fix things up right off. We all come into it with the idea the other fellow was mostly wrong and with our own ideas of what should be done. But it doesn't work out always the way we think it will. . . .

I offered to share that great liability with him, to let him use me in any way he wished in these two months. I'm rid of a lot of grief now that he turned it down — but I'm filled with anxiety about what it means. If we had shown solidarity and a united party front, it would have meant much in these debt negotiations. It might have stopped the world from its present rapid downsliding. . . . I am most anxious about it, and doubtful what may come next. We'll just wait and see.

When Misselwitz asked if Hoover had changed his mind and would write a newspaper column after March 4, the President replied, "Not a chance. I'm going to play the game with them, and make no comment in print about the new administration." [29]

Once again Hoover had won the battle of communiqués so far as newspaper editorial writers of both parties were concerned. Publicists were divided in their views. Two commentators with large followings,

Frank Kent of the *Baltimore Sun* and Mark Sullivan of the *New York Herald-Tribune*, lamented that Roosevelt would be losing two months' time. Sullivan's opposition was to be expected; along with Mills and Stimson he had helped Hoover draft the reply to Roosevelt. On the other hand, Walter Lippmann, who was even more prestigious, argued that it would be wiser to negotiate quietly through the regular channels of diplomacy rather than through a commission which would "have focussed upon it the blinding light of world-wide publicity." Roosevelt was pleased by Lippmann's comment. "The fact remains," Roosevelt remarked, "that it was the President who forced this method of negotiation [by telegram] on me. If he had presumed a more simple course he would have called me on the telephone himself and suggested that Stimson come to see me and talk things over. All of the publicity was unnecessary." [30]

Democratic leaders in Congress expressed little concern. They would have displayed no strong objection if Hoover had chosen to appoint an executive commission on his own authority, since its negotiations would be subject to congressional approval — which of course was why Hoover did not unilaterally appoint a commission. But neither did the Democrats doubt Roosevelt's wisdom in refusing to share responsibility for the appointments. It was of importance to Roosevelt's future course to hold the support of Senator Pittman, who was the ranking Democratic member of the Foreign Relations Committee, and he had succeeded in doing so. Pittman wrote his hearty congratulations. "The selection of the word 'pity' in your interview," he commented, "was not only apt but intriguingly comprehensive."

Nor was all foreign opinion hostile. The aged Lord Grey of Fallodon, who had been British foreign minister during the First World War, wrote Colonel House:

> We feel the constitutional hiatus in your Government to be very tiresome, but I realize that Mr. Roosevelt must naturally be reluctant to take responsibility before he is in office and that to share responsibility with Mr. Hoover would give him a bad start and handicap his influence and power in advance.[31]

Neither the British Foreign Office nor French officials were disposed to be generous toward Hoover, perhaps because he failed to meet their expectations that, in the aftermath of the Lausanne agreement, the United States would cut war debts to the same token level as German reparations. Had Roosevelt cooperated with Hoover and assented to the reconstituting of a Debt Commission, as Stimson's economic adviser, Herbert Feis, thinks would have been wise, the result would have been little different. When Sir Ronald Lindsay cabled from Washington on November 14, 1932, that Roosevelt was likely to allow postponement of the debt payment but to want to trade debt concessions for disarmament or trade agreements, the Foreign Office prepared a memorandum analyzing these eventualities most unenthusiastically.* They appeared to the British as no more than further obstacles on the rocky road toward ultimate cancellation of the debts.[32]

To Roosevelt, Lamont wrote at the end of the controversy, "I thought the position you took with Mr. Hoover was logical and correct." That was remarkable, coming from a Morgan partner who had played an important part in negotiating the Young plan for reparations payment. To Lamont in conversation a little later, Roosevelt made an even more remarkable statement. He said he and Moley had more knowledge of the war debts question than Herbert Hoover and Ogden Mills. There was a reason for this startling statement, even a slight possibility it might be correct: by this time, in January 1933, Roosevelt, although not yet President, was engaging in direct discussions over the debts.[33]

Roosevelt's advisers were well satisfied at the end of December with the outcome of the interchanges with President Hoover. "For people who are new to the formulation of public policy," Tugwell noted, "we have come off fairly well in this exchange with a group who have been in charge of these matters for the government for a good many years." Hoover's advisers were equally contented. Hoover's telegrams "have been dignified and on a high plane of unselfishness," wrote Stimson. "They made Roosevelt look like a peanut."

So it was that the conduct of American foreign policy seemed to be in the hands of two rival groups issuing public communiqués at each other. It was a shift that Stimson did not yet seem to grasp when Roosevelt's final telegram arrived at the White House, but he was aware that things would not again be the same. He wrote in his diary, "I brought Ogden Mills to his home in my car . . . and we both felt that it was pretty much the end of the era." [34]

Roosevelt was indeed to begin a new era in foreign relations almost immediately, and surprisingly, Stimson, chief cabinet officer in the defeated administration, was to play a vital role in bringing it into existence.

---

* In the Foreign Office memorandum, P. Nichols wrote,
  [I]t seems that the U.S. Administration are going to ask for:

  (a) Further disarmament measures (which of course means measures of a nature strictly agreeable to the United States Government), and
  (b) Trade agreements or tariff concessions — this looks like a new feature, but it is I believe nothing more than a re-hash of Mr. Hoover's harebrained scheme for obtaining debt payments *from* us by selling *to* us surplus American agricultural commodities — a scheme which, even to the European man in the street, is clearly complete and absolute nonsense. In any case how in the world is (b) to fit in with Ottawa [the 1932 agreements giving "imperial preference" to goods sold within the British Empire]? Do the United States administration think it possible that we should be ready to jettison the whole Ottawa settlement within six months or a year of its conclusion?

CHAPTER IV

The Heir Apparent and the Congressional Barons

> I hope to cooperate with the whole Congress — Democrats and Republicans alike. I expect to regard Congress as the coordinate branch of the government that it was intended to be. . . . The Constitution, however, clearly contemplated that the President might, without overstepping its proper functions, provide a degree of leadership for the varied points of view represented in the Congress.
>
> — FDR, *December 10, 1932.*[1]

Cooperation with Congress was a major theme of Roosevelt's public statements during the months before he took office, as well it might be. Unless Congress acted there would be no New Deal, and Roosevelt's presidency would become as fruitless as Hoover's. Yet if Roosevelt wished to obtain a sweeping program in a hurry he must depend upon Democratic leaders who had seldom distinguished themselves as innovators. As the seniority they built by continued election from safe districts had slowly carried them toward committee chairmanships, most of them had clung to the credo of their nineteenth-century small-town or rural upbringing. Their resistance to the Republican New Era of the twenties had come from their agrarian opposition to government favors for large business. When depression came, they were as reluctant as their conservative Republican colleagues to vote for government intervention to restore prosperity, and did so only when their constituents became desperate in 1931 and 1932.[2]

During the interregnum Roosevelt pursued a most cautious course in order not to upset these conservative Democratic leaders. He sought to build good will and confidence among them so that out of loyalty to their party and incoming President, even if not through conviction, they would in the future support his program. A score of years earlier, Roosevelt as a junior cabinet officer in Washington had witnessed with impatience Wilson's maneuvering to enlist Cleveland Democrats in the enactment of the New Freedom; now he faced a similar task. He would depend for the enactment of his program upon congressional leaders, most of whom had not wanted his nomination and who distrusted his progressive views. It was manifest that in time Roosevelt would clash with these conservative leaders, but he wished to postpone trouble as long as possible. New, more positive leadership could take over only slowly.

Pressing hard upon these conservative leaders were more dynamic men of progressive views, both Democrats and Republicans. Many of them had come to the support of Roosevelt even before his nomination, and had introduced into the Hoover Congress bills covering significant areas of the proposed New Deal. In the Senate they included men like the Democrats Robert Wagner and Edward P. Costigan; Republicans like George Norris and the younger Robert M. La Follette. In the House had been restless liberals like the Republican Fiorello La Guardia, defeated in the Democratic landslide, and numerous young Democrats from both the South and northern cities. During the 1920s, these progressives, operating across party lines, had harassed the Harding, Coolidge, and Hoover administrations. While prosperity lasted, government dedicated primarily to defense of the status quo was popular, and Senator George Moses of New Hampshire applauded as he scoffed at the dissidents as a disruptive minority, the "sons of wild jackasses." By 1931, as the depression worsened, the positive suggestions of the progressives won far more popular support and, pressured by their constituents, many moderate members of both houses began to vote with them. Previously cautious men like Cordell Hull of Tennessee joined in the demands for legislation. In the 1931–1932 session of Congress they enacted several of President Hoover's positive recommendations, and would have gone further except for his vetoes. They had seen in Governor Roosevelt a potential President who shared their views and would foster their programs. Consequently they supported Roosevelt during the campaign of 1932. The alliance between Roosevelt and the congressional progressives was manifest and continuing. During the interregnum he assured several of them privately that he still shared their views; they would be his mainstay.[3]

Whether progressives should substantially share in the Democratic congressional leadership was a touchy question that several senators raised among themselves soon after the 1932 election. William Gibbs McAdoo, President Wilson's secretary of the treasury, newly elected senator from California, made a suggestion to his old supporter, the progressive senator from Montana, Thomas J. Walsh, "It seems to me that decided concessions must be made to the liberal and progressive elements within the party," wrote McAdoo, "and that some recognition must be made also of the Republican progressives who supported us so effectively." [4]

Walsh favored a compromise course. He assured McAdoo that he would urge that three leading Republican progressive senators, George Norris, Hiram Johnson, and Robert M. La Follette, be permitted to retain their committee chairmanships. But as for the rather slow-going senator from Arkansas, Joseph Robinson, who would be majority leader, Walsh thought that despite the vociferous objections of Senator Huey Long, Robinson would be able to retain his leadership without formidable opposition. With remarkable accuracy he prophesied: "While Joe is by no means quite so progressive as you or I would like him to be, it must be said for him that he is not a reactionary and goes along with the majority though not always able to accept whole-heartedly the views of the majority." [5]

This in essence was the type of congressional leadership with which Roosevelt would have to work. He had had four years of experience outbesting the Republican majority leaders in the New York legislature, slow-footed sparring partners seldom able to parry his thrusts. The tough and adroit political warriors leading Congress would be entirely different, as Roosevelt had learned when as an inexperienced young assistant secretary of the navy he had had one or two rough bouts in committee hearings. And tactics for dealing with congressional leaders must be much more subtle and smooth, not only because they were of higher caliber, but because they were members of Roosevelt's own party. On the surface, at least, all must seem placid and harmonious. Differences must appear to be submerged in the interest of party loyalty. But beneath this bland surface there would unquestionably begin a fierce struggle for dominance, as they would seek out each other's weaknesses, and try to shape legislation to their own viewpoints. The Democratic congressional leaders would give the semblance of subservience to Roosevelt's wishes while they tried to push through the lame duck Congress a New Deal program of their own making with which to greet Roosevelt on inauguration day as an accomplished fact. It was not unlike the struggle in some medieval kingdom between the wily old barons and the supple young heir to the throne. The heir had much to learn, and was not entirely skillful at the outset, but he learned rapidly.

In the weeks immediately following his election, Roosevelt seems to have hoped that he could indeed, as people hoped, use the old Seventy-second Congress, meeting in lame duck session from December 5, 1932, until March 4, 1933, to obtain passage of a substantial part of his domestic recovery program. The House was narrowly Democratic, and the

Senate was Republican, but the Democrats by combining with progressive Republicans who had supported Roosevelt during the campaign could command adequate majorities in each house. In theory, therefore, it was possible for Roosevelt and the Democrats in Congress to begin work immediately on a new program. Roosevelt, like the suffering population, was eager to bring recovery, and to bring it quickly. But to expect much more than an appropriation bill from the lame duck Congress was a most ephemeral hope.[6]

There was scant possibility that Roosevelt could obtain basic legislation from the Congress, and a sure probability that if it differed in the least from Hoover's firmly fixed principles that the President would veto it. Until Roosevelt had the reins, especially those of patronage, firmly in his own grasp, he must consult and cajole the congressional leaders with especial finesse and gentleness.

Placing his emphasis upon cooperation, Roosevelt stopped in Washington on November 22 primarily to confer with congressional leaders, and only secondarily to meet with President Hoover concerning war debts. At 10:30 in the evening, at the end of a day which had included both the White House conference and a speech before the National Press Club, Roosevelt met the foremost Democrats of both houses in his relatively modest four-room apartment in the rear of the Mayflower Hotel. Careful of appearances, and worried about expenses, he had refused to take the luxurious ten-room State suite in the front of the hotel. It was a formidable array of Democrats who came to see him at the Mayflower, and they had incredibly little to offer. They were opposed to a special session after the inauguration, and were confident that they could push their very limited program through the lame duck session. It involved no more than legislation to balance the budget, legalize beer of a low alcoholic content, and perhaps provide farm relief. Also, of course, they were opposed to any immediate scaling down of foreign debts. Roosevelt talked to them until after midnight, and listening with apparent sympathy to their counsels, subscribed to their plans. Astutely he told them that he would not insist upon a special session if they could enact their entire program; otherwise he would have to call one. The leaders assured him they could obtain all the legislation; Roosevelt must have been privately sure they could not, especially since Hoover had told him that afternoon that he would not sign a domestic allotment farm bill. But he entrained for Warm Springs leaving the members of Congress feeling they could depend upon him.[7]

Roosevelt appeared so deferential to the Democratic leaders that one of them, Senator Cordell Hull, even envisaged a congressional advisory system — almost a regency — to aid the new President. Hull suggested to Colonel House, who informed Roosevelt:

The Governor should avail himself of the best expert assistance both in and out of Congress in dealing with each serious problem arising. . . . To avoid confusion, misunderstanding and jealousy, the Governor, in inviting and assembling persons for the purpose of conference, should ordinarily invite those in Congress according to rank, and then supplement by inviting any person or persons known to be expert on a given point or line.[8]

Both at Washington and Warm Springs, Roosevelt so convinced everyone that he was content with the congressional program and did indeed want to avoid a special session that he gave the impression that it was he who was pressuring the congressional leaders in this direction rather than the reverse. T.R.B. commented in the New Republic, "Perhaps Mr. Roosevelt is not to be blamed for his anxiety to have his first nine months in the presidency free from congressional interference." Some congressional leaders, taking him seriously, were worried by the implication that Roosevelt proposed only an exceedingly circumscribed New Deal program. One of them leaked word to the newspapers in mid-December that he had counseled Roosevelt it was high time to begin working out legislative details with members of Congress. The conservative Senator Tom Connally of Texas, conferring with Roosevelt at Warm Springs, years later professed disgust over the views he heard there. "Roosevelt still talked of balancing the budget and reducing government expenditures," Connally has reminisced. "He also stressed as a strict constructionist the constitutional limitations on the President and on the federal government. His face was tanned and rested and he puffed complacently on his cigarette. I thought it strange that a man who had campaigned as he had throughout the country would be so out of touch with reality." On the eve of the inauguration, Senator Hull, whose total program seemed to encompass only farm relief and the reduction of government expenditures, taxes, and tariffs, was still so worried for fear Roosevelt would not be progressive enough that he sent Josephus Daniels to remonstrate with the President-elect.[9]

Roosevelt was overplaying his hand in creating the impression that he was compliant toward the congressional conservatives. In so cooperating with them that he did not arouse their fears, he risked losing the confidence of the country. As it became amply plain to the nation (as it must in advance have been clear to Roosevelt) that the lame duck session would achieve little or nothing, its inadequacies weighed against Roosevelt. He could not separate himself from it, since the leaders continued publicly to visit upon him, ostensibly to ask his advice. Although Roosevelt repeatedly told newspapermen that he had no intention of dictating to the Congress, these visits fixed a considerable responsibility upon him.[10]

One after another, the leading senators and representatives called upon Roosevelt, first at Warm Springs, later in New York. One after another they talked to reporters upon leaving, usually hinting that the President-elect had looked with favor upon their proposals. The topics were the familiar ones: economy, beer, and farm relief, but not much new or concrete evolved from the interviews. An exception was Senator Robinson's statement at Warm Springs that the Senate would block further ratification of any of President Hoover's appointments, which would leave some fifteen hundred openings for the new Democratic administration to fill.[11]

Roosevelt had little choice but to emphasize economy during these weeks. He and the Democratic leaders in Congress had promised it during the campaign, and by the end of November, even before Congress met, President Hoover was putting them in the uncomfortable position of having to make good or repudiate a campaign pledge even before the new administration had taken office. The White House announced on November 19 that the President and his cabinet at an extraordinary session had devised a plan to reduce governmental expenditures by such a drastic amount, $700 million, that no new taxes would be needed. The saving would come through a government reorganization which would cut many bureaus and commissions to a skeleton or eliminate them completely. In the process it would abolish thousands of government positions which the Democrats would otherwise have been able to fill after March 4. Hoover was challenging the Democrats in Congress to cooperate with him and balance the budget, either by reducing expenditures (and jobs) or by voting additional taxes.[12]

Speaker Garner and Senate Minority Leader Robinson accepted the challenge. Hoover called them to the White House before Congress met and presented his plan as a means of lifting from the shoulders of Roosevelt, before the new administration began, the unpopular but essential task of lowering expenditures and raising taxes. Garner and Robinson agreed to cooperate.[13]

When Congress met, Hoover presented it with a budget proposing slashes of $544 million or about 17.7 percent, excluding interest and payments on the debt.* But because of uncontrollable items carried over from the previous fiscal year, it was still out of balance by $307 million. Hoover proposed that this deficit be met through a manufacturer's sales or excise tax of 2¼ percent covering practically all manufactures excepting food and perhaps some grades of clothing. Since Roosevelt

---

* The budget for the 1933 fiscal year, which had begun July 1, 1932, excluding debt items and estimated postal income, was $3,075,735,000. For 1934, President Hoover proposed $2,531,354,900 net.[14]

had made the suggestion during the 1932 campaign that the cost of federal operations be cut 25 percent, he did not challenge President Hoover's hypothesis that drastic government retrenchment was necessary.

Indeed, Roosevelt used economy as the reason for seeking in advance congressional authorization to reorganize the government. Late in December he conspicuously conferred with a conservative Kentuckian, Swager Sherley, who during the Wilson administration had been chairman of the House Appropriations Committee, and announced that he would need blanket executive authority in order to curtail federal expenditures. He wished specifically to have power over contractual relations with veterans and over executive reorganization. Curiously, he used the same argument Hoover had employed in talking to Garner and Robinson. He told congressional leaders that having been a state senator, he knew how enormous the pressure was against individual members of a legislature if they tried to reorganize the administrative offices. It should be a relief to the congressmen, he declared, if they delegated the power to him to put the reorganization into effect and let him be the whipping boy. At the same time they would retain the power to cancel any of his proposed changes. The leaders accepted Roosevelt's proposal favorably. Speaker Garner asserted Roosevelt should receive the most sweeping authorization compatible with a system of governmental checks and balances. He was ready to grant Roosevelt what he would deny Hoover.[15]

Garner was less pleased with another of Roosevelt's proposals, which was to set up parallel to the regular budget an extraordinary budget to cover certain public works expenditures. It would make Roosevelt's pledge to balance the budget — the regular budget, that is — considerably easier to attain. Garner protested that an emergency budget would be "simply a matter of bookkeeping," and would avail little. Other Democrats and many Republicans, including Undersecretary of the Treasury Arthur Ballantine, attacked Roosevelt's proposal as a false scheme which would obscure the real financial position of the government.[16]

The sharpest difference between Roosevelt and Garner developed over the question of new taxes. Garner had reason to think that he was acting in harmony with Roosevelt's wishes when he began to pressure reluctant Democratic representatives to support the Hoover tax program. Roosevelt had been telling visitors that he did not agree with congressmen who wished to postpone passage of a tax bill until after March 4. Rather he had been saying that the Republicans should offer legislation to balance the budget so that the onus of a deficit would not fall upon the Democrats. If the Republicans offered a tax bill that was reasonable and not radically counter to Democratic policies, the Democrats in Congress should cooperate to pass it.[17]

Under this rather hazy mandate from Roosevelt, Speaker Garner backed President Hoover's recommendation for a manufacturer's sales tax. Among farmers, laborers, and many retailers, the scheme was most unpopular. In the days following the President's message, the American Federation of Labor, the Grange, the Associated Dress Industries, the National Retail Dry Goods Association, and several distinguished economists all came out against the tax. In contrast, the New York Board of Trade and most prominent Republicans supported it. When reports reached Albany at the end of December that Garner was mustering support for the sales tax by assuring Democratic representatives that it had the governor's backing, Roosevelt was forced to act. If he had to choose between making good his pledge of a balanced budget through a conservative device, or of retaining the friendship of farmers and labor even at the risk of a continued deficit, he unhesitatingly chose the latter. His was also the economically sound course. Roosevelt's advisers were emphasizing to him that consumer purchasing power must be bolstered; a sales tax would inevitably have forced it still lower.[18]

Thus it was that Roosevelt, forced to take a position, let it be known emphatically through his anonymous associates in Albany that he was amazed by the news that Representative James W. Collier, chairman of the House Ways and Means Committee, was favoring the tax because he thought it the governor's wish. If need be, the Albany spokesmen asserted, Roosevelt would split with the Democratic leaders in Congress. To an old friend Roosevelt wrote:

> You are right in saying that a sales tax would be painless — but only painless to the unthinking. I think most people in this country realize that the general manufacturers' sales tax distributes the tax burden inequitably — people with less money have to pay a greater proportion than people with more money. It is the inequality of a general manufacturers' sales tax which makes it not only unpopular but also unfair.[19]

There were strong reactions in Washington to Roosevelt's firm disapproval. Speaker Garner loyally declared to reporters, "I guess that means the end of the sales tax for this session." But his private feelings came out when he went to the White House to apologize to President Hoover: "For the first time in my life I find myself unable to carry out an agreement.* Governor Roosevelt is opposed to what we have

---

* Garner's official biographer, cited by Hoover in his *Memoirs*, links Roosevelt's refusal to support the Hoover tax program with the banking crisis of some weeks later, and implies that as a result, "Scores of banks closed their doors between election and inauguration." [20]

planned, and it is a waste of time to try any legislation to which he will not agree." [21]

Agrarian Democrats were gleeful over Garner's discomfort. Representative John Rankin of Mississippi, who had led an anti–sales tax revolt the previous year, crowed that Roosevelt had "pulled some of our leaders out of a blind alley." Republican representatives helpfully rubbed additional salt into the Speaker's wounds. "Garner's statement would indicate that the crack of the whip has been heard if not actually felt," commented Fred Britten of Illinois. Britten added with unusual foresight that the manner in which Roosevelt had put a quietus on sales tax talk indicated that he "intends to dominate the next Congress with an iron hand and, if need be to appropriate the famous Roosevelt 'big stick.'" If so, Roosevelt intended to conceal the stick as long as possible behind velvet draperies. At the same time that he let be known his amazed disapproval of a general sales tax, he added that a week earlier by letter and telephone he had requested a conference with Speaker Garner.[22]

The meeting, which came to encompass the principal Democrats in both houses, was to be held in New York City on January 5. Already, before it met, the fate not only of tax legislation but of the entire Democratic agenda was in serious jeopardy. The *New York Times* on December 29 had inveighed editorially against the "do-nothing session." Consequently Roosevelt, by the time of his second conference with the Democratic leaders, was concerned not merely with taxes but with insuring that blame for inaction not be assessed against his party. He confided to Senator Pittman on December 29:

> It is my thought that if we can put the Beer bill and equally important, the farm legislation through, it will help enormously, even if either or both are vetoed. While a Special Session will probably be necessary, let us continue to make it clear that President Hoover rather than the Congress is the compelling factor in such a session.[23]

This was the argument he pursued with Garner and his cohorts on the evening of January 5.* The meeting served above all to dramatize to the press the determination of the Democrats to balance the budget and pass farm legislation in order to avoid a special session. The legalizing of beer, which only Roosevelt and Garner advocated with complete firmness, would serve to bring in considerable revenue. The remainder, the Democratic leaders proposed, should come through an increase in

---

* The group, according to the *New York Times*, was "representative of the more conservative elements in the party." It included Senators Robinson, Pittman, Hull, Byrnes, and Harrison, and Representatives Garner, Rainey, Rayburn, Collier, and Byrns. Sherley and Moley also attended. Roosevelt hinted that he would confer later with more progressive or radical leaders in the Congress.[24]

the income tax. The exemption for married persons should be lowered from $2,500 to $2,000, the initial rate be boosted from 4 to 6 percent, and the next level from 6 to 8 percent. The proposed rates would raise the income tax for those in lower brackets by a full 50 percent. In these depression years, it was a boost which would hit middle class people, but touch only a handful of farmers and laborers. At the conference, Roosevelt would commit himself no further than to withhold disapproval of the increase as a part of the budget-balancing program, a devious maneuver to avoid bearing the brunt of public protests, since actually the scheme was the handiwork of one of his Brain Trusters, Professor Schuyler Wallace of Columbia University. Moley had suggested it be sent to Senator James Byrnes, who in turn gave it to Senator Pat Harrison, who proposed it at the conference. But as might have been expected, when a howl went up from Congress, Roosevelt disavowed any connection with the scheme, and Speaker Garner reassured the potential rebels in the House that it was no more than a suggestion which would be taken up as a last resort. President Hoover, taking advantage of the dissidence in the Democratic ranks, on January 17 sent a stern special message again advocating a sales tax. The immediate response of the twelve Democratic members of the House Ways and Means Committee was to agree "off the record" to defer all questions of new taxes until a special session began. By this time they regarded it as inevitable, and expected Roosevelt to call it for April 17.[25]

Roosevelt, passing through Washington that week, again en route to Warm Springs, tried to whip some semblance of order into the Democratic ranks to try to obtain some positive legislation — if only for President Hoover's veto. There was little that either Democratic or progressive leaders, whether to the left or the right in their views, could report that was hopeful. Farm legislation that would bolster agricultural prices had passed the House but seemed unlikely to survive the onslaught of Ellison D. "Cotton Ed" Smith of South Carolina, the ranking Democratic member of the Senate Committee on Agriculture.

As for the budget, beer, and all other legislation, it was being stalled in the Senate while Huey Long of Louisiana carried on a strange filibuster, abetted by Republican conservatives, against Senator Carter Glass's bill to bolster the banks because it would allow branch banking. Through the depression there was vehement small-town sentiment against branches of outside banks or chain stores, which could undermine local banking and trade. Long was dramatizing that sentiment, and several Republican senators were happy to see Long embarrass the Democrats. "We're milling around here utterly unable to accomplish anything of real consequence," Senator Hiram Johnson complained to an intimate, placing the blame squarely upon Long, "the most irresponsible, impossible and impervious individual I have ever seen." Interestingly enough, Roosevelt in conversation with Thomas Lamont of J. P. Morgan & Co., blamed Glass for not withdrawing the branch banking section of his bill.[26]

Into this impasse came Roosevelt. Party leaders warned him in advance that he would have to exert his prestige if he wished any of the basic legislation to pass. Wisely he reiterated in advance that he would do no more than announce his general policies and leave the details to Congress. There no longer could be even a pretense that sufficient positive legislation could come out of the lame duck 'Congress to eliminate the need for a special session. Roosevelt expressed his hope after the Washington conferences that Congress would pass a compromise farm relief bill, providing domestic allotment restrictions on four major crops (although he knew that President Hoover would veto the measure if it were passed). The point had been reached when the same Democratic leaders who the previous fall had pressed against a special session were relieved to hear from Roosevelt that they could expect one in April at which he would present a balanced budget.[27]

In the meantime, Roosevelt in Washington succeeded in pleasing a wide array of visitors of differing political credos, through consulting them flatteringly, talking in generalities broad enough to embrace each point of view, and hinting of patronage. He left the antagonists Glass and Long both delighted with him. Long truculently went into his hotel room, asserting he "was going to talk turkey," and left a half-hour later with a big smile, asserting, "He is the same old Frank. He is just like he was before the election. He is all wool and a yard wide." And Senator Johnson, who was so scornful of Long, confided to a friend, "I like Roosevelt immensely. I like his good humor, his geniality, his genuine smile, and what I think was his ready agreement, generally speaking, with progressive principles." [28]

"It is a skillful, even a miraculous performance," reported Arthur Krock of the New York Times. "The only question is: How long will the unanimity last?" [29]

Roosevelt's ingratiating tactics had created an auspicious display of good will among the members of Congress. The mutual warmth between the President-elect and such diverse leaders could obviously endure only through a national emergency. As congressmen wrangled over legislation and as liberal and conservative Democrats in the House maneuvered behind their respective candidates to succeed Garner as Speaker, Roosevelt could maintain the fiction of neutrality only until he came into power.[30]

Already, he had conferred so frequently with Democratic leaders, and on the tax question had so firmly asserted himself, that the public was saddling him with some responsibility for the muddle. Their expectations were not being fulfilled, and into February, Roosevelt's prestige was waning. Even among congressional leaders, his vagueness by then was not wearing well. Senator Johnson, for all his enthusiastic admiration, admitted: "I imagined I observed that he was nebulous and uncertain about a definite program. . . . His fiddling here with his farm bill and his talk of balancing the budget, and the mode of raising taxes, have left rather a bad impression." [31]

Roosevelt's public stance did much to confirm the prejudice on the part of both congressional conservatives and many liberals throughout the land, that he was indeed what his enemies had so long charged, a lightweight, a "feather duster." It might have done him serious damage except for the incorrigible inactivity and basic conservatism of the lame duck session of Congress. True enough, behind the scenes Roosevelt was helping develop in Washington what was to become the first New Deal agricultural program, a vital and complex undertaking; * and the progressive senators and representatives were introducing bills that would form the basis for the relief program. What the public saw was that Congress was not enacting basic measures. Rather the Huey Long filibuster and lengthy proceedings against the sergeant-of-arms tied up the Senate through much of January and February. And, as the economy plummeted to new lows, Senate hearings provided a national forum for economic fundamentalism.[32]

Newspapers headlined the hearings as a "depression clinic" to guide Congress and the President-elect in formulating recovery legislation. The Republican chairman of the Senate Finance Committee called the hearings as a courtesy to Senator Pat Harrison of Mississippi, one of Baruch's inside circle, who would be the new chairman. For weeks, the nation's great financiers, industrialists, bankers, brokers, economists, and statesmen testified before it. With scarcely an exception, they reiterated the views of President Hoover and the Democratic leaders of Congress: cut government expenses, raise taxes, and thus balance the budget. Even from some of the nation's idols came the same sort of testimony. Al Smith, who was still the hero of the crowds, favored a manufacturer's sales tax sufficiently high so that the income tax could be lowered. Baruch, who had been head of President Wilson's War Industries Board, proclaimed, "Balance budgets. Stop spending money we haven't got. Sacrifice for frugality and revenue. Cut government spending — cut it as rations are cut in a siege. Tax — tax everybody for everything."

And so it went with relatively few exceptions. Most of the well-known economists were ready to say "me too." Twenty of them had

* See Chapter VI.

signed an open letter to Roosevelt recommending a three-fold recovery program: settle the war debts, lower tariffs through reciprocal agreements, and maintain the gold standard.

The only famous person suggesting a contrary course was the publisher William Randolph Hearst, who sent a written statement declaring to the committee:

> Taxation, like construction, should be accommodated to good times and to bad times.
>
> There should in bad times be more help to the community through construction, and less burden to the community in taxation.
>
> As a matter of fact, let me make the radical and doubtless unacceptable statement that taxation should be diminished in bad times. But if taxation can not be diminished it should at least not be increased.

But then, Hearst, like Al Smith, denounced the income tax as a racket, and proposed substituting a sales tax.

There were minor voices, but they did not make headlines. There was Mary Van Kleeck of the Russell Sage Foundation, who presented statistics to indicate that purchasing power had not kept up with increases in productivity. Sidney Hillman of the Amalgamated Clothing Workers testified, "Nothing else matters in this country until the millions now totally unemployed and the millions employed part time are given work at a wage that will enable them to maintain a standard of living to match our productive capacity." Ralph E. Flanders, president of the Jones and Lamson Machine Company of Springfield, Vermont, favored legislation to shorten the hours of workers and enactment of the domestic allotment plan to aid farmers. And Marriner S. Eccles, president of the First Security Corporation of Ogden, Utah, argued that the government should resort to deficit financing to stimulate the economy.[33]

Except for these few, almost all the learned specialists testifying before the "depression clinic" were unanimous in their prescription. They viewed the ailing economy as eighteenth-century physicians had their hapless patients, and recommended copious bleeding.[34]

No word of protest against either the conservative diagnoses or the congressional inaction came from Roosevelt. Yet he was the beneficiary of both. Congress seemed unable through its own leadership and internal organization to act. Nor did its members obtain much guidance from their constituents, who agreed upon little except the need for action. Representative Robert L. Doughton wrote to one of his:

> I note with interest what you say about the needs of the country. Some of us are doing the best we know how to here in order to relieve conditions. . . . [P]erhaps we do not understand just what to do, but

the same seems to be true of our constituents, as I get hundreds of letters advising what to do, but hardly any two are agreed as to what to do. We all realize the country is in terrible condition, just like doctors often realize that their patients are almost hopelessly sick, but it is not always when they realize the condition of the patient that they are able to apply the life saving remedy.[35]

Congress and the nation were awaiting the new President's program.

CHAPTER V

Planning the New Deal

It's a constant study. As Al Smith used to say, I'm getting a lot in through the ears and in spare moments
through the eyes also. I'm going ahead with a period of
intensive preparation and investigation.
— FDR, *January 11, 1933.*[1]

If Roosevelt were to initiate his own program for recovery rather than accept the schemes of President Hoover or the Democratic leaders in Congress, it was imperative that he immediately begin comprehensive planning. So indeed he did, but so quietly that very few of the public were aware of what was going on. Most headlines gave the impression that he would hew close to orthodox patterns.

Roosevelt had several good reasons for not making advance announcement of his plans in concrete detail. For one thing, he had not yet worked them out. For another he did not wish to lose support or generate organized opposition. For similar reasons, he gave little indication of the careful way in which he was establishing machinery so that he could prepare an effective program. In much of his arrangements he was so casual that even those whose support he enlisted sometimes despaired over the disorder. Some was real and some only apparent.

Until January 1, 1933, Roosevelt was able to present himself to the public primarily as governor of New York. During the previous four years, while he had worked earnestly and successfully at the governorship, he had continued to hide behind its façade to dodge uncomfortable national questions that reporters would put to him. Until the end of the year, it still provided some slight protection. What was more, he did continue to work at his gubernatorial duties, slashing estimates to drastically lower levels as he tried to leave his successor, Lieutenant Governor Herbert Lehman, a balanced budget. These duties took a good deal of Roosevelt's time.

So did the sending of letters of appreciation to some of those who had been especially helpful during the campaign, and the mere act of signing one's name to endless acknowledgments of letters of congratulations. Louis Howe continued to run the New York City "letter factory," grinding out answers to correspondence by the mail-sack full, in the same fashion that had been so effective in helping Roosevelt win the nomination and election. But Howe failed to retool the machinery speedily enough, and sent far too many answers to Roosevelt for his personal signature.

In mid-December Roosevelt protested, and set up letter-answering procedures that he was to follow substantially through the presidential years. In this instance as in others that fall, he began to develop with considerable precision new routines for handling small matters. He sent an anguished memo to Howe:

> I have just gone thru about a million of the New York letters and this business must stop! First I do not want letters prepared for my signature.
>
> What I do want is this: Acknowledge letters of congratulations as follows:
>
> My Dear. . . .
>
> The Governor has asked me to convey to you his appreciation of your very kind letter. He is grateful for your thought of him and would write you himself were it not for an amount of correspondence which makes it impossible.
>
> (signed) GUERNSEY T. CROSS
Secy. to the Governor
>
> P.S. They can be sent up here and gone thru by Missy, as she has been doing. Letters from any personal friends she will take out and the others can be signed by Mr. Cross.[2]

Roosevelt was too good a politician who had benefitted too much from close attention to his mail to neglect it now that he had been elected. Rather, he established a system through which all letters received answers, but only the most important came to his desk.*

---

* Howe's skillful letter writers devised a series of forms with which to answer most letters. After FDR's protest, they abandoned the "first person form" and substituted the one he had proposed to answer all congratulations. There were also forms for those requesting aid, those writing concerning polio, and those writing that they had named babies after FDR. The latter were the only ones FDR himself signed. Then at the end of January, there was a form letter to reply to birthday congratulations, and another to answer the increasing number of job applications. Other letters called for semiroutine replies which the letter writers dictated. Gabrielle E. Forbush, who was in charge of these writers, reported: "As you know, we have tried not to standardize these too much, in order that they may have a personal sound. We have already found this worked very well, as our correspondents show each other the letters, and [we] . . . avoid the possibility of sending exactly the same letter several times." On the last day of work in

Roosevelt's keen personal interest in the mail led him to dictate in person, for his secretary to sign, a compassionate reply to one of Hoover's more ardent supporters, Henry Holt, the publisher, who had sent Roosevelt an angry telegram on election night, followed by a contrite retraction a day or so later:

> Fortunately perhaps, in the rush of congratulatory telegrams received after election day, your telegram to Governor Roosevelt was not shown to him and now that your letter has come I am taking the liberty of sending you back your telegram without calling it to the Governor's attention. I think you would prefer that the matter be handled in this way.
>
> The Governor is the last person in the world to harbor any resentment against you and I am glad that on consideration you, like the Governor, believe it is wholly possible that all people, regardless of party, should consider the country's good.[4]

Roosevelt began to watch carefully what he said, or what was said in his name, whether it was in a letter, magazine article, or press interview. Thus it was that he cut off the flood of apparently personal letters carrying excellent imitations of his signature. He decreed after his election that no one henceforth should be allowed to sign his name; though the letters continued, they had to bear the names of secretaries. Neither could he permit the further ghosting of magazine articles. Only a few days after his election, he wrote in friendly but firm fashion to Earle Looker, who had turned out a number of *Liberty* articles for him, "Things have moved fast in this week since November eighth and it has become perfectly clear to me that future articles — at least for a long time — are taboo. Too much is involved both here and abroad for me to present the case by this method." [5]

As for the reporters, he continued to see them frequently, usually parrying their queries in a gay but uninformative way, occasionally, when he had something important to tell them, going to the pains of writing a precise statement. In the last weeks of 1928 before he had taken office as governor, bit by bit he had cleverly fed to the newspapers intimations of his future program. Complications made it impossible for him to follow so simple a procedure as President-elect. He gave newspapermen the impression that he was actively exploring with many people a number of approaches to the problem of defeating the depression. He managed to remain quite indefinite on most issues, yet give the reporters sufficient news and enough pleasant banter to retain their enthusiastic support. While Roosevelt was ensuring friendly cover-

New York at the beginning of March, before they all entrained for Washington, they did no dictation, but even at that mailed out 2,450 form letters.[3]

age by the reporters in the news columns, he was appealing to the big publishers for editorial support by inviting them to confer with him. He persuaded Eleanor Medill "Cissy" Patterson of the *Washington Times-Herald* to come to Warm Springs, and using the financier Joseph Kennedy as an intermediary, tried to lure William Randolph Hearst from San Simeon. Because of an operation, Hearst had to abandon his plan to visit, but assured Roosevelt, "I have been following your course very closely and I think I have a good general idea of your plans; and I can assure you that I am in hearty accord with those plans as I understand them to be." Hearst had already told Kennedy that he considered the success of the new Democratic administration to be so important to the nation that he intended to go to great lengths to support Roosevelt regardless of minor differences of opinion. The backing of publishers like Hearst, with his powerful chain of newspapers, would be of significant aid in launching the New Deal. Roosevelt responded politely to memoranda arriving indirectly through Hearst's editor Coblentz.[6]

In gathering and studying proposals for New Deal measures, Roosevelt was likewise all-encompassing in his interests. He listened to every viewpoint, giving the impression of sympathetic understanding in general terms that the visitor would take hopefully to mean commitment. It was a useful political technique. More than that, Roosevelt was curious about all sorts of proposals; he was genuinely receptive to a variety of ideas from both experts and amateurs. Many were ready to return the nation to the familiar progressive programs of the first decades of the century. Others went still further back, to the radical agrarian proposals of the Populists at the end of the nineteenth century. Younger men urged Roosevelt toward as yet untried devices. Roosevelt gave heed to all of these advisers and supplicants, showering upon them the same warm consideration he was showing to the congressional conservatives.

How much of the advice would he follow? Certainly more than the public could suspect, reading mostly of his courtship of the Democratic leaders in Congress. In planning the New Deal he tried to build it on as broad a base as possible.

Fundamentally, Roosevelt depended for specific planning of legislation upon the same Brain Trusters who had drafted the campaign speeches. But, skilled political leader that he was, he did not undertake to develop a program with dispassionate objectivity from the Olympian remoteness of Hyde Park and Warm Springs. True, he could assign tasks to his experts, both academic and professional, and outline to them the directions he wished them to explore. He listened alertly to their proposals. But he listened also with his politician's ear to an infinite number of spokesmen for pressures of varying intensity. Through achieving accommodations among the conflicting pressures and communicating them to his drafters of legislation, he could try to develop a viable program which would be acceptable in both the industrial areas and the farm belt, both Wall Street and Main Street. It should secure the holdings of the propertied people, yet give hope to the propertyless. In political terms, it should appeal to the Democrats who held power in Congress, yet retain for Roosevelt the, support of the millions of nominally Republican voters who had cast their ballots for Hoover in 1928, and then in despair and disgust switched to the minority party in 1932. More than a negative obeisance to Democratic conservatism was necessary if Roosevelt were to fabricate an economic and political program which by 1936 could transform the votes against Hoover of the previous election into a positive affirmation of the New Deal.

The traditions of Theodore Roosevelt and Woodrow Wilson inclined Franklin Roosevelt toward a program, progressive in its roots, which would benefit all the American people. In contrast to his public deference to Democratic conservatism, the larger part of his private planning was positive, drawing upon those who had been advocates of either the New Nationalism or the New Freedom. While he was in Washington in November, at the urging of Frankfurter he had a fifteen- or twenty-minute conversation with that staunch advocate of decentralization, Justice Louis D. Brandeis of the United States Supreme Court. During the interview, as was habitual with Roosevelt, he did more expounding than consulting, telling Brandeis a good deal that would please him — that the nation was saddled with greater debts than assets, and that the bankers had behaved in a selfish fashion. But he did not agree with Brandeis's view that America must "let up on the war debt." Brandeis wrote Frankfurter: "He seems well versed about fundamental facts of the situation — declared his administration must be liberal and that he expected to lose part of his Conservative supporters. I told him 'I hoped so.' — that he must realign . . . part of the forces in each party."

Roosevelt also emphasized to Brandeis that remedies must be pursued in an experimental and active fashion, specifically in developing the domestic allotment agricultural plan. That same day he also talked reassuringly to the farmer-labor governor of Minnesota, Floyd Olsen, advocate of a drastic farm relief program.[7]

Again, in late January when Senators Robert M. La Follette and Bronson Cutting visited him at Warm Springs, they found Roosevelt receptive to their viewpoint. La Follette reported to his brother Philip, "His attitude . . . on power, farm relief, unemployment relief, public works, was in substantial accord with the progressive position." Roosevelt told La Follette, "I think you are right in your conclusion that inflation must be a part of the program." Conversations like these, coming at the very time when Roosevelt seemed to be swinging far to the right to conciliate the congressional leaders, indicated that, even as during the 1932 campaign, he might follow his rightward tack with an equally sharp turn toward the left.[8]

There were other indications that Roosevelt's main course would be toward progressivism. His advisers with scarcely an exception were urging innovation. Rumors spread that Roosevelt's alter ego, Louis McHenry Howe, was pointing the way toward a new progressivism. Howe, who had selflessly hidden in the shadows masterminding most of Roosevelt's political maneuvers, from the progressive battles in the New York legislature of 1911 to the winning of the presidency in 1932, emerged onto front pages and radio programs immediately after the victory. Resplendent in the rather new title of Colonel (from Kentucky) and a self-embellished legend for being a picturesque sort of gnome — a romantic description of a wizened little man suffering acutely from asthma — Howe had every expectation of being the power behind Roosevelt in the White House. Howe and Howe alone was to enjoy the title Secretary to the President (although Roosevelt did not bother to tell him until shortly before the inauguration). Because Howe would be jealous of other advisers, Roosevelt did not dare put Moley also into the White House. But although Roosevelt's unbounded personal loyalty and affection for Howe never ever diminished, the fact was that Howe's personal influence was waning even while his public reputation was waxing. Partly it may have been his ill health, but largely it was because Roosevelt during his years as governor had long since fallen into the habit of looking elsewhere to various experts for advice on policy. Undoubtedly Howe had some effect upon Roosevelt's policy determination, but certainly not a fraction of what newspapermen erroneously ascribed to him. Whatever influence he had was exerted in much the same direction as that of the Democratic congressional leaders and old Wilsonians like Colonel House. Yet Howe gave the impression that he favored a sweeping return to progressivism. The United Press learned confidentially of a remarkable hour-long lecture on history and economics that Howe gave at the end of November to some twenty-five progressive or radical leaders: [9]

> He regarded the present moment as the beginning of a new phase, in which economic domination would be taken out of the hands of the financiers and perhaps the next era would be one where the country's economics would be dominated by the producers, that is, the men who made or grew things. At any rate, he indicated Roosevelt has definite ideas on how this economic domination by finance should be replaced and my informant took it that it was a program of such things as unemployment insurance and the like.

> Howe was speaking entirely in the capacity of Lou Howe and was

not posing in any way as speaking for Roosevelt. His hearers were exceedingly impressed and one might say even excited.[10]

One of Louis Howe's auditors, Frederic C. Howe, who had never lowered his progressive banner during the twenties, pledged his fealty to the new crusade Howe was proclaiming:

> If I understood the import of the suggestion . . . it involves an ambitious movement for the mobilization of the liberal minded throughout the country, not only about the President-elect, but around a new and natural cleavage in politics. This interests me very much. We are, I think, at the end of an economic era; we should adjust our political alignments to the new political era that is impending. In a radio debate with Professor John Dewey I said that one reason, and possibly the most important reason, why liberals and socialists should support Governor Roosevelt was that he was possibly the only and last stand of democratic institutions against a fascist dictator; also, that he was the only statesman that I saw in either party who seemed to face the fact that something very fundamental and something quite new was necessary to save us from collapse, a collapse that already to many seemed inevitable.[11]

Frederic Howe and others seeking drastic changes were wrong about Louis Howe, but should have been even more excited over the fact that Roosevelt continued to retain as his key adviser Professor Moley, who had so ably coordinated the speech-writing of the Brain Trusters during the campaign. The choice gave even more distinct promise of a positive program, since that was what Moley strongly advocated and he had Roosevelt's confidence. Roosevelt, according to Brandeis, "spoke most warmly of Moley's service as Economic adviser & that he wanted me to meet him."

The invitation to coordinate planning for the New Deal came to Moley when he was weary from the campaign and expecting to drop all his political activities. Moley recalls that one evening in late November, in the bedroom of the cottage at Warm Springs, Roosevelt said to him:

> I'm still Governor of New York and I face a terrible couple of weeks before January 1st finishing up that job. Meanwhile the debts thing may crop up again, and I've got to get some legislation from this Congress.
>
> I have no Cabinet yet. I can't call in many people for advice and help without inviting speculation about whether I'm going to appoint them. That will embarrass them and me. You know my intellectual commitments. You know most of the people that we've got to put to work. I'd counted on you to keep in touch with the State Department on debts for me, and to get the ball.on legislation rolling.[12]

Along with this appeal, Roosevelt offered to Moley a position without statutory duties which would leave him free to assist the President, an appointment as assistant secretary of state. Moley, who had not envisaged going to Washington, accepted Roosevelt's immediate offer to help formulate issues, but did not agree to become an assistant secretary of state until February.* Even then, he confided to one of his oldest friends that he would be in Washington only for a short while. Through the hectic winter of 1932–1933, while he was helping ready legislation and obtain acceptances to appointments for Roosevelt, he continued somehow to meet his classes at Columbia University.

Early in February, Moley made a favorable impression upon Senator Hiram Johnson, a rather prickly old progressive, telling Johnson and several like-minded senators that Roosevelt wanted their views conconcerning the war debts question and the Economic Conference. The meeting was so cordial that Johnson confided to a friend:

> He is quite the antithesis of the ordinary professor. He is sufficiently young, and apparently with some knowledge of human beings, and with a manner quite at variance with that of the ordinary member of the intelligentsia, who arrogates to himself the possession of all the knowledge upon any subject, economic or otherwise, and who looks with pity and contempt upon all others.[14]

The two former Brain Trusters most closely associated with Moley during the interregnum, Rexford G. Tugwell and Adolf A. Berle, Jr., were even more eager than Moley to obtain positive action. Moley admired both, and with accuracy differentiated between them:

> Tugwell is a young man who is a professor of Economics with exceedingly liberal tendencies. He has more of a turn for philosophical economics than anything else. Berle is much more practical. Berle is a practicing lawyer who was a sort of infant prodigy at Harvard, having been graduated at the age of sixteen. He was attached to the Peace Commission in Paris and even then manifested very independent traits. These two men have a bit of the inexperienced inadvertency of youth; but both have great promise.[15]

Both Berle and Tugwell were articulate analysts of the existing order,

* Moley explains in his memoirs:

I thought I had made it clear many, many times during the campaign that I wanted no office. I wanted to think, teach, write, and speak as a free agent, reaching an audience, however small, that accepted me on the basis of what I had to say, rather than because I was a part of a governmental machine. Impartiality and forthrightness were the price that had to be paid for such freedom. It seemed to me that honest teaching and writing about public affairs precluded not only White House cupbearing and administrative paper-shuffling, but party goose-stepping.[13]

and had written significant critiques. Berle, together with Gardiner Means, in *The Modern Corporation and Private Property* (1932), one of the most influential books of the era, had delineated the rapid growth of business concentration. Tugwell in *The Industrial Discipline and the Governmental Arts* (1933) proposed that the government take advantage of the concentration by becoming "a senior partner in industry-wide councils and [maneuvering] their member elements into such arrangements that fair exchanges could go on continuously." [16]

Essential to all three of these men was their youth and resilience. The heavy pressure under which they had worked during the campaign continued, if indeed it did not intensify. They went for weeks from early morning to early the next morning, carrying out a variety of delicate assignments, buoyed by their participation in preparing for change and their access to power. They accepted as delightful their relationship to Roosevelt, rather like that of bright young favorites in the livery of a Renaissance potentate. Not everyone Roosevelt enlisted in 1933 shared their enthusiasm. Dean Acheson, perhaps because he was the son of an Episcopal bishop, found Roosevelt's autocratic, benign airs distasteful if not degrading. "It is not gratifying," he has written, "to receive the easy greeting which milord might give a promising stable boy and pull one's forelock in return." Acheson, not present during the interregnum, entered the Roosevelt administration in the spring and left over policy differences before the end of the year. He remembered Roosevelt with admiration but not affection. Moley, who in 1936 finally broke his ties, also over policies, has always remembered Roosevelt with affection if not admiration. Tugwell, at the time and later, looked upon Roosevelt's banter as an indication of humor and warmth, relieving the tension of endless work. An entry in his diary for January 5, 1933, reads: "After my seminar in the evening I went down to [Roosevelt's] house on 65th Street. He was cheerful — whistled me upstairs shouting 'here, Rex, here Rex' and said his favorite dog had beeen called that. I told him I hoped Rex was still his favorite dog — all very merry!" [17]

Roosevelt's retention of Moley, Tugwell, Berle, and other planners during the interregnum and the early months of the New Deal made likely a translation into concrete detail of the basic policies which had appeared nebulously in the campaign speeches. Fundamentally they sought a program of government-fostered economic nationalism behind a relatively high tariff wall. In domestic policy, as in foreign affairs, other strong forces operating upon Roosevelt sought to modify the overall program. There was the phalanx of southern Democratic antitariff warriors, of whom Senator Cordell Hull was the most conspicuous example, and there were brilliant young conservative inter-

FDR leaving his New York townhouse, 1933.

nationalists, two of whom — James Warburg, scion of a New York and German banking house, and the Arizona representative, Lewis Douglas, son of a copper magnate — were among the most persuasive men around Roosevelt during the formative months of the New Deal. Already by late January 1933, Douglas, helping plan budget cuts, was laboring with grim earnestness and an absolutely clear-cut view of what he wished to achieve:

> It is conceivable that civilization itself is hanging in the balance. It can be pushed on the side of recovery or chaos. To me the primary things to be done are clear. First actually balance the budget second face the question of reviving world trade which of course means debts, stabilizing exchange, and liberalizing tariffs. Yet here men follow their normal instinct to avoid the unpleasant. They talk about inflation instead. When the logic of a situation demands taking one course the fears and stupidity of men are attempting to direct us down the other — the former leads to recovery, the latter to chaos.[18]

The fervor and logic of Douglas's views appealed to Roosevelt, and he saw no reason not to reconcile them, and Warburg's, with those of Moley and Tugwell. Both courses of action were part of his design.

The influence of Moley and the small group of experts around Roosevelt bent upon attaining economic planning must not be underrated.

Moley in years since has asserted with considerable validity that he was always a conservative, and indeed his dominant role in 1933 appears, at least in comparison with the New Dealers' attitudes toward business in 1935 and after, to have been a conservative pressure. But at the time Moley was accepting for himself the liberal label, and measured against the limited or even negative ideas of a large part of the business community, he was indeed liberal if not radical. "Nothing can save us but a party with a liberal outlook," he wrote a friend in December 1932, "and I think as things unfold you will see that that is the direction the Governor is looking toward." * Moley foresaw that the New Deal would take the American polity permanently into a new order: "I don't think the Republican party in its present form is ever coming back, because if things get much worse the identity of both parties will disappear and if they get better, the Roosevelt party will continue indefinitely." [19]

The impetus of Moley and of those experts to whom he would assign

---

* To another friend, Moley wrote, "The opportunity we now have for a liberal party is without precedent and . . . the South will go along with the West and Northwest in what ought to be the most significant party alignment in history." In February 1933, he commented to Charles A. Beard, whom he invited to send suggestions for a New Deal program, "The danger of this administration's going to the left is already disturbing the editorial page of the dear old TIMES a great deal, and I am in for a dig every chance they get."

specific pieces of planning was toward innovation. In early December, the overall outline appeared with clarity in *Liberty* magazine; one of Moley's first postcampaign tasks was to help draft a policy statement to appear there under Roosevelt's name. Although the drafting was Moley's, as with all of Roosevelt's speeches and statements, the ideas had to be those of which Roosevelt approved. Moley was an especially skillful amanuensis, always able to set forth in effective terms the thoughts that Roosevelt specified, whether or not they represented Moley's personal beliefs. It was a significant policy statement, indeed a blueprint for the New Deal, yet it received relatively little attention at the time.

At the outset, Roosevelt attested to his willingness to cooperate with Congress in developing a program to benefit all the various economic groups within the United States:

> The economic life of the country, representing as it does diversified population and interests, can best be brought into harmony through wise and judicious and temperate national leadership through the government at Washington. There have been administrations in the life of the country which have represented only a part of.this great union of interests, and, unfortunately, at times a very special and narrow interest. The character of the vote at the recent election makes it clear that the mandate imposed upon me is truly national in scope. It has been my claim that much of the difficulty through which we have passed recently is the direct result of political failure to grasp the fact of economic interdependence.
>
> The interests of labor and industry cannot be promoted at the expense of agriculture; neither can capital reach a condition of true prosperity without at the same time offering a more legitimate share to labor. Any neglected group, whether of agriculture, industry, mining, commerce, or finance, can infect our whole national life and produce widespread misery. My administration shall be devoted to the task of giving practical force and the necessary legislative form to the great central fact of contemporary American life, viz., the interdependence of all factions, sections, and interests in this great country. I believe in a higher conservation which seeks to provide work and economic security to the mass of the people in order that they may be free to live and develop their individual lives and seek happiness and recognition without inflicting injury upon their fellow citizens.

There is no clearer or more accurate statement than this of Roosevelt's approach to the New Deal. Like Theodore Roosevelt and Woodrow Wilson, he felt a strong obligation to be President of all the American people, not just a conservative faction, and to provide a balance among all the interacting and conflicting economic and political forces. Like them, he wished to enter the White House as an impartial arbiter, favoring none against the others except as it became necessary to maintain the balance. Unlike them, he conceived of his role as being positive rather than negative. They had taken office in years of prosperity when it was assumed that if the President and Congress prevented undue discrimination, a free working of the economic laws would guarantee continued rewards for the American people. Roosevelt was preparing for the presidency at a time when the nation had long endured acute depression. The business, financial, and political titans offering their diagnoses before the Senate "depression clinic" had prescribed the classic remedies of the nineteenth century: the government in time of depression should be run like a prudent household or business, cutting its expenditures so drastically that it could remain solvent, taking little or no responsibility for a sick economy that given due time would recover by itself. President Hoover, in theory clinging to the old orthodoxy, in practice offered the services of the government to aid the economy in dosing itself with mild medicines. Roosevelt was ready to reject the ancient formula that the government should remain aloof, even though he accepted the precept of sharp budget-cutting. Rather, Roosevelt was proclaiming boldly what Hoover had been inching toward, that the government must intervene positively and decisively in every sector of the economy in order to bring a quick recovery from the depression.

Roosevelt reaffirmed in *Liberty* magazine his intention of embarking upon the rehabilitation programs he had outlined during his campaign:

"The relief of agriculture and the restoration of the farmers' purchasing power" through readjustment of the debt burden and a national farm program to be devised with the counsel of farm leaders.

The rehabilitation and consolidation of railways, the establishment of a national transportation policy, proper regulation of security and commodity exchanges. . . . The task of bringing to the consumer electric power at a fair cost and, primarily in order that the rates charged . . . may be determined by scientific accuracy, the development by the national government, under government ownership and control, of the four great power resources in the four corners of the country, Muscle Shoals, the St. Lawrence, Boulder Dam, and Columbia River. . . .

The restoration of normal foreign trade . . . through reciprocal tariff agreements with other countries. . . .

A reduction in the cost of government, national, state and local. . . .

The Volstead Act must be modified.

In foreign affairs, involving great economic questions, a fair and frank, and generally friendly attitude. "We cannot wage a tariff war, for example, and expect a friendly spirit on the part of our neighbors in the world."

And, of course, unemployment relief.[20]

All that was lacking in this public statement was mention of banking legislation, already before Congress, and the social security and business recovery programs, long since being discussed by some of Roosevelt's coterie.*

In total this was the setting forth of a far-ranging positive program, first to bring economic recovery, and second to correct abuses that might lead to further depressions. Roosevelt called upon his fellow countrymen, especially the millions of independents, progressives, and liberals, to join with him patriotically in an endeavor to promote the welfare of both the United States and the world:

> We are a generation overdue in political and economic reconstruction; we confront great difficulties — many of them the result of our own past mistakes. We are about to enter a new period of liberalism and of sane reform in the United States, and we shall require unity of purpose, if not of opinion, if we are to achieve permanent and practical results.

---

* The numerous proposals of the Brain Trusters in Moley's files bear testimony to their concrete and detailed thinking about New Deal measures. On November 10, 1932, only two days after the election, Berle sent Moley a memorandum remarkable for its comprehensiveness:

> Since the results of the election will call for action immediately on inauguration, we have to consider a program which can if necessary be presented at a special session of Congress. I think the economic situation may change very much for the worse before that time, so that many of the following suggestions may have to be shifted as we go along. . . .

> ### Fundamental Legislation
> 1. The farm relief act — domestic allotment plan or some other plan designed to increase purchasing power of the farmer. . . .
> 2. (Possibly.) Industrial stabilization — limited permission to industries to get together under suitable supervision on stabilization plans, *provided* they afford reasonable probability of greater employment, protection to the consumer, and are kept in control. . . .
> 3. A relief act, which might be coupled also with an unemployment insurance program. . . .
> 4. The currency question. . . .
> 5. Funding or otherwise taking care of the floating debt. . . .
> 6. Taxation — whether by sales tax or otherwise, the budget has to be balanced. . . .
> 7. Material for tariff negotiations.

Next, Berle outlined numerous curative measures: federal regulation of security issues and of public utility holding companies, reform of banking, coordination of credit agencies, revision of federal receivership laws, and overhauling of the regulation of interstate transportation. Berle concluded:

> It must be remembered that by March 4 next we may have anything on our hands from a recovery to a revolution. The chance is about even either way.
> My impression is that the country wants and would gladly support a rather daring program.
> After your discussion at Warm Springs, we can arrange about splitting up the work.[21]

The United States has become a great nation, and its economic life functions along national lines, where our political life still clings too much to the political machinery of the past.

Roosevelt's article in *Liberty* was as close as he and the Brain Trust came to publicizing a set of principles and master plan, but there is no indication that the economic experts, the politicians, or the public paid much attention to it. There was little hint of overall planning in the press coverage, which gave larger headlines to Roosevelt's conservative overtures toward Congress. And because of Roosevelt's casual work habits, even those closest to him were likely to have the impression that the New Deal was being fabricated in a haphazard, grab-bag fashion.

Proposals for remedying the depression were pouring in on Roosevelt by the hundreds and thousands. He received innumerable plans either in the mail or brought by suppliants, and he looked upon them all with a remarkable open-mindedness. He instructed Mrs. Forbush to establish a file for them, placing each plan under its proper subject, from "agriculture" through a wide range of headings. "The distinctly crank letters I think might be kept in a regular file," he suggested, "but anything that looks as if it might have some merit might best be put in a place where it can be dragged out at the proper time." Roosevelt assigned to Moley the task of supervising the analysis of these plans. Thus a scheme to retire Liberty Loan bonds from circulation and to print non-interest-bearing United States government notes to circulate in their place — one of the innumerable inflationary suggestions — went to Adolf A. Berle, who reported to Roosevelt his skepticism.[22]

At Warm Springs, Roosevelt demonstrated a willingness to listen sympathetically to almost every conceivable point of view. Only those who tried to pin him down to a firm commitment came away disappointed. Baruch received an intent and respectful response to his pleas for drastic government retrenchment; indeed, Roosevelt devoted much of his time to planning cutbacks. But the door of the Little White House was also open to the aged General Jacob S. Coxey, who in the 1890s had led a march of unemployed on Washington to demand a public works program. Roosevelt listened to Coxey's proposal for the collection of the war debts through printing an international currency, and invited Coxey to submit his ideas in writing.[23]

On December 1, the president of the Crusaders of Economic Liberty and one of his followers presented themselves at the Little White House, and warning that they were planning to bring a caravan of hunger strikers from Columbus, Georgia, to demonstrate, requested an interview with the governor. Moley, discovering that theirs was another

"magic money" scheme, and fearing violence, tried to head them away.*
Roosevelt, on the contrary, asked to see them. Moley has recalled:

The two disturbing visitors met a smiling customer on the little
balcony at the back of the Warm Springs cottage. Roosevelt invited
them to tell him all about their ideas, and they fell to at once. After a
time, when violence failed to develop, I wandered away. Much to my
surprise when I returned a half hour later, I found that papers had
been drawn out and that the two reformers *and* Roosevelt were fascinated by one another. They talked, and he talked. The discussion went
on and on.[24]

When the delighted visitors left, they told the reporters,

The Governor was very gracious and interested in the bill. He told us
he would give it his consideration and ask Senator Carter Glass and
Representative Henry B. Steagall, chairmen of the Senate Finance Committee and the House Committee on Banking and Currency, to give it
their consideration. That's all we asked for and we were well satisfied
with the interview. There will be no demonstration here. We are going
back to Columbus, where we have 6,000 members, and hold a celebration
there.[25]

Roosevelt's cordial receptivity, in contrast to Hoover's cold refusal
ever to put up with any schemes varying in the slightest from his own
logical plans, was an indication of Roosevelt's political genius. He had
prevented the unpleasantness of a hunger demonstration, and had won
the enthusiastic support of the confused but earnest leaders of these
desperate men. There was a price, of course, and while the interview
went on and on, Moley reflected: "The economic system of the country
was cracking under the greatest strain in a generation, the agricultural
program was stymied, and a Cabinet was being selected. There were a
thousand things of importance to claim the attention of the man who
was about to become President of the United States." Earnest and hard-
working experts like Moley, who were the beneficiaries of Roosevelt's
limitless receptivity, on occasions like this had to wait helplessly, the
victims of it. They had the ear of Roosevelt, which gave them an unprecedented opportunity to transform some of their theories into reality.
But they had to hide their impatience when Roosevelt spent large
amounts of his time either in politicking, which had a value difficult for
them to appreciate fully, or simply in having fun, which undoubtedly

---

* The Crusaders sought "a new form of money to be based upon human effort"
calculated at the 1928 average pay for unskilled labor, 42.62 cents an hour. It would
be put into circulation by loans first on mortgages on real estate. In effect it was
a variation upon the favorite American scheme for inflationary relief in depressed
times from the colonial period on, the "land bank," which would circulate currency based on mortgages.

sustained his buoyancy and vitality but at times was still more difficult for them to tolerate.[26]

Moley had long since become used to working with Roosevelt, and was shrewder than most of those around him in appraising the assets and liabilities of Roosevelt's singular methods of work. For any newcomer, they must have seemed incredible. Thus Henry A. Wallace, who was to become secretary of agriculture, a quarter century later still sharply remembered his initial visit to Warm Springs as bordering on the fantastic:

> When I arrived at Warm Springs, I was quite unprepared for what unfolded. . . . I didn't want to get there *too* early so I walked out to the Little White House and got there about nine. There was a guard there although Mr. Roosevelt was not yet President. He told me that nobody was up yet, which quite astounded me.

For about three-quarters of an hour, Wallace discussed a possible cotton program with Senator John H. Bankhead of Alabama, who was also waiting. Then he was greeted by Moley, who was deeply perturbed for fear he had harmed Roosevelt's cause through a sharp remark during a party the night before. The festivities had been in the private railroad car of publisher Eleanor Medill "Cissy" Patterson, which was standing on a siding at Warm Springs. According to Moley, he and James Byrnes arrived to find Mrs. Patterson in her cups, berating a reporter:

> In the course of her rambling remarks, she told him that he was just a "cheap" newspaperman. This made me mad and I stood up and told her that she was the one who was cheap. Thereupon she shouted at me to get the hell out of the car. . . . I greatly regretted what I had done although when I told Roosevelt, he laughed and told me to send her a telegram telling her again that she was cheap.*

Wallace, hearing a more fanciful version of the altercation, recalled that it "made a deep impression on an Iowa boy":

> A little bit later word came that President Roosevelt was awake and shaving. It was about ten o'clock by that time, I guess, and would I please come in. He was seated in a chair using an old fashioned safety razor and shaving with considerable skill. . . . He proceeded to talk about the situation in agriculture.

After talking with Roosevelt, Wallace conferred with Moley and Henry Morgenthau, Jr. He found Moley a clearer thinker than either Roosevelt or Morgenthau on farm legislation: "He really discussed the political realities and the necessities . . . of these various agricultural

---

* Moley's remorse came from his fear that he had damaged FDR. He sent such handsome apologies to Mrs. Patterson that she not only forgave Moley but within a few months was trying to lure him into her journalistic enterprises.

areas, and what might be done politically to attain some legislative means of meeting these needs."

The evening was more surprising still. Wallace spent several hours watching Roosevelt parry Senator Key Pittman of Nevada. Pittman, eager to obtain Roosevelt's pledge to aid the silver interests of the West, kept trying to talk about the world-shaking importance of developing a silver program. But Pittman's first mention of silver reminded Roosevelt of buried treasure — perhaps it was silver — on Oak Island, off the coast of Nova Scotia, and of his adventures in digging for it when he was a boy. For an hour and a half Roosevelt, making himself as charming as possible to Pittman, embellished upon the story, blocking effectively any other discussion of silver.

In years that followed, Wallace repeatedly witnessed these facets of Roosevelt, especially the device of telling lengthy yarns to cut off unwanted demands. But in December 1932, it was all so new and strange that when people in Des Moines asked what Roosevelt was really like, Wallace replied that he was a daring adventurer.[27]

It was in this informal atmosphere that the New Deal program began to take on its rudimentary outlines. Roosevelt and Moley parceled out assignments in several fields to a number of people. Wallace and others were put to work on farm legislation. Berle studied the expediting of bankruptcy procedures, measures to prevent foreclosure of farm mortgages, and with William Woodin, Joseph Eastman and others, relief measures for railroads. Moley obtained suggestions for stock exchange regulation from Samuel Untermyer, who for years had sought legislation, then assigned Charles Taussig to work further with Untermyer. Senator George Norris made proposals for the development of power on the Tennessee River. And of course every Democratic leader who came to Warm Springs as did Pittman brought a full portfolio of suggestions. Silver was Pittman's primary interest, as well it needed to be if he were to retain the support of his mining constituents, but he also gave advice on foreign affairs and a wide range of domestic matters.[28]

Scores of people had the heady feeling that they were helping plan the New Deal. Some of them, quite naturally, came to overestimate their roles; many of them did participate quite vitally in laying the groundwork for legislation. All of them, directly or indirectly, were working with Roosevelt, but none could be entirely certain how much Roosevelt intended to do or how far he intended to go.

Roosevelt's techniques and thought processes were not easy for his contemporaries to identify. Nevertheless, Stimson's economic adviser, Herbert Feis, after observing him that winter during the war debt discussions, at lunch with J. Pierrepont Moffat one day in January 1933, succinctly and accurately expounded on Roosevelt's habits of mind.

"As he analyzes it," Moffat wrote in his diary, "there are three distinct characteristics: (1) a great disinclination to make up his mind, a tendency to issue trial balloons and to talk over a problem with both sides leaving them both convinced that he agrees with them, (2) a final decision made rather impulsively, (3) a considerable stubbornness in sticking to a decision once made." Only the word "impulsively" might be subject to some modification; as with Theodore Roosevelt there was more often the dramatic semblance than the reality.[29]

As for Roosevelt's basic views, also difficult at the time to determine, in hindsight, the significant kernels of thought can be separated out from the confusing chaff. He was a believer in large-scale, long-range planning, both in foreign policy and domestic affairs.

National planning, as Roosevelt conceived it, was more comprehensive and longer in timespan than the specific planning of a New Deal legislative program, with which he was engaged during the interregnum. But the legislative program could grow out of his overall view of what a national plan should be. Planning on this order was to receive his sponsorship during the New Deal. During the interregnum he was silent concerning the findings of the President's Committee on Social Trends — doubtless because it was Herbert Hoover's enterprise — although, through Moley, Professor William F. Ogburn, director of the Research Committee, offered to let him see an advance copy. But within a few months Ogburn and his scholarly associates were enlisted in Roosevelt's early New Deal, in which planners received encouragement and even greater opportunities.[30]

As for Roosevelt's own lengthy interest in planning, he wrote of it informally in *Survey* early in 1932. Publication of a New York regional plan reminded him "of that day nearly twenty years ago when Charles D. Norton and my uncle, Frederic Delano, first talked to me about the City Plan of Chicago":

> I think from that very moment I have been interested in not the mere planning of a single city but in the larger aspects of planning. It is the way of the future.
>
> Out of the survey initiated by Mr. Norton in Chicago has developed something new; not a science, but a new understanding of problems that affect not merely bricks and mortar, subways and streets; planning that affects also the economic and social life of a community, then of a county, then of a state; perhaps the day is not far distant when planning will become a part of the national policy of this country.[31]

Roosevelt as an imaginative idealist liked to think in terms of great national plans. Yet he was also a political realist who at each given point usually decided to opt for the possible, the enactable. Hence the immediate measures he came to propose were often no more than a segment or shadow of his grand schemes.

The interrelationship between his large overall thoughts and his specific recommendations to Congress later in the spring of 1933 may best be examined in this chapter and the next within the matrix of national planning. During the months before he took office, Roosevelt made substantial progress toward establishing a cluster of programs he considered essential first to restore, then to maintain prosperity: farm relief, better use of rural and forest lands, and development of hydroelectric power. Recovery, he believed, hinged upon raising farm prices. Once that was achieved, reform to bring lasting improvement called for rural and regional planning. It was out of the starting point of Roosevelt's planning ideas that eventually there developed specific immediate measures for the limited goal of increasing farm income. This transition from overall rural planning to the specifics of the Agricultural Adjustment Administration is instructive in its demonstration of Roosevelt's thought processes and techniques, and central to the first New Deal program.

Agricultural planning had been a major theme, even though the pledge to raise farm prices commanded national attention when Roosevelt had delivered his major campaign speech on farm problems at Topeka, Kansas, the previous September. At Topeka he called for a number of long-range goals: allocating lands to their best use, moving farmers off of poor, submarginal acres onto better soil, and through decentralization of industry, to encourage millions of people to return from cities to villages and the countryside. These were concepts Roosevelt had learned from many years of discussion with farm economists and rural sociologists, especially some Cornell professors. There were echoes too of Theodore Roosevelt's Country Life movement. By 1932, Roosevelt as governor of New York through speeches and legislative recommendations had made the ideas his own.[32]

Rural planning had considerable national appeal. It might meet strong opposition from commercial farmers, processors, and conservative rural congressmen, but it won warm support not only among reformers like Tugwell, but among many experts of agricultural college background — men like M. L. Wilson who had thought of themselves as Republicans and who had grown up on farms. When Professor Wilson of Montana State College came to Albany in the summer of 1932 to help in the campaign, he moved from his exposition of the domestic allotment, which he considered a temporary expedient, into recommendations for overall agricultural planning. Roosevelt listened with approval.[33]

Country life to Roosevelt was a way out of the depression and a guarantee of permanent comfort. His persistent dream was of a wholesome existence for quantities of previously deprived city people, moved to healthful country surroundings, raising their own food, and earning some income from employment in a nearby small factory. It would have been a return to the way of life in hamlets of their grandparents' day. Curiously enough, Roosevelt's familiarity with the impoverished way of life of village and country people in Dutchess County, New York, and Meriwether County, Georgia, his knowledge in the field of rural planning and his own persisting financial losses on crops — none of these seemed to dampen his enthusiasm.[34]

"Land is not only the source of all wealth, it is also the source of all human happiness," Roosevelt wrote in 1932 with all the agrarian fervor of a Thomas Jefferson or William Jennings Bryan. It was only in the large cities, Roosevelt incorrectly suggested, that large numbers of people were actually going hungry, suffering from lack of overcoats and being evicted from their dwellings. In smaller communities, and in the country, "there is deprivation; but . . . there is not the same kind of being up against it, of not knowing where you are going to sleep tonight or where you are going to get the next meal." He was sure that both food and shelter were cheaper outside of the metropolis. A New York City woman wrote him in December 1931, asking if he could not do something, since "rent is driving poor people crazy. . . . My husband is practically working for rent alone as his week has been cut in two." Roosevelt responded sympathetically that he knew the high cost of building in the past and high assessments at the present time made rents unreasonable. But the only solution he could propose was, "Have you and your husband ever thought of moving to a smaller community where the rents are a great deal lower?"[35]

Ten to fifteen million city folk must move to the country, or they would come to constitute a permanent pauper population, Roosevelt told Justice Brandeis, the advocate of decentralization, during their conversation in November 1932. Brandeis reported, "He seemed fully to appreciate the effect of a static population & that this would constitute 'a new era.'" Again, in January 1933, when Roosevelt spoke at a Boy Scout Foundation dinner in his honor, he put aside entirely his prepared manuscript, although it had already been released to the press. Instead he swung into the back-to-the-land theme:[36]

> One of the country's leading economists was telling me the other day that there are at present 12,000,000 unemployed in the country. . . . In 1929, when things were going ahead apparently at full speed, there were well over 3,000,000 out of work.
>
> If every factory wheel in the country were turning at full speed today we should still have 5,000,000 unemployed. When prosperity comes back, and it is coming back, what are we going to do with that

5,000,000? We have got to restore the balance of population, get them out of the big centers of population, so that they will not be dependent on home relief.

The quest for ways to retrain city people for rural life concerned Roosevelt. "There are hundreds of thousands of boys who only know the pavements of cities," he remarked, "and that means that they can take only those jobs that are directly connected with the pavements of cities." He had a concrete idea in the back of his mind, but was not as yet ready to reveal it. That January evening he suggested no more than that the Boy Scout movement was a means of fitting city boys for the country.[37]

What Roosevelt privately was visualizing as a main component of his recovery program was to put the unemployed to work in large numbers improving the nation's forests, and to finance their forestry work through floating a $500 million baby bond issue. He hoped many of these people would remain permanently in the country. Already he had experimented with forestry camps in New York State, and out of this idea was to come the Civilian Conservation Corps. Roosevelt continued to hope it would fit city youth for country employment. In November 1933, when CCC officials sought permission to undertake educational activities, Roosevelt approved the proposal, noting: "O.K., but stress forestry, agriculture, etc., with object of transferring life work of as many boys as possible from cities to country or small communities."[38]

In one respect, Roosevelt was perhaps correct in wanting to get people back to the countryside. It was the most shocking irony of the depression in America that while people were almost starving in the cities, foodstuffs were going to waste in the country. A penniless Nebraska farmer en route to a relief conference reported at the gathering:

In Clinton, Iowa, they told us to eat on the soup line. I didn't eat that soup. It seemed like about one onion floating in a barrel of rain water. There were children on that soup line. They were blue and pinched. Children who were ten years old looked to be six. They hadn't been properly fed for three years. There we were, who had sheep and cattle we couldn't sell, mounds of wheat and corn, potatoes and onions, and herds of pigs to put fat on those kids, and we couldn't bring it to 'em.[39]

Toward this complexity of problems requiring immediate relief and long-term planning, Roosevelt brought multiple, interrelated solutions. Within a few weeks after his election, he was thinking both of specific ways to raise farm prices and to relieve unemployment through improvement of forests and grazing lands. Tugwell, whom he put to work on farm matters, enthusiastically concurred, hoping that reforestation and land improvement could be incorporated in the overall agricultural program. After discussing these ideas at length over dinner with Wallace, Tugwell reported, "We both feel that the greatest need we have is for more trees and more legumes and he is going to try to find a feasible way of holding out a bait to farmers for this long-run improvement." [40]

Out of these interrelated strands of thought there were to come government-sponsored price supports for basic agricultural commodities, mortgage refinancing, some experimentation with rural relief and resettlement, and both soil and forest conservation programs. Action was essential, but action would depend upon reconciling differences among pressure groups and within Congress. Much of this task, essential as a preliminary to the enactment of legislation, Roosevelt supervised from afar before his inauguration.

CHAPTER VI

A First Attempt to Aid Farmers

Informed by a reporter of a mid-West newspaper that the Winter wheat crop was very light this year, Mr. Roosevelt replied that his own information was also to that effect. This led to a remark that "God was working with the new administration," and the retort that aid more than human might well be needed to solve the farm problem.

— NEW YORK TIMES, *January 27, 1933.*

Farmers so desperately needed federal aid that Roosevelt could not indulge in leisurely planning in private and postpone all action until he was well established in the White House. Rather he must take a public stand in favor of legislation before he assumed office even though he could not yet exercise effective control over Congress and could expect a Hoover veto if Congress did act. Roosevelt must at least try to marshal Democrats and farm bloc Republicans in Congress to enact a farm relief measure and repass it over the President's veto.[1]

Overproduction had forced farm prices to such pathetic lows that it was sometimes more practical to slit the throats of sheep than to market them, to burn grain rather than sell it. If production controls did not go into effect by planting time in the spring of 1933, the glut of produce would continue for still another year before controls could edge prices upward.

Debt was a critical aspect of the problem. While prices had plummeted there had been no proportionate scaling down of the farmer's obligations. He would have to deliver two or three times more cotton, pork or milk to repay his mortgage than the amount exchangeable for the dollars at the time he had borrowed them.

There was also the discriminatory disparity between farm prices and the prices of manufactured goods that led farm leaders to demand a return to an earlier more favorable ratio, to "parity." Roosevelt in his extemporaneous whistle-stop talks during the 1932 campaign had repeatedly summed up the disparity, Moley remembers, "by saying that the farmer now had to carry two wagon-loads of his produce to town to buy the same shoes, machinery, and other manufactured goods that one wagon-load would have bought in the period before the World War." Roosevelt was not exaggerating. Indeed, he would have been more correct had he said "three wagon-loads compared with 1921." A farm wife in South Dakota wrote a local editor, "My husband had to buy a pair of shoes. To pay the price ($4) we brought to town twenty pounds of butter and twelve dozen eggs. That just paid for the shoes." [2]

Nor was it invariably true, as Roosevelt sometimes seemed to think, that at least farmers enjoyed adequate food and shelter. In the single-crop areas where little was grown but cotton or wheat, even farmers could barely eat or stay warm.* And increasingly they were being evicted from their homes and fields. In the five years preceding March 1, 1932, 9.5 percent of all farms had been put up for forced sale, and 3.5 percent more at tax delinquency sales — and March 1, 1932, began a year of unparalleled further disaster. Through 1932, banks teetering on the brink of failure were foreclosing farm mortgages at a rate of 20,000 per month.[4]

Roosevelt soon learned, if he had not already known, what the abstract figures on farm sales meant in specific human terms. At the end of January 1933, Henry A. Wallace sent him a plea for help from a woman whose family, cold, starving, and deeply in debt, was being evicted. Wrote Wallace:

> Pathetic letters are coming in from the farm women. . . . I suppose that the most terrible cases of heart sickness and fear in the United States today are those of a tenant farm family where the rent cannot be paid, where eviction is imminent, and where there is not enough ma-

---

* Aubrey Williams, field representative for the American Public Welfare Association, who became a New Deal relief administrator, was trying to explode the truism that farmers continued to eat well. The governor of North Dakota told him in 1932, "These people out here are farmers, and farmers don't starve. Things get tight, but they always manage. . . . They never went down to Washington and asked to be put on the public teat and by God if it's left up to me they ain't going down there now." The governor agreed to visit farms with Williams. At the first house, the farm wife showed the governor a bare cupboard; there was only a little salt pork and potatoes to eat. The governor was shaken. At the next house, the wife showed them a large storeroom full of shelves, baskets, and cans — all empty — and explained:

> We've gotten down to living off of potatoes and a few canned beans that I was able to put up last Spring, and they are about all gone. . . . Last year I had more, four years ago, I had it full. Before that, I can't remember when I didn't have it full. We've got wheat, but we can't get nothing for it. Wheat is what's kept us alive, I guess. We even burn it for coal. I don't know what the country is coming to, it don't matter how hard they work, or what they try to do.

The governor decided to spend $50,000 on rural relief.[3]

chinery and equipment to make it possible for the family to go on another farm. The situation of these people is even more desperate than that of the unemployed in the cities.

At one time there was much talk about the agricultural ladder, — how the hired man could become a tenant, the tenant become a mortgaged owner and the mortgaged owner become a free owner. Today the ladder seems to be leading the other way and many owners are contemplating with fear the prospects in case they are unable to meet their interest and taxes.[5]

Out of desperation, farmers not only in the corn belt but here and there throughout the country were resorting to violence to try to hold onto their meagre possessions. Day after day during the winter of 1932–1933, newspapers carried accounts of forced sales and agrarian resistance, at their most serious reminiscent of the preliminaries of Shays' Rebellion, as angry farmers with gun and noose intimidated officials. The president of the Farmers' Union, John A. Simpson, in January 1933 put bluntly to Roosevelt the political purport of the agrarian distress: "My candid opinion is that unless you call a special session of Congress, after the fourth of March, and start a revolution in government affairs there will be one started in the country. It is just a question whether or not you get one started first." [6]

The relatively conservative George Peek, meeting with food processors in Chicago on December 22, 1933, jotted in his diary two news stories from the *Chicago Tribune*. One concerned a sheriff's sale at Hagerstown, Maryland, where farmers would not allow outsiders to bid: "Horses brought 5 cents each, cows and calves from 10 cents to 75 cents, and automobiles 60 cents each." The other reported that both of the two largest banks in the nation were under Rockefeller control. Peek used the news items to hammer at the processors that their fate was tied to that of the farmers. So indeed, Roosevelt would have added, was that of everyone in the country. Everyone had a stake in emergency measures to raise agricultural income and refinance farm indebtedness.[7]

The long agricultural depression beginning in the early 1920s was a national disaster. The 22 percent of the American people living on farms (compared with less than 6 percent forty years later), were a sizable part of the population who had not shared the prosperity of the New Era. Roosevelt's diagnosis of the failure of the prosperity of the twenties was in part that the persistently low crop prices had dragged down the farmers' purchasing power, in time depressing the whole economy. There were statistics to back his view of agricultural income. Gross farm income in 1919 was approximately $17 billion, in 1929, $12 billion, and in 1932, $5 billion. Net income in 1932 was less than $2 billion.[8]

Against this stark background, Roosevelt in his major farm address at

Topeka, Kansas, during the 1932 campaign rephrased Lincoln, "This Nation cannot endure if it is half 'boom' and half 'broke.' " American economic life, he believed, was a seamless web; factories could not operate at full capacity if fifty million people on farms had little money with which to buy their output. These views also formed the rationale for raising farm prices through restricting agricultural production. Even with cutbacks, farmers would produce ample food and fibers for urban people.* City dwellers would receive compensation for the slightly higher prices they would have to pay since revival of the rural market would create jobs.

During the 1932 campaign, Roosevelt committed himself firmly in general outline, without at all spelling out specifics, to the raising of farm prices. Presumably he would do so through production control — crop limitation — and definitely he would undertake a program that would not be a drain upon taxpayers. In addition, he leaned heavily toward mild inflation as a means of increasing prices, but to avoid conservative attack let no hint of inflation slip into his speeches. He was also pledged to some program of refinancing farm indebtedness, but that was not controversial. He talked too of his overall, long-range objective, rather comprehensive rural planning, which meant a great deal to him. But amid the existing distress these pledges attracted little attention. What counted both to farmers and farm leaders were prices and debts.[10]

The component of the agricultural program of greatest urgency and debate to which Roosevelt had to give the greatest attention was the raising of farm prices. Yet it was the one in which he had the least personal interest and experience. Consequently he had no firm early commitments, was flexible in his views, and ready to move toward a formula which might possibly make economic sense, and would with certainty be politically effective.

Roosevelt, ever since he had first campaigned for the New York State Senate in 1910, had proclaimed himself in politics as the friend of the farmer; his program as governor had been highly successful. But he had not had to cope with the overproduction of the great staples of the

---

* The agricultural surplus came from a drop in European purchases together with the release in the 1920s of 25 million acres previously used for producing feed for horses and mules as the nation shifted to automobiles, trucks, and tractors. The increase of food and fiber production for consumption within the United States had exceeded the population growth by 9 percent. An historian of agriculture, Van L. Perkins, concludes,

> Administration spokesmen were, therefore, quite right when they argued that, even if the predepression levels of consumption were restored, there would still be a substantial price-depressing surplus. While critics might still have argued that even the predepression levels of consumption had been inadequate for many Americans, a position that would have had considerable validity, their criticism did not usually take that form.[9]

South, the prairies and the plains. Milk production problems, the largest that New York farmers faced, could respond to state controls, since New York City was the nation's biggest market. So Roosevelt had been able to stay out of the great controversies among cotton, wheat, and hog producers over the merits of various technical devices to raise prices. It is doubtful if he had more than a superficial understanding of any of these schemes until some weeks after he had been elected President. He did understand well enough the common demand of all vocal farmers (most of whom, like him, had no real grasp of the details of plans) that the federal government must pull agriculture out of the depression.[11]

Ever since the collapse of World War I commodity prices had brought farm distress, agrarian leaders had worked for some sort of federal control program comparable to that of wartime through which to re-store rural prosperity. In 1922, George N. Peek and Hugh S. Johnson, who had both served on the War Industries Board and were at that time with the Moline Plow Company, published a pamphlet, *Equality for Agriculture*, in which they proposed that the government establish a ratio between agricultural prices and those of manufactured goods, a fair exchange value. Henry A. Wallace's father, Henry C. Wallace, who was Harding's secretary of agriculture, called a conference of farm leaders which urged Congress and the President "to re-establish a fair exchange value." Later the term "parity" was used to express this idea: the government should boost farm prices until they reached a ratio to other prices comparable to that in the years just before the war.

As a means of regaining equitable farm prices, Peek and Johnson proposed a scheme for dumping farm surpluses over the American tariff wall, compensating farmers through what was called an "equalization fee." Basically it was a protectionist scheme to make the tariff on farm products workable. A government corporation would buy up certain crops at a high figure and market the surplus overseas, charging farmers an "equalization fee" to cover the loss on sales at a lower figure outside the United States. The protective tariff would prevent farm products from other nations from undercutting the high prices within the United States. The McNary-Haugen bills of the 1920s embodied these devices.

Uniting across party lines, representatives and senators formed a farm bloc in the 1920s and twice passed a McNary-Haugen bill. Each time President Coolidge vetoed it as preferential legislation violating laissez-faire — although on the very day of his first veto he signed an order increasing by 50 percent the tariff on pig iron. Roosevelt, in 1924 an ambitious politician on the sidelines, had favored farm relief in general, but would not countenance "the artificial price fixing scheme."[12]

Since the "equalization fee" device would have stimulated still greater overproduction within the United States, and driven still lower a depressed world market, inviting retaliation from other nations, agricultural economists began to invent other schemes. President Hoover tried to solve the problem through the creation in 1929 of the Farm Board to loan money to marketing cooperatives or itself establish corporations to buy surpluses in order to raise prices. To succeed, the Farm Board would have had to persuade farmers voluntarily to reduce production, an impossibility. Consequently, during the depression crisis, it quickly spent its $500 million and did little to delay the plummeting of prices. During the 1932 campaign, Roosevelt criticized Hoover's call for voluntary crop reduction as a cruel joke, but Roosevelt himself had been slow to accept a plan for firm government regulation.

By the summer of 1932, Roosevelt on the advice of Tugwell had agreed to the "domestic allotment" scheme, which was beginning to win the backing of numerous commercial farmers, especially producers of corn, hogs, and cotton. It was a device to provide farmers with financial incentives to reduce production so that prices would then rise behind the tariff wall. Each producer of a staple should receive a "domestic allotment" — permission to grow a certain percentage of what he had produced in the past, and one or another sort of subsidy to encourage him to cut his production.

During his campaign, Roosevelt was adroit in couching his campaign generalities so that supporters of the domestic allotment scheme would read his endorsement, and those others committed to quite different proposals could also interpret approval. To the right there was still Peek and a considerable following opposed to limiting production and favoring the overseas disposal of surpluses. This group was more powerful than its numbers might indicate, since it included some large-scale farmers and many processors influential with congressmen. Baruch, whom Roosevelt respected for his congressional following, was sponsor to both Peek and Hugh Johnson. Roosevelt had no intention of offending them unnecessarily.

Another conservative group, especially appealing to Roosevelt, were the farmers of the Northeast, many of them dairymen affiliated with the Grange, who wanted as little federal economic regulation as possible yet sought higher prices. The "commodity dollar" proposals of Professor George F. Warren of Cornell offered them apparently a simple means of bringing limited inflation. Warren, an expert on prices of farm commodities, argued that if the gold content of the dollar were to be lowered, automatically prices would rise. While this idea was attractive to Roosevelt, he kept quiet about it during the campaign.

More ardently inflationary were the stricken wheat growers and ranchers on the Great Plains, vociferous neo-Populists, low in financial influence during the depression but of considerable voting strength. In good times they had been as well-to-do as corn belt farmers, but in depression years they were even worse hit and more radical. Their chief spokesman, John A. Simpson, of the Farmers' Union, full of the spirit of 1896, wanted to raise prices through massive currency inflation. Senator Elmer Thomas of Oklahoma represented this view in Congress. Moreover, Simpson backed a simple solution: the government should fix the price of farm commodities at a "cost of production" level. In practice this level would have been substantially higher than "parity." Roosevelt had given Simpson the impression of hearty sympathy; he had included a "cost of production" statement in the 1932 Democratic platform, and during the campaign told Simpson and a group of Farmers' Union leaders who met him in his railway car at Sioux City, Iowa, that he favored "cost of production." [13]

Through generalizations so inclusive that all but advocates of inflation could read their schemes into his specifications for a farm program, Roosevelt rallied strong rural support behind himself in the 1932 election. True, the specifications best fit the domestic allotment scheme, but its opponents were not offended. It was M. L. Wilson himself who had suggested to Roosevelt that he not mention "domestic allotment" by name in order to avoid alienating supporters of other devices or frightening Easterners. Gradually, through the campaign and thereafter more and more farm leaders began to accept domestic allotment.[14]

Roosevelt wished the backing of all farm organizations, and of all those farmers nationally who could not afford to belong to organizations. He was determined to retain unified agricultural support not only during the campaign but after. He spoke on farm problems not only in Topeka, Kansas, and Sioux City, Iowa, where it could have some effect upon the election, but also in Atlanta, Georgia, although southern farmers were already solidly Democratic.[15]

After the election, Roosevelt began immediately to move toward a farm program, trying in the process to retain all his rural support. He followed the same omnibus approach that had worked so well during the campaign. It was politically useful, since it forestalled potential opponents, those favoring dumping overseas, who had read this concept into the Topeka specifications, from charging that Roosevelt was now double-crossing them.* Further, Roosevelt in private had convinced Tugwell that a mixture of programs might be sound economics. Each major crop might operate under its own program. Tugwell reported that Wallace "was much struck with the Governor's idea of different heads for various crops under the allotment scheme & thought it an improvement on the rigid plan for all." [16]

* FDR did ultimately leave out "cost of production" and braved the wrath of John Simpson.

Unfortunately, part of the reason for Roosevelt's eclecticism was his failure to study carefully any of the several alternate plans; he had little real understanding of the proposed mechanisms. In time his ignorance created embarrassment. He was saved from greater embarrassment by the failure of most farmers and of the public in general to grasp the technicalities of the plans. Even the *New York Times* at one point confused M. L. Wilson's proposals with the quite different ones of John A. Simpson because each called his plan the "domestic allotment." [17]

Whatever program farm leaders agreed upon he would accept, Roosevelt told the press. There is little doubt that Roosevelt meant what he said — he was determined to avoid serious division among the farm leaders and ready if need be to experiment with several devices. As another means of achieving unity, he tried to give the impression that he was not personally taking responsibility for choosing the mechanism or mechanisms for raising prices. Indeed, the farm leaders and members of the congressional farm bloc did gain the impression for a few weeks that they were in control. For a while Roosevelt did little except engage in general discussions with them, and through agents coordinate their efforts. The authoritative accounts of New Deal farm legislation have focused upon either the leaders of the farm organizations or the agricultural economists who drafted the legislation, assigning Roosevelt only the role of a remote, distant aegis whose election had made action possible. These accounts are accurate as far as they go, and they perpetuate the impression Roosevelt wished to create at the time. Yet Roosevelt did exercise more leadership and decision-making than was apparent on the surface. His part in the drive for farm legislation therefore merits examination.

The components in the problem Roosevelt faced in seeking quick legislation were in brief:

The farmers themselves were eager for relief, and through their desperate actions becoming frightening. Congressmen were readier to legislate upon their behalf, businessmen less ready to block legislation. Yet the farmers had little notion of the specifics of the various farm plans. Some looked to inflation as the panacea, others still favored exporting, and some had begun to favor crop control. But they were desperate enough that they would accept any omnibus plan that looked as if it might be of help. Curiously enough, while they provided the pressure for farm legislation, there seemed to be no need to educate them on relief plans in order to gain their support.

Farm organization leaders, who had quarreled vigorously through the 1920s were now, because of the desperation of their constituents, readier to unite on an overall plan, as Roosevelt insisted. The election of Roosevelt gave them for the first time a genuine opportunity to obtain a federal program, and they were not disposed to relinquish it through serious dissension. Since for years these leaders had been persistent and effective lobbyists, they were the ideal group to obtain farm legislation for Roosevelt. They, in turn, were not likely to jeopardize their prestige and standing through failing to meet his expectations. "The indicated strategy" on the plan for both Roosevelt and the intellectuals, Tugwell noted at the time, was "to father it on some pressure group." [18] Roosevelt could create the impression that he was doing no more than to endorse what the farm leaders agreed upon, gain strength for his proposals as being truly agrarian, and thus blunt personal attack from conservatives. Clifford Gregory, editor of the *Prairie Farmer*, remembered that at a meeting of farm leaders in Chicago late in the campaign Roosevelt said in effect, "One of the first things I am going to do is to take steps to restore farm prices. I am going to call farmers' leaders together, lock them in a room, and tell them not to come out until they have agreed on a plan." Already before the campaign was over, the farm leaders were holding meetings. Edward A. O'Neal, as head of the most powerful organization, the American Farm Bureau Federation, was trying to assume leadership at these meetings, and as soon as it became apparent Roosevelt would be the next President, became firm in his advocacy of the domestic allotment plan because Roosevelt wanted it. In December it obtained the Farm Bureau endorsement.[19]

Farm Bureau Federation support of the program was especially vital, since the federation had already achieved the difficult task of bringing together within its organization some southern Democratic along with large numbers of northern Republican farmers, all of whom were so relatively well off that they could pay ten dollars yearly dues even in 1933.* These were substantial farmers whose views carried weight with their congressmen. Within its own membership the Farm Bureau had to some degree achieved the difficult undertaking of uniting the dairymen, corn-hog producers, wheat ranchers and cattlemen of the North with the cotton growers of the South. Its leadership was on good terms with that of the Grange, which was particularly strong in the Northeast.

Specialists in agricultural economics provided the technical background and planning that were necessary to prepare a specific, operating federal program. They sat in the meetings with the farm organization heads and journal editors, shaping much of the thinking. Richard Kirkendall labels these authorities the "service intellectuals," an interlocking group, dedicated to public service, whose success in 1932–1933

* In 1933, there were about 9,500 American Farm Bureau Federation members in the South, 98,000 in the Midwest, 19,000 in the West, and 36,500 in the Northeast.[20]

depended upon providing professional advice to the farm leaders and the President-elect. They were professors from agricultural colleges, like M. L. Wilson, or experts already in the Washington bureaucracy, like Mordecai Ezekiel, who since 1930 had been assistant chief economist to the Farm Board. It was Ezekiel who persuaded the Farm Board in December to give veiled support to the domestic allotment plan. Within this category could fit Roosevelt's representatives like Tugwell and Morgenthau, who need not distinctly bear the label of envoy but could be identified respectively as an expert on agricultural economics from Columbia University and the editor of the *American Agriculturist* who had been trained in agriculture at Cornell. Soon Henry Wallace of *Wallace's Farmer* joined them. It was a group which through bill-drafting could begin to bring shape to indistinct plans. (Frederick Lee, who had drafted the McNary-Haugen bills, was the lawyer who worked with them; Lee was on Peek's payroll that winter.) But it was also they who, even before Roosevelt was inaugurated, became the target of those jealous of their considerable power or offended by their progressivism. Peek wrote, "We called the group the 'economists' as distinguished from the 'farm' people." Even Wallace seemed to Peek a dreamy theorist who had never been "in the real rough-and-tumble of life." Already men like Peek (who had been a farm implements manufacturer) were expounding a "dirt farmer" mystique to counter the impractical "college professors" — although Wilson was a wheat grower, and Wallace a prime developer of hybrid corn. Tugwell, who came to suffer the most abuse, curiously enough was of food processor background; in his teens he had worked summers checking farmers' fields to determine the exact dates when peas and other crops were ready for his father's cannery.[21]

In Congress, the chairman of the House Committee on Agriculture, Marvin Jones of Amarillo, Texas, on the high plains, was sympathetic; the ranking Democrat on the Senate Committee, Senator Ellison D. Smith of South Carolina, was, as his nickname "Cotton Ed" suggested, interested in little beyond one crop. While each was under pressure from the farm lobbyists, each like all congressmen interested in agriculture was also under pressure from the representatives of processors and business trade associations. While Jones was cooperative in participating in meetings to plan and expedite a farm bill, some of the other congressional leaders were still jealous of their own prerogatives and ready to be divisive.

This was the background of Roosevelt's first effort to obtain legislation from Congress — while he was still only President-elect. It was a forlorn venture. Roosevelt undertook it carefully, expending little of his prestige in a cause scarcely attainable until after March 4. Soon after his election, Roosevelt openly set forth upon what appeared to be a democratic course. He began conferring with farm organization executives and congressional leaders on agricultural legislation. The first meeting was with the executive committee of the Grange on November 26. On noncontroversial proposals, Roosevelt gave his firm support. Louis J. Taber, head of the Grange, said when he came out of the meeting that Roosevelt favored credit and marketing legislation, and felt that the key to recovery was restoration of farmers' purchasing power. As to whether that could best be achieved through the export debenture (which the Grange had earlier favored), or the domestic allotment, or some other means, Roosevelt told the Grange leaders he was keeping an open mind. He did emphasize that he hoped Congress would during its short session create machinery he could put into operation immediately after he took office. And he urged the Grange officials to keep in touch with him and the congressmen.[22]

The meeting with the Grange set the pattern for Roosevelt's conversations in the days that followed with other farm leaders and key senators and representatives. Further, he let newspapermen know that he had invited Wallace, M. L. Wilson, and Morgenthau to discuss agriculture with him at Warm Springs.[23]

Wilson was not able to reach Warm Springs in time, but this was the occasion for Wallace's first visit, and the beginning of his integration into the Roosevelt administrative machinery. Wallace, reminiscing with Tugwell many years later, wondered if perhaps Roosevelt during that visit was not sizing him up, testing him as a potential secretary of agriculture. There were indications. Roosevelt threw together Wallace, with his corn-hogs orientation, and Senator John H. Bankhead of Alabama, even more than "Cotton Ed" Smith the spokesman for both cotton growers and processors of the South. Wallace was delighted, and saw the meeting as an opportunity to further the tenuous alliance between the two powerful agricultural interests. It may have been in Roosevelt's mind that since cotton Democrats would play a large role in agricultural affairs in Congress, it would be helpful if a secretary of agriculture could work smoothly, indeed enthusiastically, with them.[24]

"In retrospect I can see now exactly what they were doing," said Wallace years later. "They wanted to see what ideas I had with regard to the farm program and see how I would handle myself vis-à-vis Franklin Roosevelt; vis-à-vis Ray Moley; and vis-à-vis Henry Morgenthau; and later vis-à-vis members of the House agricultural committee, specifically Marvin Jones."

Wallace was less enthusiastic about the mission Roosevelt assigned him, to work in Washington for enactment of farm legislation during the lame duck session. Later, Wallace concluded that the real aim must have been to acquaint him with the leading farm bloc congressmen. He always felt the effort was rather quixotic:

> Somehow, knowing Franklin Roosevelt was always a realist in matters of this sort, I just can't believe that he seriously expected to have the kind of legislation that he wanted coming out of that lame duck Congress. How could you expect such legislation to be signed by Herbert Hoover? If you did get it through the Senate as well as the House, it would be a purely political maneuver and not anything that would be helping agriculture immediately. You might be putting the Republicans on the spot by showing how you were striving to get something through for the farmer no matter what. I was just not impressed with the practicality of what Franklin Roosevelt asked me to do at that time.[25]

If indeed, Roosevelt was less than sincere in trying to get agricultural legislation enacted in the beginning of 1933, he never admitted it. His moves were baffling to those he involved, but did, even in falling short of legislation, help his ultimate end. He followed his numerous general discussions by sending a group of experts of varying views to work for him in Washington: Wallace, M. L. Wilson, Tugwell, and Morgenthau. With Morgenthau part of the time was Professor William I. Myers of Cornell. Each one of these men was in time to hold important office in one or another facet of the New Deal agriculture programs. Of this array, both Morgenthau and Tugwell seemed to be speaking for Roosevelt. While they gave this impression, no one was entirely sure — nor could they always be sure. Each thought he had a mandate, and indeed so he did; it was up to him to make the most of it without getting into trouble.

An interesting example of the Roosevelt technique was the clash between Morgenthau and Tugwell over rural credit, or the refinancing of farmers' mortgages. Morgenthau considered himself an authority on the subject, and in the early New Deal came to have charge of the new consolidated farm credit program. On the other hand, Tugwell had persuaded Roosevelt to make a speech during the campaign pledging aid to debtor farmers, and after the election had enlisted D. L. Wickens of the Department of Agriculture and Mordecai Ezekiel to plan both emergency and permanent programs. Tugwell noted in his diary in January 1933 how difficulties had developed and the manner in which Roosevelt resolved them:

> After this work had been going on for some time I discovered that Henry Morgenthau was proceeding to a similar end with Wm. I. Myers of Cornell. I knew Myers and liked him but was well aware that he had *laissez faire* notions (all the people at Cornell have) and would work against any price adjustment. I therefore believed that my people were

better suited to the national situation. I was rather worried about conflict so I asked Morgenthau and Myers to come to a conference in Albany at which Ezekiel and Wilkins would also be present. This was held and it was agreed in F.D.R.'s presence that we should all proceed together. But H.M. has steadily proceeded since to disregard that agreement. I can't go here into the differences of opinion involved in this, although they are very strong and general. But it all came about, again, because F.D.R. does not realize what the issues are and is careless in his commitments. He tells several of us to do the same things even though we may have opposed views and then forgets. This is all right when it involves study and reporting to him, but when it involves handling a political situation the results are apt to be ludicrous. This is a case in point. . . .

The differences came out in the conference night before last [January 10, 1933] with F.D.R. He asked me what was going on and I told him that H.M. did not tell me and that I was afraid to mix in for fear of confusion. Moley and Berle were there. We told him our ideas about farm credits. After thinking it over, F.D.R. asked Moley to act as a sort of chairman and draw the thing together. He thought there should be postponement for a week or two until things could be formulated and then we should all agree on emergency legislation, letting the permanent set-up go over until the Special Session. . . . Moley undertook to call H.M. off and to get together a more general conference in which various views could be heard, perhaps under Senator Hull's aegis. However, last night I went to the Harrington Hotel where, I had heard, the farm leaders were meeting and found Morgenthau and Myers in full blast. I told Wickens and O'Neal on the side that the Governor had said to go a little slow and to get the thing straight before proceeding too far. At least twenty bills (including a comprehensive one by J[oseph] Robinson) had been introduced and it was going to be a considerable job to reconcile all the views since they had crystallized so far.

After a while H.M. called me into the hall and said he had had a conversation with Moley and that they had had something of a row. He wanted to be frank, he said, and not to get into any mix-up. . . . I said I had no objection to his handling farm credit matters but that there was political dynamite involved and that he had better [get] his authority straight. He said he had arranged for a meeting of a few Senators and Representatives in the morning at which there would be communicated to them the points of agreement amongst farm leaders and economists. He said he had told Moley that he had talked to F.D.R. over the phone and had been told to go ahead with this. This amounted, of course, to Moley's being superseded, but without being told. . . .

13 January 1933. . . . Henry Morgenthau had lunch with me in a conciliatory mood, evidently having made up his mind that I am honestly only a work-horse and not a rival. He professed to have the agricultural credit situation well in hand.[26]

In time those who worked for Roosevelt came to understand his technique, sometimes sloppy and confused, and sometimes effective. It could easily generate animus among contenders. Morgenthau left Moley sputtering, and both Moley and Tugwell suspected him of being over-ambitious to become secretary of agriculture. Morgenthau, for his part, having long been intimate with Roosevelt, was less disturbed by over-lapping jurisdictions and more confident of his mandate. It was Morgenthau who drew up with Representative Jones Title II of the farm bill, dealing with agricultural credit. Also it was Morgenthau who in January 1933 quietly acted as Roosevelt's envoy to Prime Minister Richard B. Bennett of Canada, preparing the way for an international wheat agreement.[27]

Roosevelt found each of his agricultural experts useful and continued to utilize them all. Actually, it was Wallace, who did not yet have the appearance of speaking for Roosevelt, who with his enthusiasm for both the domestic allotment and "honest dollar" came closest to Roosevelt's overall views.

At Roosevelt's request, his farm team conferred in Marvin Jones's office on December 3, preparing for the vital meeting with some fifty farm organization leaders in Washington on December 12–14, as an advisory committee on agriculture.

At the meeting on December 12, leaders of the Farm Bureau, Grange, and Farmers' Union (who had been holding their own preliminary meetings in Chicago) were already far along toward agreeing upon the domestic allotment. There were several staunch opponents, including Simpson of the Farmers' Union and George Peek, but they were rather on the periphery, willing for the time being not to disrupt the growing consensus. Roosevelt's experts, together with the farm economist Mordecai Ezekiel, seemed to be in control.

At the outset, Morgenthau established himself as spokesman for the President-elect, setting forth Roosevelt's program, according to the *New York Times*, as "abolition of the Federal Farm Board . . . con-solidation of all Farm credit agencies under one government bureau, and some form of domestic allotment plan." [28] The farm leaders first asserted themselves, then soon reached agreement. Tugwell noted soon afterwards:

> Things were complicated by each of the farm leaders having a pro-gram of his own. This was true also of many agricultural representatives in Congress. . . . They had to make speeches defending their own position, to read their own proposals (many of which were already in bill form — already introduced) but Morgenthau and I sat tight and listened. The general result after two days of this was that they agreed unanimously (though some of them merely came in for political reasons and could hardly be counted on) . . . and the [bill] was written.[29]

After hot arguments the draft bill that came out of the meeting included hogs along with wheat and cotton, but, in keeping with the demands of the New Yorkers, excluded dairy products. Farm leaders had won one important debate over the protests of Roosevelt's representatives. They included as Title I of the new bill a measure Jones had already introduced to give quick relief to farmers. It would have forced the federal government to buy surplus cotton and wheat — the whole year's crop outstanding — which would have been a serious drain on the Treasury. Roosevelt opposed any agricultural program which would involve heavy expenditures from general revenues. The crop reduction program would not go into effect until the second year, and then would not provide for state and county quotas and individual contracts with producers. There seemed much work remaining before a bill would meet the specifications of Roosevelt and his advisers. Tugwell was pleased, because he felt that in one important way he had improved previous proposals. He had convinced the assemblage to abandon the theory that farm prices were to be raised to a level equivalent to world prices plus the American tariff. Instead they should rise until their ratio to prices of manufactured goods was what it had been in happier days for farmers, to parity. What was really outstanding about the Washington session was the agreement on the domestic allotment plan. Roosevelt had the basic commitment he sought. Much remained to be done before it would be workable, but already the new bill bore the title Agricultural Adjustment Act.

The advisers, with the inclusion for the first time of Ezekiel, met briefly with Roosevelt on December 23 to go over the draft measure and plan strategy. It was, Ezekiel thought, the first time Roosevelt had examined the details of the proposed legislation. As yet, Roosevelt still remained in the background, and made no significant changes.[30]

As participants at the Washington meeting spread word of the bill they had drafted, opposition immediately mobilized to fight a rearguard action against production control and in favor of overseas dumping. George Peek, sitting in on the meeting on the last day, was "more firmly convinced than ever that farm leaders were being led off by economists." Peek brought pressure upon Representatives Jones and Rainey, then hurried to Chicago to attend a meeting of processors, troubled by the prospect of a farm program to be financed through a processing tax. Peek recorded in his diary, "The cotton men said that a 5-cent tax on cotton in a pair of overalls selling at 69 cents retail meant an increase in the cost of raw material entering into production of 12 cents; but that the retailer might mark up that price of 69 cents to anywhere from 85 cents to $1.00."

Bernard Baruch took a different tack, urging Roosevelt to readjust war debts and lower tariffs in order to restore Europe's power to buy farm produce. Hugh Johnson, writing from Baruch's South Carolina plantation, expressed to Moley his pungent opposition to the domestic allotment, asserting that important savings could come to farmers through eliminating the multiplicity of distributing organizations. These protests were ominous because of the power of the processors over the farm bloc, and the influence of Baruch and his men with several key senators. Gradually the conservative opponents of the domestic allotment began to coalesce in favor of a scheme of federal rental of acreage in states producing a surplus as a means of taking land out of production.[31]

The opponents also became suspicious of the President-elect, even though he was keeping himself well in the background. The chairman of the board of General Mills, James F. Bell, who had called the Chicago processors' meeting, wrote from Minneapolis in January 1933, "There is an impression here that Mr. Roosevelt has been alienating himself from his conservative friends and leaning toward the more radical elements in his party." Roosevelt and his experts continued to engage in consultations with the conservatives, neither accepting their proposals nor breaking with them. It was a muted struggle.[32]

The battle went on in Congress through January and February. Marvin Jones with the aid of Speaker John Nance Garner rounded up House votes, and on January 12 obtained passage of the farm bill by a vote of 203 to 150. Fiorello La Guardia, a defeated Republican congressman from New York City, helped deliver the support of more than a score of progressive Republican representatives. He predicted earlier to Berle that with the aid of the progressives the House could pass a measure over the President's veto. But the House did not obtain the opportunity.[33]

Conservatives succeeded in blocking farm legislation in the Senate. Several senators dragged their heels, the Senate Agriculture Committee held hearings, and both those to the right and to the left of the domestic allotment plan aired their views emphatically. Simpson made little impression from the left, but the lobbyists for the millers, meat packers, textile manufacturers and others protested that the processing tax would throw some of their employees out of jobs and oppress consumers. Peek maneuvered cautiously among the senators, some of whom responded sympathetically. The Republican sponsor of Peek's earlier export proposal, Charles McNary of Oregon (and the McNary-Haugen bills), told Peek that he had found the House bill so impossible that he had tossed it in the wastebasket. Peek had a number of amendments introduced in the Senate, one of which, to authorize marketing agreements to reduce surpluses, passed. It had the strong support of dairymen and other groups not producing the great basic staples, since it seemed to open the way for federal aid to producers of all farm commodities.[34]

Senator "Cotton Ed" Smith, who after March 4 would be chairman
of the Agricultural Committee, was in no mood to undertake the
bidding of the President-elect. On January 16, 1933, he came to New
York to spend an hour conferring with Roosevelt, then announced he
favored passage of a bill, but one that would restrict production of only
cotton and wheat. If it were successful, he announced, the price of
all other farm commodities should improve without legislation. Smith
had the committee votes to defeat supports that had been voted in the
House bill for hogs, tobacco, rice, peanuts, and butterfat. Back in Washington, Smith claimed that he had Roosevelt's approval for a limited
program.

When Roosevelt passed through Washington on January 20, he
thought he obtained agreement from congressional leaders to concur
in a conference of committees of the two houses upon a bill that would
apply the domestic allotment crop restriction to four crops: cotton,
wheat, corn in the form of hogs, and tobacco. This was as close as
Roosevelt came to obtaining Senate enactment of the farm bill.[35]

Through the month of February 1933, opponents of the domestic
allotment plan prevented Senate action. Senator McNary gave Peek an
additional reason for not acting; he said, referring to Coolidge's veto
of the McNary-Haugen bills, that he had "gone up the Hill and down
again twice by the veto route and would not do so again." Senator
Byrnes reported to Moley near the end of February that the Agricultural
Committee would make no effort to report the farm bill before the
end of the session, that according to Bankhead a majority of the committee did not favor it. Byrnes offered Roosevelt an alternative, which
Baruch had been backing, the land-leasing scheme. Bankhead had prepared a bill embodying it, and if Roosevelt wished, would introduce it.
President Hoover, Byrnes pointed out, would not be likely to veto it.[36]

The lure was interesting, particularly in the light of an entry in
Peek's diary, concerning a conversation Peek had on January 29 when
he went with Baruch to the train:

> He wanted to know what I thought of acreage rental and I told him
> "no good at this late date for this year." . . . He asked if I thought
> Hoover would sign and I said I had no idea, but I did not see how he
> could without stultifying everything he had said. B.M.B. pointed out
> that he might let it become a law without his signature, referring to
> campaign pledges of F.D.R. and election results, and then let the Demo-
> crats have the odium of administering it.[37]

President Hoover did indeed give a cautious endorsement to the
land-leasing proposal in a remarkable eight-point message on economic
recovery which he sent Congress on February 20, 1933. Hoover declared in terms certain to antagonize Roosevelt: "It seems clear that

the domestic allotment plan is wholly unworkable. It will do far greater harm than good to agriculture. . . . The plan proposed by the Secretary of Agriculture some time since for temporary leasing of marginal lands is the least harmful and the most hopeful of all the plans which have been proposed." He proposed financing it "by a manufacturers' excise tax of probably 1% to 2% upon these commodities." Hoover's outline proposal was so similar to the domestic allotment scheme and its processing tax that it is hard to see why he was damning Roosevelt's program. Subsequently in his *Memoirs* he was so confused concerning the "domestic allotment" that he described it as another name for the McNary-Haugen bill, and ascribed its paternity to none other than Hugh Johnson.[38]

Whatever the merits of land leasing, Roosevelt had no inclination to switch to it. Despite Hoover's endorsement and the enthusiasm for it of Baruch, Hugh Johnson, and the coterie of southern senators, in practice it need not have varied much from domestic allotment and might have worked about as well. There was nothing intrinsically more conservative in this proposal than in domestic allotment; details could make either of them more or less favorable to operators of certain sizes and types of farms. In any event, Roosevelt did not scrap his agreements with the farm leaders and ask Bankhead to introduce a bill, nor did Bankhead do so. The Agricultural Adjustment bill died in committee, and farm relief legislation, to no one's surprise, was put off until the new Congress could meet.

Back in Montana, M. L. Wilson observed the spectacle from afar with some irritation and bewilderment. He found it difficult to explain why Roosevelt had allowed the Senate committee to hold hearings and engage in delaying tactics; perhaps, he concluded, Roosevelt wanted the farm question to "develop into a sort of hopeless muddle," which only positive presidential leadership could resolve after March 4.[39]

The simplest explanations of historical phenomena are most often correct. In this instance Roosevelt gave every sign of feeling committed to obtain agricultural legislation as soon as possible because of the pressing need of the farmers. An indication of his seriousness of purpose are the orders he gave Tugwell on January 18, 1933 (as Tugwell noted them at the time):

> Get the farm bill through the Senate in better shape; then have several farm leaders issue a manifesto congratulating Congress and anticipating all the arguments Hoover will use in an almost certain veto message. Handle it to get headlines and show the real sources of the arguments — business interests to be hurt. Call on all farmers for support. Hoover might possibly sign the bill; then we should be so much ahead; but if not this will contribute to a better opinion for it when it does become law.[40]

The delay in the Senate seems to have changed Roosevelt's plan. In view of the opposition of President Hoover and the considerable senatorial resistance, he was apparently not willing to push friendly senators hard enough to obtain legislation that would not pass over a veto. Nor would he concede political credit to the Republicans by scrapping his own program and accepting the parallel one of Hoover, the processors, and southern senators. He would not jeopardize in advance prestige and power he would need as President.

The maneuvering in Washington had brought some useful results. It had unified dominant farm lobbyists, who together with the agricultural economists had agreed upon outlines for a farm program. Roosevelt's cohorts had softened the millers, and with the assistance of Beardsley Ruml, the meat packers, through obtaining their suggestions on administrative details, so that they would be more ready to accept the inevitable. Also a beginning had been made in persuading educated Easterners that the domestic allotment had merits. On the train to Washington one day in January, Tugwell expounded the plan so eloquently to Walter Lippmann that Lippmann subsequently publicized it with perception and sympathy.[41]

"All the basic elements of the Agricultural Adjustment Act of 1933 had been developed and had gained widespread acceptance," Van L. Perkins points out: "production control, the parity-price standard, the processing tax, the basic-commodity idea, and the idea of using marketing agreements for a number of important purposes, including the subsidization of imports." Further, Mordecai Ezekiel during these weeks had worked out preliminary proposals for the machinery of what was to become the Agricultural Adjustment Administration, and had drafted projections of how it might be expected to work. The skirmishes in the Senate had given seasoning to Roosevelt's lieutenants, and provided some indication of the formidable effort it would take to counter conservatives and obtain passage of a domestic allotment program. The lines had been drawn; the battle awaited the commander in chief.[42]

CHAPTER VII

Toward a Roosevelt Foreign Policy

> It is a pity not only for this country, but for the solu-
> tion of world problems that any statement or intimation
> should be given that I consider it undesirable to assent
> to co-operative action on foreign problems.
> — FDR, *press statement, December 22, 1932.*

Since the problems of the world could not wait for four months, circumstances were forcing Roosevelt as President-elect to develop much
of his foreign policy in advance. Contrary to general assumptions, Roosevelt despite the acute domestic economic crisis devoted considerable
attention to foreign affairs during the months before and after he took
office. Had it not been for the crisis conditions at home that deepened
after his election, he would have spent part of the interregnum visiting
western Europe, conversing firsthand with leaders there, even as Hoover
when President-elect had toured Latin America aboard a cruiser.
Foreign policy was an area of responsibility congenial to him in which
his interest never flagged. As a youth he had been excited by Theodore
Roosevelt's ventures in diplomacy and navy building; as assistant secretary of the navy he had participated at least peripherally in Wilson's
diplomatic as well as naval enterprises, particularly enjoying occasional
small ventures into diplomacy. His campaign for vice president in 1920
had centered upon a defense of the Treaty of Versailles, and throughout
the 1920s he had acted as a spokesman for the Wilsonian views, consulting from time to time with Wilson's one-time advisers. In the
campaign of 1928, it was he who prepared the Democratic foreign policy
article for *Foreign Affairs.* His only deviation from the liberal Democratic position came early in 1932 when, in response to the challenge
of William Randolph Hearst and isolationists, he declared he no longer
believed the United States should join the League of Nations. The
disavowal pained many Wilsonians, including Eleanor Roosevelt, but
was genuine on the part of Franklin Roosevelt, who insisted he had not
departed from Wilsonian principles but realistically regarded the League

as a failure. Throughout the 1932 campaign he had failed to develop foreign affairs as an issue, not through lack of interest, but rather because he accepted the general outlines of the Hoover-Stimson program. He had commented to Moley that he thought "old Hoover's foreign policy has been pretty good," and had remained silent after a verbal assurance came from Hoover, via Anne O'Hare McCormick, that Hoover would say nothing unless Roosevelt forced him to do so. Yet Roosevelt had campaigned vigorously against Hoover's international interpretation of the depression, and during the interregnum was framing a recovery program based primarily upon economic nationalism. His struggle with Hoover over war debts, as many observers both in other nations and within the United States noted at the time, involved only trivial differences concerning debt policy toward Great Britain and France. Rather it centered upon politics within the United States and the shape of Roosevelt's future program for recovery.[1]

Roosevelt held an overall coherent view of foreign policy. It was Wilsonian in origins, and differed only in particulars from that of Hoover (who after all had been one of the most loyal of Wilson's subordinates during the First World War). It was even closer to the ideas of Secretary of State Stimson (whose thinking had been formed in the Theodore Roosevelt mold). One day in late August, Roosevelt expounded some of his views to a British newspaperman, A. J. Cummings, who after the election, on November 10, 1932, published them in the London News Chronicle. The British Foreign Office took note, and sent a copy to the embassy in Washington. On January 29, 1933, Roosevelt set forth much the same ideas, covering a broader scope, to Sir Ronald Lindsay, the British ambassador, when Lindsay visited him in Warm Springs. Both Lindsay and the Foreign Office were focused upon the goal of eliminating war debt payments, but Lindsay did cable Whitehall an account of Roosevelt's full views — a remarkable indication of the direction he was to give to foreign affairs early in his administration: [2]

His general scheme is . . . a comprehensive programme in which debts and other questions will automatically fall into their proper places. He cannot contemplate piecemeal action and only by presenting Congress with prospect of curing the world as well as the domestic situation can he hope to ensure its support. He wishes to treat each subject on its merit. . . .

As regards tariffs he is most anxious that they shall be so handled as to increase international trade. . . .

He says that silver must certainly be discussed because monetary policy of India halves the purchasing power of the Far East. He also mentioned stabilization of currencies but very vaguely and I do not think he knows much about it. Indeed I should say that on all economic subjects he is rather weak.

He has a scheme for limiting production of wheat by international agreement between Canada, Australia, Argentine and United States. This is a return to scheme which was attempted about three years ago and failed owing to American objections which will now be withdrawn. . . .

He wants disarmament to be included in the programme. Not only is reduction of military expenses more than ever necessary almost everywhere to balance budgets but also Congress will never cease rightly or wrongly to connect debts and disarmament together. So far as land armaments are concerned he is generally in favour of Hoover's principle of strictest possible limitation of essentially offensive weapons such as tanks and heavy mobile guns. He is also in favour of prohibiting totally use of aeroplanes for any military purposes. They would exist solely for the purposes of commerce. I said I understood it was impossible to distinguish properly aeroplanes for commercial purposes from those for military. He said that he believed distinction could be made efficiently enough.

As to naval disarmament he suggests (1) As there will be no military aeroplanes there will be no need for aeroplane carriers thus providing a large saving in tonnages. (2) Similarly as fire of heaviest naval guns can only be directed with the help of aeroplanes, these guns will cease to have any utility and it will be possible to reduce size of battleships. He seems only partially aware of difficulty he will have over this question with American naval staff. (3) Though he cannot expect abolition of submarines he believes it may be possible to get agreement for a reduction of their size.

He wants to contribute something towards political re-settlement and therefore towards security of Europe. Though matter is in no way an American interest and only slightly less so a British one, he mentioned the question of Polish corridor which he understood was now at a point at which parties interested were [prepared to] talk and seek settlement. What he contemplated was retrocession of corridor and grant to Poland of continuous and uninterrupted independent railway communication with Gdynia. I expressed liveliest alarm at this suggestion and strongly deprecated it stating all the obvious things. I am not convinced that he has gone into the question carefully and I think that we shall hear no more about it. . . .

In regard to the Far East his view is that there is nothing to be done at present to stop Japanese government and that the question can only be solved by the ultimate inability of Japan to stand the strain any longer. His policy would be to avoid anything that would tend to relieve that strain.[3]

It was an exposition characteristic of Roosevelt — ranging from the fundamental to offhand speculation. He was firm in his basic conceptualization but vague or ignorant concerning various specifics. A detail like the war debts issue really did not concern him deeply, except as a possible booby-trap in relations with Congress; what Lindsay took to be economic ignorance was, rather, a considerable degree of political awareness. Roosevelt in his discourse was setting forth the basic policy he would pursue toward Japan for several years; his suggestion concerning the Polish corridor through former German territory was a momentary thought — but it was there that World War II began.

There was irony too, in the date of Roosevelt's conversation with Lindsay, January 29, 1933, for it was the very next day that Adolf Hitler became chancellor of Germany and rapidly rendered impossible Roosevelt's hopes for disarmament. Yet for months, and on some points for years, Roosevelt's frame of reference continued to be what he had set forth at Warm Springs. The United States along with the rest of the world was about to be swept up in a diplomatic revolution, but as yet the events of the aftermath of World War I and the depression crisis were shaping attitudes and alignments. While Roosevelt was bent upon disarmament and its monetary savings to help bring recovery in the United States, the British and French were focused upon the monetary savings they could attain through canceling war debts which they claimed morally they did not owe. Neither the British nor the French as yet were willing to make much concession in order to maintain cordial relations with the United States, nor seemed much concerned with the degree to which they might irritate the American public. Yet over the debts controversy resentments could grow which could ruffle relations between the two debtor nations and their American creditor through several critical years. Neither the Anglo-French nor Roosevelt view of the world at the beginning of 1933 would prove very workable in the decade of the dictators.

Roosevelt's starting point in foreign relations, before he began campaigning in the fall of 1932, was to build more amicable relations with the British and the French. His interview for the London *News Chronicle*, given while the Ottawa Conference was establishing imperial preference in trade relations, emphasized that he looked forward to the day when the United States, Canada, and Britain would act in concert "with a complete identity of political and economic interests and will in that way acquire the true leadership of the world." He gave a comparable interview emphasizing friendship for France for publication in *Le Matin*. It was well received in Paris.[4]

Further, Roosevelt considered visiting Europe before taking office. "I am eager to get into personal contact with leading Englishmen," he told Cummings of the *News Chronicle*, "and to find out something at first hand of modern Britain and the new spirit in Europe." When Prime Minister Ramsay MacDonald inquired of Norman Davis, the

American delegate to the Geneva disarmament conference, in October if the election of Roosevelt would disturb the highly satisfactory relations with the United States, Davis (who had conferred with Roosevelt at Hyde Park) assured him it would not, and told him Roosevelt hoped to visit Europe during the interregnum. Davis reported to Roosevelt that MacDonald was most enthusiastic. After the election, Davis cabled Roosevelt that while Roosevelt might not find the trip feasible because of troubles within the United States, it would be helpful in Europe. "Basis for solving international problems is being found more and more through cordial relationships established between heads of governments," Davis suggested. "Also trip would help reassure general continuity fundamental lines American foreign policy particularly on such questions as disarmament and Manchuria." Others discouraged Roosevelt. Frankfurter was firmly opposed, and Brandeis thought it would be a "very, very serious mistake." "Also I hope no foreign potentate will come here," Brandeis added; he thought it was hard enough to convert Americans "to the necessary international action." Reluctantly Roosevelt abandoned the idea, informing Davis in late November, "The difficulties are such that I have concluded to stay here." At the end of the year he apparently again toyed with the idea of visiting Europe; he was said to have made out a tentative itinerary. President Hoover offered (probably through Stimson) the use of a warship. Possibly all that was involved was a vacation cruise, since Roosevelt thanked Hoover, and told him he had arranged to sail in waters near Cuba and the Bahamas on Vincent Astor's yacht. Roosevelt's alternative to a trip to Europe was the very device Brandeis warned against, to persuade the European leaders to visit him in Washington soon after he took office. Through Davis and others, Roosevelt sent them personal messages.[5]

Roosevelt sometimes dabbled with adventure in the conduct of foreign policy. He was ready to make use not only of solid, reliable diplomats like Davis, but also exciting secret emissaries — in this instance William Bullitt. As it developed, Bullitt was no Colonel House, although he would have liked to have been. He did engage in feelers toward the recognition of Russia, and twice during the interregnum made tours of western Europe, carrying on discussions in Roosevelt's name. An old friend of Roosevelt's, Louis B. Wehle, a nephew of Justice Louis D. Brandeis, had convinced him during the campaign that he should obtain firsthand reports on European developments from Bullitt. A man of wealth, Bullitt gave a thousand-dollar contribution to the campaign, and met Roosevelt on October 5, 1932; Roosevelt was delighted with his quick and brilliant mind and widely ranging knowledge of European affairs. Although still a young man, Bullitt had already a remarkable background in foreign affairs. In February 1919, he had headed a mission to investigate conditions in Soviet Russia for the American delegation at the Versailles Conference; later he had strongly opposed the treaty and its instrument, the League of Nations, as vehicles which might carry Europe into a second world war. On November 16, 1932, Roosevelt agreed through Wehle that it would do no harm for Bullitt to sail, entirely on his own initiative, for private talks in London, Paris, Geneva, and Berlin.*

Bullitt sent messages back to Roosevelt via Wehle, and upon his return, went with Wehle to dine in Albany on the evening of December 27, and discuss European attitudes toward the debts. Bullitt reported, Wehle has recalled, "that the outgoing American Administration's policy, if continued by the incoming one, might cause progressive falls of European governments and resulting conditions in some countries bordering on revolution." On December 14, Premier Edouard Herriott and his cabinet had been forced out in France over the debt question. Bullitt sailed again on January 13, this time arranging to communicate directly with Roosevelt through a code they had agreed upon — a sport Roosevelt had enjoyed when he was assistant secretary of the navy.† In London, the British at first were suspicious of Bullitt. An official in the Foreign Office who knew him warned that he was "both irresponsible and dangerous," and doubted if Roosevelt had entrusted him with the mission. "Even if he has done so," the official warned, "I should recommend the greatest caution." Lindsay, who had heard in New York that Bullitt was representing Roosevelt, suggested he should be listened to, but told nothing beyond what the Foreign Office might not mind reading one day in an American newspaper. Bullitt did indeed carry credentials — a friendly personal note — from Roosevelt to Prime Minister Ramsay MacDonald, urging him to come to Washington after the inauguration. Roosevelt thought MacDonald would be more generous than his cabinet, and believed that was why the diehards in Great Britain opposed letting him go.[7]

There was a further significance to Bullitt's negotiations in England, as was evidenced by a note Bullitt enclosed in an envelope the prime minister dispatched to Roosevelt: "This paper received January 24, 1933, from Neville Chamberlain, Chancellor of the Exchequer. MacDonald added verbal assurance this afternoon, Jan. 24, that embargo on loans to Japan would not be raised." [8]

In Britain and elsewhere, Bullitt engaged in discussing both a possible

---

* FDR also received entertaining reports early in 1933 from another friend, a roving reporter for *Liberty*, Cornelius Vanderbilt, Jr.

† Among the cryptic messages was a cable sent by FDR's secretary Marguerite Le Hand to Bullitt at the Hotel Adlon, Berlin, "DELIGHTED SUGGESTION OSWALD ALL WELL." "Oswald" in the code signified Neville Chamberlain.[6]

settlement of the war debts and the placing of economic pressure upon Japan.

News soon leaked that Bullitt was acting as Roosevelt's emissary, and indeed that he was assuring the British that the President-elect favored cutting the British debt 80 percent — which created excitement in both Europe and the United States. A Republican senator from Indiana, Arthur Robinson, raised the matter repeatedly in the Senate, obtained State Department reports from American embassies overseas on Bullitt's movements, and tried to obtain prosecution of Bullitt under the Logan Act, which forbids private citizens from carrying on diplomatic negotiations with foreign powers. Senate Minority Leader Joseph Robinson and his Democratic colleagues ridiculed their Indiana colleague. Since Bullitt had technically at least gone on his own authority, Roosevelt was able calmly to deny the rumors, and Bullitt quietly came home.[9]

During these same weeks, Roosevelt engaged in some informal but direct negotiations with the French over their delinquent December 15 debt payment. Thomas Lamont, after lunching on December 31, 1932, with Emmanuel Monick, financial attaché at the French Embassy, and Jean Monnet (later famous as the father of the Common Market), reported to Roosevelt that the attitude of many people in Paris was, "We will never pay that installment to Hoover. We want to find a way of paying it to Roosevelt." An official in the French consulate in New York arranged through a friend of Roosevelt's, Florence C. Whitney (Mrs. Caspar Whitney), for Ambassador Paul Claudel to visit Roosevelt secretly at his New York home on January 10. The French commercial attaché, Mrs. Whitney reported to Roosevelt, "seemed very much worried . . . about the trend of feeling in this country towards France." It seems to have been a genuine apprehension, since the embassy expressed to the Foreign Office its fears that Americans might boycott French imports. On New Year's day, Monick suggested to Moley that the French government would be willing to make at least a token payment if it could point to some new factor which would explain to the French public why it had changed its policy. Moley was suspicious of any real intent of the French to make a payment. In any event, he insisted that a secret meeting would be folly, and that Ambassador Claudel's visit should be open, and labeled as simply social.[10]

The conversation was pleasant and productive, as Roosevelt at his urbane best courted the ambassador. Claudel, one of the greatest French men of letters of his age, sent a report to the Quai d'Orsay that read like one of the scenes from his poetic dramas, and is particularly revealing of Roosevelt's personal approach to foreign relations. It had been, wrote Claudel, a fascinating meeting with "a man of the world full of simplicity and humanity . . . a real friend of France":

I thanked the President-elect for granting me a private conversation, renewing a tradition that his immediate predecessors had interrupted. I told him that in view of the situation of the world, with France and America occupying such an important position at the converging point of such large interests, that it was impossible to exclude the possibility of direct and frank exchanges on all subjects between these two countries.

Answer:

The President-elect told me with great warmth that he agreed completely. You have seen the friction which has arisen between my predecessor and me. Mr. Hoover has a confidence in commissions and conferences which I do not share. These public conversations under the glare of publicity and under the pressure of domestic government cannot lead to any result. It is much better to speak frankly through friendly conversations on all subjects and *with all parties.*

Mr. Roosevelt underscored these words with a meaningful look on his face and added, "You have seen that in Mr. Hoover's last communication he was speaking of negotiations with *some* of America's debtors; I have said that I wanted to deal *with all of them* and I am happy that this difference was noticed in France."

. . .

Question:

This is greatly reassuring and I thank you. Often I read in the papers that America is going to discuss the issue of the debts exclusively with England and the countries who paid on time. But one forgets that until now, England has paid America with money she was getting from France and her other debtors and that, obviously this could not continue in the future. It is therefore impossible for England to make arrangements with you without consulting France and this prior discussion with us will be indispensable for success.

Answer:

On this question of the debts, I spoke with Mr. Stimson at length yesterday and I think that even before my inauguration, good work could be achieved by creating a better atmosphere and by working to educate progressively our respective publics, which in our two countries do not understand the question well. Until then, no discourses, no noisy expressions. . . .

I will give you a little history lesson. In 1777, France loaned 15,000,000 livres to America. We declared that we could not pay back either the principal or the interest and France never pressured us about it. It was not until the Restoration [of the monarchy in France?] that we were able to pay back the principal. As for the interest, the question never came up. This should never be forgotten.

We do not consider that France defaulted, added the President with force. She has not defaulted. A great people never default. This word should not be allowed to be uttered. We simply consider that France for reasons she considered very important has postponed one of her payments.

When Claudel brought the subject around to the June 1933 debt payment, Roosevelt assured him, "Do not worry, We will arrange things." He was equally optimistic concerning the forthcoming Economic Conference and the Geneva Disarmament Conference. "On all these points," he said, "I am sure that we will find common ground":

> I know that France is very concerned with her security. I talked about that sometime ago with Mr. Clemenceau and asked him what he meant by the word. He told me that security is the certitude for a child who is born at this moment not to see war on French soil before the day of his death. This statement struck me and I am ready to do everything in my power to give France the security that she wants. . . . The best way it seems to us in America is to lessen the strength of the offensive position and therefore fortify the defensive position. . . .
>
> *Question:*
> . . . The question of tariffs will also play an important role. What will America's position be on this point?
>
> *Answer:*
> An attitude of concessions on a reciprocal basis. . . . For example we could make great concessions on perfumes.
>
> *Question:*
> What about wine?
>
> *Answer:*
> Unfortunately we are not going to be able to wipe out prohibition before two or three years. At that point you will find us ready to listen to you. I was very amused and touched that in Paris even before my election, a wharf for the loading of wines was called Quai Roosevelt.

At the conclusion of the conversation, Roosevelt urged Claudel to come see him again at the end of February and they would again talk very candidly.[11]

Roosevelt was well launched upon his own direct diplomatic negotiations. But the most troublesome diplomatic relations continued to be with the White House rather than foreign nations. Roosevelt did not want to conduct a foreign policy rivaling that of President Hoover; neither did he want to accept Hoover's stand on debts, disarmament and the forthcoming Economic Conference since it could in effect mean committing himself to large parts of Hoover's program for economic recovery. Yet the differences between what Roosevelt and Hoover wanted had not been large enough to provoke debate during the campaign, and the confidence of the country, already at a low point, would obviously drop still further if the issuing of rival communiqués like those of December 22, 1932, were to continue.

A way out of the impasse did indeed exist, and it was Felix Frankfurter, the Harvard law professor, who called Roosevelt's attention to it. If indeed rival policies must be developed at the White House and at Hyde Park or Albany, perhaps they could at least be channeled through a single secretary of state when he was as patriotically above party as was Henry L. Stimson.

Frankfurter's opportunity to influence foreign policy came on December 22 when he happened to be in Albany, and with both Moley and Tugwell ill, assisted Roosevelt in drafting his final interchange of telegrams with President Hoover. Frankfurter's position was somewhat different from their vigorous economic isolationism. It was he, Tugwell thought, who influenced Roosevelt to issue the press statement deploring Hoover's position but emphasizing a willingness to cooperate in ways short of assuming joint responsibility.

The tack in direction was wholly characteristic of Roosevelt. If government reorganization were to come during the New Deal, Tugwell noted with prescience:

> . . . it will be because Democrats are pledged to economy and because some of the rest of us are interested in the reform of governmental structure rather than because Mr. Roosevelt believes it makes very much difference what kind of administrative organization there is. Everything which has to do with policy will be filtered through his mind. The difficulty will be that he will not always be careful to have continuing advice. He is apt to take it from me at one time, from Moley at another time, and, perhaps if we are not handy, from some senator or congressman who happens to turn up at an opportune moment.[12]

Tugwell's example was the advent of Frankfurter as a molder of foreign policy. Was this sheer happenstance? Perhaps, in this instance and some others, chance was the decisive factor, and Roosevelt by accident would turn for advice to whomever happened to be at hand. In part it must have been Roosevelt's technique (either conscious or unconscious) for preserving his own grip on power. No one person, not even Moley, knew all of what Roosevelt was doing, even concerning problems upon which their aid had been enlisted. Representative Sam Rayburn whispered to Moley as they were riding on a train back from Warm Springs, "I hope we don't have any ——— ——— Rasputin in this administration." Rayburn was not referring to Moley, and in any event had no cause for worry. Roosevelt's methods would not admit of any such person. It is an indication of how far he was from being under the domination of any one person or set of ideas that the British consul general in New York reported, "Colonel House is said to wield a most malign influence over Roosevelt and he is already being referred to as the Rasputin of the coming regime." [13]

So far as development of policy was concerned, Roosevelt occasionally may have acted by accident, but more often consulted those whose views were likely to fit the direction in which he wished to go. It was coincidence that Frankfurter was at Albany at the exact moment when Moley and Tugwell were ill, but the course Frankfurter proposed was one toward which Roosevelt's background and habits of thought strongly inclined him. Once embarked upon it, he pursued it, much to the displeasure of Moley and Tugwell, into the summer of 1933.

The new policy grew out of a two-hour conversation at Albany between Roosevelt and Frankfurter on the evening of December 22. The conversation apparently turned to Secretary of State Stimson. "Roosevelt suddenly out of a clear sky said, 'Why doesn't Harry Stimson come up here and talk with me and settle this damn thing that no one else seems to be able to.'" Frankfurter immediately called Stimson and reported this to him. When Stimson had served as a reforming United States attorney for the New York City area in the Theodore Roosevelt administration, Frankfurter had been one of his young assistants. A warm tie of loyalty between them had persisted. Frankfurter had assured Roosevelt that Stimson did not play politics, and Roosevelt in turn declared that he bore no ill will against Stimson * for having denounced him in a 1930 New York campaign address.

Even though Stimson had felt that President Hoover had left Roosevelt looking "like a peanut," he was ready after some thought to accept Roosevelt's assurances that there had been a terrible misunderstanding which could best be remedied through a personal meeting between the two. As proof of his willingness to cooperate, Roosevelt told Stimson that he would be glad to have British envoys come to the United States before March 4 to talk with him about debts.[15]

From the day after the Democratic landslide, Stimson had been ready to put what he considered to be national considerations ahead of the Republican party. "My whole work now," he had written a week after the election, "is towards making more easy and sure the proper transition of the work of this Administration over to the next, and that is quite an interesting job in itself." What Stimson wanted to achieve was basically the same as Hoover, to convince the incoming President that existing policies ought to be preserved. But while Hoover in his approach was suspicious and even antagonistic toward Roosevelt, Stimson was

---

* In 1931, Roosevelt had not felt so charitable. He wrote a friend, "One thing we need is a real Secretary of State, such as Owen Young or Newton Baker would make, in place of Henry Stimson." [14]

ready to be trusting and friendly. Stimson was in his own way none the less patronizing, but he was considerably more adroit. He had written in his diary just before Hoover's conference with Roosevelt: [16] "It is true that we here feel that this fear about Roosevelt and his untrustworthiness seems to be pretty well founded from information which has come from every side from people who have known him intimately; but I have found in life that the best way to make a man trustworthy is to trust him, and Mr. Hoover has not learned to do this as to Mr. Roosevelt." [17]

The unpleasant outcome of that meeting inflamed President Hoover far more than Secretary Stimson. It had been Stimson who repeatedly had tried to persuade Hoover to tone down his telegrams to Roosevelt, and on his own Stimson sent Roosevelt a letter on December 10 saying he approved of the forthcoming visit to Hyde Park by the two delegates planning the Economic Conference. Consequently Stimson had serious difficulty in trying to obtain Hoover's permission to go to Hyde Park. When Stimson talked to the President on December 23: [18]

> He by that time was crystallized very strongly against going near Roosevelt. He said that the only way that he would reopen the gate was to have Roosevelt send down two or three people of proper eminence to talk with Mills and myself. He felt that the situation was in a good political shape now so far as he was concerned, and he didn't care to reopen it. He was much influenced by the fact that every time he had had any personal interviews with Roosevelt, there had been unfavorable propaganda evidently coming from Roosevelt through the press afterwards. Mills coincided with his views.[19]

After the interview with Stimson, Hoover went to the length of sending him a written expression of his disapproval.* It made Stimson rather angry. He considered the letter unnecessary since he had no intention of seeing Roosevelt without Hoover's permission. That evening, Stimson called Frankfurter to explain that he could not meet Roosevelt.

But at about the same time Herbert Feis, economic adviser in the

---

* President Hoover wrote in part:

> I do have the feeling that our attempts to communicate with [Governor Roosevelt] through a third party have turned wholly to the disadvantage of the cause which we represent and to our relations, and that there may be no mistake in the future I am not prepared to reopen this subject in any form unless Governor Roosevelt frankly accepts the last proposition which I made. . . .
> I realize Mr. Frankfurter's sincerity and his no doubt proper interpretation of Governor Roosevelt's chagrin to you, but the idea of any meetings between representatives of this Administration and Governor Roosevelt that are not public, in view of our experiences lead us into further difficulties, as I have said, both in our relations to our own people and our relations abroad.[20]

State Department, delivered to Stimson, via Frankfurter, further evidence of Roosevelt's good intentions. Roosevelt sent word that while he felt the final agenda and policy for the Economic Conference should wait for March 4, there should be no break in preparation for the conference. Day and Williams should return to Geneva. Roosevelt's primary purpose, Feis reported, was to show the world outside of Washington that he was ready to cooperate. And the next day Roosevelt wrote Stimson of his continuing interest in conference preliminaries. "If at any time," he declared, "you would care to talk things over with me, either by telephone or in person, it would make me happy." [21]

Stimson regarded this invitation as so important that he decided to have another bout with Hoover, whom he hoped would return from a brief vacation after New Year's Day more rested and cheerful. To Stimson it was incomprehensible to deprive the incoming President of essential information about foreign affairs because of the strong prejudice of Hoover and Mills:

> I can see countless matters in which it will be important for me to have an interview with him in regard to such matters as Manchuria, the conferences and situations in Europe, about which I personally know so much and he so little, that I think it is most important for the United States and her foreign policy during the next four years that we should give this man as fair a chance as possible.[22]

While Stimson waited for Hoover's return after the holidays, Roosevelt began to make use of Norman H. Davis. Impressive in appearance, with white hair crowning his handsome face, Davis was a man of high prestige, as acceptable to Republicans as he was to Democrats. He had been undersecretary of state under Wilson, but now was serving President Hoover as an American delegate to the Disarmament Conference and a member of the commission planning the Economic Conference. Along with Newton D. Baker and Owen D. Young, he was regarded in the press as one of the most likely prospects for secretary of state. Here was another man Roosevelt could use as a liaison with the State Department. He sent word to Stimson on December 23, the day after Davis had returned from the Arms Conference in Geneva, that for certain purposes Davis would be useful, but that Stimson should not use him as a substitute for a secretary of state since Roosevelt did not have the slightest notion who his appointee would be. The use of Davis was painful to Moley and Tugwell, who heartily disapproved of his internationalist leanings, but served Roosevelt well as public proof that he was indeed cooperating in the cause of world stability.[23]

Upon his arrival, Davis had inadvertently created a problem for Roosevelt and his advisers. Roosevelt in his meeting on December 18, with the two delegates planning the Economic Conference, Day and Williams, had persuaded them to urge in Washington a postponement of both the planning sessions and the conference itself. They had not yet arranged the postponement. Davis told the press who interviewed him on the ship that the planning session would be held as scheduled in January and the full conference in April. He announced this again two days later. Next Davis telephoned Roosevelt, with whom he had been on friendly relations since the Wilson era, and arranged to have dinner with him at the Executive Mansion in Albany on December 26.

It could have been a touchy meeting, since Davis's publicly stated views up to this point coincided with those of Hoover, not Roosevelt. Tugwell had been so disturbed by Davis's statements that he had managed to get in touch with Roosevelt at Hyde Park while he was taking a bath on the morning of December 26, and had confirmed with him through Mrs. Roosevelt arrangements to come to Albany and bring Day. Davis, who insisted that Day and Williams must obtain Roosevelt's views through him rather than directly, managed to veto Day's trip to Albany. Tugwell himself hurried to Albany that afternoon hoping to beat Davis to the Executive Mansion so he could urge Roosevelt to see Day in person and insist upon postponement of the Economic Conference. But by the time Tugwell arrived, Roosevelt was already closeted with Davis, and sent word for Tugwell to return at 9:30 the next morning.[24]

At 9:30 when Tugwell was ushered into the governor's bedroom, he found Davis already there. Later, Roosevelt apologized handsomely for not having included Tugwell in the conversations the evening before; he explained he had wished to gauge Davis by letting him talk alone. The outcome could not have been displeasing to Roosevelt, since Davis's views were closer to his than those of Tugwell and Moley. He delighted Davis with the conversation. "I had a very nice & satisfactory visit with FDR," Davis wrote his intimate friend and fellow Tennesseean, Senator Cordell Hull. "He is keenly alive to the foreign situation, and I was glad to find that we are in accord as to what our general foreign policy should be." [25]

Even earlier, Roosevelt had assured Davis that he took the forthcoming Economic Conference seriously. "There seems to be some pessimism in Washington," he had written Davis, "but my personal feeling is that it can be made of the utmost importance. I particularly want to know about the proposed agenda." In Albany, he preened Davis's selfesteem by agreeing that Day and Williams should learn Roosevelt's views through Davis, and that the planning meeting for the Economic Conference should be held in January. But Roosevelt achieved his main point while preserving the good will of Davis. For it was Davis coming from the Executive Mansion in Albany on December 26, who told reporters that the Economic Conference in London probably would not be held before summer.[26]

At Davis's request Roosevelt immediately wrote Senator Claude Swanson asking that an additional appropriation be made as quickly as possible to continue the delegation, which was about to run out of funds, at the Disarmament Conference. And Davis for his part wrote Secretary Stimson lengthy reassurances that Roosevelt did indeed wish to be cooperative in any way which would not put him in the position of assuming a responsibility not yet his or hamper him in dealing with specific questions after he became President. Further, Davis pointed out, relaying a barb against President Hoover, Roosevelt "is firmly convinced that this can only be done by conversations without publicity and not by correspondence with publicity." [27]

Capping this letter, Frankfurter had a lengthy talk with Stimson, touching shrewdly upon a point which appealed deeply to Stimson's gallantry — the brave way in which Roosevelt ignored his disability from polio.* Stimson, for the first time feeling sympathetic toward Roosevelt, became even more thoroughly convinced he should see him. So it was that on January 3, Stimson again debated the question with the President. Stimson spoke "pretty seriously and I think rather impressively," explaining that he wanted to see Roosevelt and arrange for Hoover to see him alone in Washington. Hoover replied that Roosevelt was "a very dangerous and contrary man and that he would never see him alone." Stimson then explained how when he was governor-general of the Philippines he had dealt with the Filipinos, generally considered a treacherous race, by trusting them. The results had been good. To clinch his argument Stimson reasoned that, supposing Roosevelt "was as bad as Hoover thought he was, it would be worse to give him the grievance of refusing to see him than any treachery he might perform." This gave Hoover pause. He agreed to think over the problem, and the next day consented for Stimson to see Roosevelt provided Roosevelt asked Hoover first. Roosevelt complied, asking permission of Hoover, and inviting Stimson to lunch in Hyde Park.[29]

The negotiations thawed at least slightly the frozen relationship between Roosevelt and Hoover. In response to Hoover's relayed offer of the use of a ship, Roosevelt telephoned him on January 6 to express thanks.

---

* Frankfurter, in sketching his long relations with FDR, according to Stimson, particularly spoke of the courage with which Roosevelt had handled his own illness; how he had disregarded it instead of making any play upon it or any mention of it. Frankfurter had seen him go to bed or get up on his visit to Albany and spoke of the elaborate harness the man had to wear and of his shrunken legs and yet the uncomplaining way in which he went through this elaborate process at least four times a day.[28]

"Well, if I can do anything like that just let me know and I'll be glad," Hoover replied.

"Now," Roosevelt continued, "on my way to Warm Springs I may stop off at Washington, about January 19th. If anything turns up that you want to see me about I could run in to see you."

"I think that would be a good thing," Hoover responded — and put a transcript of the conversation into his files.[30]

There was one final bit of interplay. Roosevelt had wanted Stimson's visit kept secret, but Hoover announced it to the newspapers. Stimson, agitated, called Roosevelt, who said he did not mind.[31]

CHAPTER VIII

Roosevelt Takes Command of

Foreign Affairs

We are getting so that we do pretty good teamwork,
don't we?
— FDR TO SECRETARY OF STATE HENRY L. STIMSON,
January 19, 1933.[1]

Events moved so rapidly in the first weeks of 1933 that long before
Roosevelt took his oath of office he was assuming responsibility for the
shaping of United States foreign policy. Two factors within the outgoing administration made the transfer possible, President Hoover's feeling of helplessness and Secretary Stimson's willingness to serve the President-elect. And the direction in which Roosevelt began to move was far
more satisfactory to Stimson and Norman Davis than it was to Moley
and Tugwell.

After all the complications in bringing them together, when Stimson
and Roosevelt finally met at Hyde Park on Monday, January 9, they
were delighted with each other. Stimson wrote in his diary:

> The house was in a good deal of confusion from the accumulation
> of packages both during Christmas and after the campaign. . . . The
> Governor received me with great cordiality and we had a very pleasant
> interview which lasted from eleven o'clock when I got there through
> luncheon which we had entirely alone and on our drive back to New
> York, on which we were alone. . . . The Governor did everything to
> make the interview pleasant, and his hospitality was very agreeable. I
> had never had a talk with him before, but we had no difficulty in getting
> on. We both spoke with the utmost freedom and informality. I was
> much impressed with his disability and the brave way in which he paid
> no attention to it whatever. . . . I was very much pleased because none
> of the President's forebodings were realized, and even he did not have
> a word to say in criticism. We had quite a hard drive back, for the
> snow got to be quite deep, six or eight inches.[2]

As the conversation ranged the field of foreign affairs, Roosevelt agreed substantially with Stimson except that he seemed to Stimson too optimistic about the ease of settling the questions of debts, disarmament, and the Economic Conference. Stimson carried the conversation beyond these matters, which had been so long debated, into the vital area of Far Eastern policy and the question of curbing aggression.

The Japanese military leaders, as the depression had squeezed their nation's economy, in 1931 offered their nation a way out through wresting from China the potentially rich area of Manchuria. By the time Roosevelt and Stimson conferred in January 1933, Japanese troops were battling at the Great Wall of China, threatening to add the large province of Jehol to their new empire. Stimson, after a waiting period when he had hoped unavailingly that moderate Japanese civilians would regain control in the cabinet, had favored sanctions (an economic boycott) against Japan, no matter what their consequences might be. President Hoover was unwilling to go nearly so far; he suggested to Stimson that he use moral suasion against the Japanese by refusing to recognize their conquests. The resultant declaration of January 7, 1932, the Stimson Doctrine, asserted that the United States would not admit the legality of any forceful change in Chinese territorial or administrative integrity. In practice this meant a refusal to recognize the Japanese puppet government in Manchuria and a reiteration of the Open Door policy which the United States had announced at the turn of the century. The Open Door statement of 1899 had called upon the leading powers to respect the territorial integrity of China, and not discriminate against other nations within their existing spheres of influence there.

The Hoover-Stimson position of nonrecognition was no more than a tentative first step toward collective security. To Hoover the thought of going further toward economic, or ultimately even military measures, was abhorrent.* Stimson did not blink at the possibility of escalation

---

* The sharp difference between President Hoover's and Secretary Stimson's assumptions has led Richard N. Current to suggest that the mild doctrine of nonrecognition should have been labeled the "Hoover doctrine." Hoover firmly stated his contrasting views in a memorandum to Stimson, February 14, 1932:

I have insisted upon the aloofness of the United States from the League of Nations in that the sanctions of the League are those of force either economic or military, whereas the United States could not and would not enter in force measures to settle controversies among other nations under any circumstances. While such action may be necessary in Europe we felt it was not our part to engage in any such cases but in cases where our own treaties were involved we could cooperate in moral sanctions. I have also sought to build up the firm understanding that the United States would not under any circumstances enter into an undertaking which would bind it to indetermin[ant] action even of moral sanctions for the unknown events of the future.[3]

even to war. He saw in the evolving struggle between the United States, determined to maintain the independence of China, and Japan, bent on swallowing it, "an issue between the two great theories of civilization and economic methods." In the course of the struggle, he wrote in his diary, March 9, 1932, "it is, in my opinion, almost impossible that there should not be an armed clash between two such different civilizations." [4]

This was what the Stimson Doctrine meant to Stimson, and in this spirit he convinced Roosevelt that it ought to be continued. Its reiteration in January 1933 as a policy which the Roosevelt administration would further was a matter of some consequence. Rumors spreading throughout the world that Roosevelt would not endorse the Stimson Doctrine seemed likely to discourage member nations of the League of Nations just as the Assembly was about to vote on whether or not to censure Japan.

Acting on the basis of Roosevelt's assurance, Secretary Stimson a week later, coincident with the meeting of the Committee of Nineteen of the League to take up the Lytton report denouncing the Japanese occupation of Manchuria, enunciated again to European nations and the League the nonrecognition policy of the United States. He let it be known in Washington that Roosevelt would continue the Stimson Doctrine. When reporters sought confirmation from Roosevelt, sitting in the study of his East Sixty-fifth Street home in New York City, Roosevelt borrowed a pencil from one of them and wrote: [5]

Any statement relating to any particular foreign situation must of course come from the Secretary of State of the United States.

I am however wholly willing to make it clear that American foreign policy must uphold the sanctity of international relations. That is a cornerstone on which all relations between nations must rest.[6]

Roosevelt would not publicly amplify the statement; in private he told Lamont it went far beyond the Far East to indicate the necessity for all nations to keep their word. But there was no doubt to anyone that it was a clear endorsement of the Stimson Doctrine, and it brought response accordingly from abroad and at home. "Japan was not surprised," a spokesman of the Foreign Office in Tokyo declared. "It never believed a change in administrations would fundamentally alter the American policy in the Orient, remembering that it was the last Democratic administration which produced two of the sharpest notes received in Tokyo." The spokesman hoped that while the substance of American policy might not change, that the manner of presentation might become less irritating under Roosevelt.

Within the United States, the contrasting editorial comments of leading newspapers remarkably forecast the attitudes they were to assume in the great debate over collective security which opened a half-decade later. Some of the very newspapers like the *Washington Star*, which had criticized Roosevelt's failure to be more cooperative with Hoover on the war debts problem, rejoiced that "Japan's attack on mankind's laboriously constructed peace machinery has received a check." The *New York Times* pointed out that since the Japanese government was sure to try to contest and undermine the American position, it had required on Roosevelt's part "no little courage to announce that he is ready to go on with an effort and a policy which are certain not only to be troubled but trouble-making." Other newspapers like Joseph Patterson's *New York Daily News* took an ominous view of Roosevelt's interference with Japanese policy: "Well, if he wants to do that he had better begin building up the Navy the moment he becomes President. You can not make a war-provoking policy stick unless you have warlike weapons, and plenty of them — more than the other fellow has." [7]

Tugwell and Moley, who shared these forebodings of war, carried them to Roosevelt on the evening of January 18, arguing for hours against the Stimson policy as a tragic mistake. Moley has written, "Rex, always more fluent and excitable than I, elaborated the argument with all the clarity and passion of which he was capable. I listened intently, trying to discover from F.D.R.'s reaction what had motivated him." It was a remarkable colloquy that Tugwell recorded in his diary: [8]

The effort has already been felt in a firmer stand in the League against Japan. I sympathize with the Chinese, too. But I firmly believe it is a commitment which may lead us to war with Japan. I said so and registered a vigorous dissent from any such position. He, however, seemed very pleased at Stimson's cooperation with him; says he has called him on the phone every day lately and says, furthermore, that he is quite prepared to see the policy through. He has a strong personal sympathy with the Chinese; and this, added to a sudden trust in Stimson has carried him over. He admitted the possibility of war and said flatly that it might be better to have it now than later. This horrified me and I said so: I pointed out that Japan was doing what countries in trouble at home always did — creating trouble abroad to divert attention and to work up patriotism which could be used to support the military clique at home. I said that the budget was unbalanced, that there might be a financial crash there, and that things might fall of their own weight. Also I pointed out the population pressure and expressed some doubts whether Japanese imperialism was much worse than British. He said he had pointed out the financial situation to Stimson and that his answer had been that Japan was really independent financially and moreover nearly self-sufficient. A crash would merely mean resort to token money and that they could carry on indefinitely that way. I said that this seemed to me nonsense, pointed out that Japan would be glad to have war under those circumstances (at least the group of young militarists now in power would), and that we had better lean over backward not to be provocative. Both France and Britain have leaned toward Japan; we have sacrificed much in European policy to win even neutrality in our attempt to isolate Japan. We are hated for this and have lost much that we might have gained in forcing the removal of trade restrictions which is where our real interest lies. My arguments, I am afraid, had no effect, though they may cause him to be more cautious in the matter.[9]

How was it that Roosevelt felt the United States had so strong a stake in the maintenance of an independent China? Moley reports an answer — the one Roosevelt habitually gave over a period of years. It was a family tradition that coincided with that of the nation, and he was ready to accept it unquestioningly: "Roosevelt put an end to the discussion by looking up and recalling that his ancestors used to trade with China.* 'I have always had the deepest sympathy for the Chinese,' he said, 'How could you expect me not to go along with Stimson on Japan?' " [11]

The answer made Roosevelt look frivolous, but it had the advantage of turning off argument since it was irrefutable. He was to make use of it to blunt the demands of a baffled General "Vinegar Joe" Stilwell during World War II. In the same fashion Roosevelt habitually cited family tradition to explain why he cut corn off the cob before eating it, instead of giving the real reason, that one of his front teeth was artificial. No doubt family tradition had something to do with his viewpoint, but not nearly as much as his firm convictions concerning Japan and the Open Door in China which he had developed during his years as assistant secretary of the navy. It was part of his Wilsonian legacy.[12]

It was ominous that Roosevelt seemed willing to go along with Stimson if need be even to involvement in war. How seriously were these remarks to Tugwell to be taken? This was not the only time that he talked about the possibility of war with Japan; he brought it up at one of his first cabinet meetings. Surely discussions of this sort established Roosevelt as taking quite a different position from President Hoover, who felt that the United States would not and could not use force under any circumstances to settle controversies among other nations.

* The activities of FDR's grandfather, Warren Delano, were fresh in his mind at that time. Some months previously FDR had supplied some information on Delano's activities in China to Thomas Kearney, a New York attorney who was writing an article on the origins of the Open Door in China. In December 1932, Kearney sent FDR a copy of the article, which appeared in the *Chinese Social and Political Science Review*.[10]

To Roosevelt, resort to force was an option which under sufficiently serious provocation might be preferable to other alternatives. But if Roosevelt did not flinch at the thought of war, neither did speculative remarks like those to Tugwell signify an eagerness to embroil the United States; his pacific policy toward Japan during the next several years was proof of that. Rather, his seven years as assistant secretary of the navy had led him to speculate on the moves of the United States in case of a war with Japan in somewhat the same fashion that others might amuse themselves with the playing of hypothetical bridge hands. He discussed with Stimson what the "Orange" plan for possible war with Japan had been then, and how it had evolved by 1933. Responsible policy led him to endorse only the first tentative move in the direction of collective security, the mild assertion of nonrecognition of the spoils of an aggressor. The path upon which Roosevelt was continuing the United States was one of international cooperation for the preservation of the peace. It could conceivably lead to war, but to assert, as has one of Roosevelt's most vehement critics among historians, that the endorsement of the Stimson Doctrine made Pearl Harbor inevitable, is exaggeration.[13]

The tangible effect of Roosevelt's endorsement of the Stimson Doctrine was a slight strengthening of the League position as it ponderously moved toward a condemnation of Japan. Thus even before Roosevelt took his oath of office, his word was of weight on the scales of world power politics, and what effect it had was on the side of collective security.

Roosevelt, almost coincident with his subscribing to the administration Far Eastern policy, responded favorably to a message President Hoover sent Congress on January 10, 1933, urging ratification of a Geneva convention of 1925 to embargo arms bound for warring nations. Roosevelt would not comment directly upon the message nor allow himself to be quoted in specific words, but he let it be known that he had long favored the embargoing of arms shipments, especially to aggressor nations. It was an ambiguous stand, since it could please both those who felt the United States must remain aloof from all foreign quarrels and those who felt the nation could thus police aggressor nations. In the context of Roosevelt's debate with Tugwell over Japan, Moley correctly regarded Roosevelt's position as another step away from traditional isolationism. Roosevelt's inclination was toward collective security at the very time that the die was being cast for a new world crisis.

It was in that same month of January 1933 — that Adolf Hitler, head of the National Socialist party, became chancellor of Germany. Tugwell years later recalled that from the moment Hitler came into power, Roosevelt regarded him with a strong, almost religious, dislike, and considered him a serious threat.* This fellow, Roosevelt told Tugwell, was a very dangerous character standing against everything in which the United States believed. He saw Hitler clearly as a menace whose actions might tie in with those of Japan, and conceivably lead to war.[15]

Roosevelt's firm opposition to Japanese domination of China and, soon, his forebodings about Hitler, within a matter of months modified his thinking about national defense. There he faced two serious pressures. On the one side, the arguments of the peace-minded, and of far more importance, his own pledges of a balanced budget, dictated the utmost frugality. On the other, the view of American nationalists (including many who were firmly opposed to participation in collective security measures) combined with Roosevelt's own love of the navy would lead toward an expansion of armaments.

During the preceding years economy had weighed most heavily in Roosevelt's calculations. In May 1932, he had congratulated a Mississippi representative who had scaled down the War Department appropriations bill for having done a splendid job. Also Roosevelt had stood firmly for international agreements cutting the size of navies. He had commented in 1929, "If we could get the political thought of both [the United States and Great Britain] to insist on actual naval reduction it would not much matter what Admirals think, either in Washington or in London." He had been pleased that the London Naval Conference of 1930 prevented a new naval race. Even though President Hoover had saved the taxpayers some three hundred million dollars it would still cost six hundred million dollars to build to parity. Roosevelt grumbled, "The difficulty is that this parity business means that we shall be obliged to spend much larger sums on new ships during the next six years, and the average man does not see how this spells reduction." To Roosevelt a powerful navy was essential, but he was unhappy over its cost.[16]

Economy dominated Roosevelt's thinking when, at the end of November 1932, he conferred with Representative Carl Vinson of Georgia, the powerful chairman of the House Committee on Naval Affairs. After the conversation, Vinson, who had always been a "big navy" man, announced that the two causes of peace and economy demanded a less expensive naval administration. He favored slashing the $120 million per year for five years, required to build the navy to treaty strength, to a quarter of that sum, $30 million. Vinson quoted Roosevelt as believing that by reducing to a compact, small self-contained navy, the country

---

* On the flyleaf of an American edition of Hitler's *Mein Kampf*, published in 1933, FDR wrote, "This translation is so expurgated as to give a wholly false view of what Hitler really is or says — the German original would make a different story." [14]

could still have sufficient sea power for its protection, yet save $100 million per year. Vinson further proposed eliminating unneeded navy shore installations and army posts and airfields, and the creation of a central purchasing agency to serve both the War Department and the Navy Department. The retrenchment of the Hoover administration was to be followed by still more drastic cuts.[17]

The news created consternation in the naval and military establishments and their friends on Capitol Hill. Navy experts pointed out that a paring of $100 million from the budget would mean cutting in half new construction which had been planned, and closing almost all the navy yards; it would quickly drop the United States to third place among naval powers, behind both Great Britain and Japan.[18]

A few old admirals who remembered the enthusiasm with which Roosevelt had worked for the navy during the Wilson administration remained undisturbed by the news. One of the most articulate of them, Bradley A. Fiske, declared over the radio:

> Our Navy has been buncoed continually during all our history. . . . But I do not believe that the Navy is going to be buncoed now. At least I do not believe that Mr. Roosevelt is going to be party to any such malefaction. To do that, he would have to do something contrary to all his facts and sayings, while he was Assistant Secretary of the Navy. . . . Franklin Roosevelt went contrary to the ideas and policy of his chief, and made it possible to win the World War.[19]

In less extravagant terms, the retiring chief of naval operations, Admiral William V. Pratt, assured Roosevelt:

> There is one thing the Service can be thankful for. You know the Navy. You know it from top to bottom, & you were with it when it was put to the test. Thank God it came through. In many ways these are hard days & our *Navy* is the only contribution as I see it that we can make to put teeth into the Kellogg-Briand Pact [for preserving world peace].[20]

As of old, Roosevelt was quickly responsive to the navy viewpoint. Gratified by Admiral Pratt's letter, he expressed his wish that Pratt had been born a year or two later, so that he would not be retiring on March 1. He promised as soon as he decided upon a secretary of the navy to send him to Pratt for a little indoctrinating. In mid-January, he gave public evidence that his stand on slashing the navy might not be too hard and fast when he received two of the most widely known advocates of a big navy, William Howard Gardiner, president of the Navy League, and a leading lobbyist, William B. Shearer. Both had drawn the wrath of President Hoover in years past. Hoover had been angry at Gardiner for charging him with an abysmal ignorance of the needs of the navy; he had accused Shearer of trying to wreck the Geneva naval conference of 1927 on behalf of the steel and shipbuilding interests. Apparently Roosevelt received them with sympathetic cordiality, for a few days later Gardiner sent Roosevelt a copy of a new Navy League press release on "The Drift of the United States Navy to Third Place," adding the comment, "I am carrying on for you the matters of which we talked." Reporters, guessing at the purport of the conversations, asked Roosevelt after Gardiner and Shearer left if he favored a big navy. "Why don't you ask me whether I'm in favor of adequate national defense," he parried, "I'd say 'Yes.'" Favoring national defense, he remarked further, was like being for the Ten Commandments.[21]

The next day, General Douglas MacArthur, chief of staff of the army, testified before the House Appropriations Committee that in terms of military strength, the United States ranked seventeenth among the nations of the world. This news brought not a tremor throughout the United States, nor aroused the slightest responsive action from Roosevelt. There seemed as yet no possibility that any threat could come to the United States except from the sea. Germany still had only token armament, and as yet the military power of that potential giant, Russia, seemed negligible. Roosevelt had talked in November to an expert who had recently visited Moscow, apparently as a consultant to the Russian government on long-range bombing, but their conversation undoubtedly centered around the question of recognition and development of trade. That same November, MacArthur, just back from Europe, reported to Stimson that the Russian army was sunk. The materiel was no good and the generals incompetent. "They have killed off all their able men from the educated classes," Stimson recorded, "and, as MacArthur expressed it, he found in their high command Jewish commissars without the brains or requirement for command." No one was afraid of the Soviet Union.[22]

What little thought was given to the army seemed to center around a vague fear that it might become the tool of a Fascist uprising. According to Tugwell, a certain amount of wild talk was circulating and came to the amused ears of Roosevelt that if the incoming President could not pull the nation out of the depression, it would be necessary to resort to Mussolini's tactics. The choice of those favoring military control, it was further rumored, was Chief of Staff MacArthur — who most assuredly had nothing to do with the rumors and perhaps was not even aware of them — but had endeared himself to this sort of proto-Fascist by the spectacular way he had driven the Bonus Army out of Washington. Talk of MacArthur as a possible dictator, Tugwell thinks, is what had led Roosevelt to remark to him, in the summer of 1932,

A candid look at FDR at a banquet in January 1933.

that along with Huey Long of Louisiana, MacArthur was one of the two most dangerous men in America. A more serious rumor about MacArthur reached Roosevelt in the winter of 1932–1933 — that Mac-Arthur was unhappy over the result of the election and wished to resign as chief of staff. Roosevelt commissioned General Hugh S. Johnson, who had written vigorous speeches during the campaign, to sound out MacArthur. General Johnson reported back, "He never made any such remark. I find him, on the contrary, an ardent admirer of yours & much relieved that he has a new boss." MacArthur's wish to stay on was entirely satisfactory to Roosevelt * since his attitude toward all those around whom dissidents might congregate, Tugwell recalls, was, "We must tame these fellows and make them useful to us." [24]

Whatever the domestic implications, Roosevelt was keeping on a potentially powerful chief of staff of the army and was moving toward a larger navy at the same time that he was endorsing the Stimson Doctrine. In what later turned out to be the most important area of foreign policy, he was following the course already laid out by Hoover's secretary of state.

In Latin American policy, Roosevelt seemed ready also to follow the established pattern, perhaps carrying it further. As he had done during the campaign, he turned to Sumner Welles, who was to be the architect of the Good Neighbor policy, for broad recommendations. On the specific problem of festering relations with Cuba, Roosevelt suggested to one of his Brain Trusters, Charles Taussig, a sugar magnate who was hot for intervention either with troops or by means of economic force, that he consult with Stimson. Roosevelt specifically informed Stimson that Taussig did not represent him. Stimson, who regarded Taussig's ideas as "very half-baked" talked him out of the idea of sending troops, but failed to convince him that economic pressures also would be unwise.[25]

But on the question of greatest concern to President Hoover, economic negotiations with European nations to alleviate the depression, not much headway was made. President Hoover continued to make logical, arbitrary proposals which he regarded as unthinkable to modify. Could it have been suppressed anger that caused this fastidiously accurate man to scrawl at the top of a Stimson memorandum of a telephone conversation, "Stimpson Interview with Roosvelt on Jan 15th"? Or was Hoover, as is more plausible, simply a chronically poor

---

* Later when FDR unprecedentedly extended MacArthur's term as Chief of Staff, Tugwell reminded him of his earlier pronouncement that MacArthur was a dangerous man. FDR cut him off, remarking, "I know what you're going to say — why did I reappoint MacArthur. Where would you want him to be?" And after MacArthur's term had expired, Tugwell points out, FDR sent him to the Philippines.[23]

speller of surnames? He repeatedly misspelled these two. In any event, Hoover refused to accept Roosevelt's proposal to Stimson at Hyde Park that the Hoover administration invite some British statesmen to the United States to discuss the debt in Washington (with Roosevelt being willing to do no more than see the statesman and be kept informed). To Hoover this meant that Roosevelt had "not yet comprehended the problem with which the world is confronted and which we have tried to get before him." Hoover stated firmly his own view: [26]

> The question we have to meet is: Will the United States take a courageous part in the stabilization of the world economic situation? The British debt question is but a small segment of this problem. It should not be discussed except where there is to be a full quid pro quo in effort on the part of Great Britain to bring economic remedy to the world which would alter the course of economic degeneration in the United States.

What was needed, Hoover believed, was to establish a negotiating body of the best brains which would discuss for weeks or months with the British a program which they could jointly present to the World Economic Conference. If Roosevelt would nominate negotiators, Hoover would be glad to appoint them "if they are men of understanding in these questions" and would put at their disposal all the resources of his administration. But they must negotiate on behalf of the incoming Roosevelt administration, and should not meet a British delegation in the United States before March 1, or until Roosevelt had designated his secretaries of state and treasury.[27]

The new plan of Hoover's meant that, as earlier, he felt that a solution to the depression must be international. The announcement that negotiations were in course, he told Stimson, would be enough to aid the situation temporarily. But in January 1933, he had shifted to the view that whatever negotiations took place must be clearly Roosevelt's responsibility.

Roosevelt was, of course, accepting personal responsibility for the development of a foreign policy, as his statements on Far Eastern affairs and an arms embargo indicated. On European developments involving debts and other economic questions he was moving toward his own policy, which might not necessarily fit within President Hoover's large framework. Still, he could not refuse to talk once more with the President.

As a part of the cordial détente with Stimson, Roosevelt agreed to confer with Hoover a second time, on January 20 when he would again pass through Washington on his way to Warm Springs. The purpose was to consider the frequent requests of the British government through its ambassador, Sir Ronald Lindsay, for a review of the debt and a preliminary discussion of the Economic Conference agenda. Stimson telephoned Roosevelt that the British wished to send a commission, which within twenty-four hours after its arrival would want to know the American terms. Again Roosevelt invited Moley to go, and Moley accepted eagerly, since he feared the meeting would turn into an effort to jockey Roosevelt "into a policy of trading off the debts for some unrelated consideration which might or might not be of value." But this time Roosevelt also took to Washington Norman Davis, whose views were much closer to Hoover's than Moley's. And further, Stimson by this time had won the personal friendship of Roosevelt.[28]

Before they boarded the train to Washington, Roosevelt explained to Moley that he felt the British request was reasonable, but accepted Moley's view that the war debt negotiations and the Economic Conference must be kept separate after March 4. The question was whether Moley, backed by Tugwell, would be able to hold Roosevelt to this course against the persuasiveness of the others.

The initial advantage lay with Stimson, who had a long telephone conversation with Roosevelt on the evening of January 15, which seemed even to President Hoover to indicate satisfactory progress — that Roosevelt was ready to consider debts and economic matters together. Upon Roosevelt's arrival in Washington on January 19, Stimson called upon him at the Mayflower Hotel for a conversation of an hour and ten minutes' duration. Roosevelt greeted Stimson by alluding to their cooperation on Far Eastern matters. "We are getting so that we do pretty good teamwork, don't we?" Stimson laughed and agreed. Roosevelt expressed his disapproval of Stimson's proposal to send a dunning note to France, then asked to have Moley and Davis called in. Stimson eagerly agreed, and went over his proposals with the three of them. His impression was that Moley and Davis, agreeing with him at every point, brought Roosevelt to complete acceptance. Moley's feeling was that the general discussion had led to no definite agreements.[29]

That evening, while Moley in his room was entertaining some Democratic senators, Tugwell had a sharp discussion with Norman Davis, who wanted to entrust matters to the Hoover administration.* And

---

* The clash of opinion within FDR's own group of counsellors was expressed clearly by Tugwell in his diary:

The crux of the difference was that Davis . . . would have favored a single conference covering all subjects immediately. Moley was determined that nothing but preparation should take place before March 4, and that there should be no suspicion of concession on the debts. Davis represents Wall Street,

the next morning Roosevelt, although he had previously told reporters he would not take Davis to the White House, consented to let him attend the conference.[31]

Thus, at the second meeting between Roosevelt and Hoover, the President-elect brought Moley and Davis and the President was flanked by Secretaries Stimson and Mills. Again they seated themselves in a circle in the Red Room in the White House. Stimson recorded his impressions of the conference in his diary:

> The President opened up his talk after some pleasant allusions between Roosevelt and himself about the success of the Far Eastern matter, in which both expressed themselves well satisfied with what had taken place. The President opened up then on the debt negotiations with Great Britain; and before he had gotten very far, Moley, to my surprise, jumped in as the opponent of any attempt to connect the debt negotiations with assurances as to the economic situation in general. It seemed to me such a reversal of Moley's attitude of the evening before, where he had been helpful on the subject, that I could not understand it. Roosevelt became rather wobbly again, and we all took a hand, principally myself.[32]

Hoover likewise felt that Roosevelt was in an equivocal position. "I realized it was now a question of saving the Governor's face," he wrote after the meeting, "and I stated that often enough these were questions of a formula and that we might try to arrive at a formula." He suggested that the British should be informed that the administration would be glad to talk about debts, and concurrently about collateral questions. There was much pulling and hauling over Hoover's suggestion. Again Stimson intervened; he wrote in his diary: [33]

> Finally when we did not seem to get far with Roosevelt, I stood up in front of the mantelpiece and said that it was imperative that I, who had to conduct the negotiations with the British, should know where Mr. Roosevelt stood on this point, and whether he could or would not

the State Department, and the cancellationist attitude. Moley, I think, believes, as I do, that the debts are a big shadow in the background, affecting every international question; but he is against playing the Wall Street–Republican game which calls for cancellation. It is political dynamite. The Hoover administration is putting on pressure for immediacy which we suspect. If we let them move into commitments we will have to hold the bag with a hostile country and congress after they are gone. Doubtless in time the debts are going to be whittled away to nothing; this, however, will be over a period of years. Meantime we shall have to carry on a struggle, caught between the debtor nations on one side and a strong opinion at home. The Hoover administration is trying, in my opinion, to move rapidly now, so that they can say they have started the thing off and so can claim credit for it, but so that they will have none of the grief associated with the struggle over arrangements. Davis is playing their game and Moley resents it bitterly.[30]

insist upon the importance of keeping open the opportunity and getting assurances from the British which would be a return for concessions which we might make on the debts. In reply to that I finally got what I considered such assurances. He spoke of the two subjects as being twins, but he and Moley insisted that the negotiations on the subject of debts and the talk over these broader world conditions should be treated as physically two different discussions of which the results of one might be made conditional on the other. They spoke of having different representatives [to meet with the British] and holding the talks in different rooms; and in the communiqué, which Mr. Hoover drew up on the sofa while we were talking, they insisted on having language in it which would permit such an interpretation of the paper but would not make it too clear. . . . Their conditions seemed to be based upon some relics of the campaign in the shape of positions which Roosevelt may have taken; but in the light of the fight which they are going to evidently have with the British, it seemed to the President, Mills, and myself to be a highly foolish position to take. In the argument over it, I was the principal protagonist. The President was tactful and concilia-tory and finally drew the communiqué in a form which satisfied all. Mills, while making his position clear, very tactfully maintained a modest and aloof position, evidently on account of rumors that had been cur-rent about Roosevelt's personal dislike for him.[34]

To Moley it seemed as though he were having to defend his position that there must be separate negotiations on debts and on other economic matters against not only Hoover and his secretaries, but also against Davis and even Roosevelt. But in the end Roosevelt backed Moley and declared the discussions must be separate.[35]

After lunch, when Roosevelt was about to catch his train for Georgia, Stimson called and read over the telephone a statement to be sent to the British. Roosevelt withheld his approval, and instead authorized Moley to meet with Stimson to check the statement. Moley was dis-pleased, feeling that Stimson's message said precisely what Roosevelt had refused to accept, that debts and other economic questions were to be discussed together. Moley, aided by Tugwell, facing Stimson, his assistant secretary of state, Harvey H. Bundy, and his economic adviser, Herbert Feis, insisted that the statement read that debts and other eco-nomic matters must not be taken up concurrently. Stimson even read to him from his *aide-mémoire* of the telephone conversation with Roose-velt the previous Sunday evening in which Roosevelt had agreed with the remark to him of a Morgan partner, Russell Leffingwell, that in the two interrelated matters it was impossible to tell which had come first, the hen or the egg. Moley and Tugwell remained so adamant that Stimson lost his temper. "Stimson turned on me with indignation," Tug-well recorded in his diary, and denounced me as trying to tear down everything he had been working for throughout the term. . . . Evidently his little outburst was an accumulation of irritation at not having his way all day and at having to deal with people who must, to him, have seemed like sheer amateurs and upstarts. I was pretty angry and got red but managed to keep my mouth shut and take it out in glaring.

Later Tugwell wrote an alternate message to the British which Stimson reluctantly accepted.* As Stimson gradually regained his equanimity, he complained of difficulties of trying to protect a man more than he wanted to be protected, and "referred unhappily to trying to be Secretary of State for two Presidents." Feis, wearied during these days by the quibbling over untenable positions, took refuge in wit. It was the first time, he told Mills, that he had the privilege of disagreeing simultaneously with two different administrations.[36]

Regardless of whether Hoover or Roosevelt were right — if indeed either were — the consensus in Washington after the conference was that the Hoover administration had turned over to the President-elect the question of war debts, and that thereafter Hoover and Stimson would have no responsibility for them except to help prepare for discussions. On his way South, Roosevelt let it be known that he still held to his earlier policy of an open door for debtor nations who had paid their December installments. They could come discuss their obligations as soon as Roosevelt became President. The merits of the opposing positions on the forthcoming negotiations with the British were made inconsequential by Roosevelt himself, who shortly thereafter invited the British ambassador, Sir Ronald Lindsay, to Warm Springs. It would be hard to believe that their conversations on war debts and the Economic Conference fell into two neat, carefully separated compartments.[37]

At Warm Springs on January 29, Roosevelt conveyed to Lindsay views which Lindsay cabled to London and, sailing for home several days later, was able to elaborate upon in person. Within the course of the same conversation, Roosevelt told Lindsay that a debt settlement would have to be part of a comprehensive program to present to Congress, but that it would have to be treated upon its merits without being contingent upon other economic matters. Hoover had warned, Roosevelt said, that if he separated the package he would lose bargaining

---

* Stimson's draft aide-mémoire to the British read in part: "It will be necessary for the two governments to discuss at the same time [as the debts] the world economic problems and other questions in which they are mutually interested."
  The final copy of the aide-mémoire, as initialed by Stimson and Moley, read in part: "Mr. Roosevelt wishes it to be understood that any discussion of the debts which the British Government may wish to bring up must be concurrent with and conditioned upon a discussion of the world economic problems in which the two Governments are mutually interested."

power; Roosevelt on the contrary did not want to use debts to gain concessions on other matters, and wanted to get them out of the way as speedily as possible afer March 4. He would be ready to begin negotiations on March 6 through private negotiations, hoping within ten days or so to have made sufficient progress that the prime minister could come to stay in the White House and reach a final settlement.

As for the debt settlement, Roosevelt said he was ready to reduce the debts "as far as considerations of practical politics make it possible." He thought Congress would be willing to waive interest (or at least interest above a nominal charge for cost of management), regard all previous sums paid as repayment of capital, and make a new agreement to repay the remainder, a sum of $1.2 to $1.5 billion, over a long span of years — but not as much as the sixty-two years in existing arrangements.

When Lindsay countered that Roosevelt's proposals would not be acceptable, Roosevelt replied that conditions within the United States were really serious, worse than in England (which Lindsay granted), and "that Senator [Joseph] Robinson had just reported to [FDR] that it would be quite impossible to get Congress to agree to more than remission of interest and that if he and Hoover and an archangel from Heaven were all to be united in asking it for more it would not avail." Lindsay could only respond by pointing out that general sentiment in England was quite the reverse, "that obligations of honour had worn very thin and that opinion was quite ready to refuse further payment altogether." Lindsay's impression was that Roosevelt was fully aware of both British unwillingness to pay and congressional disinclination to make further concessions. Davis told Lindsay a day or two later that Roosevelt was thinking of asking Congress to give him discretion to suspend payments from debtor nations. "I can well imagine that it may be difficult for His Majesty's Government to forego final settlement," cabled Lindsay, "but I am also convinced that it will be just as difficult or even more so for Roosevelt to extort this much out of Congress where it is always said that a further moratorium is equivalent of complete cancellation." And indeed, newspapers reported that President Hoover was privately complaining that Roosevelt had thrown away the debts issue as a bargaining lever, while Senators Hamilton Lewis, an Illinois Democrat, and David A. Reed, a Pennsylvania Republican, sounded bipartisan warnings to Roosevelt against falling into Wilson's error of bypassing the Senate.[38]

Roosevelt had no intention of making Wilson's mistake, especially on a matter about which he had so little deep feeling as war debts. As Lindsay suspected, he did not wish to break off negotiations spectacularly. Rather, if a settlement were impossible, he seemed to want to place the onus upon European nations, and to make clear to Congress that he was doing everything possible to obtain repayment. Roosevelt resolved differences between Moley and Davis over debt negotiations in favor of the isolationist Moley, and sent Moley to talk to the senators. A day or two after the White House conference, when Moley reported to Roosevelt over the telephone that newspapers were suggesting that Democratic leaders wanted to replace Moley with Davis in negotiations with the State Department, Roosevelt replied (according to Moley): [39]

> I am through with Norman Davis. The incident is closed so far as I'm concerned. When he got off the train we said good-by and no mention of a future appointment was made. In the matter of debts you are my sole representative. . . . I also want you to go ahead and get Rex and two or three others to begin preparing the stuff I'll need for the preliminary economic discussions with the foreign representatives after March 4th.[40]

Moley had not won in the struggle over control of international affairs, even though Roosevelt had assigned him the troublesome European economic issues. On the remainder of foreign policy matters Roosevelt continued to seek advice and implementation from the Davises and Stimsons. Stimson left office in a few weeks, but Roosevelt on the advice of Frankfurter kept on Stimson's economic adviser, Feis. At the beginning of January, Frankfurter made a prophesy to Stimson that turned out to be closer to truth than flattery, "Indeed, it is not unlikely that out of office you will have more influence with the next Administration than you did with this one." On the other side, Moley's forebodings over accepting Roosevelt's appointment to the State Department were equally well founded; he was to find himself surrounded by a superior and colleagues jealous of him and hostile toward his views.[41]

In foreign affairs, once again Roosevelt was embarking blithely upon two contrary policies with opposing personnel, depending upon time either to blur differences or determine the final goal. Already among the men around Roosevelt there were alignments on each side of a small fissure that the gathering holocaust of the late thirties was to widen into a threatening crevasse. Roosevelt could not cement the fissure, but he was taking overall control. The ultimate power, as Norman Davis sensed, was to rest with Roosevelt himself.

Already during the interregnum, as Secretary of State Stimson had discovered, the determination of policy had shifted toward Roosevelt. In the days after the White House conference, Stimson telephoned Warm Springs to obtain Roosevelt's permission to arrange for other debtor nations which had paid their December 15 installments to have discussions with him. He had talked to the Italian ambassador, the Czech, and the Lithuanian, and was expecting the Latvian representative. Only Finland had paid and made no request. Roosevelt laughed, and said they would be along very soon. Also, Stimson sent Roosevelt a draft message to the delinquent French, subject to his approval. "We do not wish to take this step," wrote Stimson, "if you feel it would be injurious to any plan . . . you may have in mind." Roosevelt disapproved, so Stimson sent no further messages to the French. And so it went through February. If Stimson was having to serve as secretary of state to two Presidents, there was little doubt from his actions which he considered to be the most important one.[42]

CHAPTER IX

Building an Administration

I am struggling with the Cabinet, and . . . I want you as a part of my official family, not only because of my personal affection for you but also because I am very certain that the Country needs your fine idealism and your commonsense ability.
— FDR TO GEORGE H. DERN, *February 2, 1933*.[1]

In one important undertaking, Roosevelt was more the mundane traditionalist than the daring innovator; this was in the selection of his chief administrative officers. It was a task of large purport. They should be impressive figures but not so towering that they might, from independent bases of power, overshadow him before Congress or the public. They must be both loyal and competent, yet their appointments must enable Roosevelt to repay some of his political debts. They should represent diverse political and regional interests, still collectively they must implement the New Deal. Roosevelt did not forget that he belonged to a minority party, that he had been dependent upon Republican votes for his election and would need them four years hence if he were to be reelected. Neither did he overlook his future need for support in Congress, especially on the part of southern committee chairmen, if he were to obtain enactment of New Deal measures. These factors impelled him in making his chief appointments to try to obtain an effective administration and at the same time to maintain a winning political force.

The enlisting of an administration was a fairly slow enterprise in which, while Roosevelt measured candidates by standards of idealism in part, he acted even more on a basis of common sense. In its broadest aspect, making tentative suggestions for long lists of top political appointees was the sort of game in which Roosevelt reveled, comparable to his fun during World War I assigning names to warships. But this task was infinitely more serious and time consuming, involving endless sifting, negotiating and rearranging. He drew up a list of principal donors to the campaign, ranging from Jesse Jones, Joseph Kennedy, and Joseph Davies through Henry Woodring of Kansas. Most of these were men he knew himself; some were men suggested by other donors like the Wall Street plunger C. Ben Smith, or Senator-elect William Gibbs McAdoo of California. Opposite some of the names he wrote possible appointments:

> Jesse Straus — Berlin?
> Bill Woodin — Berlin
> Sumner Welles — Asst. Secy. Wash. D. C.
> Claude Bowers — Spain or Belgium
> Woodring — Mexico

Roosevelt also listed by states those who had been of especial assistance and promised to be of future value. Under Montana he wrote, "Prof. [M. L.] Wilson — Agricult. Commission." Under California he placed the name of the head of a condensed milk company with the explanation, "Mc[Adoo] promised him Min.[ister] to Switzerland." (Roosevelt sent him to Hungary).* And these suggestions:

> *Kansas* Harry Woodring — Compt of Currency
> Asst. Sec'y Treasury
> Director Vet. Bureau
> *Ohio* James M. Cox —
> Newton D. Baker — Special
> *Michigan* Frank Murphy — Vet's Bureau
> *Mississippi* Ask Rankin for loyal delegates
> *North Carolina* Josephus Daniels — Tennessee Basin

In addition, Roosevelt penciled a lengthy roster of offices, and again fitted names thither and yon. This time Woodring's name appeared as a possible treasurer of the United States, along with that of Joseph Kennedy and a third person. At this point, Roosevelt was thinking of Daniel Roper of South Carolina to be comptroller of the currency, Homer Cummings as governor-general of the Philippines, Ruth Bryan Owen to serve on the Civil Service Commission, Arthur Mullen of Nebraska to be assistant attorney general in charge of administration, Emil Hurja, the expert on election predictions, to be director of the census; Vincent Astor as assistant secretary of the navy — and Woodring as a possible third assistant postmaster general. During part of this time Roosevelt was penciling names against the many positions enumerated in his copy of the *Official Register of the United States: 1932.* It served as the Christmas list for the deserving politicians that year, but spring was to come before many of them discovered what, if anything, they were to

---

* The executive was John Flannoy Montgomery, chairman of the International Milk Company, who had been a member of the Council of National Defense during the First World War.

receive. Woodring, surviving the many paper realignments, in the end became assistant secretary of war. There were later scraps of paper also, listing additional recommendations, such as those of Senate Majority Leader Robinson, and noting:

> Letter to Mex. President about J. D[aniels].
> For Tenn. Valley Auth.
>   Nathan P. Harlan of Ore. or Wash.
>   Sen. Norris says a sound choice —
>   [James Delmage] Ross of Seattle
>   Morris L. Cooke of Pa.

Daniels did become ambassador to Mexico, but the first board of the TVA was to be made up of three quite different appointees.

These lists and scraps of paper are laconic but effective witnesses to the appointment process as it proceeded below the level of the secretaries.[2]

Meanwhile, Roosevelt was gauging where he wished to place several individuals in his cabinet. It was a peculiarly personal task. He conferred with many people, querying them with apparent candor concerning possible appointees, but talking with such sweep that the names of those whom he particularly favored were sometimes obscured by those receiving no more than the empty honor of being supposedly under consideration. He paid some attention to the reiterated recommendations of Howe, employed Farley only for a few specific errands, and assigned Moley to function more as prime negotiator than counsel. Several of the men these three recommended did receive appointments, but the choices were basically Roosevelt's own.[3]

In a fashion comparable to that in which he shaped his legislative proposals, Roosevelt solicited the suggestions of numerous advisers and political leaders. While he said nothing in public, he discussed numerous names in private, and took under consideration nominations almost beyond number. In that depression winter, appointments carried economic succor as well as political prestige, and were being sought more desperately than in decades. Roosevelt was a listener whose weakness was a tendency to appear too sympathetic, but he was also upon occasion a skillful parrier. He had at the least to pay lip service to the claims of many eminent Democrats whom he did not wish in his cabinet, and to counteract vigorous campaigns for others. He let pressures mount for those he favored as a counterweight to the pressures upon behalf of those he intended to reject. Thus he retained a substantial freedom of selection.

The first and most important decision that faced Roosevelt was whether or not he wished to build a cabinet out of the leading figures in the Democratic party, the men who had been either open or shadowy rivals of his for the nomination, or who enjoyed prestige and independence as elder statesmen. How was he to resolve the dilemma suggested by his penciled notation: "James M. Cox–Newton D. Baker — Special"? Some seventy years earlier, Abraham Lincoln, in order to cement a fragmented Republican party in time of acute crisis, had successfully appointed men like these around him. In 1913 Woodrow Wilson had felt he should appoint the most renowned Democrat, William Jennings Bryan, to be secretary of state, and three years later Bryan had resigned over a policy difference.

Newspaper speculation at first centered, as it always does, around the current galaxy of luminaries. In 1933 it would have meant a cabinet containing: the three previous Democratic presidential nominees, Alfred E. Smith, John W. Davis, and James M. Cox; Newton D. Baker, who had been Wilson's secretary of war; Senator Carter Glass, who had been briefly secretary of the treasury; Norman H. Davis, secretary of state, also briefly; Bernard M. Baruch, who had headed the War Industries Board; Owen D. Young of General Electric, who had negotiated a European debt settlement; and Governor Albert C. Ritchie of Maryland, who had been a conservative contender for the presidential nomination. Political conventionality would dictate that Roosevelt's campaign manager, Farley, become postmaster general. Otherwise this hypothetical cabinet would contain not one person who had supported Roosevelt before the Democratic convention or who would be likely to demonstrate enthusiasm for the New Deal.[4]

Roosevelt faced no such political necessity as had Lincoln to appoint rival leaders to high office, since the Democratic party was relatively cohesive through the economic crisis of the winter of 1932–1933. He was able therefore to plan a cabinet which would be more responsive to him and sympathetic toward his policies, and, as will be seen, to sidestep powerful men of contrary views. Only one of them, Carter Glass, even received an invitation to the cabinet. Roosevelt's choice was implicit rather than avowed, but was nonetheless definite.

Although there is no evidence that Roosevelt ever put his feelings into so many words, his actions indicated that although he wished his appointments to reflect a sweeping coalition encompassing both major parties, there was one group within the Democratic party he did not wish to include. These were the Democrats who had either been silent would-be beneficiaries or active participants in the efforts of eastern "allies" to stop Roosevelt at the Democratic Convention of 1932. There may have been some additional resentment on Roosevelt's part, as Moley has suggested, because many of the group had outranked Roosevelt in the Wilson administration. In any event it was easy enough to dispose of several of these people on the grounds that the public in that period of disillusion would be shocked by the appointment of men close to Wall Street. (The anti–Wall Street argument could also be used against a speculator who had been an early and generous campaign contributor, Joseph P. Kennedy.) Or, since Roosevelt was determined to retain progressive Republican support, and public power development was to them a key issue, he could drop from consideration men who were too closely associated with private utilities, like Newton D. Baker, and even a man who had been as benevolent in his neutrality toward Roosevelt as Owen D. Young.

Strong sentiment favored Young for secretary of state, and of necessity he entered into many of Roosevelt's early conversations. Of the elder statesmen, Roosevelt remarked to Berle, Young was the only one with an adventurous mind. Shortly before the convention, when Young had assured Roosevelt of his neutrality, Roosevelt had inquired what the effect would be of going off the gold standard. Young replied that while no one could tell, he could not imagine it would be catastrophic. Roosevelt could not dismiss Young lightly; neither if he appointed Young could he himself expect to dominate foreign policy. When he discussed Young with Moley, he left the intangible impression "that he didn't feel he could run around in his mental carpet slippers in Young's presence." And he added casually that Young's association with utilities would anger progressives. Young, troubled by rumors, and unable to accept an appointment because of his wife's serious illness, sent Roosevelt a letter through William Woodin on January 27, eliminating himself from consideration. He remained friendly, remarking privately in February that he had confidence in Roosevelt and did not fear radical tendencies.[5]

Relations with Newton D. Baker were less pleasant. Roosevelt told Berle he regarded Baker as "extremely honest and extremely capable, but timid about adventuring too far in economic matters." Roosevelt did not mention a factor which must have also been in his mind, that had the convention deadlocked, Baker would probably have received the nomination. Baker had not been neutral. So it was that Roosevelt told Moley that Baker simply wouldn't do as secretary of state. There were no overtures to Baker concerning any position until late in April, weeks after the new administration had been established; Baker informed Roosevelt several days later that he did not wish to hold any office.[6]

Al Smith, who had been so bitter about Roosevelt's nomination, received even more blunt treatment. At the end of January, denying rumors that he had accepted an appointment, he added with a smile, "I haven't been called on the telephone as yet." Smith's phone never rang. Smith was quoted as saying privately that he had declined being secretary of state — although the post had not been offered to him — because he expected the Democratic party to be disrupted within two years and it would then be up to him to piece together the fragments.[7]

Baruch, who had also been one of those aligned against Roosevelt at the convention, created a more delicate problem, since he had contributed $53,000 to the campaign and was closely allied to some of the most powerful southern senators. His influence was pervasive. Even before the campaign was over, he offered Berle a retainer to serve the Coolidge Committee on railroad policy. Berle queried Roosevelt, who strongly urged him to accept. There was immediate pressure after the campaign to place Baruch at the head of the cabinet. William Randolph Hearst urged through McAdoo that he be appointed secretary of state, and Glass seconded the nomination. Roosevelt commented to Moley on the evening of December 23 that Baruch could better be used elsewhere — and this was the tactic followed. Early in February when McAdoo tried to find out what Baruch knew about cabinet appointments, Baruch had to reply that during his visit to Warm Springs Roosevelt had not mentioned a single person to him or talked about Baruch's relationship to the new government. During the ensuing weeks and months, Baruch's name was linked with numerous important positions, but Roosevelt's one invitation to him was not of cabinet level — to head the farm program. Baruch declined. "F.D.R. never offered me a cabinet post," Baruch wrote years later, "which makes it almost superfluous for me to add that I would not have accepted one." [8]

Roosevelt's selection of his positive choices was equally complex. Like the plans for the New Deal, his methods undoubtedly seem far clearer from historical distance than they did to those involved at the time. The most knowledgeable contemporary was Moley, who, writing six years later, still viewed it as an almost haphazard enterprise.

Some of the factors, as Moley has enumerated them, were Roosevelt's desire for some sort of geographical balance, for representation of the progressive wing of the Republican party, for a malleable secretary of the navy, and for a woman cabinet officer. In other words, Roosevelt constructed his cabinet flexibly within only the broadest limitations.[9]

During the last weeks of the campaign, when Roosevelt was so far ahead that his election was a foregone conclusion, he must have given some thought to his cabinet. When the subject arose in the course of a conversation on October 10, Farley assured him that no embarrassing pledges had been made at the Chicago convention or elsewhere. Roosevelt, expressing his appreciation, affirmed that he also had made no commitments. Neither had he decided whom he wanted to appoint. "Right now, Jim," he remarked, "I have determined definitely on only three appointments — Louis for my secretary, George Dern for Secretary of the Interior, and you for Postmaster General." Three days before the election, when he speculated about cabinet possibilities in a conversation with Adolf A. Berle, he remarked that the average New Yorker would pick a cabinet entirely of New Yorkers, and that in any event "it was impossible for him to make any suggestions about a Cabinet now because events" might take such a turn before March 4th that by then "a quite different type of man might be needed." [10]

Roosevelt obviously had made no pledge, even to Dern, one of his earliest and most steadfast western supporters, since he did not inform Dern until February that he wanted him in Washington, and even then did not specify the position. Nor did he indicate to Howe before the election that he was to be secretary to the President, the top White House position at that time. Roosevelt may have been cautious, but it is more likely that he considered the appointment so obvious that it did not occur to him to offer it explicitly. Howe had been Roosevelt's secretary and closest adviser for twenty years. It was from Farley on the day after the election that Howe found out about the appointment.[11]

As for Farley himself, he never received an invitation more formal than that extended in October. On election night, Roosevelt whispered to Mrs. Farley, "Get ready to move to Washington." She demurred. He said nothing more until one morning a few weeks before the inauguration when Farley and Frank Walker were conferring with him while he sat in bed reading newspapers. Roosevelt, pointing to a cartoon ridiculing Hoover's postmaster general, remarked, "Frank, did you see this picture of Jim's immediate predecessor?" Farley, taking advantage of the opportunity, replied, "Thank you, sir, for the appointment." [12]

The task of assembling a cabinet began seriously in late November 1932. A considerable part of the undertaking were consultations with powerful leaders like Senator Burton K. Wheeler of Montana. Wheeler, who had been the first national figure to announce himself for Roosevelt, and a leading western progressive Democrat, received a cordial invitation to visit Roosevelt at Warm Springs. Wheeler brought with him a recommendation; for his own part and upon behalf of his ally, Senator Thomas J. Walsh of Montana (to whom Roosevelt was also deeply beholden), he urged the appointment of Edward Keating as secretary of labor. Keating, who had been a Colorado congressman in the Wilson era, for many years had edited a weekly newspaper for the railroad brotherhoods. He did not fit into Roosevelt's plans. Roosevelt pondered, then confided to Wheeler that he wished to make Walsh attorney general, and would be expected to appoint Farley postmaster general. Both were Catholics, and so was Keating. He proceeded, "I can't very well have more than two Catholics in my cabinet." That disposed of Keating. Besides, he told Wheeler, he was planning to take the unprecedented step of bringing a woman into his cabinet — either Ruth Bryan Owen, the daughter of William Jennings Bryan, or Frances Perkins. (Since the welfare activities of the federal government were at that time concentrated in the Labor Department, logically the woman would become secretary of labor.)

Roosevelt asked Wheeler to persuade Walsh to become attorney general — an appointment which could well compensate both Wheeler's and Walsh's claims. As gratuitous information, Roosevelt added that he intended to bring two western progressive Republican senators into his cabinet, George Norris of Nebraska as secretary of agriculture and Hiram Johnson of California as secretary of the interior. Presumably Roosevelt wanted to test the reaction of a western progressive Democrat like Wheeler to these suggestions. Wheeler retorted that he did not think any of the three men would leave the Senate. He and Walsh had already discussed the Department of Justice and had concluded that neither of them wished to head it. In any event, the invitation was to Walsh, not him. He left Warm Springs blocked from obtaining the appointment he had sought for Keating and charged with convincing Walsh to take an unwanted position. Several weeks later Roosevelt wrote Wheeler a pleasant note.[13]

There were numerous interviews of this sort; they may have helped Roosevelt gather needed information and certainly they flattered or placated to some degree those consulted. More than one of those whose opinions were solicited must have been secretly hoping for an invitation — and indeed more than one who in the end was asked to join the cabinet had to sit through tantalizing conferences at which Roosevelt aired name after name. Yet even in private conversation with Moley, Roosevelt was not too direct in expressing his thoughts. Early in the evening of December 23, sitting in his little study in the governor's mansion in Albany, Roosevelt discussed his plans with Moley. He would first choose someone to be secretary of state and let the rest of the cabinet fall into place around that man. Roosevelt rapidly enumerated, and eliminated on one ground or another, most of the prime contenders: Senators Pittman and Robinson, and Baker and Baruch. He talked more at length concerning Robert W. Bingham, publisher of the Louisville Courier-Journal, a sizable contributor to the campaign, and the candidate of Colonel House. He joked that the appointment of Bingham, who was not well known in the East, would be a "stiff dose for the international bankers." But Moley guessed correctly that Roosevelt was not seriously considering him — Bingham was appointed ambassador to Great Britain. The two candidates Roosevelt most strongly favored were Owen D. Young and Cordell Hull. Within a week and a half of this conversation, by January 3, 1933, he had eliminated Young, to the distress of Howe who felt that Young's neutrality at the nominating convention had entitled him to first refusal of the cabinet position. Norman H. Davis also received some consideration, and it was even whispered was offered the position, but Davis was emphatically opposed by Felix Frankfurter because of business difficulties in Cuba many years earlier, and was thoroughly disliked by Moley and Tugwell.[14]

Rather, Roosevelt even in his first conversation with Moley dwelt glowingly upon the many excellences of Hull, especially his dignity and high-mindedness. All through the 1920s, Hull had been Roosevelt's most dependable and effective southern political associate; besides, he had been Roosevelt's choice for the vice presidential nomination in 1928. Hull's was an old-fashioned southern faith in free trade as the prime consideration in foreign policy, yet he shared unreservedly the configuration of views of Norman Davis and the Wilsonian internationalists. Indeed, Davis was such an intimate that he was to be able to come into Hull's office unheralded. In Hull, Roosevelt could acquire a secretary of state of Davis's ideology without Davis's liabilities. Like Davis, Hull — with his long sober face and in his demeanor courtly, soft-spoken, yet proud and stubborn — carried himself like a secretary of state. Roosevelt remarked to Moley that Hull's appointment would please the old-line party leaders. Hull enjoyed their support, and in return could be counted upon to bring his to Roosevelt. The stinging Senate defeat of the Versailles Treaty was still a fresh memory; it would not be likely to reoccur with a prestigious cautious friend of the senators like Hull in charge of the State Department. And above all, his appointment would give prime recognition to the traditionalist Democrats of the South, so vital to a New Deal coalition.[15]

The general outlines of the cabinet soon took shape. Early on the morning of January 11, 1933, Roosevelt listed his candidates to Moley:

> State — Cordell Hull
> Treasury — Carter Glass
> War — George Dern
> Attorney General — Thomas J. Walsh
> Postmaster General — James A. Farley
> Navy — O. Max Gardner
> Interior — Hiram Johnson, Philip La Follette or
>   Bronson Cutting
> Agriculture — Henry A. Wallace
> Commerce — William Woodin or Jesse Strauss
> Labor — Frances Perkins [16]

The next task was to obtain these people, an undertaking that occupied Roosevelt and his emissaries from time to time almost until the end of February. Almost no one else seemed able to give as simple and informal a reply as did Farley to Roosevelt's equally informal invitation. Senator Hull, invited to the most important post, engaged in the most hesitation and pondering, taking a full month to give his answer. Roosevelt formally invited Hull on the evening of January 19, when he stopped in Washington on his way to Warm Springs. Hull has reminisced: [17] "I was really thunderstruck. Previously, I had not conferred with him a minute about Cabinet appointments, and I did not have them in mind. No one had informed me I was under consideration for such an appointment." [18]

Hull expressed thanks and asked for time to consider. He was a proud man, and undoubtedly had been piqued that Roosevelt had not solicited his advice in the weeks immediately after the election. Moreover, he enjoyed being a member of the Senate. He also enjoyed keeping Roosevelt dangling. To Norman Davis, whom he had consulted, Hull wrote on February 10, "I have taken no sort of steps since last I talked with you. Matters are simply floating along. I, of course, am exceedingly desirous of continuing in my present work, as you are aware." Meanwhile, on Roosevelt's orders, Moley went to Washington to brief Hull on foreign policy matters. "I was impressed by the kindliness and gentleness with which this gaunt, inarticulate man received me and heard the story of the negotiations with the Hoover administration," Moley has reminisced. But James Byrnes, Carter Glass, and several other Democratic senators who heard rumors of the offer urged Moley to warn Roosevelt that Hull would fit far better in the Treasury Department than in the State Department, since he was a specialist on taxation and knew nothing of foreign affairs. When Moley telephoned these warnings, Roosevelt's only reply was, "Well, I will be glad to have some fine idealism in the State Department." [19]

When Hull continued to delay giving a definite answer until well into February, Roosevelt sent Moley again to see him. He informed Moley that he feared the social obligations would be too great for his wife. At Howe's suggestion, Moley proposed to Hull that someone be obtained as undersecretary who would be willing to entertain diplomats. This was agreeable to Hull, so on February 11, Moley radioed Roosevelt, using a prearranged code, "Further conferences on Tennessee project [Hull] indicate possible adoption provided some other food supplying and consuming means can be found." Upon his return from his cruise, Roosevelt telephoned at about midnight one night to his old friend William Phillips, who readily agreed to become undersecretary. Hull then accepted. To a friend he explained his decision in words that were the very model of political decorum: [20] "After thirty days' consideration of [the] matter, which was not offered to any other person and which has been most insistently pressed on me by our leaders generally, I have decided to get ready to move to the other end of the Avenue on March 4. It is entirely contrary to my personal convenience, personal desires, and personal enjoyment." Hull was ready to assume the duties of secretary of state in the dignified tradition of his predecessors Charles Evans Hughes, Frank Kellogg, and Henry L. Stimson.[21]

Even more critical in Roosevelt's planning was the appointment of a secretary of the treasury. While he could brush away the claims of many an elder statesman to be secretary of state, no one seemed to the public to be so preeminently qualified to preside over the Treasury as Carter Glass. This white-maned little Virginian, originally a Lynchburg publisher, had been one of the architects of the Federal Reserve System, and during his long years in the Senate the most peppery and insistent advocate of financial conservatism. Roosevelt could not ignore the weighty influence of Glass, not only in the Senate but throughout the country. At the close of the campaign, when Hoover, quite correctly, accused the New Dealers of planning unorthodox monetary experiments, Roosevelt had enlisted Glass to deliver a fiery rebuttal.

In the public confidence that he would bring to the administration financial program, Glass would be a major asset. There was the further consideration that Senator Byrnes pointed out to Moley — if Roosevelt contemplated any inflation it would be "better to have Glass in the Treasury Department because he would be a roaring lion on the floor of the Senate." (On the other hand, conservative Treasury officials were eager for Glass to become secretary because they thought the appointment would commit the administration to sound money.) [22]

Roosevelt wanted Glass in the cabinet, but only on his own terms. During his visit to Washington on January 19, he hastily offered the Treasury Department to Glass, who immediately raised questions about the currency. Roosevelt avoided pledges, and Glass asked for time to consult his doctor. The next day Glass declared, "My doctor strongly urges me to decline the honor; and I am just as strongly inclined to follow his advice." Roosevelt insisted: "It's your duty to your party, and to your country, to assume this post. I won't take 'no' for an answer." Glass replied, "You make it difficult for me to decline but if you insist, you will have to give me more time." [23]

While Roosevelt was apparently pressuring Glass in the strongest terms to become secretary of the treasury, he significantly in these first exchanges dangled in front of Glass the very bait necessary to keep Glass in the Senate. He had been thinking of making Governor Gardner of North Carolina secretary of the navy, but assured Glass he was likely to appoint the other senator from Virginia, Claude Swanson. One of Glass's strongest incentives to accept the Treasury post would be to make way in the Senate for his effective young ally, Harry F. Byrd; the appointment of Swanson would eliminate one of Glass's prime reasons for acceptance. Glass wrote Byrd:*

Glass seemed willing to make the physical sacrifice to become secretary of the treasury only if by so doing he could ensure a continuance of financial conservatism. Not only was he opposed to inflationary schemes, but he wanted to bring in as undersecretary Russell C. Leffingwell, formerly assistant secretary, but for a decade a partner in J. P. Morgan & Company at 23 Wall Street. The House of Morgan was at the nadir of its popularity. Glass told Moley that he could understand Roosevelt's objection to Leffingwell, but that he was very much worried about future financial policy. When Moley reported these qualms by telephone, Roosevelt in Warm Springs firmly replied: "Make it perfectly clear that so far as subordinates go, we simply cannot tie up with 23." So far as financial policy was concerned, "We are not going to throw ideas out of the window simply because they are labelled inflationary." Moreover, "If the old boy doesn't want to go along, I wouldn't press it." Glass acceded on Leffingwell, but on financial policy held to a position that Moley jokingly summarized as follows: "I am not against inflation; but just you bring me any specific measure providing for inflation and see if I can't punch it full of holes." On February 8, Glass sent word through Moley that he could not accept because of his imperfect health and the social burden that would fall upon his wife. He prepared an eloquent letter of refusal, and enclosed a letter from his physician. To Roosevelt, who was yachting, Moley radioed, "Dominion definitely out." [25]

But the Glass episode was not yet finished; dedicated opponents of inflation saw in him one last means of forestalling the New Deal experiments, and persuaded him to engage in one last bit of negotiation with Roosevelt. Not only did some of Glass's friends like Admiral Cary Grayson and Baruch urge him to reconsider, but President Hoover, taking a most unprecedented step, asked him to keep Roosevelt from tinkering with gold. By this time Moley and Howe felt the appointment of Glass would be a mistake, not only because of his conservatism but because of the personal tragedy it would portend. Within a short period there would be a head-on collision and a bitter retirement. Moley turned instead in his thinking, as early as January 25, toward William Woodin.

---

* In this connection, I took the precaution to ask the President-elect if there was any probability, in the event I should feel compelled to decline the Treasury portfolio, of the appointment of any other Virginian to the cabinet. . . . He frankly said there was a strong probability of the appointment of [Senator Swanson] to the Navy. I think this will ensue, and that, therefore, the Senate will be open to you. This greatly relieves my anxiety, and makes rather certain my own action unless some unforeseen circumstance shall change my mind.[24]

Howe concurred, and on February 14 sent a cryptic radiogram to Roosevelt, purportedly referring to plans for a White House pool: prefer a wooden roof to a glass roof over swimming pool." Roosevelt puzzled over the message, then roared with delight.[26]

The charade continued, with Roosevelt preferring Woodin but still negotiating with Glass. Once more he negotiated face to face with Glass, this time aboard Roosevelt's New York–bound train as they rode from Washington to Baltimore. Once again Glass brought up matters of currency and assistants; once again he received no satisfactory answer. For several minutes the two men rode in silence. Then Glass began, "Franklin, I have made up my mind. I appreciate . . ." But Roosevelt cut him off, declaring he would not accept Glass's refusal. On February 19, Roosevelt telephoned; Glass said he had still not decided, but added that if he did not take the position he hoped a sound-money man, Swagar Sherley of Kentucky, would be chosen.* Sherley, who was at the Sixty-fifth Street house at the time, told Moley he did not want the appointment. Armed with this information, Roosevelt finally accepted a firm "no" from Glass. Turning to Moley he said, "Now call Will — and bring him here at 11 tonight." Woodin was offered the position that evening.

The refusal of Glass gave clear and unmistakable warning during the February crisis that Roosevelt would not bind himself to economic orthodoxy. Glass issued a statement firmly deriding the "mischievous report that I declined . . . on account of differences with the President-elect on fundamental economic issues." The statement (technically correct, since Roosevelt would not discuss these issues with Glass) fooled no one. Arthur Krock pointed out in the *New York Times* on February 21 that Glass in his three interviews had received none of "the assurances he required on controversial points of financial economics." [27]

Although Roosevelt failed to win over a potentially stinging critic of his financial innovations, he did succeed in obtaining a loyal secretary of the treasury of impeccable standing in the financial community. Woodin, a shy, small man, only about five feet four inches tall, was no bigger a man than Glass, and like him wiry both in body and mind. There comparisons stopped, for Woodin was notable for his quiet whimsy rather than for his vinegar. His family had made a fortune in iron casting, and he had become president of the American Car and Foundry Company. Although a Republican, he had become devoted to Roosevelt as a trustee of the Warm Springs Foundation, and had helped gather money for the Democratic National Committee in the 1932 campaign. He was a hard-headed man of figures as well as a fine amateur

---

* By this point, as will be seen in Chapter XI, the complications of the growing banking crisis were entering into FDR's negotiations with Glass.

musical composer, and above all, not dogmatic in his economic thinking. "He was the most surprised man who ever became Secretary of the Treasury, because it never occurred to him he would be," Krock has reminisced, "and, when he was appointed, he felt terribly inadequate." It was only after an hour-and-a-half cab ride through Central Park with Basil O'Connor that he accepted.[28]

With one exception, other cabinet positions did not involve such agonizing negotiation. Out of the bargaining with Glass, the Navy Department went to Claude Swanson, who long had been the Senate specialist in naval affairs, was in ill health, and happy to accept the honor. "We both recall 'the fire of battle' when he was piloting through the Three Year Naval program in the Senate," Daniels once reminded Roosevelt. The fire had long since burned out, which could not have been disconcerting to Roosevelt, since his favorite perquisite as President was to serve as commander-in-chief of the United States — especially of the United States Navy. He appointed a dynamic retired marine colonel, Henry Latrobe Roosevelt — only quite distantly related — to be assistant secretary.[29]

The appointment of Senator Swanson had a "domino effect," in part a hindrance and in part helpful to Roosevelt's future Senate relations. It did indeed bring in Governor Harry Byrd, who was to be a vehement critic, but Byrd would probably have soon succeeded the ailing Swanson in any event. Two other results were pleasant: Roosevelt's supporter, Key Pittman of Nevada, became chairman of the Foreign Relations Committee, and the Tennessee conservative, Kenneth McKellar, was blocked from the chairmanship of the Appropriations Committee.[30]

Over the attorney generalship Roosevelt got himself into the complication of offering the appointment to two men at once, but managed quickly to extricate himself. Senator Walsh had indeed felt, as Wheeler told Roosevelt, that the office "makes no appeal to me to which I am at all likely to accede." If he were able as in earlier times to argue the more important litigation of the government before the courts, he might be interested, but he asserted he was not interested in administrative and patronage responsibilities. On January 19 in Washington, Roosevelt, taking the word from Walsh as practically final, in conversation with the progressive Republican Senator Bronson Cutting offered to make Philip F. La Follette attorney general. Phil La Follette, who had just finished a term as governor of Wisconsin, was in Europe. Roosevelt made the offer to try to lure Cutting into the cabinet as secretary of the interior; he neglected to say that he had through Wheeler already offered the attorney generalship to Walsh.[31]

On the next day, January 20, when Roosevelt went through what he must have thought would be the formality of giving Walsh a personal invitation, the same warm blandishments he tried on Glass brought him embarrassment in this instance. Roosevelt put the offer, Walsh confessed, "in such a persuasive way that I shall find it hard to decline." He told Walsh that he wanted him not simply as a department head but as a "member of my advisory council." For more than a month Walsh negotiated, but there was never during this period any real doubt of his acceptance.[32]

In consequence, Roosevelt had immediately to backtrack. He confessed to Senator Cutting at the Washington station on February 20, just before he left for the South, that he had an earlier offer out to Walsh, but was sure Walsh would decline. Cutting replied that it would probably be best if he and Senator Robert M. La Follette were to have a talk with Roosevelt before Cutting decided whether to accept the offer as secretary of the interior. Roosevelt invited them to Warm Springs. During the conversation there he emphasized the progressive policies he intended to follow as President, and praised Phil La Follette. He reiterated that if Walsh declined he intended to offer La Follette the attorney generalship, adding that if Walsh accepted he would want to know what position other than in the cabinet La Follette might accept, since he needed his help in the crisis. Roosevelt's prime concern may well have been to obtain Cutting, not Phil La Follette, since Robert M. La Follette reported to his brother, "Again and again through the conversation he stated that he was very anxious to have Senator Cutting accept, but I think Cutting made it very clear to him that his decision would be greatly influenced by the decision with regard to your being a member of the cabinet."

Robert M. La Follette came to a rather cynical conclusion:

> In so far as you are concerned, two and two do not make four in this situation. . . . In any case [Roosevelt] has discussed the alternatives so far as the Attorney Generalship is concerned with enough people in the Senate, so that it is pretty generally known; and personally I have no doubt, although I have no evidence of this fact, that conservative Democrats have and will put great pressure upon Senator Walsh to accept in order to prevent what to them would seem a very unfortunate circumstance, namely, that it might be offered to you.[33]

In any event, Cutting in the end refused to become secretary of the interior, and Roosevelt, when he had the unexpected opportunity, did not appoint Philip La Follette attorney general.

In selecting a secretary of agriculture, Roosevelt in effect allowed the great conflicting farm belt forces to fight out the issue among themselves, and took the man most firmly recommended by the most powerful group, the American Farm Bureau Federation. This was Wallace, who in addition to his formidable backing was personally most accept-able to Roosevelt, and a strong political asset because of his Republican background. Wallace had felt that his November interview at Warm Springs and his assignment to work on farm legislation during the lame duck session of Congress were a sort of testing. Perhaps they were, since by early January Roosevelt was planning to appoint him. One rather embarrassing rival contender was Roosevelt's dear friend Henry Mor-genthau, Jr., who had handled New York agricultural problems for the governor. Morgenthau's father worked hard to try to gain the position for his son, but it would have been especially impolitic to appoint a secretary of agriculture from New York. Perhaps out of his affection for Morgenthau, Roosevelt went to unusual ends to squash the candi-dacy; he asked Thomas Beck of *Collier's* magazine to telegraph repre-sentative farm agencies and spokesmen on their preference: Wallace or Morgenthau. Out of two hundred replies, only one favored Morgen-thau. Roosevelt had other plans for Morgenthau, who within a year was elevated to a key position in the cabinet. Wallace accepted almost at once when he received a letter from Roosevelt on February 7, and Moley radioed: "Corn Belt in bag." [34]

Roosevelt deferred the final selection of a secretary of commerce until he had filled the key positions in the cabinet. Both his tentative choices were New Yorkers, Woodin and Jesse I. Straus, but by the time he made his final selection, Woodin was already in the cabinet, and Roose-velt had firm plans to include two other New Yorkers as postmaster general and secretary of labor. It would be awkward to include four New Yorkers in a cabinet of ten, but Straus had strong claims, and when rumors reached him, he had been pleased to think he might hold the position once filled by his uncle. Straus, the president of the R. H. Macy department store, had conducted several highly useful polls for Roosevelt in 1931 and had headed the Roosevelt Business and Profes-sional Men's League during the campaign. Geographical considerations, together with another acute political debt, took precedence. McAdoo, who had so dramatically delivered the California vote to Roosevelt at the convention, had been pressing numerous appointments upon Roose-velt on his own behalf and that of the gray figure behind him, Hearst. Most of these Roosevelt had parried, but numerous other Southerners, including Hull, Byrnes, and Daniels, were also pressing the claims of Daniel Calhoun Roper of South Carolina, who had been a first assistant postmaster general under Wilson and floor leader of McAdoo's 1924 convention fight for the presidential nomination. His appointment would be another tie with the old-fashioned southern, rural, dry forces in the Democratic party. Colonel House said he would regard it as recognition to the old Wilsonians. On the evening of February 20, only ten days before the inauguration, as Roper sat by the fire reading his evening paper the telephone rang. It was Roosevelt: "Dan, I've decided to invite you into my official family as Secretary of Commerce. I'd like to have you run up to Hyde Park next Saturday to see me." [35]

An embarrassing slip-up followed. Before Roosevelt could himself break the unpleasant news, Straus received word from his rival, the senior Morgenthau. It took much tactful explaining on the part of Moley and an ingratiating conference with Roosevelt himself to smooth Straus's ruffled feelings. In the end he was consoled and became ambassador to France.[36]

In these same last days before the inauguration, Roosevelt finally obtained a secretary of the interior who would fit his basic specification — a western progressive Republican. It was vital that Roosevelt thus reward and secure the further support of that useful wing of his 1932 coalition. He decided upon two western Democrats, Walsh and Dern, but was slow making up his mind where to put Dern. Roosevelt talked to Westerners about appointing Dern secretary of the interior, but despite his high qualifications, he did not entirely fill the political specifications. In 1924, Dern had run against the Republican governor, Charles R. Mabey, with an irresistible slogan, "We want a Dern good governor, and we don't mean Mabey." As governor, he had successfully reformed the state tax structure, and as chairman of the Governors' Conferences in 1929 and 1930 had been conspicuously friendly toward Roosevelt. Some years earlier when he was a Utah legislator he had been responsible for a mineral leasing law favorable to the state, but he was also notable as a mine owner and operator. The wounds left two decades earlier by the Ballinger-Pinchot controversy over management of the Department of the Interior were still too painful to risk appointing a man whom Republicans could attack in any manner or measure as an anticonservationist. Consequently, Roosevelt in the end placed Dern in the spot to which he had tentatively assigned him early in January, the War Department. In those years of small budgets and isolation, it was a relatively inconsequential position.[37]

As for the Interior Department, finding a distinguished Republican progressive who would accept turned out to be a trying task. Roosevelt's first choice was that formidable old progressive warrior, Senator Hiram Johnson of California. Johnson was the first of the coterie of senators to whom he offered cabinet positions on that notable afternoon of January 19 at the Mayflower Hotel. The office, he told Johnson, was of great importance, and he intended to place within it additional major functions that would make it of even larger significance. Its administration peculiarly demanded the skills and knowledge of a western man. The offer came as no surprise to Johnson, who had long since made up his mind how he would answer Roosevelt. He had confided to an intimate more than a month earlier: [38] "The Lord, I fear, made me a natural rebel. . . . I can not discipline myself, at my age to accept any views, I felt were at variance with the best interests of our people. I can not quite see myself sitting in a cabinet, for instance, agreeing to policies with which I am not in sympathy." [39]

Johnson's "no," therefore, was cordial but unequivocal.

Roosevelt accepted it as final and turned that same day to Senator Cutting. Through most of February Cutting postponed giving an answer, then declined shortly before the cabinet was to be announced. Suddenly Roosevelt found himself having to find a secretary of the interior; he turned almost casually to an Illinois Republican, a one-time Bull Mooser, Harold L. Ickes, who had organized progressive Republicans for Roosevelt during the 1932 campaign.* It was one of the rare instances, Hiram Johnson commented, "where luck finally did for a man what he was breaking his heart for." At first Ickes aspired to become commissioner of Indian Affairs, then assistant secretary, and, as Cutting spent week after week making his mind up, he began a campaign to become secretary. Although it seemed a forlorn cause, he asked friends to present his qualifications to Roosevelt. Senator Johnson was an admirer of Ickes, but felt that since both he and Cutting had been offered the position he had no right to make a further recommendation. When Moley asked for the name of a progressive-minded Republican who could participate in debt negotiations, Johnson did suggest Ickes.

It was to be looked over for this position that Ickes came to Roosevelt's New York home one day in late February and seated himself in the front drawing room along with ten or more other men, most of whom did not know each other. One of them, James Warburg, who had also been enlisted to help prepare for the World Economic Conference, vividly remembers his first impression of the governor as he was wheeled into the room — his "massive shoulders surmounted by his remarkably fine head, the gay smile with which he greeted his guests, and the somewhat incongruous, old-fashioned pince-nez eyeglasses that seemed to sit a little uncertainly on his nose."

Scanning a list in his hand, Roosevelt inquired, "Which one of you gentlemen is Ikes?"

---

* Although nominally a Republican, Ickes had voted for Bryan against Taft in 1909, and had voted for every Democratic candidate for President since 1916. In 1920 he had regarded Harding as a "double-dyed political crook." By the spring of 1932 he was so thoroughly disgusted with President Hoover that he again looked toward the Democrats. By this time he regarded Al Smith as "an enthusiastic little brother of the rich." "God knows Roosevelt is not a radical," he commented. "He is not much of a Progressive according to my way of thinking but he would suit me better than any other Democrat so far named." [40]

"Ickes, Mr. President."

"Oh, so that's how you pronounce it."

Roosevelt asked Ickes to remain until the others were gone, then embarked upon the conversation Ickes had not really thought would ever take place. Roosevelt said, Ickes recalled wittily a decade later, that he had " 'followed my career,' . . . (I wonder if he really had!) he and I had 'stood for the same things' and he had 'about concluded that the man he wanted was Harold Ickes of Chicago.' Would I come back in the morning for a final verdict? Would I!" By the time Ickes returned the next day Roosevelt had telephoned Hiram Johnson and several other progressive Republican senators; they had all vouched for Ickes as a man of ability and integrity. So it was that Roosevelt appointed him. He remarked to reporters that he liked the cut of Ickes's jib. Ickes later said Roosevelt told him "that he wanted a man at the head of Interior who could say 'No.' (And who, may I ask, can say it louder and more disagreeably than a curmudgeon, and especially a certain curmudgeon?)" [41]

And finally, Roosevelt, as he had planned from the outset, broke precedent by appointing a woman to his cabinet. Pressure from the women, who had been assuming an increasingly large role in politics through the 1920s, was becoming irresistible. In addition Roosevelt had firm confidence and warm affection for his New York industrial commissioner, Frances Perkins. As early as November, he had told Senator Wheeler he was thinking of her. Yet there were good reasons for delaying the appointment until just before inauguration. The only logical position would be as head of the Labor Department with its welfare services, but since its establishment in the Progressive era it had served as a sinecure for a union official. There was sure to be a stir — it would be less dangerous if it came in the last days, and could be overshadowed by announcements of appointments to more conspicuous cabinet posts.

Immediately after the election, the Democratic women leaders opened their campaign for Miss Perkins. "Gee! Wouldn't it be great if we could get Frances into the cabinet?" Clara L. Beyer, head of the Child Labor Division of the Department of Labor wrote to Mary W. Dewson, director of the Women's Democratic National Campaign Committee. Molly Dewson was already at work, directly recommending Miss Perkins to Roosevelt, obtaining Farley's endorsement, and using her thank-you letters as a means of launching a quiet national movement. The response among women leaders was immediate and enthusiastic; Emily Newell Blair, an associate editor of *Good Housekeeping*, wrote over seventy-five letters. Many men also gave their backing to Miss Perkins. When Senator Costigan of Colorado wrote a letter on behalf of Keating to John R. Commons, the famous historian of the labor movement,

Commons replied he had already joined some social workers in endorsing Miss Perkins. Even William Allen White, though feeling that as a Republican he had no right to give advice to the President-elect, emphasized that "Frances Perkins, as secretary of labor, would be a master stroke":

> She stands in the first half dozen of the great women of her time and her appointment would bring into the cabinet exactly the sort of woman that should be there — not the professional political woman, not the chronic female person but the broad minded, competent person who happens to be a woman as an incident of life on the planet, but the kind of a woman who has not let it bother her in doing her work.[42]

As for Frances Perkins herself, she feared as the letter-writing campaign gathered momentum and newspaper rumors increased that they might be embarrassing the President-elect. "I had read the newspaper reports about me with growing consternation," she has reminisced. "I decided to forget manners and write Roosevelt honestly." On February 1, she sent him a handwritten note: [43]

> You are quoted as saying that the newspaper predictions on Cabinet posts are 80% wrong. I write to say that I honestly hope that what they've been printing about me is among the 80% of incorrect items.
> I've had my "kick" out of the gratifying letters etc. but for your own sake and that of the U.S.A. I think that . . . some one straight from the ranks of some group of organized workers should be appointed — to reestablish firmly the principle that labor is in the President's councils.[44]

A few days later, when Molly Dewson talked to her, Miss Perkins reiterated this conviction, and added a strong personal reason for not wanting to enter the cabinet. Miss Dewson retorted that she must take the position, since otherwise generations might go by before a woman was asked again. If Miss Perkins was successful it would no longer seem strange to have a woman in the cabinet. And she added, "You've been the first woman in a great many places."

Putting her qualms behind her, Frances Perkins decided to accept if she were invited, providing Roosevelt was interested in the program she intended to propose. So it was that with a slip of paper prepared, she went on the evening of February 22 to the Roosevelt home on Sixty-fifth Street.

She has recalled:

> The house was strangely disorderly on the ground floor, showing at once that although it had been a nice, quiet private house where people lived with some elegance, it had now become a general camping ground for reporters, politicians, police men, detectives. . . . [The] little hall was . . . piled high with overcoats, hats, umbrellas, briefcases, note-

books, sheafs of paper, red envelopes, any amount of things, not only on the chairs and tables, but on the floor. There were smoking stands, ash trays, cigarette butts. The rather handsome Chinese rug on the floor . . . had wrinkled up and nobody had straightened it out.

She was ushered to an attractively furnished room upstairs, next to the President-elect's study, and was seated near a blond, bespectacled man who did not look up when she came in. He was called into Roosevelt's study ahead of her, and when, a few minutes later, she was summoned, he was sitting on the sofa there: [45] "Roosevelt gave me a friendly greeting and, extending his hand toward the stocky blond man, said, 'Frances, don't you know Harold?' " The future secretary of labor thus met the future secretary of the interior.*

When Ickes had left, Roosevelt said at once:

"I've been thinking things over and I've decided I want you to be Secretary of Labor."

In reply, Miss Perkins brought out one by one her well-rehearsed arguments: she was not a bona fide labor person; if a woman were to be secretary it should be someone who had been identified with the unions. Roosevelt parried by pointing out that she had been industrial commissioner of New York. Next, Miss Perkins remembers, she launched a different line of argument, referring to her slip of paper as she talked:

> I said that if I accepted the position of Secretary of Labor I should want to do a great deal. I outlined a program of labor legislation and economic improvement. None of it was radical. It had all been tried in certain states and foreign countries. But I thought that Roosevelt might consider it too ambitious to be undertaken when the United States was deep in depression and unemployment.
>
> In broad terms, I proposed immediate federal aid to the states for direct unemployment relief, an extensive program of public works, a study and an approach to the establishment by federal law of minimum wages, maximum hours, true unemployment and old-age insurance, abolition of child labor, and the creation of a federal employment service.
>
> The program received Roosevelt's hearty endorsement, and he told me he wanted me to carry it out.

Miss Perkins pointed out that questions of constitutionality might arise; Roosevelt thought they could be worked out when the time came. After no more than an hour's conversation, she agreed to become secretary of labor.[46]

When it became known, women's rights leaders and male sympathizers alike were delighted that finally a woman had been appointed to the

---

* There are numerous other versions of this introduction.

cabinet and that she was of the caliber of Miss Perkins. The news, Frankfurter wrote her, "exhilarates me in the way in which the anticipation of a Kreisler concert exhilarates me." For most of those in the women's movement it was an occasion for sober rejoicing. Anna Mellen wrote Margaret Dreier Robins: "Isn't it a great step forward for women that we should have a Frances Perkins to supply for a cabinet position? If only the rank and file of us could live up to her. We have a hard course before us. Sometimes I wonder if perhaps that is not going to be our salvation — that it is so hard." [47]

The cabinet apparently was complete. Curiously enough, the last two members selected, Miss Perkins and Ickes, were to be the only two who would serve through the entirety of Roosevelt's many years in office. One appointee, the elderly Senator Walsh, did not survive until inauguration day. Walsh, a widower, without confiding in even some of his closest associates, slipped away from the Senate to remarry in Havana. On the train back from Florida, he died of a heart attack. His death deprived Roosevelt of one of the most prominent and highly respected cabinet members, and faced him with the problem on March 2 of finding a replacement. He settled upon another of the old-line Democrats who had aided him loyally in the ten months before the convention and been a floor leader at Chicago, Homer Cummings of Connecticut, whom he had planned to appoint governor-general of the Philippines. Hull earlier had strongly endorsed Cummings to Colonel House:

> I have heard twelve or fifteen senators during the last week casually remark that Mr. Cummings is exceptionally well equipped to make an outstanding Attorney General. His great legal ability, which all recognize, his poise, his fine intellect, his fundamental, sane, and practical liberalism, preeminently fit him for the Attorney Generalship.[48]

By the morning after Roosevelt secured his last two acceptances, the names of his entire cabinet were being carried in the newspapers — even though he had officially announced only the appointments of Hull and Woodin. There was general disappointment that the list did not include more luminaries, and puzzled inquiries concerning some of the little-known names, like that of Ickes. There was a flurry of excitement in the Senate, which was losing three of its members, and behind the public honorifics some private detraction. Hiram Johnson confided that the years had taken their toll of Swanson so that he was physically and mentally of little consequence, and that the appointment of Dern was a haphazard compensation for the failure to make him secretary of the interior. As for Cordell Hull, Johnson continued, "To describe Hull as a tower of strength . . . whose removal seriously affects the Senate has been the subject of a good deal of laughter and joking the last couple of weeks. He is a nice man, and perhaps in the position he now has, he may develop into a great man." [49]

As was predictable, union officials in their disappointment issued wrathful manifestos against Frances Perkins. William Green, president of the AFL, announced that organized labor would "never become reconciled" to her. Miss Perkins commented that Green and the AFL were entirely within their rights. "I am glad they expressed themselves openly and frankly," she declared. "It creates a more wholesome situation and I do not regard it as an expression of ill-will against me." [50]

These sorties were of no consequence. If any fact clearly arose from them it was that the cabinet did not overshadow the President. Compared with past cabinets, Arthur Krock pointed out, its composite trait was "diligence rather than brilliance, but it contains as many elements of experience, worldly success, hard-headedness and integrity as any assemblage at the White House oval table." Some of these cabinet members never threw off their obscurity, but several were to prove themselves more extraordinary and brilliant than anyone could have dreamed at the time of their appointment, and to make their names an American commonplace.[51]

Roosevelt had put his cabinet together on a rule-of-thumb basis in keeping with most of the old party precepts. He had recognized each of the elements in his winning coalition. Those Jeffersonian-Wilsonian liberals who had worked so hard for his nomination, and who had been so disappointed at the turn of the year because he was not drawing upon their advice in planning his program, in the end included three appointees: Hull, Roper and Cummings. A fourth man, Dern, probably fitted best in this group, although his political alignment was with western Democrats. Two, both from the Midwest, represented Republican progressivism: Wallace and Ickes. The three New Yorkers were a mixed lot: Farley, the skillful political technician; Woodin, the open-minded Republican businessman; and Miss Perkins, whose appointment recognized womanhood and brought to Washington an ardent crusader for the ideals of the social justice movement. Finally, the appointment of Swanson was indirectly a concession to Carter Glass and the ultra-Jeffersonians, the new Quids. Not only the proper political formulae, but also the precept of geographical representation had been observed: two from the West (one died), two from the Middle West, three from the South, and four from the Northeast.

Most important of all, the cabinet was not one dedicated to the preservation of the old order. Although it did number Jeffersonian liberals, distrustful of positive federal action to solve the economic and social problems of the Great Depression — men like Hull, Roper, and Dern

— this group was not dominant. The large majority, including the two midwestern Republicans, was stanchly progressive in both its roots and its current credo. It was, in sum total, a cabinet which would abet more than inhibit Roosevelt's progress toward a New Deal.

CHAPTER X

An Assassin's Target

I heard what I thought was a firecracker; then several more.
— FDR, *Miami, Florida, February 16, 1933.*[1]

When Franklin D. Roosevelt left the White House after his second conference with President Hoover on January 20, 1933, another six weeks of ominous uncertainty stretched ahead toward the last of the inaugurations to take place on March 4. If Senator George Norris's "lame duck amendment" moving ahead the inauguration date had been ratified in time, he would have taken his oath of office on January 20, rather than weeks later. If ever there had been proof needed that the date should be advanced, it came in 1933, for during the weeks that dragged on into March the economy, Congress, and the outgoing administration seemed only to be marking time. And in mid-February, the frightening crack of a mentally unbalanced assassin's pistol almost deprived the nation of its new President before he could take office.

In the background were ominous daily reports from Europe, where the failure of German political and economic institutions had enabled the Nazis to come to power. Hitler was beginning to clear away the democratic rubble and lay the foundations for the Third Reich. The American government and economy still seemed secure despite the buffeting. Yet, what might continued failures and some new act of violence bring within the United States? During this interim of drift, amid the mists of depression, who could be entirely sure?

For Roosevelt these weeks began affirmatively and even optimistically. On January 21, he departed from Washington for the South to take the most positive step since his election. He visited the Tennessee Valley to reavow his campaign pledge to develop public power at Muscle Shoals. At the time it seemed a commitment more historic than forward looking, since symbolically the great dam that the federal government had built on the Tennessee River during the First World War had been for more than a decade the Verdun of the proponents of public power. It had been completed too late to be of wartime use, and had been a focal point of debate ever since. The private utilities interests mounted assault after assault against it, and while they were not successful in obtaining it, they were able to prevent public production of its power so that its great resources went largely to waste. Almost within sound of its unused waters roaring over the spillways, poverty-stricken farm families lit their kerosene lamps at nightfall.[2]

Cheap, abundant electricity seemed the means not merely to light farm homes but to redevelop and restore prosperity in one of the most acutely depressed areas in the United States. The great Tennessee Valley, cutting through portions of seven states and draining an area four-fifths that of England, was full of potential riches, yet many of its three million people were the victims of soil erosion, chronic poverty, and destructive springtime floods. Every statistic indicated relative deprivation. The average spendable income per person was less than half the national average. Although 77 percent of the people of the valley still lived off the land, compared with 44 percent nationally, the value per person of their farm products was only $154 compared with the national average of $362. In the 1920s a mountain farmer produced no more than ten bushels of corn per acre, and in the whole of Tennessee the average was only twenty-four bushels, compared with forty in Iowa. Families were large, the amount spent on each child per year of necessity only a third of the national average, and mortality rates were appalling. These were the human factors behind the struggle to develop public power and control floods on the Tennessee River.[3]

With poetic affection, James Agee described in *Fortune* the reality and the potential of the Tennessee Valley:

> The mountains and blue lapsing hills are encysted with time-wrought wealth: coal and iron . . . and, in all, not less than forty of the minerals most useful to mankind. All these await, for the most part, cheap power and the new processes that cheap power will make feasible. And the silver rivers yellowing and widening with weight of clay, which bind this valley into unity deeper than man can fence his states; a linkage and veinage of moving waters ill-kempt for navigation, capable of apoplectic flood but muscled with a munificence of power that man has scarcely touched.
>
> Steep land planted to corn, runneled and ruined with rain; flat land planted to cotton, worn and warped like a wrecked heel. . . . Cities that you would describe as provincial; towns you would describe as rube; farms so pitiable you would be sure to laugh at them.[4]

There had been no lack of proposals for harnessing the Tennessee River during the decades past, especially along the thirty-seven-mile stretch of rapids known as Muscle Shoals. During the progressive era, President Theodore Roosevelt vetoed a bill to permit private exploitation of power there; during the World War President Wilson had authorized construction of a great dam to produce power, and of enormous plants to utilize it in the production of nitrates for munitions. The war ended before the dam was completed, and the process for producing nitrates became obsolete even before one of the plants made its first test run. Yet to southern farmers, Wilson Dam and the plants gave promise of cheap power, and of a commodity that cotton growers desperately needed, cheap fertilizer. Led by Senator George Norris of Nebraska, progressives of both parties in Congress fought for public use of the Muscle Shoals resources and blocked its sale for a pittance to Henry Ford and private promoters. Norris visualized the dam as the center of a huge regional development; Presidents Coolidge and Hoover, vetoing Norris's measures, denounced his vision as socialism. President Hoover, suggesting that the states of Alabama and Tennessee rather than the federal government take action, declared in his veto message in 1931, "But for the Federal Government deliberately to go out to build up and expand such . . . a power and manufacturing business is to break down the initiative and enterprise of the American people; it is destruction of equality of opportunity amongst our people; it is the negation of the ideals upon which our civilization is based." [5]

In visiting the Tennessee Valley, Roosevelt was making more than a significant political gesture; he was reaffirming a course of action he had long proposed. As governor of New York, he had developed a public power policy which had brought him the support of a relatively small but vital following throughout the nation, of those to whom public development of power had been the touchstone of progressivism and whose idol was Norris. It was Roosevelt's acceptance of Norris's power credo that had brought him the initial support of Republican progressives. And it was an issue over which Norris and his cohorts in Congress had been able to ally themselves with substantial numbers of southern Democrats. For those southern senators and representatives to whom the recurrent flood damage and persistent poverty of the Tennessee Valley were a nagging concern, there was no issue which could more immediately tie them to the President-elect. So it was that Roosevelt, sweeping into his entourage leaders of both the public power enthusiasts and the agrarian South, journeyed from Washington to Muscle Shoals.* He was cementing the allegiance of an important part of

---

* Those in the party especially interested in public development of power included, besides Norris, Senator Clarence C. Dill of Washington, Frank P. McNinch of the Federal Power Commission; Frank P. Walsh, chairman of the New York State Power Authority, and E. F. Scattergood, builder and manager of the Los Angeles power system. The southern delegation included Senators Cordell Hull and Kenneth McKellar of Tennessee, Hugo Black and John H. Bankhead of Alabama; several representatives from each state, and John J. McSwain, chairman of the House Military Affairs Committee, which had charge of Muscle Shoals legislation.[6]

the coalition upon which he would depend for the enactment of New Deal legislation.

Partly, too, Roosevelt was moving toward the formulation of one of the most far-reaching measures in his projected New Deal. "I want to see what the whole Tennessee River project looks like," he had written Norris in inviting him to take the trip. "As you doubtless know, Senator Bankhead is chiefly concerned with the commercial development and gave me data to show the possibility of fertilizer manufacture. On this I am frankly from Missouri." [7]

It was a dramatic trip. Although the weather was chilly, Roosevelt, his daughter Anna, Norris, and other notables rode in an open car to Muscle Shoals. There Roosevelt viewed for the first time the idle auxiliary steam plant, a nitrate factory stretching along the Tennessee River for nearly a mile, and finally Wilson Dam itself, with the waters rushing unused through its spillways. The Alabama Power Company was utilizing only a minimal amount of its power under a contract in effect since 1925: in total less than five million dollars' worth. Later that day Roosevelt told a crowd, "I was not only impressed with the size of the great operation at Muscle Shoals but I can tell you frankly that it was at least twice as big as I ever had any conception of it being." He spoke of his distress and that of members of his party "that so much of that great plant had been lying in idleness all these years." Several times during the day, Roosevelt affirmed that not only would his administration utilize Muscle Shoals power to the fullest but that it would further develop hydroelectric power. As they stood by the roaring spillways, Roosevelt remarked to Norris, "This should be a happy day for you, George." With tears welling in his eyes, Norris replied, "It is, Mr. President. I see my dreams come true." [8]

Some newspapers called Roosevelt's visit to Muscle Shoals "the ride that made a 'Ruhr,' " but *Fortune* more cautiously termed it "The ride that made it conceivable that the Tennessee Valley might realize a great destiny." [9]

From Muscle Shoals, Roosevelt went farther into Alabama, expanding several times upon his theme of regional development as the means of achieving lasting recovery from the depression. "We have a great plant idle," he told a crowd of almost twenty thousand people at Birmingham, Alabama. "I propose to put it to work." After dark that night, speaking without a manuscript from the portico of the Alabama capitol in Montgomery, from the spot where Jefferson Davis had taken his oath of office as president of the Confederate States of America, he took a large, national view of the challenge in the Tennessee Valley: [10]

> My friends,
> I determined on two things as a result of what I have seen today. The first is to put Muscle Shoals to work. The second is to make of Muscle

Shoals a part of an even greater development that will take in all of that magnificent Tennessee River from the mountains of Virginia down to the Ohio and the Gulf.

Muscle Shoals is more today than a mere opportunity for the Federal Government to do a kind turn for the people in one small section of a couple of states. Muscle Shoals gives us the opportunity to accomplish a great purpose for the people of many States, and, indeed, for the whole Union, because there we have an opportunity of setting an example of planning, planning not just for ourselves but planning for the generations to come, tying in industry and agriculture and forestry and flood prevention, tying them all into a unified whole over a distance of a thousand miles so that we can afford better opportunities and better places for millions of yet unborn to live in in the days to come.[11]

Although these words were extemporaneous, they expressed Roosevelt's well-considered thoughts. In the aftermath of the visit to Muscle Shoals he elaborated upon his proposals for regional, and even national, resource development. Seated in front of the fieldstone fireplace in his Warm Springs cottage on February 2, he described to reporters his plans for "probably the widest experiment ever conducted by a government." Since the era of T.R. and Pinchot, he declared, the nation had been undertaking conservation projects in a piecemeal fashion. The time had come to tie them "into one great comprehensive plan within a given area," which would encompass development of water power, control of floods, reforestation, improvement of agriculture, and encouragement of new industry. It would, Roosevelt hoped, bring back to the land a number of those who were unemployed in the cities. Actually, as a result of the depression, the flow to urban factories had been reversed, and some of those thrown out of work had returned to try to scrape a living from worn-out fields. "The normal trend now is a back-to-the-farm movement," he said. "For those who have had experience in agricultural work I think we would do well to provide a living."

Roosevelt hoped the Tennessee Valley program altogether would employ 200,000 men in the valley, yet be self-sustaining. Although Roosevelt's notion that unemployment problems might be solved by returning families to farms was visionary, he did demonstrate a grasp of the technological factor in unemployment. Once more he declared that if the nation were to return to 1929 levels of production there would still be five million unemployed. This time he suggested more than back to the land — regional rehabilitation. If the project were successful it would "be the forerunner of similar projects in other parts of the country, such as in the watersheds of the Ohio, Missouri, and Arkansas Rivers and in the Columbia River in the Northwest." [12]

Roosevelt was making momentous announcements giving clear public indication that he would indeed innovate — that the New Deal would include large-scale regional planning centering around an enormous public power development. Unfortunately few people realized the change being heralded.

The increasing economic distress in those winter weeks distracted attention from Roosevelt's pledge to develop the Tennessee Valley. Even the *New Republic* and the *Nation*, which had crusaded so long and vigorously for public use of Muscle Shoals, found room for no more than a paragraph each of congratulations. The *Nation*, in an irony of ironies, after devoting only a few lines to hail the "recapture of Muscle Shoals," went on from brief comment on this concrete announcement of large-scale regional planning to devote a full article to Technocracy, a vaporous scheme for national planning being widely and solemnly discussed that winter. There was fairly scant editorial comment in newspapers, with most Republican newspapers of progressive leanings as well as Democratic journals expressing enthusiasm. A few like the *Washington Post*, at that time conservative, chided Roosevelt for proposing that "Congress in this period of hard times [should] waste still more of the taxpayers' money on this futile project." More typically, the *Philadelphia Record*, after describing the broad scope of the Tennessee Valley program, suggested its significance: "It gives concrete illustration of the change effected at the polls last November. It means that after twelve years of rule for the benefit of special interest the people have again won back their Government." [13]

Nor did progressives in Congress fail to grasp the purport. Roosevelt's strong promises rallied behind him the skittish progressive senators, both Republican and Democratic, who had created so much trouble for President Hoover. Edward P. Costigan of Colorado, a Democrat, wrote enthusiastically to Frank Walsh that the trip to Muscle Shoals and the statement at Warm Springs created "an immensely favorable reaction." He reported, "The feeling among Progressives in the Senate is that the power program of the administration promises incalculable benefit to the entire nation." [14]

No further major announcements were forthcoming from Warm Springs. Rather, Roosevelt, deeply involved in appointments, debt negotiations, and his legislative plans, gave reporters only a dribble of news. Most of it was of the contradictory sort intended to rally all the conflicting elements in his coalition. His first callers after his arrival were the two progressive Republican senators, La Follette and Cutting, on their serious errand to straighten out the question of two cabinet appointments. Roosevelt outlined his overall program with them, and particularly discussed possibilities for inflation. Both appointments and inflation were taboo subjects in talking to newspapermen, who learned only that the senators were seeking Roosevelt's support for a bill appropriating $500 million for unemployment relief. (La Follette barely mentioned this topic in his long report on the conference to his brother Philip.) But it was true that Roosevelt did endorse the bill. Indeed, in response to a request from the bill's cosponsor, Senator Costigan, he wired Senators Wagner and Robinson urging its enactment.[15]

Characteristically, Roosevelt spent the next day mollifying the right. He conferred with Baruch concerning the entire range of economic problems, especially means of providing temporary aid to railroads. The emphasis suddenly veered from mild inflation and heavy relief spending to drastic budget cutting. Did he still think he could reduce expenditures 25 percent, asked the reporters. "We will make a good stab at it." Again, economy dominated the conversations with Swagar Sherley, former chairman of the House Appropriations Committee, and Walker D. Hines, wartime director general of the railroads. Some savings might come from consolidation, Roosevelt was suggesting, for example, through grouping all government agencies dealing with transportation or communication into two bureaus. And Roosevelt had new suggestions for saving money through eliminating government services which might be considered luxuries in time of depression. He proposed eliminating the Naval Observatory, shutting down smaller army posts, and discharging the commercial and agricultural attachés attached to American embassies.[16]

Somehow, despite the urgent national and international problems crowding him, Roosevelt found time for some of his personal concerns. On February 2, he sent a lengthy, detailed letter to his former law partner, Basil O'Connor, concerning two Hyde Park farms abutting his own land, "which I have longed for years to own." Direct negotiations were impossible, said Roosevelt, so would O'Connor get some agent to make cautious inquiries:

> My general thought is that if old "Mr. Prosperity" comes back both . . . will be worth more money and if it does not come back land is about the only thing that does not run away. Will you put your mighty mind to work on this and see if you can find some good angel you can absolutely trust, who will investigate for the cost of a round trip ticket to Poughkeepsie and a good square meal! [17]

Roosevelt was also encouraging good angels who even in those months could write substantial checks to sustain the Warm Springs Foundation. The possibility that favors might be expected in return obviously did not bother him — and after all the heaviest previous donor had been John Raskob of du Pont and General Motors. Ben E. "Sell 'em" Smith, one of the most famous Wall Street bears, gave $5,000 for the Patients'

Aid Fund, and agreed to raise $20,000 toward meeting the deficit in operating expenses. Smith gave an additional $10,000, and checks came in for $5,000 from Tom Bragg, $2,500 from Herbert Fleishhacker, president of the Anglo-California National Bank, $2,500 from R. Stanley Dollar, president of the Dollar Steamship Lines, Inc., and $1,000 from Stuart Chevalier, a Wall Street lawyer specializing in federal taxation. Roosevelt accepted the donations with gratitude, telling Smith the checks were "the nicest possible birthday presents." [18]

There was time for some frolicking, mixed in with serious affairs. On January 30, he celebrated his fifty-first birthday by cutting slices of an eighty-pound cake for nearly ninety polio patients, many of them children, crowded around a long table in the dining room of Meriwether Inn.[19]

Several days later, on February 4, Roosevelt sailed from Jacksonville, Florida, on an eleven-day cruise aboard Vincent Astor's yacht *Nourmahal*, but of necessity the trip combined decision-making with relaxation, statecraft with horseplay. From the quarterdeck just before the ship left the dock, he gave his answer to the charges of the two isolationist senators, Lewis of Illinois and Reed of Pennsylvania, that he was going to be high-handed in settling the war debts. Not so, Roosevelt retorted; he had every intention of keeping the Senate and the House of Representatives informed. And yet it was in a holiday atmosphere that he left Jacksonville. He was met at the municipal docks at Commodore Point by his shipmates, a discreet, congenial group of gentlemen of similar social background: Justice Fred Kernochan of New York, George St. George of Tuxedo Park and New York, Dr. Leslie Heiter of Mobile, Alabama, and Kermit Roosevelt of the Oyster Bay branch of the clan.* It was the kind of coterie with which Roosevelt could relax. As they stood waving farewells from the rail, they looked like members of an undergraduate outing; St. George was bright in a striped blazer. Eyeing them glumly, Boss Ed Flynn of the Bronx remarked, "The Hasty Pudding Club puts out to sea." [21]

Under Roosevelt's leadership, the group gave itself over to much elaborate, almost ritualistic tomfoolery — ceremonies honoring Father Neptune, and joking so adolescent that a later generation of Harvard's Hasty Pudding Club would have disowned it with scorn. Through horseplay, sunning, and some fishing, Roosevelt relaxed. "I am getting a marvellous rest — lots of air and sun," he wrote his mother. "Vincent is

---

* The presence of Kermit was something of an embarrassment to his brother, Theodore Roosevelt, Jr., since it raised speculation that he was trying to retain his position as governor-general of the Philippines. When a newspaperman asked the governor-general why Kermit was yachting with the President-elect, his mother, Edith Carow Roosevelt, who was visiting, quietly interjected, "Because his mother was not there!" [20]

a dear and a perfect host. George and Kermit and Freddie and the young Doctor are excellent companions. When we land on the 15th I shall be full of health and vigor — the last holiday for many months." [22]

When the *Nourmahal* docked at Miami at seven o'clock on the evening of February 15, Roosevelt, tanned and happy, radiated the gay spirit of the outing. He informed reporters that he had had to lock up the log (repository of most of the foolishness) to keep it from their eyes. But what he told them was representative of the fun-making in which he had participated:

> I didn't even open the briefcase. . . . We fished and swam. . . . We went to a different place each day. Usually we fished in the morning and came back to the yacht for lunch.
>
> One day we had an all-day trip to the middle bight of Andros Island after bone-fish. The only difficulty is that you can't talk and fish for bone-fish. It's silent fishing and that put an awful crimp in it. We only fished for bone-fish one day.
>
> I did get one whale of a fish on my line. It took nearly all the line I had. I finally swung around and handed the rod to Dr. Leslie Heiter. The fish sounded and the line was broken on some coral at the bottom.[23]

Despite the depression Miami was crowded, and thousands of people were eager to greet Roosevelt. Later that evening he left the pier, and riding slowly in an open car, almost stopped at times by the people pressing toward him, he made his way toward Bay Front Park where he was scheduled to speak. The closeness of the people made Astor nervous; he remarked twice that it would be much too easy for a crank to shoot the President-elect. Roosevelt himself was not apprehensive in crowds. A few weeks earlier when Garner had passed on to him a congressman's warning of peril, Roosevelt replied calmly: "I think he goes a little far. I remember T.R. saying to me 'The only real danger from an assassin is from one who does not care whether he loses his own life in the act or not. Most of the crazy ones can be spotted first.' " [24]

Twenty thousand or more people jammed the benches and the area around the bandstand in the brightly lighted park. Perched on the back of the open touring car, his feet on the seat, Roosevelt gaily made a few remarks: "I have had a very wonderful twelve days fishing in these Florida and Bahama waters. It has been a wonderful rest and we have caught a great many fish. I am not going to attempt to tell you any fish stories [laughter], and the only fly in the ointment on my trip has been that I have put on about ten pounds [applause]." [25]

Roosevelt spoke for about two minutes, refused the request of news-reel photographers to repeat his remarks for them, and slid down from his perch into his seat. He chatted briefly with Mayor Anton J. Cermak of Chicago, who walked up to the side of the car, spoke to him, and then walked toward the rear. It was 9:35.

Suddenly a stubby, curly-haired man jumped onto one of the benches in the second row, and from a distance of perhaps no more than thirty-five feet pointed a pistol at Roosevelt and fired. The bench wobbled beneath him, and a horrified woman, Mrs. Lillian Cross, grappled with his arm, but in rapid succession he fired one shot after another at the President-elect. Mayor Cermak topped over; a woman standing on the bandstand, Mrs. Joseph H. Gill, was hit twice in the abdomen; three other people were wounded, but Roosevelt sat, with his jaw set, unflinching.

"I heard what I thought was a firecracker; then several more," Roosevelt declared afterward. "The man talking with me was pulled back and the chauffeur started the car." It was only then that the assassin, having emptied all five cartridges from his cheap revolver, was pulled to the ground by several men.

If the attack was too sudden for Roosevelt to react, the aftermath was not; with rapid, self-assured action he demonstrated his fearlessness and his insistence upon assuming command in a crisis. He countermanded Secret Service orders to leave immediately for fear other conspirators might renew the attack and insisted upon aiding Cermak:

> The chauffeur started the car. . . .
> I looked around and saw Mayor Cermak doubled over and Mrs. Gill collapsing. . . .
> I called to the chauffeur to stop. He did — about fifteen feet from where we started. The Secret Service men shouted to him to get out of the crowd and he started forward again. I stopped him a second time, this time at the corner of the band stand, about thirty feet further on.
> I saw Mayor Cermak being carried. I motioned to have him put in the back of the car, which would be the first out. He was alive, but I didn't think he was going to last. I put my left arm around him and my hand on his pulse, but I couldn't find any pulse. He slumped forward.
> On the left of Cermak, and leaning over him, was the Miami chief of detectives. He was sitting on the rear mudguard. He said after we had gone two blocks, "I don't think he is going to last."
> I said, "I am afraid he isn't."
> After we had gone another block, Mayor Cermak straightened up and I got his pulse. It was surprising. For three blocks I believed his heart had stopped. I held him all the way to the hospital and his pulse constantly improved.
> That trip to the hospital seemed thirty miles long. I talked to Mayor Cermak nearly all the way. I remember I said, "Tony, keep quiet — don't move. It won't hurt you if you keep quiet." . . .

The police did one quick and clever thing. When they got [the assailant] up from the ground they saw the car in which Kermit, Vincent and Moley were riding, two cars behind mine. It had just started out. They threw the man on the trunk rack and three policemen sat on him all the way to the hospital.

Roosevelt gave this statement to the newspapermen the next morning.[26]

The assailant was Joseph Zangara, a thirty-three-year-old bricklayer, only five feet one inch tall, who complained constantly of his stomach pains. He had been born in Calabria, Italy, and was a naturalized United States citizen. The immediate reaction within the United States, in keeping with the pattern of previous assassinations, was that he must be insane. Yet there was sure to be a gnawing question, especially in those times of revolution and incipient revolution throughout the world, whether his shots were the opening ambuscade in some American conspiracy. "This is the United States, not Russia," Senator Joseph Robinson remarked immediately upon hearing the news. "No fanatic, crank or revolutionist, or any number of them will be permitted to prevent the orderly transfer of power in the government of the United States."

In order to make sure that Zangara's act had been an isolated outburst of violence by a deranged man rather than part of a left-wing scheme, Moley, who was a criminologist, participated in the questioning of Zangara. By coincidence, in 1901 Moley had been at the Buffalo fairgrounds not far from President William McKinley when he had been shot by an anarchist; Zangara carried in his pocket a clipping referring to that assassination. After listening to Zangara, Moley firmly asserted that he had no political motivation.

"He didn't manifest any interest in political ideas; he was not socialistic, and gave no indication of having anarchistic ideas," * Moley declared. "He has a fixed idea of opposition to all heads of government." [28]

Zangara talked readily to his questioners, emphasizing repeatedly that his stomach hurt and that he hated all Presidents:

> After I read in the papers about Mr. Roosevelt coming here I went to a store on North Miami Avenue and bought a pistol. There was a sign in front of the store with the words on it: "Money to loan"; I paid $8 for the gun.

---

* Moley was explicit in a letter to a friend a few days later:

> I interviewed Zangara after the shooting that night and in my opinion no psychiatrist would declare him insane in the legal sense of the word. I made it very clear in my statement to the newspapers after examining him that I found no political ideas. I did this not only because it was true, but because I felt it was desirable to avoid, so far as possible, any hysteria on the subject of radicalism.[27]

I tried to get to the park early tonight so as to be as close to the President-elect as possible, but some people were there before me.

I sat there in the park waiting and my stomach kept aching more than ever. Maybe the excitement was responsible. . . .

I meant to shoot the President-elect while he was talking, but the people in front of me were standing and I am such a short fellow I didn't have a chance.

My big chance came, however, when some people got tired of standing and sat down. I stood on the bench and pointed the gun at Mr. Roosevelt.

But the people around me were pressing against the bench and making it wobbly. The gun started to shake, but I pulled the trigger anyhow — I don't remember how many times.*

I do not know whether or not I shot Mr. Roosevelt, but I want to

---

* Early in March Mayor Cermak died, and Zangara was subsequently executed as his murderer. Rumors have persisted during the years since that Zangara was aiming at Cermak rather than Roosevelt, in other words that the assassination was part of a plot rather than an irrational act. There had been reports from Chicago that Mayor Cermak and the Democratic party had been consolidating their election gains and getting tough with the Capone mob. Although Cermak had allowed the speakeasies to remain open, he was said to have closed down the gambling houses. Perhaps, it was rumored, he was preparing to run for the Senate. Various quite different and sometimes quite plausible stories began to circulate concerning the plot — rumors that came to be believed by persons as high-placed as Secretary Ickes. For example, Harry Dial, a jazz drummer, once reminisced:

> There was a joint in Cicero on Chicago Avenue where I worked in 1933. One night after I was putting my drums away I accidentally overheard some guys in the back room planning to kill Mayor Cermak. They weren't trying to kill Roosevelt as the papers wanted you to believe at that time. The guy who killed him was a dead shot. He used to come into the place all the time and shoot the antlers off the moose head that was hanging over the bar with a .45. . . . They were going to pay him $25,000 to kill Cermak, and were going to send half to his mother in Italy and give him the other half when he did the job. They knew he was going to die of cancer, that's why he was chosen for the job.

A writer, Kendell F. Crosson, has acquired a quite similar story from a man intimately acquainted with the Chicago gangs. According to this version, Frank Nitti hired Zangara, a professional gunman fatally ill with cancer, to come to Chicago from New York where he had been working for Frankie Yale. He lived for about a month in the Hawthorne Inn, engaging in target practice in the basement. After shooting Cermak, Zangara remained silent about his gang connections in return for Nitti sending money to his relatives in Italy.

Nevertheless, there is no indication that Zangara was ever in Chicago, or that he had been involved with gangsters. It is unlikely that a professional killer would undertake an assassination with a stiff, unwieldy cheap revolver. When a Florida judge asked on January 20, "Did you know Mayor Cermak?" Zangara replied: "No, not at all. I just went there to kill the President. The capitalists killed my life. I suffer, always I suffer. I make it 50–50 — some one else must suffer." This colloquy followed:

"Q. — Don't you want to live?

A. — No, put me in the electric chair.

Q. — Are you sorry only because you tried to kill Mr. Roosevelt?

A. — No, I am sorry only because I failed. . . ." [29]

make it clear I do not hate Mr. Roosevelt personally. I hate all Presidents, no matter from what country they come, and I hate all officials and everybody who is rich.[30]

Roosevelt, brushing aside thoughts of the narrowness of his escape, remained at the hospital until he could talk to Mayor Cermak and the other victims; then at about 11:15 he returned to the *Nourmahal* to spend the night. To Moley, this seemed the time of real testing; with the crowds gone and among one's companions one could react as one pleased. "The time for the letdown among his intimates was at hand," Moley has written. "All of us were prepared, sympathetically, understandingly, for any reaction that might come from him.

"There was nothing — not so much as the twitching of a muscle, the mopping of a brow, or even the hint of a false gaiety — to indicate it was any other evening in any other place. Roosevelt was simply himself — easy, confident, poised, to all appearances unmoved." [31]

Moley poured a generous serving of whiskey into a tumbler; Roosevelt downed it, became a bit silly, and at two o'clock went to bed. Several others in the party, their nerves frayed, stayed up for hours, smoking and talking. In the morning they asked the Secret Service man who had been guarding Roosevelt's stateroom whether the governor had indeed been able to sleep. "I was curious myself," he replied, "so I stole in several times. Each time Mr. Roosevelt was fast asleep." [32]

When Eleanor Roosevelt learned late that evening, after she had finished delivering a speech, that her husband had narrowly avoided being assassinated, she demonstrated similar stoicism. "Those things are to be expected," she said. She telephoned Roosevelt at once, reaching him at Cermak's bedside, and after talking to him for several minutes remarked, "He's all right. He's not the least bit excited." [33]

There were only a handful of people so bitter and alienated that they would have wished the assassin success.* There was no incipient revolu-

---

* A sociologist who was living with boy tramps in a hobo jungle reported:

About nine P.M. Boo Peep came bursting in out of the darkness.

"They got Roosevelt," he cried. "Geez, they got somebody at last, and the mayor of Chicago, and maybe Hoover too."

Everybody asked questions. Jubilation was intense. Hoping that this was the signal which would touch off the revolution, we deserted our cave and went uptown to learn the truth.

About midnight we came trailing back into the cave, very dejected. The assassin had missed. The revolution had not started, and the night was bitterly cold. . . . These boys were dejected but in a fighting mood. One of the lowly and oppressed had dared the thunder. While he had missed, his action would not be forgotten.

"Maybe this will show some of those goddam bankers and higher-ups something to wake them up," said Slim Jim. "I'd like to shoot the bastard that foreclosed Dad's home." [34]

tionary movement in the United States, even in that hard winter. Yet chance had almost eliminated Roosevelt before his term of office began. Similarly, Winston Churchill had narrowly escaped being killed by an automobile in New York in 1931. As Arthur Schlesinger, Jr., has suggested, how different America and the world would have been if these two men had been killed. Certainly the course of the United States would have been by no means the same under Vice President–elect Garner, who under the newly ratified Twentieth Amendment would have been inaugurated that March 4.[35]

Roosevelt was as fatalistic after the episode as he had been before; it did not seem to change his feelings or habits. He seemed to regard his survival as an act of heavenly intervention, gave his sympathy to those hit, and said he would pray daily for their recovery. He visited them at the hospital. Especially he was grateful to Mrs. Cross, who had spoiled Zangara's aim. He wired her, "How much greater and sadder a tragedy was averted by your unselfish courage and quick thinking of course no one can estimate. It now appears that by Divine Providence the lives of all the victims of the assassin's disturbed aim will be spared." [36]

When Roosevelt arrived in New York City on February 17 and found a guard of a thousand police turned out to protect him, his only remark was "I'm feeling fine and I've had a fine trip." Unusual precautions were soon abandoned, and when, several months later, the head of the Secret Service proposed building a high wire fence around the Warm Springs cottage, Roosevelt imposed his veto. He would accept no more than what he considered to be reasonable protection.[37]

And admiration for him grew. "Roosevelt is being praised on all hands for his courageous composure," William E. Chilton of West Virginia wrote from Miami the next day. "Of course he is that kind of a man and that is one reason why he was elected." [38]

Roosevelt's cool, even cheerful, reaction to his brush with death brought a surge of national confidence in him as had none of his other actions since the election. "People seemed to feel that their faith in the future was also the assassin's target," reported *Time;* they were buoyed by his escape and response. In those February days when frightened people were standing in long queues to withdraw their remaining savings from wobbly banks, he began to appear as a symbol of courage and hope.[39]

CHAPTER XI

The Run on the Banks

No participation by me as a private citizen could have
prevented the crisis; such participation in details would
have hampered thoroughgoing action under my own responsibility as President.
— FDR, *1938*.[1]

In the aftermath of his personal scrape with death, Roosevelt as President-
elect had to face a critical threat to the economy of the nation. Banks
throughout the United States, weakened by the long attrition of the
depression, could not withstand the heavy withdrawals and hoarding
that gained momentum in the latter half of February. "It would have
been inconceivable — if one had not seen it happening right under one's
eyes — that one hundred and twenty million odd of people should,
apparently, at one and the same time fall into terror, and rush to withdraw their deposits from the banks," Thomas Lamont, the Morgan
partner, wrote an English friend, "Yet, in effect, that is what did happen.
No banking structure in the world — no matter how strong — was
ever designed to meet an onslaught of that kind." [2]

Basically the banking crisis grew out of the exhaustion of the resources of millions of small depositors, businesses, and in turn, of banks.
It was compounded by the depositors' mistrust of banks and desperate
need for their remaining savings on the one hand, and on the other,
the heavy drain on the federal gold reserve in expectation that the incoming administration would take the nation off the gold standard and
devalue the dollar. There was a third factor aggravating the crisis: the
inability of the outgoing and incoming Presidents to cooperate.

As the pressure upon the banks became acute, President Hoover
came to believe that Roosevelt was responsible for it, and that Roosevelt alone could bring it to an end. The President-elect, only three
days after the attempt on his life and two weeks before inauguration
day, on the evening of Saturday, February 18, 1933, was sitting in the
banquet room of the Hotel Astor in New York City watching a group

of New York political reporters, "The Inner Circle," present a series of skits. The room was heavily guarded. At eleven o'clock a Secret Service operative appeared quietly at Roosevelt's side and handed him a heavy brown paper envelope bearing on its back the seal of the President of the United States. Inside was a second envelope, also sealed, addressed in President Hoover's own hand to "President Elect Roosvelt." Within was a ten-page handwritten letter. Without attracting attention to himself Roosevelt perused it, then quietly passed it under the table for Moley to read. A glance was sufficient for Moley to grasp the purport: the banking crisis was out of control.[3]

> I looked up at Roosevelt, expecting, certainly to see some shadow of the grim news in his face or manner. And there was nothing — nothing but laughter and applause for the play actors, pleasant bantering with those who sat at table with him, and the gay, unhurried, autographing of programs for half a hundred fellow guests at the dinner's end.
>
> I thought then, "Well, this can't go on. The kickback's got to come when he leaves this crowd. This is just for show. We'll see what happens when he's alone with us."

At 12:35 A.M., Roosevelt and his entourage left for his home on Sixty-fifth Street and discussed the letter for more than an hour. Roosevelt remained unperturbed despite its portentous contents: [4]

> My dear Mr. President-Elect:
> A most critical situation has arisen in the country of which I feel it is my duty to advise you confidentially. I am therefore taking this course of writing you myself and sending it to you through the Secret Service for your hand direct as obviously its misplacement would only feed the fire and increase the dangers.
> The major difficulty is the state of public mind, for there is a steadily degenerating confidence in the future which has reached the height of general alarm. I am convinced that a very early statement by you upon two or three policies of your Administration would serve greatly to restore confidence and cause a resumption of the march of recovery.

At length, Hoover outlined once more his theories, counter to Roosevelt's, of the nature and course of the depression, and to assert the view that by the summer of 1932 the United States had been pulling out of the depression, only to slip back into a state of alarm during the winter. The blame, Hoover implied unmistakably, rested upon the failure of the Democratic Congress and the President-elect to pledge themselves to a definite, conservative course. Hoover bluntly wrote out his bill of particulars, omitting nothing.

President Hoover's conclusion followed logically from his assessment. Since the crisis was due to lack of confidence in the Democratic leadership, the way to end it would be for Roosevelt to clarify the public mind on certain essentials. "It would steady the country greatly," Hoover declared, "if there could be prompt assurance that there will be no tampering or inflation of the currency; that the budget will be unquestionably balanced, even if further taxation is necessary; that the Government credit will be maintained by refusal to exhaust it in the issue of securities." [5]

President Hoover was well aware of the significance of his demands upon Roosevelt; it is not clear whether he felt that through bluntly restating his own view of the depression and placing blame for the crisis upon the President-elect and his party he could elicit positive action. Hoover seems to have known no other way to act — it was long-standing habit with him to bring as strong and as direct pressure as possible, confident that even though failure was almost inevitable he himself had been correct and in the end his opponent would have to bear the obloquy of posterity. Thus it was that the President several days later tried to bring new pressure upon Roosevelt through Democratic leaders in the Senate, sending them word through a Republican senator, David A. Reed of Pennsylvania. In a letter he gave Reed, presumably to show the Democrats, he. wrote with remarkable self-revelation:

> I realize that if these declarations be made by the President-elect, he will have ratified the whole major program of the Republican Administration; that is, it means the abandonment of 90% of the so-called new deal. But unless this is done, they run a grave danger of precipitating a complete financial debacle. If it is precipitated, the responsibility lies squarely with them for they have had ample warning — unless, of course, such a debacle is part of the "new deal." [6]

It would have taken someone with more forbearance than Roosevelt to reply favorably to a letter written in as antagonistic a tone as Hoover's. Nor was it the first time that the President had tried to force him to give up his plans for a New Deal and endorse a more conservative course. At the crux of Hoover's demands was the request that the President-elect reaffirm his intention of keeping the United States on a gold standard. One writer during those unhappy weeks referred to the departing Hoover as the "Great White Feather," a characterization as untrue as it was ungenerous, for no President since Cleveland had demonstrated such courageous, high-principled resistance on behalf of an unpopular cause. It is singular that in both instances the cause for which the Presidents so bitterly fought was the maintenance of a deflationary gold standard in time of depression.[7]

Roosevelt took Hoover's letter so seriously that he meticulously wrote on the envelope the place and time of receipt. That night, in his first discussion with his advisers, he emphasized however that whatever reply he might ultimately make, he would not mention gold. He wrote no immediate answer to the President, and in the days that followed continued to remain silent.[8]

Roosevelt's silence at such a critical time might seem a serious delinquency, or at best a frivolous failure to gauge the seriousness of the crisis. Yet there are factors which make his viewpoint understandable.

The United States had paid a heavy price for remaining on the gold standard while its principal competitors for world markets, most notably the British, had devalued their currencies. The first step toward foreign purchase of American goods was for the overseas customer to purchase dollars, and dollars had come to cost him considerably more than sterling. Between 1929 and 1932, while world trade had dropped a quarter, United States exports had declined a half. Although much more was involved besides the unfavorable valuation of the dollar, it was a contributing factor. The solution of the problem in which President Hoover and Secretary of the Treasury Mills believed seemed to them indisputably correct — through use of war debts or other bargaining levers, get the British back onto the gold standard. Hoover, in other words, wanted the British to raise the value of their pound sterling back to an unfavorably high rate and thus give up their advantage in seeking foreign trade. Hoover's was a utopian dream which in private Foreign Office officials had treated with derision.[9]

The solution Roosevelt's advisers were pressing him toward was rather for him to take the United States off the gold standard and devalue its currency to a level competitive with that of other nations. For him to have announced in advance of taking office a policy that Hoover so vehemently opposed would not only have subjected him to critical pressure within the United States but have given greater encouragement to speculators both at home and abroad to strip the Treasury of its gold reserve. While the United States was on the gold standard during the Hoover administration, dollars were freely exchangeable for gold. In the first six months of 1932, foreigners gambling that the United States would be forced off the gold standard drained away quantities of gold. The Hoover administration managed to survive the crisis, preserve the standard and even reverse the gold flow, but at the price of continued serious deflation.[10]

Roosevelt did not announce his intentions concerning gold. His last statement was the emphatic, misleading one he had made on the eve of the election, when to refute Hoover he implied that the American government would not break its covenant to keep its securities redeemable in gold. It can be argued on the one hand that Roosevelt was perpetuating a deceit, on the other that to be candid would be unpatriotic. It was a likelier possibility than either of these that Roosevelt had not thought hard about the subject and assumed that whatever was done with gold internationally, the gold clause in federal securities could be maintained. Rumors were of course prevalent that President Hoover's campaign warnings were correct, and in addition there was the downward trend of prices and production to suggest that the nation could not much longer bear the burden of deflation. By February 1933, once again gold was flowing out of the United States at an accelerating pace; quantities more were being withdrawn to be hoarded at home.

The reason why was stated one way two years later by Roosevelt's secretary of the treasury, Henry Morgenthau, Jr.: "Europeans knew that we could not maintain our currency at the old gold level without a ruinous deflation of our prices, trade and industrial activity. Facing that crisis, the previous administration stubbornly refused to take action, evidently under the impression that that was a proud achievement, when it was obviously economic suicide." [11]

And Hoover's Secretary of the Treasury Mills in rebuttal gave quite an opposite interpretation: "It was not the maintenance of the gold standard that caused the banking panic of 1933 and the outflow of gold . . . it was the definite and growing fear that the new administration meant to do what they ultimately did — that is abandon the gold standard, and their refusal to cooperate in any way with the outgoing administration." [12]

What the two secretaries were saying was that in February 1933 Hoover would not embargo gold or leave the gold standard; that Roosevelt would not announce in advance that he would keep the nation on the gold standard. The continued gold drain was thus part of the price the United States was paying for the lengthy interregnum between the two administrations.

The flight from the dollar in Europe was for the most part prudent (or speculative) in anticipation of devaluation. British banking houses were withdrawing their balances from American banks; on the continent dollars were being exchanged for pounds. London bankers emphasized, the *Wall Street Journal* reported near the climax of the crisis, "that the selling of dollars has emanated mainly from continental centers on speculative account and it is remarkable how small the flight is from the dollar by American nationals themselves." [13]

There were, of course, some conservative American businessmen and bankers who shared Hoover's and Mills's fears. Nigel Law, analyzing the crisis for the Foreign Office from the viewpoint of the City of London, cited a letter he had read from an ordinarily level-headed

American banker who was requesting a British friend to buy him $100,000 in gold and hold it in London. Law explained:

> His reasons were that he feared the new Congress would be so "radical" that it would embark on uncontrolled inflation to such an extent that neither currency nor Government securities would be safe. At the same time he feared that such heavy taxation would be imposed as to make the holding of either raw materials or equity stocks no better refuge for his liquid assets. He added that he did not consider it wise to keep gold in America lest privately owned gold should be confiscated by the Government. Personally, I think he holds an exaggerated view of the dangers ahead, but that he should think thus gives one some idea of the panic now prevalent there.[14]

Such fright was the exception rather than the rule among American financial leaders, since Roosevelt, except for his unwillingness to make public obeisance to gold, had in all of his statements and acts been following as conservative a course as the business and banking community could conceivably demand. To this extent, Roosevelt was already assuming responsibility in the area of domestic policy even as he was in foreign policy. For weeks the newspapers had been full of his own and his advisers' avowals that the federal budget would be slashed a full 25 percent and that it would be balanced. Many, if not most, banking and business leaders, including several Morgan partners, were more concerned with fiscal conservatism than the gold standard; Roosevelt's assurances on internal matters were sufficient for them.[15]

So far as the newspaper reader could see, every indication was that as President, Roosevelt would follow a program of drastic economy. None of his statements had ruffled the laissez-faire orthodoxy of Alexander Dana Noyes, the financial editor of the *New York Times*, or occasioned editorial rebuke in the *Wall Street Journal*. It was not until the week ending with the inauguration that Noyes and Krock (probably through the intervention of Hoover's friend Mark Sullivan) prodded Roosevelt to issue the three-point manifesto the President had been demanding. Rather, the financial editors had been quite satisfied with Roosevelt's demeanor, as well they might. Had he complied with Hoover's request, his three-part pledge would have marked a departure from his public position of the winter only in its affirmation of the gold standard. If he had given his pledge, he might have stemmed the gold drain, but it is questionable whether the run on the banks would have stopped.[16]

There was another secondary factor stimulating bank runs which Hoover with better reason blamed upon Roosevelt. The Democratic leaders in Congress had insisted upon publicizing the lists of recipients of Reconstruction Finance Corporation (RFC) loans; Roosevelt as

President-elect could probably have persuaded them to stop the publication. President Hoover at the time and Undersecretary of the Treasury Arthur A. Ballantine in retrospect laid emphasis upon this delinquency of Roosevelt's. A depositor who read in the papers that his bank had been forced to borrow from the RFC was likely to become nervous and withdraw his money. Yet it was Speaker Garner, himself a West Texas banker, suspicious that the loans might be used politically by the Republicans, who beginning in November 1932 forced publication of the current monthly lists, and in January 1933, of all recipients before July 1932 — altogether some four thousand financial institutions. Roosevelt made no effort to stop the lists, although he ended them shortly after he became President. He could have acted after receiving Hoover's letter, although by that time irrevocable damage had been done. He did not. President Hoover enlisted the aid of Senate Minority Leader Robinson, who introduced a bill in the Senate on February 17 that would prohibit disclosures. Shortly afterward the bill was dropped; Robinson informed Hoover that Roosevelt thought "everything should be made public." [17]

Even if Roosevelt had acted in every particular as fully as President Hoover requested, it seems unlikely he would have ended the banking crisis. Fundamentally, the millions of small depositors were not worried about the credit of the federal government or the gold standard, which seemed far-off abstractions, but about the soundness of their banks. Their faith in the federal government and corresponding diminishing confidence in banks was shown by the spectacular rise in postal savings deposits — from $150 million in 1928 to a billion dollars in 1933. In the four years prior to the crisis, 5,738 banks with assets totaling three and a half billion dollars had suspended payments. Banks, with much of their assets frozen in real estate or other property of declining value, were becoming harder and harder pressed to meet withdrawals. Yet both corporate depositors and millions of small depositors were being forced to draw even more deeply upon their accounts. Gradually banks were drained of their liquid assets; many were able to obtain RFC loans to bolster them temporarily, but the national distress was far greater than the relatively limited aid that could come from Washington. If only prosperity would return and values return to their old levels, the banks, despite certain malpractices in the twenties, would for the most part be able to function on a sound basis. After the crisis, 92 percent were able to respond. They were, above all, victims of the deflationary spiral of the depression.[18]

As for the depositors, while large speculators could be denounced, it was hard not to sympathize with the holder of a small account, dependent upon its few dollars to stay off of relief. No matter how conscientious he was, he dared not withdraw funds when a run began. One depositor has written of her decision to take her money out of Chicago banks:

> Were we helping to wreck the financial structure of the nation in trying to protect ourselves against this disaster? I suppose we were. But the small sum of money we had in those banks was all that stood between us and the bread line. We figured that it might last a year if we counted the pennies and did not get sick. My husband had been unable to find employment. Our investments had become worthless. We could not have sold the house at any price, or rented it for enough to keep us, and we could not possibly have mortgaged it. If we had lost what little ready cash we had, there was no one who would or could have paid our grocery bills or bought us coal against the blizzards.[19]

In Michigan, where the automobile workers had acutely suffered from the depression, the strain upon the banks had become intolerable by mid-February. Undersecretary Ballantine rushed to Detroit to offer a maximum RFC loan and to try to obtain private financing from Henry Ford, but deep suspicions between Ford and his old antagonist, Senator James Couzens, thwarted the arrangement. Early on the morning of Tuesday, February 14, the governor proclaimed an eight-day banking holiday.

By the end of the week when Roosevelt returned to New York, business in Michigan seemed to be weathering the banking holiday, and Wall Street did not seem unduly disturbed. After the initial upset, the stock and commodity markets throughout the country went bumping along as before at their depression lows. Cash from other states was rushed into Detroit so that retail trade continued only slightly below usual levels. Up to 5 percent of the total money on deposit could be withdrawn from Detroit banks, and only 1 percent had been taken out. Wall Streeters were ascribing the Michigan crisis to a quarrel among old antagonists in the automobile industry, and did not expect it to spread. The Sunday *New York Times*, on the street the very night that Roosevelt was discussing Hoover's letter, contained a reassuring headline, "Detroit, Recovering from Shock, Treats Bank Suspension as a Joke." In ensuing days, Louis Howe referred repeatedly to the headline, but even earlier Roosevelt was not inclined to regard the bank holiday as cataclysmic.[20]

Through the growing alarm of the final two weeks until his inauguration, Roosevelt remained outwardly unperturbed. So far as his relations with President Hoover were concerned, he remained firm in his view that there was nothing Hoover could do with his aid that he could not do without it; Hoover was still President, he as yet was a private citizen. Behind this was his experience as governor of New York in dealing with the crises that had grown out of the failure of the Bank of United States. His responsibilities in trying to regulate banks had been large; a quarter of the nation's deposits were to be found in New York banks. He had brought with him from Wall Street to Albany a belief in conservative banking practice and a willingness to depend upon leading bankers for advice. Repeatedly he had rejected deposit insurance schemes as impractical. Yet when he came to advocate moderate reform, the stubborn opposition of the bankers, backed by the Republican majority in the State senate, kindled his anger. By February 1933, he was still disposed to follow a conservative course, but was overflowing with moral indignation against the bankers. Day after day, newspapers were carrying reports of the Senate Banking and Currency Committee inquiry into the stock market and the real estate speculations of prominent bankers.*

When the bankers, who were also aware of Roosevelt's power over the Democratic senators, protested that the Senate investigation into their methods was contributing to the undermining of public confidence, he retorted, Moley remembered, "The bankers should have thought of that when they did the things that are being exposed now." Roosevelt was quite willing to see the bankers take their punishment, and seemed confident that the business of the nation could proceed relatively undisturbed, even if the banks were closed. He regarded himself as the champion of the little people, but in his anger toward the bankers he seemed to forget that the welfare of the little people depended upon the banks being open and solvent.[22]

Even while Roosevelt left Hoover's letter unanswered he authorized several differing responses to the banking community, indicating how uncertain his course was for a day or two. On Friday, February 17, the day of his return from Florida, Woodin and Howe, in the presence of Tugwell, reported to Roosevelt on the runs on banks and the hysteria of the bankers. Owen D. Young, Winthrop Aldrich of Chase National Bank, and a number of others were insistent that he take some action. George Harrison, governor of the Federal Reserve Bank of New York, wanted to talk to Roosevelt about the accelerating currency withdrawals, the unfavorable foreign exchange, and Americans' withdrawal of gold coin — as yet none substantial in dollar volume but becoming ominous. Roosevelt convinced Woodin and Young that it would be unwise for Harrison to come see him because of the danger of "con-

---

* During these weeks, the Senate committee revealed that Charles E. Mitchell of the National City Bank had received a bonus of three and a half million dollars, paid to him over three years. National City Bank had received $25 million in payment for loans to sugar companies taken over by its affiliate, the National City Company; the bank and its affiliate had jointly traded in the stock of Anaconda and other copper companies.[21]

spicuous comment." Rather, he had Moley and others meet with Harrison at Woodin's apartment on Sunday, February 19. Harrison explained to them that internal hoarding the year before had been largely a response to fear of banks; in February 1933 it reflected also a mistrust of the currency and was taking the form of gold withdrawals. Like Hoover, Harrison was anxious for Roosevelt to give conservative reassurances. Roosevelt let Harrison know through Woodin that he himself would not issue a statement. But the day before, on Saturday, he had authorized Admiral Grayson and Senator James Byrnes to inform Senator Carter Glass that he favored maintaining sound currency but could not guarantee it indefinitely. On Sunday afternoon, in response to Woodin's conversation with Harrison, he let Woodin tell Harrison he would not object, if Glass accepted his appointment as secretary of the treasury, for Glass to give a guarantee. Further, Woodin asked Harrison to bring pressure through Admiral Grayson for Glass to accept — a remarkably oblique way of doing things. Harrison did so, but when he reported back to Woodin that evening, Woodin had to suggest that it would be better to say nothing to Glass about his being permitted to make a statement. What had happened in the interim was that Roosevelt had himself telephoned Glass to plead with him a final time, had accepted Glass's definite refusal, and was about to appoint Woodin as his secretary of the treasury. Harrison, not knowing what had transpired, had to telephone Grayson a second time that night and reverse instructions. Roosevelt was moving toward no guarantees.

In talking to Tugwell on February 17, Roosevelt seemed entirely confident of the future. He "took it all smiling and could [see] no reason why he should save these bankers; it was more important, he said to us, to save the folks." In this discussion, Roosevelt, rather than concerning himself with trying to keep the banks open, talked of means of keeping currency in circulation for business purposes, perhaps through utilizing post offices and issuing scrip. Tugwell noted: "This situation is developing swiftly and may mean a tremendous change. But F.D.R. is calm and sane about it. All the bankers now want their deposits guaranteed by the government, something they fought for years. But he sees no reason, as he said repeatedly, for specially protecting this interest as against all others." [23]

Some of Roosevelt's self-assurance rubbed off onto Tugwell who, on February 25 lunching with James H. Rand, Jr., of Remington Rand, talked with surprising candor. Rand at once relayed his version of the remarks to President Hoover:

> He said they were fully aware of the bank situation and that it would undoubtedly collapse in a few days, which would place the responsibility in the lap of President Hoover. He said, "We should not worry

about anything except rehabilitating the country after March 4th. Then there would be several moves; first, an embargo on exportation of yellow chips; second, suspension of specie payments; third, reflation if necessary." [24]

Tugwell's remarks were all the confirmation Hoover needed to be firm in his belief that Roosevelt and the New Dealers were disposed to bring the economy to ruin for their own political ends.* He commented: "When I consider this statement of Professor Tugwell's in connection with the recommendations we have made to the incoming administration, I can say emphatically that he breathes with infamous politics devoid of every atom of patriotism. Mr. Tugwell would project millions of people into hideous losses for a Roman holiday." †

Through the first week after President Hoover sent his letter, the banking community seemed, outwardly at least, to be withstanding the pressure. Roosevelt left the letter unanswered. On Monday he once more conferred with the British ambassador, Sir Ronald Lindsay, concerning war debts; on Tuesday he began bit by bit announcing cabinet appointees beginning with Hull and Woodin — and Woodin was acclaimed as an advocate of sound money. The coming and going of numerous visitors to the house on Sixty-fifth Street continued unabated, and while Roosevelt received reports and recommendations on the banking crisis, he busied himself with equal enthusiasm on the details of his inauguration and a myriad of policy matters. He even found time to visit a shop on Lexington Avenue to look at some old prints.

Day by day the crisis intensified as the quantity of dollars hoarded or exchanged for the Treasury's gold mounted geometrically. The Federal Reserve was rushing additional funds to banks; large supplementary amounts were required in Michigan. On Tuesday, February 22, Roosevelt again discussed the crisis with Woodin and Moley. He pondered whether or not to issue a pledge of a balanced budget, but still vehemently opposed making any direct statement promising sound

---

* Years later, Tugwell explained concerning his conversation with Rand. "He was snooping around for information . . . I certainly did say, 'We should worry. . . .' I said it by way of evasion. I wanted to lend a light, airy tone to my conversation so that Rand wouldn't know how to take it. In other words, I wasn't going to tell him a damn thing. Hoover, who was understandably in bad shape in the lame-duck period, took it seriously." [25]

† Hoover was apparently disposed to regard Rand's report as an accurate gauge of the motivation of the incoming administration, and at some point between 1933 and 1935, mistakenly attributed the alleged remarks to Secretary-elect Woodin. He sent to William Starr Myers and Walter H. Newton for publication a log in which he had written under February 25, 1933: "Mr. Mills reported to the President that Mr. Woodin had informed him . . . that they hoped to take over the situation at the lowest point." When queried, Mills firmly asserted, "The statement . . . should not under any circumstances be published. Certainly Mr. Woodin never expressed to me any such sentiment as the words . . . would indicate." [26]

money. By Friday, Woodin was profoundly worried over the bank runs and withdrawals of gold. He and the group around Roosevelt were mulling over numerous proposals that were being urged upon them. Especially they were considering placing an embargo upon gold, or perhaps taxing gold hoarders. Friday, February 24, was the day of collapse in Baltimore; during the week depositors had withdrawn $13 million, $6 million of it on that last day. The governor of Maryland proclaimed a three-day holiday. Roosevelt on Saturday ended his silence to tell reporters he was studying banking problems. On Sunday he went to Hyde Park to work on his inaugural address. While attending services at St. James Church, a sentence came to him: "The money changers have fled from their high seats in the temple of our civilization." [27]

Drafting the inaugural had begun some days earlier. On the train to Jacksonville, Florida, Roosevelt dictated some suggestions to Raymond Moley, who on February 12–13 wrote a first draft. At this point, Howe may also have had a hand in the enterprise; in writing the editor of the *American Magazine,* he referred to the "inaugural message, as we are at present drafting it." In any event, a draft or drafts were prepared. Moley took them to Hyde Park, and in consultation with Roosevelt worked on Sunday, February 26, and part of Monday to complete the speech. At about ten o'clock Monday evening Roosevelt sent everyone to bed, and taking a pad of lined yellow foolscap he sat at a card table in the large living room, and working from Moley's draft, began writing a final version in his own hand. Now and then he would pause after copying a sentence to read it aloud and comment, "That's great." After Roosevelt had finished copying the first page, Moley walked over, picked up the page of draft, and threw it into the fire, and did so again after the second page. After that, Roosevelt threw away the draft pages one by one. Only Roosevelt's handwritten copy remained. Howe the next day dictated Roosevelt's draft to a stenographer, changing altogether about fifty words — but Roosevelt confided to Moley that he intended to change them back.* Later, before the final typing on March 3, Roosevelt added the ringing passage assailing unjustified national fear.

Despite the subsequent impression that this address was solely Roosevelt's handiwork, it was, like his other speeches, the composite of several minds, finally molded into his own pattern.[29]

---

* In the finished speech, the passages on the indictment of the bankers were of FDR's own draft, the threat to use war powers was Moley's. Moley, rather than Welles, coined the term "good neighbor." FDR gave the impression that there had been no draft prior to his by attaching to the handwritten copy this typewritten note: "This is the original manuscript of the Inaugural Address as written at Hyde Park on Monday, February 27th, 1933. I started it about 9:00 P.M. and ended at 1:30 A.M. A number of minor changes were made in subsequent drafts but the final draft is substantially the same as this original." [28]

On the same evening that Roosevelt was penning his inaugural plea for purification of banking, a gala affair in Washington symbolized the close of the old regime. J. Pierrepont Moffat wrote in his diary:

> We dined at the Spanish Embassy, — again a dinner of the Old World as I fear we will never see it again. . . . The sole was specially sent down from New York and the wines were all of rare vintages. The dinner was for the Ogden Mills and the whole table was ablaze with jewels. To realize that outside the banking situation was going from bad to worse, that Ogden Mills was being called to the telephone, that banks were closing all over the country, that confidence was shattered, made the whole episode seem unreal and almost dreamlike. I sat next to Dorothy Mills, who told me that Ogden was desperately worried and feared that the panic might assume nation-wide proportions . . . that unfortunately the Democrats were not adequately prepared to take over the Treasury. . . . All in all, a depressing situation. When it came to bridge, one of the visiting New Yorkers suggested our old times stakes. The feeling it gave you was of going to Monte Carlo. However, luck was with me. . . .[30]

The growing crisis was of necessity in the forefront of everyone's mind, whether of Mills's at the Spanish Embassy, or Roosevelt's as he worked on his inaugural address. That same morning, February 27, the *New York Times* carried an article calling emphatically for Roosevelt to issue a self-denying statement; dispatches from London and Paris echoed the suggestion. President Hoover sought through politicians, newspapermen, and Federal Reserve officials to bring additional pressure upon Roosevelt for a statement. Limitations upon banking were imposed in Pennsylvania, Delaware, Ohio, Indiana, Kentucky, and part of Arkansas. Roosevelt refused to comment, but sent Woodin to Washington.[31]

Lamont succeeded in reaching Roosevelt on the telephone just after lunch. The situation was far more critical than he had dreamed, Lamont warned; in all seriousness he did not think the emergency could be greater. Roosevelt's say-so alone, he declared, could save the country from disaster, and every hour in the next few days would count. "As the moratorium area spreads, its influence spreads precisely like the spread of an infectious disease," Lamont warned in his telephone conversation and a followup memorandum:

> Michigan was able to exist for a week or two without banks partly because its great motor companies and other great companies had large sums in New York and elsewhere outside the state to draw upon and did draw upon them and ship money in by aeroplane and otherwise to meet the payrolls. So there was some currency in circulation and some means of keeping going. But what will happen as the closed area spreads and the open area dwindles?
> It is impossible to contemplate the extent of the human suffering,

and the social consequences of a denial of currency and credit to our urban populations. Urban populations cannot do without money. It would be like cutting off a city's water supply. Pestilence and famine would follow; with what further consequences who could tell?

What Lamont requested of Roosevelt was not a self-denying statement. Rather, he wanted Roosevelt to press the Democratic leadership in Congress and the Hoover administration to take immediate positive action: 1) the Federal Reserve banks should that very day resume unlimited purchases of government securities in order to insure an ample supply of currency, 2) Congress should authorize the RFC to deposit money in weakened state and national banks without security and 3) the government should raise a billion dollars by March 15 to meet obligations. The key point would be legislation giving RFC backing to the banks.[32]

It might cost the government a lot of money to do this, Roosevelt protested. Even if the cost were a billion dollars, Lamont answered, it would be cheap compared with the alternative of possible national prostration. Apparently Roosevelt was convinced that Lamont's suggestions were impractical, since he did not act upon them. His own financial conservatism and his moral condemnation of the bankers were playing him false. Massive RFC backing of the banks could have been a significant and relatively inexpensive first step toward recovery.* Congress undoubtedly would have passed enabling legislation had Roosevelt asked for it. If President Hoover had interposed his veto the nation would have been no worse off than before, and the onus for continuing the crisis would have been shifted to Hoover.

As it was, Hoover continued to pin responsibility upon Roosevelt. A second Secret Service messenger arrived at Hyde Park at noon on Wednesday, March 1, carrying a new letter. "I am confident," Hoover wrote, "that a declaration even now on the line I suggested . . . would save losses and hardships to millions of people." Above all, Hoover wanted to suggest to Roosevelt that because of the acuteness of the panic, he should arrange for Congress to be in session quickly after March 4. Meanwhile he pledged his complete cooperation and readiness to discuss the crisis with Roosevelt.[34]

While the Secret Service agent waited, Roosevelt finally prepared a

* Moley has captured the contemporary attitude when he writes that FDR's self-confidence was

> fed by the scandalous inability of the bankers to suggest any practicable measures for blocking off the panic. . . . The bankers at first backed the Hoover idea. . . . They then threw their support behind the idea of huge loans from the R.F.C. — an idea that died aborning when it was pointed out that the R.F.C. had at its disposal only a fraction of the amount needed to take care of banks already badly shaken. Their other suggestions were equally useless.[33]

reply to be carried back to President Hoover. Alleging that his answer to the President's first letter had not been sent due to a secretary's mistake, he enclosed a letter dated February 20, saying in part:

I am equally concerned with you in regard to the gravity of the present banking situation — but my thought is that it is so very deep-seated that the fire is bound to spread in spite of anything that is done by way of mere statements. The real trouble is that on present values very few financial institutions anywhere in the country are actually able to pay off their deposits in full, and the knowledge of this fact is widely held. Bankers with the narrower viewpoint have urged me to make a general statement, but even they seriously doubt if it would have a definite effect.

And in the covering letter, dated February 28, he declared:

Now I have yours of yesterday and can only tell you that I appreciate your fine spirit of co-operation and that I am in constant touch with the situation through Mr. Woodin, who is conferring with Ogden [Mills] and with various people in New York. I am inclined to agree that a very early special session will be necessary — and by tonight or tomorrow I hope to settle on a definite time — I will let you know — you doubtless know of the proposal to give authority to the Treasury to deposit funds directly in any bank.*

In most states where banking had not yet been restricted, runs continued. The small depositor who had pulled her funds out of Chicago banks remembered:

By Thursday of that week we had done everything we could with our own affairs. Friday there was nothing to do but watch — watch the bottom drop out of the world we knew. We saw the runs on the big Loop banks. We saw the city, at first hysterical, then stunned — prostrate. I shall never see an armored truck again without a shudder at the memory of that day. "If only nothing worse happens before President Roosevelt is actually in command!" This was the thought expressed by everyone with whom we talked.[36]

That frantic Thursday and Friday, March 2 and 3, were the last two days before Roosevelt's inauguration. On Thursday the Federal Reserve issued startling figures. During the previous week, the amount of money in circulation had risen $732 million and the Treasury gold reserves declined $226 million — more than $100 million of the loss was attributed to domestic hoarding. The effect of this public exposure of

---

* The stenographic notes of FDR's replies to Hoover's letters, each on a small sheet of stationery, look as if they had been dictated at the same time. On the earlier of the two letters, the date originally written in shorthand at the top is crossed out and "20" inserted.[35]

the weakness of the banking system led to spectacular runs the next day. On Friday, March 3, $109 million in gold was withdrawn from the Treasury; more than $102 million of it for hoarding within the United States. By that evening, twenty-seven states had authorized or put into effect restrictions upon bank withdrawals.

The sanguine Wall Street expectation of the previous Monday that the worst of the banking difficulties were over had been far from realized. Nevertheless, the stock market remained relatively firm through the disasters. "There was a general feeling," reported the *New York Times* financial editors, "that confidence would begin to revive after the Presidential inaugural." Amid the holocaust of Friday, the market moved forward; stocks advanced one to four points, wheat two cents a bushel, and cotton over a dollar a bale.*

Roosevelt's mood paralleled the stock market rather than the banks. Moley later wrote,

> It was Will Woodin and I who tore our hair over the reports of the mounting gold withdrawals and the growing number of bank suspensions and who sat up night after night pondering the possible remedies. Roosevelt went serenely through those days on the assumptions that Hoover was perfectly capable of acting without his concurrence; that there was no remedy of which we knew that was not available to the Hoover Administration; that he could not take any responsibility for measures over whose execution he would have no control; and that, until noon of March 4th, the baby was Hoover's anyhow.[38]

What would transpire after noon of March 4 was another matter, and Roosevelt quietly made his preparations. He commissioned Tugwell on Monday of that week to find out from Herbert Feis of the State Department if there was not residual legal power dating from the First World War to regulate gold and currency. Feis, checking with the Treasury Department, found that apparently there was indeed authorization, in the amended Trading with the Enemy Act, which Treasury officials had thought of during the gold crisis of February 1932. The power was of doubtful legality since it might have lapsed after the war.†

---

* The *New York Times* reported:

In the face of the many adverse developments . . . the security markets retained their composure remarkably well. Steady pressure was in evidence on the bond market, reflecting in large part efforts of banks to dispose of bonds to obtain cash to meet immediate needs. The stock market throughout the week was a nervous affair. The abrupt rally in prices at the close of the week was largely due to the restlessness of shorts in the face of the current uncertainties. A general rush to cover commitments brought about a sharp rise. The exchange was closed on Saturday.[37]

† Section 5(b) of the Trading with the Enemy Act of October 6, 1917, as amended September 24, 1918, authorized the President to "investigate, regulate, or prohibit,

Roosevelt wanted a firm opinion on the legality of the law and directed Tugwell to consult Senator Walsh, who was to be attorney general. When Tugwell found that the seventy-three-year-old Walsh was away honeymooning, Roosevelt sent him to Senators Pittman and Byrnes, but they for the moment were also hard to locate. In addition, Roosevelt obtained through a partner in the law firm of Carter, Ledyard and Milburn, with whom he had started his career as a law clerk, copies of four of the state proclamations closing banks.[39]

For the remainder of the week, the forces of inertia canceled those of action. The Federal Reserve Board continued cautiously for several days more, replying on March 2 to an inquiry from President Hoover that it regarded any federal guarantee of bank deposits as dangerous, did not favor issuing clearing house certificates (scrip), and was not at that time prepared to recommend any other measure. Hoover also conferred that day with Senators Robinson and Glass, but they informed him that it would be impossible to obtain any legislation from Congress without the endorsement of the President-elect. That same evening of March 2, the Federal Reserve Board, at last alarmed, proposed that Hoover use the war power to control withdrawals of gold and deposits. The President was ready to act, but only if Roosevelt would concur. His argument subsequently was that his attorney general, William D. Mitchell, considered the war power so dubious that the only way to avoid subsequent litigation would be for Congress to give its speedy ratification; that ratification could come only if Roosevelt were to ask for it. As for Glass, he emphatically believed the power had expired with the signing of the peace treaty with Germany, if not before, and in any event did not favor such strong action then or later. He did not transmit Hoover's request to Roosevelt.[40]

This was the turn in events that Roosevelt faced when he arrived in Washington on the evening of March 2. Banks had been much on his mind that day; he had conferred with Woodin both before his departure and on the train en route. When he arrived at the Mayflower Hotel that evening, he found that Hoover wanted him to approve a proclamation exercising federal control over withdrawals of bank deposits and gold — a limited banking holiday — to last through Monday, provided Roosevelt would call Congress into special session on Monday. Hoover by this point was sufficiently ready to break with the past also to ask the Federal Reserve Board to approve an emergency guarantee of bank deposits.

Roosevelt examined the proposals cautiously. He was so careful that

under such rules and regulations as he may prescribe, by means of licenses, or otherwise, any transactions in foreign exchange and the export, hoarding, melting or earmarkings of gold or silver coin or bullion or currency."

he did not talk to Mills directly, but through Woodin in New York, then conferred for two hours with his advisers, Jesse H. Jones of the RFC and Senators Robinson, Byrnes, Pittman, and Hull. Glass was also consulted. Acting upon their consensus, Roosevelt suggested that President Hoover proclaim a moratorium until Saturday noon when Roosevelt took his oath of office; then Roosevelt would take further responsibility.[41]

President Hoover, choosing to regard Roosevelt's message as a refusal to approve, did not act. Roosevelt sent word to Speaker Garner that he did not want Congress to enact hasty legislation in its final hours; he had already sent word through Garner to members of the new Congress to hold themselves ready to be called into special session shortly after the inauguration.

On Friday morning, the day before the inauguration, Hoover and Secretary Mills seemed to think that the bank runs had abated, but appalling news arrived early in the afternoon. From the New York area there were $110 million in foreign withdrawals and $200 million in domestic withdrawals.

Hoover decided to make a last try, choosing as the occasion a pre-inauguration call that the Roosevelts would pay that afternoon. When the Roosevelts expressed their readiness to come to the White House, in keeping with protocol, Ike Hoover, the White House chief usher, had been disturbed that the President, ignoring precedent, refused to invite his successor to dinner on the night of March 3. President Hoover did authorize the chief usher to send word to the Roosevelts that they might come for tea. The President decided to make this social ceremony the occasion for a serious conference, but failed to inform the President-elect of his purpose. At four o'clock, the Roosevelts and their son James and his wife arrived. As Roosevelt entered the White House, Ike Hoover whispered to him that Secretary Mills and the governor of the Federal Reserve Board, Eugene Meyer, were waiting to participate in the discussion. Roosevelt at once sent for Moley, who was napping at the Mayflower. The tea proceeded coolly in the Red Room; everyone seemed uncomfortable. Upon its completion, in a few minutes, discussion of the banking crisis began. Meyer argued for a proclamation completely closing the banks; Hoover insisted it was not necessary, that 80 percent of the banks, measured by deposits, were still open; all that was necessary was a proclamation to regulate withdrawals. Roosevelt, as had become his custom, said he would have to discuss the proposals with his advisers. At this point there occurred a minor interchange which left Roosevelt bristling. He later recalled: [42]

> I decided to cut it short. It is the custom for an outgoing President to return the call of an incoming one. I knew that Hoover didn't want

to go through the strain involved in this custom, so I tried to give him a way out. I mentioned the custom to him, and then said, "I realize, Mr. President, that you are extremely busy so I will understand completely if you do not return the call." For the first time that day, he looked me squarely in the eye and said: "Mr. Roosevelt, when you are in Washington as long as I have been, you will learn that the President of the United States calls on nobody." That was that. I hustled my family out of the room. I was sure Jimmy wanted to punch him in the eye.[43]

Through that evening of March 3 at the Mayflower Hotel, Roosevelt discussed the crisis with Woodin, Hull, and Glass. Hoover and his administrative officers did likewise. At 11:30 the telephone rang in Roosevelt's room. It was President Hoover calling. Roosevelt informed him he was with Senator Glass, and that Glass opposed federal closing of the banks, thinking the country should temporarily resort to clearing house scrip. According to Hoover, Roosevelt suggested that governors of the states could close banks wherever necessary; he asked Hoover not to issue any kind of proclamation. A few minutes after the conversation, the clock struck midnight at the White House. Hoover said to those around him, "We are at the end of our string. There is nothing more we can do." [44]

At the Mayflower Hotel, Senator Glass inquired of Roosevelt after the telephone conversation, "What are you planning to do?"

"Planning to close the banks, of course," Roosevelt replied. Glass sputtered with indignation.[45]

The only way to prevent the resumption of the runs on Saturday morning was by governors' proclamations. At one o'clock that night, Woodin and Moley went from the Mayflower Hotel to the Federal Reserve Board room with Secretary Mills, Governor Meyers and several others. They had been calling all the governors who had not yet proclaimed moratoria, and had persuaded all except the governors of New York and Illinois. The governor of Illinois, Henry Horner, was ready to act if New York did. Governor Herbert Lehman of New York debated from ten that night until three-thirty the next morning with a group of nervous financiers. Since the New York banks were still solvent, the bankers in order to maintain their prestige wanted Lehman to declare the holiday on his own initiative. Lehman refused to act except on the strong joint request of heads of the clearinghouse and the Federal Reserve Bank of New York. From the board room, Woodin and his associates put intermittent calls through to Lehman and the conferees. As they continued to pressure the New Yorkers, Moley fell asleep. Sometime in the early morning hours Woodin awoke him, saying, "It's all right. We can go now — everything's closed." There were restrictions upon banking in every one of the forty-eight states, and the New York Stock Exchange was shut down. It was inauguration day.[46]

It was the firm conviction of Hoover and his advisers (who subsequently gave as their substantiation Tugwell's remarks to Rand) that the New Dealers had willfully allowed an unnecessary crisis to grow beyond control for the benefit of their own political ends. "It was the most senseless and easily prevented panic in all history," Hoover wrote in his memoirs. The President's loyal secretary, Theodore G. Joslin, asserted in 1934, "So far as the incoming administration was concerned, the country was to be permitted to sink to the lowest depth, so that the new administration could start from the very bottom in making its recovery efforts. That was the purpose all along." [47]

What to Hoover and his supporters seemed a deliberate plan might more accurately be described as having been the course of least resistance on the part of Roosevelt. The President, through his unconcealed distrust and dislike for Roosevelt, his concern for setting his record straight with posterity, and his insistence that Roosevelt follow his conservative course, had made joint action impossible.* Perhaps a Stimson in the Treasury department might have bridged the Hoover-fabricated gulf, but Ogden Mills's view of Roosevelt was scarcely distinguishable from the President's. Nor was Mills any less emphatic in his devotion to the gold standard. "If I were to be a dictator and could write my own ticket," Mills had written Owen D. Young in December 1932, "the first two goals which I would reach for would be the balancing of the budget of the United States Government and the return to the gold standard by Great Britain." Between the Hoover and Roosevelt forces there was not only a keen personal mistrust but also an insuperable barrier of gold.[49]

In the last week of the crisis, when not even the most ardent devotee of the gold standard could have believed that a Roosevelt reavowal would waft away the troubles, the impasse continued over a means of action. President Hoover seems not to have been in complete agreement

---

* The contemporary view of Lamont was that during the four months of the interregnum Hoover had become both powerless and unpopular, so that Roosevelt felt his effectiveness would be ruined if he joined causes with Hoover and seemed to be carrying out Hoover's policies:

> Mr. Roosevelt was apparently determined, in any event, to keep his skirts sufficiently clear to enable him on his own to accomplish something definite when he took office. Mr. Hoover, meanwhile, made the matter of cooperation more difficult, because he had the ineptitude of still trying to curry favor with the public and of attempting to get Mr. Roosevelt to cooperate with him (Hoover) in Hoover's ideas, rather than to tell Mr. Roosevelt that he (Hoover) would cooperate with Roosevelt's. In any event, the breakdown between the two was complete.[48]

with his own Treasury officials, and was sharply at odds with the Federal Reserve Board. Throughout, there was little consensus among bankers on any plan of action. The financial titans of Wall Street, who were also constantly advising Roosevelt through Woodin, would not agree until the morning of the inauguration that the New York banks should be closed. Added to their caution was Roosevelt's own faith in conservative banking rules, his refusal to believe that the national economy was imperiled, and his progressive moral judgment that the foolish bankers who had speculated in the 1920s must accept their just punishment. Given these views, the easiest, even if not the wisest, policy for him to follow was to do nothing, pledge nothing, and wait until he himself was President.

The United States was indeed sustaining a profound economic shock, but according to every index it was by no means near the breaking point. Despite gold hoarding, the dollar remained relatively strong on international markets, and American traders did little to depress it. Roosevelt through happenstance more than any deliberate plan was taking over when psychologically the nation was in a state of despair but economically still sufficiently resilient to recover. The *Wall Street Journal*, on that sober morning of March 4, hailed the change in administrations:

> Considering his personal popularity and the strength of his party in Congress on one hand and on the other the plight in which the country finds itself at the moment, the inception of Mr. Roosevelt's Presidency is literally without a parallel in our history. The very deterioration in the financial and economic position which has taken place in recent weeks has cleared some obstacles from his path. A common adversity has much subdued the recalcitrance of groups bent upon self-interest. All of us the country over are now ready to make sacrifices to a common necessity and to accept realities as we would not have done three months ago.[50]

CHAPTER XII

The Inauguration

This Nation asks for action, and action now.
— FDR, *first inaugural address, March 4, 1933.*

At one o'clock on the afternoon of March 4, 1933, the machinery of the United States seemed at a standstill, waiting for the inauguration of the new President to set it back into motion. The outwardly gala atmosphere of Pennsylvania Avenue, a mile-long ribbon of red, white and blue bunting, contrasted with the somber expectancy that was the inner mood of the half million spectators and the awaiting millions throughout the nation. The American democratic experiment appeared once more to be on trial that critical day — a testing brought on not, as in the past, by foreign war or civil strife, but by the economic crisis. The closing of the banks seemed to signal the nadir of the depression. If indeed the bottom had been reached, could Roosevelt lead the way upward? No one was very certain.

Inaugural morning, a typical Washington day in early March, had dawned gray and cold; there was a bite in the wind. Despite the festive bunting and the garlands on the inaugural stand in front of the Capitol, the flags flapping over the House and Senate office buildings were at half-mast in mourning for Senator Thomas Walsh. The bleakness of the day, the sober demeanor of the assembling crowds, and the ominous appearance of guards manning machine guns filled Edmund Wilson with foreboding.

A few days earlier in Chicago Wilson had witnessed hungry women scavenging on garbage heaps for scraps of food. On a factory wall he had seen chalked a protest against the whole awry economic order: "VOTE RED. THE PEOPLE ARE GOOFY." Not many sought a radical way out; rather the nation numbly endured the last weeks of the old administration. From Hull House in the center of distress in Chicago, so representative of the entire nation, Jane Addams lamented to a friend, "In spite of the wretched conditions this winter and the little one is able to do to alleviate the situation, one has a sense of at least 'standing by' if only to hear the stories of the unemployed. It has been like a disaster of flood, fire or earthquake, this universal wiping out of resources." [1]

At last the time of standing by was over, and the time for the new President to act had arrived. Roosevelt was aware of the popular mood; he had drafted some of the opening remarks of his inaugural address in response to it. He was cognizant, but by no means dismayed. Americans might be wavering in faith in themselves, but Roosevelt had not lost his trust in the people — and in God. His own mood as he prepared for the inaugural ceremonies seems to have been one of personal consecration to the tasks lying before him. In the preceding days his thoughts had turned to religion, to the simple tenets of his upbringing. Perhaps they were the mainstay of his serenity amidst the gloom and panic. On the train to Washington, when Farley mentioned the seriousness of the national crisis facing the President-elect, Sara Delano Roosevelt remarked, "I am not the least worried about Franklin. His disposition is such that he can accept responsibilities and not let them wear him down." And, indeed, when Roosevelt conversed with Farley during the trip, he cast aside the pressures of the banking impasse and instead discussed his faith: [2]

> He said that a thought about God was the right way to start off and he told me about his own religious training as a child. He expressed the view that, in a crisis like the one approaching, the faith of the people was far more important than any other single element and that the fundamentally religious sense of the American people would be a great factor in seeing the nation through.[3]

Eleanor Roosevelt manifested similar feelings in a different way. On the day before the inauguration, she took a taxicab, accompanied only by an old friend, to take another look at "the most beautiful thing in Washington," which she had frequently visited during the Wilson years. It was the Saint-Gaudens sculpture, "Grief," marking the grave of Mrs. Henry Adams in Rock Creek Cemetery.[4]

In a sober, religious spirit the Roosevelts began inauguration day by attending services at St. John's Episcopal Church, diagonally across Lafayette Square from the White House. Months earlier, Bishop James E. Freeman had invited Roosevelt to worship at the Washington Cathedral on the morning of March 4. Roosevelt declined because of the problem of ascending the steps, but remarked, "Personally the thought of attending a short service somewhere appeals to me greatly." He chose St. John's church, which was not only nearby but could be entered easily from the side. He arranged for Rector Peabody of Groton, the spiritual exemplar of his youth, to participate in conducting the service, and invited members of his immediate family, his secretaries and future cabinet officers and their families, some hundred people altogether. That morning, Roosevelt rode to the services in an open car, accompanied by his mother, wife, and eldest son. Peabody read appropriate selections from the Book of Common Prayer, then prayed, "O Lord . . . most heartily we beseech Thee, with Thy favor to behold and bless Thy servant, Franklin, chosen to be President of the United States." It was a brief service, only twenty minutes long. At its conclusion, Roosevelt remained on his knees for some time, his face cupped in his hands, as was customary, in private prayer. He arose, smiled at his fellow-worshipers in a benign way, and departed. As he came out, the skies were lightening, and the sun briefly streaked down.[5]

Thereafter each year on the anniversary of his first inauguration Roosevelt and his cabinet attended private services in St. John's church.

After the services, Roosevelt returned to the Mayflower Hotel to turn his attention once again to the almost nationwide banking moratorium. He conferred with Moley and Woodin and made some minor changes in the passages on banking in his inaugural address.

Then the time for the ceremonies arrived. A little before eleven o'clock, Roosevelt, garbed in the striped trousers and silk top hat of formal morning attire, arrived at the porticoed north entrance to the White House. It was the last time he was ever to see the executive mansion as a private citizen. It was a slightly depressing sight that morning, its paint yellowing and here and there beginning to peel, since as an economy measure repainting had been postponed. Huge old army trucks were lumbering in and out of the grounds taking off the belongings of the departing Hoovers and bringing the trunks and furnishings of the arriving Roosevelts.[6]

Breaking with custom, Roosevelt remained in the car while the presidential party assembled in the East Room. President Hoover and the others shortly appeared, and the President, in keeping with his office, sat himself on Roosevelt's right. Mrs. Roosevelt, dressed in her "Eleanor blue" inaugural attire, rode in the second car with Mrs. Hoover. The cavalcade of seven cars, surrounded by a hollow square of cavalry riding at a trot, paraded past the cheering thousands surging against the ropes along Pennsylvania Avenue. The outgoing and incoming Presidents, seated in icy proximity in the open touring car, seemed neither of them to be in a festive spirit. Roosevelt tried so desperately to make conversation with his uncommunicative companion that he found himself, as they passed the girdered skeleton of the new Department of Commerce building, mouthing some inanity about the "lovely steel."

During the otherwise grim ride, one final interchange took place between the two Presidents, and it was a pleasant one. Hoover told Roosevelt he was worried about his secretary and administrative assistant,

(*Above*) FDR with President Hoover en route to the Capitol for the inauguration, March 4, 1933. (*Below*) The first inaugural, March 4, 1933.

FDR takes the oath of office, March 4, 1933.

Walter H. Newton, earlier one of the leading Republicans in the House, who had resigned his seat to handle White House relations with Congress. Since Newton had no outside source of income, Hoover had nominated him to be a federal district judge, but the Senate had blocked all confirmations. Would it be asking too much for Roosevelt to provide a position? Roosevelt readily assented, and several weeks later kept his promise — although Senator Norris called it a "slap in the face to all progressive Republicans" — by appointing Newton as a Republican member of the inactive Federal Home Loan Bank Board.

Through the remainder of the ride, the President-elect tried to sit stiff and solemn, taking the view that the ovation of the spectators was for the outgoing President, but when Hoover (who quite possibly took the reverse view) remained almost completely unresponsive, Roosevelt began to raise his hat to the throngs. Happily for both men, the ride to the Capitol was a short one; after the inaugural ceremonies they never again saw each other.[7]

At the Capitol, Roosevelt slowly walked on the arm of his son James up a specially constructed ramp into the central door on the west side of the Senate wing. While President Hoover in the President's Room signed or pocket-vetoed bills and greeted senators, Roosevelt sat quietly next door in the room of the Military Affairs Committee. Huey Long started to dash in to greet him, then on the threshold turned away. Once more Roosevelt looked over his inaugural address, and wrote a new opening line, "This is a day of consecration." At twelve o'clock he started down the corridor toward the Senate chamber but had to wait ten minutes before entering to witness the inauguration of Vice President John Nance Garner. As he entered the chamber his mood was so solemn that he did no more than nod to Speaker-designate Henry Rainey, who as a member of the Inaugural Committee accompanied him, but once inside he seemed to break free from his private thoughts to smile about him. Garner took his oath and spoke extemporaneously for a minute or two. While new senators were being sworn in, Roosevelt whispered with Senator Robinson, who was to be Majority Leader. The outgoing vice president, Charles Curtis, then declared the Senate of the Seventy-second Congress adjourned *sine die*. The last lame duck session of Congress in American history had come to an end.

At one o'clock the pageantry of the presidential inauguration began. President Hoover wriggled through the jam of people at the East Door of the Capitol and joined Mrs. Hoover on the canopied inaugural stand. Eleanor Roosevelt and Sara Delano Roosevelt entered and took seats on the opposite side of the stand from Mrs. Hoover. Roosevelt soon followed. He was brought in his wheelchair to the door. A bugle sounded, and as the Marine Band struck up "Hail to the Chief," Roosevelt, bracing himself firmly on James Roosevelt's arm, shuffled down a maroon-carpeted ramp and took his place at the rostrum. The forty acres of spectators stretching out in front of him shouted their acclaim.

Facing the berobed Charles Evans Hughes, chief justice of the United States Supreme Court, Roosevelt placed his hand on the old Dutch family Bible upon which he had twice taken his oath of office as governor of New York, "a very large and heavy folio," in which he had marked the passage to which it was opened — the thirteenth verse of the thirteenth chapter of St. Paul's first Epistle to the Corinthians: "And now abideth faith, hope, charity, these three; but the greatest of these is charity." As Roosevelt had proposed, with Chief Justice Hughes's hearty approval, he departed from custom, and like a bridegroom taking his marriage vows, in a strong clear voice recited the oath after Hughes: * "I, Franklin Delano Roosevelt, do solemnly swear that I will faithfully execute the office of President of the United States and will, to the best of my ability, preserve, protect and defend the Constitution of the United States. So help me God!"

Immediately President Roosevelt turned to the assembled throng and, standing at the speakers' stand fronted by the Great Seal of the United States, launched into his inaugural address. Gone was his usual affable demeanor; not once did he smile as he spoke with force and confidence. Interpolating still another word into his opening, he began, "This is a day of *national* consecration":

> I am certain that my fellow Americans expect that on my induction into the Presidency I will address them with a candor and a decision which the present situation of our Nation impels. This is preeminently the time to speak the truth, the whole truth, frankly and boldly. Nor need we shrink from honestly facing conditions in our country today. This great Nation will endure as it has endured, will revive and will prosper. So, first of all, let me assert my firm belief that the only thing we have to fear is fear itself — nameless, unreasoning, unjustified terror which paralyzes needed efforts to reconvert retreat into advance. In every dark hour of our national life a leadership of frankness and vigor has met with that understanding and support of the people themselves which is essential to victory. I am convinced that you will again give that support to leadership in these critical days.†

* FDR had written the clerk of the Supreme Court, "The question has been raised as to whether it would be better for me to repeat the oath after the Chief Justice instead of answering 'I do.' Will you be good enough to talk this over with the Chief Justice and tell him I have no particular preference in the matter, and will abide by his judgment." The chief justice replied, "I am glad to have the suggestion that you repeat the oath in full instead of saying simply 'I do.' I think the repetition is the more dignified and appropriate course."

Unlike some of his predecessors, FDR did not kiss the Bible at the conclusion of the oath.[8]

† The renowned phrase, "the only thing we have to fear is fear itself" was Howe's handiwork, which he added to Roosevelt's draft when it had been typed. He

The crisis that faced the nation, Roosevelt suggested, fortunately involved only material things and grew out of no failure of substance but from the stubbornness and incompetence of the "rulers of the exchange of mankind's goods." The difficulties which had led to the breakdown of banking were the outcome of the "practices of the unscrupulous money changers." "They have no vision, and when there is no vision the people perish." And at this point Roosevelt launched into his almost biblical attack upon the bankers: "The money changers have fled from their high seats in the temple of our civilization. We may now restore that temple to the ancient truths. The measure of the restoration lies in the extent to which we apply social values more noble than mere monetary profit."

For the first time, the listeners applauded.

In the same vein, Roosevelt called for new national standards:

> Happiness lies not in the mere possession of money; it lies in the joy of achievement, in the thrill of creative effort. The job and moral stimulation of work no longer must be forgotten in the mad chase of evanescent profits. These dark days will be worth all they cost us if they teach us that our true destiny is not to be ministered unto but to minister to ourselves and to our fellow men.

> Recognition of the falsity of material wealth as the standard of success goes hand in hand with the abandonment of the false belief that public office and high political position are to be valued only by the standards of pride of place and personal profit; and there must be an end to a conduct in banking and business which too often has given to a sacred trust the likeness of callous and selfish wrongdoing.

Again the crowd applauded.

Restoration, Roosevelt told them, must come through a change of ethics, and through immediate positive action — putting the unemployed to work, returning some of the industrial population to agricultural pursuits, raising prices of produce, preventing foreclosures of farms and small homes, strict regulation of banking and investments, and "provision for an adequate but sound currency." It was basically a national program which must take first priority. "Our international trade relations, though vastly important, are in point of time and necessity secondary to the establishment of a sound national economy." Yet Roosevelt defended his

claimed to have picked it up in an advertisement appearing early in January in a New York newspaper — if so, it has eluded later researchers. Mrs. Roosevelt once suggested to Samuel I. Rosenman that Roosevelt had added it to the address as a modification of Thoreau's "Nothing is so much to be feared as fear." One of her friends, she said, had given her husband a copy of Thoreau's works, and it was in his suite in the Mayflower Hotel when he was polishing his speech. Whatever the immediate source, the concept was of lengthy tradition. It is to be found in Francis Bacon, *De Augmentis Scientiarum*, Book VI, Chapter III, published early in the seventeenth century.[9]

The first inaugural address.

proposed methods as "not narrowly nationalistic," but "the strongest assurance that the recovery will endure." As a corollary, he promised: "In the field of world policy I would dedicate this Nation to the policy of the good neighbor — the neighbor who resolutely respects himself and, because he does so, respects his obligations and respects the sanctity of his agreements in and with a world of neighbors."

Above all, through the inaugural address ran the promise of strong, immediate leadership. Congress would be called into special session and detailed proposals would be submitted to it. If Congress did not enact these, nor an alternative program of its own, Roosevelt was ready to go further — as far as though the nation were at war: "I shall ask Congress for the one remaining instrument to meet the emergency — broad Executive power to wage a war against the emergency, as great as the power that would be given to me if we were in fact invaded by a foreign foe." These strong words evoked the greatest applause of any passage in the address. Roosevelt paused but did not relax the grim expression upon his face. Mrs. Roosevelt, sitting nearby, shuddered at the implications. But they bespoke no intent on the part of Roosevelt to assume the role of a Mussolini or Hitler; that was too repugnant to his basic thinking. Years later, Mrs. Roosevelt remembered that once about this time she had remarked to her husband that she wished the country had a benevolent dictator who could force through reforms. He looked at her quizzically and remarked that one could not count upon a dictator staying benevolent. Rather what Roosevelt was proclaiming in his inaugural address was his readiness, if need be, to assume the powers of commander-in-chief over the nation's chaotic economy, like a Wilson in time of war. His conclusion bore out this feeling: [10]

> We do not distrust the future of essential democracy. The people of the United States have not failed. In their need they have registered a mandate that they want direct, vigorous action. They have asked for discipline and direction under leadership. They have made me the present instrument of their wishes. In the spirit of the gift I take it.

And he ended with the religious theme that had permeated his address: "In this dedication of a Nation we humbly ask the blessing of God. May He protect each and every one of us. May He guide me in the days to come." [11]

The acres of faces looking up at Roosevelt roared their approval. They had been unusually quiet through most of the address. Herbert Feis, who had left his office in the State Department to witness the ceremonies from one of the stands under the inaugural platform, has observed:

The audience, although impressed by the affirmativeness of the address and the prospect of bold action, remained grave and quiet. They did not break into his speech with loud applause but seemed rather to want to think it over before they expressed themselves. There were only a few exultant shouts. . . . On returning to my desk, where work awaited me, I still found myself cheered and assured by the positive spirit which animated the address and the man who had given it.[12]

Those closest to Roosevelt were acutely aware of the momentous nature of the address. Said Mrs. Roosevelt, "It was very, very solemn and a little terrifying." Moley turned to Miss Perkins (she remembered) and remarked that Roosevelt had turned the ship of state completely around on its course.[13]

Those who would dissent, like ex-President Hoover, whose face seemed to express wry disagreement from time to time during the address, were willing for the time being to hold their peace. Hoover hastily shook Roosevelt's hand, then slipped away to take a train for New York. In order to be fair to his successor, Hoover for some months refrained from public criticism of the New Deal. His secretary of state, Stimson, recorded in his diary private words of mistrust. That day, there were few open dissenters from Roosevelt's words. One Republican representative tartly commented, "He cuts both ways. He wants to spend money and reduce taxes. He is for sound currency, but lots of it." Otherwise, almost every congressional comment was one of praise. Roosevelt demonstrated real courage, said Senator Hiram Johnson. "We have the new era, and if we can judge from today, we have the new man."

Editorials even in nominally conservative newspapers almost without exception greeted the inaugural address with hyperbole. The *New York Herald Tribune* entitled its comment, "A Call to Arms." *The Nashville Banner* regarded the address as one more proof "that, as every great epoch has called for a great leader, so never has the nation lacked the citizen to measure to the demands." The *Chicago Tribune* said it "strikes the dominant note of courageous confidence." The program Roosevelt outlined "demands the dictatorial authority he requests," declared the *Boston Transcript*, and unprecedented though that authority might be, "such is the desperate temper of the people that it is welcome." The *San Francisco Chronicle* suggested the national consensus: "It is bold wisdom and action the people are praying for from President Roosevelt." [14]

Through both his words and tone, Roosevelt had rekindled hope in the American people. He had offered them firm, positive leadership couched in the crusading moral phrases of Theodore Roosevelt as a 1912 Progressive and of Woodrow Wilson as the wartime commander in chief. Edmund Wilson, still haunted by the faces of the starving dispossessed, had heard in the words only "the echoes of Woodrow Wilson's eloquence without Wilson's glow of life behind them." But for millions of the destitute, and fearful millions more, the words carried a promise more immediate and vital than they had known before — a promise the more breathtaking because it transcended their earlier hopes.[15]

"Perhaps the beginning of my political shift came with the first Roosevelt inaugural address," reminisced John R. Tunis, a sportswriter and novelist, to that point an unwavering Republican. Tunis had not voted for Roosevelt, regarding him as an amiable but weak man:

> That March 4 of 1933. . . . Lucy had gone to South Norwalk to cash our usual weekly check of $25 for food and expenses. The doors of the South Norwalk Trust Company were shut politely in her face. We had $3.50 in the house.
>
> Then we turned to the radio and Franklin D. Roosevelt's inaugural address. It was a talk the nation had not heard in my lifetime, and was not to hear again until 1961. I felt not merely the words — arousing, challenging, unexpected — but the tone and the great courage and the strength of the man behind them. How fortunate are those of us who lived at that time and were touched, ever so slightly, by this gigantic force in our history.[16]

A surprising number of Americans wrote directly to tell Roosevelt how much the inaugural address meant to them. One said, "It seemed to give the people, as well as myself, a new hold upon life." [17]

International radio broadcasts were as yet almost unprecedented, and listeners in Europe and even as distant as Australia were impressed by Roosevelt's forceful voice. In Paris, American bars carried the broadcast over loudspeakers. Since it came late in the cocktail hour, after much delay and many drinks on the part of would-be auditors, the words were clearer than the heads of some teary expatriate listeners. In England, Prime Minister MacDonald and King George V and Queen Mary were among the listeners.[18]

British newspapers hailed the address as heralding effective action. The Laborite *Herald* contrasted Roosevelt's promise to wage war against the depression with "the timid hesitation and Micawberish drifting of the British cabinet." The *Times*, asserting that "high and resolute militancy breathes in every line," assessed the international purport: "Its good effect will not be confined to one side of the Atlantic if his courageous words are followed by equally courageous action. Then he may lead not only his own country, but the whole world with it back to sounder and more secure prosperity."

Editors of several nations saw in the inaugural address reaffirmation of their own views. In Mussolini's Italy, *Il Giornale d'Italia* declared:

"President Roosevelt's words are clear and need no comment to make even the deaf hear that not only Europe but the whole world feels the need of executive authority capable of acting with full powers of cutting short the purposeless chatter of legislative assemblies. This method of government may well be defined as Fascist." But from Buenos Aires came the opposite and more accurate conclusion from the distinguished *La Prensa:* "We do not fear that democracy in the great Republic of the north is in danger, nor must any concealed thought be detected in the President's words that might be like a menace." [19] Without the United States as well as within, the address seemed to most of those who heard or read it to be a call for vigorous action, but only through the use of democratic means.*

Traditional celebration filled the remaining daylight hours of inauguration day. Roosevelt, in keeping with the depression spirit of economy, had wanted the day to be one of Jeffersonian simplicity, but the Democrats, twelve years out of power, were determined that it should be more reminiscent of Jacksonian revelry. Senator Robinson, chairman of the Joint Congressional Inaugural Committee, announced well in advance that Roosevelt's wish would "be respected as far as practicable," but added that "the event is taking on tremendous colorful proportions." And so the Democrats poured into Washington as though there were no financial crisis, filling hotels, overflowing the stands along Pennsylvania Avenue, and buying every available ticket to the inaugural balls, at ten dollars a couple.[21]

Roosevelt fell in with the holiday spirit, spending the rest of the afternoon as though no emergency existed, attending a buffet luncheon at the White House and reviewing the mammoth inaugural parade. It was a day of personal celebration for Roosevelt, his close friends and relatives, and staff. He had entertained them at the hasty luncheon, more

---

* With few exceptions foreign newspaper editorials on the new administration were friendly. Ambassador Joseph Grew in Tokyo reported that most Japanese newspapers expressed hope that Roosevelt would be more friendly toward Japan. The Tokyo *Asahi Shimbun*, March 6, 1933, also commented, "We hope that he will be able to overcome the financial difficulties of the United States and solve the tariff problem, which is difficult in dealing with countries with depreciated currencies." The liberal *El Sol* in Madrid, on March 5, discussed the financial and economic problems Roosevelt would face, concluding, "Reliance is placed on the frankly liberal tendencies of Mr. Roosevelt in opposition to the rigid conservatism of his predecessor." The Kaunas, Lithuania, *Lietuvos Aidas*, March 9, 1933, wrote, "The opinion is entertained in many quarters that the co-operation between the United States and Europe shall grow to considerable proportions. The only drawback is that the United States has so many pressing home problems that foreign affairs have become of secondary importance." The Bogotá *El Espectador*, previously notable for its asperity toward all things American, on March 15 declared, "Audacity, frugality and sincerity, these seem to be the fairy godmothers of Roosevelt's newborn Government." [20]

FDR arrives at the White House with Mrs. Roosevelt and James
after the inauguration.

notable for being held in the White House than for the fare. Ike Hoover had been startled when Mrs. Roosevelt informed him she wished to serve hot dogs. And it was a great day for those who had sadly gone out of power with President Wilson in 1921. Roosevelt in planning the proceedings of the day gave especial attention to those who had been close to Wilson. Not long after his election he asked Rear Admiral Cary T. Grayson, who had been Wilson's White House physician and confidant, to become general chairman of the Inaugural Committee. "We must be sure," he wrote Grayson, "not to forget to invite all of the living members of the Wilson Cabinet to the Reviewing Stand and *either* to lunch before the parade or to tea after the parade. Also, we should provide a special escort for Mrs. Wilson." So it was that Mrs. Wilson, as a guest of honor at the inauguration, wearing a gardenia corsage, had been escorted to her seat by the White House naval aide.[22]

There had been those during the two crisis days preceding who had urged cutting the parade and the balls in the evening to a minimum. Roosevelt demurred. The participants were already jamming into Washington and no good would come from disappointing them. Also it was Saturday afternoon and the business of the nation was shut down until Monday. Nor was Roosevelt's attendance a mere façade of courage in time of adversity. Roosevelt loved parades. This one, despite the economic crisis, was an outpouring of rejoicing Democrats on a scale unsurpassed since the first inauguration of Jackson. There were additional Jacksonian overtones. One commentator had referred to the address as a "Jacksonian speech, a fighting speech." And Roosevelt reviewed the parade from a stand fashioned in the likeness of the portico of "The Hermitage." It seemed, as the parade passed by for hour after hour until dark, as though every deserving Democratic worker in the nation had somehow managed to scrape together the fare to Washington to celebrate the takeover of the government. It would seem the following week as if they were all remaining to lay claim to the spoils of office.[23]

First there was a touch of military pomp and circumstance, especially appealing to the new commander-in-chief. "Preceded by well drilled motorcycles and a squadron of khaki cavalry leaning forward as they briskly canter with their sabers against their shoulders," wrote Edmund Wilson, "the silk hats and the admiral's gold-braided bicorne roll along in their open cars." There followed units of the army, navy, and marine corps, while a hundred airplanes and the dirigible *Akron* flew overhead, evoking from the one-time assistant secretary of the navy his most enthusiastic recognition. He had wished General John J. Pershing, the wartime commander of the American Expeditionary Force, to act as chief marshal, but Pershing, ill in Arizona, did not recover in time. In his stead rode the chief of staff, General MacArthur. Throughout most of the parade, General MacArthur and the chief of Naval Operations, Admiral William V. Pratt, flanked the President in the reviewing stand, sharing it with friends, relatives, and old Wilsonians.[24]

Group by group the marchers passed by, interspersed with forty bands. There were representatives from every state; marchers of every sort — real Indians and Tammany chieftains, and four Negroes pushing whirring lawnmowers down Pennsylvania Avenue as a jibe at Hoover's campaign remark that a Democratic victory would be so calamitous that grass would grow in the streets. Roosevelt for a long time greeted them all with broad smiles and vigorous waving of his own top hat. The glassed-in stand was chilly, and although Roosevelt was dressed in a fur-lined coat with an astrakhan collar (he insisted to reporters that it had been his father's), Mrs. Roosevelt feared he would catch cold, and urged him to keep his hat on his head. After a while he did so. Past him went sure friends, uneasy allies, and potential enemies. The chairman of the Democratic National Committee, Farley, led one of the four divisions of the parade. The governors of thirty-three states rode by. First there was the progressive Republican, Gifford Pinchot of Pennsylvania, a striking figure, tall, lean and mustachioed. Not far behind him, standing on the seat of his open car, was the shorter, handsome Democratic governor of Maryland, Albert Ritchie, symbol of prohibition repeal. Finally, still at a peak of popularity, evoking the loudest response from the throngs, Al Smith came striding along afoot, wearing the regalia of a Sachem of Tammany Hall and waving his famous brown derby to right and left in response to the acclaim.[25]

At dusk Roosevelt quietly left the reviewing stand to return to the White House. There a reception for a thousand guests was in progress. Mrs. Roosevelt stood between the Red Room and the Blue Room to greet the guests while they sipped tea, munched sandwiches, and listened to soft music. Lincoln MacVeagh wrote her afterwards, "It was such a pleasure to see you Mistress of the White House, and looking so lovely. It was as if a breath of fresh air had swept into the place and made it spring-like." [26]

Roosevelt hastened upstairs to the Oval Room, seated himself behind a desk, and greeted the future members of his cabinet and their families as they filed in. Already he had sent the cabinet nominations to the Senate and obtained hasty confirmation. Frances Perkins, looking around at the stately furniture in this room where in the future Roosevelt was to work so hard, remembered how impressive it all appeared at first sight: "It never looked so tidy again as it did that night. Everything was in perfect order. There were no stacks of papers, pictures and things around." [27]

Roosevelt then presided over the joint swearing-in of the entire cabinet. He called their names one by one, beginning with Cordell Hull, his secretary of state; Justice Benjamin N. Cardozo of the United States Supreme Court, who had been Roosevelt's friend in New York, separately administered to each the oath of office. The President then gave a pleasant little talk to the assembled new cabinet members, exhorting them to work together without friction for the common good of the nation. "No Cabinet has ever been sworn in before in this way," he concluded. "It is my intention to inaugurate precedents like this from time to time." [28]

Roosevelt hurried back downstairs in time to keep an earlier promise, to greet in the Red Room thirteen children on crutches who had come from Warm Springs to attend the inauguration. It was six-thirty before the last reception guests were ushered out and preparations rushed for buffet supper at eight o'clock for seventy-five relatives. After supper, Mrs. Roosevelt and the younger ones set forth in formal attire to the Inaugural Ball. Roosevelt and his secretary, Louis McHenry Howe, went to the Lincoln study where they sat talking until bedtime.

Outside, around the Washington Monument, fireworks were splashing the gray skies with flashes of color, even as the national mood had been transformed. In a single day with a single speech, President Roosevelt had won the enthusiasm of the nation and swept away in advance every obstacle to the forward thrust.

CHAPTER XIII

Reopening the Banks

I can assure you that it is safer to keep your money in
a reopened bank than under the mattress.
— FDR, *first Fireside Chat, March 12, 1933*.[1]

On Sunday morning, March 5, 1933, Roosevelt awoke for the first time
as President of the United States. It may have been an exhilarating feeling, but he did not have the leisure to savor it, since because of the
banking crisis this had to be a day of work. The responsibility had at
last become his, and he was ready to assume it. The nation, it seemed to
Roosevelt as he talked about it later, was in a state of paralysis, and it
was up to him to start it toward convalescence. Within himself he must
have felt some twinges of misgivings and lacked a bit of the complete
confidence that he had displayed publicly at the inauguration, since his
memories of that morning were that everything had been a bit strange
and wrong. He awoke in the unfamiliar bedroom, sent for the newspapers that he usually read while he ate breakfast, and they were late and
not just the ones he wanted.

Then, according to his frequent recollection to Tugwell and other
intimates, he went for the first time to the executive office, where he had
a compelling experience which seemed to him symbolic of the national
plight. His valet, Irwin McDuffie, wheeled him over to the large office
from which President Hoover had departed with all his belongings. The
walls were bare of pictures and the desk top, where Roosevelt liked a
profusion of things, empty and uninviting. As Tugwell remembered
Roosevelt relating it:

McDuffie left and there he was, he used to say, in a big empty room,
completely alone; there was nothing to be seen and nothing to be
heard. . . . Here he was, without even the wherewithal to make a
note — if he had had a note to make. And for a few dreadful minutes
he hadn't a thought. He knew that the stimulus of human contact would
break the spell; but where was everybody. There must be buttons to

push, but he couldn't see them. He pulled out a drawer or two; they had been cleaned out.

Presently he sat back in his chair and simply shouted. That brought Missy LeHand from her office on the one side and Marvin McIntyre from the reception room on the other. The day's work then began. But it had been a bad moment, one that he spoke of often. It called up reflections, among those who heard it, of his physical helplessness; but that was not what he meant to emphasize. What seemed appalling to him in retrospect was the implication that the national paralysis had struck so nearly to the center and, for that short time, had reached the vital organ of direction. What would have happened if at that instant he had been permanently immobilized? [2]

Like so many of Roosevelt's stories, this one was a bit overdramatic and his memory had slightly telescoped time. That Sunday morning he had been sufficiently unruffled to observe the customary ceremonial of a President by attending church — St. Thomas's near Connecticut Avenue. It was not until the next day that he first went to his office to encounter the shock of emptiness, and, to a paraplegic, of being helplessly stranded.

In wrestling with the problem of the banking crisis, Roosevelt did not as yet have more than a vague notion what the ultimate solution would be, but had already prepared for the first firm steps. Already before his inauguration he had started into motion the machinery to quash the crisis; if anything he was oversanguine about the possibility of keeping the economy in operation without banks. He recognized that it was slowed down to a small fraction of capacity, but did not seem to regard a standstill as imminent.[3]

In this acute crisis, Roosevelt to a surprising degree delegated the authority to negotiate solutions and himself participated little in their formulation. Rather, he seems to have limited himself at the beginning to the setting of the limits of the solution, and subsequently to the acceptance of proposals he considered viable.

At the outset, Roosevelt was so averse to taking a radical view of the emergency that, far from considering nationalizing the banks, or diverting the nation's financial business to the Postal Savings system, he continued firmly to oppose even a limited guarantee by the government of savings deposits. Whatever solution was to be evolved must be conservative; it was logical, therefore, to assign its formulation to conservative men. He delegated the banking problem to Woodin, with Moley serving as an unofficial deputy. They in turn looked to Hoover's former officials, who stayed on in Washington, and to an advisory committee of bankers. Consequently Roosevelt, just before leaving the Mayflower Hotel on the morning of March 4 to deliver his inaugural address castigating the "money changers," agreed to the recommendation originating with Mills and Ballantine that bankers from New York, Chicago,

Philadelphia, Baltimore and Richmond be brought into Washington. In this there was no inconsistency, since Roosevelt's quarrel with the bankers had been over their recklessness; he wished them to be more cautious, not more daring.[4]

In essence Roosevelt needed only to use the men who had been in the Treasury Department and the Federal Reserve at the end of the Hoover administration, and to put into effect the measures they had devised, but which Hoover had refused to utilize without Roosevelt's collaboration, in order to stem the crisis. When Woodin and Moley reported to Roosevelt on the morning of March 4, they were not sure how Roosevelt would react to the fact that they had continued negotiations with Hoover's officials after he and Hoover had come to an impasse. Roosevelt was delighted. Further, he was quite ready to give his assent to the proposals of Mills and his associates: First, Roosevelt should proclaim a banking holiday under the somewhat dubious powers of the Trading with the Enemy Act; second, he should call Congress into special session to validate the proclamation, if need be to extend the holiday, and to pass legislation to enable banks to reopen after the holiday.

What that legislation would be was not yet entirely clear. Some plan would need to be worked out which would be acceptable to both congressional leaders and the banking community. The hectic conferences continued almost all inauguration day, far into the night, and on Sunday morning. For a few moments after Secretary Woodin and Attorney General Cummings took their oaths of office Saturday afternoon, they conferred with Roosevelt. Cummings, who had missed much of the inaugural parade in order to read the legislative history of the Trading with the Enemy Act, informed the President he was ready to give an opinion that it was valid for Roosevelt's purposes. (This bit of 1918 legislation, still in effect, had been intended to enable the government to embargo gold, silver and currency transactions in time of financial crisis; it might be implied to authorize closing of banks.) Woodin assured Roosevelt that with absolute certainty he would have an emergency banking bill ready by Thursday, March 9. Roosevelt decided to call Congress to meet in special session that day.[5]

With these decisions behind him, President Roosevelt met in the Oval Room Sunday afternoon, March 5, at 2:30, with the cabinet, Vice President Garner, Speaker Rainey, Moley, and Howe. Miss Perkins remembered, "The President outlined more coherently than I had heard it outlined before, just what this banking crisis was and what the legal problems involved were. He spoke about his order to close all banks and to stop all payments on a temporary basis. The legal problems underlying that were considerable."[6]

Next, Roosevelt turned his attention to the congressional leaders. He conferred not only with the Democratic leaders of each house, but also with Senator Glass and Representative Henry B. Steagall, respectively head of each banking committee; Bertrand H. Snell, the House minority leader; and Hiram Johnson, the progressive Republican senator. He talked with them as he had to the cabinet about banking problems, and told them he wished to call a special session to take up three problems — banking, federal economy, and unemployment. They readily agreed. "The remarkable thing about him to me," Hiram Johnson commented privately, "was his readiness to assume responsibility and his taking that responsibility with a smile." In the unique diary that Roosevelt kept on this and the next day of his presidency, he noted laconically what he undertook:

> Concluded that forty-eight different methods of handling banking situation impossible. Attorney General Cummings reported favorably on power to act under 1917 law, giving President power to license, regulate, etc., export, hoarding, ear-marking of gold or currency.
>
> Based on this opinion and on emergency, decided on Proclamation declaring banking holiday from tonight through Thursday, March 9th. Secretary of Treasury to regulate partial reserves of banking facilities based on liquidity clearing house certificates and trusteeing of new deposits. Attorney General, Secretary of the Treasury, Moley and Counsel Wyatt of Federal Reserve Board at work on Proclamation until 11 P.M.* Hurried supper before Franklin, Jr. and John returned to school. Talked with representatives of four Press Associations explaining bank holiday Proclamation.[7]

Roosevelt was at his affable best in this first encounter as President with newspapermen. Stephen Early, in his new role as White House press secretary, met the four correspondents in the Red Room of the executive mansion and took them upstairs to the President's study, where Roosevelt sat at his desk, already littered with a few papers and telegrams. He shook hands with each of them, telling them that he wanted them to know what he was doing, and read them the freshly completed proclamation. Flatteringly he remarked that they were the first to hear it. He had one request, that they call it a modified or partial bank holiday, not a moratorium. As Roosevelt and his advisers worked, they seemed to Clapper to be quite unruffled:

> Secretary Woodin, a small smiling man wearing a blue shirt sat in a deep divan. Attorney Gen. Homer Cummings, tall, thin, with wide

---

* A surprising number of Hoover's officials had a hand in working upon the executive order. As early as January or February 1933, Wyatt had prepared a rough draft of a proclamation. On March 2, Wyatt, assisted by Hoover's attorney general, William D. Mitchell, prepared an up-to-date version, despite Mitchell's opposition to its issuance. After Roosevelt took office, Mills and Ballantine, consulting with Gloyd Awalt, prepared a new version. This was the draft that Roosevelt's officials and Wyatt put in final form at the White House on the evening of March 5.

eyes, peered through his glasses as President Roosevelt asked him various questions which arose regarding the proclamation. Hull, thin-faced, spare Tennessean, sat with his long legs crossed easily.

Behind the plain desk . . . looking across under the shaded desk lamp, sat the President, in a blue serge business suit. Sturdy-shouldered, smiling, calm, talking pleasantly, with an occasional humorous sally, he was a picture of ease and confidence. As he talked, he deliberately inserted a fresh cigarette in an ivory holder. It was as if he was considering whether to sign a bill for a bridge in some far away rural county.[8]

First Roosevelt signed a proclamation convening Congress into extraordinary session at noon Thursday, March 9 — as soon (Roosevelt deemed, in this era of rail travel) as Pacific Coast members could reach Washington. Next, at one A.M. on Monday, March 6, he signed the proclamation he had prepared earlier, declaring a bank holiday until Congress met.

The proclamation stated as its justification that there had been a heavy drain upon the nation's gold stocks and currency as a result of hoarding within the country and speculation abroad. Consequently it was "in the best interests of all bank depositors that a period of respite be provided with a view to preventing further hoarding . . . and permitting the application of appropriate measures to protect the interests of our people." Therefore, under the authorization of Section 5(b) of the Trading with the Enemy Act, the President proclaimed a holiday for all banks and a cessation of all banking transactions, except those that the secretary of the treasury might authorize.[9]

Somehow the faltering economy had to be kept in motion during the hiatus while the banks were closed, and the bankers and officials were debating what sort of legislation Congress should enact to reopen them on a sound basis. The New York Stock Exchange and all the securities exchanges in the country were closed, and there was a general paralysis in commerce, reflected in steel production which dropped two points below the previous week, to 16 percent of capacity. Yet businessmen seemed optimistic. Few of them could finance freight charges that week on steel, for example, but few canceled orders. On the commodity markets, prices for metals and flour advanced; American securities traded abroad remained steady in price, and American Telephone and Telegraph even went up on the London exchange.[10]

If the banks remained closed for long, the paralysis would become worse. Even before Roosevelt took office, state moratoria were having an acute cumulative effect. The president of the Schaeffer Pen Company of Fort Madison, Iowa, wrote his friend Moley on March 3: "We have today our checks returned and refused from twenty-four states and it looks as though in a few days business would be at an actual standstill." [11]

The American people somehow got through the week, the more fortunate ones looking upon the banking holiday as something of an adventure. Yet even the most well-to-do worried. No one did so with less reason than Mrs. Roosevelt, who was concerned because they had run up a large bill at the Mayflower Hotel and had no spare cash. When she expressed her perturbation to her husband, he smiled and told her he thought they could manage whatever was essential.[12]

Secretary Woodin announced regulations on Monday afternoon which would allow banks to make change, and to make loans to provide food for people and feed for animals. The Federal Reserve Board threatened to make lists of those who had withdrawn gold or gold certificates since February 1 unless they returned their hoards within five days. Altogether $300 million was returned. Retailers issued credit certificates; wooden tokens for five to twenty-five cents circulated; numerous communities printed scrip of one sort or another. Governor Lehman of New York appointed Al Smith chairman of an Emergency Certificate Corporation, which prepared to issue scrip in denominations from one to fifty dollars. The American Bank Note Company worked at top speed printing $250 million in scrip for the New York Federal Reserve Bank. It was a precedent dating from the Panic of 1907, when banks had circulated some $238 million in scrip on the basis of their credit. But it was makeshift rather than money, and was hard to transfer from one Federal Reserve district to another. Gresham's law would apply to it; scrip would drive paper money into hiding when the problem was to stop hoarding. Scrip at best was an admission of financial instability.[13]

President Roosevelt himself seemed to have no clear-cut notion on how to resolve banking questions. "Secretary Woodin reported Banker's representatives much at sea as to what to do," he noted in his diary account of March 5. Roosevelt himself appeared somewhat at sea when he undertook the rather embarrassing task on Monday of addressing the Governors' Conference in the East Room of the White House. He had called the conference early in February, not anticipating the crisis, and expecting to spend the entire day with them discussing depression problems. Because of the pressure of events he could give them only a few minutes, and had to confess that he had not prepared any formal remarks. In discussing banking, he went no further than to explain the limited fashion in which banks could function under his proclamation. As for the future, he confined himself to a few not very enlightening generalities:

We want if possible to have a general banking situation, that is to say, one covering national banks and State banks, as uniform as possible throughout the country. At the same time we want to cooperate with all of the States in bringing about uniformity. I have no desire to have this matter centralized down here in Washington any more than we can help. I don't believe there is much more to say about banking.[14]

For four days, beginning at ten o'clock on Sunday, March 5, the advisory committee of leading bankers debated on how to reopen the banks. While they could not agree upon any plan, at least they had a sense of participation. Nor had they seemed too stung by Roosevelt's inaugural reference to the "money changers." Warburg had noted in his diary, "Remarks about money changers generally considered unjust to some bankers; otherwise speech makes excellent impression." There were those who felt Roosevelt's call to the bankers for assistance was an ironic sequel to the inaugural address. Ernest Gruening, editor of the *Nation*, at that time an advocate of the socialization of banks, commented wryly to Norman Thomas, "Our information from Washington is of terrific confusion, with the money changers whom Mr. Roosevelt drove out of the temples in his inaugural congregating in the White House and telling him what to do." [15]

The feeling in the White House was that the presence of the bankers in Washington might bolster confidence — but it was thought best for a Morgan partner, one of the popular villains of the time, to be inconspicuous, and for the Brain Trusters Tugwell, Berle, and Moley, reputed radicals, to keep out of the public eye. Some of the bankers became overwrought under the strain of the crisis and the continued lack of sleep. Melvin A. Traylor of Chicago, who had been one of the Democratic contenders for the presidential nomination in 1932, was certain that the Treasury would not be able to find subscribers for its certificates when a critical refunding operation took place on March 15. When Moley suggested that as a last resort, if need be, Roosevelt could call for a public subscription through a radio appeal, Traylor exclaimed, "You're talking like William Jennings Bryan and his million men who'd leap to arms overnight!" The bankers were no more unified in their proposals than they had been before the inauguration. They made proposals and counterproposals ranging from the national issuing of scrip to the incorporation of state banks into the Federal Reserve System. They so occupied themselves in canceling each other out that the ultimate decisions fell to Secretary Woodin.[16]

On Monday evening, this quiet, flexible-minded Republican corporation president pondered the problem with Moley. He decided to accept the proposals of his predecessor, Secretary Mills, at every point except on the question of issuing scrip; he continued to mull over that until late at night. His immediate conclusions were, Moley has written:

(1) "Swift and staccato action." (Will's phrase).

(2) The stressing of conventional banking methods and the avoidance of any unusual or highly controversial measures.

(3) The opening of as many banks as could possibly be opened within the realm of safety, since the greater the number opened the greater the probability of confidence in banks generally.

(4) The blacking out of the reputedly left-wing presidential advisers (Berle, Tugwell, and myself) during the crisis.

(5) A tremendous gesture by the President and Congress in the direction of economy.

(6) A man-to-man appeal for public confidence by the President himself.[17]

By the next morning Woodin had come to the final vital decision: again, as Mills and Ballantine recommended, the government would not issue scrip. It would not be necessary. Under the authority of the Federal Reserve Act, unlimited amounts of currency could be issued against the sound assets of banks. This Federal Reserve money, unlike scrip, would not frighten people, Woodin felt. It would be money that looked like money.

These thoroughly conservative conclusions became the basis of the emergency banking legislation. Woodin and Moley rushed to the White House Tuesday morning to present them to Roosevelt. He listened attentively and gave his ready approval. "Then we were off," Moley wrote, "for forty-eight hours of wrangling over details in the meetings at the Treasury, of bill drafting, message drafting, and conferring with the congressional leaders." [18]

The preparation of the Emergency Banking Bill was a difficult technical task. Weeks earlier, Secretary Mills had worked out the basic principles in consultation not only with his own staff but also with the Federal Reserve Board and the White House. It involved, besides the issuance of new Federal Reserve notes to meet possible future bank runs, two other important devices. Conservators rather than receivers should administer banks that could not be allowed to reopen, to arrange their reorganization, merger, or liquidation. And, most important of all, banks would be authorized to issue preferred stock as security for RFC loans to underwrite their future stability.*

* Mills presented his proposals to Woodin in a memorandum of March 4 and a supplementary memorandum on the evening of March 5, when, as Mills wrote, "it became plainly evident after two days of discussions that the Advisory Committee which had been invited to consider the problem could agree on no definite program." Wyatt had dictated a rough draft of legislation weeks earlier; using it as a basis, late in the evening of March 7, he began drafting the Emergency Banking Bill. Wyatt was primarily responsible for the shaping of the bill; a number of other experts suggested modifications. Wyatt wrote in reminiscence to Ballantine some years later:

In Congress the key person was Senator Carter Glass. Despite his outburst of dismay to Roosevelt on the night before the inauguration, the acuteness of the emergency forced him to cooperate — but he exacted White House consent to several conservative amendments. Roosevelt in his vague remarks to the governors on Monday gave assurance that state banks and national banks would receive equal treatment. Nevertheless, he capitulated when Glass insisted that the legislation should not apply to state banks outside the Federal Reserve System.* On the other hand, another amendment authorized the RFC to purchase, or lend on the security of, preferred stock of state banks as well as national banks.

While one group of Roosevelt's advisers worked on the banking bill, others were preparing an even more orthodox economy measure. On Tuesday, Roosevelt hastily lunched at his desk with Lewis Douglas, his new director of the budget, to reach final agreement on the extensive cuts — and to publicize the deficits (hailed at that time as horrendous) that the Hoover administration had left behind. Douglas told Roosevelt, and the press duly reported, that the Treasury deficit on the last day of the old administration was $1,358,993,357. The deficit for the fiscal year ending the previous June 30 had been $2,900,000,000.[20]

In this preliminary stage, the drafting of the bills, Roosevelt seemed to play a relatively subdued part. The next stage was spectacular, as Roosevelt himself with rare effectiveness presented his program to Congress and the nation.

Roosevelt's initial coup was his first press conference, when he replaced the distant, formal procedures of Hoover with the jaunty give-and-take of oral questions and answers. It was a technique he had begun as assistant secretary of the navy and perfected as governor of New York. Toward the end of the Hoover administration, press relations had worn down to occasional written statements passed out to the correspondents in response to written questions they had submitted earlier. Now suddenly Roosevelt transformed conferences into sessions livelier than any that the older Washington newspapermen remembered

We completed a draft some time Wednesday morning and you took it to the White House while I flopped on a couch for an hour or two rest. You came back with a request for a lot of changes (which I thought came from the White House but some of which might have come from the [Federal Reserve] Board) and we got out another draft in time for a conference with Congressional leaders that afternoon or evening. Further changes were suggested and another draft was completed . . . and sent to the printer about 3 o'clock Thursday morning.[19]

* In consequence there was no federal control over state banks at the conclusion of the holiday. Glass insisted they not be subject to Treasury Department licensing, but be returned to state control; some states reopened banks regardless of their insolvency.

The first press conference in the V

se, four days after the inauguration.

since the days of Theodore Roosevelt. The focus of interest suddenly shifted from the Capitol to the White House in marked contrast to the Coolidge and Hoover administrations. There was a gaiety and informality at the first conference when nearly 125 newspapermen crowded into Roosevelt's Oval Office at 10:10 Wednesday morning, March 8.

There was a hint of Theodore Roosevelt too, when Franklin D. Roosevelt provoked laughter by remarking that he did not want to revive T.R.'s notorious "Ananias Club." While Roosevelt wished to talk freely, he was warning that he would deny remarks made in confidence if they were attributed to the White House. From this first conference on, despite quite firm rules, there was a mixture of frank talk and light-heartedness. Indeed, at the beginning of the conference, just as Roosevelt was about to announce the rules, in stepped John and Franklin D. Roosevelt, Jr., interrupting their father to say goodbye. As they bent over to kiss him, he remarked, "These two boys are off to Arizona," and went on to explain how he would conduct the conferences. Questions would be oral, but he would not answer "if" questions, or ones "which for various reasons I do not want to discuss, or I am not ready to discuss, or I do not know anything about." The newspapermen were not allowed to quote him directly except when his press secretary, Stephen Early, gave them statements in writing. Much of what Roosevelt would tell them he would call "background information," which they could use on their own authority in articles but must not attribute to the White House. Some would be "off the record," which they must not even report to their employers or repeat to other newspapermen not at the conference, for fear these others might use it in news stories. And thus proceeding, Roosevelt plunged into a conference which, like the thousand that followed, was exhilarating and informative to the reporters present, but was largely "background information" or "off the record." * Thenceforth, he told the reporters, the United States permanently would have a system of managed currency:

> We hope that when the banks reopen a great deal of the currency that was withdrawn for one purpose or another will find its way back. We have got to provide an adequate currency. Last Friday we would have had to provide it in the form of scrip, and probably some addi-

* Early had previously explained to Raymond Clapper that Roosevelt would limit direct quotation in part because he feared translation by foreign correspondents. He wished to limit attendance at the press conferences strictly to Washington correspondents; FDR would see managing editors and other visiting newspapermen separately. Conferences were to be held twice a week, at 10 A.M. on Wednesdays for the especial benefit of afternoon newspapers, and at 4 P.M. Fridays for the advantage of morning newspapers. Between conferences, FDR planned to give special statements to the men specifically assigned to the White House.

tional issues of Federal Bank notes. If things go along as we hope they will, the use of scrip can be very greatly curtailed, and the amounts of new Federal Bank issues, we hope, can be also limited to a very great extent. In other words, what you are coming to now really is a managed currency, the adequateness of which will depend on the conditions of the moment. It may expand one week and it may contract another week.

When a reporter then asked him to define what he meant by "sound currency" — he had promised sound currency in his inaugural address — Roosevelt responded, "The real mark of delineation between sound and unsound is when the Government starts to pay its bills by starting printing presses. That is about the size of it." And Roosevelt did not want to start the presses to rescue foundering banks at the risk of upsetting his economy program.

In consequence, because it would be costly to the federal government, Roosevelt told the reporters (as background) he was opposed to a guarantee of bank deposits. Since, in the end, Federal Deposit Insurance was to be a prime means of maintaining public confidence in banks, Roosevelt's reasoning in March 1933 is of especial interest:

> The general underlying thought behind the use of the word "guarantee" with respect to bank deposits is that you guarantee bad banks as well as good banks and the minute the Government starts to do that the Government runs into a probable loss. . . . There are undoubtedly some banks that are not going to pay one hundred cents on the dollar. We all know it is better to have that loss taken than to jeopardize the credit of the United States Government or to put the United States Government further in debt, and, therefore, the one objective is going to be to keep the loss in the individual banks down to a minimum, endeavoring to get 100 percent on them, but not having the United States Government liable for the mistakes and errors of individual banks and not putting a premium in the future on unsound banking.

In response to another question, Roosevelt expressed what was undoubtedly his firm conviction, "We cannot write a permanent banking act for the nation in three days."

When the conference adjourned at ten-forty-five the newspapermen applauded, although Roosevelt had told them almost nothing that they could attribute to him. They had little more than the exhilarating feeling of being insiders. As they left Early warned them ominously that he would make an example of anyone who violated the President's confidence.[21]

With equal success, Roosevelt won the support of the congressional leaders with whom he previewed the draft legislation that evening of March 8. From eight-thirty in the evening until almost one in the morning, he, the secretary of the treasury, the attorney general, and Moley conferred with key senators and representatives. He read them the draft bill that would be introduced the next day; it was still not in clear enough shape for them to read it themselves. At least one of those present, Hiram Johnson, confessed that no one grasped very clearly what was in it, and that the next day when they acted upon it, they knew no more than the night before. Johnson had no idea how orthodox a measure it was. At one point in the discussion he got up from his chair, placed himself in front of the President, and, complimenting him upon the strong tone of his inaugural address, proposed kicking the Wall Street bankers into oblivion and replacing them with a new banking system. Several in the room, including Roosevelt, nodded their approval.[22]

A few progressive senators did indeed favor taking advantage of the emergency to obtain a thoroughgoing overhaul of the nation's banking system and the creation of firmer federal controls. La Follette and Costigan persuaded Johnson and Norris to attend the White House meeting that night for precisely that purpose. Johnson did not seem to be urging much more than the appointment of a new Federal Reserve Board that would regulate the Wall Streeters rather than permitting Wall Street to regulate the banking of the nation. La Follette and Costigan were apparently demanding no more than that the government control whatever scrip might be issued and tighten its regulation, judging from a letter they sent Roosevelt that day. It made little difference.[23]

Earlier, according to Marquis Childs, La Follette had proposed to Roosevelt that he allow banks to reopen under only six months' licenses so that he could retain control over them while he worked out a careful permanent system of checks and balances. "Oh, but that isn't necessary at all," Roosevelt replied, "I've just had every assurance of cooperation from the bankers." [24]

When Congress acted upon the bill the next day, most of its members knew even less about it than Hiram Johnson. Roosevelt had drafted the message in longhand that morning in consultation with Governor Meyer of the Federal Reserve Board and others. It was completed and sent to the Capitol only fifteen minutes before Congress met. In the message, Roosevelt summarized the objectives of the banking bill:

> In order that the first objective — the opening of banks for the resumption of business — may be accomplished, I ask of the Congress the immediate enactment of legislation giving to the Executive branch of the Government control over banks for the protection of depositors; authority forthwith to open such banks as have already been ascertained to be in sound condition and other such banks as rapidly as possible; and authority to reorganize and reopen such banks as may be found to require reorganization to put them on a sound basis.

I ask amendments to the Federal Reserve Act to provide for such additional currency, adequately secured, as it may become necessary to issue to meet all demands for currency and at the same time to achieve this end without increasing the unsecured indebtedness of the Government of the United States.[25]

When the House met, printed copies were not yet ready, and a rolled-up newspaper symbolically substituted for a few minutes. A little later copies arrived still wet from the printing press. The new majority leader, Joseph W. Byrns of Tennessee, announced that there would be only forty minutes of debate on the bill, and that it would not be subject to amendment. The Republicans were entirely cooperative. The minority leader, Bertrand H. Snell, recommended to the House that it "give the President what he demands and says is necessary to meet the situation." The bill passed by a voice vote, apparently unanimously, and was sent to the Senate.

In the Senate the debate was little less perfunctory. Huey Long, proposing an amendment to authorize the President to declare any state bank a member of the Federal Reserve System, blamed the woes of the state banks upon the big banks, which, he charged, had loaded them with worthless paper. Long asserted he was speaking for the little people who were depositors in these banks: "You are proposing to take every dime they have away from them." Glass retorted that as it was, the bill broadened "in a degree that is almost shocking to me — the currency and credit facilities of the Federal Reserve Banking System, and largely extends these facilities to State banks which are not members of the Federal Reserve Banking System." And he pointed out that the federal government would close no state bank; it would leave them to the jurisdiction of the states. Several other senators shared Long's concern for the depositors in the state banks.

Senator La Follette warned at length against the dangerous power the strong New York banks would exercise under the legislation, and proposed strengthening national regulation. "If I could have my way," he asserted, "I would insure control by the President during the emergency." If what La Follette had in mind during the crisis was nationalization of banks, it was not apparent in his speech that day. A year later, Senator Bronson Cutting of New Mexico, writing in *Liberty*, lamented, "I think back to the events of March 4, 1933, with a sick heart. For then . . . the nationalization of banks by President Roosevelt could have been accomplished without a word of protest." But these progressive senators, if they favored nationalization, were placing the initiative for obtaining it upon Roosevelt's shoulders. The sentiment in Congress in favor of nationalization was negligible; even the traditional agrarian protest against Wall Street domination was minimal. Cutting himself voted for the Emergency Banking Bill. When the roll

FDR signs the Emergency Banking Act, March 9, 1933.

was called in the Senate, there were 73 ayes and only 7 nays — of these all but one were from the midwestern and western areas of agrarian radicalism.

The Senate adjourned at 7:52 P.M.; it had enacted the Emergency Banking Act in less than eight hours. At 8:15, Vice President Garner signed it, and rushed it to the White House. Again Roosevelt seated himself in the upstairs Oval Room in the White House; by this time its austere impressiveness had been destroyed by the disarray of partly unpacked cases of household goods. Roosevelt sat at his desk in front of the photographers, the flag of the United States to his left and the presidential flag to his right, and at 8:37 signed the measure — the first bill to come before him as President. He used only one special pen, and gave it to a White House guest, Mrs. Roosevelt's friend, Nancy Cook.*

There was scant time for ceremony. Immediately Roosevelt went to work with Woodin, Cummings, and Undersecretary of the Treasury Ballantine, preparing a new proclamation under the authority of the Emergency Banking Act, to continue the bank holiday (the embargo on gold and silver) expiring that day. Roosevelt had hoped to permit some of the banks to open the next day, Friday, but the Treasury officials could not act that soon. They engaged in a frenzied issuance of regulations and a checking of the assets of all the banks in the Federal Reserve System.

Technical difficulties hampering the reopening of the banks had been overcome, Roosevelt announced on Saturday, March 11. He had already proclaimed that all banks in the Federal Reserve System wishing to reopen must apply for Treasury licenses. By successive steps those member banks that the Treasury deemed sound would be opened on the following Monday, Tuesday, or Wednesday mornings. First those in the twelve cities possessing Federal Reserve banks would open, then those in cities with clearinghouses, and finally those in smaller cities.[27]

State banks were to return to state authority on Monday morning. The acting comptroller of the currency, Awalt, deemed this return a

---

* The Emergency Banking Act of 1933:

I. "Approved and confirmed" the President's actions under the Trading with the Enemy Act, authorized further future action in time of national emergency, and Treasury regulation of limited banking activities during a holiday.

II. Provided that national banks with impaired assets might reopen under Conservators, appointed by the Comptroller of the Currency. The Conservators could release a "safe" percentage of deposits, engage in certain other banking activities, and plan and put into effect reorganizations.

III. Authorized national banks to issue preferred stock, which the RFC might purchase. The RFC could also buy preferred stock from state banks.

IV. Authorized the Federal Reserve to issue bank notes upon the basis not only of federal securities, but during the emergency, upon 90 percent of other sound assets.[26]

mistake, but recognized that the federal government did not possess sufficient data to decide whether or not to reopen state banks. From throughout the country a number of governors telegraphed Roosevelt, urging him, in the words of Governor Guy B. Park of Missouri, to "declare for equality of treatment of state banks not members of Federal Reserve system." Governor Gifford Pinchot of Pennsylvania pointed out that 83 percent of the Pennsylvania banks, containing 48 percent of the deposits, were nonmembers of the Federal Reserve System; Governor John G. Pollard of Virginia, citing similar statistics, relayed the plea of the state banks that they should on the same character of collateral be allowed to borrow directly from Federal Reserve banks. Roosevelt responded publicly to the plea of the governors, and announced, "These banks can and will receive assistance from member banks [of the Federal Reserve System] and from the Reconstruction Finance Corporation." He made this announcement in the course of a radio address to the American people, the first of his so-called Fireside Chats.[28]

Banking was so technical, and the arrangements for reopening the banks so complicated, that many Americans had little more than a faint grasp of what was going on. This was why Roosevelt decided to address them on the radio, to explain to them in plain, clear language what had happened and what was being done to end the crisis. His was the delicate task of restoring the confidence of the depositors, to persuade them to return to their accounts the money they had withdrawn and hoarded during the past days of alarm.

It was a simple talk, unadorned with the flights of rhetoric or patriotic generalities that usually characterized presidential addresses. Undoubtedly its effectiveness lay in its simplicity and in Roosevelt's calm, earnest delivery. Too, like the press conference, it was most striking in contrast with the remote formalism of Roosevelt's predecessors, Hoover and Coolidge. As with the press conference, Roosevelt had perfected the technique of the Fireside Chat as governor of New York when he frequently went on the air to discuss vital issues with the people of the state, explaining things to them much as he might to farmers he knew in New York and Georgia. It was on the radio he put to use his technique developed in endless simple, small chats conducted from the front seat of his blue Ford roadster with his Hyde Park and Warm Springs acquaintances. Through the radio networks, he made all the American people his neighbors.

Roosevelt planned before becoming President to deliver occasional direct talks to the American people. The president of the National Broadcasting Company, M. H. Aylesworth, wrote him in December 1932, offering him the facilities of his network and urging him to speak for fifteen to twenty minutes once each week. "I fully expect to give personal talks from time to time on all kinds of subjects of national interest," Roosevelt replied, " — but I do not believe that it would be advisable to make one each week." [29]

At the time announced for the first Fireside Chat, at ten o'clock on the evening of Sunday, March 12, a large part of the seventeen million families owning radio sets turned them on to hear the President:

> I want to talk for a few minutes with the people of the United States about banking — with the comparatively few who understand the mechanics of banking but more particularly with the overwhelming majority who use banks for the making of deposits and the drawing of checks. I want to tell you what has been done in the last few days, why it was done, and what the next steps are going to be.

And in this clear, understandable way, Roosevelt discussed the nature of the crisis:

> Because of the undermined confidence on the part of the public, there was a general rush by a large portion of our population to turn bank deposits into currency or gold — a rush so great that the soundest banks could not get enough currency to meet the demand. The reason for this was that on the spur of the moment it was, of course, impossible to sell perfectly sound assets of a bank and convert them into cash except at panic prices far below their real value.

Next he outlined the measures being taken to reopen banks and re-habilitate the banking system, and sought to convince his listeners that they should return hoarded money to the banks:

> It needs no prophet to tell you that when the people find that they can get their money — that they can get it when they want it for all legitimate purposes — the phantom of fear will soon be laid. People will again be glad to have their money where it will be safely taken care of and where they can use it conveniently at any time. I can assure you that it is safer to keep your money in a reopened bank than under the mattress.

There had been a bad banking situation, Roosevelt commented, which the government had worked to rectify as quickly as possible. Nothing the government was doing, he pointed out, was complex or radical. The government was providing the machinery to restore the financial system; it was up to the people to make it work through demonstrating their confidence: "It is your problem no less than it is mine. Together we cannot fail." *

Roosevelt's reassuring talk and quick action did restore confidence. All thirty-three officers and staff members of the Columbia National

---

* Charles Michelson prepared a draft of this talk which apparently was largely discarded. Instead FDR followed a draft by Ballantine; Moley, analyzing the speech, thinks some of the phraseology characteristically FDR's.[30]

Bank in Kansas City signed a letter to Roosevelt declaring, "Hundreds upon hundreds of our customers have remarked upon the fresh understanding it gave them of the condition of the banks and the future of our country." As the banks reopened, many depositors brought back hoarded money. The banks did not have to face new runs, with the result that very little of the freshly printed Federal Reserve currency intended to meet the runs ever had to be put into circulation. The governor of the Federal Reserve Bank of Philadelphia, George W. Norris, cited to Roosevelt a concrete example of the effect of his Fireside Chat on "four old, purely mutual savings banks" in Philadelphia, which had combined deposits of over $400 million and over 500,000 depositors. When they reopened Monday morning, they had to face matured withdrawal notices amounting to nearly $10 million, but actually paid out less than a million and a half dollars. Meanwhile other depositors brought in nearly a million dollars. The net loss in withdrawals was only $441,000, and more people made deposits than withdrawals. Overall, throughout the country depositors returned more money than they withdrew. The excess of deposits was over $10 million in the Federal Reserve districts alone.[31]

The problem of determining which banks were strong enough to reopen harried federal officials for several days. It was important to the economy to open every bank that could survive, yet the officials would be responsible if they allowed numerous unsound banks to reopen. Almost on the spur of the moment they had to make many decisions vital to each city, and even to large sections of the country. It was an acute responsibility, not made easier by political pressures. After debate with the Federal Reserve Board, the Treasury established a procedure: the district Federal Reserve Board would ascertain that the assets of a member bank were sufficient to warrant reopening; the chief national bank examiner would then make his recommendation; the comptroller of the currency, acting upon it, would ask the secretary of the treasury to issue a license.

The most vital and controversial decision on the morning after Roosevelt's Fireside Chat was whether or not to reopen the Bank of America, the nation's largest banking chain, with 410 branches in California. Its failure would have been catastrophic in the West, and might have shaken banks as far east as the Continental National Bank of Chicago. Yet officials of the San Francisco Federal Reserve Bank seemed to favor keeping it closed. They apparently distrusted A. P. Giannini, who controlled the bank, a powerful and controversial figure in California finance. An examiner's report in July 1932 stated, "A continuation of existent economic conditions and the present management will place this bank in jeopardy." Giannini claimed that the San Francisco Federal Reserve Bank was making its recommendations upon the basis of outdated figures, and that the Bank of America had made a considerable recovery. This impasse seemed to have some of the overtones of the notorious Bank of United States closing that had so plagued Roosevelt as governor of New York. More traditional leaders of the banking community seemed to feel either resentment or at best mistrust of this spectacular immigrant competitor. Economic nativism seemed involved again, together with a clash of personalities and politics. Awalt and Woodin, both conservative, apolitical men, were thinking only in terms of sound banking and of the economic blow impending for the West Coast, infinitely more catastrophic than the earthquake that had hit Los Angeles that weekend. So it was that they went to President Roosevelt to recommend that the Bank of America be reopened.

Roosevelt might well have taken a political view of the Bank of America problem, as he had of war debts. He did not at the time, although both California senators were acutely distressed at the prospect of the closing; McAdoo, before entering the Senate on March 4, had been Giannini's attorney. Roosevelt declined to budge from the Treasury procedure and himself insist that the Bank of America reopen. He refused to take the initiative and responsibility, but urged Woodin and Awalt, since they felt as they did, to telephone John U. Calkins, governor of the Federal Reserve Bank at San Francisco. When Woodin first began talking to Calkins, Moley, who was present, remembers that Calkins insisted that the Bank of America should remain closed. Woodin quoted the bank examiner's figures, and finally asked Calkins if he would take responsibility for keeping the bank closed. Calkins declined to take the responsibility, and Woodin retorted, "Well, then, the bank will open." Woodin stepped into the anteroom where the two California senators, Johnson and McAdoo, were waiting. To their immense relief, in their presence he signed orders reopening the Bank of America and a lesser rival institution, the Anglo-California Bank, which Calkins had also initially decided against.[32]

Apparently had Governor Calkins remained adamant, Roosevelt would not have overruled him, regardless of both economic and political implications for California. Yet in the months and years ahead, the Bank of America not only recovered but flourished, resuscitated in its difficult periods not so much by the Federal Reserve as by large loans against its frozen assets — mostly mortgages — that Jesse Jones provided through the Reconstruction Finance Corporation. Roosevelt reaped much political benefit. Giannini, unlike most bankers, became a staunch supporter of his administration. And while there were those who credited Hearst or others, rather than Awalt and Woodin, with the rescue of the Bank of America, it was Roosevelt who was generally regarded as its savior.

By the end of May 1933, Roosevelt had incorporated a heroic story

about the rescue of the Bank of America into his large repertoire. At
tea in the White House one day, while two of his grandchildren were
playing on his knee, he told J. F. T. O'Connor, a California lawyer
whom he had appointed comptroller of the currency, the Roosevelt
version of events: When Calkins reported that the Bank of America
was forty million dollars in the red, said Roosevelt, he told Calkins
that in that event no banks could open in the San Francisco Federal
Reserve district until they had been examined. Calkins then called back
to say that Bank of America was forty millions of dollars solvent and
was okay. "It was," said the President, "the same old crowd trying to
destroy competition." O'Connor wrote Roosevelt admiringly, "You
saved a situation which could not have been corrected in fifty years
had any other course been taken." And Giannini urged O'Connor to
run for governor of California.[33]

Within a month the Treasury finished its initial licensing of banks.
The shaking out of weak banks was over. A little more than 70 percent
of the nation's 17,796 banks, 12,817 with deposits of $31 billion, were
fully open. Of the five thousand others, some three thousand ultimately
reopened; the remaining two thousand were reorganized under new
names, consolidated with existing banks, or closed permanently. Together with the numerous bank failures prior to the crisis, the number
of closings had been enormous.[34]

For the moment, the Roosevelt administration had remarkably restored public confidence, as the flow of hoarded funds back into the
banks demonstrated. On the morning after Roosevelt's speech, Monday,
March 13, when official foreign exchange resumed, the dollar bounced
back spectacularly in relation to other currencies; the franc and pound
fell. On Wednesday, when stock exchanges reopened, trading reached
a volume unsurpassed since the bear market of the previous September,
and prices advanced a sensational 15 percent over the previous closing
prices of March 13. There had never been such a sharp rise in a single
day. The offering of $800 million in Treasury certificates that week,
which bankers like Traylor had feared earlier would not be taken, sold
at the highest interest rates since the First World War. Banks immediately oversubscribed for the certificates by more than 100 percent.[35]

The most useful device for retaining confidence in the banks would
be the insurance of deposits up to a limited figure. For weeks after the
banking crisis, Roosevelt continued to oppose insurance. In the end he
gave way.* During the struggle with Congress in June, to obtain
completion of his legislative program, he reluctantly accepted an insurance program.[36]

In March 1933, Roosevelt also faced the problem of maintaining the

* See Chapter 26.

solvency of banks when so many of their assets, especially their mortgage holdings, could be liquidated into cash only at distress sale well below their normal value. In part, the Federal Reserve banks could meet the need for cash through the provision of the Emergency Banking Act enabling them to issue currency to banks upon some of these assets. This provision was little used. Basically the underwriting of the banks became the task of the RFC. The banking legislation specified that the RFC could purchase or loan money on the basis of preferred stock in banks.

At first Jesse Jones, chairman of the RFC, wished to go slowly. He has written in his memoirs:

> In approaching the bank repair job, I discussed it freely with the President and recommended that we should not be too open-handed or too quick about the government putting in all the needed capital, because if we did so the government would soon own control of too many banks. I told him we should try to interest people in the various communities in reestablishing the banks by putting some of their own money in the stock. He agreed, and we decided that we would be liberal in valuing the assets of the banks.[37]

Jones's caution gave Acting Comptroller Awalt, and presumably the Treasury Department, the impression that he did not favor the purchase of preferred stock. This impression remained, even though Jones publicly was urging the reluctant bankers to accept capital from the RFC so that they could adequately run their banks. Only four banks sold stock to the RFC in the first three weeks. On April 28, 1933, he asked the American Society of Newspaper Editors to help persuade the bankers to sell preferred stock to the RFC in order to increase their capital. At the beginning of August, Jones repeated his pleas over the radio and before newsreel cameras. On September 5, speaking before the American Bankers Association, he admonished them, "Be smart for once. Take the government in partnership with you in providing credit which the country is sadly in need of." The bankers were hostile since they feared sale of their stock to the RFC would lead to national control of the banks. That evening when they insisted he speak again, he told them off the record, "Half the banks represented in this room are insolvent; and those of you representing these banks know it better than anyone else." These blunt words were effective. Banks in considerable numbers began to sell their stock to the RFC, which by this device provided them with capital.[38]

In mid-October, when it was clear that several thousand banks would have to receive new capital to qualify for Federal Deposit Insurance on January 1, 1934, several of Roosevelt's advisers became fearful that the RFC could not complete the task successfully. Roosevelt resorted to a favorite device: on two occasions he brought Jones into his office and let him debate the problem with Eugene Black, governor of the Federal Reserve Board, Director of the Budget Douglas, and Henry Bruere of the Bowery Savings Bank, who in the fall of 1933 was a special consultant to the President. All three feared another banking crisis in January 1934, when the deposit insurance program began, unless two thousand open but insolvent banks were bolstered with some $600 million in new capital. They did not think the RFC could provide the funds quickly enough. Jones retorted that the banks would need more than double that sum, and that the RFC could indeed provide it quickly enough. Roosevelt after listening to both sides remarked, "Boys, I am going to back Jess." Roosevelt instructed the four of them to work out a plan, but the RFC alone completed the refinancing. It poured a billion dollars into six thousand banks within the allotted time.[39]

As the banking crisis abated in mid-March 1933, what was most apparent was that Roosevelt had succeeded in enlisting the enthusiastic backing of the American people. The banks were for the most part open and again functioning. The economy had suffered further serious damage, not generally recognized until April. And as yet the federal government had not so strengthened the banks that a repetition of the collapse of February could confidently be avoided. That was to require the infusion of capital through the RFC and the establishment of the Federal Deposit Insurance Corporation. In the end these two reforms, which Roosevelt during the February crisis had been too conservative to accept, did stabilize both state and national banks within and without the Federal Reserve System. The stabilization came later than was necessary and at a far higher price in liquidated banks and losses to depositors. Ballantine felt fifteen years later that "the calamitous and humiliating episode might have been avoided." The irony was that it had not been avoided, and that it was remedied so quickly in March 1933 that the nation showered upon President Roosevelt its admiration and gratitude. The *Wall Street Journal* declared on Monday, March 13:

> Last week marked an end to three years of a nation's drifting from bad to worse, an end to helpless acceptance of a malign fate which halfhearted, half-way measures gave hope of averting. . . . For an explanation of the incredible change which has come over the face of things here in the United States in a single week we must look to the fact that the new Administration in Washington has superbly risen to the occasion. It and the country still have incalculable tasks to perform before they can afford so much as to pause for breath. But together they have made a good beginning and there are times when a beginning is nearly everything.[40]

CHAPTER XIV

Economy, Reorganization—

and the Veterans

Our Government's house is not in order and for many
reasons no effective action has been taken to restore it
to order. . . . National recovery depends upon it.
— FDR, *March 10, 1933*.[1]

The slashing of federal expenditures, balancing of the budget, and reorganization of federal agencies to make them more efficient were all
integral components of Roosevelt's overall recovery program. He gave
them first priority.

The economy recommendations following the emergency banking
measure made Roosevelt during his first few days in office appear to
some progressives and radicals as singularly conservative. It seemed as
though his Pittsburgh speech of the previous fall attacking the extrava-
gances of the Hoover administration was to set the theme of his presidency, and the "cut-expenses-to-the-bone/balance-the-budget" recommendations of Senator Pat Harrison's "depression clinic" hearings were
to serve as his blueprint. It could be argued that Roosevelt was shifting
his administration somewhat to the right of the Hoover program, to take
it back to the dogma of the nineteenth-century Democratic Presidents,
Martin Van Buren and Grover Cleveland, who had believed that the
prime duty of the government in time of depression was to preserve
its solvency. Roosevelt in a time of acute deflation seemed bent on
pursuing a still more deflationary course.

The President, as became apparent in the next several weeks, had a
great deal more planned. He was well aware of the deflationary aspects
of the economy program and expected to counter them with mildly inflationary measures. Tugwell had impressed upon Roosevelt the previous
December "that we ought not to attempt to either inflate or deflate
exclusively." The economy phase of the New Deal was not an aberra-

tion but one aspect of the overall program in which Roosevelt never lost faith, but which came to clash with other phases and to be overshadowed.[2]

During those March days when the New Deal seemed to be a program of retrenchment and further deflation, businessmen, bankers, and old-line political leaders applauded loudly. They seemed to have in the White House a cheerful Cleveland, a states'-rights, limited government, penny-pinching Democrat. There was not as yet even any clear indication that he was actually taking the nation off the gold standard. The Treasury bonds issued during his second week in office bore the pledge that they would be redeemable at maturity in gold coin at the current standard of value.

Yet many progressives and liberal Democrats equally approved. They too were convinced that the federal government was inefficient and had been wildly overspending, especially in its benefits to veterans. They or their parents had been dismayed by the inflationary demands of the Populists in the 1890s, and had seen their apprehensions confirmed in the runaway German inflation of the 1920s. Excessive indebtedness and inflation could, they feared, send the dollar careening up the same path the mark had taken. The basis for their thinking and Roosevelt's was entirely different than that of later generations. After all, when Roosevelt had gone to Washington twenty years earlier, in 1913, to become Wilson's assistant secretary of the navy, the federal budget was less than three-quarters of a billion and the national debt not much over a billion dollars. During the 1920s, federal budgets by latter-day standards were exceedingly small and grew little; the debt declined from its post–World War total of over $25 billion to $16 billion in 1931. Then the depression brought deficits unprecedented in peacetime, and by the pre–World War I standards which many people would have still liked to consider normal were nothing short of horrendous. In the worst of the Hoover fiscal years, 1932, it was nearly $2.5 billion. Adolf A. Berle, considered one of the most advanced of the Brain Trusters, warned Roosevelt in a memorandum that the mounting debt threatened the credit of the government. Roosevelt was being serious, and was taken seriously, when in his economy message he asserted, "For three long years the Federal Government has been on the road toward bankruptcy." And it was this same sort of continued public view of federal deficits which gave such powerful ammunition to his opponents throughout the later New Deal. Roosevelt's generation never learned to look at heavy deficits with equanimity; neither did he.[3]

Roosevelt, like most progressives, was firmly of the opinion that the Republican administrations in Washington during the 1920s, especially under the aegis of Hoover, had become wastefully lavish in providing services to business.* In his campaign speech on the federal budget, Roosevelt had specifically attacked Hoover for his expansion of the Department of Commerce, "now housed in that great marble building which is facetiously called in Washington the 'Temple of Fact Finding,' which cost the people considerably more than the Capitol of the United States." [5]

Hoover's monumental contribution to Washington architecture was the federal triangle of massive public buildings along Pennsylvania and Constitution avenues. These not only lent majesty to the capital but could be justified as large-scale public works to counter the depression and as a means of saving the government millions of dollars in rental of office space. Yet the impression they gave, like a Cecil B. de Mille spectacle of imperial Rome, was one of conspicuous waste. "Somehow or other," Moley has pointed out, "Hoover had always seemed to be an expensive President." Hoover was so unpopular that any reversal of his policies could win approval. There was no general outcry when the new Secretary of the Interior Ickes decided that the great dam arising on the Colorado River, which had been known (as it is officially today) as Hoover Dam, should rather be called Boulder Dam. "The President chuckled and told me he was glad I had done this," Ickes wrote in his diary, "but that he was also glad I had done it without consulting him." And, however unfairly, Roosevelt could gather support for his economy and reorganization proposals in part from the reaction against President Hoover.[6]

If there were to be any real savings, a large part of the budget cuts had to be at the expense of veterans. During the 1932 campaign, Hoover in rebutting Roosevelt's budget speech had pointed out that even if Roosevelt cut in half government services other than armaments, he would have to halve the funds veterans received, "a gross injustice." Expenditures for veterans in the 1933 fiscal year accounted for almost a quarter of the total budget — $946 million out of $3.6 billion — paid out to 1 percent of the population. Yet Hoover himself had been scathing

* As a means of gauging the nature of this attack and its compatibility with national planning, note the views of the outstanding progressive historian, Charles A. Beard, in 1932. Beard enumerated a long list of government services to business: regulation of railways, improvement of waterways, subsidies to shipping companies and airlines, building of highways, the seeking of foreign markets through commercial attachés at American embassies — and numerous others, especially the pork barrel and protective tariff. One significant thing about Beard's enumeration is that he was less interested in proposing that other interest groups such as farmers receive comparable benefits than in suggesting that the federal government cut back its favors to businessmen. He considered his enumeration proof that "rugged individualism" was a myth. Rampant individualism of a "devil take the hindmost" sort was, Beard believed, responsible for the plight of western civilization. What was needed was planning, which would mean restraints upon the business community.[4]

toward Congress in his message of May 5, 1932, for authorizing "enlarged expenditures in non-service-connected benefits." It could be argued on the one hand that veterans had a valid grievance in that they could not persuade the government to pay them in advance their promised bonus, which most of them badly needed during the depression. On the other hand, for twelve years the veterans' organizations had lobbied irresistibly, gaining benefit after benefit in piecemeal fashion. It had become, the British ambassador reported to London, "the greatest and oldest 'racket' in America." By way of comparison he pointed out that of the two million British wounded in World War I, a half million received disability allowances; only 234,000 Americans had been wounded, yet 776,000 veterans received compensation.[7]

Reduction of Civil War veterans' pension payments through veto of private bills had built President Cleveland's fame. The cutting or elimination of pensions for disabilities not connected with military service seemed the only way Roosevelt could make good on his promise of economy. Yet the American Legion lobbyist boasted that at his signal, legionnaires in more than ten thousand posts all over the nation would dispatch a hundred thousand telegrams to their congressmen. When Lewis Douglas as a Democratic representative from Arizona led a fight against pension increases, only three Democratic representatives voted with him. On the other hand, Douglas, running for reelection in a state where 20 percent of the voters were veterans, won by a substantial margin.[8]

Speed was essential, since Roosevelt could expect almost irresistible pressure upon Congress to oppose decreases in both governmental and veterans' expenditures and in administrative reorganization. He reasoned that he must send these measures to Congress without advance notice at the very beginning of his presidential honeymoon while Congress was still disposed to vote for whatever he requested. In this first vote he must obtain full authorization to make whatever budget cuts and undertake whatever reorganization of the government he wished. He could reason that he was thus removing from Congress the onus for measures which although popular in their overall purport would certainly be unpopular in their specific applications. This applied both to veterans' benefits and governmental agencies.

One of the basic reasons why Roosevelt needed blanket authorization — which unfriendly critics could call dictatorial powers — was to circumvent the enduring ties and powerful community of interest between congressional committee chairmen and bureau chiefs. As Roosevelt had discovered in the Wilson administration, Presidents and cabinet officers came and went, but heads of committees and government bureaus usually enjoyed long tenure, cordial relations, and in consequence a power almost impervious to direction not only from the office of an assistant secretary but even from the White House. In 1919 while assistant secretary of the navy, Roosevelt recommended at a congressional hearing a greater centralization of authority and the creation of a Bureau of the Budget to safeguard that authority. In 1922 or 1923 he planned a book on government in which he proposed chapters on "The Crying Need of a National Budget" and "A Revision of Departmental Functions." He never wrote more than the preface, but in that he stated, "If American governments were private corporations they would go into the hands of a receiver in about twenty-four hours." * As governor of New York, he fought energetically and with some success to exercise effective executive power.[9] As presidential candidate he said:

> We can make savings by reorganization of existing departments, by eliminating functions, by abolishing many of those innumerable boards and those commissions which, over a long period of years, have grown up as a fungus growth on American government. These savings can properly be made to total many hundreds of thousands of dollars a year.[10]

Although subsequently Roosevelt felt that reorganization was primarily important as a means of obtaining greater effectiveness in the government, in March 1933 he planned it as a means of cutting costs. Roosevelt was ready to act immediately, since he had been preparing his economy moves since shortly after his election. In December 1932, he gave Congressman Douglas the prime responsibility for working upon the economy program.[11]

Douglas was eminently suited for the undertaking. He was himself a veteran who had been cited by Pershing for bravery and a member of the American Legion, yet he had fought diligently against the American Legion lobby. Both his brilliance and social charm were renowned in Washington, and he possessed the youthful resilience essential to meet the interminable demands of the New Deal. He was thirty-nine. "Prior to the inauguration," he wrote his father, "I was working with Swagar Sherley, a man of great character but very sensitive and very slow and very talkative. The result was that I never ended a day

---

* Owen D. Young suggested to FDR in December 1932 that simple government was essential to maintenance of simple business organization. FDR sent Moley for possible future use, a "pretty good" statement "Young scribbled . . . off while sitting at my desk":

> One of the chief objectives of government regulation is to keep our business organizations simple enough so that the public can understand them too and feel an effective intelligent check on their operations. To accomplish this objective the governmental organization itself must be simpler and understandable. Sprawling bureaus in government bring irresistible complexity in the business groups with which they come into contact.

until midnight." After the inauguration, although Douglas no longer was held back by Sherley, his work load became even heavier and the days longer. He was so close to the center of power that he confessed to his father something of an awe-stricken feeling:

It seems queer to telephone at any hour to a President, to go into his bedroom at one in the morning, in fact to have the entré at any time and to be writing a Presidential message to Congress on the budget. . . . How strange for an insignificant young man from Arizona to be in such a position. When I stop to think about it all it is quite frightening.

Along with his humility, Douglas possessed the self-confidence and independence that could come through being born into a wealthy family. They stood him well in his relations with the new President, whom he had not as yet entirely gauged. The money did not make him a political liability to Roosevelt since it had come from Arizona copper; there was no damning taint of Wall Street about it. The feeling of independence was so strong that Douglas could comment privately, "Eventually I might be compelled to resign either because I might not be able to go along with [the] President on some now unknown wild scheme or because if we did a good job I might have to resign to protect the President." [12]

Douglas not only delighted Roosevelt but charmed the Brain Trust, he was so perceptive and wide-ranging in his thinking. While his prime responsibility was the deflationary balancing of the budget, he was articulate on the dangers of deflation and eager for countermeasures. "Douglas very intelligent: liked him a lot and wondered at it in a congressman," Tugwell noted in his diary. "Later discovered him to be an Amherst man, etc." Douglas did not reciprocate the feeling toward Tugwell, deeming his advocacy of the farm program very silly.[13]

Along with preparations for economy, Douglas planned reorganization. Roosevelt had recognized during the interregnum that little reorganization was possible without firm prior authorization from Congress. He hoped to get it from the lame duck session. While riding back to Albany from Hyde Park one night late in December 1932, Roosevelt (according to Tugwell) asked Douglas

to attach a clause to the appropriations bill giving the President leave to reduce personnel, abolish functions, transfer, etc., his idea being that he might carry out a reorganization (which Congress will never do) and have it done months before Congress comes back. Members could then unload the burdens on him and simply recognize a *fait accompli*. A new President, he said, can do this and get away with it, if Congress will come through with blanket permission.[14]

The Democrats did indeed act during the lame duck session, and tacked onto one of the appropriation bills authority for Roosevelt to reorganize and consolidate agencies, subject to congressional veto. Like the wartime Overman Act of the Wilson administration and earlier legislative authorization to Hoover, the measure allowed the President to issue executive orders which could go into effect after sixty days, provided one or the other house of Congress did not vote negatively in the meanwhile. In order that Roosevelt might be free to reorganize agencies as he pleased, Democrats in the House had refused Hoover's recommendations for the consolidation of fifty bureaus and commissions into a few agencies.[15]

As Democratic leaders in Congress knew, Roosevelt was directing Douglas to plan considerable reorganization. The congressional leaders assumed that he would make his principal economies through consolidation or elimination of agencies. They were startled, therefore, when on the evening of March 9 they were summoned to the White House an hour after Roosevelt had signed the Emergency Banking Bill. He explained the economy bill to them, telling them that he wanted power to reduce government salaries by more than $100 million, and revise the veterans' pensions to save more than $400 million. By delegating power to him to make the cuts, Roosevelt argued, members of Congress could avoid the wrath of the veterans' lobby; he was ready to be their whipping-boy and take the blame. "Shortly after midnight" the leaders departed, wrote Ernest Lindley, "a mixture of dazed, determined, and angry men." [16]

The next morning, March 10, 1933, Roosevelt sent Congress a brief, strong message, and with it the economy bill. Douglas, its chief draftsman, gave it an effective title, "A Bill to Maintain the Credit of the United States Government." * Its contents were of the sort that would have led Congress in more normal times to bury it in committee. Not only did it give the President power to reduce or even eliminate veterans' pensions, but also to reduce all government salaries by as much as 15 percent, including their own, according to a cost-of-living yardstick. Roosevelt's argument, foreshadowing "parity" for farmers, was that during the depression prices had fallen drastically, and that salaries should likewise drop, at least to a floor 15 percent below their earlier level. He took 1928 prices as the base point. For congressmen this meant that a vote for the economy bill was a vote to bring their own salaries down from $10,000 to $8,500, and in addition to bring down upon their heads the wrath of the veterans' organizations. So drastic was the measure that Roosevelt estimated it would reduce by nearly 13 percent the 1934 federal budget that would go into effect July 1, 1933.[17]

* Others who helped draft the bill were Swagar Sherley, Dean Acheson, Representative John McDuffie of Alabama, Representative Clifton A. Woodrum of Virginia, and General Frank Hines, adminstrator of Veterans' Affairs. As for the accompanying message, Douglas drafted and Moley revised it.

Assuredly the cuts would hurt some citizens, Roosevelt declared in his economy message, but failure to lower expenditures would injure all citizens. As for reorganization of pensions, Roosevelt implied that he did not intend to neglect the welfare of veterans and their families with legitimate claims to aid. "We are unanimous in upholding the duty of the Government to care for those who suffer in its defense and for their widows and orphans." The danger to the government necessitated subordinating benefits for some to the needs of all. He pledged, "If the Congress chooses to vest me with this responsibility it will be exercised in a spirit of justice to all, of sympathy to those who are in need and of maintaining inviolate the basic welfare of the United States." [18]

Federal solvency was essential to the national welfare, Roosevelt insisted. "Too often in recent history liberal governments have been wrecked on the rocks of loose fiscal policy." These were views with which almost every national commentator of stature — Walter Lippmann, Mark Sullivan, Frank Kent and others — heartily agreed.

Congressional leaders were not so unanimous. The economy bill evoked instant encomiums from Senator Harrison and all who had admired the testimony of Baruch and other ardent budget-balancers before his "depression clinic." Harrison emphasized the recovery factor: "The very fact that the short-term paper of the Treasury sold less than a year ago bore only 1 per cent [interest] and that the issue the other day had to go above 4 per cent is proof enough that something has got to be done and done now to demonstrate to the world that the credit of this government is to be maintained."

Senator Glass, who would have likewise agreed that the way to recovery was economy, struck at the most vulnerable point of the existing pension program, payments to men whose disabilities had no service connection. Said Glass, "I am not paying one dollar to any one who never heard a percussion cap or saw the Atlantic Ocean."

With conservatives solidly arrayed behind him, Roosevelt faced opposition from those long the supporters of veterans, some of whom were also ready to back liberal or even radical domestic legislation. Representative John E. Rankin of Mississippi told a cheering gallery that the veterans should not be penalized for the mistakes of the bankers. Senator Huey Long declared, "I didn't go to war and urged against it. But they haven't compensated the people who did go. Talk of balancing the budget! Let them balance the budget by scraping a little off the profiteers' profits from the war."

House members, many of whom depended upon American Legion support, were especially reluctant to accept the economy bill. The previous year they had voted down the mild pension cuts President Hoover had recommended, and most of them had received Legion aid in winning reelection. Some among them were inflationists who favored immediate payment of the World War I bonus in greenbacks, printing-press money. At their backs was the powerful Legion lobby which had never previously failed. One of the lobbyists used to tell each congressman, "If you don't support this bill, your successor will." Someone tipped off the lobby a day in advance that Roosevelt was about to send the economy bill to Congress. It telegraphed all Legion department adjutants and executive committeemen: "Wire your congressmen and Senators immediately opposing Congress abdicating its constitutional responsibility by granting to the President authority to repeal or amend existing veterans' laws without approval of Congress." [19]

There were initial signs that the lobbyists might once more carry the field. Two House Democratic leaders defected. The newly elected floor leader, Joseph W. Byrns of Tennessee, would not sponsor the bill. When Speaker Rainey assembled the Democratic representatives in caucus on the morning of March 11, the assistant floor leader, Thomas Cullen of Brooklyn, and some of the Tammany congressmen joined with western and southern agrarians to block the two-thirds vote which would have bound all Democrats to support the measure.

It took the energetic management of the chairman of the House Economy Committee, Representative John McDuffie of Alabama, and his conservative cohorts to win unimpaired passage of the economy bill. In the caucus and later on the floor of the House, McDuffie fought down an amendment that would have blocked the President from discontinuing any pension or from cutting any pension more than 25 percent. On the floor of the House on the afternoon of March 11, McDuffie worked in alliance with the Republican John Taber of New York, allotting only two hours to debate, and keeping opposition to a minimum. The result, with substantial Republican support, was a resounding victory for Roosevelt. The House passed the economy bill 266 to 138. Sixty-nine Republicans voted for the measure, and 92 Democrats against it; 62 percent of the Republicans and 68 percent of the Democrats voted for the measure.[20]

There was the possibility that the economy bill might run afoul of its enemies in the Senate, with its tradition of unlimited debate. It was not a large danger, but Roosevelt forestalled it, or at least so Washington newsmen thought at the time, by suddenly sending to Congress a highly popular proposal which the Senate could not approve until the economy bill was out of the way, a measure to legalize beer of 3.2 percent alcoholic content.

"I think this would be a good time for beer," Roosevelt told several friends who were with him at the White House on Sunday evening, March 12, waiting for him to make his Fireside Chat on the opening of the banks. He had obtained an opinion immediately after the election that the Volstead Act could constitutionally be amended to permit malt beverages and perhaps wine of limited alcoholic content. After Roosevelt delivered his radio talk, he took a copy of the 1932 Democratic platform, and quoting its pledge almost word for word, wrote a seventy-two-word message, perhaps the shortest ever to go to Congress: [21]

> I recommend to the Congress the passage of legislation for the immediate modification of the Volstead Act, in order to legalize the manufacture and sale of beer and other beverages of such alcoholic content as is permissible under the Constitution; and to provide through such manufacture and sale, by substantial taxes, a proper and much-needed revenue for the Government.
> I deem action at this time to be of the highest importance.[22]

Members of the House assembling the next noon greeted the message almost literally with a whoop, several of them shouting as the clerk finished reading the proposals, "Vote, vote, vote." They had planned to adjourn until the Senate had acted on the economy bill, but with enthusiasm began work on the new business, which urban Democrats knew would be highly popular among their constituents. Nor need House members with dry constituencies quake. The beer was (they were solemnly told) to be nonintoxicating because of its low alcoholic content, but would bring $100 million or perhaps even $150 million per year in taxes. Beer took over some of the headlines—a popular diversion which could be labeled a recovery measure.[23]

From March 13 to 15, the Senate debated the economy bill. An indication of its overwhelming support came early when a motion to refer it failed 60 to 20. The American Legion sought a compromise, offering to accept a straight 25 percent cut in pensions, but Senators Pittman and Robinson, who were managing the bill, saw no need to compromise. Indeed, the offer highlighted a main reason why not only much of the public, but indeed a considerable part of the Legion membership, sympathized more with Roosevelt than with the lobby. The lobbyists were ready to accept a serious cut in the income of those disabled in war and the widows of those killed in order to keep on the rolls those whose claims had no wartime origin. It stuck in the craw of many veterans that the lobby was most zealous in protecting the pension of the man who fell off a ladder in his own basement in 1926, who often had been receiving more compensation than widows. Cynics pointed out that dead men had no votes. In March 1933 the mood of many live men had changed. The national commander of the Legion, Louis A. Johnson (who in 1937 was to become assistant secretary of war), on March 5 declared, "The Legion wants nothing more than to be of service to America in this situation as our members were in 1917–1918." Through the debate over the economy bill and the attacks on pension cuts that followed, Johnson stood by his statement, and persuaded many Legion members and posts to support the President. Lobbyists admitted that mail to congressmen ran three to one in favor of economy. And much of it came from veterans.

In the Senate debate, opponents brought up the serious charge that the Legion lobby had implied, that the delegation of authority to Roosevelt would make him a dictator.

The conservative Josiah Bailey of North Carolina defended the President. "Our country will never stand for a dictator," he told the Senate, "but from the days of Washington, down through the times of Lincoln and Woodrow Wilson, it always has looked to a leader in times of stress. We are now spending $3,000,000 a day in veterans' benefits. Those who vote against this bill must vote for $500,000,000 in new taxes."

Nevertheless, Senator Champ Clark of Missouri returned to the argument that adoption of the economy program would mean that Congress would be abdicating its functions. He hastened to add that his opposition had "no faintest trace of lack of confidence in President Roosevelt."

Singularly enough, congressmen said little about the effect of the bill upon their own salaries or those of federal employees. Senator Borah of Idaho fought against reducing the pathetically small salaries of the many government workers receiving $1,000 per year or less, but his amendment was voted down.

On March 15, 1933, the Senate passed the economy bill 62 to 13, adopting only a few minor amendments. Four Democrats, including Long, Clark, and Pat McCarran of Nevada, voted against the bill; one was paired against it; one, Carl Hayden of Arizona, failed to vote because of previous commitments to his constituents.

The Democratic ranks in the Senate had held almost solid, yet Roosevelt and his legislative managers tried to repair what might develop into a broadening breach. His friends and advisers, Arthur Krock reported, assured worried senators that Roosevelt intended to respect the separation of powers between the executive and legislative branches of government and not request laws involving "constitutional dictatorship."

The question of whether the quick voting of blanket authorizations to the President was a move toward dictatorship could not easily be brushed aside in the spring of 1933. The issue of *Time* covering the inauguration of Roosevelt bore on its cover a picture of Adolf Hitler, who in a rigged election was consolidating his power in Germany and beginning to crush all opposition. Whether the United States was witnessing in their early stages parallels to Hitler, Mussolini, and Lenin was a serious enough question that the august General John J. Pershing publicly addressed himself to it. Pershing, writing in the *American Magazine*, said he had not been surprised in Europe a few months before when he was frequently queried whether the United States was drifting toward dictatorship. He was startled upon his return to find some Americans of importance engaging in the same kind of talk. To all such suggestions, Pershing's answer was an emphatic "no," that American democratic institutions were far different from those in European nations where dictators had come into power. What was happening in the United States in 1933 was distinctly in keeping with the nation's traditions:

> There is a method, staunchly American and tried by experience, by which we may attain speed and decisiveness for the period of the emergency. We have seen it applied in war and in peace.
>
> Faced with the necessity of speedily mobilizing the entire military and industrial resources of the nation, President Wilson asked for and obtained extraordinary powers. . . .
>
> Under this regime mistakes were made, of course, but the nation as a whole *did* move forward, steadily and irresistibly, toward its goal.
>
> In recent months we have been faced with an emergency just as real as that of 1917. More serious, indeed, because in war we at least know who our enemies are. . . .
>
> With a national crisis pressing hard upon us, it was a time which cried aloud for speedy, decisive action. Congress with its time-honored and complicated procedure, plainly was not equipped to give us such decisive action. . . .
>
> Here, certainly, it would be thought in Germany, Russia, Italy, or the Balkans, dictatorship was inevitable.
>
> But Americans don't do things that way. The American people understood, as did their President, that decisive action was necessary. The necessary power, therefore, was quickly concentrated in the Executive. He was given a free hand to deal with the banking crisis. He was given broad authority to reorganize the government bureaus and cut governmental expenditures. He was able to act with the speed and efficiency of a dictator.
>
> He was not a dictator, however, in any true sense of the word. His powers were not seized, but granted voluntarily. They were, furthermore, definitely limited in extent. The procedure, in fact, is democracy's own method of acting quickly in time of crisis.[24]

General Pershing's analogy to President Wilson's assumption of unusual powers in the First World War was widely echoed, and indeed reflected what many in Congress wanted of Roosevelt and what he himself was ready to undertake. It was a useful device, but also one mischievous in several ways, as William E. Leuchtenburg has pointed out; it could lead to slipshod emergency action rather than carefully planned, permanent undertakings. But emergency action was inevitable in the spring of 1933, and the drawing upon the experience of World War I not only speeded action but seemed patriotic and therefore more palatable to a basically conservative electorate. It was cautious men in both the Senate and House, seeing Congress divided and ineffective, who had felt by the end of the lame duck session that the President ought to assume special powers — to achieve traditional ends. Representative Robert L. Doughton of North Carolina, a powerful iconoclast on the House Ways and Means Committee who had fought Hoover's 1930 tax proposals as executive aggrandizement, on March 14, 1933, wrote a constituent in words that summed up congressional majority sentiment on the analogy to war and the issue of dictatorship:

> I do not think that anyone need be alarmed about the granting of powers to President Roosevelt to effect necessary economies, being exercised in a "Dictatorial" way. We are now at war with poverty, distress and suffering, and unless we have some leadership, we will never end the war. I think the entire country has faith in President Roosevelt — that he will be fair to the citizens of the nation — and I am therefore following his leadership in matters to get us out of our present economic distress.[25]

No reassurances, no matter how prestigious the source, could convince a certain number of those alarmed by Roosevelt that he was not on his way toward dictatorship. What were the forebodings of a handful in March 1933 continued as the dark predictions of a minority throughout the entirety of Roosevelt's presidency.

Roosevelt attracted little public attention in the other, and perhaps more important, aspect of his economy program. Quietly he worked all through the spring of 1933 with the budget director in major reductions of departmental personnel and expenditures and minor reorganization or elimination of agencies. There was surprisingly little outcry from the congressmen who customarily protected these agencies. Perhaps they were being kept too busy with the avalanche of proposals for new emergency agencies. Perhaps it was because Roosevelt was withholding most patronage until the session ended, and the new agencies would provide ample openings for loyal followers. In any event, Roosevelt and Douglas trimmed away at every department.

The President's premises remained clear enough. During the years of the fatted calf when Republicans had run the administration, departments had become too big and the number of free services to business had become outrageous. It was a view that could emerge from a reading of *Our Wonderland of Bureaucracy* (1932) by the arch-conservative James Beck or the fat, descriptive *American Leviathan* (1930) by the liberal Charles A. Beard. Already the government was frighteningly large and wasteful compared with what the generation of 1933 had known in its youth. The irony is that it was not rendering a fraction of the services that a later generation expects of the federal government, thanks in considerable part to Roosevelt.

Roosevelt's prejudices against the Republican services to business directed his aim. That Hoover's Department of Commerce was a prime target was no secret even before inauguration day. Secretary Roper knew, it was publicly reported, that he had been chosen to preside over its sharp contraction. Hoover's pride had been a corps of commercial attachés, operating from the Bureau of Foreign and Domestic Commerce, attached to American embassies to develop overseas trade. Roosevelt cut the budget of the bureau a third and dispensed with most of the commercial attachés. "There are two hundred and fifty of them running all around the world having a grand time," Roosevelt remarked at a press conference in June 1933. "Now, where is the saving on that? It is in eliminating all but about fifty of them." These fifty Roosevelt attached to the State Department. Business should pay for whatever services it received from the government — even shippers toward whom, like everyone nautical, Roosevelt had always been partial, in theory should not receive subsidies. He had thought in January of asking for special taxes or tolls to reimburse the government for $60 million per year it spent on maintaining waterways and navigational facilities. When he faced political reality, Roosevelt prudently did not act.[26]

The National Bureau of Standards, which saved businessmen many millions per year (business estimates had been $300 million) through its scientific services and promoting standards of types, did during the New Deal obtain nominal income ($108,500 in FY 1938) from its testing fees. The Census Bureau, which provided inestimable aid to business through its statistical data, was able to collect small fees ($11,500 in FY 1938). Both sustained deep cuts; the Bureau of Standards budget dropped by half in two years, throwing numerous scientists out of work. Some later obtained employment on relief projects at work for which they were ill-suited, often at stipends not substantially lower than their previous nominal salaries. Scientific work lagged, and the Bureau of Standards did not again reach its 1931 level until 1940. Gaps appeared in statistics, for instance, through the dropping of completion of statistics for 216 cities and the compiling of financial statistics of the states. Some of these gaps in statistics could never later be filled.

By June, Roosevelt was able to boast to newspapermen that the

Department of Commerce expenditures were dropping from $41 million to $29 million through "lopping off employees and stopping the spending of money." Secretary Roper even laid off his half-brother.[27]

Roosevelt planned no New Deal for science, as was apparent to Tugwell from his earliest conversation on reorganization with Roosevelt and Douglas. In mid-January 1933, Tugwell enlisted the aid of Harold G. Moulton of the Brookings Institution and Charles E. Merriam of the University of Chicago, two of the most distinguished experts on public administration, to prepare memoranda on research work in the various departments. Fearing that "there is apt to be a good deal of slashing here and there," Tugwell was concerned that "this should be as intelligent as is possible under the circumstances."

Tugwell feared that research agencies would suffer most under undiscriminating attack and that they could be least spared in the long run. Roosevelt implied to him that the agencies would be cut, and laughed at Tugwell's mournful expression. Later, when Tugwell was assigned to the Department of Agriculture, he conferred with Douglas, promising cooperation but asking to be allowed his own procedure. Tugwell had scant success; 567 workers on scientific projects in the department lost their jobs, and many others had their salaries cut to not much above a subsistence level.[28]

Other services of the government received rather more consideration. Secretary Ickes mourned when he found he would have to cut $5 million from the Interior budget that it would be a tough nut to crack. He received some sympathy when he and his fellow cabinet officers took up the subject in a cabinet meeting on April 4, 1933, pointing to what would happen to the Indian Bureau, National Parks, and some Negro activities. Vice President Garner gratified Ickes by commenting that he thought it would be an error to reduce services to Negroes.[29]

Although Roosevelt loved the navy, he cut into its appropriation and that of the army. Indeed, next to what he recouped from veterans' services he made his greatest economies in the regular budget there, since that was the only other branch of the government with relatively large expenditures. Years later, ex-President Hoover, representing himself as the friend of defense, pointed out that "at a time when Hitler, Stalin, the Japanese and Mussolini were loudly threatening the peace of the world," Roosevelt cut the defense budget from $752 million in FY 1932 to $531 million in FY 1934. But Roosevelt was able to charge some 1934 defense expenditures to the emergency budget; the reduction there was not so large as it seemed.[30]

Overall, Roosevelt was able by the beginning of June to boast to newspapermen of the "billion dollars that we are already saving through lopping off of functions." Of course, parallel to these economies in the regular budget, there were the billions that he was persuading Congress to pour into the emergency budget. This involved no hypocrisy on Roosevelt's part. Before his inauguration he had planned the emergency budget to carry the temporary burden of relief, hoping that with the rapid return of recovery that budget could quickly be eliminated and that overall he could keep the government finances in balance.

Roosevelt's tinkering with the reorganization of the federal administration attracted less attention during the spring of 1933. The press all but ignored Title III of the Economy Act of March 1933, which extended for two years the President's authority to reorganize through executive orders. The orders were to go into effect after sixty days if neither house of Congress disapproved.

Through the spring, Roosevelt day by day talked to Douglas about one or another aspect of reorganization; what developed were changes here and there rather than any comprehensive overhauling. By June he was ready to present a list of minor proposals to Congress. Reorganization, he explained at a press conference, would save relatively little money. In the case of the Commerce Department, for example, it would amount to no more than a million and a half dollars. Rather, its major importance was to bring about greater efficiency, which he asserted was being achieved rapidly:

> That is being done particularly by intradepartmental orders that do not have to go to Congress. Those are coming right along; I suppose I sign one almost every day. . . . Then there are orders affecting interdepartmental work. Part of that can be carried through without submitting it to Congress. Then there will be others which will be submitted to Congress before they go home. —
> So that the reorganization . . . is proceeding in a perfectly orderly way.[31]

On June 10, 1933, just before Congress was scheduled to adjourn, Roosevelt sent to the Capitol Executive Order No. 6166 "consolidating and abolishing many governmental agencies."[32]

It was an unspectacular list, containing some useful recommendations such as the consolidation of disbursing under the Treasury Department and the abolition of minor commissions, including an oddity that caught the eye of newspaper readers, the elimination of the National Screw Thread Commission, one of Hoover's agencies for standardization which after its demise in 1933 was later revived. At the end were significant recommendations that would normally never run the gauntlet of Congress: the cutting by 25 percent of costs of aid to vocational education, agricultural colleges, experiment stations, and extension work — the great national empire of the Farm Bureau.[33]

There were cries of outrage from the Senate. Reed of Pennsylvania called the message "a contemptuous gesture." La Follette, Long, and Hiram Johnson all expressed their displeasure. Nevertheless, Roosevelt obtained what he wanted.[34]

Through 1934, Roosevelt continued to make a few minor transfers and economies. In the fall of 1933, his eye even fell upon the United States Geographic Board. "There exist in the United States thousands of cases of duplication of names, and this involves not merely geographical units such as lakes, mountains, rivers, etc., but also a great many towns," he wrote Douglas. "For instance, a lot of mail must get misdirected today because of name duplications of postoffices. It occurs to me that the U.S. Geographic Board would be the agency best fitted to look into this. What do you think? Mac [Marvin McIntyre] suggests that this also would give the Geographic Board something to do!" Douglas replied that the Geographic Board already was doing some of this work, but he feared a presidential assignment might give it an excuse to expand and cost more. Rather, Douglas suggested, it should be abolished and its work turned over to the Library of Congress. The upshot was that it was indeed abolished, but its functions went to Secretary Ickes's growing Department of the Interior. There were immediate protests from geographers and map manufacturers who feared that the Interior Department under political pressure might assign irrelevant names. After all, Ickes had without consultation changed the name of Hoover Dam to Boulder Dam. All this attention of the President, the director of the budget, and geographers was focused on a commission whose total expenditures during the fiscal year, including the printing of a report, came to less than $11,000.[35]

There were larger schemes being discussed in the spring of 1933. Roosevelt proposed changing the name of the Department of Labor to "Department of Labor and Welfare," authorizing the Children's Bureau to use the services of the Public Health Service, and perhaps transferring both the Public Health Service and the Office of Education into the Labor Department. Nothing materialized.[36]

Not until his second term did Roosevelt turn toward major reorganization of the executive branch and reduction of government expenditures so drastic that the emergency as well as regular budget would be brought into balance. Meanwhile, through the early months of his presidency, for a few minutes almost every morning while he was still in his bedroom, Roosevelt saw his director of the budget to talk over specific economies, and discuss larger programs. In the aftermath of the "great victory" that the economy bill represented, Douglas was most enthusiastic. "Roosevelt has been magnificent," he commented to his father. "He flirts with ideas, has imagination, is rather slow to come to a definite decision, but when he finally does is willing to go through to the end. This at least is my experience so far." Roosevelt for his part, commented to Moley one morning after Douglas had departed from the presidential bedchamber, "In twelve years he would be a good Democratic candidate for President." [37]

Gradually the warmth between Roosevelt and Douglas cooled, but economical, efficient government continued to be Roosevelt's ideal throughout his presidency. It was not an aberration or enthusiasm limited to 1933. His efforts in 1933 were in some respects misdirected and a failure. He went too far in budget-cutting and not far enough in reshaping the administration. Concerning Roosevelt's sincerity there can be no doubt. He returned to the Treasury 15 percent of his own first salary check as a symbol of what he thought everyone ought to be doing, in and out of the government. When Josephus Daniels urged him to speak up on behalf of schoolteachers and university professors, who were in desperate straits, his reply was obtuse, considering the drastic salary cuts and nonpayment of educators, but it was in keeping with his firm beliefs in March 1933:

> One of the difficulties is that most of the College Presidents and Commissioners of Education have been unwilling to cut costs in proportion to their enterprises. In most parts of the country the past decade has seen a very large increase in teachers' salaries, and even if all teachers were cut 15%, like government employees, they would still be getting relatively more than in 1914.! [38]

Viewed in the setting of the spring of 1933, Roosevelt's efforts seemed valiant rather than hard-hearted. Sir Ronald Lindsay, who was later far from enthusiastic toward the President, reported to the Foreign Office on March 15,

> It remained for Mr. Roosevelt to lead the attack on . . . scandalous abuse and thereby demonstrate his ability to govern in the national interest and his determination to defeat political privilege, whether that of the veterans or the moneyed interests. . . .
> I think there is little doubt that this vigorous and determined assault on the national problems has already induced a revival of confidence throughout the country.[39]

Although conservatives would have been happy to stop at this point, already Roosevelt was moving on toward other aspects of recovery programs.

CHAPTER XV

Employing an Army of Youths
in the Woods

It is essential to our recovery program that measures immediately be enacted aimed at unemployment relief.
— FDR TO CONGRESS, *March 21, 1933.*

During Roosevelt's first days in office, while he was pursuing economy,
he also faced the imperative need to aid the twelve or thirteen million
unemployed. A large program would easily cost billions of dollars, and
it was some weeks before he made up his mind whether he could foster
aid on so large a scale. There were rumors, which in mid-March he
denied, that he would float a half-billion-dollar bond issue. Meanwhile,
one segment of his relief proposals promised not to injure seriously his
budget tightening, and this he rushed through Congress before the
end of the month. It created the Civilian Conservation Corps, to send a
quarter million unemployed youths out of the cities to improve the
forests. Incidentally this action gave him several additional weeks to
decide how expensive a public works program he would accept.[1]

Those counseling Roosevelt had long engaged in a running debate
whether massive public works construction of the sort Senators Wagner,
La Follette, and Costigan demanded would be a wise means through
which to seek relief and recovery. The pressure from the progressives
was considerable, but from the outset of the depression, Roosevelt (while
governor of New York) had taken a wary view of public works construction as a palliative. His criticisms of President Hoover's program
had been more than campaign opportunism. Roosevelt's ideal, like
Hoover's, would be a public works program that would ultimately repay
the cost of construction. While the progressive senators would have
liked to pour $5 billion into public works, Roosevelt thought Hoover
had been able to find only about $900 million worth of self-liquidating
projects, and that only a limited number existed. Reinforcing Roosevelt's
conservatism was Budget Director Douglas and economists like Ralph

Robey of the *New York Post*, who felt that a balanced budget was essential if business confidence were to be restored. To be sure, they recognized that heavy federal spending would stimulate the economy, but they felt that it would be a very small stimulus compared with that of business resurgence — and that deficit spending would prevent business recovery. The articulate, informed young banker, James Warburg, thus presented the case early one March morning at Moley's office. According to Moley's diary: [2]

> As a conservative, [Warburg] is tremendously concerned lest the government enter upon a huge public works program. The expenditure of billions of dollars, he says, will be only a drop in the bucket — and put only an infinitesimal portion of the population back at work. Something more fundamental must be done to right the balance. Further, he says that wild talk about huge projects will surely cause the bottom to drop out of the bond market and make impossible further government borrowing.[3]

Moley, while feeling that as an assistant to the President he must bring to Roosevelt the arguments of Senator Wagner and his colleagues and of Brain Trusters like Tugwell, also told Roosevelt that he sympathized with Douglas, Robey, and Warburg. Yet Moley felt something must be done for the unemployed, and Roosevelt regarded it as imperative. This was the problem Roosevelt faced, and as usual he tried to solve it by reconciling the two recommended courses of action and proceeding along a line between them.

For some days, Roosevelt did indeed toy with the idea of asking for only a half-billion-dollar program, which he would finance through floating an issue of baby bonds to bring small hoards of dollars out of hiding. He would use this money not for large construction projects, but to put people to work immediately. There were numerous schemes being pressed for his attention. Frances Perkins has reminisced that there were over two thousand plans on her desk and as many more on Roosevelt's. One, which the governor of Florida had brought to his attention, he had Ickes, Wallace, and Dern, his secretaries of interior, agriculture, and war, look into on March 7. It was a proposal to move some of the unemployed onto unused agricultural lands he would obtain from the State of Florida. The Florida scheme went no further, but Roosevelt acted immediately in other directions, and on March 9 supervised the drafting of a bill.[4]

When Frances Perkins saw the bill she was troubled, and over breakfast with Raymond Moley on March 14 explained her objections. At nine that same morning Moley took the criticism to Roosevelt, who for the first time expounded to Moley his proposal, not simply to give men public works jobs, but to assign an army of unemployed youth to re-forestation. Moley, dazzled, immediately thought of William James's essay "The Moral Equivalent of War," and asked Roosevelt if perhaps his thought was not a result of the influence of James upon him at Harvard. Roosevelt confessed he had known James only as a famous professor with abundant whiskers, then said, "But look here! I think I'll go ahead with this — the way I did on beer." Roosevelt meant he wanted to send a message and bill to Congress without further ado.[5]

The brilliant impulsiveness that Moley thought he saw in Roosevelt that morning was in reality only the President's theatrical streak. He had not only personally been giving a good deal of time and thought to the reforestation scheme, but had consulted a number of experts in the process. He simply had not informed Moley of what was going on, and enjoyed popping it to him as though it were an improvisation.

The idea had been prevalent throughout the country, as Roosevelt well knew. He later sent this word to someone who was sure he had first thought of the scheme, adding that there should be credit enough for everyone. Indeed, said Roosevelt, he himself as governor of New York had decided as early as the fall of 1929 to ask the legislature for "additional funds for conservation work to be used primarily to employ people out of work." By 1932, he had ten thousand men from relief rolls planting trees. Several European nations had opened conservation camps for the jobless. He expressed no pleasure when Tugwell, who helped him with planning in the winter of 1932–1933, called Mussolini's efforts to his attention. The camps in Germany after Hitler came into power became notorious paramilitary units, abhorrent to American liberals and a perversion of Roosevelt's vision — but that came later. In his acceptance address at the 1932 Democratic convention, Roosevelt had promised to put a million men to work fighting soil erosion and timber famine. After he was elected, he involved both state and federal forestry experts in preliminary exploration of several approaches. Especially he was interested in federal purchase of cut-over or second-growth land which with much work and many years' growth could become valuable forest. As President he obtained appropriations to buy land.[6]

Somehow, during his first week in office, on March 9, Roosevelt fitted in time to draft a bill incorporating his reforestation scheme.* He summoned the secretaries of war and interior and their legal officers, together with several others, for a conference. He asked few questions and did most of the talking himself, laying before them in considerable detail plans to employ 500,000 men in public service, to plant trees, protect and improve forests, and engage in flood control. Financing was

---

* FDR also found time on March 8 to draw up detailed instructions for the spring planting of trees at Hyde Park.[7]

to come through a bond issue. Turning to the two legal experts present, the solicitor of the Interior Department and the acting judge advocate general of the army, he handed them a one-page memorandum and asked them to draft a bill by nine o'clock that evening. When they returned, they found Roosevelt in his upstairs study with the cabinet officers, several congressional leaders, and his secretary, Howe. Roosevelt read the draft and pointed out that it failed to provide for the condemnation of private property; Howe suggested striking out the word "enlistment" because it was a military term. The lawyers made the changes.[8]

It was the provision in the bill that the unemployed receive housing and sustenance but only a dollar a day in wages that worried Frances Perkins, secretary of labor, who had not been included in the conference. That was all well and good so far as reforestation was concerned, she told Moley, but flood control was another matter, since, she said (according to Moley), "when it is applied to public works such as levee building, drainage work, etc., it tends to bring down the price of free labor to the same level. And this is a most pernicious thing." [9]

Miss Perkins had indeed identified a serious objection to Roosevelt's plan, which, as it then stood, could include public works in general. In fact, Ickes had described it in his diary as a public works bill, even though the only specifics he mentioned were reforestation and flood control. Organized labor would strongly object to a dollar-a-day wage for public works.

Further, Roosevelt, in hurrying only this bill to Congress, might dismay his progressive supporters in the Senate who had long sought billions for public works, and his secretary of labor, Miss Perkins, who had been preparing a bill to authorize federal grants-in-aid to states for direct relief. Advocates of both measures might feel eliminated unless they were included in discussions of the scheme.

Immediately after taking office, Miss Perkins had met to plan federal welfare grants with William Hodson, director of the Welfare Council of New York City, and Harry Hopkins, head of the Temporary Emergency Relief Administration, which Roosevelt as governor had established in New York State. She then worked with Senators Costigan, La Follette, and Wagner to draft a bill. On the morning of March 14, she had asked Moley if Roosevelt would be willing to consider it.[10]

Of course Roosevelt would. He accepted Moley's suggestion that he refer the relief matter to appropriate cabinet members, and this time included Miss Perkins along with Dern, Ickes, and Wallace. He asked them to constitute themselves an informal committee to coordinate plans for the proposed Civilian Conservation Corps, including suggestions on various sorts of public works. The next day they reported back to Roosevelt that they believed the CCC should be strictly limited to forestry and soil erosion projects in order not to depress wage levels and undercut job opportunities. They also recommended that the two other aspects of the unemployment relief program should each be proposed in a separate bill: federal grants-in-aid to states for direct relief work, and a large labor-producing public works program. When Roosevelt met the next day with Miss Perkins, Hopkins, La Follette, and Costigan, he promised them he would include a promise of both grants-in-aid and public works in his message.[11]

On the morning of March 15, while the cabinet members were sitting in Ickes's office deciding upon their recommendations, Roosevelt was holding a press conference at the White House. He delivered a graphic disquisition to the reporters on the ways in which 200,000 unemployed men could improve woodland through clearing out scrub growth, thinning saplings, and cutting thirty- or forty-foot-wide fire breaks.[12]

The question of a dollar a day came up immediately; Roosevelt would not confirm it. The reporter who made the query was not appalled at the smallness of the wage but at the largeness of the projected federal expenditure. "Even at a dollar a day for a year," he remarked, "that is enormous . . . a half a billion or one billion . . . on this one item."

"These people would be people who are today on the dole," the President responded. "They are performing no useful work." [13]

In the next several days, Roosevelt penciled a draft message to Congress in which he promised that both Federal Relief aid to states and a public works program would be forthcoming a little later, and asked immediately for the Civilian Conservation Corps.* On March 19, Roose-

* FDR's handwritten first draft compared with the final version of the message gives a glimpse of how he wrote and revised, and something of Moley's contributions.

Here are the first two paragraphs of the draft:

Work Bill

The other legislation I ask is related to the giving of occupation to many of our unemployed. The time is too short to permit me to submit at this moment to you a large practical labor producing program of useful construction projects that would not burden future budget demands. This we must act on as soon as full consideration has been given to its details.

Nor do I feel it advisable at this moment to ask for an immediate further appropriation for grants in aid to States for relief work. I am informed that the balance appropriated to the R.F.C. is sufficient to carry on with until May. However, I suggest setting up at this time a Federal Relief Administration to coordinate relief work with and among the several States & Territories and the District of Columbia. . . .[14]

By comparison, the same passages in the final message read:

It is essential to our recovery program that measures immediately be enacted aimed at unemployment relief. A direct attack on this problem suggests three types of legislation.

velt gave the draft to Moley to revise and expand. He then shortened Moley's new version, and twice polished it.[16]

The message Roosevelt sent Congress on March 21 accompanying a bill authorizing the Civilian Conservation Corps followed the recommendations of his cabinet officers. The CCC was to engage in "simple work, not interfering with normal employment, and confining itself to forestry, the prevention of soil erosion, flood control, and similar projects." It would also conform for the time being with his emphasis upon a balanced budget; he asked no new funds, saying that unobligated funds previously appropriated for public works would be sufficient to carry it for several months. Then, with enthusiasm, he stated his long-held views on the worth of the program:

> More important, however, than the material gains will be the moral and spiritual value of such work. The overwhelming majority of unemployed Americans, who are now walking the streets and receiving private or public relief, would infinitely prefer to work. We can take a vast army of these unemployed out into healthful surroundings. We can eliminate to some extent at least the threat that enforced idleness brings to spiritual and moral stability. It is not a panacea for all the unemployment but it is an essential step in this emergency.[17]

Several days later at a press conference, Roosevelt at last began to talk about the inescapable question of how he hoped to balance the budget yet spend sums that would almost at once run into the billions on feeding and giving work to the unemployed. The formula was the one that Moley had suggested to him the previous May, and which had been aired in January — the establishment of an emergency budget parallel to the regular budget which he insisted he would balance:

> Q. With reference to the budget: Is it fair to ask whether it will be possible to balance it in any particular year?
> THE PRESIDENT: There . . . you have to go into a long detailed explanation of what you mean. . . . What we are trying to do is to

The first is the enrollment of workers now by the Federal Government for such public employment as can be quickly started and will not interfere with the demand for or the proper standards of normal employment.

The second is grants to States for relief work.

The third extends to a broad public works labor-creating program.

With reference to the latter I am now studying the many projects suggested and the financial questions involved. I shall make recommendations to the Congress presently.

In regard to grants to States for relief work, I advise you that the remainder of the appropriation of last year will last until May. Therefore, and because a continuance of Federal aid is still a definite necessity for many States, a further appropriation must be made before the end of this special session.

I find a clear need for some simple Federal machinery to coordinate and check these grants of aid. I am, therefore, asking that you establish the office of Federal Relief Administrator, whose duty it will be to scan requests for grants and to check the efficiency and wisdom of their use.[15]

have the expenditures of the Government reduced, or, in other words to have the normal regular Government operations balanced and not only balanced, but to have some left over to start paying the debt. On the other hand, is it fair to put into that part of the budget expenditures that relate to keeping human beings from starving in this emergency[?] I should say probably not.

Q. That might be taken care of in the bond issue?

THE PRESIDENT: Yes. . . . It is very important to differentiate between normal running expenses of the Government and emergencies. For instance, suppose the City of New York was destroyed overnight by an earthquake and you had a loss of seven million lives and a great many billions of dollars of property. Should the reconstruction of the city and relief of the relatives of seven million people killed — should that come out of the ordinary running expenses of the Government? That is an extreme case, but it illustrates the point. You cannot let people starve, but this starvation crisis is not an annually recurring charge.[18]

At the end of March 1933, since large appropriations had not yet commenced, Roosevelt's explanations, given as background to reporters, did not seem very important news.

With national attention focused upon the farm relief bill that had been introduced five days earlier, even the CCC bill attracted relatively little attention. Labor leaders and some liberals denounced the proposal. The ordinarily bland president of the American Federation of Labor, William Green, raised not only the protest Miss Perkins had expected against the $30 per month pay, but also against the backdrop of Mussolini and Hitler raised the specter of army regimentation: "We cannot believe that the time has come when the United States should supply relief through the creation of a form of compulsory military service." Socialist Norman Thomas declared: "Such work-camps fit into the psychology of a Fascist, not a Socialist state." In the House, the chairman of the Committee on Labor, William P. Connery of Massachusetts, echoed these misgivings.[19]

Roosevelt made a blunt, cogent retort at his press conference the next morning, but would not allow himself to be quoted directly because he did not want to seem to be answering William Green:

In the first place, they all talk about military control and militarization, but that is just utter rubbish. The camps will be run just like those in any big project — Boulder Dam or anything like that. Obviously, you have to have some form of policing. In other words, you cannot allow a man in a dormitory to get up in the middle of the night and blow a bugle [laughter]. You have got to have order — just perfectly normal order, the same as you would have in any kind of a big job. That is so much for the military end.

Then, on the point of interference with work. . . . This is not competition, because these fellows have no chance to get a job at the present time and 250,000 men . . . is a mere drop in the bucket. It is just a little step toward the relieving of 12 million people, but it is a practical step.

Then take the other point about competition. To be sure, they are to be paid only a dollar a day but it costs the Government another dollar a day to take care of them, and, in the area in which most of these people will work and in which the work would be done, a $2 a day wage for that kind of work would probably be higher than in a great many places than what labor is actually paid, or has been paid. You take down in the State of Georgia where I know something about outdoor labor, even in 1929. In 1929 their pay was about $1.50 or $1.75 a day with no quarters, no food, no clothing. From that you will see that it is not so much out of line with the existing wage schedule for that type of work in those localities.

Of course, any skilled labor that is brought in from outside the ranks of those boys will be paid the normal rate for labor.[20]

Roosevelt's remarks are an indication of how able and informed he could be in extemporaneous discourse. He must have said much the same things to the members of the House and Senate labor committees when he invited them to the White House that evening. The objections were utter nonsense, he told them, and by the end of the conference most of them agreed. He failed to convince Connery, who continued to demand higher wages and shorter hours, but won the chairman of the Senate committee, David I. Walsh of Massachusetts, who helped rush the bill through joint hearings. At the hearings, Miss Perkins defended the proposal in such a clear unequivocal fashion that she gained additional congressional support. Others testified that the Department of Labor, not the army, would select the men, and Chief of Staff Douglas MacArthur assured the committees there would be "no military training whatsoever." As a conciliatory gesture toward Connery and the labor leaders, the Senate committee amended the bill to delete the $30-a-month provision, but gave the President such broad powers that he could run the program as he pleased and pay what he wished.

After two days' debate, the CCC bill passed the Senate on March 28 by a voice vote. There was opposition in the House, not only from Connery and several supporters of organized labor, but from Republican conservatives, together with two southern Democrats, Lister Hill of Alabama and John J. McSwain of South Carolina, who opposed granting Roosevelt further unrestricted power. The House made one vital amendment to the bill — the proposal of its only Negro member, the Republican Oscar De Priest of Illinois — "that no discrimination shall be made on account of race, color, or creed . . . under the provisions of this Act." The House also passed the measure by a voice vote; the Senate accepted the House's amendment, and the bill went to the White House. Roosevelt signed it on March 31.[21]

Acting as though the Civilian Conservation Corps were his personal New Deal agency, Roosevelt lavished much time in creating its rather complex machinery and rushing it into operation. His secretary, Howe, devoted even more time to its details, especially in the first three months. For its head Roosevelt, in a conciliatory gesture toward the AFL, chose one of the vice presidents of the International Association of Machinists, Robert Fechner, from the Boston area. Roosevelt and Howe had become acquainted with him when he came to Washington to help settle labor disputes during World War I, and during the 1932 campaign he had brought Roosevelt the backing of the Machinists' Union. Roosevelt's acquaintance with him was so slight that on April 3 when he sketched a scheme of organization for the CCC, he jotted at the head "Fechter." But the choice turned out to be felicitous. Fechner, a simple, old-fashioned man, thought of himself among the Brain Trusters as "a potato bug amongst dragonflies," but in a loyal and affable, even if a rather unimaginative way, he ran the CCC throughout its existence.[22]

Drawing organization charts was one of Roosevelt's favorite pastimes, even if he paid little attention to them once they went into operation. He thought of calling the head the director of Reforestation Activities, then (perhaps because it was more politic), scratched that out on the executive order and wrote "Director of Emergency Conservation Work." That title stuck. Under Fechner were lines running to five assistants and four departments: Labor was to handle enrollment, the War Department would handle outfitting, housing and medical care; Interior and Agriculture would be in charge of the work.[23]

"I want *personally* to check on the location scope etc of the camps, size [,] work to be done etc.," Roosevelt wrote under the diagram. For some weeks he and Howe did make it their personal function. When General Hines informed him that the Veterans' Administration had supplies in depots that could be used, Roosevelt queried Budget Director Douglas, "This sounds good. How shall we take advantage of it?" Douglas began a canvass of all departments for surplus supplies. The War Department sent a cost estimate on food and shelter; Howe gave it a preliminary okay, but Roosevelt wrote on it, "This figure of $1.92 a day, not including transportation or wages, is absurdly high — it must be greatly reduced." [24]

Enrollment in the CCC began quickly. Roosevelt set aside $10 million to provide for 25,000 young men for six months, and issued initial quotas to enroll 2,500 from several eastern and midwestern cities, ranging from 7,500 for New York to 400 for Kansas City. Despite the latitude of the enabling legislation, they were to be for the most part single young men from families on relief, willing to serve six months and to send home $22 to $25 of their $30 monthly wages. The first man to enroll was typical, Fiore Rizzo, an unemployed nineteen-year-old New Yorker from a family of thirteen whose father had been out of work for three years. He passed an army physical examination, signed over $25 of his pay to his family, and took an oath. At an army camp in New Rochelle he received an issue of olive drab army work clothes, blankets, and a mess kit. After two weeks of physical conditioning and learning to obey camp rules — but no military drills — he went off to work in a National Forest.[25]

The personal but not necessarily careful scrutiny that Roosevelt and Howe tried to give every detail of the CCC in the spring of 1933 was at one point an embarrassment, and continually created a bottleneck. The embarrassment came when Howe approved the offer of some promoter to sell 200,000 mess kits to the CCC, at the ostensibly money-saving price of $1.40 each. A Republican senator denounced the deal, declaring the army would have provided the same kit for 32 cents. A hearing before the Senate Military Affairs Committee ensued; it exonerated Howe of corruption but not negligence.[26]

The bottleneck became intolerable. Despite their interest, Roosevelt and his secretary were both too busy to give daily attention to the details of the CCC. Papers piled high, unsigned, on Howe's desk, and at one point there had to be a frantic search for some vital memoranda that needed immediate approval. Through his own overcaution, Fechner added to the delays as he felt his way into his job. Further, too many of the campsites Roosevelt did approve were in the West and too few in the East, where most of the workers were being recruited. While many of the new CCC workers awaited assignment to camps not yet built, there were unresolved disputes about camp construction and a myriad of unsettled administrative details. Roosevelt's goal of 250,000 young men by July seemed impossible. At this point of crisis on May 12, the army representative, Colonel Duncan Major, proposed abandoning existing policy and delegating authority. The Labor Department should provide the War Department with 8,540 men per day which it should move to camps. Roosevelt gave his approval, and the CCC began to burgeon. The army assumed far more authority than had first been contemplated, and by July 1 it had constructed 1,300 camps, filling them with 274,375 men, thus, Colonel Major reported to Roosevelt, breaking "all American war and peacetime records." [27]

As the CCC took shape, it became useful to Roosevelt in several unexpected ways. In April, he extended its benefits to 14,400 American Indians, whose poverty had been compounded by years of drought; most of them were married men who continued to live at home rather than in camps. He also authorized hiring 24,375 "local experienced men" at Civil Service wage scales, most of them former foresters or lumbermen, to supervise and train the workers. Employment of these local unemployed relieved resistance to the camps and increased the enthusiasm of their congressmen.[28]

The CCC provided Roosevelt with a workable solution to the politically embarrassing problem of what to do with unemployed World War I veterans who in the spring of 1933 once again marched on Washington to demand payment of their bonus for wartime service, not due until 1945. The Bonus Marchers' spectacular occupation of Washington, and Chief of Staff MacArthur's even more spectacular dispersal of them, had contributed to the unpopularity of President Hoover in the summer of 1932. Roosevelt had no desire to unbalance his budget through paying the bonus immediately, nor did he wish to mistreat the veterans.

When nearly a thousand men of an average age of about forty arrived in the second Bonus Expeditionary Force in May 1933, Roosevelt had ready for them 600 tents with latrines, showers, mess halls, and provided three meals a day at an old army camp near Mount Vernon. And, at the suggestion of General Hines, he offered to enroll 25,000 veterans in the CCC. At first the men were not interested in the prospect of work at a dollar a day. "Not for me," said one of them, although he had been long out of work, "It's like selling yourself into slavery." [29]

When Roosevelt was asked if he planned to visit the men, he parried, "You know I have been working really day and night. I don't believe I can get off." Rather, one afternoon Howe drove Mrs. Roosevelt down to the camp and dozed in the automobile, while she, unannounced, walked over to the line of men awaiting food and introduced herself. She followed them into the mess hall and spoke briefly to them of her visit to the battlefields in France just after the war. "I never want to see another war," she said, "I would like to see fair consideration for everyone, and I shall always be grateful to those who served their country." After joining them in singing an old army song, "There's a long, long trail awinding," she plodded through the mud, checking into the kitchen and infirmary just as she had on innumerable inspections for her husband when he was governor of New York. It was a familiar routine for her, and she was in no way nervous over being unprotected and unaccompanied. After about an hour she departed, waving farewells. One veteran remarked, "Hoover sent the army; Roosevelt sent his wife."

The Bonus Army bomb was defused. Within the next several weeks over 2,600 of the veterans joined the CCC, leaving only a die-hard 350 to drift home.[30]

Although there were small percentages of veterans, woodsmen and Indians in the CCC, it was predominantly an organization of unemployed white city youths averaging nineteen years of age. There had to be considerable pressure upon some southern officials to persuade them to recruit Negroes; ultimately 10 percent of the CCC men were black and usually served in segregated camps.

The CCC men, in addition to their forestry and flood control work, undertook the construction of what came to total 12,000 miles of telephone lines and 40,000 or 50,000 miles of horse and truck trails. When a serious forest fire broke out in Montana, the CCC helped fight it, and thereafter served frequently in disaster relief. The corps, as its contributions became manifest, grew rapidly in public esteem.[31]

In a holiday spirit, Roosevelt one August day in 1933 went on an 180-mile drive along the crest of the Blue Ridge Mountains in Shenandoah National Park, Virginia, inspecting five of the camps. He took with him not only Howe, Fechner and several of his cabinet, but also President Green of the AFL, who had been the most vocal critic of the CCC. Green, flattered by his inclusion in the tour, counted it a pleasing experience, and later assured Roosevelt he "could not help but view the whole project in a most sympathetic way." Thereafter there was no serious opposition from unions.[32]

At each camp Roosevelt saw a neat line of army tents set up along a company street and about two hundred tanned young men who stood at attention until an army sergeant dismissed them so they could rush up to the President's car and shake his hand. "The only difference between us," he said to one group, "is that I am told you men have put on an average of twelve pounds each. I am trying to lose twelve pounds."

Roosevelt was delighted with what he saw. "All you have to do," he remarked, "is to look at the boys themselves to see that the camps . . . are a success." [33]

It was a personal success for Roosevelt, since the CCC more than any other New Deal agency embodied his own ideas and his own plan of organization. When someone warned him that the complex assignment of functions through several departments would not lead to efficient administration, Roosevelt, according to the memory of Frances Perkins, responded, "Oh, that doesn't matter. The Army and the Forestry Service will really run the show. The Secretary of Labor will select the men and make the rules and Fechner will 'go along' and give everybody satisfaction and confidence." To some extent that was what happened. Perhaps more important was Roosevelt's willingness to delegate authority and speed operations when a bottleneck developed in the White House, together with his good fortune that both the army officers and foresters possessed precisely the competence to run CCC camps effectively.[34]

CHAPTER XVI

Roosevelts in the White House

If you can come, I trust that you will stay with us at
the White House and bring with you any of your
family you may desire.
— FDR TO PRIME MINISTER RAMSAY MACDONALD,
April 6, 1933.

There had not been such a change in the White House since the Theodore Roosevelts moved in. Suddenly on the afternoon of inauguration
day there was laughter, an air of excitement, and while Roosevelt swore
in his cabinet in the second floor Oval Room, there was the noise of
children romping on the stairway. Colonel Edmund W. Starling, head
of the White House Secret Service detail, returned from Union Station
where he had bade farewell to ex-President Hoover to find the house
"had been transformed during my absence into a gay place, full of
people who oozed confidence. . . . The President was the most happy
and confident of them all." [1]

The White House drapes were drawn back and there were lights and
bustle as people came and went, many of them young, and many of
them newcomers, of a sort who never in previous administrations had
received invitations. "I never thought I should be dining here," confessed
someone Mrs. Roosevelt had asked on the spur of the moment. The
President laughed and responded, "You have nothing on me." The
answer was not really so, since Roosevelt had known both the rollicking
White House of Theodore Roosevelt and the quieter dinners during
the Wilson era. Then the Roosevelts had been one of the dashing young
couples among the Washington elite, mentioned with great frequency
in the society notes of the local newspapers.[2]

Now, those whom protocol demanded be dinner guests — diplomats,
cabinet officers, congressional leaders, and Supreme Court justices —
plus quite a few of the elite, including Eleanor Roosevelt's cousin, Alice
Roosevelt Longworth, still received invitations. But the White House
atmosphere, sniffed one old Washingtonian, had become that of "Satur-

day night at a country hotel." Long ago, the "best people" had made similar observations about the White House upon the advent of Jackson and Polk.[3]

The Roosevelts, without detracting from the majesty of the White House, made it their home, living in it gracefully, excitingly, and largely publicly. Long since they had subordinated their private lives to their political existence without losing their self-assurance and the comfort of their daily routine. They brought to the White House the way of life they had developed at Hyde Park and at the governor's mansion in Albany, but both the scale of entertaining and the public attention were far greater. Eleanor Roosevelt, whose problem it became to manage the White House, wrote after less than a month:

"I confess that I was not a little worried at the prospect of how a house which was partly public and partly private on such a large scale as the White House could be run in order to provide for a family real peace and quiet and home life and still give the public all the rights which they should have." [4]

With her customary efficiency, Mrs. Roosevelt planned in advance how she wished to make use of the White House. She accepted Mrs. Herbert Hoover's invitation to visit in advance, and, declining the use of an official car, arrived on foot on the morning of January 28. She toured the building, according to Ike Hoover, the usher, calm and composed, attentive but apparently little interested as Mrs. Hoover described with considerable detail the many changes she had made in the public rooms. Mrs. Roosevelt, bent on economy, did not intend to make any alterations in these rooms. Rather, her interest intensified when Mrs. Hoover took her to the kitchen and living quarters, for which she already had many plans — nor were her inner thoughts entirely solemn. Several days later, sitting next to Claude Bowers at a dinner in her honor, she confessed her "almost irresistible impulse to laugh on being shown the Lincoln bed of teakwood, black and heavily carved, with the headboard looming toward the ceiling. The picture had flashed upon her of the plight of the occupant if the headboard should ever collapse." [5]

Mrs. Roosevelt's problem was to fit a rather large household into the relatively small living quarters and to carry out her husband's request to cut the running expenses, like everything else in Washington, by 25 percent. She reduced expenses by discharging some of the staff, hoping that with White House recommendations they could find new positions. Perhaps she thought whites could more easily obtain employment, for she discharged all the white servants and kept the Negroes. She brought in as housekeeper Mrs. Henrietta Nesbitt from Hyde Park, who operated on a tight budget and served less-than-lavish meals.[6]

The White House cuisine, which occasioned some complaints, reflected economy and Mrs. Roosevelt's interest in American dishes. In the spring of 1933 she attracted national attention through serving on at least one occasion a seven-cent lunch of hot stuffed eggs with tomato sauce, mashed potatoes, prune pudding, and coffee. She explained to an inquiring woman, to whom she sent the Cornell University menus, that she would find this low figure possible only if she purchased a week's food supplies at a time. Even the President ate the seven-cent lunch in order to dramatize Mrs. Roosevelt's point, that it was possible for people with small incomes or on relief work to obtain "a balanced ration on which a child or an adult can not only live but do ordinary work." [7]

While Mrs. Roosevelt left the public rooms unchanged, like every newcomer she modified the upper two floors to meet her family's needs. Since her daughter Anna Roosevelt Dall and her two children were to spend most of their time at the White House, she turned two of the third floor rooms into nurseries for Sistie and Buzzy Dall. She gave the former housekeeper's rooms to Roosevelt's secretary, Marguerite LeHand, who had lived with the family for years.

On the second floor, Mrs. Roosevelt introduced a few pieces of early American furniture from her Val Kill factory. From the storerooms she rescued some comfortable old sofas and easy chairs, slipcovered them with cretonne, and put them in the end of the upstairs hall as a lounge for young people. The family sitting room, which had been called the Monroe Room, contained a few pieces of furniture from the period. Fearing it would be hurt, Mrs. Roosevelt arrayed it along the hall, and filled the room with their own comfortable belongings. Afternoons she served tea there to friends and family. [8]

It was President Roosevelt who wrought the greatest transformation in the living quarters. The Oval Room, which served as his study, came immediately to look like his overflowing studies elsewhere. Over the mantelpiece he placed a painting of the destroyer *Dyer*, upon which he had crossed the Atlantic during World War I, and flanked it with two companion naval paintings. He brought in two desks, one a reproduction of Jefferson's revolving desk that Mrs. Roosevelt had her artisans make for him, and the other from the timbers of the *Resolute*. In his bedroom, adjacent to the study, he hung more pictures and placed mementos. His bed, an extra long one, came from the Val Kill factory.

Like her predecessors as First Lady, Eleanor Roosevelt occupied a suite of rooms next to her husband's. The bedroom was so large that she transformed it into a sitting room and put her bed into the former dressing room.

The President and Mrs. Roose

e White House study.

Even into the President's office Roosevelt brought his own touch. Sitting like his predecessors with his back to the French windows opening out into the gardens, Roosevelt did not, as they had, gaze at bare walls. He broke with tradition by hanging some of his marine and Hudson River prints where he could gaze at them, and in time added to the room several good-sized ship models. Although he had a fascination for historic things, there was nothing special about the desk in his office, unlike those in his study. Again economizing, he took the one he found there and used it throughout his more than three terms. Curiously enough, according to an inscribed plate on it, the furniture manufacturers of Grand Rapids, Michigan, had presented it to President Hoover. The desk was clean at first, but day by day as visitors brought gadgets and souvenirs it became more crowded. The grandchildren were fascinated. Altogether, it was a Roosevelt White House in appearance and spirit, and the President felt at ease, as though he had always lived there and always would.[9]

As a public edifice, the White House was politically useful. It was a showcase for the Roosevelts; their informal, even light-hearted way of life in the mansion cheered the nation, giving vicarious pleasure to millions even as it began to anger traditionalists with a love of older ways.

Invitations to tea, to dinner, and to stay overnight were, in ascending order, part of the currency of politics. More than one high-salaried figure whom Roosevelt wished to enlist in the New Deal was softened into accepting a low-paying position through an invitation to stay at the White House. Early in his administration, Roosevelt began the policy of inviting prime ministers like Ramsay MacDonald to stay in the White House, placing them in the best guest suite, the room in which Lincoln had signed the Emancipation Proclamation. Less important figures had to stay in their nation's embassies. Since there was only one other guest suite and three additional guest rooms, it was not easy to extend the accolade of an invitation to stay overnight, especially when the children were home. Occasionally there were slipups. In the fall of 1933, the wealthy Wall Streeter, Ambassador Norman Davis, arrived when the regular guest rooms were full, and was taken to a small room on the third floor. Davis was so upset that he insisted he would go to his club, but was placated when he found his dinner clothes laid out for him in the Green Room.[10]

Especially in the spring of 1933, the cordiality and the relative informality of the Roosevelt White House were an effective contrast to the stiff protocol of earlier Presidents. It had been a quiet refuge for the beleaguered Hoover, the scapegoat for the depression, who had followed the ritual Washington expected of him. When he dined alone with Mrs. Hoover, at eight o'clock he dressed for dinner and ate in the State Dining Room. Roosevelt disliked the dressing ritual, and ate informally in a business suit whenever he could.[11]

Even the newspaper correspondents were hard to break away from the old customs. When Roosevelt accepted their invitation to the Gridiron Dinner that spring, he tried to persuade them to let him come in a dinner jacket, but they insisted upon the dignity of a white tie and tails. At the dinner, he entered into the fun, off the record, rather than remaining a rather formal ornament.* The traditionalist Frank Kent thereupon complained to Baruch, "The Gridiron dinner was good, and our Peerless President made a poor and puerile speech. This was not only mine, but the unanimous opinion." [13]

One permanent change toward greater informality that Roosevelt introduced to Washington was the use of first names. President Hoover after four years had continued to refer to the secretary of state (whom he disliked) as Stimson, and even addressed the secretary of the treasury (for whom he had warm feelings) as Mills. In contrast, Roosevelt immediately greeted everyone from the cabinet members to White House staff by their first names. Through his administration he continued the habit, addressing in this familiar fashion both friends and foes.

What others called the President was a somewhat different matter. Respect for the office was involved. He made it a point to insist to Josephus Daniels and a few others that he was "still Franklin," but it became clear that outside of family and the rare camaraderie of yachting trips he was not. Several years later when James Roosevelt became a White House secretary, he instructed James to call him "Mr. President" in public. To a few intimates he was "Governor" rather than "Mr. President," but he expressed to others his annoyance in the spring of 1933, when Berle sent him several letters rather curiously saluting him as "Dear Caesar." [14]

During his first week as President, Roosevelt broke another tradition, flouting what Hoover had said to him a few days before, that a Chief Executive pays no calls. On March 8 he honored Justice Oliver Wendell Holmes on his ninety-second birthday by driving to his Georgetown home. It was an extraordinary tribute, since it was no easy or quick matter for Roosevelt in his braces to make his way up the steps.

* At the National Press Club dinner, several weeks earlier, just before the legal 3.2 beer appeared, FDR made it the central theme of his talk, saying he and Secretary of the Navy Swanson had discussed whether it could be served on naval vessels. They had decided they could not ban it since legally it was nonintoxicating. There were loud cheers, but Roosevelt stopped them, and continued saying that Secretary Hull had informed him that the displacement of naval vessels was fixed by treaty. To take on board beer would increase the displacement, therefore beer would be forbidden in order to uphold the sanctity of treaties.[12]

Holmes, although his age had become a burden, was still mentally alert. When Feis had seen him a few days earlier: "There wasn't a thing ashen about him. His face was pink and his eyes clear. True, he sits back deep in his chair and it is almost as if the mental and physical effort of coming forward were sometimes a little too much. He invited chatter about what was going on, even though he said he no longer tried to follow affairs." [15]

Holmes was in a convivial mood; earlier in the day he had drunk champagne, and he chatted with the President — of all things, about John L. Sullivan and pugilism.* When Roosevelt asked his advice on the crisis, he replied, in the metaphor of a Union officer of the Civil War, "Form your ranks and fight." As Roosevelt left, according to the anecdote Alexander Woollcott was soon repeating, Holmes commented, "A second-class intellect — but a first-class temperament." [17]

The routine that Roosevelt established in the White House was much like that he had followed previously in Albany. Since it did not bring him into the executive office until 9:30 to 10:30 in the morning, some Washingtonians jumped to the unwarranted conclusion that he was much too leisurely a President. After all, Hoover had arrived at his desk at 8 o'clock, and Coolidge at 7:30. In the case of Roosevelt, he was shaping his day's activities in keeping with his seldom-mentioned infirmity, and had cleared away some of his important work before he arrived at the office.

The President began his day at 8:30, his mood, Henry Pringle reported, a shade indigo until he had consumed his breakfast tray of orange juice, eggs, toast, and coffee, and lit the first cigarette. He would insert each cigarette in an ivory holder with a long detachable quill stem which he held between his teeth at a jaunty angle.† By this time he was usually cheerful and skimmed through five morning newspapers — the *New York Times* and *Herald Tribune*, the *Washington Post* and *Herald*, and the *Baltimore Sun* — paying especial attention to editorials

* Afterwards Holmes sent a note:

My dear Mr. President and Mrs. Roosevelt
Your kind thoughtfulness in coming here the other day sets me free to express my congratulations and good wishes to you. They are very sincere, and follow what seems to me a most fortunate beginning of the term. Old age has made it hard for me to write so that I must confine myself with this brief expression of confident prophecies for the future
with deep respect I am
Your obedient Servant
O. W. Holmes [16]

† In the course of a day the President went through two packages of Camels. His use of the long holder with its soft end was a characteristic cartoonists made famous, and which led some Republicans to jeer in 1936 that he was theatrical even in his smoking habits. Roosevelt's long holders, according to the tobacconist who supplied them, were designed for him because he had tender and receding gums.[18]

and to the columnists, Walter Lippmann, Frank Kent and others. It was the *New York Times* that commanded most of his attention; at first the *Washington Post*, until Eugene Meyer began to build it into a formidable paper, merited little of his attention. In addition, soon Howe was supervising the assembly of a digest from innumerable papers from throughout the country, jokingly known as Louis Howe's *Daily Bugle*, which provided a much broader view of the press. Roosevelt never depended upon shortcuts.

While Roosevelt was checking through the newspapers he was also going over the key problems of the day with several advisers. Throughout the spring the pair at his bedside almost every morning were Moley and Lew Douglas; by fall it was usually Morgenthau and Jesse Jones. Roosevelt would give orders and Moley would jot them in his little notebook, within a few minutes telephoning instructions to others.

Next Roosevelt would give a few minutes to Marvin McIntyre, appointments secretary, lining up appointments, while Steve Early, the press secretary, tried to get some bits of information for his 10:30 meeting with the White House correspondents. During this time, Mrs. Roosevelt, Anna, or Howe might come into the room for a few words, and Roosevelt might be shaving himself while he talked. He conducted presidential business and chatted with family in his bedroom, garbed with a democratic simplicity worthy of Jefferson, who had once worn carpet slippers when he received the British minister. Roosevelt, to the disgust of his mother, refused to use his new pajamas, and instead, economically and comfortably, continued to wear mended ones with cut-off sleeves.[19]

There were days when Roosevelt, who was a chronic sufferer from sinus trouble and pulmonary disorders, felt unwell and exhausted, the rings dark under his eyes. He would announce he had a cold, cancel official appointments, then continue to transact considerable important business in bed, or perhaps from the pleasant Oval Room upstairs in the White House. Mrs. Roosevelt, whose candor continued undiminished after she moved into the White House, informed one solicitous woman: "You must remember that the word 'cold' is very often used when one really means that one wishes merely to take a rest. My husband does not have quite so many colds as the papers would indicate." [20]

The President made his way from his bedroom to the executive office, as was his usual means of behind-the-scenes locomotion, pushed in a small wheelchair. It had a little attachment on the side to hold an ashtray, but no arms, so that he could swing himself into the seat behind his desk.

Once at his desk, Roosevelt was immobilized for hours at a time, often until nightfall. He could not pace around, or even stand gazing out onto the terrace. Until one o'clock he saw visitors, ordinarily at fifteen-minute intervals. McIntyre pared from the appointment list as many as possible of the innumerable official delegations or personages come to pay their respects for whom seeing the President, and if possible being photographed with him, is the equivalent of attaining the lower reaches of the royal honors list in Britain. There were still appointments enough of governmental or political import, and frequently Roosevelt let them run overtime, ignoring secretaries signaling from the doorway. Conscientious visitors, knowing others were waiting their turn outside, nervously broke away as soon as they could. Some of the callers were ones whose presence Roosevelt wished to hide from the omnipresent White House correspondents. These would enter secretly through a tunnel from the State-War-Navy Building across the street (now part of the executive office of the President).

At first there was a considerable informality in seeing visitors. Roosevelt summoned whomever he wished and often paid little attention to the appointments list on his desk. Or he allowed people to overlap, so that Ickes might find himself having to discuss some topic with the President while someone not even remotely concerned with the subject sat in the office. Dean Acheson later remembered going to the White House with some other Treasury people to see the President in the Oval Room. The door was open so that he could see Roosevelt within, surrounded by advisers to whom he listened, jotted down some notes, signed a paper thrust before him, and chatted over the phone; then seeing Acheson's group outside his door he shouted, "Come on in. We're doing a land-office business." [21]

Even at lunchtime Roosevelt did not leave his desk, but had a meal sent in for himself and one or two important visitors. At first the White House kitchen could not provide hot lunches, so that he and his guests, although they used elegant china, had to make do with fare which was not only simple but cold. After a while hot lunches came from the kitchen on a portable steamtable, and thanks to the many gifts of food to the President, the meals became less austere. Mrs. Roosevelt remarked in 1933 that the President's favorite food was scrambled eggs and that she thought he would happily eat them three times a day if they were placed before him. But by early 1934 McIntyre was saying:

> Well, he usually has a very light lunch. He might start with clams or a clear soup, and then eat a chop or some broiled trout. You know that's his favorite dish, broiled trout. A good many of his friends know of his fondness for it and send in messes very frequently. . . . He'll eat a few light vegetables, very light dessert and then have coffee. But the conference — and not the luncheon — is the important thing to him.[22]

The food did indeed make little difference to Roosevelt or the visitors, for the talk was continual. Indeed, Tugwell found that the best way to set forth the problem which had led to a luncheon appointment was to eat before arriving, wait until Roosevelt's mouth was full of food, then start in. Roosevelt enjoyed holding forth, and while he sometimes used his steady flow of anecdotes and ideas as a word barrage against an unwelcome subject, for the most part he had no ulterior motive. He was taking advantage of the fact that ordinarily no one cuts in on a President's discourse or complains about the repetitiousness of the stories. But to emphasize only Roosevelt's talkativeness is to give a false impression. Stimson, who was of the old school, came back from an hour-and-a-half luncheon at the President's desk on March 28, according to Moffat, with unconcealed admiration:

> Time and time again they were interrupted by people coming in on urgent matters, and he said that the versatility of the President and his ability to reach the kernel of a problem was astounding. His mind is not that of a lawyer or scholar, and he rarely is familiar with past history or detail, but none the less he showed that he could grasp the essentials, reach a decision and complete action with speed and clarity.[23]

After lunch, from two to three, Roosevelt would dictate letters and sign official documents. Incoming letters and telegrams were averaging four to seven thousand a day. A considerable staff handled the mail, directing most of the correspondence to various agencies. Every letter was read by someone and even crank mail was carefully filed. Letters which were either significant or potentially interesting to the President by ten o'clock each morning went onto the desk of Grace Tully, who gave them a further winnowing, so that when he rang she was ready with an armful of letters and her stenographer's notebook.[24]

Roosevelt was not a great letter writer in the tradition of Theodore Roosevelt or Woodrow Wilson. Other pressures upon him were too heavy, but in any event it was not his inclination or talent. He handled a good bit of business through brief memoranda, explaining to reporters in March 1933: "I am using the chit system which I invented in the Navy Department. They are these little slips — I use them. If I want to inquire about something from the Secretary of War or any one of the Cabinet officers I just send one of these things over written in longhand." [25]

That first spring many were in his own hand; later large numbers went out typed, with his penned initials, "FDR" at the bottom; and still later considerable numbers bore only his typed initials. Early described in 1933 how Roosevelt handled the larger part of his correspondence.

The President goes through his mail with a stenographer sitting along side of him. He will read the letter and say, "Take a memorandum." The memorandum will say something like this: "Prepare reply." Then the President indicates the nature of the reply, i.e., "Yes" or "No."

The phrase "Prepare reply" means the letter is to be prepared for the President's signature along the lines he indicates. You would be surprised at the rapidity with which he can clear up a heavy mail in this fashion. In the evening and on Sundays he does a lot of this work and, in many instances, dictates his own letters.[26]

Many of the replies to official letters that departments prepared for him received only his signature, but sometimes he would revise them to modify their meaning, or to add a personal touch. At first he could even find time to write a friendly "thank you" to Judge Samuel I. Rosenman, so long his assistant in Albany, who had remained on the bench in New York, or an explanation of some of his policies to Colonel House. There were innumerable political thank-yous, and in time Roosevelt assigned most of these, and even some personal notes, to members of his White House staff to draft. But he dictated quantities of important official letters, and sometimes relaxed by dictating notes to friends and relatives. His personal letters reflected his conversation, a combination of earnest high-mindedness and rather amateurish wisecracks. When Ambassador Breckinridge Long wrote him of his ceremonial call upon Mussolini, riding to the palace in a procession of four carriages, one of which was empty, Roosevelt responded, on June 16, 1933, that the supposedly empty carriage was in fact "occupied by GREAT CAESAR'S GHOST," then went on to make some serious remarks. The informal style served as an assurance that the letter was directly from the President, and not one laboriously drafted in the State Department. (In later years, several of Roosevelt's secretaries became skilled in turning out these light, informal letters.) [27]

Roosevelt also liked to write direct personal letters to royalty, as was his privilege as more than a prime minister, himself the chief of state. He checked with the State Department for the proper form of address before sending a note to the king of the Belgians. The State Department had to hunt in its archives back to the days of Theodore Roosevelt and his correspondence with the kaiser before reporting the obvious answer, "Dear King Albert."

The august George V of England was also the recipient of a personal letter and an accompanying packet of envelopes. One morning, Undersecretary of State Phillips, calling at the White House, was ushered into the presidential bedroom where he found Roosevelt sorting over a file drawer of envelopes which had been strangely addressed to him in one way or another. Roosevelt was selecting those from various parts of the British realm to send George V, whom he was sure as a stamp collector would be amused. The king, either out of bafflement or respect for the limitations upon his royal power, sent the letter, which included pleasant remarks about the war debts problem, to the Foreign Office, which drafted a reply for him.[28]

Roosevelt was also entertained by some of the letters he received. One, from a farmer's wife, supposedly authentic, can be identified with more certainty as the sort of joke that appealed to the President's sense of humor: "Our neighbor, Pete Smith, loaned us $25 on our team. He says he'll take the mules away unless he can come to see me when my husband is away. How can I save the mules?" [29]

After handling his correspondence, Roosevelt in the afternoons would return to conferences, or once a week to his meetings with the cabinet. The cabinet meetings were informal, but especially in that first spring, when he did not know or depend upon most of the cabinet officers, not especially productive. He would give each an opportunity to speak up in sequence, starting out by turning to the secretary of state and asking, "Well, Cordell, what's on your mind today?" Often afterwards one or two would stay behind to transact the important business they did not wish to share with the group.

Twice a week there were the press conferences, from a quarter-hour to half-hour in length, almost entirely off the record and surprisingly informative. There Roosevelt often said the same things that he had been telling his cabinet, advisers, or congressional leaders within the past twenty-four hours. Especially in 1933, and continuing for a year or two, there was little of the adversary relationship between him and the White House correspondents. They were delighted that their previously dull posts, secondary to Capitol assignments, had become the prime source of news. At the end of Roosevelt's first year in office, Edwin L. James, the managing editor of the *New York Times*, estimated that it had published a million words of presidential stories.[30]

Roosevelt treated the newspapermen as though they were all junior members of an exclusive club, something like the Fly Club had been at Harvard — but with him presiding as the benign senior, ready to join in the fun, but just a trifle aloof. He was so relaxed with them that one warm evening while waiting for a communiqué from a conference inside, several of them together with McIntyre stood on the portico of the White House singing "Home on the Range" in close harmony. When NBC persuaded them to repeat their performance over the network, Roosevelt listened in, then, disguising his voice, telephoned the studio, offering them a contract. When their spokesman on the phone asked who was calling, he replied, "I'm the advertising manager of Cascarets" — a famous laxative. Roosevelt thought so well of the joke that he repeated it at his next press conference, announcing they were resigning because "they had a very handsome offer to sing on the Cascaret Hour." On the following evening he and Mrs. Roosevelt had the quartet appear at the White House in a "command performance." [31]

In addition to the joshing there could be a remarkable give-and-take in the press conferences without Roosevelt letting them forget very often that his was the presidential authority. If someone persisted in questioning, he would put on a warning smile and remark, "Remember, no cross-examination!" If he were playful, the correspondents roared with laughter. What in print looks rather commonplace or awkward at the time seemed hilarious coming from the President of the United States.

One bit of repartee came not at a press conference but on a June afternoon when the Roosevelts were chatting informally with the White House correspondents. One asked Mrs. Roosevelt,

"How would it be if we grabbed our racquets and got out on the White House tennis courts sometime?"

The First Lady readily gave her assent. Next a reporter asked,

"And, Mr. President, what about the swimming pool some of these hot afternoons?"

Roosevelt responded,

"Yes and there's also those sand boxes we've put out there for the children. You might try them, too." [32]

The White House swimming pool was an essential for Roosevelt. He sorely missed the pools he had used at the governor's mansion in Albany and at Warm Springs. For several months that spring he suffered from lack of exercise except for conventional therapeutic exercises and massages, and Charles Hurd, the *New York Times* correspondent, has thought that his disposition and weight also began to be the worse for it. The *New York Daily News,* later to be one of the most vehement critics of Roosevelt, quickly raised $10,000 in contributions of pennies from schoolchildren to provide him with a pool. By June 2 it was ready, tiled, with lighted water and diving boards, enclosed in a pleasant pavilion beside the corridor between the White House and the executive offices. Roosevelt, delighted, upon the completion of the pool shook the hand of each of the workmen, many of them Negroes, and spoke to them briefly:

> I built a pool once myself, and did all the designing and all the work and when I had completed it the pool fell in. The pool that you built will stand up.*
>
> I want you men to know that this pool will be a big help to me, as it

* President Nixon transformed the pool into an elegant room for the White House press corps.

will be about the only air I can get. It will be one of the greatest pleasures for me during my stay in the White House.[33]

Several times weekly Roosevelt would swim in the pool, sometimes with his secretaries, or his wife or daughter, demonstrating his powerful butterfly stroke and tossing a ball. If a visitor like Nicholas Roosevelt, back from serving as minister to Hungary, called and was invited for a swim, the conversation was relatively subdued. If it was his children, he led in the hilarity and horseplay.[34]

Before Roosevelt left his desk, he would often recapitulate the day's activities with his staff. Borrowing the term that Ray Moley had given to similar meetings with his assistants, Roosevelt called these the "children's hour." Although often serious matters came up at these sessions, Roosevelt gave them a light-hearted touch. Missy LeHand remarked that first year in the White House, "It has always been so much fun working with the Roosevelts." [35]

At one session with the staff soon after he became President, Roosevelt expressed his concern that they not lay themselves open to charges of profiting from their inside knowledge of economic developments. In a rather embarrassed fashion he warned his secretaries against investing in the securities of railroads, steel companies, utilities, or other industries that might be affected by administrative or congressional action. Someone asked what sort of security was permissible, giving Roosevelt an opportunity to joke, looking at the women, that cosmetic stocks should be a stable investment.

Roosevelt was circumspect in his own investments. In addition, in March he suspended his already inactive partnership in the law firm of Roosevelt and O'Connor, and in July, after hearing rumors that the name was being used to solicit law business, gently and firmly asked Basil O'Connor to drop the Roosevelt name. The change in no way affected Roosevelt's continuing cordial relationship with O'Connor.[36]

The President did allow those around him to earn extra money through radio broadcasts and writing. Moley received permission to write articles and even a column. Louis Howe was especially active as a writer, and for a time delivered fifteen-minute Sunday radio broadcasts, remarkable neither for their delivery or contents. The *Forum* criticized the vagueness, and noted his "oldish, dark-brown voice; he says 'pa'-ticu'ly' 'purty soon,' 'I s'pose so' and, all in all possesses a genuinely up-country tang." Roosevelt responded to the editor that he thought Howe's broadcasts had improved since the first two. It might have been embarrassing to have denied Howe and Moley permission to earn extra money, since Roosevelt himself received royalties from *Looking Forward*, and Mrs. Roosevelt fees for editing, writing, and lecturing.[37]

There was also the possibility that his sons might benefit from the position of their father. Rumors were afloat about James Roosevelt's insurance business in Boston — rumors that defenders of Roosevelt's son said came from disappointed office-seekers. When twenty-two-year-old Elliott Roosevelt headed west to try to establish himself on a ranch, he declared he was having to leave the advertising business because almost every account that came his way might have Washington strings attached. The children were subscribing to an ideal which it was almost impossible to maintain in practice.[38]

For both Roosevelt himself and members of his family, the office he held and his leadership in the Democratic party impinged upon almost all of their affairs. That was why it was so important to maintain a private family life on the second and third floors of the White House. In their mature years, the Roosevelt children have felt that their parents were successful in this endeavor. On the frequent occasions when the children all assembled there, they were relaxed and noisy, James Roosevelt recalls. "One of the great things about the White House is that the second floor really isn't like a museum," he says. "This is a family home, and this is where the family feels . . . not under public scrutiny."

One of the few family times of the day for Roosevelt came before the eight o'clock dinner, when he would often stretch on his bed to rest, read the evening newspapers, and have his legs massaged. It was an interlude when his children could see him easily, and privately. "I know some of my brothers have said they remember definitely resenting having to make appointments to see father," Anna recollects. Franklin, Jr., has added:

> We used to kid him, and say, "Well, I suppose I need an appointment to see you." This wasn't exactly true, We could always see him before dinner in the evening . . . and we could talk about things that were happening in the world and in the country. Sometimes we would talk about our own personal problems. And he was always very interested, and very warm about the relationship between himself and his family. He was a great family man.

While the children were away from the White House, Roosevelt carried on an irregular correspondence with them through scribbled or dictated notes, and immediately telephoned if there were family problems. They usually heard from him once or twice a month, and from their mother a good bit oftener. When one of his sons came to Washington, Roosevelt tried to rearrange his luncheon appointments so that he could eat with him. Several summers he took them with him on extended sailing vacations.

"The presidency invariably places restrictions on families staying closer together," Elliott Roosevelt reminisced years later, "but I feel that both my mother and my father made great efforts to keep the family a close-knit unit." [39]

Yet when Roosevelt was President there were times of acute stress for the children, when Mrs. Roosevelt felt he did not give them the advice and comfort they needed. The brunt of serious problems fell on her.

It was she who had to make a hurried trip to the West in June 1933 to see their son Elliott, who had left his wife and child in the East. She returned with the news that Elliott was not only divorcing but immediately remarrying. There are stories that Roosevelt, when he arrived on the *Amberjack* at Campobello at the end of June, was taking it quite hard, and that it contributed to tension between the Roosevelts. There is no doubt Mrs. Roosevelt was upset. The story bears repeating as some indication that Franklin Roosevelt, as well as Eleanor, behind his outward façade was a person of deep feeling. Roosevelt could not always discuss openly with his children problems of theirs about which he cared intensely, nor was he very good about discussing them with Eleanor Roosevelt. In consequence he sometimes gave an impression of callousness, even to her. With an intimate whom he trusted he later fell into the habit of pouring out his worries and even anguish about his sons. Yet when one of his sons with a critical personal decision to make came to see him in the White House office, his response was to pick up a paper and show it to the young man, remarking upon what an historic document it was. In day-by-day relations with his children he was warm, affectionate, accessible, and even a boisterous playmate, yet at a point of crisis he could withdraw. [40]

This was the enigma about her husband with which Eleanor Roosevelt grappled throughout her marrige — the friendly, laughing extrovert with the intense inner reserve, even toward those he most loved.* In December 1933, *Fortune* entitled an article on Roosevelt "The Enigma," and repeated the anecdote of a Washington correspondent on Campobello Island, who one foggy day at the end of June 1933 was strolling through the woods with a young woman:

> And all at once, not five yards off in the thin fog, there was the President's Ford. . . . And there beside the car was the President. He was sitting on the trunk of a tree, his legs folded out in front of him, his hands over his face. And suddenly, before they could move, the

* Years later Mrs. Roosevelt suggested to her son James, "His was an innate kind of reticence that may have been developed by the fact that he had an older father and a very strong-willed mother, who constantly tried to exercise control over him in the early years. Consequently, he may have fallen into the habit of keeping his own counsel, and it became part of his nature not to talk to anyone of intimate matters." [41]

hands came down and there were his eyes looking straight into their eyes just a few steps off and not seeing them at all . . . there was a kind of drawn grimace of his mouth and over his forehead like a man trying to see something in his mind and suffering. And then all at once they could see his eyes focusing . . . the smile came back over the look in his eyes and he called out: "Hello there, Billy. Picking flowers?" They turned and got out of there. They could hear his big laugh back of them in the spruce.[42]

Perhaps it was in reaction to her husband that Eleanor Roosevelt, despite her shyness, was so candid in talking and writing about much — not all — of her inner life.

As for Roosevelt, what could be painful at times within his personal life was one of his most useful assets in public life, to be genial, warm, but automatically reserved, carrying a certain air of mystery about him, as, even in most of his recreation, there was a mixture of the public and the private.

The President enjoyed getting out of the White House on spring afternoons or weekend days aboard the *Sequoia*, heading down the Potomac to Chesapeake Bay, or up the Rappahannock, York, or James rivers. Occasionally he fished, with little success; sometimes he enjoyed the sun and the breeze upon the deck; and almost invariably he took along with him figures who would be impressed with the honor, or with whom he wished to confer seriously. He had declined the use of a friend's yacht, saying he preferred the *Sequoia*, which had been used by the Coastal and Geodetic Survey, although it was "not much more than a glorified house boat . . . because she only draws five feet of water." The shallow bottom was no asset when they hit thunderstorms and the *Sequoia* pitched and rolled alarmingly. Secretary of the Treasury Woodin, upon his return from a weekend trip with the President at the end of May, told reporters that although he had been in two or three train wrecks and on ocean liners in trouble, the greatest scare of his life had been the night before when for twenty or thirty minutes they had not known whether or not they could ride out a heavy squall. "I know the President, who is a yachting man, realized our danger thoroughly," Woodin declared. "The storm kept up nearly an hour, but for thirty minutes of it we didn't know whether it was the end or not." Roosevelt made no comment.[43]

Entertainment at the White House could be fun for the President, but also useful, whether it were letting the public onto the grounds for the annual Easter Monday egg rolling or presiding over a formal dinner. The egg rolling on April 17, 1933, brought 47,100 children to the south grounds of the White House. Roosevelt came out on the portico to wave and call out to the applauding children.[44]

A more vital occasion came in late May when the Roosevelts gave a garden party for more than six hundred disabled veterans from the Washington hospitals. It was almost five o'clock before he could break away from a conference with a Japanese envoy to stand with Mrs. Roosevelt under a great tree near the White House. It was a hot afternoon, and occasionally he wiped his face with his handkerchief as he stood in his braces, with one arm grasping that of his naval aide, with the other shaking hands, smiling and making friendly remarks to each of the veterans as they came by, some on crutches, some in wheelchairs.[45]

Washington habitués like the J. Pierrepont Moffats were equally pleased with the Roosevelt hospitality. When they went to one of Mrs. Roosevelt's teas on April 7, 1933:

> It was all very simple, but there was an atmosphere of cordiality that was distinctly lacking in the last regime. There were some two hundred people present, most of whom knew each other, with a judicious sprinkling of the Judiciary, Congress, the Executives, and Washington society, all of whom gathered in the East Room. When Mrs. Roosevelt came down, the line passed through the Blue Room to the Red Room, where she was receiving. She spoke with everyone a few sentences. . . . All in all a well done show.[46]

A few days later, Moffat was seated at a dinner next to Anna Roosevelt Dall, and found her a very pleasant companion as she regaled him with amusing stories of happenings on the second floor of the White House. After attending a White House musicale at which the Hampton choir sang, he noted, "there is a happiness and cheerfulness which probably has not been seen since the days of the great Theodore." [47]

White House dinners that spring, when Roosevelt was pressing Congress to enact legislation of a nature at variance with their beliefs and at a speed equally contrary to traditions, became an essential way to hold support. The freshness and friendliness of the Roosevelts' manner did much to preserve voters for the New Deal measures. Hiram Johnson wrote his son on April 1 after he had dined with the Roosevelts:

> The whole atmosphere of the White House is different. It used to be we were like so many sticks when we arrived, herded into one of the rooms, where we stood about looking at one another, until the announcement of the President and his wife. When we entered this time, immediately we were shown into the room which in the past we have been familiar with, and where we expected to stand, first on one leg, and then on another, and wonder who was standing next to us, but as we entered, there was Mrs. Roosevelt herself insisting on presenting each guest to every other one, and herself going from group to group, pleasantly and sweetly. The President himself was a bit late, but as soon

as he came down from the elevator, Mrs. Roosevelt said, "You must come and meet my husband now," and we all trooped out where he was smiling, with a pleasant word for everybody, and we went into dinner. The stiff formality of former days was utterly absent, and it was much more like dining with intimate friends than indulging in a state dinner. In one thing, confidentially, they failed, and that was in the dinner itself. The ordinary meal I have at home at night was infinitely superior to the meal there served. But always in instances of this sort, the menu is of little consequence, and in the inbred courtesy of our hosts and the enjoyment of being with them, we forgot what we were eating . . . we had a very indifferent chowder first, then some mutton served in slices already cut and which had become almost cold, with peas that were none too palatable, a salad of little substance and worse dressing, lemon pie, and coffee. Afterwards we had a movie, and we reached home a little before eleven. I think I saw signs of weariness in the President's face, but he assured me he enjoyed the work, and that meeting the innumerable people he did, and dealing all day with intricate subjects, was his greatest enjoyment. Rather pathetically, he said, "You know I can not play tennis or golf and get about in the fashion the ordinary individual does, and my pleasure is in meeting human beings and dealing with problems." I commented to Mrs. Roosevelt upon his equanimity, and the patience I had seen him exercise in the conferences that I had attended, and his unfailing good humor, and I asked her if he ever got mad. She said really he never did, and she then gave the reason that we have often heard here concerning him, that he went through such a fiery ordeal in his extraordinary and terrible illness, that it gave him stability, and he had learned patience and toleration.[48]

At informal dinners, Roosevelt was even more relaxed and genial. On Sunday evening, Mrs. Roosevelt customarily scrambled eggs in a chafing dish and Anna Dall served the guests, who included friends, notables and newspapermen. Even at these, it took some six months for the White House secretary who sent out the invitations to accept the President's assurance that he did not want the guests to appear in black tie. On the steaming hot evening of June 3, when the Roosevelts gave a dance for newspapermen and their wives, the word had gone out that it was a black tie affair. While the reporters were sweltering in dinner jackets, Roosevelt was dressed in a white silk suit. He punned to one of the ladies, "I see the men wore black ties and nothing else." In the course of the evening, a young woman walked up to one of the newspapermen and told him the President had asked her to dance with him. Later she took him over to Roosevelt who, gazing at him, remarked, "Well, he looks all right to me." Afterward Roosevelt said it was the liveliest White House party since the marriage of Alice Roosevelt and Nick Longworth.[49]

The relaxation after dinner was often motion pictures, at which several times a week Roosevelt joined family and guests in viewing. He took great pleasure in them, especially if his mother and some of her elderly friends were present, since he would then make rakish remarks about the physical attributes of the actresses. Yet even at the movies, Roosevelt was being practical, since in these pretelevision days it was during the evening sessions that he viewed the newsreels. These brought him pictorial and sound impressions of events ranging from the alarming scenes of Nazi book burnings and attacks on Jews to his own public appearances and addresses (which he abhorred hearing).*

After the movies it was back to work until late. Or, if the pressure slackened, he might take time to work on his stamp collection. On the night after his inauguration, after signing the proclamation closing the banks, Roosevelt asked Assistant Secretary of State Wilbur J. Carr to remain after the others, then inquired,

"Wilbur, don't you get a good many interesting foreign stamps?"

"Yes, many."

"I should appreciate it greatly if you would sometimes bundle up a few and send them over to me."

Thereafter, every Friday manila envelopes came from the State Department containing foreign stamps. Ickes discovered two remaining sheets of Department of the Interior stamps for him. In addition, Roosevelt had the pleasure of helping decide upon new American commemorative stamps, and obtained the first sheet of each issue. Farley as postmaster general catered to the President's interest — always, of course, paying for the stamps. He wrote Farley that the first copy of a Newburgh commemorative stamp, the first issued in his administration, would always have "the greatest personal historic interest" for him, and thought an N.R.A. stamp issued that summer was grand:[51] "The honest farmer, who looks like me; the honest businessman, who looks like Grover T. Whalen; and the honest blacksmith, who looks like Lionel Barrymore, are magnificent. But Oh Heavens what a girl! She is wearing a No. 11 shoe, also a bustle, and if recovery is dependent on women like that I am agin recovery." [52]

As a proposer of stamp designs, Roosevelt in response to a suggestion queried the third postmaster general whether Whistler's Mother could be reproduced on a stamp to commemorate the hundredth anniversary of the artist's birth. She was.[53]

---

* When Vincent Astor wrote FDR he wished he could send him a recording of his last radio address, it was so good, FDR responded: "I just want to say that I would listen to a siren or even to Gus [Gennerich, his bodyguard] singing close harmony, but I will not listen to my own voice come out of a tin can! I might even add, if you are very good, that I will let you sing to me but I hate the sound of my own preserved voice!" [50]

It was usually not until midnight or later that Roosevelt retired to the privacy of his bedroom, where he might chat with his wife or read for an hour or more before going to sleep. The reading matter was less often detective stories than reports and recommendations to mull over, or serious magazines to thumb through. Then to sleep, but since he was a paraplegic, unlike other Presidents, the bedroom doors remained unlocked.

One day, Gerard Swope of General Electric expressed his admiration at lunch for the calm and poise with which Roosevelt carried the burden of those hectic days. Roosevelt replied: "I'll tell you, Gerard, at night when I lay my head on my pillow, and it is often pretty late, and I think of the things that have come before me during the day and the decisions that I have made, I say to myself — well I have done the best I could, and turn over and go to sleep." [54]

A friend of Hoover's who had known Roosevelt during the First World War and had not seen him again until March 1933 marveled: "He is no more like the man who was here in Wilson's time than the capital is like the city it was then. . . . I attribute the change to his physical disability. Having overcome that, he is not afraid of anything. . . . This man functions smoothly because he has learned to function in chains." [55]

CHAPTER XVII

A Most Extraordinary First Lady

Off the record, strictly off the record, I will have to ask
my wife.
— FDR TO NEWSPAPERMEN, *March 24, 1933.*

Eleanor Roosevelt provided one of the greatest surprises of that startling
spring, as the American people discovered that in addition to a dynamic,
optimistic new President they had acquired a most extraordinary First
Lady. Soon people were comparing Franklin D. Roosevelt to Wilson,
the first Roosevelt, or even Jackson. They could make no similar comparisons among first ladies, since none of them, even the hospitable
Dolley Madison, had undertaken a fraction of her responsibilities or
made such an impact upon the nation. Her immediate predecessors,
Grace Goodhue Coolidge and Lou Henry Hoover had been gracious
hostesses, vigorous in good causes; Mrs. Hoover had been national
president of the Girl Scouts. But their activities in no way approached
in degree or dimension those Mrs. Roosevelt began to undertake after
she arrived in the White House. To one admirer that spring who felt
she deserved some special title, she wrote: [1] "I have never felt that I
had any official position or that I was entitled to any official title because my husband was elected President. I feel that my job is to help
him as much as possible and to do whatever falls within my scope." [2]

It was a considerable mandate she gave herself, and she undertook it
spectacularly. Indeed, by that fall a notable American historian, Mary
Ritter Beard, in reviewing one of Mrs. Roosevelt's books, *It's Up to
the Women*, gave her the unfelicitous title "The Great White Mother."
Mrs. Roosevelt was amused.[3]

The appellation Mrs. Beard gave Mrs. Roosevelt was not far from the
mark. She was, like her predecessors, a wife and mother, manager and
hostess in the White House, and to a greater degree than they involved
in voluntary affairs. In addition, she had her own staff, held her own
press conferences, through her pronouncements was becoming a national counsel on all manner of troublesome women's and family con-

cerns, was a power in the Democratic party, a driving force in obtaining significant appointments for women, and slowly becoming an influence in the New Deal — all this in the first few months. Even in the beginning, in her private chats with her husband she may have been a major influence; at a critical point at the end of June 1933 it is clear that she helped tip the balance in his mind against Moley. In all this she was indeed, as she wrote her admirer, loyal to her husband's great ends, yet she maintained her independence of mind, holding to her own convictions which sometimes differed from, or were less politically viable, than his. And into the White House she brought her own separate life-style which she had been developing painstakingly for the previous fifteen years. The prospect of becoming First Lady had appalled her, but she assumed the role with immediate grace and effectiveness.

For some weeks after the election she had continued as best she could her old pattern of life, teaching at the Todhunter School and involving herself in her well-established enterprises. The publicity she received intensified; her students no longer could regard her in the same way. It was apparent that she would have to embark upon a modified existence, and she was still unsure she would fit. As late as the dinner in her honor on February 8, she told Claude Bowers, "As the time draws near and I think of the terrible condition of the country, and of the high expectation from the change it frightens me." [4]

Yet she proceeded with her customary efficiency to make ready for the inauguration and life in the White House. She spent several days in Warm Springs planning the family details of the inauguration with her husband, who also liked to involve himself in these matters. They found the family party of Roosevelts and Howes would be nearly thirty, too large for them to accept the invitation to stay with Sumner Welles, but rather that they should occupy a number of rooms at the Mayflower Hotel. (Their bill at the Mayflower, although there was no charge for Mr. and Mrs. Roosevelt or Howe, totaled $687, an enormous sum in that depression month.) In the same quick, efficient way, upon her return to New York she selected her inaugural wardrobe. It took her less than thirty minutes to select a most fashionable stock model from a Fifth Avenue shop, Le Mouchair, to be made up in a unique hue, "Eleanor blue," a shade of hyacinth blue which she said was the favorite shade of her favorite color. She also bought nine dresses from Milgrim's and four hats from Lilly Daché. The shops gave her low prices, since they were eager to have the First Lady display their clothes. But in the fall of 1933 she made it clear to Milgrim's that she could not shop there again until the ILGWU strike against them had been settled to the satisfaction of both sides. Herman Milgrim wired her several days later that the strike was over. Mrs. Roosevelt was happy to wear attractive clothes, but not to exploit garment workers.[5]

In February 1933, having acquired a new wardrobe, Mrs. Roosevelt decided that she would travel to Washington in characteristically simple fashion. She would load her roadster with belongings and drive down with a woman friend. This was too much for Roosevelt — the only occasion upon which Moley ever heard him make any complaint about his wife. Roosevelt lamented that it was too bad that on this one occasion the whole family could not take the train together. Eleanor Roosevelt gave up her plan to drive.[6]

What the personal relationship was between the two energetic, strong-minded, charming Roosevelts during the White House years is hard to fathom from the outside. A considerable part of the time they went their separate ways, but this was true of many married couples of upper class background. Mrs. Roosevelt traveled so much that an unkind, and obviously untrue, story went the rounds in the summer of 1933 that Roosevelt had rung for the head usher one day to ask if Mrs. Roosevelt could see an old former servant who was calling, only to be told that she had been out of town for three days. Intimates of Mrs. Roosevelt have since reminisced that she was still suffering from the hurt of her husband's romance at the end of World War I with Lucy Mercer. Gossip about that romance was floating around Washington in 1933, and came to the ears of at least one newspaperman, Raymond Clapper. Whatever Mrs. Roosevelt's private thoughts may have been when she was in a dark mood, or whatever her husband's even more private feelings, outwardly they seemed to have, if not an all-absorbing relationship, a healthy, happy one, full of tenderness and strong family feeling. There was no touch of the Gothic or of Edith Wharton in their daily living in the White House. Roosevelt had been President for less than two weeks on the occasion of their twenty-ninth wedding anniversary, on March 17. He sent her a check, and with it a typical note: [7]

Dearest Babs:
    After a fruitless week of thinking and lying awake to find whether you need or want undies, dresses, hats, shoes, sheets, towels, rouge, soup plates, candy, flowers, lamps, laxation pills, whisky, beer, etchings or caviar

I GIVE IT UP
!

And yet I know you lack some necessity of life — so go to it with my love and many happy returns of the day!

F.D.R.[8]

Eleanor Roosevelt considered her husband the custodian of the family genealogy, hers as well as his. The subject bored her. When someone inquired about her line of descent from the famous Chancellor Edward Livingston, she queried him, and he replied on one of his chits: "Tell the lady you are descended from the Chancellor's elder daughter, who married Edward P. Livingston." [9]

Roosevelt twitted her occasionally upon her appearance in pictures, a sore point with her. She was not as shy about them as she had been when her husband had run for vice president, but nevertheless wrote a painter, "I am sorry I can not agree to have my portrait painted, but portraits and photos are things which I do not like very much." Yet her husband's consideration became apparent when they sat on the sofa by the fireplace in the President's study for a joint portrait to appear on their Christmas card. Roosevelt appeared well in all of the proofs, but he chose not the one most flattering to him but to his wife.[10]

Whatever it might be in private, the Roosevelts' marriage was a political partnership of unparalleled success. Mrs. Roosevelt came to the White House long since a significant and successful public figure. Her stature and influence steadily grew, and for her as well as her husband, the White House became what her uncle, Theodore Roosevelt, had called a splendid pulpit.

As hostess at the White House, Mrs. Roosevelt seemed to operate with effortless efficiency making guests feel at ease. Some of them were women friends and associates, veterans of the Social Justice movement of the Progressive era and active in politics, whose deep commitment she helped bring to the New Deal. Roosevelt might occasionally grumble about the "do-gooders," but Eleanor Roosevelt had long used them to educate him, and they were of continuing service to him. Large numbers of those who attended teas and garden receptions were ordinary people, toward whom Mrs. Roosevelt demonstrated an unfailing kindness and interest. At the annual garden party for wounded veterans, when an eighty-eight-year-old Civil War veteran told her he had shaken Abraham Lincoln's hand, she replied: "I do much of my work in the same room that President Lincoln used for his study, and often I think of him, pacing up and down that room in the long hours of the night in those hard days while you were at the front." [11]

Mrs. Roosevelt handled the White House social arrangements and courtesies, from sending roses to the comptroller general when he was ill to the arrangement of state dinners. That first year, when she sent out invitations early in the season for a dinner in honor of the vice president, Mrs. Garner inquired if the dinner could not be canceled so that the vice president, who did not like dinners anyway, could stay in Texas until after Christmas. She talked over the problem with Roosevelt and replied there was no reason why the schedule could not be arranged to move the dinner to January. And sometimes suggestions came to her from the President. He sent on to her a letter from one of their dear friends of the Wilson era with the notation, "Sometime when we have a free afternoon I think it would be nice to motor out to see Edith Eustis at Oatlands. I have acknowledged the letter." [12]

On two touchy subjects involved in White House entertaining that spring, cigarettes for women and the serving of 3.2 percent beer, she took firm stands without reference to political expediency. It was only just becoming respectable for women to smoke, and the White House had been considered much too formal a place for an American woman to light a cigarette. On the other hand, the wife of a European diplomat could light a small cigar without censure. At once Mrs. Roosevelt, although she herself did not like to smoke, firmly obtained equality for women. When she noticed one of her guests wondering whether or not she dared light a cigarette, Mrs. Roosevelt asked for a cigarette, lit it, and took several puffs. In answer to a report someone sent her that she and her daughter had been seen smoking on the rear platform of a train — still an unpermissible vulgarity — she denied this unladylike conduct, but added: "My daughter does smoke cigarettes occasionally and I occasionally take a cigarette if I am in a group where I feel they would be more comfortable if I did so." [13]

The question whether the White House would serve beer was one Roosevelt would not answer reporters, although on occasion he had offered bootleg whiskey to individual newspapermen he had taken up to his study late at night. Rather, he told the correspondents they would have to ask his wife. Everyone knew she had been a prohibitionist; when one of her husband's Georgia friends had turned up at Warm Springs that winter with a jug of corn liquor, he inquired if Mrs. Roosevelt was there before presenting it. Eleanor Roosevelt abhorred heavy drinking as only the daughter of an alcoholic could, but she felt moderation, not total abstinence, was the answer. Several days after the reporters queried her husband, she issued a mimeographed statement:

> When it is legal to serve beer in any government house, it will naturally be proper to do so for any one who desires it at the White House.
>
> I hope very much that any change in legislation may tend to improve the present conditions and lead to greater temperance. There has been a great deal of bootlegging in beer, and, once it is legal, this will be unprofitable, and I hope that a great many people who have used stronger things will be content with legal beer, so that the cause of temperance will be really served.[14]

The first two cases of legal 3.2 percent beer arrived with great fanfare at the White House in a truck with a huge sign proclaiming, "President Roosevelt, the first real beer is yours." The time was 12:04 A.M. on April 7, 1933, and despite a light rain, a crowd of eight hundred people on the sidewalk cheered. As he had promised in advance, Roosevelt sent the beer to the National Press Club. Mrs. Roosevelt did indeed allow beer to flow at the White House, but only in moderate quantities. At one party for her children's friends, she provided enough for them to have two glasses apiece.[15]

One woman wrote Mrs. Roosevelt protesting that she, not the President, should set the temperance standard in her household, and make her husband and children conform. Mrs. Roosevelt replied energetically, going beyond the question of beer to her view of her role in the family:

> I am amused at your suggestion that my husband is a guest at his wife's table. I should have reversed the process for after all the man is still the head of the household.
> I am not afraid of having my children drink beer or anything else in moderation. I am afraid of all excesses of any kind. Personally I do not drink anything but that is a personal conviction and I think that total abstinence can only come as a question of personal conviction. You cannot legislate with such questions and have it accepted by the great mass of the people. Neither can you in your own family announce ultimatums for the entire family. Individuals must have the liberty to make their own decisions. The only result I have found in families where any one member insists on certain standards, is at best lip service and a certain amount of deceit. I far prefer being responsible only for myself and allowing each person to be honest as to what they do and able to make their own decisions in their family group.[16]

Eleanor Roosevelt announced her decision to serve beer at a press conference of her own. One of her innovations had been to inaugurate her own press conferences, the first any First Lady had ever held. On March 6, she met thirty-five newspaperwomen in the Red Room of the White House, "with fear and trembling, trying to cover my uncertainty by passing around a box of candied fruit," and answered questions, many of which touched upon the way the economic crisis affected the women of the nation. Mrs. Roosevelt had no especial headline-making remarks, even though unlike her husband she allowed direct quotation of what she said. She had no message for women as women. The inaugural address, she said, had been a message to all the American people, and that included women. "This time is one that requires courage and common sense on everybody's part." [17]

Although Mrs. Roosevelt's first press conference did not generate much news, it was encouraging to women reporters, who in those years, with only a very few exceptions like Anne O'Hare McCormick, were confined to reporting news of particular interest to women. The White House and Capitol were men's domain (and, it should be added, a lily-white domain). In advance, Mrs. Roosevelt set only one rule, that she would not answer questions on political subjects, and that whoever asked them would not be invited again. She also modestly described the press conferences as an experiment. "If the newspaper women find it a bore after a while," she said, "we can always stop." Not everyone was enthusiastic. One woman correspondent, presumably one with whom Mrs. Roosevelt did not have pleasant relations, was quoted as remarking in private, "Mrs. Roosevelt doesn't hide her light under any bushel; if she had a bushel she'd burn it to add to the light." [18]

The conferences never stopped, for Mrs. Roosevelt's line against political questions was a very shadowy one, and as her concerns grew so did the areas of legitimate questioning and the news she generated. She soon became a prime news source, second only at the White House to the President. As she boldly set forth to make social justice a prime component of the New Deal, news of her interest in aid to the poor and improvement in the position of women and Negroes helped test public sentiment. Sometimes it gave the President an indication that he could safely advance. Bess Furman wrote, "At the President's press conference, all the world's a stage; at Mrs. Roosevelt's all the world's a school." Miss Furman's remark is an indication of the partisan loyalty Eleanor Roosevelt was developing among newspaperwomen, for actually both Roosevelts performed the same task through their press conferences. Roosevelt too, through his off-the-record lectures, was performing primarily as a teacher, painstakingly preparing the way for change.[19]

It was generally assumed that Mrs. Roosevelt had influence on her husband, and many people began to seek access to him through her. Admiral Richard E. Byrd, who for the previous nine months had been promoting government economy, in April sent her a note. "Franklin is doing superbly," he wrote, and enclosed a letter to him. Presumably Byrd felt otherwise the letter might not get by the secretaries; Mrs. Roosevelt did deliver it to her husband.[20]

Before the end of 1933, Mrs. Roosevelt was receiving about five hundred letters a day. Some like the one protesting the serving of beer in the White House raised questions in which she was interested and might stimulate her to reply personally. But if the question was one that came to her over and over again, she left the letter to her secretary for a response. To one indignant woman who protested against hearing only from a secretary, she explained: "My secretary knows my attitude on questions such as old age pensions as well as I do and that is why she answered your letter, also in the White House any letter which I sign I have to pay the postage on, whereas when my secretary signs it it is official and needs no postage. This amounts to a great deal when you get hundreds of letters each day." [21]

Many of the letters to Mrs. Roosevelt came from distressed people asking help from her or her husband, and most of these she routed (as was about four-fifths of her husband's mail) to the relief, agricultural, or other agencies where the problems could receive direct attention. A few she tried to attend to herself. Soon she was serving as an informal national ombudsman.

In keeping with her interest since her teens in helping poor people, Mrs. Roosevelt continued on a national scale her efforts to obtain legislation, enlist private philanthropy, and to help personally. Her first public undertaking, in March 1933, was to tour the almost indescribably squalid, disease-breeding alleyways of Washington where black people lived in misery, in some instances in sight of the Capitol dome. She herself drove through the alleys, accompanying the eighty-one-year-old Charlotte Everett Hopkins, a Washington aristocrat who had long tried to wipe out these shocking conditions. Mrs. Roosevelt assured Mrs. Hopkins that her husband would help get legislation through Congress, perhaps even by taking some members of Congress through the alleys, but she had to report later that Roosevelt thought it would be impossible to get any local bills of any kind through the special session. Roosevelt reassured her that at the regular session the legislation could be passed, but for decade after decade since many of the alleys have continued little improved.[22]

With greater success, since she did not have to depend upon Congress to act, Mrs. Roosevelt took up the cause of unemployed women. She not only helped obtain a camp for young women comparable to those of the CCC, but persuaded Harry Hopkins to make use of unemployed schoolteachers through the emergency relief program. Grosvenor Clarkson, who had been one of Wilson's wartime administrators, commended her for her aid to unemployed women in words reminiscent of the Progressive crusade. It was, he said, "one of the finest things to come out of the great tapestry of doing since March 4th," and he reminded her "how T.R. used to react to O'Henry's stories about the New York shop girl working for starvation wages." [23]

Rural poverty also deeply concerned Mrs. Roosevelt, who before long was traveling to see for herself conditions in the soft coal mining area of West Virginia. Soon, with the active cooperation of Howe, she was trying to launch an ambitious experiment there with federal funds to establish a model community and provide work for its members. She also wanted to do what she could out of her personal resources for one or another poor family whose plight particularly touched her heart.[24]

> The day that I was in Morgantown one of the case workers took me to see a family who lived in a camp up on the side of a hill. She said it was one of her worst families and that they were in pretty bad condition.

The little boy had a bunny to which he seemed very devoted and the question of using the bunny as food came up and the case worker told me that the little boy objected strenuously. I wonder if a hundred dollars would really help that family out. I have an offer of that amount of money, but I felt that they were so shiftless that, unless someone would be responsible for the spending of the money, it would be of little real help.[25]

In this instance it was William Bullitt, to whom she had related the story at dinner, who had rescued the pet bunny from the stewpot, but most of the money that Mrs. Roosevelt found for countless desperate people came largely from her own lectures and writing. She never talked about what she herself gave, but she came under severe criticism because as First Lady she continued to earn sizable sums. When she entered the White House she was editor of a magazine for Bernarr MacFadden, *Babies, Just Babies;* within several months it foundered. Mrs. Roosevelt then contracted to prepare a monthly feature, answering letters for the *Woman's Home Companion,* but quickly switched to the *Ladies' Home Journal.* Each of these positions also included a salary for her daughter Anna, who was separated from her husband. In 1933, Mrs. Roosevelt also served on the editorial board of the Junior Literary Guild, receiving $100 per month for helping make selections.[26]

Mrs. Roosevelt was a bit sensitive to criticism, and explained to the *Writer's Digest,* but not for publication, that while, granted, she had received invitations to edit and write because her name would attract attention, that she had not been putting anybody out of work (since *Babies, Just Babies* continued to employ an expert editor). Besides, she had had considerable experience in editing a paper for Democratic women in New York, "even to the pasting up and preparing the dummy, so I did know my job in a small way." While she could not very well "divorce myself from my name," she insisted, "I always honestly try to do every job to the best of my ability."[27]

Among feminists, except perhaps ardent Republicans, there was pride rather than disparagement over Mrs. Roosevelt's many activities. They gloried in her achievements, and benefited from her efforts to advance the status of women, in both large ways and small. Eleanor Roosevelt was one of them. "She was very much a woman's woman," Frances Perkins has reminisced. "There wasn't any of this waiting for the men to come in after coffee."[28]

Both as First Lady and as a leading woman figure in the Democratic party, Eleanor Roosevelt was active in pressing Roosevelt, Farley, and anyone else she could persuade, to give more and better positions to women. Roosevelt was cooperative, and indeed one day in March delighted her by reporting that another senator had called up to say how well fitted Miss Perkins had shown herself to be. Some of the other men were less cooperative, and she aided and abetted Molly Dewson of the Woman's Division of the Democratic party in keeping after them. Miss Dewson allowed Farley no rest, and, if she could not get a good post for an important Democratic woman, on occasion compromised by obtaining one for her husband. Mrs. Roosevelt herself tried to persuade an able woman to become one of the regional directors for the Woman's Division of the Democratic National Committee.[29]

At one of her early press conferences, Mrs. Roosevelt did her best to counter the depression policy of firing married women from government jobs. She reinforced Secretary of Labor Perkins's protest, declaring that it would be a "very bad and very foolish thing" for the government to dismiss women because they were married, the more so because government salaries "in most cases are so small as to be hardly enough to support more than two persons, and certainly not enough on which to educate and rear a family." [30]

Again to call attention to what women could achieve, on an evening in April after a dinner party she flew over Washington in one of the big new Curtiss-Condor planes of the Eastern Air Transport Company with Amelia Earhart at the controls. "It does mark an epoch, doesn't it," Mrs. Roosevelt remarked, "when a girl in evening dress and slippers can pilot a plane at night?" The *New Yorker* was snide enough to point out that regular pilots had taken off and landed the plane. "We men don't give up without a fight." [31]

Some men might smile, but women who had been in the forefront of the fight for their rights were thrilled by all Eleanor Roosevelt was undertaking, and by the outstanding women the President was appointing to service. The matriarch of the women's rights movement, Carrie Chapman Catt, wrote: "For some time I have had a collection of statesmen hanging upon my wall, but, under the new administration, I have been obliged to start a new collection and that is one of stateswomen. Now it is ready and you are the very center of it all." [32]

It was Judge Florence E. Allen of the Supreme Court of Ohio who emphasized the most remarkable aspect of Mrs. Roosevelt's achievement — "to have your courageous self in the White House, willing to speak your own thoughts and live your own life in spite of the slavery which that position entails upon the 'first lady.' " [33]

CHAPTER XVIII

Launching a Recovery Program

We seem to be off to a good start and I hope to get through some important legislation while the feeling of the country is so friendly.

— FDR, *March 13, 1933*.[1]

As public confidence soared during the first few days of Roosevelt's presidency, he faced the imperative of stimulating quick recovery. The nadir in national morale had come in the weeks before his inauguration, but the closing of the banks had dealt a still further destructive blow to the economy, and through March 1933, indices were still bumping along to the bottom, well below figures of a year earlier. Roosevelt had to act positively and speedily to meet the challenge that John Simpson of the Farmers' Union, put to him: "There is just one test of whether any legislation is beneficial or not and that is did it put any money in the pockets of the poor people of the Country, laborers and farmers. Unless the legislation being passed by Congress results in doing that, God pity those who are responsible." [2]

These were stark words to address to a President at the peak of his popularity. Never before or since has one achieved so much in his first few days in office as had Roosevelt. He had broken the long, dreary deadlock between President and Congress that had marred most of the Hoover years and amidst general acclaim obtained a burst of legislation. He was a hero to Republicans as well as Democrats and had restored hope for the future. But that future inevitably involved a return to bitter partisanship. To some who admired him in March 1933, he had undertaken all that was advisable. The restoration of confidence, according to their credo, was sufficient to start the automatic working of the economy, and they believed that providing there was no further tinkering, prosperity would spontaneously return. Roosevelt, although benefiting from the favor that these orthodox believers in laissez-faire briefly bestowed upon him, by no means shared their economic views. He wished to satisfy them as long as possible, as indeed he sought general approval, but was fully aware that hope alone does not fill empty stomachs nor stop evictions from homes and farms.

Nor had restoration of confidence alone been sufficient to stop the downward march of economic statistics. Moody's financial service reported that freight carloadings, electric power and steel ingot production had all dropped during the bank holiday. In mid-February, steel production had been 22.3 percent of the 1928 level; it fell to 19.2 percent in the week ending March 4, and to 16.7 percent in the week ending March 11. Both the bank closings and the economy legislation were likely to stimulate further deflation unless Roosevelt countered them. Employment figures continued to drift downward. William Green, president of the American Federation of Labor, had announced in January that the number of unemployed had increased some 800,000 to an estimated 12,700,000, and on March 10, after conferring with the President, he declared, "I am sorry to say that the situation is not improving. The banking situation has set back what little bit of recovery had been noticed, and that was very slight." [3]

Both the farmers and unemployed urgently needed relief, and could not be expected to wait patiently through a congressional recess or long debate. For some weeks, Roosevelt had been considering both programs to help them and more drastic and speedy measures to counter the deflation and economic decline. A serious drawback to the relief measures he was ready to recommend in the latter part of March was that even if they were speedily enacted they would not stimulate the economy for some months to come.

There was nothing particularly positive about the three pieces of legislation so far before Congress, the emergency banking, economy, and beer bills, Roosevelt remarked to reporters as background information on March 15, 1933. Only the beer bill might be considered partially constructive. While Congress was still in session, he told them, there were two other measures he wanted to initiate which would be really constructive:

> The first is a definite effort to put people to work . . . Like all big projects, it is in a sense experimental, therefore we don't want to launch it on too big a scale until we know how practical it is. . . .
>
> Then the other measure is not only a constructive measure but if it does not go through at this time, it might as well wait until next Winter. That is the effort to increase the value of farm products. The reason for haste on that is perfectly obvious, for if we defer consideration of it until April we probably would not get through until May or the end of April anyway, and a large part of the crops would already be in the ground. If we are going to have it apply to this year's crops, it ought to be put through immediately.[4]

For a day or so, Roosevelt departed from his original schedule only so far as to advocate passage of farm and unemployment bills before a recess. By March 16, he was thinking of keeping Congress in continuous session until he obtained all his legislation. He conferred with Joe Robinson, the Senate majority leader, then raised a trial balloon. The President's impression, newspapers reported, was that the American people did not favor a long recess, rather "that the psychological effect would be better to have Congress on the job even should there be some delay in presenting the completed administration program." [5]

Congress was already anticipating several New Deal measures. Senator Norris once again dropped his Muscle Shoals bill in the legislative hopper. Also, Roosevelt suggested that the Banking and Currency Committee continue its investigation of banking practices, and he informally asked the Senate Foreign Relations Committee to reintroduce an arms embargo resolution. Within the White House, Moley remembers, Roosevelt effortlessly slipped from the assumption that Congress would adjourn to the decision to keep it in session: [6]

> F.D.R. himself scarcely stopped to recognize that he faced a choice. He allowed that the congressional leaders must be somewhat tuckered out by the winter's work. He granted that they'd all looked forward to a week or two of respite. But, he said, figuratively thumping his chest, *he* wasn't tired. *He* was full of pep. *He* was rarin' to go. The thing to do was to strike while Congress was hot.[7]

As was good politics, Roosevelt on March 17, in explaining to the press the decision to continue, gave credit to the congressional leaders for the shift in plans. He said he had been consulting them for the past three days and that

> there was a rather distinct feeling on their part, with which I went along, that, now that they are here, if the Administration can anticipate this legislation and the definite lines of policy and get them in a good deal more quickly, that the Congress would prefer to stay right on and see if they can get the legislation through by the end of April or the early part of May.[8]

There can be little doubt as to Roosevelt's sincerity in his early disarming statements that he would present major bills, including farm legislation, only after a recess of several weeks. He so informed Simpson on March 6. Later he had to write apologetically to the furious Simpson, who, taking Roosevelt at his word, left Washington and missed the prestigious conference on the farm bill.[9]

There can be no shred of doubt that Roosevelt was well aware of the unique nature of his opportunity. Not 'for long could the nation remain at such an emotional pitch or feel that desperate emergency justified

Roosevelt's measures. As soon as conditions improved, the acute pressure for action would slacken. Nor for long could he expect heavy majorities in both houses of Congress so speedily to pass bill after bill. Franklin D. Roosevelt, as one who had undergone his political apprenticeship in the Progressive era, had learned to discriminate between the shortcoming of the talented but frenetic Theodore Roosevelt, whose sustained exhortations in the end wearied many among the electorate and in Congress, and the skilled political timing of Wilson with his intermittent pressures, who had gained his ends — until the Senate failed to ratify the Versailles Treaty.[10]

For a brief period, Roosevelt enjoyed overwhelming public enthusiasm, and he was ready to act rapidly while it lasted. In his first twelve days in office, he received 14,000 laudatory telegrams. A midwestern labor leader sitting in the White House anteroom remarked, "Out in my country there are no Republicans or Democrats. We are all for Roosevelt." William Allen White, the Kansas editor, had expressed his disgust in January when Roosevelt failed to intervene strongly with Congress: "Nero fiddling was vastly wiser." But on March 11, White confessed to Ickes: [11] "It doesn't matter much what your man Roosevelt says. It is what he is doing that is pleasing the American people. So far so good. If he would keep this up for four years I am ashamed to think what will happen to us poor benighted Republicans if there are any left." [12]

Roosevelt could fire that enthusiasm through stimulating a favorable press and the final expedient of talking directly to the people through the radio Fireside Chats. Further, he could channel public feeling toward Congress. Few members of the House (with an election only a year away) wished to struggle against it; even a large part of the senators were carried along.

There were additional factors working upon Congress. Many of those who had gone through the fruitless lame duck session were rather confused and demoralized, ready to accept the discipline of Roosevelt's leadership, even if their confusion continued and they did not really understand or approve his proposals. One harassed senator, Josiah Bailey of North Carolina, in January 1933 had described to a political associate the conditions that gradually wore down many a strong-minded independent or conservative to the point of bowing to accept the President's yoke after March 4:

> Dictatorships act upon reason and democracies act upon necessity. It is not difficult to get one man to decide on the course but it is very difficult to get five hundred men to decide on anything, and this is especially true in the present state of the public mind. Members of Congress are flooded with remedies and really have no time to read the

documents submitted. At the same time, they are besieged with people seeking office, not as a means of honor but as a means of livelihood. Besiegers are so numerous that one cannot leave his room to go to the office after nine. I find myself very badly broken down but quite hopeless of getting any relief from the pressure. I am down here tonight dictating letters, wholly because I am not permitted to do anything in the day time. What we do we have to do on the fly.[13]

The Roosevelt administration would indeed have jobs to dispense. The knowledge of that fact led hundreds of thousands of needy supporters to pressure representatives and senators that spring, and led them in turn to look eagerly to the White House. There would be about 25,000 places to fill not subject to Civil Service, including 15,600 postmasterships. Including minor technical positions, day labor, and seasonal jobs, the patronage open to Democrats when Roosevelt took office totaled almost 100,000 positions. The creation of each New Deal agency that spring opened still more positions exempt from Civil Service controls. During the "hundred days" Roosevelt filled only major positions; there was only a skeleton crew of New Dealers in his administration during the weeks that he was pressuring through his legislative program. The significance of withholding patronage until the end of the special session was not lost upon Congress. Already when some House members had shown signs of rebelling against the economy bill, one leader had told them publicly in the House chamber, "When the *Congressional Record* goes to President Roosevelt's desk in the morning he will look over the roll call we are about to take, and I warn you new Democrats to be careful where your names are found." The rebels hissed and groaned, but voted for the administration.[14]

In point of fact, most of the new Democrats, who were numerous indeed, were more willing to vote for New Deal measures than were some of the long-time members of Congress. After March 4, a sizable part of the membership of both houses of Congress was new — 14 senators and 144 representatives, most of them swept into Washington on the Roosevelt landslide. They were inexperienced, sometimes bewildered, and had every reason to grasp for the security of Roosevelt's leadership and the tangible rewards it carried. There were others not much more seasoned than they. Nearly a quarter more of the members had initially been elected in 1930. In consequence, more than half of the Congress had first been sent to Washington in response to the depression, and might be expected to favor positive action.[15]

There were exceptions, of course, and Josiah Bailey of North Carolina, who had been elected to the Senate in 1930, was one of them. He welcomed Roosevelt and at first supported him, then gradually voted more and more often against New Deal measures and turned into a vitriolic critic. Yet, coming from a state whose voters were fanatically pro-Roosevelt, Bailey never repudiated the President in an election year.[16]

Bailey's reaction to Roosevelt was rather more vehemently conservative than that of most of the veteran Democrats in Congress. Some in the opposite fashion, like Representative Robert L. Doughton, also of North Carolina, were energetically pro-Roosevelt and pro–New Deal. In the middle were those regulars delighted that the Democratic party was back in power for the first time since March 1921, and pleased to have in the White House a President so popular with the voters. They might not understand much of what they were asked to vote upon in the spring of 1933, and not approve of what they did understand, but the habit of party loyalty was strong. Added to that was their personal loyalty to the Democratic leaders promoting the legislation, and the loyalty of these leaders to a President with whom most of them had been on friendly personal terms. The leaders cherished the committee chairmanships they had waited for many years to attain, and being members of the minority party, shared Roosevelt's interest in obtaining the support of a majority of the electorate for the Democrats so that they could retain their power and perquisites. Whether leaders or part of the rank-and-file, the Democrats were susceptible to the range of means or persuasion that Roosevelt utilized, from the flattery of personal attention or cajolery to the lure of patronage once the legislative program was enacted.

Additional backing came to Roosevelt from the Republican progressives, especially in the Senate, whom he courted so assiduously both before and after the election. Together with the Democratic progressives they shared a considerable following among the electorate. They were independent in their voting, and as they demonstrated during the first week, did not hesitate to oppose measures of which they disapproved. In the Senate during the 1920s they had been a force capable of disruption well out of proportion to their numbers. They did like and had long advocated parts of the program that unfolded during the spring of 1933; indeed, they could claim to have originated impressive segments of it. Roosevelt readily incorporated proposals of the Republicans Norris and La Follette, as well as of the Democratic progressives Wagner, Costigan, and others, into his grand design. The progressive senators of both parties, as long-time advocates of lost causes, found it exhilarating to have their ideas recognized and transformed into law. The change in administration elevated them from frustrated outsiders into honored prime-movers. The Republican Norris, whom Hoover labeled a great master of demagoguery, was hailed by Roosevelt several years later as "one of the major prophets of America." [17]

In turn, Norris and some of the other progressives saw Roosevelt as the President who could make their dreams come true. During the Progressive era, theorists had pointed out that the progressive capture of Congress was not sufficient to bring about reform. It was also essential, reasoned Herbert Croly, Walter Lippmann and others, to elect a powerful, sympathetic leader. In Franklin D. Roosevelt these remaining progressives in Congress had found another T.R., a new Wilson, and in the spring of 1933 they rejoiced.*

"There has never been a president in the history of our country who has had thrown in his lap at the beginning of his term so many difficult governmental questions as President Roosevelt has had to face," Norris wrote on May 1 to Ellery Sedgwick, the conservative editor of the *Atlantic Monthly*. "Regardless of party, and regardless of every other consideration, it seems to me that every patriotic citizen should help him in every way." This was the course that Norris himself followed, supporting Roosevelt with enthusiasm, although as he confessed in the fall of 1933, he had not agreed with many of Roosevelt's partisan ideas.[19]

Roosevelt was emerging as a strong President, in contrast not only to his predecessor Hoover, but to the image he himself had created during the interregnum. At the time he had paid the penalty of seeming relatively colorless, flabby and directionless as a leader; after his inauguration he appeared positive and dynamic. He had not only kept his options open but also had kept expectations at a relatively low level before he took office. Part of his magic during the "hundred days" was the way in which he threw off his early guise and surpassed all predictions. It was hard for the men in the Capitol to resist him.

The House was particularly well organized for the enactment of the New Deal program, since Henry T. Rainey of Illinois, an enthusiastic supporter, succeeded in winning the Speakership. During the lame duck session, an undercover struggle had gone on between Speaker Garner and the Roosevelt forces. Garner, reluctantly leaving his position of power to become vice president, had tried to rally the House Democrats behind the conservative John McDuffie of Alabama, reputed to be tied to large corporate and utility interests. Jouett Shouse, who as chairman of the Democratic National Executive Committee had helped organize the Allies against Roosevelt at the 1932 convention, had also quietly tried to gather support for McDuffie. Roosevelt, who had a large stake in the outcome, was too shrewd a politician to appear involved. In late December 1932, after Garner told him the contest had narrowed to

* Subsequently, some of the progressives in Congress, though never Norris and Wagner, turned against FDR. Among the sum total of progressive leaders in the United States, as Otis Graham has pointed out, a considerable part came to sour on the New Deal.[18]

McDuffie versus Rainey, Roosevelt warned James A. Farley it would be bad policy for Farley to show his hand at that time. To one of the minor contenders, Representative John J. O'Connor, Roosevelt would comment only that Rainey was popular and that he hoped for the sake of party harmony there would be no fuss. Farley publicly announced his neutrality; there was no fuss, and the result was quite favorable to Roosevelt. It would be difficult to believe that Farley did not engage in considerable covert negotiation, but the outcome had already seemed likely by the first of the year. Garner had told Roosevelt that the third serious candidate for Speaker, Representative Joseph W. Byrns of Tennessee, of whom Roosevelt spoke well, would throw his support to Rainey. That was what happened. When the Democrats caucused, they chose Rainey as Speaker, and Byrns as floor leader. Doughton, who had opposed McDuffie, became chairman of the Ways and Means Committee. It was a result highly favorable to the incoming President.[20]

Speaker Rainey, a seventy-four-year-old white-haired patriarch who dressed like a cartoonist's version of a congressman, expanded his devotion to William Jennings Bryan to encompass Roosevelt. He was the first Democrat from a northern state to become Speaker in more than a half century; Democratic representatives from recently Republican districts were responsible for his victory. He had promised them in advance that he would democratize the House machinery through organizing a Democratic steering committee. "Failures in the last Congress have been due to the fact that the determination of policies has come entirely from the speaker's chair; it will now come from the party," Rainey announced. "We will put over Mr. Roosevelt's program." In operation, the steering committee was a rather confusing apparatus, lessening the control of House leaders, and heightening the influence of Roosevelt.[21]

The techniques President Roosevelt used in sending legislation to Congress were familiar to those who had observed him as governor of New York, but a novelty to the rest of the nation. First he conferred with Democratic congressional leaders. Then he would send a brief, dramatic message to Congress calling for a specific piece of legislation, and an hour or so later a bill would follow. Various congressional leaders with whom Roosevelt had made arrangements would introduce the measure and help expedite its passage.

Roosevelt "displayed remarkable skill in manipulating the attention of Congress and of the public," wrote a political scientist, E. Pendleton Herring, at the close of the session:

> His messages to Congress were strategically timed and positive and specific in character. Disagreement with his proposals was interpreted

by the general public as obstructionism. His swift pace, his boldness in assuming responsibility, and his definite recommendations not only stimulated popular support of his policy, but likewise branded as dissenters and critics congressmen holding to different policies.[22]

The Democratic machinery in the House at first passed Roosevelt's bills in almost routine fashion, giving members little time for debate or opportunity for amendment. These tactics led one member at the time of the passage of the economy bill to complain against the Rules Committee, "Now we are nothing but rubber stamps!" As weeks went by and the sense of urgency diminished, the House operated less as a rubber stamp, and the Senate began to reassert its customary checks against White House proposals. In order to obtain passage of his program, Roosevelt had to utilize subtle additional methods, not as apparent to the casual observer as the carrots-and-sticks of patronage and kindred devices.

Roosevelt was flexible rather than doctrinaire, ready to ride congressional movements he favored, and to allow Congress to make significant contributions to the shaping of New Deal legislation. When need be, he accepted modifications to his proposals, since he did not feel as Hoover so often had that deviations were necessarily unsound and must be rejected. What went on in the Capitol that spring was by no means the rubber-stamping of White House bills but the shaping of both executive proposals and congressional initiatives into finished measures.

The very nature of the bills Roosevelt submitted to Congress made modification easy. Because of the many pressures converging upon him and because he was by no means certain what would work, he usually had them drafted to be quite broad, containing numerous options, and reflecting a consensus. Readily enough he would accept amendments if they did not threaten the fundamentals. On the other hand, Congress was disposed at times to give him even greater discretion than he had requested.

Another part of the compromise process operated outside of the specific measures themselves. On occasion Roosevelt reassured cautious elements in Congress by letting them know in advance that he would appoint a conservative administrator they trusted to set into operation an untried program. It comforted Bourbons when they learned that Baruch men were to head both the agricultural and industrial experiments. Another element of compromise was involved in the handling of legislation. There were some bills that Roosevelt either did not have introduced that spring or allowed to remain in limbo because they might have jeopardized support for his major measures.

Much mystery and drama surrounded the introducing of the New

Deal program measure by measure. In part this was Roosevelt's political calculation, in part the fact that some bills were not yet drafted. Even those upon whom Roosevelt depended to expedite his legislation sometimes had little notion what future weeks might bring. "I have been hoping that the program would develop so that I can have some idea as to the length of the present session," Senator James F. Byrnes explained privately on March 25. "However, from day to day the program is enlarged, and no one can now make even an intelligent guess as to when we will be able to adjourn." It was a complex, frequently confusing undertaking to draft and 'enact the legislation of the "hundred days." [23]

The top priority went to agriculture, because crops would not wait, and Roosevelt seemed to consider it the key to recovery. So much work had already been done that Roosevelt was able to send a farm bill to Congress less than two weeks after he took office. There had been sufficient advance preparation that Roosevelt was able to focus on a number of other issues and give relatively little of his time to the farm bill during the days of its final assembly. Even Moley, the prime coordinator of most of the legislation of the "hundred days," was scarcely involved. As a matter of fact, Moley was appalled at the bill, regarding it as so cockeyed that he thought it would never pass.[24]

The farm bill developed almost in the automatic way Roosevelt had earlier suggested — putting the contenders together until they could emerge with a consensus proposal. On the evening of March 8, when Wallace and Tugwell asked Roosevelt if they could take advantage of the national wave of approval and proceed immediately with farm legislation, he told them to go ahead. Wallace and Tugwell feared the disagreements persisting among both farm leaders and congressmen over proposed remedies. They hoped they could take advantage of the excitement for the New Deal and encompass these differences, as they had the banking legislation, in an omnibus bill that would grant the President broad powers. Since everything would depend upon the approval of the pressure groups interested in agriculture, they did not feel they themselves could draw up such a measure. Rather, Wallace began immediately by telephone to invite numerous leaders of farm organizations and editors of farm papers to Washington for a bill-drafting conference to meet on March 10. As he talked to each of them he tried to plant the suggestion that the solution to differences might be blanket authorization. He was so subtle that several of the Midwesterners en route from Chicago to Washington were thereafter certain that it was they who conceived the idea. On the train they debated all afternoon, then in Ohio obtained newspapers containing reports of the bank bill. "There was the answer to the problem," one of their number,

Clifford V. Gregory of the *Prairie Farmer*, has written, "a broad grant of authority to an administrative agency. Before the last of the farmers went to bed that night the plan of the new relief act had taken definite shape." [25]

In order to obtain some sort of quick legislation, the fifty or so representatives of farm organizations and publications compromised during their day and a half of meetings in Washington. The old basic divisions were still there, with those favoring overseas marketing of surpluses, the one-time McNary-Haugenites, taking the view that they were dirt farmers and fighting against the production controls of the "domestic allotment" scheme. "The farm leaders," Peek declared bitterly several years later, ". . . muffed their big chance and left the field open to the professors." Peek's complaint was not over exclusion of his export proposals; the bill would include them. Rather he was angry because he could not eliminate the domestic allotment. But — just as had been true in Roosevelt's great omnibus farm speech at Topeka the previous September — the discussions were so sweeping that everyone, including Peek, seemed through the forthcoming legislation to be gaining at least authorization for his specific farm plan. The exception was Simpson of the Farmers' Union, who missed the conference, and whose impossible "cost of production" plan was left out. A member of the Farmers' Union executive committee was present in his stead.

Because the McNary-Haugenites were essential to a viable coalition, Wallace maneuvered to keep Peek and the conservatives involved. He consulted Peek, and sent for Peek's one-time close friend and associate, General Hugh Johnson, to participate in discussions. Once again, Fred Lee, who had drawn up the McNary-Haugen bills, was enlisted to help draft legislation. Wallace's friendliness toward Peek was beyond question. After all, as Peek knew, Wallace had written Roosevelt in November nominating him for secretary of agriculture. Also, Wallace favored export programs in addition to crop restrictions. Yet Peek was in an ill temper, which in part, his biographer Gilbert Fite thinks, may have come from a reason Peek would not admit to himself, that Roosevelt had not appointed him secretary. At the conference Wallace immediately took a vital step to neutralize Peek by asking him to run the new farm program. Peek declined vigorously and nominated Baruch, but Wallace continued the overtures.[26]

The powerful positive support that Roosevelt and Wallace needed in framing and enacting the farm bill came from the dominant organization representing commercial farmers, the Farm Bureau Federation. Indeed, they thought of the bill as their handiwork, looked upon Wallace as their secretary of agriculture, and even felt that Roosevelt was under their tutelage. The president of the federation, Edward A.

O'Neall, an Alabama gentleman farmer who had succeeded in uniting the southern and midwestern farmers within the federation, was also certain throughout his life that it was he who had persuaded Roosevelt to dump Morgenthau and appoint Wallace. Roosevelt never disturbed O'Neall's further belief that, in the early New Deal years, as a one-time economist for the Farm Bureau, John Kenneth Galbraith once reported he was "the President's private tutor on farm affairs — and considered the President a promising student." *

The farm leaders' meeting went speedily without much rehashing of familiar arguments, since everyone agreed oñ the need to act. "The proposal to grant broad authority to the Executive fell on receptive ears; but there were also words of caution," Wallace has written. The principal debate concerned which plan would best suit specific crops — representatives of wheat growers favored the domestic allotment; cotton men, crop leasing; dairymen were skeptical. "The upshot of the discussion," Wallace declares, "was the proposal to make the legislation so flexible that the Secretary could apply whatever scheme seemed best adapted to a given commodity." [28]

Roosevelt authorized the drafting of a bill when a committee from the conference presented proposals to him on Saturday, March 11. There followed four hectic days and nights of pulling and hauling as the bill took shape. There were conflicts within conflicts as the representative of each interest battled for his viewpoint. The economists, with the Farm Bureau and the Grange behind them, wanted to write in the domestic allotment, and succeeded. Peek, backed by Hugh Johnson and Baruch, above all wanted export marketing agreements, and also succeeded. Peek for a while during the debates seems to have favored also levying a tax on imports to raise funds for acreage rental. Marvin Jones, chairman of the House Committee on Agriculture, wanted only to take acreage out of production through rental. A provision for acreage rental went into the bill, but the other possibilities still remained.

As usual, Roosevelt kept his options open as long as possible, acting only as final arbiter. The conservative Peek ironically got the impression that Roosevelt was in danger of making too many concessions to the processors, bankers, and speculators. He lectured Wallace, telling him that the "President could not lean two ways; one toward the farmer, the other toward the old gang." Tugwell told Peek this kind of talk should be presented to the President, and together with Wallace and Johnson went to the White House on March 15. They returned to inform Peek that the President stood with Wallace.[29]

---

* In retrospect, Galbraith feels this states precisely O'Neall's attitude toward FDR, whom he greatly respected and perhaps even loved. "In later times, Southern planters have not thought so well of liberal Presidents," writes Galbraith. "O'Neall was, however, in many ways, a remarkable man." [27]

In the two arguments that Roosevelt himself had to resolve, curiously enough the interests of Wallace, the economists, and Peek seemed to coincide. The first concerned a struggle between some of the economists and Morgenthau, who wished to finance the scheme through a sales tax on the finished products rather than a processing tax. A sales tax would have been much more acceptable to the processors, but Roosevelt decided against the unpopular sales tax and in favor of a tax which processors must pay. The other debate was whether the bill should be of a truly emergency nature and limited to one year. Wallace and the economists presented to the President a memorandum arguing forcefully that surpluses were so large that it would take three or four years to dispose of them, and the imbalance between farm production and consumer demand "cannot be corrected without continued control of supplies until such time as surplus workers are disposed of in urban industry and land utilization programs." Roosevelt retained the emergency phraseology, which could help bring enactment of the bill, but accepted a program that would be indefinite in duration. The legislation would remain in effect until the President proclaimed the agricultural emergency at an end.[30]

On the day before he presented the bill to Congress, Roosevelt was still so indefinite about it that off the record he told reporters, first, that it would be like the Smith cotton bill, a device for taking land out of production through leasing, then a few minutes later, that it would "probably vary in accordance with different crops." When he was asked whether it was permanent legislation, he gave a reply which touched at the crux of the matter: "No, obviously a farm bill is in the nature of an experiment. We all recognize that. My position toward farm legislation is that we ought to do something to increase the value of farm products and if the darn thing doesn't work, we can say so quite frankly, but at least try it." [31]

The bill was broad enough both to enlist a variety of supporters and to permit an array of experimentation. As Russell Lord has suggested, "The measure as drawn sought to legalize almost anything anybody could think up." [32]

At noon on March 16, Roosevelt again saw Wallace and Tugwell, gave the bill his final approval, and jotted on a yellow legal pad a few words to serve as a message to Congress. That afternoon he sent the bill and message to the Capitol. This "new means to rescue agriculture," he told Congress, was "of definite, constructive importance to our economic recovery." He emphasized once more the stake of all American society in agricultural recovery. The bill, he said, "seeks to increase the purchasing power of our farmers and the consumption of articles manufactured in our industrial communities." [33]

The American people, still filled with relief that the banking crisis had been brought to a conclusion, were, if one is to judge by the press at the time, not particularly excited over the farm bill. There seemed no especial awareness of a sharp break with the past in the momentous proposal to introduce federal planning into a major sector of the economy, agriculture. Nor did there seem to be urban resistance, even though the *New York Times*, counseling Roosevelt to go slowly in farm experimentation, asked, "what will the great mass of consumers think of this form of sales tax, resting heavily on food?" The response, during the House debate several days later, was what the President wanted. Representative William Patrick Connery, Jr., a Massachusetts Democrat, asserted: [34] "The farmers will have a bigger income. With that, they can repair their buildings, purchase new farm machinery and new equipment for their homes, so that industrial workers will be able to obtain employment in the factories." [35]

So far as the general electorate was concerned, a comment by Herbert Feis on March 15 seemed to apply: "The outside public seems to behave as if Angel Gabriel had come to earth." That too seemed to be the reaction of the rank and file of farmers. They had little understanding at first of the farm bill, nor even, so far as the single seriously flawed postal card poll at the time would indicate, any affirmative desire for the specific formulas it proposed, but they wanted quick government action. This their flood of mail to Washington made clear beyond question.[36]

Congress would no longer act instantaneously, although as spring advanced the need for farm legislation was as urgent as the banking and economy bills, and should have been regarded as more vital than the thirst that brought Senate passage of the beer bill on March 16. Roosevelt and his lieutenants may have hoped that agricultural legislation would be enacted in the course of several days, but the way in which the Senate had battered, then abandoned, the farm bill during the interregnum session had given indication that nothing short of a miracle would bring its quick passage in March 1933. Already some of the compelling sense of urgency had evaporated; the mounting popular faith in Roosevelt would not suffice. Although the rank and file of both houses of Congress were ready by an overwhelming margin to accept Roosevelt's recommendations, key figures in the Senate would respond only slowly.

Even in the House the farm bill received an inauspicious reception. Chairman Jones of the Agriculture Committee declined to introduce it, saying that although he would not oppose it he did not approve of some of the provisions. He hoped to simplify the measure, and meanwhile left its introduction to the second-ranking Democrat on the committee. The Agriculture Committee made several minor changes in the bill, among them, eliminating appointments under the bill from Civil

Service regulations. Democrats defended the change as essential if the new program were to be established quickly, or to be liquidated if it did not work. Republicans charged it was a patronage grab.

Speaker Rainey and the Democratic leaders in the House, by applying the "gag rule" limiting debate to four hours and prohibiting amendments from the floor, succeeded in rushing through the farm bill almost as rapidly as its predecessors. The brief debate was significant only because Republicans presented a preview of the forthcoming line of attack upon the New Deal. The conservative James Beck of Pennsylvania declared that the only justification for the bill was the emergency, "and in Germany, with the same excuse, they are voting power today to Hitler." Joseph Martin of Massachusetts warned against the "army of tax-gatherers and spies" who would deploy under the "czarlike power of the Secretary of Agriculture," to put Americans "well on the road to Moscow." Others elaborated upon the Communist theme, Michael Hart of Michigan credited Tugwell and Mordecai Ezekiel with authorship of the bill. Tugwell, he charged, was a member of the American Civil Liberties Union, which "defends anarchists when they shoot somebody." Both Tugwell and Ezekiel had spent time in Russia, said Hart, and "I am not going to follow communism." From this point on, conservatives plastered Tugwell with the Red label.

Some of the critics in the House raised sober questions. Martin asserted it would saddle poor consumers with a billion-dollar tax bill. Numerous farm bloc representatives either preferred the radical "cost of production" scheme, or felt the most urgent need was to refinance farm mortgages and through one or another inflationary scheme to bring up farm prices. Most of these representatives were ready nevertheless to vote for the measure. William Lemke, although he favored "cost of production," asserted, "Normally there are not enough Democrats in my State to fill the [postmasterships]. But we gave Franklin D. Roosevelt a 160,000 majority. We had confidence in Franklin D. Roosevelt; we still have confidence in Franklin D. Roosevelt." [37]

On March 22, only six days after Roosevelt sent Congress the farm bill, the House passed it 315 to 98.* Hearings began in the Senate two days later.

The Senate was more deliberate in its consideration of the farm bill. On the afternoon of March 16, as soon as it had passed the beer bill, "Cotton Ed" Smith, apparently in a cooperative mood, asked the unani-

---

* The vote on the bill was 273 Democrats, 38 Republicans and 4 Farmer-Laborites for; 24 Democrats, 73 Republicans, and 1 Farmer-Laborite against. These figures can be interpreted as meaning a Democratic victory. Edward O'Neall, breaking down the figures by region rather than party, could point to the overwhelming vote for the bill of 106 to 26 among midwestern representatives, and 109 to 4 among Southerners, and take credit for the Farm Bureau.[38]

mous consent necessary for immediate introduction and announced a meeting of his committee for the next day, Saturday, so that it could report the bill to the Senate on Monday. Several southern senators, including Huey Long, immediately objected. Richard Russell of Georgia protested that he did not want to "have to vote tomorrow on one of the most important bills without even a chance to read it." Both Smith and Majority Leader Robinson had to promise there would be time for full consideration of the bill in order to obtain unanimous consent to introduce it.[39]

Deliberation in the Senate threw off Roosevelt's timing by giving opponents of the measure an opportunity to rally against it. "We had hoped to get the thing through before lobbyists of the processors could descend on Washington"; wrote Tugwell while it was still before the Senate, "but we immediately met with strong opposition. The packers, millers, and spinners are quite adequately represented in Congress. It seems impossible, in that group of small-town lawyers, to find anyone with the slightest interest in farmers or workers. They represent business interests for the most part." [40]

Spokesmen for the millers, meat packers, cotton brokers and textile manufacturers immediately assailed the program at its weakest point, the new tax it would impose in those deflationary times. It was bearish, they declared, and would cut consumer demand. The former president of the New York Cotton Exchange wired Roosevelt that it would "demoralize all markets for agricultural products owing to the oppressive and almost confiscatory tax it proposes to levy on processors." A prominent member of the Chicago Board of Trade labeled it "the most fantastic bill ever proposed by any country in peacetime," and the president of the Omaha Grain Exchange asserted it "reflected the policy of the same crowd of professional farm racketeers who presume to represent agriculture in Washington."

Farm pressure for the measure was, contrary to Tugwell's lamentations, far more powerful than that of the processors. The conservative president of the Illinois Agricultural Association, Earl Smith, praised the bill as "the most feasible, practical farm measure presented in Congress in recent years." The governor of Mississippi announced that a conference of the governors of cotton-growing states supported the proposal to reduce cotton acreage.[41]

A minority in the Senate, some of it in strategic positions, wanted a limited, cautious farm bill. A majority, representing the farm states, continued the farm bloc of the 1920s, and wanted to go much further than the administration to accept Simpson's "cost of production" scheme and some form of inflation in order to bring about an instant increase in farm prices. Elmer Thomas of Oklahoma, the prime inflationist in the Senate, on March 29 wrote: "I am giving the President every possible support and will continue to do so. We have the so-called farm relief bill pending now. I realize that no permanent relief is possible until the masses have buying power; in other words, the unemployed must have jobs and farmers must have cost of production before the country can begin to be prosperous." [42]

Roosevelt's task was to pursue a middle course which would preserve the bill from being emasculated by "Cotton Ed" Smith and conservatives or being inflated into an unworkable chimera by the western agrarians. It was easier to neutralize the former McNary-Haugenites and the processing interests than those demanding "cost of production" and substantial inflation.

Out of the contest among contending interests came the likelihood that the Senate would considerably modify the farm bill. A Republican leader proclaimed Roosevelt's legislative honeymoon to be over. Even Roosevelt's ally, Key Pittman, president pro tempore of the Senate, while predicting passage in a week, labeled the bill a potpourri which the Senate would greatly modify in a conservative direction. "Cotton Ed" Smith announced he would move to strike out everything in the bill after Section 1, which was his own "cotton clause." The ranking Republican on the Agriculture Committee, Charles L. McNary of Oregon, wanted to limit the programs to wheat and cotton.[43]

For several days, the Agriculture Committee held hearings, allowing some proponents and many opponents of the farm bill to testify. Not only were there lobbyists for the processors, but also critics like Simpson of the Farmers' Union who, with Senator George Norris backing him, once more was demanding "cost of production." Simpson struck at a vital weakness when he declared, "These farmers are not producing too much. We need all this. What we have overproduction of is empty stomachs and bare backs." [44]

While the Senate Agriculture Committee continued its hearings, sentiment throughout the country was overwhelmingly favorable to passage of the measure, ranging from enthusiasm on the part of a few to a widespread feeling that whatever its shortcomings, it should be tried. There was little vehement opposition, even from urban consumers' interests. Lippmann, mildly favorable, was of the view that the legislation would not have much effect, and should be passed quickly so Congress could proceed to more vital measures. Most newspaper editorials reflected acquiescence and if not faith, at least hope. Farmers' letters to Wallace, according to Gilbert Fite, who has surveyed them, demanded federal aid to raise prices, differing only over means, not the end.[45]

The one aspect of agricultural relief upon which almost all farmers and members of Congress were united was the demand for refinancing of farm mortgages. Few farmers were able to keep up payments on the heavy mortgages carrying 6 to 8 percent interest that they had incurred when commodity prices were higher. Senator Borah expressed his disappointment that the farm bill did not contain a plan for rural refinancing.[46]

Roosevelt as he had promised earlier had every intention of proposing legislation to refinance farm mortgages. Through his authority to reorganize the executive branch of the government he expected to consolidate the eight farm credit agencies. On March 27, he sent Congress an Executive Order creating the single Farm Credit Administration, which would provide greater uniformity in agricultural credits and result in an immediate saving of more than two million dollars. It was a beginning toward "meeting the credit needs of agriculture at minimum cost." Roosevelt appointed Morgenthau to serve as governor of the new agency.[47]

As for mortgage refinancing, Roosevelt on March 22 told reporters it would probably be the subject of the next message and bill to go to the Hill. He added that similar legislation for the relief of small homeowners would accompany it or shortly follow. The problem with which Roosevelt wrestled was how to reduce mortgage interest rates drastically, yet be able to sell at par the bonds of the Federal Land Banks through which to raise money for the mortgage funding. By April 3, Roosevelt had solved the interest problem; while he and his advisers would have liked 2 percent, they had to settle for 4½ percent. He informed Congress: [48]

> That many thousands of farmers in all parts of the country are unable to meet indebtedness incurred when their crop prices had a very different money value is well known to all of you . . . [T]he Federal Government should provide for the refinancing of mortgage and other indebtedness so as to secure a more equitable readjustment of the principal of the debt and a reduction of interest rates, which in many instances are so unconscionably high as to be contrary to a sound public policy, and, by a temporary readjustment of amortization, to give sufficient time to farmers to restore to them the hope of ultimate free ownership of their own land. I seek an end to the threatened loss of home and productive capacity now faced by hundreds of thousands of American farm families.

The program, Roosevelt pointed out, would impose no heavy burden on the Treasury. He added a significant promise: "Also, I shall ask the Congress for legislation enabling us to initiate practical reciprocal tariff agreements to break through trade barriers and establish foreign markets for farm and industrial products." [49]

The message was an opening public salvo in Roosevelt's bombardment of the Senate on behalf of the farm bill. His mortgage proposal, to be embodied in the measure, brought strength to it. The promise that he would seek reciprocal trade legislation would help disarm McNary-Haugenites and blunt somewhat the processors' attacks. It also may have helped weaken Peek's protestations that he did not want to head the proposed agricultural agency — for the very next day Peek discussed with Baruch the bargain he might strike with the President if he accepted the appointment.

Roosevelt's discussions with Peek settled everything and nothing; he cajoled Peek into becoming an administrator but left policy differences smoothed only on the surface. On April 5, accompanied by Wallace, Peek saw the President and urged him to appoint Baruch. Roosevelt parried that he had talked to Baruch and that he would not take the appointment. Peek then said he could not accept unless a lot of things were understood, since his views were in conflict with those of Wallace. The secretary of agriculture agreed that they disagreed. Peek then handed Roosevelt a five-point statement recommending that agricultural exports be favored over industrial exports and that industrial plant capacity be reduced. Roosevelt congratulated him for getting his statement on one sheet, and arranged a further meeting. Two days later when Peek returned to the White House with Baruch and Frank Lowden of Illinois, Roosevelt told Peek he agreed with the five-point memorandum, that their difference was over restriction of farm production as a national policy. Peek pushed that point no further, but instead, assuming acreage reduction would take place, urged Roosevelt to finance it through a tariff on agricultural imports like blackstrap molasses and vegetable oils rather than a processing tax. Roosevelt said he would not object.

Peek gave in to Roosevelt's persistence and well before the passage of the farm bill agreed to become its administrator. This foreknowledge that Peek would run the program was one of the most potent influences in breaking down resistance among cautious senators and processors' lobbyists.* But in exchange for an immediate legislative advantage,

---

* The agreement of Peek to accept appointment also neutralized Baruch and Baruch's lieutenant, Hugh Johnson. Several days earlier, Johnson, writing FDR at Baruch's request, warned that he regarded the bill as "clearly unconstitutional as an invalid appropriation and an invalid delegation of the taxing power." To Moley he complained that the bill had been drafted without consulting either Baruch or him until it was so far set that they could obtain no modifications to make it practicable. It "nearly breaks my heart," he declared, but, "We have refused to discuss it even with members of Congress or anybody else because while we think we have the right to fight in the bosom of the family for what we think is right and sound, we do not think we have a right to snipe or to sabotage anybody outside." [50]

Roosevelt had chosen an administrator of a key program who disapproved of its main means of seeking recovery.

Roosevelt was eager to get the farm bill out of the Agriculture Committee and through the Senate. When the hearings carried over into a second week, he summoned "Cotton Ed" Smith and his committee to the White House to demand that they report the bill at once. Smith gave in, abandoned a substitute bill he had written, and on April 5 reported the administrative measure. The committee had added several significant amendments. One of these was Roosevelt's farm mortgage proposal which would make the bill easier to enact; farmers could refinance their mortgages at 4½ percent and mortgage holders could exchange their mortgages for Federal Land Bank bonds paying 4 percent interest. Another significant amendment gave promise of trouble for Roosevelt, the Norris-Simpson "cost of production" scheme, which in theory would have sent farm prices disproportionately high.[51]

As soon as it became apparent that the Senate would act only deliberately upon the farm bill, Roosevelt, with his eye upon other impatient segments of the electorate, began to submit to Congress others of his proposals. Action upon these slowed the debate in the Senate on the farm measure, as spring rapidly advanced from the Deep South into the northern tier of states. Already the cotton plants were shooting up and the sows were farrowing their pigs. Only bad crop conditions in the wheat belt gave promise of preventing a calamitous surplus there.

Throughout the Middle West and the Great Plains, simmering agrarian discontent threatened to come to a quick boil. Pressure was becoming enormous for mortgage relief and a quick rise in commodity prices. A professor of rural sociology at the University of Chicago, Arthur E. Holt, upon returning from a tour of Wisconsin, Minnesota, Iowa, and the Dakotas, declared on April 11: "Everywhere we found farmers taking definite steps toward a united action in protest against existing conditions. There is developing a class consciousness among the farmers, and unless the Roosevelt farm relief measures become immediately effective, a general farm strike is certain to result." [52]

Simultaneous with the debate in the Senate, antiforeclosure disorders and threats of farm strikes were endemic. The desperate mood of the farmers may have had little direct effect upon the course of debate, since from the outset it was clear that a decided majority of the senators favored legislation, and many of them favored some instant palliative. Simpson's "cost of production" formula, under the prestigious sponsorship of Senator Norris, received some support, since it would have authorized the Department of Agriculture to set immediate high prices. But production would have soared, and as Senator Bankhead of Alabama pointed out, the huge supplies of wheat and cotton in the hands of middlemen who could sell them at low prices would have kept producers from receiving benefits for one or two years. Roosevelt was sufficiently alarmed over the "cost of production" amendment that he drafted a letter to Senator Robinson opposing it. At Wallace's recommendation, Roosevelt withheld the letter. Despite the arguments of Wallace, Bankhead, and others, the Senate adopted the amendment on April 12 by a vote of 47 to 41.[53]

Rather, Roosevelt's means of coping with "cost of production" was to accept limited inflation. During the debate, the pressure for remonetization of silver or some other form of inflation, which members of the farm bloc hoped would bring a quick rise in commodity prices, became contagious. A contemporary reported that in the excitement the Senate all but forgot the farm bill.

CHAPTER XIX

Going Off Gold

Orthodoxy may not be the only method for nations any
more than for individuals, to get to Heaven.
— FDR, *July 27, 1933*.[1]

Compelling reasons, both national and international, led Roosevelt in
April 1933 to make the moves he had so long contemplated, to take
the United States definitely off the gold standard and undertake controlled inflation. From overseas there was the immediate threat of a
renewed gold drain and the long-standing disadvantage compared with
Britain in competing for world markets. At home, the measures that
Roosevelt was sending to Congress one by one were likely, as with the
farm bill, to take some time to pass, and in any event contained no
sudden stimulus that could send the economy upward that April. Roosevelt was continuing to cling close to his pledges of thrift, and had as
yet submitted no proposal that would require large-scale public spending. Rather, he still hewed to budgetary orthodoxy, and as a means
of preserving it, turned to the mild monetary unorthodoxy that Westerners in Congress, agrarians, and even some merchants, manufacturers,
and financiers were urging upon him.

Well into April almost every weekly index figure gave additional
bad news to the President as the economy limped along not much above
the low points of March 1933 and well under the level of April 1932 a
year before. Prices had risen somewhat when Roosevelt took office, in
part perhaps because of hints of forthcoming inflation; by April they
were slipping. Business activity was increasing, but only very slowly,
according to the Dun & Bradstreet index, from 44.2 percent of the
1928–1930 average at the low point on March 22, up to 46.4 on April 5,
and to 48.4 by April 19.[2]

The answer to gold raids from abroad and the price decline at home
seemed to be to drop off the gold standard and obtain authorization to
inflate currency and credit. There were those who argued that it also
might improve Roosevelt's bargaining position with European leaders

coming to confer with him that April, and strengthen the United States at the World Economic Conference. It would not add to the federal deficit but would placate agrarian senators unhappy about the farm bill. Thus it seemed to offer the solution to several of Roosevelt's immediate problems.

The persisting acute deflation, creating a sharp disparity between existing price levels and property values on the one hand, and on the other, of debts incurred when prices were much higher, also worried Roosevelt. He had long felt that there must be some restoration of balance. A few months later, in explaining the reasons for his monetary actions he stated this problem succinctly:

> In talking with people about our basic economic troubles I have often drawn for them a picture showing two columns — one representing what the United States was worth in terms of dollars and the other representing what the United States owed in terms of dollars. The figures covered all property and all debts, public, corporate and individual. In 1929, the total of the assets in terms of dollars was much larger than the total of the debts. But, by the spring of 1933, while the total of the debts was still just as great, the total of the assets had shrunk to below that of the debts.
>
> Two courses were open: to cut down the debts through bankruptcies and foreclosures to such a point that they would be below property values; or else, to increase property values until they were greater than the debts.
>
> Obviously, the latter course was the only legitimate method of putting the country back on its feet without destroying human values.[3]

Roosevelt has sometimes been presented as only reluctantly capitulating to the demands of Senator Thomas of Oklahoma and the western inflationists in order to forestall passage of measures requiring much more serious inflation. Quite to the contrary, there is every indication that for many months, even as Hoover had been informed, Roosevelt had planned mild inflation. The demands of the agrarians if anything were of help to him in giving him an excuse to act against the advice of the gold standard advocates. On April 5, before more than light pressure had developed in the Senate, he wrote Colonel House:

> While things look superficially rosy, I realize well that thus far we have actually given more of deflation than of inflation — the closed banks locked up four billions or more and the economy legislation will take nearly another billion out of Veteran's pay, departmental salaries, etc. It is simply inevitable that we must inflate and though my banker friends may be horrified, I still am seeking an inflation which will not wholly be based on additional government debt.[4]

Two days later, in more guarded terms, Roosevelt told newspaper-men off the record that since so much of the legislation of the spring had locked up money or prevented its flow, he faced the problem of offsetting the deflationary effect in some way. He suggested no means, except to retort to a reporter who asked if the administration would print currency, "We are not going to start the printing presses. That is silly." [5]

For months some relatively conservative eastern financial experts and businessmen had been urging Roosevelt to abandon the gold standard. A retired banker, Rene Léon, had suggested to Roosevelt during the winter that the President had the right to stop the flow of gold to Europe by invoking World War I legislation still in effect. Then he could force the price of the dollar downward on the free market. During his first interview with Roosevelt, Léon has recalled:

> I remained standing. As I was about to leave Roosevelt asked me "one last question": did I believe that the Pound Sterling, then about $3.30, would fall to $2.50 or even $2.00? I answered that I couldn't say what the Pound would do until his inauguration, but that hereafter it would go wherever Roosevelt determined in its relation with the Dollar. Roaring with laughter, Roosevelt said, "Of course you don't mean that." Not alone did I mean it but I would demonstrate it to him any time he wished. "No time like the present," said Roosevelt. Inquiringly I turned to Moley who said "Sit down." [6]

At the conclusion of the conversation, Roosevelt told Léon he would accept the plan provided Léon could satisfy him as President that he had the power to act. Léon subsequently provided Roosevelt with a brief setting forth his power as President to embargo gold under the Trading with the Enemy Act of 1917. Léon, like many of those ad-vising Roosevelt on money, drew a narrow line between what he ad-vocated and abhorred. Léon believed in trading the dollar down and the pound up, but subsequently regarded raising the price of gold as Roose-velt's worst blunder.

The most prestigious group pressuring President Roosevelt toward mild inflation was the Committee for the Nation to Rebuild Prices and Purchasing Power. It advocated exactly that panacea, inflation through manipulating gold. Its chairman was James H. Rand, Jr., and it included in its membership the president of the National City Bank, Frank A. Vanderlip, and both the president of Sears, Roebuck, General Robert E. Wood, and the chairman of its board, Lessing P. Rosenwald. Rand, head of Remington Rand, Inc., was typical of the group in that he sought recovery through slight inflation, yet feared other methods as dangerous; he had lunched with Tugwell in February, then de-nounced him to President Hoover. [7]

Among Roosevelt's academic advisers were a number of moderate inflationaries, including the economists George F. Warren of Cornell and James Harvey Rogers and Irving Fisher of Yale. Fisher even suggested to Roosevelt a scheme for raising revenue and at the same time speeding circulation of money by issuing a billion one-dollar bills, each of which at the end of each week would have to be validated by affixing a two-cent postage stamp to its back. Roosevelt was sufficiently impressed to take it up with the cabinet committee on unemployment, Secretaries Dern, Ickes, Perkins, and Wallace. Undoubtedly the money would move fast, since no one would want to be caught with it at the end of a week, but it also became apparent that it would place an impossible burden upon users, and would be deflationary rather than having the desired result. The scheme was dropped.[8]

Inflationary proposals of all sorts came from everywhere. Will Rogers, acting as a self-appointed court jester, aboard one of the primitive airliners of the time tapped out a letter to the President on his portable typewriter. It began with a dubious pun (that several years later Mussolini used in speeches), and contained a rather more acceptable suggestion:

> I like your middle name Frank since I learned the accent was on the first syllable. But I just want to tell you Delano, that I have written you a lot of letters on the monetary question. . . . Your President now and Dictator and you ought to have all those 20 Billions of Government bonds corralled and you know what to do with them. If you don't tear them up and turn them into currency the minute you lay your hands on em, Im coming down there, if I have to hyke and talk turkey to you. I'll do worse than that but I'm afraid to say it in written. Im in the air and have no stenographer to blame it onto if the words aint just legal. But Arthur Brisbane [Hearst's columnist] is with me now, and if you dont do as we say — hell write underhanded things about you and Ill tell two faced Jokes about you — and you wont like it.[9]

Roosevelt toyed with this idea, which had come from numerous sources, and in the end it was one of the inflationary schemes he received authority with some modifications to undertake, up to a $3 billion limit.

The silver inflationaries, persistent and politically forceful, were for the most part like Senators Pittman of Nevada and Wheeler of Montana, from the mining and plains states. An exception was the most vocal national publicist for silver, at that time an ardent Roosevelt supporter, Father Charles Coughlin, the Michigan priest, who weekly harangued a radio audience of millions. An increase in the price of silver from its depression low of 25 cents an ounce would be a subsidy for the mines, which produced silver as a by-product of copper and other metals, but the silverites extolled the merits of the metal with all the hyperbole of William Jennings Bryan. Wheeler had spent a long evening in February setting forth the virtues of silver to Moley and Woodin; after Wheeler left, Woodin composed a little tune he titled "Lullaby to Silver." Pittman had several opportunities before Roosevelt took office to urge a silver program upon him. Senator Clarence C. Dill of Washington wrote Roosevelt on March 24 that one of the most constructive ways to stimulate trade both in the United States and throughout the world would be to raise the price of silver: [10]

> If we can increase the value of silver we will multiply the buying power of that billion people in the world who have no money except silver money with which to buy anything, and they will immediately start buying from the United States.
>
> I note in the Seattle newspapers that already as a result of the recent increase of five cents per ounce in the price of silver our Pacific Coast business men are receiving new orders from the Orient. Of course, if the price of silver drops, those orders will be cancelled.[11]

The silverites' reasoning seemed sound to Roosevelt, and within a few months he responded to it concretely and positively. Meanwhile he assured Dill he was working hard on the silver situation. Professor Warren's gold commodity dollar proposals were even more appealing to Roosevelt, and most in keeping with the views of Wallace, Morgenthau, and a good many of the farm-state senators.

Both metal schemes, the raising of the price of gold and of silver, had the advantage of being limited. It was frequently remarked that having a little inflation was like being a little pregnant, and there were forebodings among the sound money men that the United States if it began inflation might wind up with runaway devaluation like that of Germany in the 1920s. Roosevelt had confessed in private conversation early in January that while he felt the United States really needed inflation he was fearful of most schemes because they possessed no terminal point that could be counted upon. The finite supplies of gold and silver, unlike the unlimited possibilities to proliferate paper money, would provide safeguards.[12]

In total the monetarists and inflationaries formed an important wing among those seeking to shape the emerging New Deal. In 1934, Moley gave a sophisticated appraisal of them:

> Their concern is in the readjustment of money and credit in order to provide a just means of compensation for the decline of prices and the increasing burden of debt throughout the country, particularly among the farmers. They believe, if I understand them correctly, that to relieve this burden of debt will restore a general degree of prosperity that will carry on the individualistic economics of the past.

Included in this group, of course, are innumerable people — some as naively simple in their economic views as was Bryan. . . . But it is only fair to say that the men . . . in this group advocate, in the large, simply a permanently managed currency in order that the stability of prices and debts may be maintained.

During the campaign, I observed a reluctance on the part of the group who were helping to formulate policies — and this applies particularly to Berle, Tugwell and Johnson — to place much dependence upon an exclusively monetary policy. They believed that the way to economic justice was a much more complicated way than the one suggested by Professors Warren and Rogers. As the President developed his monetary policy, however, it was apparent that it was only one aspect of an infinitely broader and more complex policy.[13]

To Roosevelt, as to at least one of his advisers, Tugwell, monetary policy with its promise of inflation was a vital counterbalance to the deflationary effect of some of the other New Deal measures, including the processing tax at the heart of the farm program. Monetarism seemed not a sole panacea but a viable corollary to economic planning.[14]

Yet it was with a continued fascination that Roosevelt gave heed to Warren of the Cornell agricultural faculty, with his numerous charts setting forth index numbers on gold and selected commodities and his endless talk of the "commodity dollar." To Warren the answer was simple and easy; he never tired of propounding it before large groups and small, even to Mrs. Roosevelt in February when he caught her at a home economics conference at Cornell. Warren was gratified at her "real understanding," but confessed that she was "quite able to put an economist on the rack if he disagrees with her." If one accepted Warren's views, the indices were simple to understand. He regarded gold as a commodity comparable in its market fluctuations to those produced by farmers. Drive its price up in the world markets and that of wheat, cotton and other staples would follow (even as the value of the dollar declined). Roosevelt liked this sort of index and talk. James Warburg, who had no sympathy for Warren, remembered that the President was fond of using cotton, wheat, silver, and gold as illustrations in his conversation. "Those were the four commodities," Warburg explained, "that had political pressure behind them and they were always the ones that came up." [15]

Roosevelt seemed on the brink of putting Warren's ideas into effect late on the night of his second day in office when he signed a proclamation not only declaring a bank holiday but assuming control over gold and silver. Morgenthau had dinner with Warren, his one-time professor, that evening, and told him the President had said he was absolutely right. At 10:30 P.M., Warren saw Roosevelt at the White

House, and found him indeed an apt pupil. The President, Warren noted in his diary, "showed me the debt and wealth comparisons for 1909 and had the relationships straight. He recognized that deflation cannot be gone through with." Later that night, while Warren watched, Roosevelt signed the proclamation, and declared gleefully, "We are now off the gold standard." Afterward, to the bafflement of Cordell Hull, he discoursed with Warren about revaluation and index numbers. Hull, wrote Warren, "evidently did not understand what we were talking about and innocently asked whether supply and demand did not govern prices." As Roosevelt talked on and on, James Roosevelt, after repeated efforts, gave up trying to get his father to bed, kissed him goodnight, and left. Yet amidst his exuberance of the evening, Roosevelt displayed caution. When his secretary, Marvin McIntyre, said the newspapermen wanted to know whether or not the United States was off the gold standard, Roosevelt replied he did not want to comment on that question, saying, "Tell them to ask a banker." [16]

For the next several weeks, Roosevelt proceeded carefully, telling reporters on March 8 that in some respects the United States was still on the gold standard and in some ways it was not. As authority he read to them a technical exposition by a conservative economist, Ralph Robey of the Columbia School of Business and financial editor of the *New York Post,* who had worked for Roosevelt during the campaign. Whatever Roosevelt's intent had been when he talked to Warren, neither his proclamation prohibiting gold export nor the subsequent emergency legislation more than slightly depressed the dollar on foreign markets. The inflationary effect was nil. Even on April 5, 1933, three weeks later, when Roosevelt issued a new proclamation forbidding the holding of gold or gold certificates in amounts more than $100, except in coin collections, the dollar remained steady in the foreign exchange market at 99.75 cents.[17]

Quietly Roosevelt and his advisers were preparing for both complex and sophisticated and simple and politically expedient inflationary moves. On the sophisticated side, Roosevelt was employing the skills of James Warburg, the youthful but experienced member of a famous international banking family, as a planner for the World Economic Conference. Warburg, a man of dazzling talents, put them to use in clever observations upon his contemporaries and in brilliant recommendations for limited forays from a base of financial fundamentalism. He had a conservative respect for gold and international stability, but felt the United States should temporarily engage in tactics to drive down the dollar on world markets to a competitive level. The device should be a large fund comparable to the British stabilization fund with which the United States could, through buying and selling dollars, manage its rate of exchange. Warburg, after developing his ideas with Fred I. Kent, one of the most prestigious older New York bankers, presented them in Washington on March 15, first in conversations with Moley, Feis, and Hull, then to the President.

Warburg, accompanied by Hull, Feis, and Charles Taussig, saw Roosevelt in his executive office at 5:15; the President took them into the White House proper where they would not be interrupted, and over tea discussed the alternatives with them for an hour and a half.

Some of the points that Warburg had been suggesting throughout the day were:

That the United States not decide at that time whether to raise the gold embargo and return to a gold basis in the immediate future or at some later date, but do no more than state broad intentions and rely upon the cooperation of banks to prevent a gold drain.

"That the widely held opinion, that a firm dollar in the exchange markets is a great sign of strength and a great thing for the country, was, in fact, erroneous; that it is to our interest at the present moment to have a cheap dollar in terms of the other exchanges," because it would thwart the interests of Britain and France, strengthen commodity prices, and relieve some of the pressure for inflation. "Unless some account is taken of this pressure and some concession made to it, Congress cannot be held in line."

As a means of implementing his recommendations, Warburg suggested establishing a large stabilization fund at once, arguing that its mere existence might so overawe speculators that it would not be needed. He added:

> Irrespective of whether we ever use the fund, it is a very much healthier way for us to sit down at the table with the British if we have a gun on our hip so long as we know that they are coming with a gun on their hip. It is very much easier to suggest that we both unbuckle our belts and lay the guns on the table than for us to make this suggestion to the British if they know and we know that we have no gun.[18]

Roosevelt, according to Warburg, "asked a considerable number of very searching questions," and concluded by saying he thought the suggestion had much merit. He asked Warburg to pursue it energetically at once.[19]

With Roosevelt's specific or tacit approval, Warburg during the next several weeks was active in planning international currency policy. He developed a proposal to establish a currency stabilization fund to operate out of the foreign exchange section of the Treasury Department, and took it up several times with the President. He also, with the authorization of Moley and Woodin, discussed monetary matters with the British and French representatives in Washington. They left open whether or not the gold content of the dollar should be reduced, but agreed that the three countries should cooperate in stabilizing their currencies and eventually in operating on a gold standard. On the evening of April 4, when Warburg went over his monetary proposals with Roosevelt, including the provision for the ultimate return to gold: [20] "I read the gold clause verbatim and asked the President point blank whether he wanted to leave the devaluation question open" as Warburg had in the clause. "He said the clause was exactly what he wanted." [21]

Simultaneously, Roosevelt was acting conciliatory toward the silverites. One of the provisions in Warburg's monetary memorandum was that nations should agree to increase their silver holdings and reliance on silver coins to send the price of silver upward "as a corollary to a general rise in the price of commodities." The silver section, Warburg noted on April 4, "seemed to please the President very much." [22]

Already Moley (accompanied by Hull and Feis) had pursued this line of reasoning in the first detailed discussion of economic problems that the new administration undertook with the British, on March 27. Moley gave what Ambassador Lindsay regarded as a rather curious reason for taking up silver first, that the question raised less difficulties and might be an easy subject for initial agreement. Lindsay tried to counter Moley's arguments on behalf of a rise in the price of silver by suggesting that China was normally an importer of silver, and that a rise in the value of her silver currency units would not improve her capacity to import goods. Moley replied that an increase in the value of silver might bring private hoards onto the market for export from China and India. He gave notice that the President would especially appoint one of the delegates to press the silver issue at the World Economic Conference.[23] Lindsay soon concluded that the Americans were less interested in improving world trade than in bettering the lot of American silver producers.

There was also the main thrust toward gold manipulation. In early April, Professors Warren and Fisher were in Washington drafting legislation for the Committee for the Nation and the leaders of the farm organizations. O'Neall of the Farm Bureau Federation, Taber of the Grange, and Simpson of the Farmers' Union were able to unite among themselves and join with Rand and the business leaders of the committee on behalf of dollar revaluation. On April 6, a delegation including Rand and Warren called on Secretary of State Hull, who told them that for reasons he could not fathom the administration measures had not brought the expected price increases. Twice in the next several days, Warren together with farm and business leaders talked to Roosevelt.[24]

In his conversation on April 12, Roosevelt rather frivolously passed on to the committee a suggestion he said someone had made that the gold clause in securities could be kept intact through a strange device: "If one were called on to supply gold, he might borrow it from the Treasury for a few minutes, pay it to the man who asked for it, and a Secret Service man could stop the man from taking it out of the Treasury."

Roosevelt asked Warren the figure in relation to gold at which the committee proposed to revalue the dollar, and what the amount would be in grains of gold. He jotted down the figures, and told the committee members to continue their activities. The conversation seemed like so many others Roosevelt had undertaken in the previous few weeks, a conciliatory gesture toward some of those advocating mild inflation, which might ultimately lead to some careful and limited undertaking.[25]

Yet a week later Roosevelt took sudden, dramatic action. Two simultaneous crises impelled him to move — the impasse over the farm bill in the Senate where inflationaries were coming to command a majority, and a new gold crisis in the international money markets. Combined, they caused him to modify his course slightly toward less economic cooperation with the British and French and greater response to inflationaries at home.

In the policy Roosevelt had been developing through Warburg, he was trying to keep the United States nominally on a gold standard with the prospect of future stabilization in relation to sterling and the franc, probably with a more favorable value to the dollar. Thus, while he did not authorize the free flow of gold out of the United States, his executive order of April 5 calling for the return of hoarded gold, issued on the authority of the Emergency Banking Act, also authorized the secretary of the treasury to issue licenses to export gold for trade purposes. Almost immediately international speculators tested the order; the dollar weakened on April 11, and on April 13 fell sharply to the point where it would be profitable for speculators to buy gold with dollars, ship it abroad, convert it into foreign currency, and reconvert the currency into dollars. New York bankers applied for licenses to export approximately $10 million in gold. There was a debate in the Treasury Department over whether to keep up the price of the dollar through allowing gold to be shipped overseas; Hoover's undersecretary of the treasury, Arthur A. Ballantine, who was still serving, wanted to grant licenses. Roosevelt agreed. The Treasury announced it was authorizing a shipment of gold to Holland on the *Statendam* that day, and the price of the dollar rallied.[26] Roosevelt was assured that only small shipments would be necessary to bolster the dollar, and that night was in a cheerful enough mood to tease Warburg by saying that he had authorized Warburg's Bank of Manhattan to ship $600,000 in gold, that he had told the

Treasury Department to issue this one license and no more. Warburg, embarrassed, explained to Roosevelt that he himself had opposed granting permission, and thought it very foolish to issue licenses.[27]

In the next several days the European raids on the dollar intensified, and the dollar fell briefly on April 15 to 96 cents. The requests for licenses to ship gold mounted heavily. Roosevelt heard that speculators in Amsterdam were operating with a pool of $125 million to drive down the dollar. One of the cabinet officers insisted, erroneously, that the British were responsible; rather, the British were using their fund to depress the pound, which would send up the dollar. There were other serious reports for Roosevelt to consider. Foreign investors held $750 million in short-term balances in the United States that they might try to withdraw in gold; American capitalists fearing inflation were trying to send gold abroad. There might be acute gold losses and a new crisis. On Saturday night, April 15, Roosevelt decided to abandon his defense of the dollar. He made no public announcement but did tell Secretary Woodin he would issue no further export licenses except those already orally promised. The Treasury issued these remaining licenses on Monday and Tuesday, April 17 and 18, seemingly continuing the old policy, and making more dramatic Roosevelt's statement of April 19, turning policy around.[28]

It was the flight of gold that made Roosevelt's action imperative; during the brief period of licensing the United States lost $100 million of its gold reserve. But national attention focused upon the inflationary excitement in the Senate which seemed to most observers at the time, and many historians since, to be the prime reason for abandoning the gold standard.

The rise in sentiment for inflation among the senators was in response to the despair of their constituents. At a dinner party on April 12, Senators Wheeler of Montana and Elbert D. Thomas of Utah expressed their pessimism to Secretary Ickes, telling him that economic conditions were blackening and that there would be serious repercussions unless there was quick action. They were primarily impressing upon Ickes the need for a large, immediate public works program, but Wheeler was also fighting in the Senate for an amendment to the farm bill that would require the President to remonetize silver at a ratio of 16 to 1 to gold.[29]

On Monday, April 17, as the drain of gold to Europe was continuing, the Senate voted on Wheeler's silver amendment to the farm bill. In January, Wheeler had been able to obtain only 18 votes for a similar amendment, but by April Roosevelt was worried that Wheeler might have a majority. He sent word through Majority Leader Robinson that he would veto the farm bill if it contained the Wheeler amendment.

William E. Borah of Idaho, swayed by Roosevelt's opposition, voted against the amendment although he was favorable to it. Carl Hayden of Arizona did likewise. On the morning of the vote, Hayden arranged with Moley to absent himself until the roll call was almost completed; if the amendment seemed certain to lose, he would then vote "aye." He wrote Moley the next day, "I waited until the tally showed over 30 votes for 16 to 1, and then voted 'Nay.'" Roosevelt's intervention, according to Moley's calculation, caused at least ten senators to vote against the Wheeler amendment. There was a majority in the Senate in favor of inflation. The administration, Moley's diary notation indicated, did not want the Wheeler amendment to pass, but did want it to make a good showing. Roosevelt was firmly opposed to mandatory legislation like Wheeler's and was determined to be in control of whatever future inflationary moves there might be.[30]

At once Roosevelt assumed command over the inflationary forces. Whether he did so out of necessity is debatable; Moley and Warburg thought so at the time, and it was a convenient explanation with which to fend off opponents of inflation. On the day he announced his actions, Roosevelt referred reporters to a column of Lippmann's of that morning: "Either the Administration . . . will take charge of the inflation and manage it, or Congress will produce the inflation by statute. . . . But there is no choice any longer between inflation and no inflation. This choice has been abolished by economic developments and by the political sentiments which they now reflect." [31]

The question of necessity is of little consequence, since Roosevelt had long been maneuvering toward limited inflation, and had no intention of allowing Congress to force action upon him. The backing of Congress and even some pressure from it helped justify his actions. The Senate ayes on the Wheeler amendment demonstrated the pressure; the nays indicated that his influence over the Senate was sufficient to modify its actions. The leaders of the inflationary attack, Burton K. Wheeler of Montana, Huey Long of Louisiana, and Elmer Thomas of Oklahoma, were powerful and persistent, with a considerable following among the progressive bloc in the Senate. They were also thoroughly disliked by an even larger part of the senators, especially the conservative Democrats. When Thomas, a tall, earnest one-time campaigner for Bryan, declared on the Senate floor that his proposals would "take $200,000,000 from the hands of those who have it, including the bank depositors, and give it to the debtors," his colleague from Oklahoma, the witty, blind Thomas P. Gore, retorted, "If we must inflate the currency, why don't we license all the counterfeiters? That would get the money into the hands of the people." It was the kind of situation ready-made for Roosevelt, who, like T.R. in the battle over railroad regulation, was ready to play the progressive forces against the conservatives to obtain what he really wanted, something in the middle. Roosevelt's reaction in the spring was high-spirited — and he could well have written then as he did in November to Hiram Johnson, when the inflation controversy was at its height, "It's a grand place I'm in! The old line bankers and Wall Street on one side and the Farm Holiday bombers on the other! You are like me — best when in action." [32]

Tuesday, April 18, became a day of spectacular action for Roosevelt. Early that morning, Moley had two telephone calls from senators, warning him that an inflation amendment Thomas had introduced the previous day was likely to be adopted. It was a clever device, of exactly the sort Roosevelt himself was employing that spring — an omnibus measure to capture all those who like Wheeler and Long favored silver, together with those who favored other means of inflation. Further, Thomas made the proposal palatable by authorizing, but not requiring, the President to use any or all of the plans at his discretion.* Contrary to popular impression it was not mandatory even in its early stages. James F. Byrnes reported to Moley that John Bankhead of Alabama, who had voted against the Wheeler amendment to the farm bill, was ready to give the Thomas amendment a try; even some farm belt Republicans were attracted to the measure.

Byrnes went to the White House with Moley and at breakfast convinced Roosevelt that he would be wise, if Thomas would water down his amendment, to approve of it. Roosevelt wrote a memorandum to serve as a basis for Moley's and Byrnes's revisions. Later that day Byrnes brought Thomas to the White House. Roosevelt told him he would accept the amendment but that it must be carefully rewritten. The President was so ingratiating that Thomas agreed to accept most of the administration draft in place of his own. Thomas has reminisced:

> Two points respecting the amendment appealed to the President. One that the powers proposed to be conferred on the Chief Executive would, if exercised properly, increase prices. And, two, with such powers in his hand he would be free to act without further legislation by the Congress. . . .

* Thomas has written,

Knowing that I had to secure at least a majority of each House to support the amendment, I prepared the legislation with such end in view. While either of the plans proposed, if properly administered, would have produced an increase in prices, yet I knew that if only one plan was suggested that each of the other plans would be offered either as substitutes or as additional programs to accomplish the end all supporters had in mind; hence, in order to secure the maximum support I joined all of the plans for increasing the circulation in one amendment and then proposed to leave the exact plan or plans to be used to the discretion of the President.[33]

During our conference I casually suggested that if the amendment was adopted and became the law that he would then have all power over money and that with such powers he would be able to definitely agree to, if not dictate, terms at the London Conference without having to make treaties which would have to be . . . ratified by the United States Senate, whose membership in the main know little about the intricacies of the science of money.[34]

That evening, Roosevelt had planned a meeting with several of his advisers to go over the plans for meetings with Prime Minister Ramsay MacDonald and a British delegation who were en route to Washington. First Moley, Bullitt and Warburg arrived, then a half-hour later, Pittman, Hull, Feis and Taussig, and finally Woodin and Lewis Douglas. As each person came in, Roosevelt in a jocular way would make some remark like, "Congratulate me. We are off the gold standard," enjoying the auditor's reaction. To Warburg he seemed in an ugly mood. Roosevelt's decision was not open to change; he had informed Woodin the previous Saturday that the Treasury was not to issue any further export licenses for gold. Then Roosevelt talked about the need to consolidate power in his hands to inflate credit as a means of raising the price level, and announced the second startling piece of news, that he had agreed to accept, with revision, the Thomas amendment. According to Warburg:

He said that the reason for the amendment was that unless something of this sort was done immediately Congress would take the matter in its own hands and legislate mandatory law instead of permissive. He then read us the bill which, in brief, authorizes the President to bring about inflation by one of four methods or any combination of the four methods.[35]

It was this statement of Roosevelt's, taken at face value since, that has caused the widespread impression that he accepted the Thomas amendment to avoid a mandatory inflationary measure. As Van Perkins has pointed out, mandatory legislation was never imminent.[36]

Roosevelt's proposals created sharp division among the advisers. Moley, acting as a technical expert, did not argue, but took out his little black notebook and began jotting down the President's instructions. It was his task to supervise revision of the Thomas amendment. Woodin, who was later commended by Roosevelt for having been a good sport, whispered to Moley, "What's a Secretary of the Treasury to do when he's presented with a *fait accompli?*"

Two hours of vehement debate followed, as Douglas and Warburg, according to Warburg, "carried the brunt of the attack with a certain amount of support from Hull, occasional wavering support from Pittman and Woodin, and a few timid observations by Feis." At one point in the discussion, Roosevelt, trying to make the point that the value of money depended upon people's faith in it, amused himself by pulling out a ten dollar bill, looking at it, and remarking, "Ha! Issued by the First National Bank of Pipeville. . . . That's in Tennessee — in your state, Cordell. How do I know that's any good? The fact that I think it is, makes it good." Hull looked as though he had been stabbed in the back; Pipeville, Tennessee, was nonexistent except in Roosevelt's imagination.[37]

As for Warburg:

> At the risk of being impudent I went so far as to say that I considered the passage of such a bill completely hairbrained and irresponsible, and that unless it were accompanied by a statement from the President that he had no intention of using the powers conferred, it would result in uncontrolled inflation and complete chaos. . . . He and Moley took the position, more or less agreed to by Pittman, that at any time they could reverse the machinery and thus control the inflation — a view which I can only characterize as King Canute.

Douglas was even more upset, but it was he who did most to turn back the inflationary tide:

> It was a thoroughly vicious bill. Finally when the President asked that it be somewhat changed I was on the point of resigning. But at any rate I worked almost all night and by noon of Wednesday had the bill which is now known as the Thomas Amendment. So much better than the original. When the President agreed to it . . . I couldn't very well resign. Finally the President asked me to appear before the Banking Committee of the Senate to explain it. Awfully embarrassing for me, but I am sure that I must stay on until a real overt act has been committed.

When Douglas and Warburg had left the White House for sleepless labor and lamentation through the night, Douglas supposedly asserted, "Well, this is the end of western civilization." If so, after Roosevelt had accepted the modifications, Douglas was more sanguine: "It is pretty discouraging but it might be worse. Of course I do not believe that the President will use either the greenback provision or the power to devaluate the dollar except as a result of an international conference." [38]

For his part, Roosevelt made the Thomas amendment sound a good bit less than earthshaking when he talked to the reporters and his cabinet the next day. He had come down with a cold which made even a cigarette taste bad, and met the press in his Oval Study in the White House proper. Despite his cold, he graphically and in detail explained to them the significance of his moves. He had decided to quit competition to keep up the price of the dollar, and the result should be an increase in commodity prices. He did not want those prices to become too high. He wanted them up to a recent level but not the 1929 level. The move was constructive, he said, since it would reduce the value of the dollar to an equitable level with other currencies. Then he hoped "to get the world as a whole back on some form of gold standard." In other words like those of Warren of Cornell, which would be reassuring to farmers, he explained how his move would raise commodity prices within the United States: "There are a good many commodities which are sold in terms of world trade. Well, for instance, cotton. Cotton is sold on a gold basis and, with the dollar where it has been, it works out to a certain number of cents. Therefore, if the dollar were to sell off 10%, the price of cotton in terms of dollars would go up 10%." [39]

Roosevelt devoted his entire cabinet meeting that afternoon to a discussion of devaluation, saying that it might mean fluctuation for a while, but the nation would benefit if the dollar were not maintained at an artificially high value. [40]

Ickes, listening to Roosevelt's discourse to the cabinet, granted to himself that he did not have an economic mind and that he would do better to let those better qualified than he determine policies. Bullitt had taken a similar view during the furious debate the night before. Most of the public felt the same, but there was a minority whose expertise in monetary matters might be as lacking as that of Ickes, but whose passions ran high, either for or against the President's actions. True believers in the gold standard never forgave him; to many conservatives, from this point on Roosevelt was abhorrent. Their anger was compounded when Roosevelt on June 5, 1933, signed an act of Congress abrogating the gold clause in public and private contracts.

On April 22 Baruch drafted a letter to his friend Senator Byrnes, lashing out at him for supporting the President's policies. Then, perhaps because Baruch did not wish to relinquish his toehold at the White House, he did not send it. The draft letter set forth clearly the case for avoiding a fluctuating dollar:

It may interest you to know that about a month ago things had commenced to improve. After the Banking Holiday, people were getting their courage back and money was commencing to creep into employment.

Of course you must know that when you give the president the power to cut the gold content of the dollar as much as $.50, that immediately stops all investment and long time business operations cease. The only one who could now sell bonds will be the United States Government, and it can sell them only to itself. . . .

As you know, I have seen no one while the discussion of the various bills has been going on. So far as I know, no one wants to see me to discuss these things because there are a lot of new ideas based upon a new system of economics, and a new era, and a new deal." [41]

There were similar cries of outrage from the City of London. Brendan Bracken lamented to Baruch, "He has driven a coach and four through the sanctity of contract, and appears to be anxious to destroy the vital spring of the capitalist system — the free market." Moffat, on the western Europe desk at the State Department, thought the experiment worth trying, and was startled at the bad spirit the British displayed. "For a year and a half now, they have been off the gold standard and vaunting themselves on its advantages, using an equalization fund to play with our exchange and keep the pound down," Moffat noted. "Now we follow suit, at least to the extent of letting the dollar find its natural level and lo and behold, a chorus of rage from one end of the British Isles to the other." [42]

On the other hand, the great international banker, J. P. Morgan, issued a statement welcoming the reported action as a means of combatting deflation. Nor did Roosevelt's two advisers among the Morgan partners, Thomas Lamont and Russell C. Leffingwell, seem at all disturbed. [43]

As for the Thomas amendment, Roosevelt's advisers quickly modified it in more conservative directions. First Moley worked at the Capitol with Senators Byrnes, Pittman and others, while Warburg and Douglas drafted another modification to deflate the bill. Roosevelt was in an amenable mood, and to the relief of Warburg and Douglas accepted the changes. The principal one, replacing a provision that the President could issue almost unlimited greenbacks(paper money not redeemable in gold or silver), provided instead authorization to arrange with the Federal Reserve Banks through open market operations to put $3 billion in new currency into circulation; if the Federal Reserve refused, he could issue $3 billion in greenbacks. Warburg convinced himself that, "from a position twenty-four hours ago which meant the practically certain beginning of uncontrolled inflation, we have now covered up the worst features of the measure to a point where there is very little danger." [44]

When the senators acted on the measure they strengthened the silver provisions, but did vote down amendments providing for mortgage relief and the payment of the soldiers' bonus. Wheeler was angry because Roosevelt had not summoned him to the White House along with Thomas and the others. Roosevelt assigned Frank Walker of Montana to placate Wheeler. Wheeler retorted to Walker that Roosevelt could go to hell, but subsequently relented and accepted an invitation to the White House. Roosevelt, waving his hand, said, "Burt, I want to talk to you about silver."

Wheeler tartly responded, "Mr. President, I don't deserve this kind of treatment from you. . . . You called in all these people, none of whom was sincerely interested in the fight I'm making to remonetize silver."

Roosevelt replied, "Burt, Bryan killed the remonetization of silver in 1896."

And then, with the aid of Senator William H. King of Utah, Roosevelt persuaded Wheeler to draft a compromise proposal, allowing but not requiring Roosevelt to remonetize silver. It became part of the Thomas amendment parcel.[45]

As for Huey Long, who also had not been consulted, he chose instead to announce victory, that the President "swallowed our demand, hook, line, and sinker." [46]

On April 28, the Senate approved the Thomas amendment by a vote of 64 to 21.* In its final form it permitted but did not require the President to undertake six different ways of inflating credit or currency.

Passage of the Thomas amendment prepared the way for the Senate to enact the farm bill that same day, April 28, by a vote of 64 to 20. Only four Democrats voted against it. There was still a fight over the Norris-Simpson cost-of-production amendment, which the Senate had passed April 13. Senator James B. Frazier warned that unless it were retained, farmers throughout the nation would go on strike. Simpson urged Roosevelt and Wallace to let the amendment remain in the bill, arguing that like the Thomas amendment, its powers were discretionary. Roosevelt refused, sending word to the House leaders to eliminate cost of production from the bill in conference. Norris was unable to rally the senators to vote it back in; Roosevelt had sufficiently placated the inflationary senators. On the other hand, the Thomas amendment had not alienated the more conservative farm leaders, who were well pleased that Peek was to head the agricultural agency. Peek himself seemed little bothered by inflationary schemes. "I don't care what we use for money," he once said. "We can use gold or brass or tin or buffalo chips." So it was that Congress enacted the omnibus Farm Relief Act, combining the Agricultural Adjustment Act and the Emergency Farm Mortgage Act. On May 12, before a considerable group of those involved in the fight for the legislation, Roosevelt signed the measure.[48]

The United States had finally taken the momentous step of undertaking peacetime national planning of agriculture. In the legislation,

* The Thomas amendment in various technical ways with various safeguards authorized the President to (1) issue up to $3 billion in additional paper money; (2) reduce the gold content of the dollar by no more than 50 percent; (3) fix the weight of the silver dollar in relation to gold — i.e., remonetize silver; (4) accept silver in payment of war debts; (5) issue paper money (silver certificates) on the basis of this silver; (6) permit the Federal Reserve Board to increase or decrease reserve requirements.[47]

Roosevelt had obtained everything he wanted, and was given the option to undertake a good bit additional. Both houses of Congress had, far from rubber-stamping their approval, modified the legislation substantially; one house or the other had added a total of eighty-five amendments by the time the bill went to the conference committee. In some practical ways involving specific programs, Congress had made the measure more workable. Also, the two months of discussion had helped inform and prepare the nation for a farm program. Roosevelt's leadership in obtaining the measure, when compared with the fiasco during the lame duck session, was an effective political feat; during the pulling and hauling he lost little support.

As for the farmers, they could only hope that out of the bundle of conflicting plans would come a better living for them. Their attention shifted toward the administration of the measure, already controversial because of the proposed appointment of Peek to head the program. Meanwhile, even the most radical farmers were ready to wait and see. Milo Reno canceled the Farmers' Holiday Association strike scheduled to begin the next day.[49]

Roosevelt's move off of gold and acceptance of the Thomas amendment eclipsed the farm bill in popular attention on April 19 and for several days thereafter. There were even rumors on Capitol Hill that the endorsement of inflation altered the necessity for the agricultural and other recovery programs. They were serious enough to cause Wallace to point out to Roosevelt that while inflation might materially reduce fixed charges on the farmer such as taxes, interest, and railroad rates, it would have almost no effect on problems growing out of unbalanced production. Indeed, it might stimulate overproduction. Roosevelt for his part at once emphasized the point in a press conference. "It is just as important to curb over-production the balance of this year and next year as it is to keep farm prices up," he said, "because obviously, if everybody goes to planting 25 percent or 30 percent more acreage, it is going to cause a reduction again in farm commodity prices."[50]

The immediate effect of going off of gold and the prospect of inflation was to cause not only farm prices but all prices to rise moderately. On the first day, silver went up three cents an ounce and the pound at one point soared to $3.85; the stock market enjoyed a five-million-share day. The dollar dropped 12 percent below its gold level. Prices of commodities, both of farm products like wheat and metals like copper, rose with minor fluctuations until mid-July. Other factors, especially the anticipation of an industrial recovery program, contributed to the rise. For the week ending May 3, the Dun & Bradstreet business activity barometer was up to 51.1 percent of the 1928–1930 average, compared with 46.4 a month before — but on May 4, 1932, the figure had been 54.0. Steel production was up to 32.1 compared with 26.5 the year before. Within the next several weeks, economic indices were finally beginning to show some substantial increase, not only above 1933 lows, but above corresponding levels of the year before.[51]

Roosevelt was obtaining a modest degree of quick recovery, in part through going off gold, and in part through creating the possibility of future inflation. It was by itself no solution to depression problems, but a short-term panacea which gave Roosevelt time to get his recovery program through Congress.

CHAPTER XX

A Thrust of Reform:
The Securities Act and TVA

What we seek is a return to a clearer understanding of
the ancient truth that those who manage banks, corporations and other agencies handling or using other people's
money are trustees acting for others.
— FDR TO CONGRESS, *March 29, 1933.*[1]

Despite the urgency of both relief and recovery measures, Roosevelt
found time in the spring of 1933 for a thrust of reform. It was sufficient to prove the earnestness of the moral fervor running through his
inaugural address, and to give notice that when the nation was back on
a more satisfactory economic course, he would turn to an agenda of
reform to try to eliminate the causes of future depression. The two
conspicuous reform measures of the "hundred days" also indicated
how firmly Roosevelt's ideology was implanted in progressivism and its
two main courses of thought. One of the reforms was in the tradition
of Theodore Roosevelt's New Nationalism, involving as it did regional
planning and development. That was George Norris's Tennessee Valley
Authority. The other was equally in the tradition of Woodrow Wilson's
New Freedom and the ideology of Justice Brandeis, with its emphasis
upon policing the "money trust." It was the Securities Act of 1933.
Both were unfinished pieces of progressive reform, of keen interest to
Roosevelt and relevant in 1933. What they had in common, in the
view of the President's progressive supporters, was corporate exploitation of the American public through the marketing of securities at over-
inflated values and the sale of electric power at excessively high
charges. Both the "Truth in Securities" Act of 1933 and the TVA
production of power as a "yardstick" to measure private rates were
aimed at preventing future fiascos like that of the Insull utility empire.
The previous year, Samuel Insull's utility holding companies extending
into thirty-two states, and built on power profits, had collapsed, bringing loss and bitterness to countless stockholders.

It was deceit and the betrayal of trust that angered Roosevelt rather than the taking of a legitimate but quite risky chance for high gain. He himself as an investor had held blue chip stocks and sound bonds, but with small amounts of his capital he had dabbled in highly speculative enterprises. There was an oil company that struck only gas too far from a city to be salable, and on the other hand there was the first frozen food company, which became a success. He had not gambled on margin in the stock market, buying and selling for quick return, and his first reaction to the 1929 crash was to consider the losses a punishment for those who had. Later, as scandal after scandal among corporations and financial houses revealed the way in which executives had marketed securities for their own gain far beyond any possibility of fair return to investors, he shared in the general indignation.[2]

Utility holding companies forced consumers to "pay exorbitant rates, measured not in terms of reasonableness for legitimate investors but rather in terms of speculative profit," Roosevelt had told the New York legislature in 1931. The piling of holding companies one atop the other led to "stock which is not always represented by actual investment." A year later he had extended his criticism to all securities, declaring to the legislature: "It is time to differentiate between prospects and true values, or at least to tell an unskilled public the whole truth about the contents of what in the past has been a package too often sold only because of the bright colors on its wrapper."[3]

The Democratic platform in 1932 called for a filing of financial statements before issue of stocks and bonds, and for the regulation of holding companies, utility rates, and securities and commodities exchanges.[4]

Roosevelt made regulation one of his campaign issues, and moved toward implementing it soon after his election. He authorized Moley to invite Samuel Untermyer to draft legislation that would regulate securities issues. The seventy-four-year-old Untermyer, for decades one of the most publicized New York lawyers, with a *Who's Who* sketch almost two columns long, had served as counsel for the famous congressional investigation of 1912, the Pujo Committee, which publicized J. P. Morgan and a so-called "money trust." The investigation prepared the way for the creation of the Federal Reserve System during the Wilson administration. It did not lead, as Untermyer would have liked, to federal supervision of stock and bond issues because of doubts of constitutionality, but it did stimulate states to enact regulations. These state measures came to be known as "blue sky" laws because one legislator had warned that unless there were restrictions, promoters would unload on the gullible everything but the blue sky. But the state laws were confusing and ineffective. Untermyer in 1914 tried to resolve the constitutional question by drafting a bill, introduced in the Senate, that would give exchanges the option of complying with state law or accepting Post Office regulation, under penalty of losing use of the mails. There could be no doubt that the mails operated in interstate commerce, which Congress had authority to regulate. Wall Street fought the measure, President Wilson withheld his blessing, and it died in the Senate. Through the years that followed, Untermyer had not lost his zeal for reforming the securities market and punishing corporate malpractices; he had recently become counsel for bondholders who had been swindled by Ivar Kreuger, the Swedish "matchking." [5]

Untermyer did little more than resurrect for Roosevelt what he had not been able to persuade Wilson to accept. Through the interregnum he was in touch with Moley, sending him letters and memoranda; but remembering earlier constitutional controversies, he confined himself to recasting his 1914 measure. Constitutional questions did not disturb Roosevelt unduly, but Jim Farley's Post Office Department, a service agency of the administration concerned with the delivery of mail, seemed a less than satisfactory locale for the policing of securities.

Roosevelt, without informing Moley or Untermyer (through absent-mindedness, Moley charitably thinks), turned as soon as he took office to another veteran of the New Freedom, Secretary of Commerce Daniel Roper, who with his staff undertook to draft a bill. Roosevelt also enlisted one of Wilson's assistant attorney generals, Huston Thompson, former chairman of the Federal Trade Commission, to help shape the legislation. Howe may have had a hand in the maneuver, since he led Thompson to believe that he had favored him for attorney general. Politically the switch was useful, since it gave Roper — and for that matter, the old Wilsonians — some positive involvement in the New Deal legislative process. There were no serious ideological differences between Untermyer and Thompson. Thompson, a Westerner in origin, also distrusted Wall Street. Basing his draft on state "blue sky" laws and British statute, he proposed placing regulatory authority over the issuing of securities in the Federal Trade Commission rather than the Post Office. When Moley discovered that both Untermyer and Thompson were working on securities bills, Roosevelt expressed dismay, and fell back on his customary procedure. He invited them both to a conference at the White House to soothe feelings and reconcile their two drafts. It was not one of Roosevelt's more successful afternoons, although he tried to convince Untermyer and Thompson that there was no real conflict between their two bills, that Untermyer's involved sales in stock exchanges, and Thompson's the issuing of securities. Thompson wrote in his diary: [6]

> In the morning I was requested . . . to call upon Mr. Samuel Untermyer at the Shoreham Hotel at ten o'clock. I found Mr. Untermyer in

bed. He was in an irritable mood and suggested that I would be hostile to his bill. I laughed and said I knew nothing about his bill and felt sure there was no conflict between our bills and soon demonstrated this fact, leaving a copy of my bill with him.

In the afternoon at four o'clock, at the request of the President, I met in a room on the second floor of the White House with the President and Messrs. Moley, Untermyer, Cummings, Roper and Taussig, an economist, and several others. . . .

The President directed most of his conversation to Mr. Untermyer and myself. He had a draft of Thompson's and Roper's proposed bill before him and discussed it. He criticized its length and detail, suggesting that we cut down both. . . . He distinguished clearly between our bill and Untermyer's and said there was no conflict, the latter covering sales on stock exchanges.

Thompson, according to Moley, attacked Untermyer's Post Office idea, and Untermyer retorted that his bill was perfect, and Thompson's a mess. Yet in Thompson's view Roosevelt had reached a workable reconciliation:

After an hour's discussion we retired to tea in an adjoining room where [the President's] daughter, her children and some British lords were present. I had a separate discussion with Messrs. Roper and Cummings and we all agreed to keep our bill entirely apart from Untermyer's bill. I had a talk with the President and he also agreed to this.

The President asked me to make the changes in the bill and bring it back in two days. He seemed in [a] very good mood and handled Mr. Untermyer cheerfully and successfully.[7]

Moley was not happy with Roosevelt's solution, since it meant that Thompson's bill on the issuing of securities, which did seem to have serious deficiencies, would go to Congress immediately, and Untermyer's on regulating the exchanges not until later. The immediate danger in the spring of 1933 was of speculation in the exchanges, where indeed a boomlet was soon underway, and not in the issuing of new securities, which was likely to be nil. Roosevelt parried that there was plenty of time for both measures, but by the time he received Untermyer's bill he had decided to postpone asking Congress for exchange legislation until its 1934 session.[8]

On March 29, when Roosevelt sent a message to Congress asking for securities regulation, Thompson's bill was ready to introduce, and the President still assumed the measure to regulate exchanges would be ready in a week or ten days. Nevertheless, the message covered only issuance of new securities, and declared that bills providing regulation of exchanges and prevention of unethical and unsafe banking and corporate practices would follow. In order to emphasize the constitutional basis of regulation, he began the message, "I recommend to the Congress legislation for Federal supervision of traffic in investment securities in interstate commerce." Moley's draft of the message had been even more explicit — but rather unwieldy — "under powers vested in Congress by the Constitution in relation to Interstate Commerce." Using words similar to those Thompson had suggested to him, he declared, "This proposal adds to the ancient rule of *caveat emptor*, the further doctrine 'let the seller also beware.' It puts the burden of telling the whole truth on the seller." [9]

The bill, Roosevelt warned newspapermen, provided "publicity rather than any guarantee to the investing public":

> Well, the simplest example is this: If a company is organized to develop a gold mine and they have got what they and the engineers honestly believe to be a perfectly good speculation and it is not over-capitalized, there is no reason why they should not get a license to operate provided it is said to the public that it is, like most gold mining operations, a speculative venture. Of course, it must be started in good faith. In other words, what we are trying to do is to get the kind of publicity information as to each issue before the investing public so that, if they then invest, they will know at least that the representations that have been made to them are true.[10]

Newspapers spread the catchy phrase, "let the seller beware," and even the *Wall Street Journal* approved the objectives of the bill. In the House the legislation came under the powerful aegis of Sam Rayburn of Texas, chairman of the Interstate Commerce Committee. Since his early years in the House during the Wilson administration he had favored securities regulation and, indeed, had succeeded by 1920 in placing control over railroad financing with the Interstate Commerce Commission. Unfortunately, it became the consensus during two weeks of hearings that Thompson's bill was confusing and seriously flawed. It would force the filing of information concerning a corporation and its securities with the Federal Trade Commission before the securities could be issued and would put the force of federal law behind existing state statutes. But it was thirty-five pages long and uneven; Thompson seemed to expect it to be largely self-enforcing. Legislators who wanted firm, clear regulation joined financiers who really wanted no regulation in protesting against the bill. A liberal businessman, Averell Harriman, told Moley his associates considered it impossible. Moley relayed the criticisms to Rayburn.[11]

"It'll have to be thrown out," Rayburn told Moley. "I want you to get me a draftsman who knows this stuff to write a new bill under my direction. And you've got to persuade the Chief that this Thompson bill won't do."

Since the bill was in congressional committees, Moley took the view that the administration must not interfere, that while he could inform Roosevelt, he would have to act on Rayburn's authorization, not the President's. On this basis, technically as an agent of Rayburn's, Moley telephoned Felix Frankfurter for help. Frankfurter was a shrewd choice on Moley's part because he was one of the most distinguished proponents of the New Freedom type of regulation. He stood high in the regard of Roosevelt, who had tried to persuade him to become solicitor general, and even higher in that of Brandeis. On the surface there would seem to be no break between what Untermyer and Thompson advocated and what Frankfurter stood for.[12]

In practice there was a generation's difference. Untermyer and Thompson had their roots deep in the states'-rights constitutionalism that gripped the Democratic party up into the Progressive era. They feared and distrusted bigness and centralization, both in Wall Street and Washington; their proposed remedies were cautious and rather negative, within a rather strict construction of the Constitution and vested little power in Washington. In their thinking, they were much closer to Brandeis than to his devotee Frankfurter, or, for that matter, to Roosevelt, who bowed to Brandeis as "Isaiah," and then looked forward toward more energetic solutions to the modern complexities. For, though it would have been heresy to have said so around Frankfurter and his group, that spring Brandeis was proposing specific solutions that seemed limited and naive. Like Holmes, he was becoming an ancient monument, revered more than followed. On the one hand, Frankfurter reported his every triumph to Brandeis, as he would to an all-wise father. On the other, he rushed to engage three of his young protégés, James M. Landis, Thomas Corcoran, and Benjamin V. Cohen in the drafting of a new securities bill. All three were of the Brandeis-Wilsonian tradition, but ready to move well beyond the New Freedom. As had Adolf A. Berle and Gardiner C. Means in their book, *The Modern Corporation and Private Property* (1932), they had adjusted their thinking to encompass the revolutionary growth, bureaucratization and dispersal of ownership in corporate and financial structure that had burgeoned during World War I and the New Era of the 1920s. They would not prescribe horse-and-buggy remedies in an automobile age. In the spring of 1933 they were a bit fumbling and tentative but they were to bring modern concepts of federal regulation to Washington. Within the next several years they made their mark on the New Deal as distinctly as did Moley, Tugwell and Berle.

Of the trio, Landis was professor of legislation in the Harvard Law School and had been exploring problems of regulation, especially state "blue sky" laws. He had served a year as Brandeis's law clerk and was full of reforming zeal. Cohen and Corcoran had both worked in New

York law firms as specialists in corporate reorganization. Corcoran, who had been law clerk to Holmes, had already come to Washington in 1932 to serve as the lawyer for the Reconstruction Finance Corporation. In appearance and personality, Cohen and Corcoran were a contrast: Cohen, gentle and quiet, a bit disheveled in appearance; Corcoran, ebullient and ready to inject himself into the hurly-burly of politics. All three were brilliant legal craftsmen ready to work day and night for weeks on end.[13]

Incessant labor, a Washington prerequisite that spring, awaited Frankfurter's protégés. Moley had thought when he phoned Frankfurter for help (telling him, incidentally, that the President wanted him to come down) that it would be a weekend patching job. Frankfurter had already read the bill and thought more than a little tinkering would be necessary, which was why he immediately involved Landis and Cohen. When he arrived in Washington he talked to Roosevelt, then Rayburn, explaining to them that it would take time to develop a satisfactory bill. Over the weekend, Cohen, Corcoran, and Landis under the guise of preparing "perfecting amendments" drafted a tentative new measure, based on the English Companies Act. In order not to offend Thompson and his supporters, it included a number of the provisions of Thompson's bill, which later were eliminated in the legislative process. But it contained the core of the Securities Act of 1933.[14]

Weeks of maneuvering followed, in which Roosevelt's hand from time to time appeared, before an acceptable securities bill passed Congress. First there was the problem of keeping Thompson, who had a considerable following for his bill, from realizing the full extent of the modifications and becoming offended. Thompson was a good deal more amiable than Untermyer, but also had far more support in Congress.

On April 7, the same day Roosevelt saw Frankfurter, he also summoned Thompson to the White House. It was a balmy spring day and Roosevelt was seated in his second floor study with a door open and a breeze from the Potomac blowing through the room. "The President was in high feather," Thompson noted in his diary. For an hour and a half he talked cheerfully of various matters of state, ranging from farm legislation to European affairs, and let Thompson report on the progress of the securities bill. Then he told Thompson he had an additional assignment for him, that at Muscle Shoals power companies had been obtaining power free or stealing it with the apparent approval of the Army Engineers. Ickes had employed Louis Glavis, famous as the investigator who in the Taft administration had precipitated a great controversy over an alleged grab of coal lands in Alaska, to check into private use of Muscle Shoals power. Glavis had reported evidence of wrongdoing, and the President wanted Thompson to handle a lawsuit on behalf of the government.[15]

A few days later Thompson did take the case, and also a second one involving Henry Ford and Muscle Shoals. Marvin McIntyre, one of Roosevelt's secretaries, was also flattering, asking Thompson's advice on a letter Roosevelt was thinking of sending to the Republican head of the Federal Power Commission, George Otis Smith, asking for his resignation. Thompson suggested the letter not be sent, and rather that Jim Farley summon Smith to his office and orally ask him to leave. Roosevelt decided the person who could best carry out this delicate mission was Thompson himself, and persuaded him to call upon Smith and tell him the President wished him to resign.[16]

Apparently Roosevelt was not trying to dump Thompson and get him out of town (as has been suggested), but was simply trying to make him feel appreciated, and reconcile him to the changes in the bill. It is even possible that Roosevelt himself did not as yet know how drastically Rayburn wanted it rewritten. On Monday morning, April 10, Landis, Cohen, and Corcoran, after their hasty weekend drafting session, had breakfast with Thompson and told him they had been preparing amendments to his bill. Two days later, Thompson asked the President to persuade Rayburn to iron out differences between the House and Senate bills with the chairman of the Senate Committee on Banking and Currency, Duncan U. Fletcher of Florida. Roosevelt obliged by penciling a memorandum to Rayburn, asking him to see "Sen. Fletcher & try to reconcile the Security Bill." [17]

No reconciliation took place. Rayburn asked Frankfurter's team to remain in Washington to perfect their draft. Frankfurter returned to Harvard Law School and met Landis's classes for him while Landis remained and for weeks worked with Cohen, Corcoran, and Middleton Beaman, chief legislative draftsman for the House of Representatives.

There was considerable support for Thompson's bill. The seventy-four-year-old Senator Fletcher preferred it, and so did Secretary Roper and those of his staff who had worked upon it. By late April, Thompson was becoming aware of what was going on. He lamented to McIntyre that he was afraid the Brain Trust crowd had ruined his bill. McIntyre replied consolingly, "Well, I bet they haven't caused you any more trouble than they have caused me." When, on May 5, Thompson finally learned the full truth, "that from the time Frankfurter appeared I was apparently superseded," he took it philosophically, and still hoped the House and Senate bills could be reconciled.[18]

It was Rayburn who insisted that Landis, Cohen, and Corcoran work in secret on numerous quite technical problems until they had a draft ready that the House subcommittee could report out to the full committee. Word leaked to Wall Streeters that they were preparing a dangerously drastic measure — the same complaint as against Thompson's bill. Once again there was pressure upon Moley, who this time persuaded Rayburn to give a group of New York lawyers who were experts on securities an opportunity to discuss the bill before his subcommittee. Rayburn reluctantly agreed, with the stipulation that Landis and Cohen should be present to defend their bill. John Foster Dulles, not too well prepared, led the attack. "Rayburn . . . exhibited considerable annoyance . . . at Dulles' allegations that Rayburn was sponsoring legislation that would undermine our financial system," Landis has recalled. "Rayburn insisted that all that was being demanded was that the system should live up to its pretensions." The other two experts suggested some useful technical alterations which the drafters made in the bill.[19]

There was little disposition on the part of most members of Congress to share the financiers' alarm over the securities bill. Wall Street prestige, which had been at a low ebb, was dropping even lower that spring as Senator Fletcher threw most of his energies and that of his Banking Committee into an investigation of Wall Street malpractices. With Ferdinand Pecora, a master of the dramatic, as its counsel, the committee summoned J. P. Morgan to its hearings, and drew from him lists of personages, including Bernard Baruch, William Gibbs McAdoo, William Woodin, and Norman H. Davis, who in 1929 had been invited to buy stock issues at preferential prices.* Morgan and his partners looked upon the list as a means of sharing an equity risk with underwriters; Pecora gave it a less pleasant interpretation. McAdoo protested that he had lost $2,500 on his stock purchases, but it was not easy for any of the Democrats to explain away their names on the lists. Morgan, with his beetling brows and aristocratic airs, tried to maintain his dignity even when a circus press agent posed a twenty-seven-inch midget on his lap and was fairly successful. Pecora uncovered no proof of serious misconduct comparable to that of the National City Bank officials investigated earlier, but the mighty were being humbled, and the way prepared for securities regulation. While working on the bill, Landis and Cohen were staying at the same hotel as Morgan and his

---

* The three common stocks, in holding companies Morgan helped form, were United Corporation, Alleghany Corporation, and Standard Brands, Inc. Morgan, rather than sell the stocks to the general public, disposed of them privately to financial organizations, and to the public figures. A Morgan partner thus offered Woodin 1,000 shares of Alleghany common at $20 per share, the cost to the firm, which Woodin could sell whenever he wished. At that time, the stock was selling for $35–$37 per share. Personages receiving such opportunities included former President Coolidge and Charles A. Lindbergh. Morgan insisted there were no strings attached.[20]

staff, and were glad Morgan did not recognize them when they shared the same elevator.[21]

As soon as the House bill was in final form, on May 5, Rayburn rushed it through under a special rule allowing no amendments. Landis reported, "Rayburn did not know whether the bill passed so readily because it was so damned good or so damned incomprehensible." Rayburn had persuaded Joe Robinson to hold up the Senate bill until the House measure had passed. The Senate on May 8 enacted Thompson's bill, with an amendment added that was the particular concern of Hiram Johnson. It would create a Corporation of Foreign Security Holders to negotiate with foreign governments to try to obtain some return for some 700,000 American individual and institutional investors holding nearly $3 billion in defaulted foreign government obligations.[22]

The differences between the Rayburn-sponsored and the Fletcher-sponsored bills created no serious problem in the House and Senate Conference Committee. Rayburn became chairman, and although he was fully considerate toward the senators on the committee, at every point except the Johnson amendment the finished bill came to embody the handiwork of Frankfurter's drafting team. As for the Johnson amendment, it was a political hot potato they tossed back to the White House.

On the one hand, President Roosevelt was assiduously courting Johnson that spring. Johnson's cause, to retrieve moneys small investors, and in some instances churches and hospitals, had lost in purchasing foreign (most often Latin American) government bonds, was a popular one. The average holding was only about $800. On the other hand, Herbert Feis on behalf of the State Department vigorously opposed the establishment of a new independent federal agency authorized to deal directly with foreign governments. Moreover, Secretary Hull was eager to begin a policy of conciliation and increased trade toward the Latin American republics. Roosevelt expressed his sympathy and concern to Johnson, but to Johnson's sorrow also wrote congressional committees in the vein of Feis's objections.[23]

While the conference committee was preparing the final version of the bill, Rayburn asked Johnson, who was sitting on the committee, to obtain definite instructions from the President whether or not to include the Johnson amendment. As the committee neared the end of its work Johnson had received no word, and could only suggest that Rayburn telephone the President. Roosevelt in this instance could come to no conclusion except to tell Rayburn to use his own judgment. Landis, who had accompanied Rayburn to an adjoining room and listened in on the conversation, suggested to Rayburn the formula by now familiar, but which on this occasion had not occurred to Roosevelt: give the

President optional power. Johnson's amendment should go into effect only when the President deemed it to be in the public interest and issued a declaration. Landis quickly drafted the provision for the conference committee, and to his surprise Johnson accepted it. Roosevelt never exercised the option, but did encourage the ultimate formation of a private bondholders' association which in its membership came closely to resemble a government agency.[24]

The House and Senate both passed the securities bill as reported out of conference, and on May 27, Roosevelt signed it. "If the country is to flourish, capital must be invested in enterprise," he declared. "But those who seek to draw upon other people's money must be wholly candid regarding the facts on which the investor's judgment is asked." [25]

"Don't worry about the new Securities Bill," Roosevelt had tried to reassure a financier friend shortly before final enactment. "As passed by the House it will not hurt any honest seller of securities and some of them are seeing things at night!" Nonetheless there was a crescendo of protest. Wall Streeters, as they had through the weeks since the bills were first filed, acclaimed the principle behind the legislation but denounced the specifics as being harsh, unreasonable, and certain to inhibit the flow of capital into business. Although some critics in Congress had asserted the measure was too lenient, they said that the civil damages that could be recovered were too harsh; each underwriter was liable for the entire total value of the issue, regardless of the percentage he had floated. There were criticisms of other provisions as being either too severe or too expensive. Six months later, the president of the Investment Bankers Association stated that the law was hindering recovery, that it had almost completely stopped new corporate underwritings. The attack was exaggerated; lack of demand for funds was a prime reason why few new stock and bond issues were appearing. But the act was flawed, despite the weeks that had gone into its gestation. A friendly critic, William O. Douglas, evaluated the measure years later, saying it was no model of draftsmanship. But it was sound at heart, and after a few amendments in 1934 it became a workable statute.[26]

The administration of the Securities Act of 1933 fell to the Federal Trade Commission until, thirteen months later, the Securities and Exchange Commission came into existence. From the outset, Landis was involved in putting it into operation. The Securities Act would not have curbed the speculative boom and stock crash of the 1920s, but it was the first of several steps Roosevelt had in mind.[27]

The development and distribution of federal power at Muscle Shoals was to be only in part a "birch rod" or "yardstick" to police private utilities; the regional planning, development and conservation it would involve were even more exciting in Roosevelt's mind. One night not long before the bill went to Congress, Roosevelt invited Norris to dinner and talked to him until a late hour projecting the potentials of the program.

"What are you going to say when they ask you the political philosophy behind TVA?" Norris inquired.

"I'll tell them it's neither fish nor fowl," Roosevelt replied, "but, whatever it is, it will taste awfully good to the people of the Tennessee Valley." [28]

Like the dams that Roosevelt planned in the Tennessee Valley, his plans were multipurpose. He was ready to combine Norris's prime concern with power production and utility regulation with the emphasis of various southern congressional leaders upon fertilizer production, together with his own overriding interest in regional planning. Roosevelt earlier had consulted Arthur E. Morgan, president of Antioch College, who had made his reputation as a flood control engineer and become an advocate of social redevelopment. He had asked Morgan the question in the forefront of his long-range thinking: "Is it possible, especially down in this region, where people never have had adequate incomes . . . for us to develop small industries, where the people can produce what they use, and where they can use what they produce, and where, without dislocating the industry of America, we can absorb a lot of this unemployment, and give population a sound footing on which it can live, possibly with restricted standards, but still live soundly and in a self-supporting way until we can work our way into a new economy?" [29]

The TVA to Roosevelt meant primarily regional development. "He talked about an hour about its possibilities, and there was scarcely a mention of power or fertilizer," wrote Morgan a year later. "He talked chiefly about a designed and planned social and economic order. That was what was first in his mind." [30]

In effect, Senator Norris, prime mover for so many years for power development on the Tennessee River, acted as bill drafter for the President. Roosevelt wrote him on March 13, "We must decide very soon on procedure," suggesting the bill should be ready in a few weeks. Although Roosevelt was ready to go further than Norris had earlier envisaged, Norris drew up an all-encompassing bill, and went over it with Roosevelt and others on April 1 and 7. At the meeting on April 1, Roosevelt conferred for almost two hours with Norris, Ickes, Wallace, and two congressmen, John J. McSwain of South Carolina, chairman of the House Military Affairs Committee, and Lister Hill of Alabama. Although McSwain and Hill had opposed the CCC as giving too much power to the President, they were advocates of the TVA — but in a more conservative form than Roosevelt and Norris wished.

McSwain later took credit for having thought of the name, Tennessee Valley Authority, but in April 1933, rather than cosponsoring Norris's bill, introduced a somewhat different one of his own in the House.*

To the dismay of Moley, Roosevelt went further than he had in the campaign and fully accepted Norris's position on power. Speaking at Portland, Oregon, Roosevelt had referred to possible federal transmission and distribution of power as a "birch rod" in the cupboard that the federal government would use only if private companies failed to provide "reasonable and good service." † Roosevelt by April 1933 was ready to accept authorization to build transmission lines, which Norris had included specifically in both this and his previous bill. In contrast, President Hoover had insisted that at Boulder Dam on the Colorado River the federal government should go no further than to produce the power, delivering it to private companies at the "bus bar" on the generators.[33]

On April 10, Roosevelt sent Congress one of his most eloquent messages, representing his own views, and upon which he had put the final polish in his own hand:

> It is clear that the Muscle Shoals development is but a small part of the potential public usefulness of the entire Tennessee River. Such use, if envisioned in its entirety, transcends mere power development; it enters the wide fields of flood control, soil erosion, afforestation, elimination from agricultural use of marginal lands, and distribution and diversification of industry. In short, this power development of war days leads logically to national planning for a complete river watershed involving many States and the future lives and welfare of millions. It touches and gives life to all forms of human concerns. . . .
>
> Many hard lessons have taught us the human waste that results from lack of planning. Here and there a few wise cities and counties have looked ahead and planned. But our nation has "just grown." It is time to extend planning to a wider field, in this instance comprehending in one great project many States directly concerned with the basin of one of our greatest rivers.
>
> This in a true sense is a return to the spirit and vision of the pioneer. If we are successful here we can march on, step by step, in a like development of other great natural territorial units within our borders.[34]

Just as in the winter when Roosevelt had first announced the Tennessee Valley program, in the spring it was still so overshadowed by

---

* Representative John E. Rankin of Mississippi introduced Norris's bill in the House, but the House considered neither McSwain's nor Rankin's, but a bill Lister Hill introduced on April 20, which emphasized nitrate production.[31]

† FDR's concept had come from a by no means radical source; it was Owen D. Young of General Electric who suggested to him that if consumers could not obtain satisfactory rates, municipalities establish their own power companies.[32]

other events that it attracted relatively little attention. Both its fame and the controversy over it developed with time. Only the House held hearings, listening to the protests of the private power company executives. Wendell Willkie, newly appointed president of the Commonwealth and Southern Corporation and a Democrat, took a position much like that of the financiers on the securities bill. He praised the general principle of regional development, but criticized the specific authorization for federal transmission lines. These would duplicate those of private companies, and threaten their $400 million investment.

Transmission lines were at the crux of the debate in both houses of Congress, since if the private companies could obtain federal power at the bus bar, there would be little threat to their rates and control. The federal government would be serving them. The House version of the bill placed limitations on the building of transmission lines. Norris held the Senate firm, but even after bills had passed both houses, he was fearful that the conference committee might submit to the power interests and specify that the TVA could not construct transmission lines until it had obtained permission from local power companies. Ickes helped enlist Roosevelt's support. The President took a keen, detailed interest in the work of the conference committee, and stipulated specifically that he favored no limitation on the TVA's authority to transmit power.* The TVA was enabled to build transmission lines if

---

* An indication of FDR's detailed interest and intervention is the memorandum he sent the conference committee on May 9, 1933:
Senator Norris and Chairman McSwain asked me for my opinion on the bills — Here it is:

1. O.K. on merely typographical or grammatical changes in Senate Bill —
2. O.K. on officials (in Senate Bill)
3. On fertilizer I think the Norris wording is better as the basis, with slight verbal changes on which Senator Norris and Mr. McSwain agree. The purpose is (a) to operate primarily for experimental purposes but also (b) to sell the products of these experimental runs.
4. Section 10 Senate bill is better than Section 11 of House Bill.
5. Section 11 Senate and Section 12 House, O.K.
6. Section 12 Senate — Section 13 House [.] Rates may take zoning distances into consideration provided the differentials are approved by the corporation. I strongly favor the wider powers for transmission lines in the Senate bill. The restricted House provisions means that the United States is buying a series of law suits.
7. Senate Section 18 — House 16 [.] The transmission line from Cove Creek to Muscle Shoals should be authorized as well as any other transmission line to connect any and all Corporation power development.
8. O.K. to give me power to investigate.
9. Not very keen about bond guarantees.
10. Civil Service Compensation should apply.
11. Civil Service appointment not to apply.
12. Any fair wage provisions applying to government contracts shall apply to this work.[35]

it wished, and, in keeping with strong southern interest, to experiment with the production of fertilizer. "It was a glorious fight right up to the very end," Norris's secretary wrote a friend, "with President Roosevelt standing firmly behind Senator Norris in every particular." [36]

For both Roosevelt and Norris, the signing of the bill on the afternoon of May 18 was a particularly joyous occasion. Norris stood at the President's left in the group arrayed behind him at his desk. Roosevelt, thumbing through the pages of the lengthy bill, questioned whimsically if he should read it before affixing his signature. Someone retorted in kind that since Senator Norris approved of the measure, that was not necessary.

"George, are the transmission lines in here?" Roosevelt asked. Norris said they were.

Looking around the room, Roosevelt then made a mock inquiry for the representative of the Alabama Power Company.

With these good-humored preliminaries out of the way, the President, using several pens, signed the measure, giving to Norris the one with which he wrote "Roosevelt." [37]

CHAPTER XXI

Two Roads in World Policy

The domestic situation is inevitably and deeply tied in with the conditions in all of the other Nations of the world. . . . We can get, in all probability, a fair measure of prosperity to return in the United States, but it will not be permanent unless we get a return to prosperity all over the world.

— FDR, *second Fireside Chat, May 7, 1933.*[1]

In the spring of 1933, President Roosevelt tried to regain for the United States the leadership in world affairs which the Senate had forced President Wilson to relinquish. His aim was to initiate international action to restore prosperity and protect threatened nations from military aggressors, yet not upset his domestic recovery program or frighten isolationists.[2]

Second only in Roosevelt's thinking to the economic crisis at home was the growing military crisis in the world, the gathering storm that was to burst into World War II only six and a half years later. The American people were aware of the threats of aggressive military powers; they shuddered over the newsreels of Japanese troops battling across northern China, and feared war for Europe. Few could have believed that America could become involved in another world conflict; if it came their concern would be to stay out.

Roosevelt shared their concern, and felt he could best promote the nation's welfare by throwing the influence of the United States into the prevention of war and the promotion of economic recovery. Yet he must do so without disturbing domestic arrangements. He must limit himself to the sort of international cooperation that would not undercut agricultural, industrial, or financial recovery policies, nor cause him to run afoul of Congress. The Senate's humiliation of Wilson in blocking American entrance into the League of Nations was too recent for Roosevelt ever to overlook. Hence from the very outset, Roosevelt formulated foreign policies aimed at global effect yet circumscribed by domestic realities.

Roosevelt at once committed his administration to a foreign policy of internationalism even while step by step he was building a domestic structure of economic nationalism that spilled over into foreign affairs. Simultaneously Roosevelt, listening to Moley, Tugwell, and the architects of much of his domestic program, authorized nationalistic measures in the realm of foreign policy to implement the recovery programs, and also, listening to Secretary Hull, Stimson, and Norman Davis, pursued policies aimed at restoring world prosperity and reducing the threat of war. One of the most precise observers, Anne O'Hare McCormick, pointed out in the *New York Times* on May 7:

> The administration is not only moving in two directions at once in the domestic field; it charts two opposite roads in world policy and proceeds to follow them both. Mr. Roosevelt drafts tentative plans for a possible state of economic isolation in which the United States will sustain itself and as far as possible contain itself. At the same time he has spent one month out of his two in conference with the representatives of other governments.

That same evening, Roosevelt in his second Fireside Chat bore out Mrs. McCormick's analysis. In his brief talk he set forth first his plans for agricultural and industrial recovery through raising prices and wages, which could succeed only by keeping out competing foreign imports, then emphasized the necessity for international cooperation to end the depression. "The international conference that lies before us must succeed," he declared. "The future of the world demands it and we have each of us pledged ourselves to the best joint efforts to this end." [3]

It was more difficult to reconcile conflicting goals in foreign policy than domestic affairs. The cleavage between opposing advisers was much sharper and more distinct; there was little or no common ground between Moley and the economic nationalists on the one hand and Davis, Hull, and the internationalists on the other. Roosevelt, to judge by all he said and did at the time, hoped he could somehow combine both courses of action — temporarily follow nationalistic policies, especially concerning money, and then in the long run promote monetary stabilization and stimulate foreign trade. Similarly, he would temporize with congressional isolationists (perhaps better called nationalists) on those methods of fostering international security to which they objected, so long as their votes were helpful in obtaining his domestic program. In addition, he so carefully phrased his pledges of international cooperation that they could not well object. He innovated, then insisted he was merely carrying out the foreign policy of his Republican predecessors, to which the Senate had given its approval.

No doubt Roosevelt was consistent in his pursuit of long-term goals, but his improvisations in the early months of his presidency seemed at times wobbly if not downright erratic. In retrospect, a consistency in his overall course is apparent, and some of his oblique moves can be compared to a yachtsman tacking against the wind. Some wobbles still remain. He veered a good bit, not always gauging the consequences in advance as he tried within a loose framework to accommodate incompatible personnel and conflicting policies. In his concepts and actions that spring there was much that was visionary as well as realistic to a certain degree. As bit by bit he made accommodations, his working policy became incompatible with his overview, and the outcome by the summer of 1933 was temporarily one of economic nationalism.

Some of Roosevelt's nationalistic actions were to avoid conflict with Congress. Since his long-range foreign program was secondary to the immediate enactment of domestic legislation, he did deliberately modify or postpone some items on his agenda in order not to jeopardize votes or risk filibusters that could delay or threaten recovery bills. He immediately took steps to avoid a clash with congressional isolationists over two organizations they particularly abhorred, the League of Nations and the World Court. While he remained professedly a Wilsonian, he could not be drawn into favoring American membership in the League. He did not want to alienate those members of both houses of Congress who, while isolationists, were voting for much of his domestic program, nor to unleash the invective of the temporarily friendly Hearst chain of newspapers. More than that, he genuinely believed, as did most informed observers, that the League was malfunctioning. The unwillingness of its members to undertake any effective collective action to stop the Japanese invasion of Manchuria left little room for illusion about the League's future role. To the irritation of idealists who could not face the realities at Geneva and tried in advance to dissuade Roosevelt, he reprinted in his book *On Our Way* his 1932 strictures on the League.[4]

At the time of the initial furore over Roosevelt's statement, in February 1932, he sent a retort in the form of a fable to a woman critic who felt that he "could not be sound on the economic [question] if he were unsound on the question of international relations." It was a justification of the tactics Roosevelt came to employ as President:

> Two men started at the same time to race each other around the world. Their goal was the same and each one of them started out in a nice new car. A few days out one of the men died and his place was taken by a friend who got it into his head that the objective was to circle the globe in the same car with which the race had been started. He got mired in some low country and his car was smashed up many times in crossing the first range of mountains, necessitating months of repairs. Because he stuck to the old car he had to take slow freighters instead of passenger ships. When he came to the desert he nearly

starved to death amid nomad tribes and when he came to the jungles he came down with fever and was often at the point of death. At last after forty years he came back home — with what was left of the old car. It was a heroic journey and he attained his end.

The other man, realizing that the attainment of the goal in the shortest possible time was the true object of the race, bought new cars when he got stuck, used fast ships and aeroplanes, avoided the deserts and the jungles and reached home in one year. He too had attained the goal.

As old William Cobbett said a hundred years ago: "That is a bone for them to gnaw on!" [5]

Nor would Roosevelt even risk stirring debate over American entrance into the World Court, although all three of his Republican predecessors, even the hypercautious Coolidge, had recommended it. At the end of December 1932, when Senator Pittman had thought he could get approval through the lame duck session of Congress, Roosevelt expressed gratification. "It would be a great help," he wrote, "getting this subject definitely and permanently out of the way." Pittman failed, leaving the issue to plague Roosevelt. In late March 1933, Senator Hiram Johnson was upset because Joseph Robinson at a meeting of the Foreign Relations Committee demanded the question be reported favorably on the floor of the Senate. When Johnson sat down for dinner at the White House a day or so later, Roosevelt leaned across to him, grinned, and said, "Now Senator I want you to enjoy your dinner. I know you will enjoy it when I tell you that the World Court will remain for the present at least in the Foreign Relations Committee." [6]

To others Roosevelt displayed his internationalist side. Only two days before he entertained Hiram Johnson at dinner, he ate lunch on his flattop desk with former Secretary Stimson, and in the course of an hour and a half conversation convinced Stimson of his soundness on foreign policy questions.

Stimson's impressions of Roosevelt's foreign policy views were those of the State Department officers. The President seemed indeed to be carrying out the internationalist policies of the Republican Stimson and interestingly to be facing the united opposition of the Republicans in Congress. That same day they had lunch, a House subcommittee by a strict party note, with every Democrat favorable and every Republican opposed, accepted Roosevelt's proposal for an arms embargo, which Hoover and Stimson had been urging upon Congress for several years. When Moffat saw Stimson later that afternoon:

> I then talked over . . . the tendency we had all noticed that the Republican party, unable to make headway against the President's domestic politics, was endeavoring to fight him on foreign affairs and to

revert to the old time isolationist, anti-League, anti-Court, anti-coopera-
tion stand which had won them a victory in 1921. Mr. Stimson was
scathing and remarked somewhat jocularly that if such were the case
it would make him a Democrat.[7]

There was a good political reason for the Republicans to fight Roosevelt on foreign policy: they could augment their numbers with Democratic isolationists.

Roosevelt's appointments demonstrated that he basically favored international cooperation. With a single conspicuous exception, his staffing
of the State Department corroborated what his cordial talk with Stimson
and his appointment of Hull as secretary of state and Norman Davis as
ambassador at large seemed to indicate. Both advice on foreign policy
and its execution were the responsibility of men committed to cautious
international cooperation. It was Stimson, incidentally, not Colonel
House, who was the gray eminence encouraging the Roosevelt administration toward internationalism. House, like Howe, was primarily representative of bygone days and old loyalties, who received no more than
an occasional note from Roosevelt and a brief visit in June 1933. Stimson
was an energetic presence and moral force in Washington, who saw
Roosevelt occasionally and Hull frequently. Stimson's estate Woodley
was Hull's refuge where he and his subordinates relaxed, playing croquet once or twice a week. State department officials continued to brief
Stimson and consult him on delicate matters — as well they might since
they revered him and could be sure of the President's approval. Roosevelt left undisturbed at their State Department desks Stimson's chief advisers: Feis as economic adviser, Moffat in charge of western European
affairs, and Stanley Hornbeck in charge of the Far East. They continued to function as they had under Stimson, and indeed, during Hull's
regime gained in influence and power. It would be an exaggeration to
say that after Hoover left office Stimson continued as before as Roosevelt's shadow secretary of state, but during the spring Frankfurter's pre-
diction seemed to be coming true that Stimson was more influential out
of office than he had been as Hoover's secretary of state.[8]

Another old Wilsonian was the undersecretary of state, William
Phillips of Boston, who had been a good friend of Roosevelt's during
the First World War, and who fitted well into the small corps of professional diplomats with their similar elite backgrounds and loyalties to
each other. There was a bit more than this to Phillips. Along with his
Brahmin gentility he carried something of the heritage of Wendell
Phillips, the abolitionist and reformer. Feis noted that he was more
tolerant of those of other races and religions than most of his peers.
That spring he was especially sympathetic to Robert R. Moton,

principal of Tuskegee Institute, when Moton came as one of a delegation to urge that the United States replace the League and again undertake a dominant and benevolent role in Liberia.[9]

Most of the Foreign Service officers remained unaffected by the change in administration except for the disastrous cuts they suffered in their salaries and allowances due to the Economy Act. Word went around the State Department before Roosevelt took office that he did not think the creation in the 1920s of a career foreign service had worked well, and that he intended to remove some of the senior career diplomats whom he felt had grown out of touch with American developments, but the changes were few. Competent Republicans, even those known as Hoover's men, suffered little, except perhaps to be moved out of the most desirable European missions. Roosevelt was insistent that Hugh Gibson, ambassador to Belgium, who was particularly close to Hoover, be transferred. Gibson, who found himself en route to Brazil, took the change in good grace, and by 1937 was back in Belgium.[10]

One of Roosevelt's concerns was to ensure that envoys spoke the language of the country to which they were assigned. He pondered what to do about Joseph Grew, who had been sent to Japan only a few months earlier, and whom he knew well enough to address in a note as "Dear old Joe." Lamont had pointed out to him when he inquired about Grew's suitability that Grew did not speak Japanese. But in the end Roosevelt asked Grew to remain in Tokyo.[11]

In his political appointments, Roosevelt sent distinguished men to the more important posts. They might have contributed heavily to his campaign, but they also commanded respect and were sympathetic to the leadership and ideas in the State Department. To London he appointed Robert Bingham, and to Paris, Jesse I. Straus. In his first days in the White House, he penciled a note to Hull: "How about inquiring if Judge Bingham will be acceptable as Ambassador to Great Britain? If OK I can appoint him at once & the quicker he goes over the better — don't you think so?" [12]

Secretary Hull did indeed think so, for he had strongly urged the appointment, and in Bingham gained a staunch supporter in a key embassy.

Rome created something of a problem for Roosevelt, since so many Democrats with strong claims were interested. One of Roosevelt's friends tried to undercut the aged James W. Gerard, who had been Wilson's ambassador to Germany, by reporting to Roosevelt that Gerard wanted the position only for a year, and only so he could write about the experience in his memoirs. Colonel House was urging the colorful mayor of Boston, James Michael Curley. Roosevelt had held grievances

against Curley for many years, and instead offered to send him to War-
saw. Curley declined. There were two other formidable claimants. One
was Breckinridge Long, once an assistant secretary of state under Wilson, who refused to become one again because of a personality clash
with Phillips. The other was Clark Howell of the *Atlanta Constitution*,
long a political supporter. Roosevelt offered Howell first Brazil, then
Argentina; Howell declined both. At this point, Roosevelt sent a note to
Hull and Moley: [13] "Why not cut the Gordian knot in regard to the
Argentinian Ambassador by asking Breck Long if he will take it?" [14]

The scheme did not work. Roosevelt patiently offered two more posts
to Howell, first Turkey and then Poland, at which point Howell
dropped out of the ambassadorial sweepstakes. Howell's final request
was to be appointed a delegate to the London Economic Conference,
but Roosevelt did not grant it. Several years later he sent Howell as a
special ambassador to the coronation of George VI. Breckinridge Long
went to Italy, and at once began to send Roosevelt enthusiastic letters
about Mussolini and his Fascist regime. [15]

Finding a suitable ambassador to send to Berlin was a delicate matter
which took several months. It had been a comfortable but expensive
post, one that William Woodin had coveted because of his love of
music. The coming into power of the Nazis quite altered that, and
Roosevelt sought someone who was of great distinction and moral
force, who could take a firm but discreet position against the anti-
Semitism that was beginning to engulf the Jews of Germany. His first
offer was to James Cox, who declined. Then at one point in the early
weeks, not yet fully aware of the seriousness of the Nazi onslaught, he
tentatively thought of sending Jesse Straus, a distinguished Jew, but
concluded that would be impossible. Late in April, Roosevelt queried
Hull concerning Newton D. Baker, but Hull reminded him that Baker
had been Wilson's secretary of war, and it would be necessary un-
officially to sound out the Germans first. In mid-May, Roosevelt told
Morgenthau he was thinking of his old friend Adolph Miller of the
Federal Reserve Board and President Glenn Frank of the University of
Wisconsin. Frank, one of a slate of several university and college presidents, was eliminated because of the mistaken notion that he was a Jew.
Morgenthau suggested Harry Emerson Fosdick, a notable clergyman,
and Roosevelt expressed interest. For no other diplomatic appointment
were so many candidates so carefully considered. Finally Roosevelt
selected a man Daniel Roper had nominated, Professor William E. Dodd
of the University of Chicago, an historian full of Jeffersonian and Wilsonian fervor who had taken a doctorate at the University of Leipzig. [16]

Another exponent of Jeffersonian ideals, the journalist and historian
Claude Bowers, who had labored long and effectively for the Demo-

cratic party, went to Spain, where Roosevelt thought he would have the leisure and quiet for writing. The outbreak of the Spanish Civil War quite altered that, and Bowers subsequently spent many years in Chile. Roosevelt gave his one-time superior, Josephus Daniels the post he wanted, Mexico, forgetting about the naval and marine interventions during those years. The Mexicans soon forgave the charming, shrewd Daniels. Neither Bowers nor Daniels ever learned to speak Spanish and neither was a professional diplomat, yet both were to be among the most popular and successful envoys in Latin America.[17]

Some of the juggling to find positions abroad for political appointees who did not fit into subcabinet spots in Washington turned out well. Roosevelt received credit for appointing the first woman envoy, Ruth Bryan Owen, daughter of William Jennings Bryan, to be minister to Denmark. In 1936, she married a captain in the Danish Royal Guards. Concerning the high qualifications of Laurence A. Steinhardt, whose mother was an Untermyer, Roosevelt penned a longhand note to Hull: "I have the man for you for Asst. Scry in charge of legal work — . . . excellent lawyer — knows a lot about world affairs — I think this is the best choice." Instead, Steinhardt became minister to Sweden and was launched upon an outstanding diplomatic career.[18]

Roosevelt regarded all these envoys as his personal ambassadors, as indeed technically they were, and urged several of them to write to him directly. Lengthy letters came to the White House regularly from Bowers, Daniels, Dodd, Long and others. Yet there was nothing of importance on foreign policy that they did not also communicate to the State Department. When George Earle III saw the President before leaving for Vienna, Roosevelt informally asked him to make calls upon the American envoys in Rome, Berlin, Prague, and Budapest. After arriving at his post, Earle discreetly queried Moffat, "Will you be kind enough to tell me what I should do in the matter of the President's oral orders. . . . They certainly were direct orders to me, but they were not written. Must I take the time doing this out of my leave and do I get my expenses?"[19]

The personal relationship Roosevelt enjoyed with many of his ambassadors did not disrupt the control the State Department hierarchy exercised over the diplomats. Nor did Roosevelt overhaul the Foreign Service. About 50 percent of the appointments went to career officers. His actions as President led Grew to comment after some months, "Isn't it fine the way the President is supporting the career diplomats? Some day that will cease to be a term of opprobrium in the United States." Routine continued much as under Secretary Stimson, and the orientation of both the State Department and the Foreign Service continued to be toward mild international cooperation.[20]

The one spectacular exception in the spring of 1933 was Assistant Secretary Moley, who maintained an enclave of economic nationalism and was responsible only to the President. Moley's presence in the State Department was like that of a second queen bee in a hive, and not only Secretary Hull but almost everyone connected with the department, even newspapermen assigned to cover it, rallied in the common cause to try to eject him.

Moley was the prime exponent of Roosevelt's other road in world policy. There were vital ideological reasons as well as personal animus and jealousies that made him unacceptable to that small closed society, with its social as well as professional ties. Yet Roosevelt had assigned Moley there not for ideological or mischievous reasons, but rather because it was a useful spot to provide office space and a salary for his chief adviser. There was as yet no allocation of funds for White House assistants; that did not come until 1939. Had there been, Roosevelt still could not have provided for Moley under the same roof with Louis Howe. There is the further possibility that Roosevelt was making a concession to the nationalistic chairman of the Senate Foreign Relations Committee, Key Pittman, and to Hiram Johnson. It was reassuring, particularly to Johnson, to have Moley in the State Department and in charge of war debts.

Moley was fearful that the State Department assignment might be a trap. He had wanted to accept Secretary Woodin's invitation to become assistant secretary of the treasury, a fitting spot because of his responsibilities over war debts, a Treasury function. But Roosevelt thought urgent Treasury duties would take up too much of Moley's time.

Since Moley thought of his position as only a temporary one, as his correspondence at the time and his continuing his Barnard College classes show, the post could not have seemed too important. Moley's long-range interest was in journalism; he was already engaged in the negotiations which led to the founding of *Today*, and with Roosevelt's permission contracted to write a newspaper column. He gave little attention to State Department routine, not assuming the considerable burdens of his predecessor. On the other hand, Farley delegated to him responsibility for diplomatic appointments, an area in which Roosevelt took keen personal interest. It involved Moley in constant struggles with Undersecretary Phillips, who opposed Democratic worthies like Bowers. Moley felt Phillips was favoring socialites and rather elegant, pro-British career officers, of the sort newspapermen dubbed "cookie-pushers." Phillips and the career men regarded Moley distrustfully as being too political. Again, Feis was critical because Moley did not demonstrate much interest in being briefed by even the more talented of the officials.

But it would have been difficult for Moley to find the time, he was so swamped with White House assignments. The fact that he also seldom found much time for sleep must have lowered his capacity to suffer lengthy intricate explanations running counter to his own strong views. Like Roosevelt, his concern was with overall basic policy, not shadings of detail, and he must have been continually exhausted. There were occasions when he was abrupt or when his temper flared. When it did, there were those not only at the State Department but throughout official Washington who noted it with satisfaction, watchful as they were for any sign of weakness that could lead to his downfall.[21]

Lines were drawn quickly. The British ambassador, Sir Ronald Lindsay, who was on warm terms with the State Department professionals, on March 30 jotted down his private estimate:

> Mr. Hull, the Secretary of State, is an elderly gentleman, amiable and courteous. I should not call him very practical and he certainly is not a man of action. He is diffident and timid and he hardly dares to come to the point, so that he spends much time in beating about the bush and making a speech of almost senatorial dimensions. But his views are excellent and he is as nearly a free-trader as an American could possibly be. If his views are ever realized, it will be due to the President rather than to himself.
>
> Professor Raymond Moley is a less attractive figure, rough and incisive; indeed, in the interviews we have had, he has more than once intervened energetically to put a point to us in a blunt manner which the Secretary of State has been stating with circumlocution. Moley is not a true economist but he thinks himself one, and he likes to be thought so. He is of professional character and his knowledge savours of the midnight oil. He regards himself as a White House man and not as a State Department man, and apparently he is still giving lectures at Columbia University which takes him away from Washington at least one day every week. We may manage to get on with him all right but I think that he is probably rather a strange and foreign element in an organization like a government office and I should think that there would be difficulties in the offing with the permanent officials. I should be rather inclined to bet a small sum that sooner or later, when the President's debts of gratitude have been discharged, it may be found necessary or advisable to eliminate Professor Moley.[22]

Lindsay's sketch was no estimate of Moley's abilities, which were extraordinary. Although the loyalties of J. Pierrepont Moffat were not with Moley, he had come by mid-May to admire the effectiveness of Moley and others of the Brain Trusters in participating in conferences and preparing statements. "Moley is undoubtedly the strongest and most practical of the group," wrote Moffat, "but he plays a lone hand, makes no attempt to conciliate anybody, and does not fit into an organization."[23]

Within the State Department Moley, while devoting a large part of his time to domestic issues, fought for foreign policies of economic nationalism against two adversaries who, although apparently slow-footed, possessed strong backing, Secretary Hull and Norman Davis. Hull found himself in a most unhappy situation, not only because Moley dealt directly and constantly with the White House without keeping him informed, but because Undersecretary Phillips also had better access to the White House, and especially since President Roosevelt, acting as his own secretary of state, only infrequently consulted Hull and seldom kept him informed. Behind his mild, apparently forgiving exterior, Hull smoldered and waited.

As for President Roosevelt, oblivious of the dynamite he had stacked in the State Department, he zestfully gave as much attention as he could spare from the domestic crisis to the pursuit of foreign affairs. Contrary to the general impression in decades since, he devoted a considerable part of his time and thought to foreign policy even in the spring of 1933.

Roosevelt, succeeding a cautious President who had restrained a dynamic secretary of state, instantly reversed the order of things. Nevertheless he was more conservative than he appeared. He was indeed impressionable concerning foreign as well as domestic matters, but followed the same course of procedure in both areas. Again and again he would set forth sweeping, spectacular suggestions on the basis of a single conversation. He liked to play with new ideas, and would try out snap assertions, more speculative than binding. Then after much consultation and long private mulling, he would finally arrive at a rather prudent decision. Some of his fliers were so wild that they were amusing — but they may have shaken the confidence of auditors.

What was spectacular in Roosevelt's assumption of responsibility for foreign policy was the way in which he took over control in the White House, instructing American envoys, holding conversations with foreign representatives, and often not bothering to inform Secretary Hull or the State Department of his actions. Part of Moley's troubles with Hull doubtless stemmed from the fact that Roosevelt assigned Moley responsibility for war debts and at one point asked him to carry on some conversations with the British without informing anyone, even the secretary. Hull found out about the conversations only when Sir Ronald Lindsay inadvertently came to him and brought up some of the questions to which Hull had no answers. Yet Roosevelt was equally ready on occasion to keep Moley in the dark when he himself carried on conversations about debts. Moffat informed Hugh R. Wilson in Geneva:

> You have no idea of the White House control over foreign affairs now. To do so you must go back to the regime of the great Theodore.

Not only are there personal negotiations between the President and Ambassadors, but telegrams go over by the score and return with notations in the President's handwriting. Every telegram from Norman Davis has gone straight to the President. The system has its advantages and disadvantages. It gives a distinct finality and I think a degree of consistency to our policy that will bear fruit. On the other hand, it is extremely difficult to know what has gone before and this doubt of knowing background extends even in high circles.[24]

Foremost among Roosevelt's concerns over American security when he took office was the rising hostility of Japan, which because of the domestic crisis the American people scarcely noticed. Although he did not often talk about it and gave it less of his time than European affairs, it was his overriding worry in foreign policy that spring. He had taken Stimson's briefings seriously, and according to Farley, warned his cabinet the first time they met that there could be war with Japan. Prime Minister MacDonald reported to the British cabinet after his conversations in April that concerning world security "Mr. Roosevelt's great preoccupation was Japan." [25]

During those weeks, as the Japanese swept through the last remaining Chinese territory north of the Great Wall, they faced the prospect that the League of Nations and the United States might embargo arms and munitions of war bound for Japan. Their reaction, as Ambassador Grew repeatedly reported, was largely against the United States. Grew had been startled at the number of bellicose articles appearing in Japanese publications, hypothecating attacks upon the Philippines, the Panama Canal, and Pearl Harbor. During January and February 1933, when Japan came to suffer League censure and withdrew from the organization, the anti-American campaign grew in intensity. Ambassador Grew on February 23, 1933, sent a cable which gave the incoming Roosevelt reason for serious thought: [26]

By the decision of the Cabinet to secede from the League of Nations Japan has prepared to burn her most important bridge with the outside world. This step indicates the complete supremacy of the military and a fundamental defeat for the moderate elements in the country. . . . There is no bluff in her attitude. The military themselves, and the public through military propaganda, are fully prepared to fight rather than to surrender to moral or other pressure from the West. . . .

[A] large section of the public and the Army has been led by military propaganda to believe that eventual war between the United States and Japan or Russia and Japan or both is inevitable. The military and naval machines are in a state of high efficiency and are rapidly being strengthened. They possess complete self-confidence and arrogance. The Navy is becoming more bellicose. In the present temper of the Army and Navy and the public there is always the risk that any serious incident tending to inflame public opinion might lead Japan to radical steps without counting the cost thereof.[27]

Roosevelt, inheriting this potentially dangerous problem when he took office, continued Stimson's policy of cautious cooperation with the League of Nations yet avoidance of any dramatic move that might cause alarm in Japan. Stimson had only with difficulty persuaded Hoover not to issue a public declaration that it would not "ever engage in sanctions other than that of public opinion," but rather to permit the State Department to endorse the League's censure of Japan. The British, on the other hand, at once embargoed war supplies to both Japan and China and began consulting other governments to see if an international embargo could be applied.[28]

During Roosevelt's first weeks in office there seemed to be some opportunity for much stronger action, for the United States to join with the League in an arms embargo against Japan. Hoover had repeatedly sought legislation from Congress to give him the discretionary power to forbid the export of arms and ammunition to any country or countries where war threatened or had broken out. Congress did not act. When Roosevelt took office, he had a new embargo message drafted, then decided to act more quietly. In answer to a reporter's query, he denied there was any need for speed. Rather than a message, he sent letters to the chairmen of the Foreign Relations committees, then decided that even these might be too strong and ordered the State Department to withdraw them. Next William Phillips arranged to testify before the House committee, but canceled his appearance. Isolationists dominated the House hearings, but with little effect.

Thus far, Roosevelt's strategy of avoiding alarmist headlines worked well. He so thoroughly dominated the House that on April 17 it passed an arms embargo resolution by a vote of 253 to 19. The resolution authorized the President, whenever he found conditions in any part of the world such that the shipment of arms and munitions "may promote or encourage the employment of force" in a dispute among nations, "after securing the cooperation of such governments" as he deemed necessary, to prohibit the export or sale for export of arms to any country or countries he might designate.[29]

While Roosevelt was working quietly for permission to embargo arms he was also downgrading news that the United States would cooperate with the League committee on the Far Eastern situation, which the British had asked to consider an international arms embargo against Japan. Roosevelt authorized Hugh R. Wilson, minister to Switzerland, to participate in the committee's deliberations but not to vote. How directly and carefully the President himself directed these delicate matters became apparent when Moley called to his attention a press release from the pen of Stanley Hornbeck of the Far Eastern division which, in Moley's view, "would have lent itself to wide misinterpretation of our relations to the League." Roosevelt crossed out a section detailing past American cooperation with the League, and told Moley to reduce the draft to a few lines. Roosevelt's instructions, which Moley jotted down, were, "We don't want a big story made of our 'closer' coop[eration]." In his own hand, Roosevelt softened the words of the draft, changing "Participation of the United States" to "Presence of the United States" and adding, "The representative of the United States cannot take any action binding this country." In this bland form the statement could scarcely give umbrage to American isolationists or Japanese militants.[30]

At the end of March, Wilson cabled from Geneva that the American government would be the determining factor in the imposition of a joint arms embargo against Japan, whether it wished to be or not. Other nations were waiting to see what the United States would do. Wilson did not add what was obvious to Roosevelt and the State Department. The members of the League had been so slow and cautious in coming even to the rebuke they administered in approving the Lytton report, that regardless of American action there was scant chance they would vote an arms embargo or other effective sanctions against Japan. Already the British, having unilaterally imposed an embargo, in mid-March revoked it, taking the position that only action in concert could deter Japan. Roosevelt, talking off the record to Robert J. Bender of the United Press after his January conference with Stimson, had both expressed his concern over Japanese militarism and his disappointment with the vacillating and dilatory tactics of the League. At that time he expected no concrete achievement; there was little reason for him to think differently later that spring.[31]

CHAPTER XXII

Assuming Leadership
toward World Order

The world faces a crisis of the first magnitude. If normal life is to be resumed, the World Economic Conference must be made a success. . . .

We agree that political tranquillity is essential for economic stability; that economic disarmament can take place only in a world in which military disarmament is possible.

— JOINT STATEMENT BY FDR AND ITALIAN MINISTER OF FINANCE GUIDO JUNG, *May 6, 1933.*

Prosperity and peace on a world basis — these from the start of his administration were the goals of Roosevelt, as indeed they have been of every American President since. They have seldom seemed more distant and unattainable than in 1933, yet in the face of growing militarism and economic nationalism in many nations, and of isolationism at home, he sought to salvage the two great international conferences, the one on disarmament and the other on the world economy, and turn them toward these ends. The likelihood of persuading nations to sacrifice or limit their immediate interests to vitalize the year-old Geneva Disarmament Conference or to reach major agreement at the forthcoming World Economic Conference was slim indeed, but Roosevelt was willing to risk his sudden, spectacular international prestige in the effort.[1]

As early as January 1933, Roosevelt began considering ways in which he could dramatically assert American leadership in the cause of peace, to reverse the drift toward international anarchy and war. His options were limited, since the League had not only proven a weak vehicle, but was politically unacceptable within the United States. Part of Roosevelt's task was to rally American public opinion behind international action. Consequently he must choose acceptable means. Fortunately for him, his Republican predecessors of the 1920s, in developing alternatives to membership in the League of Nations, had made international conferences and one acclaimed but empty international agreement so respectable they were immune from isolationist attack. President Harding had summoned the Washington Arms Conference of 1921, and since then the United States had participated in other conferences outside the League structure. Roosevelt therefore could urge action in both the Disarmament Conference and the World Economic Conference without violating the orthodoxy the Republicans had established. Further, he could make use of a vague treaty outlawing war as an instrument of national policy — the Kellogg-Briand Pact of 1928, that bore the name of President Calvin Coolidge's secretary of state linked with that of a French foreign minister. Almost every nation had subscribed to it without impairing its national interests; it carried no effective means of enforcement. Perhaps Roosevelt could provide for its implementation. In any event, he was careful to propose building upon what Moffat in the State Department referred to as "the two cornerstones of our foreign policy, (a) the sanctity of the Kellogg-Briand Pact and (b) the observance of our independent judgment in any circumstances that may arise." (There was a third strong point which Roosevelt wished to utilize, the Monroe Doctrine, which he would modify into a Good Neighbor policy.) [2]

Events in Germany and Japan had already by the spring of 1933 eliminated any possibility of effective disarmament; the likelihood of economic cooperation was little better. Hitler had already, like Bismarck, chosen the iron dice of war — or the threat of war — as the means to his ends, and would only wait until his armed forces had gathered strength and his victims appeared vulnerable before making his cast.

At the time the prospect seemed disheartening but not hopeless, and Roosevelt's actions gallant rather than quixotic. After all, Mussolini's earlier bellicose pronouncements had turned out to be bombast, and Italy, advocating a Four Power security pact in the spring of 1933, was in the forefront of the struggle for collective security. Was not the same likely to be true of Hitler? There is an unreal quality, consequently, to the statements that respected statesmen and high-ranking military officers were making during those months, growing out of assumptions of the 1920s. It took time for them to grasp and then act on the frightful new realities; there were shocking predictions aplenty in 1933, but responsible leaders still hoped to prove them false, and in consequence they continued their earlier routines of decision-making.

When the Disarmament Conference at Geneva, which had met and deadlocked in the first half of 1932, reconvened in February 1933, it resumed the earlier line of discussions despite the Nazi accession of power in Germany. It was, unfortunately, a line of argument upon which the Nazis could capitalize as long as there remained uncertainty as to their plans. Debate had revolved around the twin themes of disarmament and compensating security guarantees. The representatives of the Weimar Republic had been demanding an easing of the restrictions the Versailles Treaty had placed upon Germany. The French and their East European allies, fearing the resurgence of Germany, opposed general disarmament except with strong treaty guarantees of military aid. The British and Italians, with whom the Americans sympathized, wished more drastic disarmament but were unwilling to make as firm guarantees of security as the French wished. In February the French introduced their plan at the conference, and the British another. By March, the conference seemed once again deadlocked and on the verge of disintegration.[3]

As the President of a still secure, isolated United States, Roosevelt entered the discussions. The American people could look with horror but no fear of immediate attack upon threats of war in Europe. Their view was across an ocean they commanded with a strong navy and which only occasionally a daring Lindbergh traversed by plane. Thanks to the navy bulwark the land army need be only a skeleton establishment which there would be ample time to enlarge in time of emergency or war. The United States was already virtually disarmed. Roosevelt was commander in chief of a regular army of 140,000 men (including 6,500 Philippine Scouts), operating on a budget of less than $229 million. In order to economize, Roosevelt planned a drastic reduction among the 12,000 regular army officers, but the transfer of 3,000 of them to duty in CCC camps made it unnecessary. The army was so little mechanized that the cavalry horse and army mule still performed essential service; of the 6,000 trucks, 4,000 were left over from World War I. "This is below the point of safety," warned the chief of staff, General MacArthur.[4]

When MacArthur went to the White House with Secretary of War Dern to protest against the cuts in the army, he recalls engaging in bitter debate with Roosevelt:

> The President turned the full vials of his sarcasm upon me. . . . For the third and last time in my life that paralyzing nausea began to creep over me. In my emotional exhaustion I spoke recklessly . . . to the general effect that when we lost the next war, and an American boy, lying in the mud with an enemy bayonet through his belly and an enemy foot on his dying throat, spat out his last curse, I wanted the name not to be MacArthur, but Roosevelt. The President grew livid. "You must not talk that way to the President!" he roared. He was, of course, right. . . . I said that I was sorry and apologized. But I felt my Army career was at an end. I told him he had my resignation as Chief of

Staff. As I reached the door his voice came with that cool detachment which so reflected his extraordinary self-control, "Don't be foolish, Douglas; you and the budget must get together on this."

When they got outside, Dern exclaimed gleefully, "You've saved the Army." But, MacArthur remembers, "I just vomited on the steps of the White House." [5]

Roosevelt still saw no necessity to pour large sums of public works money into the army as he would into the navy. As for MacArthur, he was making surprising proposals for the American delegation to the Disarmament Conference: give up all heavy mobile artillery and abolish naval and military aviation.[6]

For some years Americans had worried about the intransigence of the French in refusing, unless they received strong guarantees, to reduce the powerful and expensive army they maintained behind the apparently impregnable fortifications along the Alsatian frontier, the Maginot line. The German army of 100,000 men with no offensive weapons was no immediate worry; Italy's Fascist regime seemed relatively benign. Soviet Russia scarcely entered into the calculations.[7]

To American experts, the key to European disarmament seemed to be France; the key to world disarmament was to circumvent the problem of Japan versus the United States. From Geneva, Hugh Wilson as delegate to the Disarmament Conference was strongly recommending a regional approach as a means of getting around the Japanese refusal to cut the size of its armies while they were engaged on the Asiatic mainland. Europe would constitute one region, and European powers should then reduce their land armaments in relation to each other. When Norman Davis, whom Roosevelt sent as the new head of the American delegation, joined Wilson in Geneva, he agreed and sent lengthy cables to Washington seeking approval for the regional plan. Roosevelt, preoccupied with his domestic program and wishing to make no decision until he had conferred with MacDonald, jotted a note to Hull, "I think we can defer making decision till end of week — it will be clearer by then — & the P.M.'s visit may be a substitute." Meanwhile he did express his feeling that a regional approach should be effective in Latin America. Whatever Roosevelt himself decided to propose as a disarmament plan depended upon his preliminary conversations with the British and the French.[8]

In March 1933, Hitler's alarming actions caused Roosevelt to place disarmament foremost among his foreign policy concerns, but he instantly discovered that much as he would like to keep it separate, he must discuss it concurrently with questions of international economic rehabilitation and a war debt settlement. As had been the case since hi first telegram from Hoover, they were so intimately interrelated that he could not deal with one without becoming involved in the others. And all three led back to worry over the possible future course of Germany and Chancellor Hitler.

The Nazi revolution was exploding in Germany in March 1933 and frightening the rest of the world. Following a great act of arson gutting the Reichstag, the Nazis began to sweep away not only the Communist party but all opposition; in a final free election they won control of the Reichstag, and in the succeeding days threw out of office all those who were not Nazis or Nazi sympathizers. They suspended the constitutional guarantees of civil liberties and property rights. Gangs of uniformed young Nazis raced through the streets raiding Jewish-owned stores and wielding steel springs with balls on the end with which they could inflict painful bruises without breaking bones; they beat hundreds of Jewish victims. Seven were United States citizens, but the American embassy received only "official regrets" in response to its protests. Perhaps, commentators suggested, there was no cause for alarm. "A dictator," Time explained, "once he feels secure in the saddle, always tries to curb and discipline his followers who have invariably run more or less amuck." [9]

The British were so nervous over Hitler's immediate outright violation of the Versailles Treaty that Prime Minister MacDonald hurried to Paris to consult with Premier Edouard Daladier, then to Rome to see Mussolini. Hitler was adding 60,000 so-called auxiliary police — storm troopers and the like — to the authorized German army of 100,000, and was moving some of them into the demilitarized zone close to the French border near Strasbourg. Daladier told MacDonald on March 10 that there was great anxiety in the French parliament. The threat drew them closer to each other and caused them both to look with fresh expectations toward President Roosevelt and the United States. They pledged full candor and confidence to each other in their forthcoming negotiations with the United States. Up to this time, the French Foreign Office had not rated the United States very high among its interests, if one is to judge by its American section (covering both North and South America), which among its small staff could boast only one man who spoke English — he had an English grandmother — and not one who had ever been to the United States. The tone of the meeting was quite different. Daladier emphasized the French desire "to continue the closest collaboration between France, Great Britain and the United States, the three great democracies, with the object of maintaining peace." [10]

MacDonald had come to Paris in part to inform Daladier of a new compromise disarmament proposal that he hoped might bring agreement in time to stem the demands of Hitler and rapid German rearmament. He urged Daladier to accompany him to Geneva. Daladier hesitated, and then belatedly went to the Disarmament Conference to lend support (if not approval) to MacDonald's presentation. At the conference, on March 16, 1933, MacDonald proposed revising the Versailles Treaty, "not at the point of the bayonet but at the point of reason." He declared, "Either Germany is given justice and freedom or Europe will risk destruction." It was the beginning of a long era of making concessions to Hitler to rectify what some considered the inequities of the Versailles Treaty, in the hope he would turn out to be reasonable. The strategy came to be called "appeasement," which because it failed carries an unsavory connotation.

In his plan, MacDonald tried to provide reassurances to France along with concessions to Germany. The compromise proposals were closer to the French disarmament plan than previous British suggestions. They would provide the Germans double the army they possessed, 200,000 men, and cut the French army in Europe down to the same number. But MacDonald did not guarantee the French the treaty protection they sought, nor hold out to the Germans any likelihood of boundary revisions.[11]

Shortly before MacDonald rose to speak in Geneva, the British ambassador, Sir Ronald Lindsay, called on Roosevelt at the White House to inform him of the plan and assure him that the British were "acting in the most unselfish spirit possible for solution of an dangerous crisis." According to Lindsay, the President replied that he "was all in favour of the most drastic possible action and . . . was therefore quite inclined to support the line taken by His Majesty's Government." He hoped the rumors were true that MacDonald was planning to visit Rome, since he thought Mussolini for the moment held the key position in Europe. Roosevelt also suggested MacDonald visit Berlin, since he "was very anxious to know what Hitler's intentions really were, especially whether he was seeking merely to appear a success or whether he meant mischief." Finally, he expressed the wish that the prime minister would round off his tour of European capitals by visiting Washington. Lindsay reported:

> I admitted [the] great importance of a meeting between himself and the Prime Minister over disarmament but I felt very strongly that it would not be possible to arrange it without having to discuss debts and economic questions as well. . . . He admitted this point but suggested that possibly the Prime Minister if he came over here in this manner, might engage in discussion of all these questions and possibly arrive at a settlement while here. I said that I felt confident that [His Majesty's Government?] would regard this as far too dangerous. The

economic questions could not be settled without the most careful previous exploration and to attempt to settle them offhand might result in
dangers equally serious for the United States and for His Majesty's
Government and indeed for the whole world. He rather admitted
this. . . .[12]

In this informal fashion, without careful preparation, Roosevelt moved
into the limelight of world affairs in the noble cause of trying to reverse the trend in Europe toward war. Disarmament and security arrangements were the issues of most importance to him, and coordinated
action with Britain the first step. But immediately the discussions he
sought with Prime Minister MacDonald carried over into the questions
of debts, tariff truces and the like, concentrating upon the agenda for
the World Economic Conference.

It took some persuading before MacDonald agreed to come. His
position as prime minister was precarious as the head of the Labour
party in a coalition government in which Conservatives were dominant
and perhaps even working quietly to topple him. The cabinet was reluctant to let him come, and indeed it was important to him to be sure
of substantial results. And that brought the focus back upon that tired
topic, the war debts. The British were seeking as an immediate goal a
moratorium on the June 15 payment, arguing that the price for a
MacDonald visit to Washington should be an assurance of deferment
of the payment. Sir Frederick Leith-Ross, the financial expert, was
recommending that if MacDonald saw Roosevelt he should explain
that unless the United States suspended war debts the World Economic
Conference could not meet. On the other hand, Hull told Ambassador
Lindsay that unless the prime minister visited and evoked the sympathy
of the American public, a debt solution would be hard to reach; Moley
more bluntly said that unless MacDonald came it would be impossible
to get a moratorium through Congress. But neither Roosevelt nor anyone in his administration could guarantee a moratorium. For his colleagues in the Foreign Office, Sir Orme Sargent summed up the quandary: [13]

> If we want a moratorium in June Mr. Roosevelt tells us that the
> Prime Minister must come out himself and fetch it.
> If by making this journey he was quite sure of bringing back the
> price there would be no two questions about his going, but the snag is
> that even if the Prime Minister does go out he must be ready to face
> the prospect that even so Mr. Roosevelt will in the end not be able to
> deliver the goods.[14]

At every point, the British came around to the question of the debts.
They met several times with Norman Davis when he arrived in London

concerning the MacDonald visit and kept returning to the topic, although Davis had been instructed not to discuss it. Davis urged MacDonald "to put debts completely in the background for the time being and to concentrate on ways and means for recovering from the depression." Debts were Moley's domain; Moley complained to Roosevelt, and the President sent a memorandum to Hull saying he heard Davis was "talking debts and economics. This is *not* his job!" Davis had no choice; day after day the discussions centered around how reluctant the rather Conservative cabinet was to let MacDonald go unless the June 15 debt payment were deferred. Finally the British cabinet decided to take the risk and authorized MacDonald to go, but sent two of their most effective experts to accompany him, Sir Robert Vansittart, permanent undersecretary for foreign affairs, and Sir Frederick W. Leith-Ross, chief economic adviser to the government.[15]

To compound the excitement and problems, Roosevelt unexpectedly decided to invite the French and top officials from other governments to come to Washington for informal conversations. Ernest Lindley wrote not long afterward:

Something had to be done about the French. They were the key to the continental impasse. . . . Beginning with our post-war refusal to guarantee the French domination of Europe, our sympathies and active help had swung slowly over toward the side of the dissatisfied nations. Mr. Roosevelt's family and wartime associations made him naturally sympathetic to the French point of view. Most of his close associates thought Mr. Hoover had badly mishandled the French. Mr. Roosevelt felt evidently that with kindly understanding of the French he could get somewhere with the European situation.[16]

The first Secretary Hull and Undersecretary Phillips knew of the decision was on the morning of April 5 when they took to the White House the draft of the formal invitation to MacDonald. The President, propped up in bed, took his pencil and added a personal ending to the letter. Then he asked Phillips to call in various ambassadors and tell them that he would welcome the heads of their governments. He explained that the day before, in saying farewell to the departing French ambassador, Paul Claudel, Roosevelt had suggested that a preliminary meeting with the French, Italian, and perhaps the German experts to discuss the agenda of the Economic Conference might be a good idea. Claudel inquired whom Roosevelt might suggest sending. The President replied that while, of course, anyone the French government might designate would be welcome, that Edouard Herriot, until recently premier and who favored paying the war debt, would be a popular choice in the United States. It was Herriot, conspicuously friendly, but scarcely able to commit the French government, who subsequently came.[17]

Hull and Phillips were startled, for this was the first they knew of the invitation to the French, or indeed of President Roosevelt's desire to receive other missions. He had not even told Moley, to whom he had given responsibility for planning for the Economic Conference. They suggested diplomatically that it would be helpful if Roosevelt would send them a memorandum on his conversation with Ambassador Claudel. "This seemed a new thought to the President," Moffat noted, "but he agreed to prepare and send over such a record." He never bothered to do so. The State Department was in a flurry of considerable confusion through the afternoon. The next day, Phillips returned to the White House and obtained more concrete instructions from the President. He told Phillips to invite the representatives of nine nations in addition to the British and French.* Subsequently the envoys in Washington from every other nation represented there also participated in discussions.[18]

Roosevelt's purpose, according to notes Moffat received from Phillips, was "largely to educate public opinions in the different countries and to prepare the ground sufficiently to prevent disagreeable surprises in the actual conference." He wished the talks "to be kept bilateral and to arrange nothing that might savor of a preliminary conference unless it be of experts." After Moffat prepared a cable informing American missions in Europe, he noted in his diary, "I fear we are doomed to many improvisations from this regime, but the country is thriving on them." Moffat had no notion how far improvisation was taking Roosevelt in this case. The President did not add in his remarks to Phillips that one of his prime objectives was to prepare American opinion for a vigorous role in the world.[19]

Security rather than debts was Roosevelt's major reason for wanting to see Herriot as well as MacDonald. Further, what seemed later to be mistiming on the part of the French was part of Roosevelt's plan; he wanted their visits to overlap. Claudel's final dispatch from Washington reporting the private conversation with Roosevelt carries a quite different emphasis from Roosevelt's briefing of Phillips. The President did talk about debts, and urged that the French make their overdue December 15 payment so that in the eyes of the public they would be on an equal footing with the British. Then Claudel quoted the President on his basic concern:

> The situation is alarming. Hitler is a madman and his counsellors, some of whom I personally know, are even madder than he is.
> *France cannot disarm now and nobody will ask her to.*
> I would like to talk about the general political situation with Mr. Herriot at the same time as with Mr. MacDonald.
> At the same time I will be talking with Mr. Herriot I will be glad to

* Italy, Germany, Japan, China, Canada, Mexico, Argentina, Brazil, and Chile.

see a French expert, for example, Mr. Monick, whom I appreciate very much.[20]

The discussions in Washington served some useful purposes, but there was also the risk that they would be a buildup to a fiasco. They gave Roosevelt his first opportunity as President to engage in personal diplomacy, and he reveled in it. He was charming, reassuring, and sometimes unintentionally misleading, as he greeted the eminent foreigners who country by country made their way to the White House from late April into early June. There were informal luncheons, state dinners, sails down the Potomac on the *Sequoia*, and intimate conversations seated on the broad sofa by the fireplace in the President's office. The talks ranged over the problems that were plaguing the world from debts to the rise of Hitler. Undoubtedly these talks were useful in enabling Roosevelt and the representatives of other nations to gauge each other and to explore their mutual concerns. In this sense they were educational as Roosevelt had hoped, and indeed vital for the troubled future.

There were serious liabilities as well. Roosevelt was not able to set aside sufficient time from his extremely overcrowded schedule to enter the conversations well prepared and firm in his own views. In addition to his uncertainty over what he wished policies to be, his propensity for appearing accommodating caused him to leave impressions and perhaps enter into commitments contrary to his subsequent actions during the World Economic Conference. Worse still, the highly publicized meetings, seeming to indicate that leadership in world affairs had returned to Washington, stimulated exaggerated expectations both within the United States and in other countries. At home, Roosevelt, even as he was fabricating a nationalistic domestic program, was creating the illusion that the solution to the depression would come from the World Economic Conference. For the moment he seemed the miracle worker. If he had restored confidence in the United States in the past six weeks, might he not within several months show Europe the way out? Moley, a chief participant in the talks and firmly skeptical of an international means of recovery, wryly recalls, "Day after day the headlines featured the discussions with the foreign statesmen. Peace — it was wonderful! Prosperity — it was going to be negotiated at London in June." Yet little took place to justify the fine-sounding but vague joint communiqués that blossomed into these headlines, for both sides were cautious.[21]

The meetings with the British began inauspiciously; indeed, had there not been a commitment and the delegation on its way, they would not have begun at all. MacDonald and his retinue arrived in something of a state of shock, for while they were aboard the *Berengaria*, on April 19, without advance warning, they received word that Roosevelt had taken the United States off the gold standard. They had expected that Roosevelt, like Hoover, would offer inducements to them to return to gold as a means of achieving stabilization of currencies. (Their expectations had been solidly founded. In a draft reply, unsent, to an unofficial letter from MacDonald, Roosevelt in February had written, "Concurrently we should attempt to devise ways and means to enable countries, which today have depreciated currencies, to return to the gold standard." When MacDonald on shipboard asked Leith-Ross's advice, he recommended that when they reached New York they immediately return to England on the *Mauretania*, sailing that same day, since "the American action made nonsense of all the plans for the Conference." Of course, MacDonald would do no such thing, since like Roosevelt he was an optimist, hopeful that face to face they could reconcile differences.

Meanwhile, Roosevelt studied the MacDonald arms plan and prepared for the meetings. Phillips tried once again to persuade him to keep the State Department informed. A day or two before, he had spent an hour with the incoming French ambassador, his old friend from the Wilson era, André de Laboulaye, and had told no one in his administration what was said. (Officials at the Quai d'Orsay knew, for Laboulaye reported the President was planning a radical disarmament proposal.) Phillips admonished Roosevelt; he must keep adequate records of the conferences and moreover, he should not rely upon his rather creaky French in negotiating with Herriot. Roosevelt agreed.[22]

On a hot April afternoon, a cavalcade of automobiles carrying Prime Minister MacDonald, his daughter Ishbel and the British party drew up to the White House portico, where Roosevelt, leaning on the arm of his naval aide, together with Mrs. Roosevelt and their daughter Anna, greeted them with a warmth and informality unprecedented in state visits. MacDonald was given Lincoln's study as his bedroom; he recalled that during his previous visit it had been Hoover's study. The spirit of informality carried over into their conversations, which ranged over their large mutual problems as each man expressed sympathetic understanding with the other. Neither was well prepared to deal with complex details of economic questions, nor could either make binding arrangements — Roosevelt, the new man of power, because of the congressional check; MacDonald, a waning figure, because of the conservative domination of his government.

Close in the wake of MacDonald came Herriot, who, although no longer premier of France, was president of the Commission on Foreign Affairs of the Chamber of Deputies. He declined State Department suggestions that he come on a later ship (for reasons only one American,

Roosevelt, could grasp), stayed quietly at the Mayflower Hotel, and for a day or two alternated with MacDonald in conversations at the White House. On the afternoon of April 24 when Herriot and his delegation first formally made their appearance, Roosevelt had to excuse himself from MacDonald to put on his cutaway, and the departing British and arriving French (not to mention the also arriving Canadian prime minister) encountered each other in the corridor.

It was an indication of the pressure under which Roosevelt was operating that he held his first formal meeting with the French delegation at ten-fifteen that same evening, April 24. The President delivered a little welcoming speech in French, which Bullitt and Warburg had drafted. The Harvard-Groton accent of Roosevelt's French grated on Warburg's sophisticated ear, but cheered the French:

> It was very bad French, but it was so nicely said, so warm and the mere fact that he would take the trouble to do it, worked so that we had very little trouble with the French delegation thereafter. That completely won their hearts. . . . [H]e went on into the agenda and got about three paragraphs in French before he said, with a grin, "Well, I guess that's as far as I have to use my bad French." [23]

Roosevelt ran through the agenda, impressing Warburg with his extraordinary skill in stressing the right things and sliding over the wrong ones. Then, because of the lateness of the hour, he suggested the experts meet the following morning — but the French, eager to begin discussions, moved with the Americans into another room of the White House where they conferred until midnight. As for Roosevelt, he entered into a private discussion with Herriot on armaments.[24]

Roosevelt personally took over negotiations on what to him were the critical issues of disarmament and European security, seeking an accommodation among the British, French, and Americans. It was a bold move, since from Norman Davis's three recent telegrams totaling about twenty-five pages, which he had not yet answered, and from his State Department briefings, he knew full well that Davis was insistent upon a regional approach rather than the British global program, and that Phillips, Moffat, and presumably Hull had strong objections to the MacDonald program.[25]

There is little likelihood, therefore, that it was by accident that Roosevelt omitted taking Secretary Hull or Undersecretary Phillips, or indeed any of his advisers except the faithful Howe, with him on a Sunday outing on April 23. The Roosevelts and the MacDonalds, forming a family party, cruised for seven hours on the *Sequoia*. Howe seems to have occupied himself in witty banter with Ishbel MacDonald, leaving Roosevelt to go below the chilly decks accompanied only by

MacDonald and Vansittart. There they negotiated for hours, going over the MacDonald plan section by section. In the evening when they returned to the White House, the family atmosphere continued as Mrs. Roosevelt scrambled eggs for them in a chafing dish.[26]

What took place in the cabin of the *Sequoia* brought dismay to Phillips and Moffat when they learned the details of the conversation not from Roosevelt but the British undersecretary, Vansittart. Roosevelt was in general accord with most of the British plan, but he wished more careful international inspection; it should be continuous and automatic. Roosevelt had already conversed with Herriot, and knew the French wanted the inspection section strengthened.

The serious difficulties, Roosevelt explained, began with the security provisions of the plan; if the United States subscribed to them in the form of a disarmament treaty, there would be difficulty in getting it ratified by the Senate. Rather, Roosevelt proposed that he issue a unilateral declaration, which would have the validity of the Monroe Doctrine. It was a device acceptable to MacDonald, and had been to Herriot when Roosevelt broached it, but might be hard to sell to the French government. The declaration Roosevelt proposed was:

> Following a decision by the conference of the Powers in consultation in determining the aggressor — a decision with which on the basis of our independent judgment we agreed — , we would undertake to refrain from any action and to withhold protection from our citizens if engaged in activities which would tend to defeat the collective effort which the States in consulation might have decided upon against the aggressor.

Vansittart's conclusion was more than a bit of pious optimism:

> Finally the fact that the President and the Prime Minister are at one, broadly speaking, on the rest of the Convention [that is, the plan] is a fact of real significance and hope and the Prime Minister trusts that it will be possible to turn it to good effect at this critical, and probably final, stage of the Disarmament Conference.[27]

Phillips and Moffat, staunchly opposed to Roosevelt's acceptance of the British plan, were upset the next morning when they received instructions from Roosevelt to cable Davis at Geneva in its support.*

---

* The objections were:

[N]ot only would acceptance of Part I [the security section] of the British plan involve us far deeper than at present, but [there were] various deficiencies of the MacDonald plan: (1) it permits a large measure of rearmament by Germany; (2) it liberates Germany at the end of five years from all armament control and puts her in a far better position to begin the armaments race than would be the case if she got her freedom today; it gives Russia more men than Poland and Rumania combined; it is filled with jokers favoring British needs

They protested to Secretary Hull when he arrived, and Hull authorized them to draft tentative alternative instructions to Davis embodying their thesis. Roosevelt sent for Hull and Phillips and had a brief conversation with them — not time enough for Phillips effectively to present his objections — while MacDonald paced impatiently in the next room. Phillips then had the further unsettling experience of sitting in his office in the State Department while Vansittart wrote his report to London on the conversations that had taken place on the *Sequoia*. For an hour Vansittart debated his views with Phillips and Moffat without convincing them. The next day he gave them a copy of his *aide-mémoire*, which became the only State Department record of Roosevelt's conversation with MacDonald, and appears in *Foreign Relations of the United States*.[28]

The President's only concession to Phillips was to let him sit in that night while Roosevelt discussed disarmament with MacDonald and Herriot. Security was of prime concern to Herriot; he was not impressed with the MacDonald proposals, but said that an American statement that the United States would not interfere with collective action against an aggressor would be valuable. He urged Roosevelt to attach the declaration to the Kellogg-Briand Pact, but the President countered that the United States would make the pledge only in return for real disarmament.

The next day, Phillips made one final effort to persuade Roosevelt to modify the instructions to Davis in Geneva and endorse the regional European approach to disarmament excluding Japan. He found frank conversation difficult, since Roosevelt was with MacDonald and Vansittart. MacDonald expounded what might be considered the reverse of a domino concept, a dragon's teeth theory — he "remarked that if Japan would not disarm, Russia would not disarm, and if Russia would not disarm, Germany would rearm." Roosevelt would not budge. He saw Phillips for a few minutes in private, made some changes in the State Department telegram to Davis, stating the new American security doctrine, then in longhand wrote a further telegram to Davis, setting forth his overall disarmament policy. It is a statement significant for its expression of Roosevelt's comprehensive views, even if it expressed hopes that were to be blasted: [29]

> Please be guided by the broad policy of United States in consistently pressing for immediate and practical actual disarmament. Our ultimate goal is two-fold: First, reduction of present annual costs of armament

from beginning to end. We also made the point that for us to espouse the English plan hook, line and sinker would probably so upset the French at being once more confronted by their bogie of an Anglo-American understanding that they would bolt the reservation.

maintenance in all national budgets and, Second, arrival at a goal of domestic policing armaments in as few years as possible.

To arrive at these by cutting the power of offense and thereby increasing the power of defense, thus also diminishing danger of surprise attacks, should do more than any other thing to lessen war dangers.

You can make it clear that we regard the MacDonald Plan as a definite and excellent step towards the ultimate objective, but that it is a step only and must be followed by succeeding steps. We do not ask that the MacDonald Plan be amended to make it stronger at this time because we do not want to jeopardize it as a whole by offering amendments, except the amendment to make the inspection machinery continuous and automatic. But at the same time we shall press at a later Conference for additional limitations on the weapons of offense or of surprise attack. This position is an answer to any German effort to increase armaments now, for in effect we ask them to stay as they are and that other nations will reduce to their level by steps.

Please let me have your opinion as to the advisability of a public statement by me covering the ultimate objective and laying stress on the necessity of concrete action at this time.[30]

When he talked to Herriot the next day, Roosevelt showed him both the telegrams to Davis, and emphasized the State Department instructions that the United States would not abandon its neutral rights until the conferees had reached substantial agreement on disarmament. Herriot defended the need for a large French army on the grounds that it was essential to support the British navy, since the British did not possess a large army. Roosevelt was amused, saying it was a new idea for him.

There seemed to be no sharp differences between Roosevelt and Herriot. Rather, they seemed to share a common concern over war breaking out in Europe. Herriot thought the most dangerous spot was the Polish Corridor running through former German territory to the sea. Roosevelt wondered if it would not be possible for Germans to traverse the corridor either by air, elevated railways, or even tunnels. Herriot pointed out that it was already easy to cross by train or on a highway — and indeed did not feel there was any solution to the dangerous problem, which Hitler was already agitating. The initiative was in Berlin, not Paris, London, or Washington. Furthermore, Herriot pointed out, France did not have much influence over Polish decisions.[31]

On economic issues, Roosevelt was less successful in arriving at clear-cut policies that could lead to constructive future action, since there were serious differences between the national economic interests of the United States and Great Britain, France, and other nations. These differences were becoming greater as the New Deal domestic program unfolded, and it was difficult to derive formulas that could reconcile these differences yet not threaten the recovery measures. To a considerable extent, Roosevelt depended upon his experts in trying to arrive at formulas: Moley or Douglas took the lead on debts, Warburg on monetary stabilization, and, because everyone became weary with Hull's lengthy, rambling, high-sounding speeches, Feis as often as possible on tariffs. Bullitt and Taussig were also active in the conversations. They felt their way through to formulas with the British and French which gave some reason for hope that the Economic Conference could bring some results, constructive if not spectacular. As they continued their presentations over and over again to delegation after delegation they became so polished and persuasive in their arguments that occasional auditors like Moffat were impressed.

There was, first in attention and time given to it, the festering problem of the war debts. MacDonald was no more conversant with its intricacies than Roosevelt, but Leith-Ross came armed with impressive statistics indicating that the British had received far less favorable treatment than other nations, particularly Italy, in the 1920s. They owed 40 percent of the total debt, and had made 84 percent of the overall payments; on Italian terms they would be paid up to 1956. There were the further arguments that they could not afford to pay, since under the Lausanne agreement, German reparations had been cut to token level, and the British government was in economic straits. Roosevelt's response was to assure MacDonald that the Lausanne agreement was the finest step taken since the Versailles Treaty, and to promise repeatedly that he would obtain permission from Congress to allow the British to defer their June 15 payment pending a final settlement. As for the final settlement, for days he had been discussing a clever scheme, the handiwork of James Warburg, which he came to call informally "Jimmy's bunny." It was a device through which an initial gold deposit and minimal settlement that debtor nations were to deposit annually for twenty years in an international bank were to be invested in United States bonds. Interest on the bonds accruing during the twenty-year period would give the illusion that the debtors were paying far larger sums than they were in actual fact. (Warburg gave it an additional appeal for domestic consumption by providing that this money could fund a great public works program within the United States.) Not only was Roosevelt intrigued with the idea; the British gave it serious consideration and discussed among themselves variations upon it that might be acceptable. It might in the end have brought some nominal contribution toward war debts from the hard-pressed British Treasury, which was trying hard to avoid the stigma of default. But by the end of 1933 Roosevelt had let "Jimmy's bunny" quietly disappear forever, presumably because leaders in Congress like Hiram Johnson would have immediately seen through the camouflage and pointed out that the main contributor over the years would have been the United States Treasury, paying interest on its bonds.

Rather, in the voluminous interchanges that continued until June 15, Roosevelt began to back away from asking Congress for deferment of the British payment, and instead to suggest that a token payment in silver, that metal so politically potent in the United States, would be acceptable. The British reluctantly delivered $10 million in silver, at an inflated valuation Congress had established, which they had purchased from India for considerably less. Senator Pittman was delighted, and the negotiations for a permanent debt settlement put off until fall.

With the French, Roosevelt and his experts took a rather different tack on debts, trying to persuade them to pay the delinquent December 15, 1932, installment in order to obtain an opportunity to participate in Warburg's "bunny" scheme. Herriot was affable, since indeed he had favored making the December 15 payment, which France had been financially able to meet. The Daladier government, capitalizing upon the political unpopularity of the debt payment issue, leaked to the press a garbled version of the Warburg scheme, and thus ended the matter.

Roosevelt may have felt some continued moral indignation toward the French, but what he was succeeding in doing through the lengthy and rather empty discussions of the debt that spring was to go far toward defusing the issue. He did not dare ask Congress, when things became difficult late in May, even for postponement of June 15 payments, but on the other hand, he heaped no righteous wrath on defaulters. There was much more of the same in the fall of 1933 as Roosevelt, the British, and to a lesser degree the French lavished attention on the debt issue, all with lessening public attention. In 1934, Congress enacted legislation forbidding Roosevelt to accept further token payments; no more were forthcoming — only regular full payments from Finland — and the debt question finally petered out.[32]

Currency stabilization was quite a different and more serious matter. In going off gold, Roosevelt almost ended the Economic Conference before it began. Warburg, himself a banker in good standing among the financiers of both the United States and Europe, was particularly worried that continued fluctuation among the dollar, pound, and franc could make the conference impossible. Although the New Dealers considered him conservative, Warburg was attracted toward Keynes, and in his own thinking felt in retrospect that he was partway between the conservatives and the experimenters. He was also a man of extraordinary ingenuity, and once again, as with the war debt "bunny," he came up with a complex scheme to assure de facto, even if not official, stabilization through the conference. On April 24 he found an opportunity to express his concern to Roosevelt:

> I said that I thought we should try within the next few days to work out a plan for tripartite cooperation to bring about the de facto stabilization provided we could agree on a price for the pound. I pointed out that this would not close the door on eventual devaluation of the dollar but would, on the other hand, give a firm foundation on which other discussions could be based. . . . The president took to this suggestion more quickly than I had expected.[33]

With Roosevelt's approval, Warburg persuaded Fred Kent to take the night train from New York to help work out a stabilization device that the British and French would accept. When Warburg took Kent into the President's study, Kent, who was very deaf and carried a large, cumbersome hearing aid with him, inadvertently frustrated Roosevelt who for once did not dominate the conversation. He turned off the hearing aid and began to hold forth, talking through the President every time Roosevelt tried to say something. Several times Roosevelt opened his mouth, then stopped, realizing Kent could not hear him. Finally Warburg reached down, turned on Kent's hearing aid, and said, "Shut up. The President wants to talk." [34]

Since the French were on the gold standard, their expert, Charles Rist, was ready to take the view that stabilization involved the dollar and pound, not the franc, and there was no need for France to share the risk by contributing to a stabilization fund. Warburg countered that if the United States were to attempt de facto stabilization at a disadvantageous time in order to help the world in general and France in particular, France should certainly share in the risk of the operation.

Warburg, Moley, and Pittman then took the problem to Roosevelt in the White House, since he had to decide, if there were to be de facto stabilization, what the level of the dollar should be. Roosevelt suggested that, with necessary reservations of the American right to change the figure, it should be at a discount of between 25 and 15 percent. Warburg convinced Roosevelt that it would require a huge stabilization fund to drive the dollar lower than a 15 percent discount on the world market, and that figure was agreed upon. Upon this basis the Americans developed a plan for a fund which they submitted to the French and the British. When Warburg reported to Roosevelt on the stabilization discussions, he "was delighted with the way in which from having been on the spot we have now put the French and British on the spot as regards exchange disorder in the world." Yet the whole arrangement was no more than tentative, and Roosevelt later was sure he had made no commitment to stabilization.

The French position was vital, since ultimately it was over French insistence that there be temporary stabilization of the dollar and Roosevelt's refusal that the World Economic Conference foundered. Some recollections of Bullitt's have created confusion; he has asserted that the French finance minister, Georges Bonnet, twice refused to accept the stabilization proposal, and at the time of the second refusal when the French asked Roosevelt to keep the offer open, Roosevelt refused. There is no indication of this point in either French or American published diplomatic documents. Rather, the French continued to urge stabilization of the dollar, and indeed by mid-May to insist upon it as a requisite for the opening of the Economic Conference.* At the same time they were reluctant to participate in a stabilization fund, which they continued to feel was an Anglo-American, not a French, responsibility.[35]

Warburg's most difficult selling job was to persuade the President to continue to favor stabilization. "He became unstuck periodically before we went to London," Warburg remembers, "but I could stick him together again." [36]

The projected temporary currency stabilization for the duration of the Economic Conference was not to take place until the conference began. Shortly beforehand, representatives of the American, British, and French Treasuries and central banks were to meet in London to establish the relative rates. Roosevelt did not commit himself upon what he would do after the conference, and indeed there was the possibility that when the conference began he might again, in Warburg's words, "become unstuck."

On tariffs, on the other hand, Roosevelt not only was ready for the United States to take the lead in obtaining a tariff truce for the duration of the Economic Conference. He was also talking broadly of reciprocal trade, and of a favorite idea that Charles Taussig, erstwhile president of a molasses corporation and his tariff adviser, had sold to him. This idea, which fascinated Roosevelt, probably because it was so bizarre, was known as the "President's lamb." Despite the efforts of Feis, Warburg, and others to destroy it, Roosevelt kept broaching it. Robert Lincoln O'Brien, the Republican chairman of the Tariff Commission, whom Roosevelt kept on in the office, remembers his introduction (several months later) to a curious variation of the "President's lamb":

---

* The French position as outlined in a Foreign Office memorandum of May 9, 1933 was:

    a. Favorable to a prompt stabilization of the dollar and the pound;
    b. unfavorable to the principle of the common fund and
    c. inclined to consider . . . the question of the rate of stabilization of the dollar and the pound as a problem mainly Anglo-American;
    our representatives have agreed that the question of the stabilization fund will be the object of a technical study, our freedom of choice being totally reserved.

The President said that this was an Administration of experimentation, of trying to do things in a new way; that it was important that we should build up our international trade, imports as well as exports, and he thought that it might be a good idea to decree that in ships coming into the Port of New York, let us say, the goods in one ship in every seven — not to be known in advance by the parties interested — were to be admitted duty-free. This theory he expatiated at some length. I told him it was not a good idea; that it was a clear, sheer lottery and that to it all the objections to a lottery would apply. He was exceedingly gracious, saying that quite likely I was right, very probably I was right; other persons whom he did not name had told him the same thing. That was the last I ever heard of it.[37]

In the spring of 1933, Roosevelt was suggesting to the delegations that as a means of reducing tariffs they admit 10 percent of the goods they imported free. After Taussig had expounded the concept to Guido Jung, the Italian minister of finance, Jung commented to Warburg that the idea would not be practicable unless the United States were to establish a control monopoly over foreign trade like that of the Soviet Union. Warburg explained that it was a pet idea of Roosevelt's "and that possibly he had something in mind that none of us had as yet been able to catch on to." No one ever caught on, for Roosevelt had not thought through the implications of the scheme, or even of Hull's reciprocal trade program which he was also advocating. Nor, perhaps, did he expect to be taken seriously on a lottery, or 10 percent free, scheme. But he did expect somehow to fit Hull's reciprocal trade device into the New Deal, and was genuine in his advocacy of a tariff truce.[38]

The tariff truce carried disadvantages for the British, who had been particularly active in developing trade within the empire and raising barriers against imports from the rest of the world. MacDonald encountered strong resistance from his government, which was as energetically engaged in economic nationalism as was Roosevelt's. In the end, the British agreed, and at a May planning session Norman Davis succeeded in obtaining a truce to run from May 12 through the end of the conference. Roosevelt only technically kept the United States within the bounds of the truce, since before the conference met, he signed an executive order establishing the AAA cotton-processing tax, which automatically raised the tariff on cotton products.[39]

The only clear-cut agreement that Roosevelt easily reached with MacDonald and Herriot was on the site and time of the Economic Conference. Roosevelt earlier had rather wanted it in Washington, where presumably he could have dominated it, but MacDonald and Daladier had not felt they could come and stay long. Since European conditions were so unstable (and maybe because their own tenures were so precarious) they both wanted it in London. Even before MacDonald arrived, Roosevelt had decided the conference should begin between June 1 and 10; he readily agreed to June 12 and to London. Moley was dismayed, since he had hoped that Roosevelt would abide by his thinking of the winter, and not consent to the conference until the domestic program was well underway.[40]

During the meetings with MacDonald and Herriot, Roosevelt seemed convinced that an international recovery program would by no means create problems for his domestic measures. Further, disarmament and security were in the forefront of his thinking. The cheerful, optimistic joint communiqués that he issued upon the departure first of MacDonald, then Herriot, undoubtedly represented his earnest expectations at the time. The British and Americans had not arrived at definitive agreements; that had not been the intent, his joint statement with MacDonald declared:

> But they showed that our two Governments were looking with a like purpose and a close similarity of method at the main objectives of the Conference. . . . There should be a constructive effort to moderate the network of restrictions of all sorts by which commerce is at present hampered, such as excessive tariffs, quotas, exchange restrictions, etc. . . . The ultimate re-establishment of equilibrium in the international exchanges should also be contemplated. We must when circumstances permit re-establish an international monetary standard.[41]

All these formulas appeared also in Roosevelt's statement with Herriot, and in most of the subsequent statements as one after another of the foreign delegations concluded their visits to Washington.

There was another theme that ran through the communiqués too — in effect, that through its domestic measures the New Deal was setting a model for the depressed nations of the world, and that recovery depended upon the coordination of the several domestic recovery programs with a single international program. The Roosevelt-MacDonald statement asserted, "The achievement of sound and lasting world recovery depends on co-ordinating domestic remedies and supplementing them by concurrent and simultaneous action in the international field." The Roosevelt-Herriot statement contained the same idea and in addition declared more specifically, "We have examined . . . the remedies which may be brought forward to attack the menacing problem of unemployment and the stagnation of business by the execution of programs of public works to be carried out by the different governments."

At the end of April, Roosevelt seemed to be participating in planning a New Deal for the world, and to be preparing for the propitious time to assert publicly American leadership in disarmament and security. That time was to come in May.[42]

CHAPTER XXIII

The Initial Skirmish with Hitler

A profound hope of the people of my country impels
me. . . . This hope is that peace may be assured through
practical measures of disarmament and that all of us may
carry to victory our common struggle against economic
chaos.
— FDR TO HEADS OF NATIONS OF THE WORLD,
May 16, 1933.

The shadow of Hitler continued to fall across Europe and even the
United States during the first spring of the New Deal. On May 15, 1933,
Morgenthau, at lunch with Roosevelt, inquired what the likelihood
was that Germany would go to war.

"A very strong possibility," Roosevelt replied.

"Will the U.S. have to go in and defend its treaty rights?"

"We won't have to send any men abroad anyway." [1]

The President was not indulging in exaggeration to shock Morgenthau.
Rather, Hitler with dramatic speed and thoroughness was crushing all
opposition, taking over all economic controls, degrading Jews to a ghetto
level, and assembling the largest army in Europe. Together with these
internal measures he was bringing pressure to absorb Austria, and perhaps the Polish Corridor. His violation of treaty restraints and discard
of the tenets of modern European civilization, the dual threats of aggression and repression, did raise the question of war. Would Hitler
strike his weak neighbors? Would the French again march into
Germany (as they had in 1923), this time to forestall rearmament while
there was still overwhelming military force on the French side? These
were grim questions, and not wholly hypothetical.

For Roosevelt there was already, by the beginning of April 1933, an
additional horrible question to which he never gave a satisfactory
answer, and which he had to face again and again during the remainder
of his career: What would he as President of the United States do to
aid the Jewish victims of Nazi oppression?

It was not a clear-cut question in April 1933, nor was it entirely
clear until much later. There were pressures and counterpressures upon

Roosevelt within the United States, and that first April, Hitler (as in his other maneuvers) was able to make it appear that he could be persuaded into being moderate, that it was a mob of Nazi followers that had caused the trouble. Nazi mobs had indeed been responsible for the hundreds of beatings after the Reichstag election at the beginning of March, and perhaps for some of the smashing, picketing, and boycotting of Jewish-owned stores. But it was already unmistakably Hitler's policy to throw Jews out of government, the professions, business, education, and the arts.

There was worldwide protest, and within the United States meetings in three hundred cities. In New York, an impressive array of notables, ranging from Rabbi Stephen Wise to Al Smith, attended the gathering. Rabbis throughout the country proclaimed a day of fasting and prayer. Most non-Jewish Americans, including many of German ancestry, who had been sympathetic toward Germany, shared the feeling of abhorrence. "It seems to me a complete relapse into barbarism, and has killed for the present every desire I have to be of help to them," lamented Oswald Garrison Villard, publisher of the *Nation,* and son of a famous German immigrant. "I think they are in a state of absolute insanity at the present time, and must be treated as such." [2]

Nazi leaders reacted to the protests with amazed indignation. Herman Goering gave an hour-long interview to foreign correspondents in which, according to *Time,* he insisted that there had been no reign of terror and it would stop at once. Goering protested, "There is not one person in all of Germany from whom even one fingernail has been chopped." Secretary Hull, trying to calm the apprehensions of Jewish leaders demanding State Department action, declared, after reading dispatches, "Mistreatment of Jews in Germany may be considered virtually terminated." Hull meant that physical violence had ceased. [3]

The Nazi party announced that on April 1 it would begin a boycott of all Jewish business establishments, and a fresh wave of alarm swept over the United States, even into the State Department. Secretary Hull conceived of his task, according to Moffat, as being "to try and calm down the situation created by a lot of extremists in Germany and inflamed by a lot of extremists in this country." He commissioned Moffat to draft an appeal calling for mutual understanding and tolerance, but Moffat had no sooner done so than a cable came in from the calm, competent *chargé d'affaires* in Berlin, George Gordon, stating that rapidly deteriorating conditions made his reports of a few days earlier no longer true, that he feared Jews again would be beaten. Hull threw away the draft. The next day the German ambassador called to suggest to Phillips that Roosevelt and President Paul von Hindenburg of Germany issue a joint statement. Moffat tried to draft a message, but found it "out of the question to prepare anything that could be used in both countries." [4]

Rabbi Wise sent the State Department officials off on a different tack. He called during the afternoon to inform them that a retaliatory boycott was being planned, and convinced them they should make an appeal to the German government. Hull telegraphed Gordon in Berlin directing him to inform the German foreign minister, Baron Konstantin von Neurath, that while the United States government could involve itself only in the international aspects of the boycott, the friendly feelings of the American people might be affected. Hull instructed Gordon to inquire if there were not some way the two governments could ease the tensions — a very cautious way of trying to persuade Neurath to call off the Nazi boycott.

While President Roosevelt was at dinner that night at the White House, Governor Herbert Lehman of New York called him to urge him to forward to Neurath through government channels a message of vigorous protest from the Jews of America. Roosevelt countered Lehman by telling him the State Department had already sent a message.[5]

Word came back from Berlin that Neurath and one or two other moderates had persuaded their colleagues that if the United States issued a statement minimizing news stories from Germany and opposing an American boycott as harmful to economic relations, the Nazis should rescind the boycott order. Moffat drafted a statement for Hull, but Neurath was not able to get the boycott canceled. However, the Nazis ran the boycott in a relatively nonviolent fashion for only nine hours. They pasted black and yellow posters reading "quarantine" on almost every Jewish-owned shop, then later removed them. The boycott, they insisted, was in protest against untruthful atrocity stories being spread by foreign Jews, its mildness supposedly a demonstration to the world that Jews were receiving no physical harm. Then, in succeeding weeks, they continued systematically to remove Jews from almost every aspect of German life — and to bar foreign reporters from hospitals where Jewish victims of violence were receiving treatment.[6]

Thus far, Roosevelt was remaining publicly silent. His assumption, which the State Department would not let him forget, was that maltreatment of Jews, much as he might abhor it, was a domestic matter, and the United States must not interfere in the internal affairs of other nations. It was still not entirely clear that Hitler would be much more of an adventurer than Mussolini; he was clever during these troubled weeks in making the violent aspects of anti-Semitism seem to be a failing of his unruly followers, who were about to be pulled into line. The State Department in its internal policy discussions compared Hitler's anti-Semitism with that in Rumania in the 1920s: It was an old, unfortunate malady, flaring up from time to time in central and eastern Europe, with which the United States government simply must not tamper.[7]

There was also a certain degree of anti-Semitism within the United States. The Roosevelts had certainly outgrown the family feeling against Jews which was part of their heritage as American aristocrats, and Secretary Hull's wife was Jewish. Nevertheless, the elite in the United States still had at least a mild sympathy with the repression of Jews. Anti-Semitism was not confined to the poor and the ignorant. All too many of the Foreign Service officers in the State Department belonged to clubs or took vacations in resorts that barred Jews. For that matter, most Jewish leaders and organizations did not push Roosevelt and the State Department too hard for fear there would be an outburst of virulent anti-Semitism in the United States. At least one of the brilliant young Jewish lawyers who had come to Washington that spring worried with some reason on these grounds because so much of the talent on the second echelon of the Roosevelt administration was Jewish. And, indeed, as Roosevelt and Secretary of Labor Perkins began to exert themselves on behalf of Jews in Germany, anti-Semites throughout the United States began to whisper that they were Jewish (neither of them were). Roosevelt, several years later, in response to one query, wrote that in the dim past the Roosevelts might have been Jews, Catholics, or Protestants, but he was more concerned with whether they were good citizens and believers in God; he hoped they were both.[8]

Conspicuously, Roosevelt and the State Department, while treating the persecution of Jews as an internal German matter, were not providing a haven for them in the United States. The failure led Hitler to jibe in the course of one of his addresses early in April:

> America, which of all other lands has taken it upon itself to set up a movement against our methods of self-defense, has the least excuse for such action. The American people were the first to draw practical and political conclusions from differences among races and from the different value of different races.
>
> Through its immigration laws it has prevented the entry of those races which seemed unwelcome to the American people. And America today is by no means ready to open its doors to so-called refugee Jews from Germany.

In publishing Hitler's statement, *Time* added a damning comment, "Under his hand Germany proceeded openly to reduce her Jewish inhabitants to the social and political position occupied by Negroes in the southern U.S. and Orientals in the West." [9]

In gingerly fashion, Brandeis and Frankfurter undertook to persuade

Roosevelt to lower immigration restrictions to permit Jewish refugees from nazism to enter the United States without providing the difficult proof that they would not become public charges. The State Department was opposed, on the familiar basis that it would be interference with German domestic policy, and through Assistant Secretary Wilbur J. Carr persuaded the House Committee on Immigration not to report out such a measure. Brandeis was so cautious that in an hour's discussion with Roosevelt early in April, he did not find an occasion to slip in a few words. Thereafter, Brandeis repeatedly urged Frankfurter to act:

April 13: Ought not FDR do something re German Jews [?] We are falling very far behind Western Europeans.
April 18: Hope you have gotten FD to act re Jews.
April 26: I hope F.D.R. will act soon.
April 29: F.D. has shown amply that he has no Anti-Semitism and his appointments of Straus and of Steinhardt . . . are distinctly helpful. But this action, or rather determination that there shall be none, is a disgrace to America & to F.D.'s administration. You could have doubt-less decided before this whether it would be well for you to see F. D. again: if yes, it should be done immediately.[10]

As for Frankfurter, he seemed to share the same caution; he did not mention the issue in the more than a dozen letters he wrote Roosevelt that spring (which have subsequently been printed).[11]

Rather, Brandeis and Frankfurter gained an ardent and effective advocate in Miss Perkins, who undertook to sell Roosevelt on lowering immigration restrictions to let in refugees from religious persecution. On April 18, she raised the question in a cabinet meeting; immigration was within her domain of the Department of Labor at that time. Hull mildly objected, and thought he had ended the matter. But the next day Roosevelt telephoned Phillips to inquire why the State Department had not prepared the requisite Executive Orders for him to sign. Phillips expressed his opposition, and convinced Roosevelt that since the immigrant quota was not full there was no need to act. Roosevelt asked him to explain the situation to Miss Perkins. That was easier said than done, according to Moffat:

She said that it was in accordance with our traditions and with our policy to be of free entry to refugees of all forms of persecution, that whether or not this was agreeable to the [American] Federation of Labor or whether or not it would affect our economic conditions was a matter for her Department to decide and not ours. The only place in which she was interested in our opinion was whether or not such a policy would affect our foreign relations. Furthermore, she said that she was going to press for an immediate decision and if she did not get favorable action by the Administration within a day or two, there would be unleashed upon us the most formidable instance of Jewish pressure. In fact she quite blew our poor Under Secretary off his end of the telephone.[12]

Secretary Hull, primed by Phillips and Moffat with several arguments, successfully withstood pressures from both Jewish organizations and the White House. The State Department officials had found President Wilson's message vetoing the Illiteracy Exclusion Bill of 1917, which had also made special provision for victims of religious persecution. Wilson had asserted that for an American consular officer to ascertain whether or not persecution existed would be to pass judgment on a friendly foreign nation and open the way to endless complications. They also armed Hull with the warning that Catholics were demanding that as much be done for victims of religious discrimination in Mexico. So it was that when Hull on April 21 faced the president of the American Jewish Committee and the general secretary of B'nai Brith he quietly informed them that the State Department had repeatedly pointed out to Germany the danger of inflaming American opinion, and had done much to modify the Nazi boycott.* To the satisfaction of his subordinates, Hull held off the Jewish leaders. They also managed to keep Roosevelt from letting in additional numbers of Jewish refugees, even though month by month the Nazis tightened the thumb screws. Frankfurter lamented to Miss Perkins at the end of 1933, "It will be an eternal black mark against our State Department that they frustrated the wise plan of the President." [14]

If the State Department professionals were correct that it would ill serve the United States government to become openly anti-German, they were soon frustrated. Roosevelt boasted of the way he expressed his hostile feelings during his meetings with the special representative Hitler sent to discuss preparations for the Economic Conference, the president of the Reichsbank, Hjalmar Horace Greeley Schacht. Despite his unusual name, an indication of his father's political leanings in the presidential campaign of 1872 during a sojourn in the United States, Schacht was a most useful agent of Hitler, ready to assure Warburg he was not anti-Semitic, yet to explain to others the Nazi program with

---

* Moffat and his colleagues felt that they had done all that was necessary, and indeed had been effective. George S. Messersmith, consul general in Berlin, corroborated their view:

> The energetic protests which we had to make here because of the attacks on American Jews, the way in which we did it, and particularly the opportunity which it gave us to point out in a friendly way what the real effects of this upon the new regime would be both at home and abroad, were, I believe the principal elements in stopping these physical attacks and had a good deal to do in bringing about a more moderate attitude toward the Jews generally which is already showing itself in many ways.[13]

sympathy. With his round face rising from above a high collar, Schacht bore a marked resemblance to the Georg Grosz caricatures of the Berlin burghers of the twenties; he was sure to be a target of demonstrations.[15]

At the outset, Roosevelt greeted Schacht at the White House portico with the same apparent warmth he had shown MacDonald and Herriot, and as they entered the Blue Room the Marine Band struck up "Deutschland über Alles." After luncheon, he made a short welcoming speech recalling his weeks of study in a German public school, and toasted President von Hindenburg. In private conversation he immediately moved into the allied questions of Nazi mistreatment of Jews and rearmament. If Roosevelt hoped in this fashion to get a firm message to Hitler, he failed, at least in what Schacht reported in his dispatch to the Foreign Ministry:

> After dinner, exactly half an hour remained for a private conversation between the President and me. He began with the Jewish question, which had undoubtedly done a great deal of harm, probably not out of particular sympathy for the Jews, but from the old Anglo-Saxon sense of chivalry toward the weak. But he did not elaborate on this theme and said that this hurdle would be cleared even if its importance should not be underestimated. The American people were also unfortunately not quite sympathetic when they saw in the motion picture theaters the marching, uniformed columns of Nazis. The Americans considered every uniformed formation as such a military one. . . .
>
> Both at the table and afterward, the President gave indication of undoubted sympathy for the person of the Reich Chancellor, and stated that he hoped to see him sometime soon. He once made use in his conversation of the expression that when it came to the speedy execution of governmental measures, there were not everywhere such efficient managers as (literally) Mussolini, Hitler, and Roosevelt.[16]

Either Schacht glossed over unpleasantness in his dispatch or Roosevelt could not bring himself to be blunt and stern even with an envoy he disliked from a chancellor he detested.

Afterward Roosevelt sent to the State Department for chapter and verse to show Schacht that Germany through its Treaty of 1921 was as much bound to the United States to honor the military clauses in the Treaty of Versailles as it was to the Allies. Roosevelt was trying to convince Schacht that by treaty, Germany was responsible to the United States on the matter of armaments; therefore he had a right to discuss the topic. It was his only conversation among all those preliminary to the Economic Conference which he followed with an *aide-mémoire* to the secretary of state:

> I talked this afternoon with Dr. Schacht for one half hour and made it perfectly clear that the United States will insist that Germany remain in status quo in armament and that we would support every possible

effort to have the offensive armament of every other nation brought down to the German level. We discussed only land armament and not naval. I intimated as strongly as possible that we regard Germany as the only possible obstacle to a Disarmament Treaty and that I hoped Dr. Schacht would give this point of view to Hitler as quickly as possible.[17]

The President tried out on Schacht a possible disarmament scheme — that the powers would agree that they would send no military personnel or weapons beyond their boundaries provided none of them increased their armaments. What he was trying to devise was a means to guarantee Germany against unprovoked attack yet prevent her from increasing her military strength. Roosevelt asked the State Department to draw up a technical statement that he could use either as a declaration or a convention, but the idea was stillborn.[18]

Schacht had not come to Washington to agree to continued disarmament, but rather (it transpired as economic negotiations unfolded), his purpose was to give notice that the German government was going to stop payment in foreign currencies on external obligations — that it would force default on the German federal, local, and industrial securities that American private investors had purchased to a total of $2 billion during the 1920s. "I began slowly to prepare Roosevelt for the fact," Schacht recalled years later; and subsequently at a meeting which Ambassador Hans Luther and Hull also attended, he bluntly informed Roosevelt. "I myself expected an indignant outburst on the part of the President. To our astonishment there was nothing of the sort. Roosevelt gave his thigh a resounding smack and exclaimed with a laugh, 'Serves the Wall Street bankers right!'" Roosevelt's reaction had been absolutely calm, Schacht cabled the Foreign Ministry; therefore he requested quick action.[19]

When Warburg and the experts discovered what was going on, they were as indignant as Schacht had anticipated. Not only would the losses to small American investors be staggering, but if Schacht announced the default after talking to Roosevelt, it would appear as though the President consented. After all, as Feis pointed out, during the 1932 campaign Roosevelt had attacked security houses for their unscrupulous sale of foreign bonds to American investors. That night, Schacht had an angry conversation with Warburg, which disturbed Warburg even further. The basic purpose of Schacht's trip, Warburg believes, was "to default under our umbrella." [20]

When Secretary Hull and the negotiators carried their warning to President Roosevelt the next day, he had them draw up a memorandum for Hull to give Schacht, declaring that the President was "profoundly shocked." Warburg objected to the pun and wished to substitute "gravely disappointed," which would have been more near to the truth, since Schacht had already informed Roosevelt and the President had expressed no objection. But the other advisers wanted to retain the word "shocked," and Roosevelt remarked that while Warburg was probably right, from a political viewpoint it was better to retain the word. He then instructed Hull to receive Schacht coldly and hand him the memorandum.

"I went right to the point, and with some anger," Hull wrote in his *Memoirs*, describing the dressing-down he claims he gave Schacht. "I felt outraged at such a bald attempt to involve this Government in so odious an act by Germany." [21]

Either Hull's dressing-down was milder than he thought or Schacht chose to ignore it, for he made no mention of it in his report to the Foreign Ministry and in his memoirs speaks only of a brief, formal conversation following his receipt of the note. Schacht did react to it by cabling most urgently to the Foreign Ministry that "the mood has changed completely since yesterday, because the fear has arisen that the Government here has to a certain degree approved our step or even intervened." Therefore Schacht postponed for some days the default on German securities. Both in his official cables and his recollections, Schacht gave the impression that Roosevelt had treated him cordially. In their final interview, Roosevelt again emphasized disarmament, and, sitting alongside Schacht on the sofa, put his hand on Schacht's knee and said, "You made an excellent impression by your frankness." So reported Schacht.[22]

Roosevelt boasted that he and Hull had given Schacht a very bad time. "I wish you could have been present when I was talking with Dr. Schacht," he wrote Irving Lehman, concerning Nazi mistreatment of Jews. "At last the German Government now knows how I feel about things. It is probably better to do it this way than to send formal notes of protest because, frankly, I fear that the latter might result in reprisals in Germany." [23]

Later, with relish, Roosevelt described his instructions to Hull and the ensuing scene to his departing ambassador to Germany, William E. Dodd. Undoubtedly for both Roosevelt and Hull there was much emotional satisfaction in thus venting on Schacht their pent-up feelings about the Nazis. Not only did they feel that Schacht was trying to involve them unfairly in the German default, but while the conversations were still proceeding, Roosevelt received a long report on what Schacht was saying privately about Jews in Germany.* He sent the report on to

---

* Samuel R. Fuller, Jr., a rayon manufacturer with important connections in Germany, and an old friend of Roosevelt's, reported (on the basis of notes he and his wife made) his conversation with Schacht on the S.S. *Olympic*, May 8, 1933:

Regarding the Jews: Dr. Schacht stated that the Jewish situation had been much exaggerated in the American press. No one had been killed; no persecu-

Hull. The secretary thought that through his stern interview he had led Germany to moderate its financial course, but from the standpoint of the German Foreign Ministry as well as the State Department, the only significant outcome of Schacht's visit was to heighten mutual distrust.* It increased rather than alleviated Roosevelt's and Hull's worries about Hitler.[25]

The question of German rearmament still most concerned Roosevelt. At the beginning of April, immediately after the anti-Jewish boycott, Roosevelt personally decided that Norman Davis nevertheless should go ahead with a visit to Berlin, making it clear to the public that he would discuss only disarmament and the date of the Economic Conference. The necessity to bind Germany in an arms agreement seemed to outweigh indicating disapproval of Nazi anti-Semitism.[26]

The meetings with Schacht took place at a time of growing crisis. Germany was persecuting Jews, burning proscribed books in public bonfires, and objecting to the proposed tariff truce for the duration of the Economic Conference. What was most ominous, Germany was deadlocking the Disarmament Conference by insisting that the quasi-army of veterans, the Steel Helmets, and other similar groups must not be considered part of the German army. If other nations accepted the German interpretation, Germany would possess by far the largest standing army in Europe.

The prognosis of many of those with whom Roosevelt talked was that war was likely, sooner or later. Fuller thought war quite probable, since "Germany, a nation which loves to be led," was "again a marching nation." Bullitt felt at all costs Germany must be kept from rearming,

tions had taken place in the sense that the Jews were made to suffer personal violence.

A large number of Jews entered Germany after the War. These had joined, to a great extent, the Communists' party. The Government for the past 10 years had been filled, in the bureaucratic places to a very large extent by Jews. The majority of places were held by Jews. Germany is not a Jewish nation. The appointed judges of the Courts were largely Jewish. The ministry of Education was filled with Jews. The Chief of Police of Berlin was a Jew. 2600 out of the 3200 Berlin lawyers were Jews. In the University of Berlin 3 per cent to 4 per cent of the student body were Jews, and 40 per cent of the Professors were Jews. Germany felt this was wrong; and they put them out and filled their places, or places where necessary, with Gentiles. "But," said Dr. Schacht, "there were many unnecessary places in the Government . . . the Gentiles were removed the same as the Jews. . . ."

Dr. Schacht said the people of the world must realize that this is a revolution, a glorious revolution for Germany. He repeated at intervals the phrase "glorious revolution." [24]

* Gerhard Weinberg concludes on the basis of a careful study of German archival materials, "Schacht apparently noticed the fact that the American position against rearmament had stiffened. He also recognized the strong effect the German anti-Semitic measures had on American public opinion, and he directed Hitler's attention toward it."

that the Nazis wanted five years of peace only to give themselves time to gird for eventual war.[27]

Viewing the European threat, Roosevelt could see that the likelihood of decisive Anglo-French action was slight; the MacDonald plan was foundering at Geneva. This seemed to be the time for him to cast his own prestige onto the balance on the side of peace-keeping. James G. McDonald, chairman of the Foreign Policy Association, returned from Germany emphasizing the remarkable standing of Roosevelt in Europe: "Everywhere I went I heard the President spoken of in the highest possible terms. . . . It is no exaggeration to say that he, more than any other statesman, has helped to lighten the prevailing pessimism." [28]

On the evening of May 1, McDonald spent nearly two hours in conversation with Roosevelt, telling him that Hitler was gaining in strength, and urging him to talk with brutal frankness to Schacht, whom Hitler knew well and trusted. Roosevelt did indeed talk to Schacht, but that was not enough. On May 9, when Morgenthau lunched with him, Roosevelt in bantering fashion betrayed his anxieties: [29]

> He greeted me in German. I asked him about Schacht, and he swung his arms around and said, "Why, he is terrible. I am in an awful jam with Europe," and jokingly remarked, "I may have to call up the Army and the Navy as Great Britain and France respectively disown MacDonald and Herriot. They are a bunch of 'bastards,' " he said — referring to European statesmen.[30]

Behind this facetious façade Roosevelt was preparing for the bold step he had so long contemplated, a direct call for disarmament and security. On the afternoon of Sunday, May 7, he talked to Frankfurter — upon whom he could always depend for instant laudatory reassurance — of his idea of "appealing, through the heads of state, to the peoples of Europe to save the Disarmament Conference." It might not work, Roosevelt realized. And from Frankfurter came encouragement, lauding the scheme in noble terms: "I was particularly heartened by your remark that it would not matter if you did 'fail.' . . . In any event you would tap new forces for peace and recovery. Such courageous assertion of leadership in behalf of right and reason would set in motion the latent forces of right and reason in men." [31]

By the following weekend, the German crisis had risen to such a peak that some alarmists feared it was a repetition of 1914. The Disarmament Conference was at the point of collapse, and the British, fearful that Germany would withdraw from the League and rearm, were warning of reprisals. Their negotiations with Hitler's special representative, Dr. Alfred Rosenberg, chief of the Foreign Politics Division of the Nazi party, were chilling. It was ominous that Hitler would send such an envoy, for Rosenberg had once said, "On every telegraph pole from Munich to Berlin the head of a prominent Jew must be stuck." Lord Hailsham, the minister of war, arose in the House of Lords to point out that Germany was still bound by the Versailles Treaty, and that Britain might have to resort to sanctions. Vice Chancellor von Papen retorted at a Steel Helmet rally in rhetoric that particularly upset Roosevelt: "Today, as in 1914, not only the military but the moral isolation of Germany is being accomplished. . . . First, we should attempt to make clear to the world that the German nation of January 31, 1933, blotted out from its vocabulary the term pacifism. . . . The battlefield is for a man what motherhood is for a woman!"

Von Papen's speech might well have been a prelude for Hitler's manifestoes, for the chancellor suddenly summoned the Reichstag to meet in special session on May 17 to hear a statement on armaments and foreign policy.[32]

It was imperative for Roosevelt to act immediately if he were to modify Hitler's course of action. On Saturday afternoon, May 13, he summoned Hull and Phillips to the White House and spent the entire afternoon with them, preparing a rough draft of a statement to the nations of the world. He wanted the State Department to go over it with a fine-tooth comb to get it into shape to transmit on Monday, May 15. On Sunday, Hull, Phillips, Bullitt, and Moffat labored inter-mittently into the early evening, weighing every word. They were anxious for the President to omit a proposal for a nonaggression pact be-cause there had been no study of its effects upon Latin American and Far Eastern policy. That evening, Roosevelt went over their draft at the White House, reinserting the nonaggression proposal and com-pletely rewriting one page. By this time it was a hodgepodge in need of restyling, a task which Moley performed the next morning. "We talked over the general tone to be used and decided that with a message from sovereign to sovereigns, it should have the full mellow notes of a pipe organ and not the lighter tone of string instruments," Moffat noted. "He accordingly locked himself up and turned out a superb bit of work."

On Tuesday morning, Roosevelt, well pleased with the final draft of the letter, prepared to release it to the heads of the fifty-four nations attending the Disarmament Conference. He included, despite the strong protest of Phillips, the Soviet Union, asserting that the letter would not constitute recognition. It was one of the most serious of his undertakings thus far as President, yet with as much frivolous satisfaction as though he were displaying a new set of stamps for his collection, he remarked to Huston Thompson that here was a letter going out to all the rulers of the world, and the first name was King Zog of Albania. But a few minutes later he cut short his conference with Thompson and others to work on an explanatory message to Congress; his appeal was so much in the forefront of his mind that he could not concentrate on anything else. It was the most vital step he could take toward preservation of peace, his own idea, and, despite the many rewritings, for the most part in his own words. Roosevelt's purpose, as Moffat explained to Hugh Wilson in Geneva, was this:

"[T]he time has gone by for hesitating, maneuvering, trying at all costs to keep the conference alive. It seems that the time has come for plain speaking and for a realization that a rearmament by Germany would sooner or later lead to European trouble." * In other words, the President's message was an attempt to cure the illness rather than improve the outward symptoms.

As for himself, Moffat candidly added that he thought the message might do some good, but he remained skeptical. "At any rate," he declared, "Hitler's speech tomorrow should tell the story very quickly." [34]

Roosevelt's message was a noble call for international security against military threats and joint efforts to improve living conditions:

> To these ends the Nations have called two great World Conferences. The happiness, the prosperity, and the very lives of the men, women and children who inhabit the whole world are bound up in the decisions which their Governments will make in the near future. The improvement of social conditions, the preservation of individual human rights, and the furtherance of social justice are dependent upon these decisions.

Once again he spoke of the need for international stabilization of currencies, freeing of world trade, and action to raise price levels, then focused on the grim problem of armaments:

> If we ask what are the reasons for armaments . . . it becomes clear that they are two-fold: first, the desire, disclosed or hidden, on the part of Governments to enlarge their territories at the expense of a sister Nation and I believe that only a small minority of Governments or of peoples harbor such a purpose; second, the fear of Nations that they will be invaded.

The way to eliminate this fear, said Roosevelt, was for nations to agree to eliminate entirely the possession and use of aggressive weapons. That must be the ultimate goal. Meanwhile, the Disarmament Conference should take a first step through accepting the MacDonald plan, decide upon the time and procedure for further disarmament, and that while disarmament was proceeding no nation should increase its existing armament beyond treaty limitations. Finally, to assure peace during the

---

* In his diary, Moffat wrote even more strongly that the President was convinced "that the German reacts better to a perfectly blunt statement than to a tenuous appeal." [33]

period of disarmament, he proposed that all nations enter into a pact of nonaggression, reaffirming their obligation to reduce armaments, and pledging "that they will send no armed force of whatsoever nature across their frontiers." [35]

More tersely, Roosevelt explained to Congress the purport of the message: "The way to disarm is to disarm. The way to prevent invasion is to make it impossible." [36]

There was nothing to do but await Hitler's reaction. That evening, Warburg arrived at the White House from New York while the Roosevelts and some dinner guests were watching a blood-and-thunder deep sea movie. During the picture, Roosevelt whispered, "Have you heard about my note to all the crowned heads?" Warburg had not. The picture was not over until eleven o'clock, but Roosevelt took Warburg, Moley, Doc O'Connor, and Howe (who promptly fell asleep) into his study to speculate upon the outcome.[37]

In the Chancellery in Berlin, Hitler, alone with his secretary, waited until a translation of Roosevelt's message arrived before putting his speech into final form. (He also received a telegram from Mussolini to take into consideration.) With Roosevelt's plea in hand, he could take advantage of the opportunity to avoid the opprobrium for wrecking the Disarmament Conference by appearing reasonable and cooperative. Neurath sent him a memorandum showing him how he could appear receptive to the request without deviating seriously from German rearmament plans for the next five years.

So it was that Hitler solemnly read his speech to the Reichstag on the afternoon of May 17, avoiding the flamboyant rhetoric with which he so often aroused crowds to the point of hysteria. In the White House, Roosevelt, seated at his radio with Moley and Howe, could catch enough of the drift of Hitler's speeches to translate aloud key phrases—"Germany is ready to join a solemn non-aggression pact. . . . Germany would be ready to dissolve its whole military establishment if. . . . The German Government sees in the English plan a possible basis. . . ." He then listened to an abbreviated translation of the entire speech before turning to other problems much enheartened. Hitler declared that Germany "is ready immediately to endorse . . . the American President's magnanimous proposal to put up the powerful United States as a guarantor of peace." [38]

In London, Ramsay MacDonald, addressing the Pilgrim Society, rejoiced that "America has boldly and openly cut her moorings on the quays of the New World." In words much like Roosevelt's he declared, "The cardinal point in the policy of Great Britain is to get into active, not quiescent, cooperative relationship with the United States in everything relating to peace, world prosperity and human progress." [39]

As the German delegate returned to the Disarmament Conference, there was general acclaim of Roosevelt, who received credit for the mildness of Hitler's response.* In his exuberance, Roosevelt remarked to Morgenthau, "I think I have averted a war," and declared he had given the Nazis an additional private warning: "I sent word through the German Ambassador to Hitler that I was going to send a message and that if his message was of the same character as [that of] Von Papen that I would not blame France if she went to war. . . . I think that sending that message to Hitler had a good effect." [41]

Only the Japanese and the French regarded the message sourly. The Japanese ambassador called at the State Department asking if he could assume the message was primarily for European consumption, and received no such assurance. When a reporter asked Roosevelt if he was aiming his message at Europe, the President responded, "The whole world; it is aimed at the whole world situation." The French were hostile. The secretary general at the French Foreign Office suspected it of being a British trick, and said the French did not feel at that time as though they could scrap even one of the ancient cannon at the Invalides. News that a message was forthcoming had leaked to the French, and they were disappointed that it did not contain the security guarantee Roosevelt had promised Herriot. Roosevelt assured the French ambassador he was standing by his word. Five days later at the Geneva conference, Norman Davis embodied in a most significant speech the unilateral statement which Roosevelt hoped would be as august and effective as the Monroe Doctrine. Davis declared: [42]

> [W]e are willing to consult the other states in case of a threat to peace with a view to averting conflict. Further than that, in the event that the states, in conference, determine that a state has been guilty of a breach of the peace in violation of its international obligations and take measures against the violator, then, if we concur in the judgment rendered as to the responsible and guilty party, we will refrain from any action tending to defeat the collective effort which such state may make to restore peace.[43]

There was rejoicing both in the United States and abroad among those who had hoped to see America assume leadership in maintaining security. Roosevelt's bold moves seemed to scrap isolationism and make the dreams of the internationalists come true. Many of them believed that the absence of the United States had been the reason for the failure of the League. The Republican *San Francisco Chronicle* declared, "President Roosevelt has taken a great and dramatic step to return America to the world and the world to sanity. This is the end of isolation, or it is nothing." The London correspondent of the *Christian Science Moni-*

---

* FDR was so proud of the responses from the chiefs of state that four years later he published them in his *Public Papers and Addresses*.[40]

tor cabled that observers there believed "the United States will now finally assume full obligations of membership in the League of Nations without actually becoming a member." The foreign secretary, Sir John Simon, told the House of Commons, "The American people are prepared to abandon a tradition which they have most jealously guarded and have made a fundamental change in their country's position." [44]

If American pledges and European treaties could stem military aggression, indeed a miracle had been wrought, for along with Roosevelt's appeal and Davis's statement, Mussolini persuaded Germany, France, and Great Britain to join Italy in a Four Power ten-year pact to keep the peace. There was a break in the clouds, but only momentary.

The threat of war in Europe would end only if Hitler were genuine in the assurance he gave in his Reichstag speech. Immediate State Department reaction, as the experts listened at a radio in the file room, was that while the tone was moderate the changes in German viewpoint were more apparent than real. Moffat noted, "However, we have won the first round, which was to prevent Hitler from breaking up the conference, and have at least achieved a truce." Both in the State Department and in the American Embassy in Berlin, there was the feeling that Hitler had acted cleverly but not necessarily sincerely. From Berlin, Gordon raised the question, "[I]s this merely a tactical move to shift the responsibility for a possible disruption of the Disarmament Conference onto France?" and answered, "However that may be . . . [Hitler] must resort to a flexible foreign policy in order to gain time for the necessary internal political consolidation." [45]

The inconsistencies between Hitler's categorical rejection of war and the Nazi glorification of it were all too apparent. So, too, was the conspicuous appearance of uniforms throughout the Reich — marching Steel Helmets and other paramilitary units, drilling with heavy packs, carrying on secret practice with army rifles, the large aviation units with their distinctive uniforms (although military aircraft were banned), and the well-organized motor corps — all of which the Germans at Geneva were asserting must not be considered part of their armed forces. Hitler already had 1,600,000 men both within Germany and in Austria and other adjacent countries who were under Nazi discipline.[46]

These realities were what made the French government unwilling to trade its heavy armaments for weak treaty assurances and for Roosevelt's guarantee, to which Congress had given no endorsement. Already in March, Winston Churchill from the back bench in the House of Commons had asserted, "During this anxious month there are a good many people who have said what I've been saying for years: Thank God for the French Army!" It was scarcely a propitious time to dismantle that army, whether or not the French had to take the onus for disrupting the Disarmament Conference. The French foreign minister, Joseph Paul-Boncour, announced at Geneva that when the proper time came France would not favor destroying its so-called weapons of defense, but would want to turn them over to an international police force — and again and again the other members of the conference had shown a total unwillingness to join in creating a police force. Roosevelt commented off the record, "If you are going to eliminate guns, it is better to keep them about 5,000 fathoms. That is the best and safest place for them." The Japanese created a further complication by declaring that they would not accept the MacDonald plan unless an amendment were adopted which would in effect give Japan naval parity with the United States and Great Britain.[47]

The Disarmament Conference, deadlocked, adjourned until the fall — when it would again meet, again helplessly. The cause of disarmament was dead, despite all of Roosevelt's extraordinary efforts. Amazingly, he clung to some hope of disarmament into 1935. It remained only for Hitler before the year 1933 was out to renounce openly the Versailles Treaty, withdraw from the League of Nations, and at top speed strengthen his military machine. The martial spirit was engulfing everyone in the Reich — even the small daughter of one of the American diplomats, who at five o'clock every Wednesday afternoon at her school in Berlin had to practice throwing dummy hand grenades.[48]

In May 1933, Roosevelt along with accolades from internationalists received brickbats from isolationists. He sought at once to soften the blows. On the day after his appeal to the heads of states he issued a White House statement emphasizing that the very proposals that he was trying to interpret abroad as vital peace-keeping measures placed no obligation upon the United States unless other nations agreed to eliminate weapons of offensive warfare, and in the case of violation of agreements, only the obligation to consult with other nations. It was "no change from the long-standing and existing policy." That was exactly what the French feared, but isolationist alarm was renewed and emphatic when, almost simultaneously, Davis announced at Geneva that the United States would relinquish its traditional rights of neutrality on the high seas, and not act to defeat collective effort against an aggressor — that is to say, sanctions in the form of an arms or economic boycott. Almost simultaneously, the Senate Foreign Relations Committee thwarted Roosevelt's efforts to obtain authorization to declare an arms embargo against an aggressor.[49]

As for Roosevelt, having failed to stem armament building, and coming under attack from the isolationists, he moved toward more politically viable positions. The opposition came at a time when Roosevelt's vital industrial recovery measure and several other major bills had not yet passed Congress. He did not want to jeopardize them.

As for Hitler, Roosevelt remained relatively optimistic for some months, not facing the fact that he had lost in this first skirmish. One of the tragic aspects of Hitler's thrusts toward his adversaries was that each country, through giving priority to domestic considerations, played into his hands. Hitler, the most vicious of all nationalists, profitted the most from the nationalistic and isolationist impulses in other countries. Roosevelt's America was no exception.

CHAPTER XXIV

Toward Planned Industrial Recovery

The organization of the American economy had become so closely knit, and each part of it had become so
entirely interdependent, so thoroughly welded in the
whole, that each and every element in it had to receive
the active attention of Government.

— FDR, *November 1, 1937* [1]

When President Roosevelt signed the National Industrial Recovery Act
in June 1933, he proclaimed its significance in extravagant terms — "a
supreme effort to stabilize for all time the many factors which make
for the prosperity of the Nation, and the preservation of American
standards." Yet only two months earlier he had been by no means
certain he would propose any industrial recovery measure that spring.

True enough, during the interregnum and the first weeks of the New
Deal, Roosevelt had authorized several persons and groups to explore
the question of industrial recovery. On March 9, Hugh Johnson, riding
to Washington with Moley, had emphasized that it would be fatal to
recovery not to accompany the agricultural program with a parallel
industrial rehabilitation scheme. Moley, impressed with the logic of
Johnson's argument, took it to the President, who assigned James Warburg to work with Moley in exploring possibilities.[2]

Nevertheless, for weeks Roosevelt gave little outward indication that
he was planning more than aid to railroads plus a rudimentary twofold program, a modification of the thirty-hour-week bill together with
a public works proposal that might be attached to some other measure.*

---

* FDR sent a confidential memorandum to Vice President Garner on April 19,
1933, enumerating the state of various pieces of legislation before Congress, including the thirty-hour bill. He wrote:

In addition to the above there will probably be (1) a simple railroad bill —
(2) a bank bill. Neither has yet been introduced.
There is also the problem of a public works bill but it is my present thought
that this can be tacked on to one of the other bills in the form of a broad
appropriation, the details of which will be left to the Administration.
Finally, sometime later there will probably be two important Resolutions —
one on Tariff and the other on Debts.[3]

As late as April 26, he told reporters "as far as I can tell now, there is only one more major thing going up [to Congress] and that is railroads." [4]

Roosevelt did indeed, as he had asserted in his campaign speeches, look forward to some long-range program of cooperation between government and business, but he had not as yet decided what precise form it should take. Nor did he seem to deem it essential to rapid recovery. Rather, he seemed to be counting upon a combination of mild inflation and a limited amount of public construction, together with the restoration of agricultural prices, to bring a sharp, immediate upturn in the economy.

The same threatening indicators, early in April 1933, that precipitated Roosevelt's decision to go off gold also made irresistible the innumerable proposals for one sort or another of an industrial recovery program. The threat of a new economic collapse augmented the pressures from outside the administration from both businessmen and workers, and culminated in a congressional stampede toward the thirty-hour-week bill. The President responded by modifying his plans spectacularly and authorizing a grand scheme for the national planning of the economy.

There is no clearer indication of how little need Roosevelt felt to be ideologically consistent than the way in which he clung to a policy of minimum interference with business while he enthusiastically advocated regional planning, with somewhat less enthusiasm accepted agricultural planning, and took for granted firm federal planning for railroads. Tugwell, the most advanced proponent of industrial planning among the Brain Trust, looks back at the Roosevelt of that spring as too much an heir to Wilson's New Freedom, too difficult to move in the direction of T.R.'s New Nationalism. Both Moley and Tugwell drew upon their firm grounding in the economic theory of the Progressive era to press the President — both of them from their study of Charles R. Van Hise's *Concentration and Control* (1912), and in the case of Tugwell, also from the teachings of Simon Patten.[5]

Tugwell was not very successful during the first weeks in moving Roosevelt toward government regulation and rationalization of the economy. That spring he published *The Industrial Discipline and Governmental Arts*, in which he recommended that the federal government supervise reorganization of industry to control prices, eliminate excessive competition, and allocate capital. "We possess every needful material for Utopia," Tugwell wrote, suggesting that the way to organize that material was through national industrial planning.[6]

In his private counseling of Roosevelt, Tugwell urged drastic remedies. He noted in his diary on April 21:

> The government really ought to take over immediately large blocks of paralyzed industries, in my opinion, to make certain that production

is set going, especially in the heavy industries. At the very least it ought to take them on lease. . . . Prices have increased some 10%. But the bottom will drop out of this unless something solid is furnished in the way of support. This ought to be a public works program and the leasing or taking over of the industries now working at 15 to 25% of capacity.[7]

Tugwell was undertaking that spring to convince Roosevelt not to be an atomizer in the Brandeis tradition, but to foster "concentration and control." But the President paid little attention to Tugwell, the prime advocate of economic planning among his advisers, and would go no further for some weeks than to authorize Tugwell to investigate also the question of a program.

While Roosevelt continued cool to industrywide economic planning, for months he had been making preparations for new, tighter economic controls over railroads to rescue them from incipient or actual bankruptcy. Although the outcome was to be trivial in the overall pattern of the New Deal, the question of railroads occupied a significant amount of Roosevelt's attention, and must have done much to prepare his thinking for the National Recovery Administration. There were, as a minor factor, personal reasons for his keen interest in the plight of railroads; he himself was the son of a railroad executive and never lost his boyhood zest for traveling slowly around the country in a private Pullman car. It was to be one of his greatest delights as President. But transcendent in his calculations was the central role of railroads in the economy, and the dependence of both large trust funds and small investors upon blue chip holdings of railroad stocks and bonds.

Operating revenues had declined by half since 1929, and railroads had cut their dividends 70 percent. Insolvent lines were defaulting upon bonds (although overall, interest payments by railroads were up). There was another statistic, translatable into even more human misery; railroads had cut their payrolls also by half and had reduced the number of workers by more than 750,000. Sadly enough, in all the deliberations over the plight of the railroads, the emphasis was upon the threat to security-holders, not to railroad employees.[8]

No one was surprised that Roosevelt was planning new controls over the railroads; so had the Republicans. Railroads were the one area in which, already in 1920, the precedent was firm that the federal government should engage in economic planning and regulation to bolster a depressed industry.

If Roosevelt's thinking on federal economic control was far from clear, perhaps even muddled, so indeed had been the evolving pattern of relations between the federal government and business, with special reference to railroads. Although antitrust laws were federal statute, Congress in 1920 enacted legislation to encourage consolidation of distressed railroads, and even stipulated that railroads must place part of their earnings over 6 percent into an Interstate Commerce Commission loan fund for weaker lines. Neither provision was effective, but the principle was unchallenged that federal policy toward railroads, far from being antitrust, should be one of rigorously regulated monopoly. Wartime precedent had been even more rigorous; the government had leased the railroads and run them through a Railroad Administration under McAdoo as a single unified line. The most obvious result had been remarkable efficiencies in untangling previous tieups and delivering war supplies to Atlantic ports.[9]

The chairman of the Interstate Commerce Commission, Joseph B. Eastman, whom both Republicans and Democrats hailed as the nation's greatest transportation expert, had repeatedly expressed himself in favor either of continuing government operation of railroads or moving toward government ownership. During the depression, he favored drastic overhaul of the railroads, and in private suggested that one alternative would be for lines in distress voluntarily to transfer their ownership to the federal government. Yet Eastman was a protégé of Brandeis, the advocate of decentralization and smallness, and it was Frankfurter who commended him to Roosevelt. On January 11, 1933, when Eastman met with Roosevelt, Moley, and Tugwell, he talked primarily about government operation of railroads. His views are an indication of how impossible it was to separate distinctly the supposedly contrasting Wilson versus T.R., antimonopoly versus economic planning, approaches in the spring of 1933. Eastman wrote Frankfurter a few days later:

> For a long time I wavered in my views upon competition. There are impressive evidences that competition is a stimulus to alert, aggressive management, while monopoly may lead to an indifferent and unprogressive management. However, I am now convinced that the evils and wastes of competition outweigh its advantages, and I believe that a monopolistic management can be saved from dry rot. This points to the conclusion that competition among railroads should be eliminated and that they could be operated as a unit. But I do not believe the country will stand for that without Government ownership, and it is also clear that this is the simplest road to unification.[10]

The greatest pressures for drastic railroad reorganization were coming from financial groups whose investments were evaporating. In 1932, major lines fell $250 million short of earning their fixed charges; the Reconstruction Finance Corporation had already loaned them a third of a billion dollars, and lines operating 40,000 miles of track were already in receivership or facing it. Roosevelt had aimed his campaign speech on railroads toward reform of receiverships and reduction of wasteful competition. One of the few achievements of the lame duck Congress, one in which Adolf A. Berle and Eastman were involved, was to enact the more satisfactory Railroad Bankruptcy Act of 1933.[11]

Since bankruptcy legislation was out of the way, Roosevelt had only to concern himself with devices to force or encourage railroads to become more efficient. In this area he could draw authority from the report of the National Transportation Committee, which several insurance companies and major universities, heavy holders of railroad securities, had financed. Former President Coolidge was chairman of the committee until his death in January 1933; Baruch received much credit for its findings when they appeared in February, even a wire of congratulations from Winston Churchill. The report was the work of Harold G. Moulton, head of the Brookings Institution; Berle was deeply involved in it, and many of its views reflected Eastman's ideas. It recommended drastic efficiencies and firmer regulation to encompass the entire transportation system. Of its prestigious members, only Al Smith expressed some reservations; he favored abolishing the Interstate Commerce Commission and establishing a Department of Transportation. Fright had driven nominally conservative creditors this distance toward government regulation. By comparison, Roosevelt's expansive plans seemed modest, and he soon limited them.[12]

At first, before he took office, Roosevelt considered the idea of establishing federal regulation over all transportation, from railroads to airlines to pipelines. That continued to be his ultimate goal, but he decided that in the spring of 1933 he would seek emergency measures that would apply only to railroads. When he came into office, the railroads seemed so close to bankruptcy that it was logical for him and his advisers to think of quick expedients for their rescue rather than long-range balanced reform.

At the outset, Berle was Roosevelt's prime expert on railroads, not the prestigious but quite independent-minded Eastman. In the fall Roosevelt had authorized Berle to serve on the staff of the National Transportation Committee; he kept Roosevelt informed of its actions and of progress toward bankruptcy legislation. At the time of the banking crisis, Berle then took over from Woodin the chairing of conferences with railroad executives to discuss coordination. On March 9, out of one of the conferences came the proposal by Carl Gray of the Union Pacific that the railroad executives at once form coordinating associations in each region. These regional associations, Berle reported to Roosevelt, would "eliminate duplicating facilities, run trains over one of two parallel tracks where this could be done; provide for joint use of bridges, tunnels, etc.; and generally treat the systems within the co-ordinating areas as single systems, working out a division of saving as compensation." Gray pointed out that the government would have to scrap antitrust laws and to take a strong hand with the railroad men.[13]

The pressure, Berle apparently persuaded Roosevelt, was to come through the Reconstruction Finance Corporation, which held staggeringly large notes from the railroads, several of which would mature that summer. Berle favored continuing some of the loans for those railroads that were in relatively good shape, letting some of the least efficient "go through the wringer." In April, Roosevelt appointed Berle special assistant to the RFC board to serve as railroad credit manager. In this role he was to persuade the railroads to deflate their capital structure so that they could meet interest charges, and not to loan them more money than they could repay. Control over RFC loans to railroads was to be the stick to force refinancing and coordination.[14]

The drafting of a bill to coordinate railroads proceeded in more methodical fashion than most of the other legislation that spring. Roosevelt appointed a committee with the famous Eastman as chairman and Berle as one of its members, placing it under the aegis of the Department of Commerce. It came to be known consequently as the Roper committee, although the role of Secretary Roper seemed largely that of trying to gain for his department whatever control over transportation the new measure might specify. Later Roosevelt appointed a second, broader Roper committee to consider the first committee's proposal.

In his initial meeting with the committee on April 1, Roosevelt examined four plans. He was attracted at first to one of these, a financiers' plan to consolidate all railroads into seven major systems, the scheme of Frederick H. Prince, a Boston banker. Moley has suggested that it caught Roosevelt's imagination because it was a new idea; he was "interested in anything novel." A second generalization about Roosevelt was equally true; he was repelled by whatever would upset the budget. When Eastman and others pointed out to him that the Prince plan would involve federal loans of nearly two billion dollars, Roosevelt lost all interest. He turned to the other three plans, which involved a proposal that Berle and representatives of security-holders had devised for a coordinator of the railroads, and two modifications of this proposal, one by Eastman and associates, the other by railroad executives. Thereafter work centered around the coordinator plan. What ensued was the familiar pattern that bill drafting followed that spring. Earl Latham has written: [15]

> Out of the welter of conferences, caucusses, committees, notes, plans, memoranda, draft proposals, messages, letters, and replies six principal coalitions of interested groups emerged and the final product was the result of their mutually influential activities. These were the bankers,

investors, shippers, railroad managers, railroad unions, and government officials.[16]

As Roosevelt let the contenders thrash out their differences, one characteristic particularly distinguished this undertaking from others that spring. Secretary Roper was eager to gain control over either all or segments of the Interstate Commerce Commission as part of the executive reorganizations then underway. President Roosevelt himself wanted greater power over transportation, as indeed he was ready to make his authority felt in other independent regulatory agencies. He was bringing into Washington a struggle he had already carried on with state agencies in Albany. In Eastman, Roper faced a formidable adversary who overwhelmed him. After one committee session, Eastman exploded to Roosevelt, "Mr. President, the Secretary and I just don't speak the same language. I can't learn his, and he doesn't want to understand mine!" It soon became apparent that Eastman and Roosevelt also did not speak the same language, but they respected each other. Eastman was a prestigious ally, at the outset admiring, but never willing to subordinate the ICC to the White House. After Roosevelt at a conference in April had mentioned that he was contemplating an Executive Order to reorganize the transportation activities of the government, Eastman expressed his frank misgivings over placing under the control of an executive department matters that should receive judicial or quasi-judicial settlement. Roosevelt at once backtracked. Since Eastman never compromised this principle, Roosevelt's relations with him were cool. Nevertheless, Eastman's reputation was so high that the President utilized him throughout three terms as another of the appointees who could reassure conservatives.[17]

The railroad bill that Roosevelt finally sent to Congress on May 4 was the product of two Department of Commerce committees and numerous compromises. It had started as a security-holders' and railway executives' measure; it was they who were seeking thoroughgoing federal planning as a way out of their difficulties. Their conservative journal, *Railway Age*, even complained in mid-April because progress had been so slow in drafting the legislation. Latham has suggested that in part the executives were trying to forestall Roosevelt from acting too rigorously; in larger part they were eager to obtain legislation before representatives of shippers and railway labor could force modifications. Roosevelt included shipper and union representatives on the second committee, but the finished draft of the bill that Roosevelt made public on April 28 was basically beneficial only to railroads and the holders of railroad securities. George Harrison as spokesman for the Railway Brotherhoods remonstrated with Roosevelt at the White House that he had failed, as he had earlier promised, to include guarantees for workers in the bill. Roosevelt gave Harrison reassurances, but on

May 4 sent the bill to the Capitol unchanged, accepting the argument of advisers that Congress could publicly modify it to protect the interests of labor. At the heart of the bill was provision for a coordinator. Roosevelt informed Congress: [18]

> As a temporary emergency measure, I suggest the creation of a Federal Coordinator of Transportation who, working with groups of railroads, will be able to encourage, promote or require action on the part of carriers, in order to avoid duplication of service, prevent waste, and encourage financial reorganizations. Such a Coordinator should also, in carrying out this policy, render useful service in maintaining railroad employment at a fair wage.[19]

At first glance Roosevelt seemed to be seeking to create what newspapers liked to call a "czar," a federal dictator over railroads. Yet even cursory examination indicated little real strengthening of government control; it would broaden ICC criteria for rate-setting to include effect on movement of traffic, and extend ICC authority over railroad holding companies, most notably the new Van Sweringen empire, the Alleghany Corporation. As for the coordinator, although the expectation from the time the bill was made public was that it would be Eastman, he received little real power. The bill would establish three groups of railroads — eastern, southern, and western — each of which would elect a committee of five railroad men. To these committees went the initiative to decide upon the pooling of rolling stock and terminals and the elimination of competing service within their regions. If they failed to act, the coordinator could order them to carry out his recommendations or face a $20,000 fine, but they could appeal to the ICC. In practice if not statute, the fundamental power seemed to lie with the railroads; they were obtaining legislation to regulate themselves. It is not surprising that representatives of motor and water carriers sought to be included in the bill so that they too could eliminate competition without risk of facing federal suits under antitrust laws. The House Committee on Interstate and Foreign Commerce refused the request.[20]

Union leaders protested that the bill would enable railroads to lay off from 50,000 to 500,000 more workers. Donald R. Richberg on behalf of the unions persuaded the Senate committee to amend the bills to protect workers' employment.* Since any real economies in railroad

---

* The sympathies of Eastman, whom Roosevelt did indeed appoint coordinator, were with the railroads. "Labor executives are drunk with power!" he commented to a friend. To Eastman the railroad layoffs would be as essential as the layoffs in federal employment, which removed 500 experts from his small ICC staff: "If I understand the theory on which the Administration is now proceeding, it is that all waste and nonessential expense should be eliminated in Government service and elsewhere, and that along with this policy should go companion measures which will stimulate business activity and provide for increase in employment in useful, needed work." [21]

operation depended upon eliminating "feather-bedding" and consolidations that would wipe out large numbers of jobs, the purpose of the bill — to enable railroads to save money — was negated in advance. Roosevelt, not daring to offend the strongly unionized Railway Brotherhoods, assented to modification of the bill. He thus protected railroad workers from a drastic elimination of their jobs during the same weeks that he was forcing his new administrators under the Economy Act to dismiss quantities of government workers.[22]

Railroads took almost no steps toward efficiencies during the duration of the legislation. Nor was the RFC able to persuade many of them to reorganize and squeeze the water out of their securities. Berle soon left the RFC. The fundamental reasons for so little change went beyond the guarantee of railroad jobs; already by the time the legislation was enacted, in May 1933, carloadings were up and railroads were beginning to enjoy larger revenues. Their interest in accepting reform, even cartelization, under government auspices vanished.[23]

In several fundamentals the ingredients that went into the Emergency Railroad Transportation Act of 1933 indicated the way in which industrial recovery legislation was to develop several weeks later: self-regulation to promote efficiencies and eliminate competition under the benign surveillance of a federal "czar" with little real power. Secondarily there was to be some protection of organized labor, and even a gesture in the form of representation on committees to the consumers (in the railroad instance, shippers). All this in the case of railroads should involve no increase in federal appropriations; the coordinator and his staff were to be financed by an assessment against every railroad of $1.50 for each mile of its lines.

Yet it was only slowly and without visible enthusiasm that Roosevelt moved toward an overall industrial recovery device. Perhaps it was because he first eliminated several formulas that appealed to him less than the railroad scheme.

The first, undesirable in Roosevelt's eyes because it would involve large federal expenditure, came, curiously enough, from the conservative James Warburg with the backing of the even more conservative Lewis Douglas. Warburg had fallen heir to all the many plans that had come to rest in Moley's files since the election. Somehow he found time, despite his concentration on financial matters and planning for the World Economic Conference, to devise a scheme. He talked to the economist Harold G. Moulton, head of the Brookings Institution, Fred I. Kent, the elderly, prestigious New York banker, Adolph Miller of the Federal Reserve Board, and Douglas. From Kent he adapted a plan through which the government would stimulate production through underwriting the output of producer's goods, giving guarantees against losses in return for a pledge of a share in profits. When he took the idea to Roosevelt, the President expressed most concern about the cost. Warburg assured him that it could be met through payment of the guarantees in long-term government bonds. Nevertheless, Roosevelt thought it might be expensive for the government and he was firm in his insistence upon budget-balancing. (He was even afraid of an alternate proposal to lend RFC money to industry, although in the course of events the RFC did in fact become a prime recovery agency). Further, Warburg failed to make his plan politically attractive. With an obtuseness incongruous in so brilliant and sensitive a man, he attached to his report of April 4 a draft message for the President to send Congress referring to the proposed measure as "a bill for the regimentation of industry." [24]

Above all, countless persons were showering upon the President the suggestion which was most obvious, that the way to wage war upon the depression was literally to return to the Wilsonian concept of the War Industries Board. Roosevelt himself was thoroughly familiar both with the WIB and its successors of the 1920s, the private trade associations. His own ideas on industrial planning need be traced back no farther than his experiences in Washington during World War I. Then, through industrial committees of the WIB, largely manned by executives on leave from business to serve the government at a dollar a year, the government had stimulated (or inhibited) production, eliminated wasteful duplication or competition, and regulated prices. And for labor, with which Roosevelt had been most closely concerned, there had been the setting of wages and hours and adjustment of disputes through the War Labor Board. These operations looked more effective in retrospect than they had been at the time, when they had been more dependent upon moral suasion than the clout of federal enforcement. There had been little real control over soaring prices, wages, and profits. After the war when Herbert Hoover, who had headed the Food Administration, became secretary of commerce, he sponsored trade associations through which he tried to retain wartime setting of standards and industrywide efficiencies. Trade associations set codes of fair procedures and standards, but also, to Hoover's dismay, tried to post uniform high prices.[25]

Roosevelt had become head of one of the associations, the American Construction Council. The construction industry was anarchic, suffering from seasonal fluctuations and, in some cities, from criminal connivance between contractors and labor leaders. Through the six years he headed the council, Roosevelt tried to promote long-range planning to postpone construction at peak periods and stimulate it in slack times. But the council failed to bring order, indeed functioned little at all, except for Roosevelt's communiqués, because there was no way it could enforce its proposals. It did not have behind it even the mild federal sanctions that had given some effectiveness to the War Industries Board.[26]

No sooner had the depression hit American industry than some businessmen, among them former dollar-a-year men, proposed one or another form of peacetime agency analogous to the War Industries Board to direct business out of the depression. Gerard Swope of General Electric, who had served in Washington during the war, in the fall of 1931 suggested the idea, and by 1932 Henry I. Harriman, president of the United States Chamber of Commerce, was advocating it. President Hoover rejected the proposal as sheer fascism which would create a gigantic monopoly destructive of American industry.[27]

For some time after he took office, Roosevelt was not sure whether he favored a new agency. On April 13, in response to a vigorous memorandum from his uncle, Frederic A. Delano, proposing the essentials of what became the National Recovery Administration, Roosevelt, referring the suggestion to Secretary of Commerce Roper, commented that he thought his uncle "right but perhaps a little ahead of his time." [28]

Already when Roosevelt made this comment, the growing pressure for Senator Hugo Black's thirty-hour bill had become so great that either the President would have to accept the Black bill in some form or recommend to Congress some other industrial recovery plan in the spring of 1933. The option to wait until January 1934 no longer existed.

The Black bill was a simple formula for increasing jobs through spreading the work. Even before the depression, organized labor had begun to advocate a shorter work week as a means of countering technological unemployment. With the coming of the depression, the emphasis changed to forestalling layoffs through cutting hours. During the lame duck session of Congress, Black introduced a bill prohibiting a work week in industry of more than five days or thirty hours. In order to bring the measure within the Constitution, the enforcement device was the prohibition of the shipment in interstate commerce of goods from noncomplying factories. Unions backed the proposal, and William Green of the AFL threatened a general strike to obtain its enactment. After Roosevelt took office, Black reintroduced the measure, asserting that it would create six million jobs. Countless workers wrote congressmen pressuring for the Black bill. The president of the China Grove, North Carolina, local of the United Textile Workers of America laboriously penned an appeal to his representative, Robert Doughton. The body of the letter sounded as if it had been copied from a standard union statement:

> No effort that is made to stimulate employment and relieve distress
> will be of any permanent value until we regulate industrial production

so that it roughly corresponds to current rates of consumption. Passage of the 30 hour bill is therefore in the nature of laying a foundation for economic recovery. Regulation of hours is only one of many steps toward recovery but it is the first; the establishment of minimum rates of pay is the second step and one which must accompany the first. One is largely useless without the other. Therefore the success or failure of the present administration will depend on its ability to solve the economic difficulties which now confront the American people.

Variations upon this appeal piled high on congressional desks. And at the end of the communication from China Grove, North Carolina, were words unmistakably those of the writer, the local union president: "I say, that almost anything that can be done is better than the present policy of Industrys own Regulations. God, knows we the laborers of the South cant stand much longer heres hoping for a New Deal." [29]

A southern congressional leader like Doughton seldom felt moved to act upon behalf of factory workers, especially those who were union members. Doughton liked to be referred to as "Farmer Bob"; he was widely known as "Muley." He did not answer the textile union president, but did respond to one of the other workers in China Grove — beginning his letter in a mood of indignation, then softening the tone, as indeed pressure was causing so many on Capitol Hill to modify long-held views:

> You state that you are working from Monday morning until Saturday noon and sometimes more each week. I am just wondering if it is not a lot to be thankful for to have an opportunity to work as there are so many million people in the United States unemployed.
>
> In my work for the Public I never work less than 15 hours each day, sometimes much longer and then I am unable to keep up with my duties. Of course I do not want to see those who labor work such long hours, but I am certainly glad to know that your mill is running. I am hoping that business will soon pick up so we can all find ourselves in better circumstances.[30]

As sentiment for the thirty-hour bill gained momentum in the Senate, Roosevelt became worried. He was sympathetic with the objective of putting more people to work, but felt it would not solve unemployment. Nor would it fit rural industries with which he had long been so familiar, like canneries at peak season or the daily routine of a dairy. "There have to be hours adapted to the rhythm of the cow," he told Frances Perkins. Further, the attorney general advised him the bill was unconstitutional, and he agreed.[31]

The President sent word to the Senate that he doubted the constitutionality of the thirty-hour bill and considered it too restrictive. At the very least he wanted it amended to expand the limitation of hours to thirty-six per week and eight a day. Nevertheless, the Senate defeated his amendment and on April 6 passed the bill 53 to 30.

What the answer might be was not yet entirely clear to Roosevelt, but the Senate action served notice that pressure for some sort of measure had become urgent. It must not be the Black bill with its serious flaws. Merely to shorten the work week without keeping a floor under wages would be to spread the national misery. Yet it was also true that to shorten hours and maintain existing wage levels without any increase in business would threaten manufacturers with bankruptcy. Roosevelt authorized several people to engage in different courses of action simultaneously.

Publicly, Miss Perkins gave expression of administration sympathy for the objectives of the thirty-hour bill by appearing before the House committee holding hearings upon it and giving it support — with amendments to make it more flexible in hours and to establish minimum wages through industrial boards representing management, labor, and the government. In keeping with her background as well as her position as secretary of labor, her deepest concern was with the plight of workers.* Roosevelt strengthened her thrust by wiring a number of governors of industrial states asking them to seek minimum wage legislation comparable to that just enacted in New York.

The support Roosevelt gave Miss Perkins was limited and from the background as he waited to see how Congress and the nation reacted. She herself was not engaged in a legislative feint, since she genuinely sought legislation separate from any industrial recovery scheme to improve the working conditions and income of labor. Had her proposals won congressional support and generated enthusiasm throughout the country, Roosevelt undoubtedly would have backed her, and, as he had been remarking to newspapermen and congressional leaders, the administration measure of that spring would have been a modification of the Black bill, a recovery measure specifically for workers. Miss Perkins was having her turn, as did so many others, to demonstrate what she could achieve. She failed, since businessmen immediately expressed vehement objections that it would give federal officials power over wages and hours that belonged to experienced, responsible executives. Henry I. Harriman of the United States Chamber of Commerce insisted wages and hours regulation should be a component of the overall fed-

* The Labor Department of Pennsylvania found in a survey that April that some ten thousand woman needle workers were earning an average weekly wage of $5.61; a quarter of these earned less than $4. A girl working in Lebanon, Pa., in a shirt factory for ten hours a day for five and one-half days received $2.73 in a pay envelope bearing on the outside the admonition: "If you would have freedom, be thrifty. Slaves are as plentiful today as they were before Lincoln delivered his Emancipation Proclamation. Are you hampered in your freedom of action? Just knock the 'l' out of slave." [32]

erally sponsored "industrial self-government" he had been advocating. So great was the furor that Miss Perkins's recommendations served Roosevelt only as part of a useful holding operation as he moved on toward an overall piece of apparatus. And, as the administration shifted, Miss Perkins, was by early May, in the eyes of her solicitor, through clinging to earlier views, "(though she does not appreciate it) . . . outside the whole circle of developments here." [33]

The time had come for others. During the weeks before the Senate passage of the Black bill precipitated action, they had, with Roosevelt's specific or tacit approval, been working on recovery proposals.

CHAPTER XXV

"Twin Efforts—Public Works and Industrial Reemployment"

> History will probably record the National Industrial Re-
> covery Act as the most important and far-reaching
> legislation ever enacted by the American Congress
> — FDR, *June 16, 1933*.[1]

The National Industrial Recovery Act evolved out of Roosevelt's response to a multitude of pressures. To a number of those persons and
groups who had urged him in the spring of 1933 to move toward an
industrial recovery program, his response had been to invite them
cheerfully to go ahead and to explore the question and perhaps even
draft a bill. One after another of the proposals or drafts met with his
disapproval; others, rumored about Congress or in the press, failed
to survive the "trial balloon" stage.

Perhaps, as some have suggested, Roosevelt was being no more than
absent-minded in authorizing so many people to look into the industrial
problem; in later years he was habitually forgetful and consequently
notorious for giving overlapping assignments. It may be that his ready
authorization in March or early April 1933 was the easiest way to
parry discussion of a topic to which he did not as yet give top priority.
Or, in keeping with his avowed trial-and-error approach, he was seeking
useful answers. The possibilities were not mutually exclusive; all or
several might have been involved. There was one further factor, beyond
Roosevelt's deliberate reliance upon the "trial balloon" to deflate politically unviable proposals. The numerous inquiries generated articles
and a good bit of discussion which helped prepare the public for a
major recovery measure.

In April and early May 1933, three main interacting groups engaged
in planning what became the National Industrial Recovery Act. Altogether, the list of those who in one way or another became involved in
shaping proposals reads like a catalog of New Deal planners curiously
intermingled with labor and business figures. Roosevelt specifically in-

structed Moley to get in touch with the Brookings Institution, where Moulton was already active, and with the United States Chamber of Commerce, whose head, Henry I. Harriman, had long favored the NRA idea.

Senator Wagner, who headed one of the three main bill-drafting groups also liked the plan that Moulton was advocating in association with another Brookings Institution economist, Meyer Jacobstein, who had been labor manager for a Rochester, New York, firm. On April 22, with Roosevelt's consent, Wagner called a series of conferences to draft legislation based upon the Moulton-Jacobstein plan.* It would permit trade associations to draw up codes, and grant labor wages and hours protection and the right to bargain collectively.

Within the administration, Roosevelt assigned responsibility for planning industrial recovery to the Department of Commerce. Assistant Secretary John Dickinson headed this second major planning group.† Frances Perkins and Rexford G. Tugwell associated themselves with it. Several members also had close ties with members of Wagner's group, and by early May the two sets of planners were working jointly to produce a single draft bill. Tugwell succeeded in writing into the draft his scheme for enforcement — the levying of a processing tax like that in the agricultural program. From time to time the federal government was to distribute the proceeds of the tax among those firms which had complied with code provisions. A strong economic incentive would thus force companies to cooperate.

The third bill drafting group came about, according to Moley, through a fortuitous accident. On his own initiative, Moley late in April commissioned General Hugh Johnson to draft a recovery bill when he ran into Johnson and Baruch in the lobby of the Carlton Hotel, freshly arrived from a hunting trip to Baruch's Hobcaw plantation in South Carolina. Moley asked Baruch if he would loan Johnson, and Baruch assented. Whether or not Moley had sounded out Roosevelt in advance, it was a shrewd move, since like the enlistment of George Peek in the farm program, it almost guaranteed the support of Baruch's

---

* In addition to Moulton and Jacobstein, the "Wagner group" included Fred I. Kent, James H. Rand, Jr., Virgil Jordan of the National Industrial Conference Board, W. Jett Lauck, a United Mine Workers economist, Representative Clyde Kelly of Pennsylvania, who had earlier proposed legislation to stabilize the coal industry, David L. Podell, a trade association attorney, and Malcolm C. Rorty, an industrial economist. Wagner assigned Moulton, Podell, and Lauck to draft a bill.[2]
† Tugwell enlisted for it two economists associated with farm problems, Louis Bean of the Department of Agriculture, and Jerome Frank, who was to be counsel to the new AAA. Bean had been working with Jacobstein. Frank brought to the task a young lawyer, Leon Keyserling, who soon joined Wagner's staff. Dickinson and Frank were the chief bill drafters in the Department of Commerce group. Dickinson, who had been an economist with the War Trade Board in 1917, had earned both a Ph.D. and a Harvard law degree. He had practiced law with McAdoo, then became a law professor at the University of Pennsylvania.[3]

conservative admirers in the Senate. It was the opportunity for which Johnson had been longing, and he began work immediately in Moley's office. "Indeed," Johnson wrote two years later, "I never went back to New York from that day to the end of my service except to get my clothes and rarely even so much as saw my own family." Donald R. Richberg, who had been legal counsel for railroad unions and helped draft the Railway Labor Act of 1926, worked with Johnson on the labor clauses of the legislation. Lew Douglas said that the President wanted a brief, broad bill, so Johnson drafted one on a pair of sheets of legal foolscap.[4]

The final bill was not to be so short, for Roosevelt employed the same tactics as in the drafting of agricultural recovery legislation. He encouraged work on an omnibus bill that would incorporate all of the recovery schemes — the shorter work week and a guarantee of collective bargaining for labor, the War Industries Board sort of production controls for industry, and a public works spending program to stimulate the economy. The two basic drafts, that of the Wagner-Dickinson groups, and of Johnson and Richberg, were not too far apart, but reconciling differences was not easy. Tugwell noted a few days later:

> Of course nothing could be settled really without the President. I liked the draft worked out by Frank and Dickinson which I had constantly talked over with them and which, in fact, embodied my ideas. But Johnson had more power in his bill — with clearer compulsions — and I like this part of his if we cannot have my own method of making compliance profitable. But Johnson and Dickinson came to loggerheads and we finally took it to F.D.R. Each side told a story and he too leaned toward shorter and quicker action but his mandate was to go away and agree.

That was on May 10. It was not until this meeting that Roosevelt decided to combine all the recovery components into one big bill.

> Wagner, Dickinson, Frances Perkins, Johnson and I fought over the thing in Lew Douglas' office for some time. I failed to get them to adopt my tax and reserve-fund scheme. I argued for it strongly but dropped it for the sake of harmony. But I sided with Johnson in his demand for more teeth in the penalty provisions if we could not have the tax. Dickinson was compelled to give way.[5]

Of the three major components in the recovery package, the one business had been seeking seemed to create the least debate during the planning sessions. The federal government was to sanction trade association self-regulation of industries through codes of fair practices, backed by some sort of penalties. That was the part of the package that almost exclusively interested General Johnson, and seemed to be the chief concern of Tugwell and Dickinson.

What businessmen eagerly sought was the prohibition of unfair competition so that they could raise their prices to a profitable level. In effect, they wanted the federal government to allow them to engage in price-fixing, and to suspend prosecution against it under the antitrust laws. In the 1920s the Supreme Court had decided against the maple flooring association on the grounds that it was engaging in illegal price-fixing.

Roosevelt was no more ready than Hoover openly to sanction price-fixing or to guarantee the suspension of antitrust laws, but as Wagner announced in the Senate, the recovery legislation would allow industries to file lists of their prices and their terms of sale without danger of prosecution. Out of this open pricing could come uniform price schedules. Critics of the NRA code system were to attack it as government-sponsored monopoly.[6]

Rather, in his initial thinking about the NRA code system, Roosevelt regarded it as an essential way to distribute orders for manufactured goods — the reverse of monopoly. It should be a business counterpart of the thirty-hour-week bill, he suggested to newspapermen on April 12, 1933. The question in his mind was "whether the Government should try to spread work within a given industry over the whole industry and to prevent the concentration in the hands of any one or two units of the industry of all the work."

In explanation he resorted to one of his simple fables, which he fabricated around a small plant operating not far from Hyde Park in Washington Hollow, New York. It was a sweater factory, he said, where the employees, like those in other sweater factories were practically starving because the factory received only orders enough so it could operate six weeks a year. The employees agreed to take a one-third cut in pay so that the factory could lower its prices below those of competitors. As a result the factory obtained sufficient orders to run three shifts a day for six months, but two other sweater factories were forced out of business.

"Now," concluded Roosevelt, "that brings up the question as to whether we can work out some kind of a plan that will distribute the volume of consumption in a given industry over the whole industry . . . It might be called the regulation of production or, to put it better, the prevention of foolish over-production."[7]

Foolish overproduction, in two related areas, bituminous coal and petroleum, leading to waste of natural resources and starvation wages, were also concerning Roosevelt during the period of gestation of the recovery program. On March 27, together with Secretaries Ickes and Perkins, he discussed with John L. Lewis and several of the officials of the United Mine Workers possible remedial coal legislation. By late

April, some operators also were asking for federal control over wages, output, and prices, so that producers in Illinois and Indiana, where miners received $5 per day, could compete with those in other fields paying as little as $1 per day. When a reporter asked Roosevelt early in May if he had any plans for stabilization of the bituminous coal industry, he replied that he thought it the most difficult subject in the United States, and had made no progress in dealing with it. Control over bituminous coal production was to be one of the major facets of the NRA.[8]

In point of fact, the problem of petroleum controls was a far more difficult problem for Roosevelt and Ickes than one like coal that ultimately fell under the jurisdiction of the NRA. At one of the first cabinet meetings, on March 14, Roosevelt asked Ickes to telephone the governors of the three major oil-producing states, Texas, Oklahoma, and California, to ask them to come or send representatives to a conference in Washington to try to limit production. The price of crude oil had dropped from as high as $2.31 per barrel in 1926 to as low as 10 cents in the flush new fields of East Texas by the end of 1930. Several of the oil producing states had imposed production quotas, and the federal government, a substantial tariff that reduced importation of oil by about 65 percent. But by March 1933, prices, which had risen to above a dollar a barrel, were again plummeting as operators in defiance of state quotas were marketing "hot oil" for as little as 10 to 25 cents a barrel in the Mid-continent field.[9]

When the oil industry representatives met in Washington late in March, spokesmen for the major oil companies and factions of the smaller independent producers quarreled bitterly over proposed remedies for the spectacular fall in prices and allegedly acute overproduction.

The only governor to attend the conference was Alf Landon of Kansas, the fourth largest producer of oil among the states, who became chairman of a committee representative of the conflicting groups. Landon was himself a major leader of the independent producers as well as an investor in Sinclair and Standard Oil, and had shown himself an imaginative and compassionate leader in seeking to bring order and to rescue submarginal producers. Far from appearing as a Republican challenger to Roosevelt, as he was to be in the 1936 presidential campaign, he was eager in the spring of 1933 to cooperate with the New Deal. By participating in the conference, he announced, he was acknowledging the appreciation the people of Kansas felt for "the courage with which President Roosevelt has attacked the depression." It was "one way in which a member of that species thought by many to be extinct — a Republican Governor in a Mid-Western state — can aid in the fight, and I now enlist for the duration of the war." [10]

Landon and the conferees agreed that the states could not success-fully enforce quotas for oil production and purchasing. The federal government must intervene, for, Landon declared, "even the iron hand of a national dictator is preferable to paralytic stroke." The oil men requested Roosevelt to ask the governors of the major oil producing states to close all flush pools — those that were highly productive — until April 15, and that he should ask Congress for legislation prohibiting interstate shipment of oil produced in violation of state laws.

Roosevelt had no desire to add control over oil production to his powers. While he kept his options open, he disarmed the quarreling oil men with his friendliness. He met with a dissident group of inde-pendents who were arguing vigorously that there was no overproduc-tion within the United States, only unwarranted importation by major oil companies. They wanted not quotas but a ban on foreign oil. One of them has recalled:

The President reclined easily before us, his left elbow on the arm of his chair, his head leaning on his left hand with its long middle-finger stretched alongside and deeply imbedded in his left cheek. He was almost boyish as he asked us to reverse in our minds the ordinary con-ception that "one teacher usually teaches many pupils." Today, he laughingly declared, he was *the pupil* — we were the teachers . . .

We presented to him the several recommendations . . . We also spent about fifteen minutes in discussing our recommendation for a divorcement of oil pipe-lines from their present major oil company ownership.

Of all our recommendations, each of which we considered to be of major importance, Mr. Roosevelt, strangely enough, seemed in-trigued at the pipe-line divorcement suggestion and showed the greatest and most avid interest in our argument regarding the matter. To my surprise, on our concluding the pipe-line presentation, the President, with a rather grandiose, flourishing toss of his head, said, and very seriously, "I think you are right. I am going to recommend it." [11]

Roosevelt did indeed ultimately favor legislation to separate pipelines from other oil enterprises, as the group of independents wished, and did, as Landon's committee requested, support federal prohibition of "hot oil." But he was chary about asking governors to close down pro-duction of flush pools. When a newspaperman at a press conference asked him on March 31 if he would order pumping suspended, he re-plied that would be unconstitutional.

"How about a request — " the reporter persisted.

"A request?" parried Roosevelt. "I will have to consult with Thomas Jefferson as to how far — ." At this point the newspapermen broke into laughter.[12]

Although Roosevelt promised the oil men he would ask Congress for legislation, into early May, despite repeated pleas, he failed to act. On May 5, Ickes took into a cabinet meeting a telegram he had just received reporting the sale of crude oil in East Texas for 4 cents a barrel. Although the governor had declared martial law in the Texas fields to try to curtail production, oilmen were pumping double the quantity of crude oil that the Washington conferees had recommended. And the price was so low that a barrel of oil was selling for less than a bottle of the newly legal 3.2 percent beer.

Roosevelt, being buffeted by pressure against as well as for federal regulation, would only tell Ickes that he was preparing a letter to Congress. Finally, on May 20, 1933, Roosevelt did ask Congress for legislation, suggesting that it might incorporate regulation of the oil industry in its general industrial recovery program. "Hot oil" and pipeline provisions did constitute Section 9 of the National Industrial Recovery Act.[13]

The conflicting demands of major and independent oil producers, of importers and their beneficiaries in New England, and those who opposed both importation and restrictive quotas within the United States, created irreconcilable political problems for Roosevelt. He could not take any course of action that would please everyone, and gave the impression that in the end he acted only because the pressure for him to do something was considerably greater than the negative forces.

The quandary Roosevelt had faced over oil production was symptomatic of the problems that an overall NRA code system would produce. Inevitably it would favor some segments of any given industry at the expense of others. Nevertheless, by the beginning of May Roosevelt had decided definitely that he would undertake the experiment. In addressing 1,200 members of the United States Chamber of Commerce, he talked in general terms of the need for cooperation:

> You and I acknowledge the existence of unfair methods of competition, of cut-throat prices and of general chaos. You and I agree that this condition must be rectified and that order must be restored. The attainment of that objective depends upon your willingness to cooperate with one another to this end and also your willingness to cooperate with your Government.
>
> In almost every industry an overwhelming majority of the units of the industry are wholly willing to work together to prevent overproduction, to prevent unfair wages, to eliminate improper working conditions. In the past success in attaining these objectives has been prevented by a small minority of units in many industries. I can assure you that you will have the cooperation of your Government in bringing these minorities to understand that their unfair practices are contrary to a sound public policy.[14]

The business leaders cheered Roosevelt heartily; *Time* referred to the address as "a businessman's brief talk to businessmen."

Of the 49 speakers at the Chamber of Commerce convention, 27 favored a greater degree of government intervention, and only 9 were diehard exponents of laissez-faire. Henry I. Harriman, president of the chamber, declared, "I am confident that if trade associations in conference with labor and the Government were permitted to promulgate fair rules for industry . . . covering limitation of hours of operation, minimum pay (and) prices . . . and the setting up of reserves for accident, sickness and old age . . . the serious economic problems which confront us would soon vanish." The convention before adjourning adopted a resolution proposing that trade associations in each industry in cooperation with the government "be permitted to promulgate fair rules for industrial production and . . . to improve the status of labor." [15]

Almost simultaneously with this cheering news, on May 6, 1933, newspapers carried Secretary Ickes's indignant protest because when he opened ten sealed bids for 400,000 barrels of cement for Boulder Dam, he found them all to be an identical $1.29 a barrel, up 20 cents from March. He requested the Federal Trade Commission to investigate whether there had been illegal price-fixing. Thus thin from the outset was the line between cooperation and collusion.[16]

Even thinner were the promises in response to Roosevelt's request to the Chamber of Commerce members that they not cut wages, but rather increase them in conformity with rises in commodity prices. While Roosevelt was offering advantages to businessmen, in return he was expecting concessions from them. While he was offering more than President Hoover and the Republican party had been willing to grant, the numerous Republican favors to business in the 1920s had not required corresponding responsibilities. Many business leaders found the shift in governmental attitude difficult to accept, even though the potential favors were larger than those of the "New Era."

The labor provisions of the draft bill, Section 7(a), went further than the paternalistic protection of workers that Roosevelt had requested in his address to the businessmen — further than Roosevelt and his secretary of labor, with their progressive outlook, had really favored. The section included in indefinite form the fundamental stipulation "that employees shall have the right to organize and bargain collectively through representatives of their own choosing." This was what union leaders sought and were to obtain as their part of the overall bargain. Most employers, while disposed to make concessions to their workers, including wages and hours guarantees, were still true believers in nineteenth-century business fundamentalism, and would not willingly accept unions. When the National Association of Manufacturers learned what was in Section 7(a), it sent representatives to Roosevelt to seek modification. Roosevelt fell back on the device of insisting that Senator Wagner and the drafting committee, not he, the President, were preparing the legislation, and sent the delegation to them. Wagner would not budge.[17]

Simultaneously, Roosevelt engaged personally in the debate over the degree of public works spending that was to fuel the recovery scheme. Throughout the discussions, he leaned toward the conservative side, against quick, heavy spending. It was not that he and his advisers were ignorant of the embryo views that were to mature into Keynesian doctrine. One of the economists they most respected, Alexander Sachs, director of research for Lehman Brothers (who was to become chief of the Division of Economic Research and Planning of the NRA), repeatedly counseled Johnson and Moley that the fundamental spending thrust must come from the private sector of the economy, but nevertheless that government efforts were important. Sachs wrote Moley on April 15:

> I have converted into quantitative terms the significance of government spending on public works for direct and secondary employment along the lines of a formula that was developed by a Fellow of Kings College, Cambridge, now in this country, who, at the suggestion of his teacher, Mr. J. M. Keynes, came over to see me. For the United States, due to the bare subsistence level of the unemployed, the repercussions of additional employment would be considerably greater than has been calculated as true for England.
>
> My conviction . . . is that the combination of public works and independent coordinate action of industry with the aid of consumer credit released by them — which I have been discussing with officers of General Motors — should serve to turn the tide.[18]

General Johnson and the other draftsmen of the industrial recovery bill, with the exception of Budget Director Douglas, felt that public works spending was essential to generate new buying power. Otherwise the wage increases, Johnson has pointed out, would lead to raising the prices of goods to consumers without lifting consumer purchasing power. The result would be an ultimate drop in consumption, manufacture, and employment. "There is no doubt in the world that there is much here to give us pause," Johnson wrote two years later. "We relied, however, on [the Public Works Administration] to activate the heavy industries at once and thus increase the *total number of available purchasers*." *

---

* Johnson went on to say, "We relied on AAA to increase farm purchasing immediately and thus still further add to the *number of purchasers*. These added to NRA additions would so far increase *volume* that we thought (and I still think)

Yet President Roosevelt's approach to public works continued to be that of the frugal builder whom only political exigencies could push toward what he seemed to regard as waste of the national patrimony. The new solicitor of the Department of Labor, Charles Wyzanski, at that time a quite conservative young man, fresh from serving as clerk to Judge Learned Hand, was rather awe-stricken and heartened by Roosevelt's performance at a key conference. Since Frances Perkins had commissioned Wyzanski to redraft the public works bill, at Ickes's suggestion he accompanied them to a meeting of the subcommittee of the cabinet on April 29, which assembled upstairs in the White House:

> In a few minutes the President was ready to see us in another room, the one that he has fitted up with pictures of sailing vessels etc. . . .
>
> The conversation lasted for two hours and a half. The President began by reading aloud my draft of the bill. You can imagine how little I know about grants or loans to public works projects and the inauguration of an Administration of Public Works, so you understand that my draft was nothing more than a rehash of other bills such as Senator Wagner's. The bill called for 5 *billion* dollars in *grants* to public bodies. Of course Miss P was all for it, since she is heart-and-soul for some immediate relief. (I suspect that she has nothing like so good a head as she ought to have.) Wallace was all for the proposition too, although he wondered whether subsidies should not be to private enterprises not of a public nature, since it was important to let factory workers work in factories not on buildings. Wallace is quite definitely a Western liberal. The President handled the situation excellently. He had Douglas talk about the budget. — Douglas is charming, has real brains and is the soundest man I've met in Washington. I think that he is first rate. Then the President asked to see a list of the proposed projects. He took the New York part, went through the whole list, commented on each project and showed a remarkable knowledge of every single item. It was a masterly demonstration, and he convinced everyone how unsound most of the projects were. This graphic dealing with particular projects and his informal way of calling the male members of the cabinet by their first names won the day. He reduced the proposed expenditure to 1 billion, emphasized that the Public Works Administrator should have power to lend as well as grant, asked to have provisions covering slum clearance projects, explained that he favored public works which (1) are useful to a large number of persons, (2) offered opportunity for increased employment, (3) are capable of completion in a short time, (4) allow a larger expenditure for services than for goods and (5) are as near as possible self-liquidating.
>
> I felt much greater confidence in the President than I had expected and Douglas was the real back bone of the conference. I'll bet that some day he becomes one of the great leaders of the country.[20]

the increased labor cost could be absorbed without much increase in price. The President specifically asked industry to take this gamble." [19]

Secretary Ickes, with less admiration noted in his diary that he had never seen the President so critical and perhaps captious. He felt a bit sorry for Miss Perkins, although she had handled herself capably, and wondered if the President was feeling nerve strain from the extra burden of conferences with foreign dignitaries he had been carrying.[21]

By the time the bill was ready for Congress, Roosevelt capitulated on public works, probably out of need for political compromise rather than economic conviction. He accepted an overall figure that the Bureau of the Budget experts thought could be financed and that Wagner set as encompassing available projects — a total of $3.3 billion.

It included $2.75 billion for the projects the Construction Council and Committee of Architects had recommended, even though Roosevelt had questioned the utility of part of the list. It also provided an item which must have been far more palatable to Roosevelt, $238 million for naval construction. Through this specification, he was able to start building the navy toward the strength allowed by the Treaty of London of 1930 without pushing a special bill through Congress or upsetting the balance of his "regular budget." [22]

The scheme of assigning emergency public works money to shipbuilding did not originate with Roosevelt. The navy had already obtained $15 million from Hoover's relief funds for ships and use in shore establishments. Soon after Roosevelt's election, the Navy Department supplied Carl Vinson, chairman of the House Naval Affairs Committee, with data on the way ship-building could stimulate the national economy. Vinson brought the arguments and figures to bear upon the President-elect. Through relief funds the navy would enable shipyards that would otherwise slow down to continue operations and rapidly spend considerable sums on both labor and materials. It would augment substantially the aid to seaboard areas, especially New England, that would not benefit much from dam-building and other public works proposals. Thus Roosevelt, through an expedient as simple as including a few phrases in the public works section of the recovery bill, repeating the formula of 1932 legislation, could begin building the new navy he believed the nation needed, stimulate recovery, and make more certain that representatives and senators with navy yards and private shipyards in their districts would vote for the recovery bill. The shipbuilding clause that Johnson inserted into his original recovery bill draft survived unquestioned into the final bill. Indeed, two weeks before the bill went to Congress, Secretary of the Navy Swanson announced after conferring with Roosevelt that the public works program would include an immediate $46 million, and $230 million over five years to construct thirty new warships: twenty destroyers, five light cruisers, four submarines, and one aircraft carrier.[23]

One acute quandary remained to occupy Roosevelt and his advisers for some days. What sort of taxes should he ask Congress to vote in order to raise an extra $220 million per year to pay interest on the emergency indebtedness? His assumption, with which Douglas had come to agree, was that the heavy borrowing for public works would not imperil the credit of the government providing taxes covered the interest. Yet here again, Roosevelt would have to make a recommendation both deflationary and unpopular. He debated what sort of tax it should be. One of the possibilities was a "breakfast tax," on tea and coffee. Again and again, deliberations came back to the perennial proposal, a manufacturer's sales tax, which this time would bear a more glamorous name, "re-employment tax." Several evenings Roosevelt debated the pros and cons of the sales tax with congressional leaders. Representative Doughton, chairman of the Ways and Means Committee, who the previous year had led the successful congressional sales tax revolt against President Hoover, was loyal enough to say only to newspapermen that he "reserved comment." The sales tax revolt had been uncomfortably recent, and Roosevelt himself had been responsible for killing a sales tax proposal during the lame duck Congress. The tax was not likely to be any more popular in May 1933, yet when Roosevelt returned on May 14 from a cruise on the Potomac, he sent word he favored it.[24]

At this point the congressional leaders rendered Roosevelt one of their most effective services of the session; they persuaded him to leave the question of taxes to them.* To be sure, they conceded to him, he could obtain the "re-employment tax," but only if he led a personal fight for it. But if he made no specific tax recommendations, they would obtain new levies for him.[25]

On May 17, Roosevelt sent a message to Congress recommending a three-part bill: the NRA code scheme, the $3.3 billion public works program, and a blank section for Congress to fill in with $220 million in new taxes to service the borrowing for public works.[26]

The nation was amply prepared for the recovery measure, which newspapers had been predicting with quite accurate details since mid-April. In his second Fireside Chat of May 7, 1933, Roosevelt himself set forth clearly the premises and principles:

> It is wholly wrong to call the measures that we have taken Government control of farming, industry, and transportation. It is rather a partnership between Government and farming and industry and transportation, not partnership in profits, for the profits still go to the citizens, but rather a partnership in planning, and a partnership to see that the plans are carried out.

* The leaders were Speaker Rainey and Representatives Joseph Byrns and Doughton; Senators Robinson, Harrison, and Reed.

Let me illustrate with an example. Take the cotton-goods industry. It is probably true that 90 per cent of the cotton manufacturers would agree to eliminate starvation wages, would agree to stop long hours of employment, would agree to stop child labor, would agree to prevent an overproduction that would result in unsalable surpluses. But, what good is such an agreement if the other 10 per cent of cotton manufacturers pay starvation wages, require long hours, employ children in their mills and turn out burdensome surpluses? The unfair 10 percent could produce goods so cheaply that the fair 90 percent would be compelled to meet the unfair conditions. Here is where the Government comes in. Government ought to have the right and will have the right, after surveying and planning for an industry, to prevent, with the assistance of the overwhelming majority of that industry, unfair practices and to enforce this agreement by the authority of Government. The so-called anti-trust laws were intended to prevent the creation of monopolies and to forbid unreasonable profits to those monopolies. That purpose of the anti-trust laws must be continued, but these laws were never intended to encourage the kind of unfair competition that results in long hours, starvation wages and overproduction.[27]

As Roosevelt worked on the Fireside Chat with Moley, the section on partnership between government and the economy was such a sharp departure from the Wilsonian concepts that Moley felt Roosevelt should make absolutely certain he wished to make the commitment. As had been his habit, he informed Roosevelt where he himself stood, then reviewed the conflicting 1912 views of Theodore Roosevelt and Wilson. "You realize then," Moley concluded, "that you're taking an enormous step away from the philosophy of equalitarianism and laissez-faire?"

Moley has recalled: "F.D.R. looked graver than he had been at any moment since the night before his inauguration. And then, when he had been silent a few minutes, he said, 'If that philosophy hadn't proved to be bankrupt, Herbert Hoover would be sitting here right now. I never felt surer of anything in my life than I do of the soundness of this passage.'"

Writing seven years later, after his break with Roosevelt, Moley ruefully added: "It was a statement I was to recall many times as I watched his administration lurch between the philosophy of controlling bigness and the philosophy of destroying bigness, between the belief in a partnership between government and industry and the belief in trust busting." [28]

Indeed, Roosevelt was not choosing between two clear-cut ideologies, but rather employing what in his mind were interrelated means toward the end of recovery. Inconsistencies and conflicting cross-currents in the recovery bill, and indeed in his larger program, were not a major concern. He was being innovative when he talked of a peacetime partnership between government and the economy, but he by no means thought of himself as exclusively undertaking economic planning. It was to be one more of the numerous experiments he was establishing in the New Deal laboratory.

CHAPTER XXVI

Enacting the Final Measures

I want to convey . . . my thanks for making possible
. . . a more sincere and whole-hearted cooperation between the legislative and executive branches . . . than
has been witnessed by the American people in many a
long year.
— FDR TO CONGRESS, *June 16, 1933.*[1]

In a final hectic, sweltering month, between mid-May and mid-June
1933, Congress enacted the remainder of the Roosevelt program and
finally went home. Roosevelt bade them farewell with a letter thanking
them for their cooperation which, coming at the rancorous close of the
session, seemed not quite candid. When a few vacation days had passed,
and both he and the members of Congress became a good bit cooler
both in body and spirit, the message seemed more accurate. For indeed, that spring both in the White House and at the Capitol there had
been a spirit of cooperation and compromise and a willingness to innovate that helped make the special session of the Seventy-third Congress
one of the most fruitful in the nation's history.

The last weeks were so difficult that its exhausted members would
have scoffed in derision if they had been accused of operating as a
rubber stamp to approve Roosevelt proposals. The sporadic charges,
usually leveled against the House, only with the passage of time grew
into the standard critical stereotype of the "hundred days" Congress.
As a matter of fact, during the disorderly, drawn-out conclusion of the
session, newspapers were full of colorful reports, describing the Senate
as being on the brink of revolt and far from acquiescent. As economic
indices turned upward, the national mood moved toward greater caution, perhaps even a touch of skepticism. More and more senators began
to assert their basic independence and conservatism. Roosevelt had
reason to ram through his final measures before the slight trend toward
reaction swelled into a tide. There was the danger that the handful of
representatives and senators who had been crying communism and voting
against White House measures since March might increase into a majority. In response, Roosevelt had to intensify his tactics of cajolery

and to generate public enthusiasms. His Fireside Chat of May 7, a warm, friendly explanation of what he was trying to achieve and a reassurance that nothing frightening or totalitarian was being planned, was effective. Congressional support continued, but it was no longer certain. The normally testy and obstructionist Republican Senator Hiram Johnson, whom Roosevelt had won so wholeheartedly to the New Deal, in his weekly letters home accurately delineated the mixed feelings of a large part of his colleagues by mid-April:

> We're fiddling along with more legislation than any one man or any legislative body can accurately digest. I am still in the mood of trying anything that may be suggested, and the country is still in the mood, in my opinion, of following Roosevelt in anything he desires. He is likely, however, to come a cropper at any time. I hope not, but he is attempting so much that all can not succeed. The Farm Bill we have been discussing is really the most bizarre thing that was ever suggested to a set of sentient beings. If it were not for the feeling that most of us have toward the President, it would not have a corporal's guard supporting it in the Senate.[2]

Nothing could stop the farm bill, which had passed both houses before the end of April and soon received final approval.

Republican leaders and Democratic dissidents sought other measures to oppose, ones less essential in the emergency, to which Roosevelt would have more difficulty in rallying support. By early May, obstructionists had identified several of these, and were falling back upon economic nationalism as their defensible line. It was a shrewd strategy, since Roosevelt was depending upon the votes of many of the most stalwart economic nationalists, like Hiram Johnson, even while in economic matters he was moving in both nationalist and internationalist directions. Hence Roosevelt's solicitude toward Hiram Johnson's interest in protecting holders of defaulted foreign bonds. At lunch on May 15, at Howe's suggestion Roosevelt called up Rayburn and asked him to do something about Johnson's proposal. After Roosevelt hung up, Howe suggested, "Now if you really want to make Hiram Johnson happy, call him up and tell him what you told Congressman Rayburn." Roosevelt did so; it was one of many small maneuvers that spring through which he retained Johnson's loyalty.[3]

Opponents in Congress organized to try to block the President from winning permission to scale down the war debts or negotiate lower tariff rates — powers which they expected he would request to strengthen the American bargaining position at the World Economic Conference. One Republican spokesman, who asked the reporter not to use his name, vowed that the Republicans would throw every impediment possible in the way of debt and tariff authorizations and force

Congress to remain in session until late summer. On debts, he said, the Republicans would have help from Senator Ham Lewis of Illinois and that redoubtable filibusterer, Huey Long. Democratic leaders lent some credence to this talk by predicting that there would be a stiffer fight to obtain whatever was not of an emergency nature, including Senator Glass's banking legislation, which was not on Roosevelt's legislative agenda, and approval of the St. Lawrence Waterway treaty, which Roosevelt had always strongly favored.[4]

For several days the Republican offensive against Roosevelt on the debts issued continued. It was one way in which they could win Democratic allies. Some congressmen, according to Arthur Krock, expressed fear that Roosevelt's announced Fireside Chat of May 7 would focus on debt revision, even though Roosevelt himself was letting it be known that he would defer a debts message, that he thought the nation must first be reeducated. Speaker Rainey was so alarmed by the rumors that he announced there was not the slightest chance Roosevelt would cancel the debts, then the next day declared emphatically:[5]

> All talk about Democratic leaders in Congress being ready to "call the hand" of the President, of warning him that he is committing "political suicide," smacks very much of political propaganda. The President has never suggested the cancellation or reduction of these debts with any member or members of the House, and I am certain this is also true of the Senate. . . .
>
> We hear it solemnly whispered about that if the President sends a message asking authority to cancel or reduce the debts a storm in Congress will follow. That's true, just as would be the case if President Roosevelt asked for authority to give Alaska back to Russia or to surrender to some other power control of the Panama Canal.[6]

Nevertheless, Krock returned to the theme in the *New York Times*, suggesting that the majority of leaders expected Roosevelt to appear before a joint session of Congress to ask authority over the war debts as a means of guaranteeing success in the World Economic Conference. Roosevelt responded off the record at his press conference by urging newspapermen not to be stampeded by news coming from London of impending debt rearrangements. When one of the reporters suggested that the public might be more stampeded by headlines on stories from Washington, and asked Roosevelt to clear it up, the President resorted to satire:

> I have forgotten which story it was this morning, but one of the stories — I guess it was the Times [laughter]. Oh, I know, it was Arthur's story. . . .
>
> Why, he talked to — I wish they would put the names down, it would be so much clearer. He says that an Administration leader today — oh,

come on and tell me what his name is — and then a whole paragraph about the impression the Administration leader is supposed to have conveyed. Then he goes on to say that an Administration leader of almost equal rank had another idea and then he gives another paragraph.

For example, there was a story — what was it, three weeks or a month ago — that said there was a possibility that I would send a message to the Congress on debts. Now, I suppose I could have stopped it by saying there is also a possibility that I will send no message to the Congress on debts. Well, that is still the situation. I don't know. I don't know any more than you do whether I will send a message or, if I did send a message, what would be in it. Now, that is literally true, I don't know.[7]

What Roosevelt was learning was how high feelings of economic nationalism were swelling. During the weeks ahead, as he labored to obtain enactment of major legislation, he kept deferring the matter of debts, and showed signs of irritation when newspapers engaged in speculation about his plans. On May 31, when reporters asked him if they could use as background his statement that there was no change in the debt situation, he agreed, then went on rather tartly:

Of course, it depends a little bit on how you use it for background. Here is a story that says, here is the lead [reading from the New York Times, May 31, 1933]: "The White House refused to concede publicly that there had been any definite program adopted by President Roosevelt for dealing with the war debt problem." . . . It is [like] a story one day that the President had murdered his own grandmother and the next day saying that President had refused to concede that he had murdered his own grandmother [laughter]. That is not clean ball.[8]

In the end, Roosevelt did not send a message on debts to Congress.

The tariff was a more vital and complex matter, since it was avowedly on Roosevelt's legislative agenda. In his message to Congress of April 3, asking for farm mortgage legislation, he had appended at the end, "Also, I shall ask the Congress for legislation enabling us to initiate practical reciprocal tariff agreements to break through trade barriers and establish foreign markets for farm and industrial products." The lowering of tariffs was the first priority in Secretary Hull's thinking, and had been much involved in Roosevelt's discussions with foreign delegations preparatory to the World Economic Conference. On the other hand, Moley and others of the planners felt that economic rehabilitation could take place only behind tariff barriers to keep out imports that would undercut American prices and wages. A resurgence of this classic sentiment was sweeping Congress as it prepared to consider the economic recovery legislation. Day by day it became politically more difficult for Roosevelt to move with Senator Wagner and Baruch's devotees toward economic nationalism and with Secretary Hull, Lewis Douglas, Warburg, and the old-fashioned free-traders toward economic international-ism. Yet Roosevelt slowly worked toward his tariff request to Congress. After the introduction of the industrial recovery bill, Secretary Hull said that only one more conference with Roosevelt would be needed to perfect the tariff bill. Speaker Rainey explained that it would be only a simple joint resolution to authorize the negotiation of reciprocal agree-ments.[9]

At the end of May, Roosevelt admitted off the record at a press conference, "I still have not made up my mind definitely." He said he was working on a complicated tariff proposal, to authorize possible increases and decreases during the summer and fall before Congress returned. The first draft had been sixteen or seventeen pages long; he had boiled it down to three and a half pages, and hoped to reduce it to a page and a half. "I want to make it simple and as little controversial as possible," he explained: "If I can get something . . . that there won't be very much controversy about, not more than one day's debate . . . I will send it up . . . [W]hen I get it down, I am going to talk to the leaders of both Parties up there and see whether they like it." [10]

That was as far as Roosevelt carried the tariff question. On June 9, with the senators becoming increasingly refractory, he told news-papermen — still off the record — that he was not going to send Congress a tariff message. There was still the right under existing law, he had decided, for increases or decreases through Executive Order if the Tariff commission would recommend them. Besides, it would take some months to work out a reciprocal trade agreement, which would have to go to Congress for approval in January anyway. Therefore, he reasoned, there would be little loss in time. By this point, Hull had left for London and could not press Roosevelt for one more item of legislation that might delay adjournment of Congress.

"Congress would never give me complete authority to write tariff schedules," Roosevelt remarked.

"Well," a newspaperman retorted, "they have given you everything else." [11]

Roosevelt was equally pragmatic in dealing with the ratification of the St. Lawrence Waterway treaty. Senators from the Great Lakes area strongly favored it, but those from eastern seaboard areas were equally firm in their opposition. Eight midwestern governors urged Roosevelt to place it upon his agenda; Senators La Follette of Wisconsin, Arthur Vandenberg of Michigan, and others added their pleas, telling him they could muster a two-thirds majority for the treaty. When reporters queried him on May 24, he told them candidly (not for publication):

[I]t presents really a question of fact as to whether they are right in saying they have the votes for it. . . . There is no question about my being for the St. Lawrence Treaty and if we have the votes for it, it means cloture in the Senate. I would like to see it go through now. On the other hand, if it means two weeks of debate with the question of whether it goes through in the end in doubt, I think it better not to take it up.[12]

Roosevelt went no further than to send La Follette a letter on June 8, saying that he favored the St. Lawrence treaty and that construction of the waterway could become an essential component of the public works program. He thus placed the onus for ratification upon La Follette; as Roosevelt had suspected, La Follette could not persuade Senate leaders to bring the treaty to the floor for a vote.[13]

Toward another impending congressional action, the Glass-Steagall banking bill, Roosevelt employed similar cautious tactics to avoid being caught in a bitter contention among Democrats. It was a ramification of the old quarrel between central and small-town bankers, between Wall Street and the grass roots. Senator Glass, who considered himself the father of the Federal Reserve System, wished to bring into it in one way or another the numerous state banks operating under forty-eight different sets of regulations, most of them laxer than federal law. Representative Henry B. Steagall of Alabama, chairman of the House Banking and Currency Committee, championed the state bankers, determined to maintain their competitive advantage, even though their rate of failure had been disproportionately high. In both houses, most Democrats from the South and the West opposed extending the Federal Reserve controls, just as they fought the extension of chain stores within their states. They were defenders of the local banker and merchant against outside interference. Huey Long had been their most vociferous spokesman, filibustering the Glass bill to death in the lame duck session.[14]

As for Roosevelt, on the one hand he continued his respectful obeisance toward the famous Glass, even though Glass was already fulminating against several facets of the New Deal program. On the other, he delayed for weeks taking a stand on banking legislation. "You cannot say that we are for or against any one feature of the Banking Bill," he remarked on April 12, "because we have not got there yet." [15]

Roosevelt did not want to offend either of the contending Democratic forces, nor did he agree entirely with either. He preferred, like Glass, greater Federal Reserve control over all banking, a prime means of augmenting the safety of banks. On the other hand, while Glass insisted that the Federal Reserve System should be responsible to the banks and free from political interference, Roosevelt sought Treasury control. The issue of executive control was to grow into major proportions by 1935.

The major quarrel over banking between Roosevelt and Congress in

May and June 1933 was an ironic one. Various of the congressional conservatives demanded, while Roosevelt and Glass fought, a federal deposit insurance system. The President continued to insist it was impractical. Representative Steagall, and behind the scenes, Vice President Garner, were prime movers for deposit insurance. The ordinarily cautious Jesse Jones of the RFC abetted them, and the Republican Senator Vandenberg was their instrument.

On the day before inauguration, Garner had urged Roosevelt to give his assent to the Steagall deposit insurance bill, which had passed the House and was in Senate committee. He assured Roosevelt the Senate would pass it and President Hoover sign it. Roosevelt protested that it wouldn't work, that the weak banks would pull down the strong ones. After the banking holiday, Jones informed Garner that he had found in conversation with Vandenberg that he favored deposit insurance. While he was presiding over the Senate on May 19, Garner arranged with Vandenberg to introduce an amendment to the Glass bill, assuring him Glass would not fight it too hard. By a lopsided margin the Senate immediately adopted the Vandenberg amendment, temporarily insuring bank deposits up to $2,500.[16]

At a cabinet meeting on May 23, Roosevelt expressed his dismay over both the Glass and Steagall bills, which he considered to contain several unsatisfactory provisions, especially their guarantees of deposits. He hoped through parliamentary tactics to defeat them, but events dictated otherwise. Perhaps the prime factor was the popularity of the sensational Senate hearings probing into the workings of the House of Morgan, which Roosevelt himself had encouraged. His intention had been to prepare the way for firmer regulation of private banking, but one result was that on May 25, the Senate, reacting in part to public sentiment, by a voice vote passed the Glass bill, which would require private bankers either to stop accepting deposits or to leave the securities business. Although Roosevelt continued to encourage the investigation of private bankers, he persisted in fighting the provision for deposit insurance in the Glass and Steagall bills. When a Senate-House committee met to reconcile differences between the two houses on the bills, he threatened a veto unless they removed deposit insurance. The committee refused.[17]

Accepting the inevitable, Roosevelt wrote privately, "There seems to be no question that we shall have some form of bank insurance. I am trying to have it made as sound as possible." Already Roosevelt had been moving in that direction. On June 1 he met with both Glass and Steagall, together with his new undersecretary of the treasury, Dean Acheson, the new governor of the Federal Reserve Board, Eugene Black, and Comptroller of the Currency J. F. T. O'Connor. Both Glass and

Acheson were opposed to deposit insurance, but Glass was forced to accept it, and thus retain the support of many small bankers, or see his entire bill again fail. Consequently, Glass joined with Roosevelt in seeking a means of making it sound. Besides, Glass's pride was somewhat offended by the sheaves of form telegrams opposing deposit insurance that the American Bankers' Association was inspiring. "I have been in Congress thirty-two years," Glass complained (according to O'Connor), "and [have] never known bankers to do anything but protest [against] any legislation."

The conferees debated where to obtain an insurance fund to back the system. Governor Black objected to providing $150 million from the Federal Reserve. Roosevelt proposed raising money by taxing depositors somewhere between $\frac{1}{4}$ and $\frac{1}{16}$ of 1 percent. "I am interested," he said, "in establishing the principle of [the depositor] paying something." The proposal ultimately died, since no one but Roosevelt and O'Connor favored it.[18]

Subsequently Roosevelt assented to the use of deposit insurance coverage as a device to lure state banks into the Federal Reserve System. Day by day he worked toward decisions. O'Connor recorded the process in his diary:

> June 6, 1933 . . . I told the Pres. we should not compel state banks to join the Fed Reserve in order to get insurance. He said new amen[dment] now in conference. He said about 5,000 state banks would ultimately be eliminated. Jim Farley was present part of the time. . . .
>
> June 7. Went to White House with M. H. McIntyre. — the President was shaving. Went back to his office and discussed the Insurance feature of the Glass bill. the Pres. agreed that a reasonable time should be given for State banks to qualify in Federal system. . . . Conference (at 12) with Pres. [,] Woodin, Glass, Acheson, Gov Black and myself. We agreed on giving State banks until Jan 1 –'36 to qualify under Fed Res. Acheson suggested delay. I told meeting we must act — people were impatient and demanded security on deposits. . . .[19]

Nonetheless, the Glass-Steagall bill in its final form probably would not have passed had not other differences with Roosevelt kept Congress into session for some days extra. In the final rush, the banking bill as it had come back from conference went through the House by a vote of 262 to 19, and the Senate by acclamation. Roosevelt accepted the measure in good grace. He telephoned Glass his congratulations, saying that it was the best banking legislation since the Federal Reserve Act. When he signed it on June 16, he remarked, "This bill has more lives than a cat." [20]

In retrospect, Roosevelt did well to accept his defeat with grace. The

Banking Act of 1933, because it created the Federal Deposit Insurance Corporation, was one of the major achievements of the spring.* It was generally regarded as one of the New Deal reforms, and the President reaped political credit for it.

Into the latter part of May, Roosevelt was not meeting serious difficulties as he reaped a large part of his legislative harvest. On May 12, Congress gave final approval to both the farm bill and the emergency relief bill; on May 18, to the TVA; and on May 27, to the securities bill. There remained only the bills to rescue railroads and small homeowners, and, Roosevelt's chief concern, the recovery measure.

At first there was every indication that the recovery bill could proceed through both houses without much difficulty. Roosevelt had helped prepare the nation for it through the trial balloons in the press and his address to the Chamber of Commerce and Fireside Chat. The bill was such an omnibus structure, offering so much to several pressure groups and constituencies, that it seemed assured of far more than majority support in Congress. Newspapers reported that labor and capital joined in hailing the bill.

There were signs that some business lobbyists and congressmen would object to the concessions to labor. While the director of the Steel Founders' Society of America said, "Now the trade associations are getting the green light," others were alarmed that labor also was getting a green light. Harriman of the Chamber of Commerce, standing by his alliance with the administration, did not publicly assail the labor provisions. Indeed, Harriman predicted that within six months after the act went into effect the wages of at least ten million workers would increase. It would be, said Harriman, the "Magna Charta of industry and labor." On the other hand, Robert L. Lund of the National Association of Manufacturers, commenting that "no legislation has carried such possibilities of good and evil," warned that the labor provisions might "destroy the welfare organizations for sickness insurance, group life insurance, and such things now common in industry, and might further serve to force employers to deal with communistic or racketeering organizations." [22]

There were also numerous indications in the press that recovery was coming. The upturn was in part a response to Roosevelt's inflationary moves and in some measure in anticipation of the NRA. Early in the month, reports from Buffalo, Chicago, and Los Angeles had all indicated business improvements. Roosevelt's message proposing the NRA led brokers to urge their clients to reinvest in industrial stocks and bonds;

---

* The divorcing of private investment bankers from deposit banking led to great changes in the securities markets, but, Vincent P. Carosso suggests, "reduced drastically the amount of capital available to float new issues." [21]

businessmen began to place orders for goods and manufacturers to increase production. They were acting in the belief that the depression would soon be over, and some were trying to beat the anticipated rises in labor costs and prices. An NRA boomlet was in the making. A *New York Times* headline four days after the bill reached Congress proclaimed, "Recovery Signs Over Nation Grow." Yet economic improvement could make both businessmen and some congressmen less certain the country needed the recovery bill. Ernest K. Lindley wrote later in the year: "In two weeks the revolt, in business and in the Senate, became formidable. . . . The psychology of employers underwent a sudden and wondrous change. Laissez-faire boldly raised its voice. Business and banking pundits proclaimed the arrival of recovery from 'natural causes.' "[23]

Roosevelt was less fearful of effects upon Congress than that the boom might develop too rapidly and capsize into a recession. At lunch on May 22, when Morgenthau showed Roosevelt his business chart, the President was delighted to see that construction was increasing, but when he looked at the steel activity chart he exclaimed, "That is going up too fast." A week later at another lunch with Morgenthau and Baruch he set forth his mild inflationary views, then said, "I do not want to see the stock market go up too fast." The market did go up with spectacular speed; between April 1 and June 1, the value of stocks rose 64.8 percent. As stocks rose the pressure upon Congress declined.[24]

Humid summer heat had returned to Washington, adding to the discomfort of fatigued congressmen; their tempers grew short. With impatient political lieutenants plaguing them for jobs, they became increasingly irritated over Roosevelt's tactic of withholding most patronage until the session was over, meanwhile allowing only a trickle of appointments. These few had to carry Farley's approval. Further, in filling some major positions, Roosevelt had not consulted senators from the appointee's state. "Cotton Ed" Smith complained to Morgenthau that Hoover had treated him better than Roosevelt. "Mark you, Morgenthau," he stormed, "if they do not change their method of distributing patronage the President will soon have a revolution on his hands." In the House, the day after Roosevelt sent his NRA message the Democrats for the first time openly attacked him for the delay in providing offices. An Arkansas representative on the patronage committee complained that instead of assets the House Democrats were receiving only liabilities — and himself received a round of applause.[25]

Nevertheless, for the first few days the recovery bill fared well. There was still enough aura surrounding Roosevelt for a Texas congressman to orate, "This is the President's special session of Congress. He is the Moses who is leading us out of the wilderness." Roosevelt tried to reinforce confidence by letting word leak from the White House that General Johnson would be administrator of the bill. That same day Roosevelt officially appointed Harry Hopkins to be relief administrator and the conservative Krock wrote a column for the *New York Times* hailing the President for bypassing the professors when he chose those who were to run his programs, relying instead upon the practical men like Johnson and Hopkins.* It was not a view of Hopkins that Krock would always hold. The point Krock made was an important one, that Roosevelt's selection "served further to persuade those who have feared the ascendancy of educators in this administration that the President is drawing a distinction between planners and executives." [26]

There was some grumbling in the House because Roosevelt had left to Congress the unpleasant task of deciding upon new taxes to fund the $3.3 billion loan for public works, but on the other hand, the discussion over taxes so occupied the representatives that they offered little other objection to the bill. Director of the Budget Douglas submitted to the House Ways and Means Committee four possible tax programs. A general manufacturers' sales tax of either $1\frac{1}{8}$ percent or $1\frac{1}{5}$ percent headed Douglas's proposals, and he gave the impression that it was the one the administration preferred. Doughton's committee firmly rejected the sales tax, and turning to the other three plans, selected from them an increase in the normal income tax rates, the extension of these rates to corporate dividends (which had been exempt), and an increase in the gasoline tax. [27]

The proposed increase in taxation led to minor opposition in the House. The proposal came in the same days that the Senate hearings were publicizing that J. P. Morgan and his partners, through claims for capital losses spread out over the depression years 1931 and 1932, were able to avoid all income taxes. They would still be able to apply against 1933 taxes what remained of these capital losses. It also became public knowledge that the junior partners in the firm had been receiving a minimum of $100,000 a year. Why, protested indignant congressmen of both parties, should citizens of small means be forced to pay higher taxes when the Morgan partners were able to avoid all taxes? The opposition was so widespread that the Democratic leaders succeeded only by a close majority of 213 to 194 in enacting the special rule for the speedy consideration of the recovery bill. Roosevelt was stirred into action and conferred with Secretary of the Treasury Woodin and Undersecretary Acheson on ways to plug the revenue leaks. Administration leaders in the House agreed to include in the bill restrictions

---

* Krock failed to note Roosevelt's appointment, also that same day, of the president of Antioch College, Arthur E. Morgan, to be chairman of the Tennessee Valley Authority, but did cite Peek, Eastman, Fechner, and Lewis Douglas.

upon tax deductions through capital losses. As finally enacted, it limited claims to the year in which the losses had been incurred.[28]

There was no serious clamor against the taxes on the grounds that they would be one more deflationary force in that spring when the chief problem was to increase the buying power of American consumers. Only later would economists emphasize that factor.

There was also one final skirmish on the manufacturers' sales tax which forced Roosevelt to switch back to his January position of un-equivocal opposition. Republicans in the House, looking for an issue with which to gain political leverage, joined with some Democrats in pushing for the tax. A Democrat, John W. McCormack of Massachusetts, proposed a tax of 2.5 percent, but Senator James Byrnes, acting as liaison with the White House, met with Roosevelt, then announced that he was sure Congress would not enact a sales tax in any form. McCormack's proposal was defeated, and the other tax increases voted.

There were also charges that the recovery bill was unconstitutional. Strangely enough, considering the mildness of the enforcement provisions, both proponents and opponents joined in the view that it would give the President dictatorial powers. The chairman of the House Rules Committee said it would make the President for the time being a benign dictator. Representative Beck responded, "You might as well talk of a peaceful murderer," and went on to characterize the public works appropriation as "the thirty pieces of silver by which the liberties of the American people are to be delivered." The opposition was not vehement; even Beck conceded "the charming personality and high motives of the President of the United States." When the vote on the recovery bill came in the House on May 26, it passed 323 to 76.[29]

Serious trouble developed in the Senate where for too long Roosevelt had been trying, in the view of some members of that highly independent body, to obtain rather too much too precipitately. Hiram Johnson observed to his sons on June 4:

> We're going at top speed in order to adjourn early. This adjournment has been fixed tentatively for Saturday next. I am inclined to think we'll be driven to it. . . . Roosevelt wants the Congress out of the way. He is losing a little of his astounding and remarkable poise, and I rather think a bit of his extreme good nature. There is a revolt in the air in the Congress, too. Men have followed him upstairs without question or criticism. Some individuals have been mute concerning their most cherished ideas in order that they might contribute what little they could in aid of the President's efforts in this economic crisis. These men have about reached the limit of their endurance. Roosevelt, clever as he is, senses that fact, and before there is an actual break, he wishes us out of the way. I think he is wise in his decision.[30]

Already, by the end of May, several senators were making the charge against Roosevelt that he was obtaining too much power, applying the accusation first to cuts in veterans' benefits and extending it to the recovery bill. Before they were through they had inflicted a stinging defeat upon the President and threatened his recovery program.

"How much longer are we going to continue this delegation of power?" declaimed Senator Lester J. Dickinson of Iowa, the Republican keynoter of 1932, when the Senate began debating veterans' affairs again on May 31. Borah followed in like vein, saying that he was not making a personal attack upon Roosevelt, but "no one man can execute all the powers we have given to him." [31]

How far Roosevelt's authority over veterans' pensions fell short of making him a dictator became clear before the middle of June 1933. Through that spring, since the passage of the Economy Act, the political forces that the organized veterans could enlist in their behalf recouped strength. The veterans' lobbyists had lost an opening battle with Roosevelt, not the war. During the struggle over the economy bill, Colonel John T. Taylor, chief lobbyist for the American Legion, had sent a warning to each legislator: "The members of Congress might transfer their authority to the Executive, but they cannot transfer the tremendous responsibility that will rest upon them for the results of their action." With congressional elections due again in 1934, many congressmen who had voted for economy in March in subsequent months were ready to veer back toward support of the veterans. The pressure for economy was momentary; the barrage upon behalf of the veterans continued through the spring.[32]

When President Roosevelt on April 1, 1933, announced the new regulations for veterans' pensions that Douglas and General Hines had worked out, he asserted that he did not want any veteran to feel that he was being singled out to make sacrifices, rather that every department and agency of the government was equally contributing. But the changes were even more drastic than the American Legion had expected. Under a new, more equitable, and simple rating of disabilities, some pensions increased and others lowered. Most pensions for non-service-connected disability were dropped, except for those totally disabled, and for aged veterans of the Spanish-American War. Altogether the reductions increased from the estimated $383 to $460 million.[33]

Pensioners, frightened by the lobbyists' warning that disabled veterans would receive only 30 percent of their previous stipends, appealed to Congress and Roosevelt. Roy Roberts of the *Kansas City Star* sent word to Stephen Early that the cuts in pensions of men that were actually wounded or gassed overseas were creating a furor among veterans. He enclosed a memorandum from one of his reporters stating that war-connected cases were being cut not the expected 25 percent in pensions, but 40, 50, or even 60 percent. Early sent on the letter and evidence to veterans' administrator Hines, telling him that Roosevelt and Howe had seen them: "We all think it is an accurate presentation of the picture and deserves careful reading." [34]

Even before Roberts's startling information arrived, Roosevelt sought to quiet the veterans by conferring on May 10 with Commander Lewis Johnson of the American Legion and Budget Director Douglas, then issuing a White House statement: "As a result of the application of the veterans' regulations, it now seems that the cut in compensation of service-connected World War Veterans with specific injuries has been deeper than was originally intended. The regulations and schedules in this respect will, therefore, be reviewed so as to effect more equitable levels of payment." [35]

Roosevelt also tried to spike rumors that veterans' hospitals were to be closed. But he failed to counter the congressional reaction against drastic pension cuts.

Veterans' organizations had a second chance at the Capitol in June 1933, thanks, ironically, to President Hoover's pocket veto at the end of his term of the $946 million veterans' appropriation in the Independent Offices bill. As a result, Congress had yet to appropriate funds for the Veterans' Administration for the fiscal year beginning July 1. The pressure upon Congress intensified, as newspapers carried articles describing the plight of disabled veterans. The Socialist Norman Thomas repeatedly stated his disapproval. Even the conservative Arthur Krock asserted in the *New York Times* that "down many Main Streets go armless veterans who used to get $94 a month from the Government, and now get $36." Senator Bronson Cutting of New Mexico brought into the Capitol a veteran suffering from an advanced case of tuberculosis who had lost his pension. At eleven o'clock one night at the White House, President Roosevelt met a legless veteran whose pension had been reduced. Obviously many disabled veterans were suffering injustice or at least hardship, but in both of these dramatic examples, case files indicated no probable connection between their disabilities and wartime service.

No matter. The veterans' lobby was clamorous, the genuine sympathies of many congressmen enlisted, and the proposal of $3.3 billion for public works made the original economy drive seem remote. When the Independent Offices bill came before the Senate in June, irritated senators sought to modify it by limiting cuts in pensions of war-disabled veterans to 15 percent, a figure modified to 25 percent. The Senate voted 42 to 42 on the amendment; Vice President Garner broke the tie by voting for it. The amendment would restore $170 million to veterans.[36]

Simultaneously, the Senate was harassing Roosevelt over the recovery bill. The Finance Committee seriously battered the measure, adopting by a vote of 12 to 7 McAdoo's proposal to strip it of its enforcement power, the licensing clause. It also voted an amendment running counter to the President's preparations for the London Economic Conference, an embargo on all imports that would interfere with operation of the recovery program. Further, it had failed only by the narrow margin of 8 to 10 to adopt Senator Bennett Champ Clark's amendment to strike out the entire bill except for the public works provisions. Ominously, seven Democrats had joined the Republicans in opposing the administration.*

The guarantees to labor again came under attack. A thousand delegates to the National Association of Manufacturers' convention in Washington favored the Senate Finance Committee's amendments, and wished it to go further and dilute Section 7-a. Before the Senate could act, Green of the AFL warned that he would urge friends of labor in Congress to vote against the bill if 7-a were modified.[38]

Roosevelt, eager for Congress to adjourn on June 10, before the World Economic Conference sessions began, day by day jettisoned or postponed less vital parts of his program. He also marshaled Democratic leaders to squash the revolt. The leaders were not optimistic when he met with them on the evening of June 4. They told him that Congress should have adjourned a month earlier, and that he should bring the session to an end as quickly as possible, even if he had to shelve his industrial recovery program. Speaker Rainey, depressed, told reporters that "plans for early adjournment of Congress have all gone blooey," and predicted it would remain in session until July 1. Roosevelt rejected pessimistic warnings; while he would make concessions he had no intention of abandoning the NRA. While the debate went on in Congress, General Johnson, although not yet officially appointed administrator, was opening headquarters, hiring personnel, and inviting key businessmen to serve on the national board.[39]

The Senate did indeed submit to Roosevelt's discipline, and on June 8, although the temperature soared high in the nineties, deliberated for thirteen hours. The next day it passed the recovery bill. The debate went well, although there were some attacks. Senator Borah denounced the bill as a monopoly device, and Huey Long warned it would wreck the small "molasses maker and country sausage packer down in my country." But a majority favored the measure; they restored the enforcement provision and made optional the embargo of competing imports.

---

* They were Josiah Bailey of North Carolina and Harry F. Byrd of Virginia, already in the forefront of Democratic opponents of New Deal legislation, and Champ Clark of Missouri, Tom Connally of Texas, Thomas P. Gore of Oklahoma, William H. King of Utah, and McAdoo of California.[37]

They shared the feelings of representatives concerning tax loopholes for the wealthy, and while defeating a sales tax proposal, voted not only to tax the income of previously exempt bonds, but also La Follette's amendment to publicize income tax returns. Then, using the recovery bill as a convenient omnibus to carry whatever else they wished enacted before the end of the session, they tacked amendment after amendment on it, until the total reached about a hundred. The bill passed 58 to 24, with only 4 Democrats voting against it. The House and Senate bills went to conference where speedily most of the amendments were deleted; state and municipal bonds retained their tax exemption.[40]

Roosevelt seemed to have gained his way, and on Saturday night, June 10, Congress was on the point of adjourning. Budget Director Douglas arrived at the Capitol and established himself in the office of the secretary of the Senate, so that he would be there to advise the President when he arrived a little later to sign bills. The House had already completed its action on all bills; the Senate seemed ready to follow. Several senators voiced their objections because they had not been consulted about Roosevelt's appointment of the three directors of the TVA, but nonetheless they were confirmed.

Then came unexpected trouble. There arrived a final message from the President transmitting for approval an Executive Order consolidating or abolishing several government agencies. The changes were relatively minor; the saving would be an estimated $25 million. "Please let me tell you simply and frankly that in transmitting this Executive Order at this late hour," wrote Roosevelt, "I have had no thought of taking what might be considered an advantage of Congress." But that was exactly how the senators received the Executive Order, and several of them in protest began a filibuster. Senate Majority Leader Robinson urged the President to withdraw the order, pointing out that it did not need congressional approval to go into effect.* Fatigue was apparently taking its toll on Roosevelt also; his "Dutch was up," and he refused. The Senate, its members in an irascible mood, adjourned until Monday.[41]

By continuing in session, the Senate left the way open to pass Glass's banking legislation and to increase still further the benefits to veterans. Roosevelt had already accepted a compromise over the compromise amendment to the veterans' appropriation. During the weekend he

---

* The trouble arose, Early explained to Clapper, over a slipup in a prearranged maneuver. The White House was to send over the Executive Order after the Senate had agreed to the adjournment resolution. Robinson telephoned to go ahead, leading to its premature submission. Johnson, Borah, and others rebelled and refused to let the Senate adjourn. Robinson then promised them he would persuade the White House to withdraw it — without consulting the President. Roosevelt, irritated that Robinson had acted without permission, balked. It was, Clapper commented, the first bad muddle of the session.

summoned Democratic leaders to the White House to warn them he would veto the bill unless they made further modifications. He did agree to Byrnes's amendment to provide $15 per month for elderly Spanish-American War veterans if they were substantially disabled and needy.[42]

For several wretched days more Congress remained in session, wrangling with the President. While attention focused on the quarrel over veterans' payments, the senators also took advantage of the opportunity to pass the banking bill, and to express their displeasure with the recovery bill as it had returned from the conference. The National Industrial Recovery bill passed in final form by only 46 to 39, with 11 additional Democratic senators voting against it. And again the Senate passed a version of the veterans' measure unacceptable to Roosevelt. It was not an easy week for him. "He looked very tired and his face was drawn with fatigue," noted Morgenthau on June 12. "I have never seen him look more exhausted." [43]

In the end, Roosevelt came out rather well. He hinted to newspapermen that he would give the veterans' bill not a pocket veto like Hoover, but a "good worded veto," but did not have to do so. As the Senate sought to adjourn, debate went on until 1:20 A.M. on June 15. Weariness, and perhaps the presence of the dispenser of patronage, Jim Farley, sitting in the gallery, led the senators finally to pass the bill in a form acceptable to the President. Together with eight other Democratic senators, Hugo Black of Alabama switched to the support of Roosevelt's compromise. Black declared, "I am not willing to be responsible at this time for continuing a useless and futile contest." The bill as the Senate approved it added $100 million to the cost of pensions, but had the merit of establishing review boards to investigate disabilities presumed to be of wartime origin.* It was more equitable to disabled veterans even after the compromise, and the total number of veterans receiving aid dropped from 998,000 to 581,000.[44]

Congress demonstrated that when it wished it could effectively check the powers of even a President as popular as Roosevelt. Yet the setback they gave him did little to tarnish his glamor, even at the Capitol. Hiram Johnson wrote home:

> We adjourned last night sometime after one o'clock. . . .
> The latter part of this session has been terrible. We're all tired and many are disgruntled. The last fight was on veterans. The Bureau of the Budget has acted in the most shameful, outrageous, and cruel manner. The attempt was made by the Senate to right this, not by a return to

---

* FDR did drastically lower expenditures for veterans' services, from $985 million in the 1932 fiscal year to $557 million in 1934 — a reduction of $428 million. In 1935 expenditures went up to $607 million.

old expenditures, but reasonably. Something has been accomplished, but not what is right. The Director of the Budget is a young man, Lewis Douglas, of Arizona, born to the purple, loves the English and their ways, and has a heart of stone.[45]

It was Douglas not Roosevelt who served as the whipping boy. President Roosevelt had made the most of the approximately hundred days that Congress had been in session, and long after the rancor at the end of the session had been forgotten, the achievements continued to attract attention. Through the next day, Roosevelt signed bills, hailing the recovery measure as a monumental achievement.[46]

By seven o'clock, Roosevelt had kept his last appointment at the Executive Office. He took a swim in the new White House pool, then went to board a special train for Boston and his vacation. At the station he said he felt "tired but happy that Congress has ended its important legislative session so successfully." [47]

President Roosevelt had obtained his fundamental recovery measures; the first legislative phase of the New Deal was at an end. Now the national attention turned toward administration as headlines proclaimed the inception of the National Recovery Administration and the first sweeping crop control measures of the Agricultural Adjustment Administration. In anticipation, prices were already rising — would buying power follow? June 1933 was an optimistic month when, with Roosevelt in the White House, all good things still seemed possible.

CHAPTER XXVII

A Tack toward Nationalism

I am squarely behind you and nothing said or done here
will hamper your efforts. There is no alteration of your
policy or mine.
— FDR TO SECRETARY CORDELL HULL IN LONDON,
June 11, 1933.

Roosevelt's maneuvers in foreign affairs and politics were sometimes like those of a yachtsman who, unable to sail directly toward his destination, tacks against an unfavorable wind. At times there were minor inconsistencies when the hand at the tiller seemed unsure, but his major shifts back and forth in order to arrive at a long-range destination, especially in foreign policy, were by no means accidental. Since sailing was his favorite sport, it is even possible that he consciously applied yachting techniques to his statecraft.[1]

In any event, it was in the early summer of 1933 that Roosevelt, after spending days skippering a small schooner along the New England coast, dramatically altered the course of his foreign policy from one of international cooperation to one emphasizing economic nationalism. He sent what in familiar metaphor is known as the "bombshell message" to the World Economic Conference in London. A more accurate description would be to call it a political tack, and to take him at his word when he insisted that he was by no means abandoning his earlier goal.

The tack began in May 1933. It began to appear that Roosevelt, despite his many dramatic meetings with foreign envoys and his appeal for disarmament and security, was failing to find solutions to problems. More critical still, he was heading into serious conflict with his domestic program and into difficulties with Congress.

The shift began first on the security question, as the Disarmament Conference deadlocked despite Roosevelt's appeal to the heads of states, and Hitler all too openly began a military buildup. Both Roosevelt and his spokesmen tried to give the impression that they had never ever strayed from the isolationist policies of the 1920s. Senator Robinson assured the American Iron and Steel Institute that the appeal to fifty-four nations by no means obligated the United States to use other than moral force. The President himself calmed Senator Hiram Johnson by telling him privately, quite contrary to fact, that Norman Davis in his speech at Geneva had exceeded his instructions.[2]

The President went to some pains to quiet the fears in the United States concerning Japan. The greatest worry of Americans was not Hitler, whom they assumed did not have the military strength to strike, and who was not likely to embroil the United States. Rather, they were nervous about involvement in East Asia, in part because Roosevelt asserted that his pronouncements were not confined to Europe but were worldwide in application. He seemed to be aiming his policies, and particularly the embargo power he sought, against Japan. Public and congressional concern over the dangers of involvement with Japan weakened Roosevelt's power to back European nations confronting the Nazi menace.

One gesture came in late May when Roosevelt engaged in a friendly conversation, which newspapers described as "heart-to-heart," with a special envoy from Japan, Viscount Kikujiro Ishii, whom he brought to a press conference. Viscount Ishii in a subsequent radio talk declared he was "profoundly impressed by the candor, the sincerity, and the generosity" of the President.[3]

Roosevelt's major change in policy was to concede to the Senate that it need not grant him the embargo power to support sanctions against aggressors. Already in early May, the embargo resolution was running into considerable objections in the Foreign Relations Committee, which resisted giving the President authority to embargo munitions destined for one warring power or group of warring powers for fear a discriminatory embargo might involve the United States in war.* Especially they feared Japan would take affront if they passed the resolution.[4]

If a President wished to stir up war, the State Department replied to the committee, he already had authority to do so through many "simpler and more expeditious means." As for the embargo, "This is a peace measure and it would be used to promote peace." The State Department declared that it did not expect the League to move toward an embargo against Japan, and if it did so, the United States would not join unless it received substantial guarantees against the possible effects

---

* Curiously enough, the Senate Foreign Relations Committee, like that of the previous Congress, worried about the American munitions makers: "What good will be accomplished, it is urged, if the United States manufacturers refrain from shipping arms to a country or countries in question if ample munitions of war are supplied from some other country? In such a case would not our manufacturers and our producers of raw material that enter into the manufacture of munitions needlessly suffer?" Within another year or two as the Nye Committee's investigation of munitions makers took over the headlines, such a query became unthinkable.

of Japanese retaliation. Further, an embargo would be ineffective because of Japan's substantial munitions industries. Rather, the State Department wanted the embargo measure voted so that certain European nations could not place upon the United States the onus for failure of the League peace machinery.[5]

Senator Pittman, chairman of the Foreign Relations Committee, proposed to Roosevelt a compromise amendment Hiram Johnson was backing, the handiwork of a great conservative American authority on international law, John Bassett Moore. It stipulated that "any prohibition . . . shall apply impartially to all the parties in the dispute or conflict. . . ." Roosevelt reluctantly accepted it. Secretary Hull protested to the President that the proposal was directly in conflict with the American position at the Geneva disarmament conference, and suggested that if "certain extremists among the Senators" wished to prevent adopting "the policy of peace that is being pursued by every other enlightened nation, they might be given the privilege of tying up proposed peace legislation over the next few months." [6]

The Johnson amendment, which the Senate Foreign Relations Committee nonetheless voted, did indeed destroy Roosevelt's primary aim, to invoke the arms embargo against aggressor nations as part of a world security system. Yet Roosevelt was cautious, and making no statement of his own, followed the strategy Hull suggested. He instructed the Democratic leaders in the Senate not to bring it to the floor during the special session, but to wait until the January 1934 session to urge its enactment in its original form. It was a preview of Roosevelt's struggles with Congress over neutrality legislation through the 1930s, as it tried to bind him with mandatory legislation and he strove for discretionary powers through which he could further collective security.[7]

By the beginning of June 1933, Roosevelt could let drop for the time being the question of embargo legislation, since the Japanese armies, after rushing to within thirteen miles of Peiping, on May 31 negotiated a truce with the Chinese. The truce, which gave Japan an opportunity to extend its influence in China, created a demilitarized zone thirty to forty miles wide, extending south of the Great Wall almost to Peiping. On the advice of Hornbeck, the United States had declined in the preceding weeks to become involved in mediation, but rather allowed events to take their course. Hornbeck seemed to hold rather a "paper dragon" view of the Japanese armies, thinking they would become overextended in China and have to pull back after their weakness became clear. Roosevelt during these weeks seemed to let the State Department make policy, which meant, Dorothy Borg has pointed out, that the influence of Hornbeck and his Far Eastern division became stronger than before.[8]

Hull was no Stimson, and Roosevelt was focusing his attention else-where when in May he talked to T. V. Soong, the Chinese finance minister. Soong came seeking help to bring an end to the fighting, but the best he could obtain from Roosevelt was a $50 million loan to enable China to buy American wheat and cotton. Just before the end of his meeting with Soong, Roosevelt remarked to Jesse Jones of the Re-construction Finance Corporation, "Do not make the Chinese pay too quickly for this transaction and do not make the interest rates too high." The Chinese foreign minister interpreted the loan as "moral assistance," and the Japanese authorities agreed, expressing their dis-pleasure to American diplomats and taking measures to deny China its benefits.[9]

As for the truce, neither Roosevelt nor the State Department pro-tested it, although it was highly unfavorable to China. Rather, the President, the secretary of state, and Ambassador Grew all began to labor toward improvement of relations with Japan. Grew was especially active, and began to feel optimistic when before the end of the summer a moderate became foreign minister.[10]

Simultaneously, Roosevelt began a program to build the United States Navy toward the strength that the Treaty of London of 1930 authorized. In mid-March, when he was worried about tensions in Japan, he said he had not thought about a navy program, but by mid-May admitted that naval construction would be a part of his public works program. It was not until June 16, after the Japanese-Chinese truce, that he formally announced he was allocating funds to construct thirty-two new vessels. These would include two cruisers 10,000 tons in size and carrying eight-inch guns, of longer range and greater fire power than any existing cruisers, obviously designed primarily for defense of the Pacific. Concurrently Roosevelt continued to enforce drastic econ-omy upon the navy, threatening cuts of officers and enlisted men. In June 1933, when he went to Annapolis to address the graduating class at the Naval Academy, there was a somber undertone to the festivities. To save money, the navy and marine corps awarded commissions to little more than half of the 432 midshipmen.[11]

Roosevelt's timing may have been coincidental, but the purport of the building program extending over several years together with the immediate contraction of naval personnel was clear. He did not fear an immediate threat but was safeguarding future security.* The Japanese

---

* Even had there been no tension with Japan, and despite his strong interest in disarmament, FDR undoubtedly would have favored modernizing the navy and building it toward treaty strength. In 1930, he praised for "its common sense and clearness" an article favorable to the results of the London Conference, then added: "However the country does not understand the Naval Conference at all. Most

did not react with shock, but expressed, Grew reported, the expected indignation. "To the Japanese people," he wrote, "American naval construction means a threat to Japan and the first step toward an armament race." [13]

Toward Japan Roosevelt was willing to try, and continued to attempt, the internationalist approach of collective action and naval armaments agreements. Already before he took office both had proven nearly impossible. The Japanese government was insisting upon naval parity, although it had only one ocean to defend, and the United States two. The Senate difficulties over the arms embargo resolution as a collective security device were an indication of future opposition within the United States. On the other hand, some of the isolationist nationalists, whether senators like Johnson and Borah, or newspaper publishers like Hearst and Colonel McCormick of the *Chicago Tribune*, were pleased that Roosevelt was strengthening the navy. The potential risks in sanctions frightened them, but not those from a naval race. For two years, as Roosevelt authorized naval building toward treaty strength, he continued to work toward further naval limitations with Japan.

There was a subtle shift rather than a sharp redirection of policy toward international economic stabilization during the several weeks before the Economic Conference opened in London. Gradually the sessions with foreign dignitaries petered out, and along with them Roosevelt's focus of interest. His enthusiasms were usually of fairly short duration, and the novelty of negotiating with heads of states gave way to the tedium of endless repetition of the same statements. The time-consuming negotiations over the June 15 war debt payment may also have eroded Roosevelt's goodwill toward the British and French. All the many hours of cordiality and willingness to make concessions that he had brought to that exhausted subject had failed to bring compensation, either personally or politically. It was easy to slip into suspicion of the goodwill, not of MacDonald and Herriot, but of the governments refusing to back them. There had been the tart remark to Morgenthau about those British and French cabinet members — "a bunch of 'bastards.' " Along with his strong fraternal feelings there had always been a fear that the United States as the younger brother might be a victim of sharp practice. On May 22, 1933, he wrote a cordial note to MacDonald regarding debts and the forthcoming conference, suggesting he would be willing to accept a part payment in silver of the June 15 installment, but declaring, "I am disturbed lest the deliberations of the Conference be unduly affected by the desire of the debtor governments

people realize merely that as a result of the Conference we shall have to build a lot more ships at a vastly increased cost than we have been doing during the past few years. This does not sound like reduction in naval armament." [12]

to bring about a new settlement of the debt question, even though this question does not form a part of the Agenda." [14]

There were also slight realignments around Roosevelt which might indicate either a changing emphasis in his thinking, or in the influences upon him. In the days after he failed to bring a solution to the impasse in the Arms Conference, he saw less of Hull and Phillips and read fewer cables from Davis. On the other hand, he was insisting that Moley handle war debts exclusive of Hull, although Hull (as Moley noted at the time) was becoming more and more unhappy. In connection with domestic matters, he was continuing to see much of Moley, Tugwell, and increasingly of Morgenthau. As the agricultural program was developing, Wallace, with his firm stand in favor of economic nationalism, was also involved. And both the excitement of starting the agricultural program and the exigencies of obtaining passage of the industrial program through a somewhat irritable Congress forced Roosevelt's attention toward economic nationalism.[15]

Secretary Hull was becoming quite depressed. "I'm sure Hull doesn't know half of what goes on," Tugwell wrote in his diary. It was all too true, and what hurt most was that Moley did know, and on occasion Roosevelt specifically charged him not to tell anyone. Phillips expressed his shock and concern to Warburg over the lack of liaison between the President and the secretary and the impossibility for the State Department to find out what the President and Moley were undertaking. As for Hull, he did not hide from those close to him his loathing of Moley, but dared vent his feelings toward the President only by referring, with his slight lisp, to "That man acwoss the stweet who never tells me anything." [16]

On the question of lowering trade restrictions, Moley as well as Hull was becoming quite uneasy. Moley thought the President's intention was to let Hull deliver fine-sounding speeches and in the end he would make no moves that would impair his recovery measures. But Moley, even at the time, was not entirely sure. In point of fact, Roosevelt was giving encouragement to both Hull and Moley, and if in the end the irreconcilable could not be reconciled, then the hard choice could come. Meanwhile there was ambiguity, and for both Hull and Moley, embarrassment. News correspondents and foreign policy analysts put side by side the statements of the secretary and assistant secretary of state, and pondered.

Hull, in an address on May 2:

> It is now clear that no nation can live and thrive by itself. The proponents of the policy of economic isolation . . . are still unable to offer any basic remedy for business recovery except this broken-down

and discredited policy. They can only point to its colossal failure as a guaranty of its future ability to improve business conditions.

Moley, in an address May 20:

> It is overwhelmingly clear that a good part of the ills of each country is domestic. The action of an international conference which attempted to bring about cures for these difficulties solely by concerted international measures would necessarily result in failure. In large part the cures for our difficulties lie within ourselves. Each nation must set its own house in order, and a meeting of representatives of all the nations is useful in large part only to coördinate in some measure these national activities.[17]

The President had not only given his approval to the article upon which Moley based this talk, but remarked upon reading it, "As a matter of fact, this would be a grand speech for Cordell to make at the opening of the conference." [18]

The temper of the nation and Congress also made Hull apprehensive about his program. On May 13, Hull in discursive fashion lamented to Ambassador Lindsay the national preoccupation with recovery legislation: "He said that deflation caused by [the] banking crisis had inflicted the most acute distress and had created a fertile field for activities of demagogues both of the press and of Congress. Latter was now in a highly sensitive mood and required the most careful handling." [19]

The prevalent expectation in Washington, Lindsay reported the next day, was that the Economic Conference would be a failure — "and this condition of affairs is not improved by the fact, if Americans were prepared to admit it, that failure will be due to their own departure from gold." And Lindsay (referring, as almost always, to debt payments) summed up the confusion in the capital concerning Roosevelt's intention on economic matters:

> I believe that if the President decided to use all means of pressure at his disposal on Congress he could bend it to his will. Meanwhile what his intentions are is wrapped in complete obscurity and every statement of them, whether by himself or by his spokesmen, is evasive. Whenever a phrase is used of which publication is allowed it is worded so as to be susceptible of two interpretations at least — the result is much uncertainty. . . .
> [The] President has now had statesmen from a dozen countries to consult with him about economic questions. His two speeches last week emphasized the necessity of making [the] conference a success; only yesterday [the] official communiqué about discussions with [the] German delegation put international cooperation forward as a necessity; he seems to me to be committed to it. If he now tries to reverse his path, and refuses to make any effort to remove an obstacle in the way of international cooperation [i.e., postpone the June 15 debt payment],

though he may thus send his Congress home in a good temper, he must know he will not escape all blame even in America for results which must speedily ensue.[20]

Lindsay reported that the expectation that the Economic Conference would fail was so marked that some State Department officials had considered sending only a second-class delegation in order to discount failure in advance. But they had decided to send the strongest possible group. There was nothing to the rumor; it may have started because Moley did not want to serve — he neither wanted to be tied up in London for the summer nor to be discredited if, as he expected, the conference was a disappointment.[21]

The delegation was Roosevelt's own choice; he savored the selection of the delegates and technical experts. In March he had suggested to Hull the need "to get in new blood . . . more representative of this country" when choosing delegates to conferences. The Americans Roosevelt sent to London were new blood without a question of a doubt; not one had ever attended an international conference before. Collectively they reflected neither expertise nor a single ideology — rather a paying of political debts and a respect for the power of Congress.

It had been Roosevelt's intention to send the prestigious Baruch as chairman of the delegation, even though Baruch's sound money, high tariff ideas ill fitted New Deal international thinking of the spring. Rather, since it turned out that Secretary Hull wanted to go, the secretary took precedence, became chairman, and prepared to depart with a single overriding concern, to lower tariffs. Roosevelt, ever mindful of the fiasco following the Paris Conference of 1919, wanted strong congressional representation. He invited the Democrat Key Pittman of Nevada, chairman of the Senate Foreign Relations Committee. The choice of a Republican senator was difficult. Roosevelt urged that famous isolationist, Hiram Johnson, to join the delegation, but Johnson, much as he wanted to see London, decided he could not compromise his principles and declined. After he refused to go, he entertained Moley and Bullitt at dinner. They expressed their regret, giving Johnson the impression they would have liked him to destroy one after another of the foreign conferees and perhaps even break up the conference. At the last minute Roosevelt invited the Republican Senator Couzens of Michigan to join the delegation. Roosevelt's other appointees were Samuel D. McReynolds of Tennessee, chairman of the House Foreign Affairs Committee; James M. Cox of Ohio, Democratic candidate for President in 1920, and Ralph W. Morrison, a wealthy Texan.[22]

A competent staff of technical experts and advisers accompanied the delegation. Bullitt was chief executive officer, the only reward of significance he had been able thus far to obtain for his trips to Europe on behalf of Roosevelt. Earlier, Roosevelt had assured Bullitt he was to be the first American delegate, and in charge of preparations for the conference. Feis was chief technical adviser, and Warburg, financial adviser. Roosevelt wanted Moley and Tugwell to serve as liaison; first the one, then the other, were to go to London for several weeks to take a fresh look.

The delegation was split between low tariff advocates, most of whom favored sound money, and high tariff men, who tended to be monetarily unorthodox. On the one side were Hull, Cox, McReynolds, and Morrison; on the other, Pittman and Couzens. The balance was with Hull, but that would suggest a unity seldom to be found among the delegates.

In Washington, the balance was against Hull. There were Moley, Morgenthau, and for the moment Baruch. When Warburg protested against placing Baruch on the delegation, Roosevelt agreed to ask Baruch to stay to advise him on the continued instructions to the American delegation. Later, when Roosevelt went on vacation, he left Baruch in the glorious but rather empty role of appearing to be in charge in Washington. Newspapers hailed Baruch as Acting President, but he had little authority. What there was would be on behalf of the fledgling NRA, which he had declared necessitated high tariffs.[23]

Through the last days before the American delegation sailed, Roosevelt continued to insist that there was no need to choose between the domestic recovery program and international economic cooperation. A reporter asked him on May 26 if he saw any conflict between some of the basic New Deal measures and the program of breaking down trade barriers. Roosevelt replied there was not, that he was trying to frame emergency measures in order to promote international trade:

> Q: But wouldn't they tend to foster an isolation policy? Wouldn't they require for their successful operation a rather closed door and a policy of isolation?
>
> THE PRESIDENT: Oh, no, not necessarily. Of course, our hope is that we will raise commodity prices not only here but all over the world. That is the real international objective. . . .
>
> Q: Mr. Baruch has said that under the Industrial Recovery Bill, which would raise wages, that higher tariffs would be necessary to protect the American market?
>
> THE PRESIDENT: Not necessarily; it depends entirely on the individual product and, if commodity prices are raised in proportion in other nations at the same time, the present tariff will be equally [protective].[24]

These remarks reflected accurately enough Roosevelt's thinking at that time. Earlier that day he had held a lengthy meeting with advisers and delegates to the Economic Conference at which he had approved a set of fine-sounding instructions to the delegates, in which Warburg (and Feis on the tariff) had summarized the American positions during the meetings a few weeks earlier with the representatives of several nations. Roosevelt suggested only including a clause endorsing balanced national budgets, and accepted the addition of a resolution proposing international production controls over basic commodities, especially wheat. He expressed his pleasure with the instructions, and according to Warburg said they "were not only just what he would have wanted to say himself, but that I seemed to have stolen his language." Since Roosevelt accepted the Hull proposal for lowering tariffs, it followed that he must obtain power to negotiate changes in the tariff from Congress. The bill to permit reciprocal trade agreements, which Feis was preparing, was to be ready to send almost immediately.[25]

Still, Hull did not feel that Roosevelt was clear on the specific action on trade barriers that the American delegation could undertake at London. Three days later, on May 29, Warburg, sitting in Hull's office, wrote a clear-cut call for a low tariff and international economic cooperation. It concluded with the declaration that

> all nations collectively and individually are now faced with the decision of a choice between a broad policy of practical international, economic cooperation for purposes of business recovery with the resulting increase of profits and wages and living standards in every country, or of embracing in still more extreme and impracticable forms the present policy of world economic warfare.

The purpose of the memorandum was to force Roosevelt to commit himself one way or the other. Warburg and Hull took it to the White House, where Roosevelt met later that day for two and a half hours with Moley, Baruch, and the delegates and experts bound for London. Warburg suggested that trade policy needed clarification, and as a basis for discussion handed the memorandum to Roosevelt:

> He read this out loud and made the following comment: that he would say what was in the memorandum to any individual nation but not to a group of nations; that he definitely agreed with the substance but that it could not be expressed in this form at the Conference. I said that I had no idea of expressing it in this form at the Conference but merely wanted to make sure that we would not be preaching one gospel while the cohorts of protectionism were carrying out another behind our backs. This led into a lengthy discussion of the proposed tariff bill as submitted by Feis and Pittman, which was then also approved by the President. Baruch said that he did not want to argue for raising tariffs but merely wanted to point out the discrepancy between our Economic Conference policy and our domestic policy. It was then agreed that there was not necessarily any discrepancy if the administra-

tion of these two measures was carried out along the lines of reducing rather than increasing trade barriers. This comes closer to a definition of our tariff policy than anything we have had yet, although I have no illusions as to what will really happen.

Moley, who saw eye to eye with Baruch on the tariff, remembers leaving the conference almost literally sick to his stomach.

Warburg left the White House that day for London, feeling much the same queasiness over stabilization. At the initial meeting, Roosevelt had talked of a rather unclear plan for an international currency which Louis Howe had been trying to sell him, but did not insist it become the delegation's proposal. At the second meeting, after the long tariff discussion, when the conversation finally changed to temporary stabilization — the exchange truce that the French wanted above all — O. W. M. Sprague interrupted before the President could speak. Sprague, a Harvard economist, had been handling stabilization for the Bank of England, and Roosevelt had just obtained his services for the Treasury Department. Sprague informed Warburg, the financial expert for the Economic Conference, that stabilization had nothing to do with the conference; it would be handled by representatives of the Treasury and Federal Reserve. Warburg noted:

> I asked the President whether this met with his approval and he said that it did. I asked him whether I was to understand that if the French and British tried to discuss this with me upon my arrival I was to answer that special representatives were coming over for this discussion and say nothing further. He said that he would be glad to have me transmit their views as soon as I could get them. I said that in this case I could take no responsibility either for producing de facto stabilization before the Conference or for convincing the French that stabilization prior to the Conference was not essential to the success of the Conference. Inasmuch as several people were talking at the same time and the President's lunch was being put on his desk, I did not feel at all certain that a clear understanding had been reached on this subject, particularly as Moley had left some minutes before.[26]

So it was that Roosevelt sent off his delegation and experts to the Economic Conference, armed with eloquent exhortations on behalf of international economic cooperation, and almost no concrete authority. In part it may have been the extreme pressure he was under from Congress, giving him little time to think through what he really wanted to do, but his positions then and later really changed relatively little. When he did change, he did so in response to American economic and political conditions. It may have been his tendency to let subordinates undertake what they could on their own, and if they succeeded reward them, if they failed, repudiate them. There was some of that.

Part of the later difficulties came because none of his experts and delegates saw precisely eye to eye with him on everything.

Secretary Hull was going to do something about lowering the tariff, and while Roosevelt was sympathetic, he did not want duties lowered which would compete with domestic recovery.

Warburg wanted a stabilization of exchange, considering it essential to international economic recovery. Those hostile to him in Washington regarded him as an agent of big bankers, threatening through international agreement to end Roosevelt's options to inflate under the Thomas amendment. Roosevelt was willing to accept some sort of stabilization if it became necessary to prevent a runaway boom, but did not want to abandon future options.

Senator Pittman came closest to Roosevelt's views, but his single interest was a silver agreement, which would have great political appeal. Letters bearing numerous and weighty signatures had come to Roosevelt from both houses of Congress urging that the silverite Father Coughlin be sent to London.

As for the President himself, he had considerable interest in international agreements to regulate production and prices of commodities ranging from wheat through sugar to copper. Above all he wanted to bring international price levels up. If he succeeded in doing so, then permanent tariff and currency stabilization agreements would not be harmful to the United States. To arrive at his goal would require intricate maneuvering, if indeed it was in any way possible.

Other major nations at the conference had only a secondary interest, if any at all, in Roosevelt's basic goal. The prime concern of the British was specifically the June 15 war debt payment and the elimination of war debts as soon as possible. Despite their pledge that they would not bring up the debt question at the conference, its president, Prime Minister MacDonald, mentioned debts in his opening address. The British talked a good bit about stabilization, but wished it at a level advantageous to themselves. As for tariffs, it would be futile to try to pry them away from the Imperial Preference they had brought home from the Ottawa Conference. They had some interest in international commodity arrangements, but not a great deal. As for the French and the other gold bloc nations, their single concern, upon which they were ready to hinge the continuance of the conference, was currency stabilization. In sum, what the major nations at the conference would have liked from the United States was virtual elimination of war debts and a restoration of the dollar to an exchange level favorable to the other nations. There is scant indication that they were willing to make any concessions in return.

As for the United States, it was well, considering the odds against satisfactory agreements, that Roosevelt was keeping his options open.

These options day by day carried him in the direction of immediate American economic self-interests since the nation seemed launched toward unilateral recovery. Prices and production were both rising spectacularly as the boom in anticipation of the National Recovery Administration controls moved toward its peak.

In early June, Roosevelt was undergoing his greatest tensions with a preponderantly nationalistic Congress, and prudence, if nothing else, dictated that he not add to his difficulties by trying to obtain permissive legislation on the tariff. He decided definitely against sending Congress the trade agreements bill. From Hull on the high seas aboard the S.S. *President Roosevelt*, he received a plaintive query. Roosevelt immediately replied that the situation in those closing days of Congress was so full of dynamite that immediate adjournment was essential. He tried to reassure his secretary of state by telling him he had full authority at London to negotiate general reciprocal commercial treaties, which could be submitted to Congress for approval as soon as it reassembled. Hull could not so easily be put off; he knew perfectly well that under the pressure from lobbyists the Senate had never ratified trade treaties, which, after all, required two-thirds approval. The only way to lower tariff barriers within the United States was to get blanket approval in advance, and he had hoped, armed with the American bill, to win concessions in London. Roosevelt's message, he has written in his *Memoirs*, "was a terrific blow. It swept from under me one of the prime reasons for going to London." [27]

A new blow fell upon Hull when he arrived in England. He discovered from the London *Times* that Roosevelt was not only withholding the reciprocal trade bill, but accepting an amendment to the National Industrial Recovery bill bestowing upon him far-ranging discretionary power to raise tariffs and impose import quotas upon whatever articles (covered by NRA codes) might compete with domestic recovery. The news threw Hull into such a temperamental state that he seemed on the verge of resigning. However, Hull confined himself to sending a mild inquiry to Phillips, who went to Roosevelt. Phillips sent the reassuring news that the President had telephoned Senator Pat Harrison, who agreed immediately to get rid of the amendment. And in response to a distressed cable from Cox and Bullitt, Roosevelt sent fresh reassurances to Hull: [28]

> Please do not worry about situation here in regard to tariff reductions and removal of trade obstacles. The eleventh hour rows in Congress over domestic problems made general tariff debate dangerous to our whole program.[29]
>
> I am squarely behind you and nothing said or done here will hamper your efforts. There is no alteration of your policy or mine. Remember

too, that if we can get treaties signed we can call special session of Senate alone in the autumn to consider ratification.

Nevertheless, the amendment to the National Industrial Recovery Act stood. Despite his repeated promises to Hull, Roosevelt had allowed the session to end without obtaining authorization to negotiate agreements lowering tariffs, and had accepted fresh power to raise tariffs and impose import quotas.

Even as Roosevelt was sending Hull this bland reassurance, he was seriously editing the draft of Hull's proposed address to the Economic Conference, which seemed too full of criticism of the "trade barrier," too long, too mumbling — and too optimistic.*Nor, as Moley points out, was it any more than sophistry on the part of Roosevelt to suggest that the Senate could meet in special session that fall. His kind dispatch was compounded of his characteristic unwillingness either to hurt or face the fact and "his disingenuous habits when it seemed essential to escape the consequences of a hard decision." [31]

Hull in London felt utterly betrayed and circumscribed. Moley's view on the tariff, not his, had prevailed, so that Hull could do little but pursue endless talks on international agreements on commodities. Even there, wheat was out of his jurisdiction. He had already been humiliated in Washington by having to confess to the British ambassador his lack of knowledge of war debt negotiations. In London he had no authorization to discuss either debts or monetary stabilization. He did not resign, but he did act humble and passive. In private, Cox complained a few days later, he and Mrs. Hull talked obsessively about a single subject — Moley.[32]

Roosevelt's course of action on stabilization paralleled that on the tariff. The fall of the value of the dollar in relation to the pound during the month of June was much greater than he had expected, and he was not disposed to stem the decline at a time when it seemed so favorable to the United States. Nor did he wish to back stabilization through the export of gold, which would enable speculators in Amsterdam or elsewhere to renew the threat of April to drain a sizable quantity of bullion from the United States. Through the rapidly moving events, Roosevelt was wary, moving at times toward agreement and at other times shying away.

At the outset of these critical weeks, on June 7, talking off the record

---

* Moley carefully refrained from editing the speech, and it was Roosevelt himself who made changes, and (writing in the third person) instructed Hull to recast one paragraph: "It is at variance with the President's campaign speeches, notably that at Louisville, wherein he differed with President Hoover as to the latter's theories that other nations were responsible for the world depression. The President throughout the campaign maintained the view that the United States was the first offender." [30]

to reporters, he commented on the efforts since April to attain temporary stabilization, particularly on the part of the French. "We have felt," he explained, ". . . that the time is not ripe . . . because we do not know as yet the status of the currency of each country in relationship to . . . the individual price level of a country." He hoped within the month of June that the relationship between a nation's currency and prices would be fairly well fixed so that discussion of stabilization could proceed. The objective of the Americans at London, he declared, would be to seek stabilization for the sake of international trade and to eliminate the speculators — "those fellows in Amsterdam and Antwerp." [33]

After making these remarks at a press conference, Roosevelt seems to have become immersed for more than a week in his struggle with Congress, and to have paid little attention to the first phase of the stabilization negotiations in London. Beginning June 9, Sprague of the Treasury Department and George Harrison, governor of the New York Federal Reserve bank, with Warburg acting as liaison with the American delegation to the Economic Conference, met with British and French representatives. Warburg on June 13 sent a lengthy cable to Roosevelt detailing a proposed stabilization agreement toward which the negotiations were moving. Roosevelt received it that same day, and perhaps in the rush of activities forgot it, for he mentioned it to none of his advisers, nor to the Treasury Department. This was the day that the recovery bill finally passed, and the Senate was still trying to restore cuts in veterans' pensions. Warburg, receiving no reply, assumed Roosevelt did not object and the conferees continued their work.

When word leaked from London on June 15 that de facto stabilization was about to be reached, it caused the dollar to rise and commodity and stock prices to fall. Roosevelt, Secretary of the Treasury Woodin, and Moley were alarmed. Woodin issued a denial, which rallied the stock market, and Roosevelt sent a sharp cable to London: [34]

> All kinds of wild reports here about stabilization at some fixed rate, some reports saying around 4 dollars [per pound] and other reports at other rates. I feel sure all these reports are not founded in any fact. Of course any proposal must in any event come here for approval or disapproval by Treasury Department and me.[35]

Roosevelt's attitude continued to be critical, since he feared any temporary stabilization arrangement might impair recovery within the United States. A lengthy cable came in from Sprague outlining a proposal to stabilize the dollar for the duration of the conference at a middle rate of $4 per pound, and commit $60 million in gold to be expended if need be in bolstering the dollar to that level. Warburg endorsed the proposal, and warned Roosevelt that though doubtless he would be flooded with protests from inflationary groups like the Committee of the Nation, the alternative would be to lose leadership in seeking economic peace among nations. The cables caused much excitement at the White House. Roosevelt was preparing to leave for his vacation, but spent much of the morning with Moley and Acheson drafting an answer. (Secretary Woodin was too ill to participate, but approved the conclusions.) At first Roosevelt suggested in the draft a rate of $4.25 in relation to the pound, and the export of from $50 to $80 million in gold to maintain it, but in the hope of driving a hard bargain, he eliminated these terms from his instructions. If the pound rose to an excessive point, he cabled, the United States would consider unilateral action. If the exchange went the other way, he wished to reserve freedom of action in order to prevent commodity price declines. It was a clear-cut statement, Moley believes, of Roosevelt's view at that time and later. "He was not at all impressed by the position of the French and British that temporary stabilization was an essential prerequisite for a successful conference. And he was now a little nettled that the American negotiators were out of accord with his domestic objectives." [36]

There was also reason for Roosevelt to be concerned over the undisciplined way in which the American delegates were functioning. Secretary Hull, his morale low, was failing to exercise control over it, and individual members were issuing such contradictory statements that Phillips sent an admonitory cable warning that the picture in the United States was one of lack of unity of purpose. Senator Pittman, Robbins wrote Roosevelt, "went on a beeno and only got back to normalcy yesterday." * There was every indication that the most pessimistic predictions about the delegation and the conference were coming true. [37]

---

* There are lively impressions of the conference and the delegates in Herbert Feis, *1933: Characters in Crisis* (1966), pp. 169–258.

CHAPTER XXVIII

The Bombshell

I would regard it as a catastrophe amounting to a world
tragedy if the great Conference of Nations, called to
bring about a more real and permanent financial stability
and a greater prosperity . . . should, in advance . . .
allow itself to be diverted by the proposal of a purely
artificial and temporary experiment affecting the monetary exchange of a few nations only.

        — FDR, *July 2, 1933.*

President Roosevelt sent the bombshell message to the Economic Conference at the culmination of a two weeks' vacation sailing along the
New England coast. While the American delegation was floundering in
London, he left Washington in mid-June for his first real rest since he
had taken office. First he visited Groton School to see his sons, Franklin
D. Roosevelt, Jr., and John, then headed across Massachusetts to Marion,
where years before he had undergone strenuous treatment to try to
recover his leg muscles. In the years when he had frequently visited
Marion he had attracted little attention, but now as President of the
United States, traversing Boston and its suburbs by automobile on
Bunker Hill Day, he was cheered by as many as a quarter million people along his route.[1]

At Marion Roosevelt boarded the forty-one-foot schooner *Amberjack
II.* Acting as skipper, and with his son James and several of James's
friends as the crew, he headed up the New England coast. For several
days as he made his way around Cape Cod the weather was bad and the
progress of the boat slow, but Roosevelt was thoroughly enjoying himself, demonstrating his seamanship and his ability to weather a blow. In
accompanying boats, newspapermen, some of them with queasy stomachs, were witness to his prowess. The captain of one of the boats, before the heavy wind began, commented, "I don't like to criticize the
President of the United States, but if he would set the foresail to the
starboard, he'd get a better full." Not long afterwards the newspapermen
saw the sail set on Roosevelt's boat. Roosevelt had to abandon course
temporarily when a gale set in, and take his pitching craft into Nan-

tucket harbor. When the reporters drew alongside, they found him grinning behind the wheel, his face unshaven, an oilskin over his sweater. "We were worried about you," he said. "We decided it was better to study the weather here than off the cape." [2]

Although Roosevelt was playing the role of old sea dog, with dried brine glistening on his slicker, he was still keeping a finger from afar on stabilization negotiations in London. Sprague and Warburg (with Cox by this time associated with them) were trying to arrive at a figure that both Roosevelt and the British and French would accept. On June 18, they inquired if he would accept a 10 percent spread in the sterling-dollar rate, of $3.80 to $4.20. From Nantucket, Roosevelt replied that he feared that if there were a range, London and Paris would probably combine to keep the dollar at the lower end. But Roosevelt was still ready to drive a bargain:

> Why not probably try suggestion of our willingness during Conference to keep pound from going above 4.25. You can make it perfectly clear that the 4 dollar medium point is in my judgment too low especially at this time of year with tendency of trade balance favorable to us during next few months depressing pound still further.
>
> Talk to Baruch and Moley about advisability of suggesting to Cox a final medium point of 4.15 with maximum point of 4.25 and minimum 4.05. I hesitate to go even that far but it is worth considering.[3]

The next day Moley arrived to spend two hours on the *Amberjack* talking to Roosevelt as they rounded Cape Cod toward Provincetown Harbor. Moley had been convinced by Marvin McIntyre and James Byrnes that he was courting serious trouble by going to London, but felt the only way he could get the orders countermanded was by seeing Roosevelt in person. The President could not be reached by telephone, so on his own initiative Moley went to the President. He flew to Martha's Vineyard in a navy plane, then was ferried by a destroyer to the *Amberjack*. Roosevelt may have groused subsequently over Moley's visit, but greeted him in high spirits. The President insisted Moley should go to London, was apparently little concerned over the enormous newspaper attention the trip would undoubtedly create, and indeed even joked about making it more spectacular by sending him by destroyer to intercept a Europe-bound liner. As for instructions, Roosevelt still seemed ready to accept temporary stabilization at a ratio that would not harm the United States. Moley was ready to be cautious also, and remembers suggesting that he felt some apprehension over too rapid, too speculative a price rise. "Perhaps we could devise some sort of action that would somewhat slacken the rise without impairing our recovery and would at the same time check speculative excesses." Roosevelt was not yet firm in his own thinking. He penciled a fresh cable to Hull, for Moley to dispatch from the destroyer, reconfirming his instructions of June 17. The last two sentences suggested the direction of Roosevelt's thoughts: "Remember that far too much importance is attached to exchange stability by banker-influenced cabinets. In our case it concerns only about 3 per cent of our total trade as measured by production." [4]

In his conversation with Moley, Roosevelt again put considerable emphasis upon the idea Howe had been pressing, that what was needed was some sort of international version of the commodity dollar, and an international unit of exchange that would not vary in value (to be called the dinard).* Moley departed for London believing he should promote these ideas on behalf of the President.

Before Moley left the *Amberjack*, he handed Roosevelt a memorandum summing up arguments against stabilization that Herbert Bayard Swope, a New York newspaperman who was accompanying Moley to London, had prepared the evening before. "F.D.R. took the memorandum," Moley recalls. "I no more dreamed of its ironical consequences than de Maupassant's villager foresaw the consequences of picking up the pieces of string." [6]

As Roosevelt sailed on up the coast, Moley, the focus of international attention, returned to New York to embark with Swope on the *Manhattan* for London. Joseph Kennedy stopped by at Moley's hotel in New York to warn him that Roosevelt was growing jealous of Moley's prominence and that he had better watch out. Yet Roosevelt had insisted Moley go to London. Although he armed Moley with written instructions making clear that he was no more than a liaison man, the *New York Times* editorially expressed its incredulity. Inevitably the rumors spread that Moley was coming with a plan to save the conference. Roosevelt, consummate showman that he was, liked to operate in an air of mystery and excitement, and seems to have been willing to let attention center on Moley for some days.

---

* FDR had two different ideas. One was that within countries there should be a currency which would always have the same buying power in certain basic commodities. The other, the dinard idea, he explained to newspapermen on June 7:

> For example, if you and I are trying to make an international contract — you are an Englishman and I am an American — it is difficult to make it today because you and I don't know what either the pound or the dollar is going to be a year from now when the payment is due. This particular school of thought says, "if we had an imaginary coin, you as a Britisher, would not have to think of the dollar, you would merely have to think of the coin in its relationship to the pound and not as to the dollar. . . ." The imaginary coin would always be fixed in terms of gold or gold and silver, whereas, as it is now, you and I have to think of the pound going up and down and the dollar going up and down or of the two going up together or coming down together. You have six possibilities if you work it out with paper and pencil.[5]

With FDR, Jr., and Sara Delano Roosevelt in Groton,
Massachusetts, June 1933.

FDR on *Amberjack II*, cruising from Marion, Massachusetts,
to Campobello, June 16–29, 1933.

While Moley was on the high seas, negotiations lagged and Hull fumed. The secretary's prestige, already low, sagged further. Some days earlier, Louis Howe's correspondent son Hartley had written his father, "In the more frivolous diplomatic circles our chief delegate is apparently referred to as 'Miss Cordelia Dull.'" But the diplomats began to close ranks against Moley. All the resentment toward the professor, who was neither professional politician nor diplomat, began to come to a focus. The Republican editor from Kansas, William Allen White, as he later boasted, led the jeering from London before Moley could even arrive. White cabled home the rumor that Moley was coming to take over the American delegation and quoted the gibe, "Moley, Moley, Moley, Lord God Almighty." [7] Meanwhile, Roosevelt, sailing along the foggy Maine coast, sent for Norman Davis, who rushed up on the destroyer *Bernadou* to give a most optimistic report on developments at Geneva. While Moley was bound for London, his prime opponent in foreign affairs, Hull's staunchest ally, was cruising with Roosevelt.

Contrary to some sardonic later accounts, and Hull's oversensitive impressions, Moley, aware of the perils facing him, leaned over backward when he arrived in England to defer to the secretary. While on the *Manhattan* he had received a message from Roosevelt. The President approved of a press statement Moley wished to issue at Plymouth, in which Moley quoted Roosevelt's own words that he was to "act in a sense as messenger or liaison officer." The message contained a further sobering thought indicating that he might be concerned about his aggrieved secretary of state. Roosevelt wired Phillips: "I am inclined to think that from now on [Moley] should give out no further statements or talk with press because he is under the Secretary and is not a member of the delegation. The same should apply to Swope. You might suggest this to Moley and inform the Secretary." [8]

At Cobh in Ireland, Moley received a confidential letter from Hull, informing him that the hostile British and French press had been heralding the view that Moley was "to be virtually in charge of United States interests in London," and asking Moley to set forth the limits of his authority in his first press statement. [9]

In consequence, when Moley arrived at Paddington Station in London, he followed Roosevelt's instructions so carefully that he made only the third page of the *New York Times*. He refused to be photographed or to make a statement, saying he had to see Hull first. He explained, "I am bringing to my . . . chief, Secretary of State Hull . . . a report on the latest economic and legislative developments in the United States." [10]

Secretary Hull introduced Moley at a press conference the next day as "also of the State Department." Moley emphasized Roosevelt's high confidence in the American delegation, and in its distinguished head. He said he was in London to render whatever service he could to Hull, and would issue no further statements except, "following an appropriate custom, through my chief, Secretary Hull." Frederick T. Birchall wrote in the *New York Times*, "Of the day's incidents the Conference debut of Professor Moley was the most interesting and provocative of the most comment, all favorable to the newcomer." Moley was relieved to feel that he had "dispelled the idea that I had come as a savior." [11]

Moley's sense of relief was misplaced; his very presence in London made him the focus of attention and left Hull feeling as he had throughout the long Washington spring, as if he were a figurehead on the periphery. When MacDonald, continuing his habit of that spring in Washington, sought to reach an agreement, he turned to Moley (who, obtaining Hull's permission to talk, thought he was acting within Roosevelt's instructions). Hull was deeply hurt because when MacDonald had asked the secretary if he could talk to Moley, he had added that Hull could come along if he wished. Hull acquiesced, and added the insult to his dossier of evidence. While Hull used the metaphor that he was giving Moley rope, more precisely he was quietly gathering these bits one by one preparing for the day when he could go to Roosevelt and demand a death warrant.[12]

As for Roosevelt, he did not wish either Moley or Hull to be his surrogate at London; he wanted to run the American negotiations himself, while he was resting and relaxing, sailing in and out of patches of fog, east of Mt. Desert Island. It would have been hard enough to have conducted the complex, delicate affairs on the spot in London. Roosevelt compounded his difficulties through depending upon ill-coordinated Navy and State Department communications linking him to the State Department in Washington, and thence to the delegation in London. Further, as he made subtle shifts in his thinking, the two groups of advisers, in Washington and in London, much better informed but of different opinions than his, tried to shape his orders to meet their own views and the realities as they saw them.

These orders and the confusion focused upon the question of temporary stabilization, which the French and other gold countries considered a prerequisite if they were to stay in the conference. Roosevelt continued to feel it was not even a part of the function of the American delegation, but a matter to be handled separately by the Treasury and Federal Reserve representatives, preferably through unilateral American action. The American delegation followed his instructions, issuing a press statement declaring that the greatest immediate contribution the United States could make to world recovery would be its efforts to raise prices, and that the ultimate aim was worldwide stabilization.

Warburg cabled Roosevelt on June 22 that the point of crisis was past, that there was no need for temporary stabilization in order for the conference to continue. He did hope that Roosevelt would authorize the Federal Reserve, without making any declaration, to limit undesirable fluctuations in the value of the dollar. "The worst crisis of the Conference has been passed," Cox cabled. "If you love us all don't give us another week like this one." [13]

"Delighted way things are going," declared Roosevelt in a cable to Hull and Cox:

> The real trouble of first week lay I think with French and British press trying deliberately to discredit us for certain objectives. . . .
> Do not worry about attitude of a few papers like *New York Times*. Prestige of delegation is generally excellent at home and most people are saying you were all clever enough to avoid an obvious trap.

The cables from Warburg and Cox gave Roosevelt the impression that by standing firm he could avoid a temporary stabilization agreement, and that he could prevent disastrous exchange fluctuations through authorizing unilateral Federal Reserve action. He asked Phillips, Baruch, and Woodin in Washington to see if he should take this step to prevent the pound from fluctuating violently above \$4.25.[14] So nominal a commitment, Roosevelt hoped, would be unnecessary.

On the contrary, on June 27, Hull reported a fresh crisis to Roosevelt. MacDonald had assembled the American delegation to warn them that France, Holland, Switzerland, and Belgium, the gold countries, were warning that they would be off gold in perhaps as little as a week if the rapidly softening dollar were not stabilized. On June 28, speculators momentarily drove the dollar down to 76.3 cents in gold. Roosevelt refused to be frightened. He prepared a cable to Hull stating that he thought it questionable whether France would stay on gold under any circumstances. Further, "I do not greatly fear bad setback to our domestic price level restoration even if all these nations go off gold." And in the cable he once again emphasized that there must be only private action by central banks under any tripartite agreement; the Treasury must not participate. A final admonition sounded as though Davis, who had reached the *Amberjack* that day, might be influencing Roosevelt: "I suggest that special care be taken by delegation and Moley and those close to it to insure no publicity of any kind except through Secretary Hull."

These vital instructions never reached Hull! In his covering dispatch to the acting secretary of state, Roosevelt asked Phillips to discuss them with Acheson, Baruch and others, and send them as soon as possible if there were "no serious disagreement." There was disagreement, since as Undersecretary of the Treasury Acheson wired Roosevelt, if the gold bloc nations devalued their currency, they would thus force up the value of the dollar and depress American commodity prices. Unilateral action by the Federal Reserve would not be adequate to stabilize the dollar; only tripartite action would suffice. Roosevelt replied to Acheson he would not object if Governor Harrison entered into a purely temporary *modus vivendi* with the central banks of the European nations; that "would not be a function of the government so long as no government action were implied or required." [15]

Acheson, Baruch, and Phillips held up Roosevelt's second set of instructions to the delegation because word came in that Sprague and Moley were working on a proposal in keeping with Roosevelt's cables of June 17 and 20. Had Moley received Roosevelt's new instructions, he could have dropped or modified the agreement he was negotiating.

Moley on his second morning in London had learned from Bullitt that the representatives of the gold countries seemed to have abandoned their demand for temporary stabilization and were ready to settle for a statement of ultimate objectives. They had approached MacDonald, who had suggested involving the United States. Moley was intrigued, and, informing Hull in advance, took responsibility for helping shape a statement that could go to Roosevelt for approval. If the President could accept "some sort of innocuous, non-binding compromise," he has reminisced, "it might cure most of the confusion in which the delegates had been immersed since their arrival." [16]

The statement Moley helped draft was indeed on its face one of innocuous generalities, in keeping with Roosevelt's frequently reiterated views and instructions. It was concocted largely out of the original instructions to the American delegation and the subsequent policy on unilateral control. Sprague in London, and Woodin, Acheson, and Baruch all approved the resolution. Moley, in wiring the final version, declared, "Really believe success even continuance of the Conference depends upon United States agreement." [17]

The statement, which the United States and Great Britain were to sign along with the five gold bloc nations, affirmed that "stability in the international monetary field be attained as quickly as practicable," with gold the international medium of exchange. This was the long-range objective.* As for temporary stabilization:

> Each of the governments whose currencies are not on the gold standard undertakes to adopt the measures which it may deem most appropriate to limit exchange speculation and each of the other signatory governments undertakes to cooperate to the same end.

* FDR's instructions to the American delegation had provided: "That it is in the interests of all concerned that stability in the international monetary field be attained as quickly as practicable; That gold should be reestablished as the international measure of exchange values. . . ." [18]

Each of the undersigned governments agrees to ask its central bank
to cooperate with the central banks of the other signatory governments
in limiting speculation in the exchanges and when the time comes in
reestablishing a general international gold standard.[19]

While Moley and the American delegation in London waited with
growing tension, Roosevelt decided upon a reply. The messages from
London and Washington reached him at Campobello Island, which
he was visiting for the first time since he had left on a stretcher, a polio
victim, twelve years before. He was back in the summer home where
he had frolicked as a boy and suffered intense pain and despair in 1921.
It was a gathering of the family and friends, with Eleanor Roosevelt,
Franklin, Jr., Howe, and Morgenthau all there — the sort of gathering
he had so frequently known and relished in earlier years, this time augmented by the excitement among the people on the island over being
hosts to the President of the United States. It was in this setting that
Roosevelt ratified the conclusions he had already reached on the *Amberjack*.

There were pressures both pro and con. When Colonel House had
come aboard the *Amberjack II* at Gloucester on June 21, he had handed
Roosevelt a long letter from a disciple of Warren emphatically opposing
temporary stabilization. House also gave Roosevelt a copy of an important new British treatise, Sir Basil Blackett's *Planned Money*. On
the other hand, Norman Davis, according to Howe, had been strongly
urging Roosevelt to stabilize the dollar. Howe himself was opposed,
and urged Morgenthau to work on Roosevelt, since "the trouble with
this idea is that there are no limits to how much money they might
need." [20]

Eleanor Roosevelt was also involved, not concerning stabilization but
Moley. Herself a strong League of Nations internationalist, she may
not have liked Moley's ideas. There was an additional concern in her
mind — her husband's independence. In 1928 she had warned Roosevelt
he must think seriously before taking Al Smith's brilliant but domineer-
ing aide, Belle Moscowitz, to work for him. In 1933 she may have
shared Howe's apprehension over someone being as close and influential
as Moley had become, and felt that once again Roosevelt must decide
if he were to be his own man. Morgenthau noted that Eleanor Roosevelt had said to her husband on Thursday evening, "It seems to me that
it is a mistake to have Moley go over to London, and that it is belittling
to Hull and must weaken Hull's position." Then, according to Morgenthau:

F.D.R. tried to explain to her that this was not so, but he was not
very convincing about it. Eleanor Roosevelt followed me to my room
and talked to me about 15 minutes. I told her that I had agreed to what

she said about Moley. She made a most startling statement. She said, "I made that statement about Moley for two reasons—one, I wanted to get it over to Franklin and, two, I wanted Missy [LeHand, Roosevelt's secretary] to hear it as I know she will repeat it to Moley." I said, "I thought Missy didn't like Moley." She said, "She pretends not to but Moley takes her and Grace Tully out to tea and makes a big fuss over them." Eleanor said, "You know I see and know what is going on around Franklin, but he seems to be entirely oblivious to all of it." [21]

There is no reason to think that Howe, Morgenthau, or Mrs. Roosevelt played any critical role in Roosevelt's decision on the London statement, although they may have contributed to the vehemence of the bombshell message he sent two days later.

About one in the afternoon of June 30, according to Roosevelt's later memory, McIntyre came ashore from the cruiser *Indianapolis* to inform Roosevelt that a long message was coming in from London. Roosevelt went on to an informal luncheon on the beach where Mrs. Roosevelt entertained a hundred guests, toasting hot dogs.[22]

In the afternoon while the Roosevelt family went for tea on the *Indianapolis*, Roosevelt entertained the reporters in his Campobello living room. "He was dressed comfortably in his favorite vacation costume of slacks and a worn sweater. He was not wearing his braces," Hurd recalls. "No one could look more the part of a loafer than he did at the moment." It seemed to be an informal visit, since he had assured them that "the news lid is on," and so for a while it was as he told them stories about the Bay of Fundy, and played a few hands of cut-in bridge. As he played, the problem of how to answer the incoming message from London, which had not yet reached him, must have been in the back of his mind, for he suddenly turned the card game into an informal press conference and (without a stenographer present to take down his remarks) gave the correspondents in advance the word he was planning to send the American delegation, apparently assuming that Moley's message would be a stabilization proposal. Hurd's recollection years later was:

> [T]he President pushed back his wheel chair and said, "I think it might be more interesting just to talk for a while." . . . Roosevelt was off and running on a "conversation" that must have been conceived as spontaneously as a message to Congress. Etiquette of the day forbade us to take notes; we listened. . . . Roosevelt might be an internationalist, something of an Anglophile through family and friends, a cosmopolitan; but at this stage he was determined that the United States was not to be pushed around.
>
> Out came tumbling all of Roosevelt's resentment against the debtor nations' refusal to pay their obligations, which wound up hurting

Americans who held worthless or depreciated bonds. Out came also his feeling that changes in tariffs must not make possible dumping on American markets, and in conclusion came his firm statement that this was not the time for currency stabilization.

It was a major story, Hurd and his colleagues realized, and they asked the President if it was for publication. He told them it was "off the record," but made clear in subsequent remarks that he would not authorize, but also not object to, whatever they might send with a Campobello dateline.[23]

On the front page of the *New York Times* the next morning, July 1, 1933, Hurd's story appeared: "President Roosevelt will not obligate the United States at this time to any form of stabilization of the dollar, it was learned on high authority. . . ." The Associated Press story that followed dispensed with the circumlocution and attributed the statement directly to Roosevelt. London newspapers and the press of the world carried the flat statement, based on remarks Roosevelt made to reporters before he had even read Moley's message.[24]

It was the night of June 30 before Roosevelt received the message and prepared his reply. The message was garbled through transmission and decoding troubles, and by the time it reached Roosevelt his mood may not have been at its best. For a second day in succession he had presided over a jolly cocktail party, and apparently had upset Mrs. Roosevelt by serving a cocktail to Franklin, Jr., still in his teens. When the assemblage arrived at the dinner table a half-hour late she talked to her husband, according to Morgenthau, as though he were a small boy. Roosevelt retorted, "You can't scold me this way. It is not my fault and I didn't know what time supper was." [25]

In the course of the evening the dispatch from Moley finally arrived. McIntyre inquired what answer to send, and Roosevelt said, "Send word to Hull to say nothing, do nothing and agree to nothing." When Moley in London received this dispatch, it added to his nervousness; there was little doubt what would follow. At the cottage on Campobello, an often-described scene took place. For several hours, Roosevelt sat talking with Morgenthau, Eleanor Roosevelt, and her two friends, Marion Dickerman and Nancy Cook. Howe, stretched out on a couch half asleep, did not take part in the discussion as Morgenthau once again expounded with charts the familiar Warren and Pearson commodity dollar ideas. In addition, he discussed with Roosevelt a lively but superficial article that Garet Garrett had just published in the *Saturday Evening Post*, denouncing the iniquities of "Sterlingaria." The evening may have confirmed Roosevelt's views; it is not likely the discussion modified them. He did not show Morgenthau the dispatch from London; at nearly midnight he sent off a lengthy answer in which he set forth his already familiar views, not all of them relevant to the proposed agreement that Moley had submitted: [26]

"In regard to suggested joint declaration I must tell you frankly that I believe the greatest part of it relates primarily to functions of private banks and not functions of government." By this he meant temporary stabilization. "Other parts of declaration relating to broad governmental policies go so far as to erect probable barriers against our own economic fiscal development." Roosevelt had in mind his option to modify the gold content of the dollar and not return to gold unless or when he wished. He concluded:

> It would be well to reiterate fact that England left gold standard nearly two years ago and only now is seeking stabilization. Also that France did not stabilize for three years or more.* If France seeks to break up conference just because we decline her dictum we should take the sound position that economic conference was initiated and called to discuss and agree on permanent solutions of world economics and not to discuss domestic economic policy of one nation out of the sixty-six present. When conference was called its necessity was obvious although problem of stabilization of American dollar was not even in existence.[28]

As the message finally started to arrive in London, Moley caught Hull on his way to spend a weekend with Lord and Lady Astor at Cliveden. Hull refused to delay his departure, but had a copy of the message sent out to him at the Astors'. There, to the surprise of the British, he expressed open satisfaction, even though Roosevelt's message made it almost impossible for him to continue his work at the conference. He interpreted it as a humiliation of Moley, and to Hull that was what seemed to count most. Several of the Americans at the house party also rejoiced, and for the same reason. It was also a victory for the professional Foreign Service. Moffat reported to a fellow Foreign Service officer afterward:

> The Service (with one exception) stood by [Hull] loyally at London and he is well aware of the fact. Jimmie Dunn tells me that the camps were so sharply divided within the delegation at London that there was no possibility of being neutral, smiling to everybody, and going your own way. You had to declare yourself on one side or the other.[29]

So it was that the Americans rejoiced at Cliveden. Not all the rejoicing was out of hostility to Moley; Pittman, who favored stabilization, continued to be Moley's advocate. The hollow laughter of War-

---

* In phrases like this, the words of Swope's memorandum that he had left with FDR came back to haunt Moley. Swope had written: "Your attention is directed to the fact that England left the gold standard a year and nine months ago, and only now is she seeking stabilization. France did not stabilize for something like four years (verify period)." [27]

burg and Bullitt expressed less a lack of enthusiasm for Moley than the
irony of the way in which their work was destroyed. Warburg shortly
resigned and returned home. But as for those who were exclusively
concerned with Moley's defeat — "little did they realize that the rug
had been jerked from beneath their feet, too," Moley has reminisced,
"that the country they represented had been grievously injured in the
eyes of the world." [30]

Loyally Moley replied to Roosevelt, "Personally bow to your judgment with no inconsiderable relief," by which, he has explained, he
meant, "It is your baby now." (Both Moley and Hull lavished congratulations and assurances of fealty upon Roosevelt in the next several
days.) Then Moley, baffled at Roosevelt's assumption that the agreement had involved immediate stabilization and the President's "fantastic
economic reasoning," withheld the dispatch from the press. Rather, he
had the press officer simply announce that Roosevelt had rejected the
declaration in its present form. Hurriedly, Moley and Swope, with the
assistance of Walter Lippmann, drafted an explanatory softening statement for the American delegation to issue on Monday morning, July 3.
Before they could issue it, Roosevelt sent his own statement.[31]

Roosevelt wrote the message on the *Indianapolis*. On Sunday afternoon, July 2, his vacation over, he departed for Washington in the way
he relished most, as Commander in Chief, aboard the cruiser. He rode
to the Welchpool, New Brunswick, wharf, and between flanking lines
of scarlet-coated Canadian Mounted Police was piped aboard the destroyer *Ellis*, which took him out to the *Indianapolis*, its white-uniformed
officers and crew awaiting him. As he came aboard to the sound of
four ruffles and flourishes, the band struck up the "Star Spangled Banner," unfurled the President's flag, and an American flag so large it
dipped into the water. Roosevelt then received a twenty-one-gun sa-
lute.[32]

A little later, established in the captain's cabin, Roosevelt took off
his coat, sat at the desk, and wrote a statement to send to London. There
were no newspapermen aboard, only Howe, Morgenthau, and Franklin, Jr., and a friend. Roosevelt had before him a draft of Howe's, and
characteristically took the first sentence, then rewrote the rest. When
he had finished, he read the draft to Morgenthau and Howe, made a
few slight emendations, and dispatched it. Proud of his handiwork, he
gave Franklin, Jr., the handwritten original, and signed a copy for
Morgenthau. There was no group of advisers and speechwriters from
outside his inner circle to suggest revision of concepts and phrasing,
only Howe (who had been wanting to have a hand in foreign policy)
and Morgenthau, who was unwavering in his adulation. It did not
take Roosevelt long to prepare; he had not boarded the *Indianapolis*

until about 4 P.M. and the statement went off by radio at 6 o'clock. There was nothing soothing or reassuring in Roosevelt's words.[33]

> The Economic Conference should not allow itself to be diverted from its large purposes through concern with temporary monetary stabilization, affecting only a few nations.

> I do not relish the thought that insistence on such action should be made an excuse for the continuance of the basic economic errors that underlie so much of the present world wide depression. . . .

> The sound internal economic system of a nation is a greater factor in its well being than the price of its currency in changing terms of the currencies of other nations.

Then he launched into his own internal program, and the dogma of the Warren commodity dollar:

> It is for this reason that reduced cost of government, adequate government income, and ability to service government debts are all so important to ultimate stability. So too, old fetishes of so called international bankers are being replaced by efforts to plan national currencies with the objective of giving to those currencies a continuing purchasing power which does not greatly vary in terms of the commodities and need of modern civilization.

Finally, he turned to his ultimate goal:

> Our broad purpose is the permanent stabilization of every nation's currency. Gold or gold and silver can well continue to be a metallic reserve behind currencies but this is not the time to dissipate gold reserves. When the world works out concerted policies in the majority of nations to produce balanced budgets and living within their means, then we can properly discuss a better distribution of the world's gold and silver supply to act as a reserve base of national currencies. Restoration of world trade is an important partner, both in the means and in the result.[34]

The message arrived in London for the American delegation early in the morning. When the delegation met, Warburg professed not to know what it meant. Moley described his last conversation with the President in which he had emphasized the commodity dollar, and suggested Roosevelt wanted them seriously to discuss and consider it. As for stabilization, Roosevelt left no doubt in Hull's mind (if indeed there had been some lingering ambiguity) when he talked to Hull by transatlantic telephone on July 5. He expressed in no uncertain terms what he thought of the agreement Moley had submitted to him: [35]

> Make it perfectly clear that this particular flare-up over gold related to private agreements between five or six nations and that the agenda for the conference had nothing in it about this particular subject and

that we have not taken up any of the really big things in the agenda and that on the temporary monetary paying problem we are perfectly willing to have the other four or five nations concerned do what they want to do. We are not blocking London, Paris, and Rome from making some agreement. I have heard over here — we have pretty good information that if that plan had gone through originally and we had approved it, they would have ear-marked a half a [billion] of gold in this country and if they had done that there would have been a flight of gold from the dollar and we would have been morally compelled to stop gold exports again.[36]

Roosevelt's message blew up the moribund conference. It did continue for three weeks more (mainly for the sake of appearances), but any possibility of achievement seemed gone on Monday, July 3. Whatever euphoria Hull enjoyed during his weekend at Cliveden had subsided into despondency; MacDonald received the news stoically on Monday morning, but by evening was thoroughly dejected. "When a man says something with which you can disagree, even if he says it unpleasantly, you can argue with him," MacDonald lamented to Warburg. "But if he says nothing in a hurtful way, there is nothing you can say." Later he told Moley that the message "doesn't sound like the same man I spent so many hours with in Washington." [37]

MacDonald's sorrowful points were the ones that came up again and again as the leaders of the major European nations debated whether or not to continue the conference. Warburg kept notes on a meeting in the prime minister's room on July 4. As he arrived, Prime Minister Hendrik Colijn of the Netherlands, chairman of the economic committee, had just reported that because of Roosevelt's message all the subcommittees had refused to continue deliberations.

> COLIJN: Apparently all the knowledge about monetary affairs is on the other side of the water and we here know nothing. Perhaps that is correct, but I scarcely think so. In any case, progress on the economic side is absolutely impossible except perhaps in a few isolated things like wheat.
> MACDONALD: The wheat thing is stuck again.
> COLIJN: What I meant is that a few sub-committees on a restriction of production of commodities might continue their work, but continuing the whole Conference would be a pure waste of time.

Cox suggested that since frankness was requisite in the discussion, he would be glad to withdraw if his presence restricted what others might say. MacDonald assured him he should remain, and there was no lack of candor in what followed. Jung of Italy and Bonnet of France also thought it would be idle to continue. Bonnet asserted he had consistently felt that without some degree of monetary stability there could be no progress in financial or economic deliberations. According to Warburg, Bonnet said:

> that Herriot and Roosevelt had agreed on the ultimate reestablish-
> ment of a gold standard and the necessity for monetary stability, but that
> Roosevelt's yesterday's message marked a complete departure down a
> new road. . . .
>
> MacDonald: I was not going to bring up the question of conversations
> that took place in Washington, and I do not intend now to discuss
> them except to say that Roosevelt and I considered currency problems
> when I was there and that the position he took in his yesterday's
> message is quite contrary to the position Roosevelt then revealed to me.
> There is no doubt at all that the message of yesterday was a very serious
> one. We do not want to interfere with the internal policy of the
> United States. It would ill-become us to make President Roosevelt's
> task any more difficult than it already is, but what we rightly expect of
> Roosevelt is that he should not make our task any harder. He ought
> to be a cooperating negotiator, helping us to find an arrangement which
> will not bring chaos on Europe as the price of American success. I
> still hope that he will cooperate in this way, but what hurts me about
> his yesterday's message is that the tone is that of an outsider, — of one
> who has no interest in the affairs and troubles of the rest of the world.
> That is why this crisis has arisen. . . .
>
> Jung: About the Washington conversations I need only say what was
> stated in my joint declaration with the President, which certainly was
> not an agreement along the lines indicated yesterday. . . . I think we
> should keep the fire alive by keeping such committees at work as can
> profitably continue, but should adjourn the Conference without general
> discussion.

Chancellor of the Exchequer Neville Chamberlain, who had joined the meeting,

> said, that in view of the Roosevelt message, it seemed to him quite
> futile to continue the Conference but that he dreaded the effect of its
> dissolution. . . . He suggested adjourning until October 1st, and Mac-
> Donald added, "or until there is reasonable hope that the chief obstacles
> to progress have been removed." [38]

The Europeans had a plausible grievance against Roosevelt, who was in July by no means what he had been in April and May. Indeed, he had been again different in January and February when the United States was still on the gold standard and he was eager for the conference to meet early, primarily to persuade the British to return to gold and stabilize the pound — to remove the disadvantage American exporters were suffering in the world markets.

Defenders of Roosevelt could retort that the shoe was on the other foot. Fundamentally, the President did not want stabilization because it would cost the United States some of its gold reserve, which could be a political even if not an economic disaster. Further, it would interfere with his plans for a managed currency, whether the "commodity dollar" or some other more sophisticated scheme. They could accuse the French and the gold bloc nations (and to some degree the British) of seeking only currency stabilization and ultimate American return to the gold standard in order to regain their lost advantage. Feis, who was never overly fond of Roosevelt, in his economic analysis a generation later concluded that the President was indeed averting the peril of a drain of a half billion dollars in gold, which could have had painful effects in the United States over a period of years.[39]

Contemporary comment on Roosevelt's bombshell message within and without the United States bore the marks of national bias and attitudes toward the gold standard. Within the United States, nationalism was the prevailing note. Conservative papers, which were soon to assail Roosevelt's "baloney dollar," hailed the President for running up the stars and stripes on the banks of the Thames in defiance of the selfish Europeans. In England there was a mixed press, and support from Winston Churchill and John Maynard Keynes. Keynes and Lippmann aided Moley in preparing a masterful defense of Roosevelt's policies for the use of the American delegation. On the continent there was vehement criticism in gold standard countries. The *Journal de Genève* in Switzerland went so far as to assert that the collapse of international confidence was due to two individuals — Hitler, who had paralyzed the Disarmament Conference, and Roosevelt, through his egoistic and incoherent policies, the Economic Conference. After taking office, Roosevelt had raised the hopes of the Old World, and the disillusion was all the more cruel.[40]

Roosevelt had overreacted in his dispatch rejecting the resolution and in the bombshell message. Only slowly during the months since January had his thinking clarified so he could see the inconsistencies between managed currency, perhaps the commodity dollar, at home and a tripartite stabilization agreement with Britain and France. (He still would not admit to the inconsistency between the AAA and NRA on the one hand, and Hull's trade program on the other.) While circumstances and his own concepts were changing, his habitual affability and skill in generalizing his way across serious differences gave the impression that he was still reaching accommodations. As a result, in his meetings with the British, French, and Italians in the spring, he had falsely given the public the impression that the Economic Conference would work miracles. He had seemed to promise stabilization to the French, but the French, British, and Italians really had pledged nothing to him. In private the officials of these nations remained skeptical that much could come from the conference. It is probable too that the wearisome debt negotiations had irritated Roosevelt.

In discussions with his financially more orthodox advisers, as with foreign envoys, Roosevelt had talked in general enough terms to accept their positions. He had made it amply clear to Warburg in their final discussion that he was excited about the commodity dollar, but Warburg did not feel himself bound to promote the idea in London. With these advisers too, strong in their views and at times argumentative, his patience also may have become strained. There is also the possibility that Kennedy was right, that he was becoming jealous of Moley (and other experts), and that Mrs. Roosevelt's urging caused him to feel that he could in his own right, without their modifications, take a strong, effective stand.

At Campobello and on the *Indianapolis* Roosevelt was away from all the usual restraints which led him to be accommodating — both the foreign leaders and his own advisers. Had the conference met in Washington, where, with his experts beside him, he could have dealt face to face with the foreign representatives, there would have been no bombshell message, but rather a new round of optimistic but empty resolutions. And in the aftermath there might well have been accusations of bad faith against Roosevelt. But all the restraining forces were in London, and his patience was at an end. He had rejected two stabilization proposals. The third mild compromise statement that Moley sent him (containing no stabilization formula whatever) led to a blast against the whole idea of stabilization and the conventional operation of gold among nations. Moley years later prepared a devastating analysis of Roosevelt's dispatch showing how far it overshot the statement submitted to him; it was possible to question whether Roosevelt had even read it carefully. Perhaps not. It made no difference. Roosevelt was breaking loose from accommodation toward the British and French, and, it turned out, from reliance on Moley and Warburg.

Yet Roosevelt, having seized world leadership for himself and the United States, through his overkill of the dying Economic Conference threw the leadership away. He had created false expectations, sent a wildly disparate delegation to carry them out, given only sporadic supervision from the *Amberjack II*, and then repudiated those who to the best of their ability were trying to carry out his instructions. He brought down on the United States the onus for the failure of a conference which few if any experts either then or later have believed could have stabilized currencies, lowered tariffs, or raised international prices.

Roosevelt's own reactions were twofold. He sent an explanatory

After a vacation at Campobello, the President boards the
U.S.S. *Indianapolis* to return to Washington, July 2, 1933.
Captain John Morris Smeallie, commander of the *In-
dianapolis*, greets him.

statement to the delegation intended to demonstrate that through its domestic recovery program the United States could best work toward international economic cooperation and recovery. And he began boasting of his remarkable feat in thwarting the selfish designs of the European powers. The more apparent it became how seriously he had undermined his own and his country's prestige, the more, like President Theodore Roosevelt when he blundered, Franklin D. Roosevelt proclaimed that his action was both necessary, effective — and a great coup. Four years later, in February 1937, he told Arthur Krock of the *New York Times* that the United States at London was about to be "had" by the Bank of France and the Bank of England. As for the bombshell message, said Roosevelt, "I'm prouder of that than anything else I ever did." Yet in August 1933, he was pleased to receive a clipping of a favorable article in the London *Times:* "I was a little afraid that they still felt that I was a sort of pirate who had torpedoed their pet schemes at the Economic Conference!" [41]

CHAPTER XXIX

The End of the Beginning

The government of the United States sees no inconsistency between its program for economic recovery
and international cooperation for the purpose of restoring prosperity throughout the world.
— FDR TO AMERICAN DELEGATES TO ECONOMIC CONFERENCE,
July 4, 1933.

Both advocates and adversaries could agree as they began a reevaluation
in the aftermath of Roosevelt's bombshell message to the London Economic Conference that a significant change had taken place. It marked
an end to the beginning of the New Deal and a change in tactics and
focus, even though Roosevelt proved over the course of the subsequent
years what he insisted at the time, that there had been no change in
his ultimate goals.

Roosevelt, not wishing to bear responsibility for the collapse of the
Economic Conference, urged Secretary Hull and the American delegation to do all they could to keep it functioning. He tried to set for it
a new main objective, to achieve higher price levels. In his guideline
statement for the delegates on July 4, he explained that the tariff and
quota restrictions, mandatory in the agricultural recovery program and
optional in the industrial program, existed only to prevent the exploitation of workers and a "lowering of living standards throughout the
world." If other countries paid wages and farm prices comparable to
those in the United States there could be a free flow of trade and no
need to invoke the NRA and AAA restrictions.[1]

As a means of avoiding censure, either direct or implicit, Roosevelt
wanted the conference to continue. He cabled Hull:

An adjournment of 60 days is in my judgment a defeatist gesture
and we should oppose it. We cannot in any way admit or agree that no
progress can be made on economic problems until temporary exchange
fluctuations are first settled.

The people and press here are united in praise of our stand and regard
the French position as wholly selfish and ignoring utterly the big objectives of Conference.[2]

Roosevelt followed the dispatch with a telephone call to Hull. When Hull told him that the delegation's plan was to take a recess subject to the call of Chairman MacDonald, he retorted, "That might be six months. That was intended to nail us to the cross." [3]

In response to Roosevelt's urging, Hull did manage to hold the conference together, dropping his passivity and for several days asserting positive leadership over his delegation. Like Roosevelt, he basked in commendatory messages. But it was a futile undertaking, and as it became clear that almost nothing could be accomplished, Hull relaxed his control. Feis wrote despairingly on July 17:

> The Secretary has practically ceased his effort to direct the delegation. His hands have lost all guiding forces against the difficulty of managing this collection of difficult personalities. Resentful impatience closes in on him. . . . The Secretary is so shaken and shocked by his experiences that he is unwilling to express an American position on any point without explicit authorization. Only the calculating silver man from Nevada does anything.[4]

Once again the members of the delegation went their own way, several of them seldom bothering to attend meetings. The total achievement was not quite zero, thanks to Senator Pittman. After the conference, Charles Ross, a St. Louis newspaperman, remarked to Feis that Pittman had seemed drunk nine-tenths of the time. "You're wrong," retorted Feis. "He was drunk all the time." Yet Pittman succeeded in obtaining an international agreement that would raise the price of silver.[5]

For the rest the operations of the conference were negative, which did not upset Roosevelt unduly. In suggesting that the delegation continue to work toward world production limitations, he had Phillips cable a little joke at the expense of his Tennessean secretary of state: "In regard to wine production limitation the President does not believe we can enter into any agreement which would limit our right to make domestic wines. This, he holds, is a domestic industry of great potential value and is in line with our national effort to increase temperance by substitution of beer and wines for Tennessee and Georgian mountain dews." [6]

There was an appropriateness to Roosevelt's reference to Appalachian customs, for Hull, with the tenacity and virulence of the head of a mountain feuding clan, was still gathering bits of evidence on Moley day by day. From his secretary, Hugh Cumming, he obtained a memorandum of a conversation on July 1 in which Moley, trying to assure Cumming he did not wish to undermine Hull, allegedly made the incredible statement that had he ever wanted to be Secretary of State, which he had not, "he supposed that he was at one time in a position to work to that end." [7] At Hull's request, Bullitt on July 2 wrote another memorandum, declaring that Moley at his own request had taken over discussion of exchange fluctuations — a charge that Hull considered so serious that he himself countersigned the statement. In addition, Hull urged the multimillionaire Texas delegate, Morrison, to talk to Roosevelt, and may well have inspired messages from Ambassador Bingham to the receptive Howe. All these became mere supporting evidence when Hull obtained from the embassy a copy of a cable Moley had sent Roosevelt listing the agenda for a telephone conversation. It contained two damning sentences:

> Topic 2. On personal side Pittman is only member of delegation able intellectually and aggressively to present your ideas to Conference. . . .
> Topic 4. Reconstituted delegation would be helpful in view of developments. . . .[8]

Judge Hull's case was complete. Moley had just departed for the United States after the conventional exchange of assurances of fidelity and high regard. There followed one of the greatest performances of political drama since James G. Blaine had "read" the incriminating Mulligan letters on the floor of the Senate. Folding back the top of the letter, with the offending paragraphs before him, he held forth to the delegates and experts. Warburg, arriving back at his room late at night, found a note summoning him to the secretary's presence. Hull in his dressing gown declaimed: "That piss-ant Moley, here he curled up at mah feet and let me stroke his head like a huntin' dog and then he goes and bites me in the ass!" [9]

During subsequent years, Hull frequently referred to Moley's cable and his reading of it to the assembled delegation. Feis in his analysis of the conference confesses that before he himself in his research saw the cable: "I too had been led by Hull's account to think that it contemptuously criticized each and every member of the delegation by name. On reading it much later, however, I found it unjust but I did not find it as harsh as I had conceived it to be or its purpose as unworthy." [10]

Hull was ready to break his silence to Roosevelt. Bingham had already telephoned Howe several times, and the President was prepared for the long, indignant cable:

"It is most painful . . . to have to report an attitude and course of conduct on the part of Professor Moley which has been utterly dumbfounding to me. . . ." And the full bill of particulars followed, from Moley's radio speech of May through his direct negotiations with "MacDonald and other Prime Ministers." In contrast, Hull pictured himself as the true defender of the President's interests and honor, at the very time of Moley's prime betrayal. When the delegates of the gold nations were about to vote a resolution charging Roosevelt with wrecking the conference and recommending adjournment, Hull wrote:

> The chances seemed ninety-nine to a hundred that this course would be taken. Many of the Delegates were frozen towards me as I strove to quiet and compose them at the meeting called expressly to carry out this adjournment program. At any rate, while it so happened that I was in the position of undertaking to deal with this crisis singlehanded, and was lucky enough if I may say so to be the chief single factor in pre-serving the life of the Conference and in saving you from the outrage of being branded as its destroyer, Moley was secretly sending code messages to you about my incapacity to function here.[11]

As was characteristic, Hull ended with no overt ultimatum — but it was clear enough. Roosevelt had to choose between a secretary of state whom he had infrequently seen and less often kept informed and the chief of his advisers to whom he had entrusted the pursuit of numerous vital projects and the drafting of almost all his major speeches and statements. Yet to have dropped the secretary would have been more explosive than the bombshell message, a signal for revolt among hard-pressed conservative southern Democrats. Hull was not Carter Glass, who as secretary of the treasury could have made Roosevelt dance, but his coercive power was considerable.

Besides, Roosevelt as usual seems to have convinced himself there was no need for a clear-cut choice. He could not move Moley into the White House because of the jealous Howe, but he could send him out of Washington for a while, out of the spotlight. (Perhaps he too had not relished seeing Moley's picture on the cover of *Time*, or the wisecrack of the spring that one had to call up Roosevelt to get an appointment to see Moley.) It was easy also for Roosevelt to slip into criticism of Moley's course of action, he was hearing and reading so much of it both from Hull's coterie and from conservatives, who as yet did not dare turn their guns on the President. Arthur Krock sent Baruch a column by the right-wing Frank Kent sizzling Moley, and commented, "You see Frank was much rougher than I. Yet it's all true." [12]

For several weeks Roosevelt did not make his mind up. He greeted the apprehensive Moley upon his return without any reassurance, which was depressing for Moley. Rather, he talked as though nothing had happened and everything would go on as before — and boasted of his own role in the conference. The cynical Swope wrote Baruch, whom he served, that Moley had been forgiven, but that he was so shaken that he would not be useful as a conduit. At the end of July, with Hull about to return, Roosevelt had to come to a decision. He sent Hull a cable expressing his "affectionate regard for and confidence in you," and other words of high commendation, and inviting Hull and Mrs. Hull when they arrived in New York to come to Hyde Park to stay overnight. Then he confided his plans to Morgenthau.[13]

> F.D.R. told me as a deep secret that it was absolutely necessary for him to get Moley out of Washington before Hull returned as Hull would kick up such a terrible fuss. F.D.R. said that after Moley was in London two days he started dealing direct with some of the countries which, naturally, made Hull furious. He said, "I am thinking of sending Moley to Hawaii to make a study of conditions there, and in this way get him out of the path of Hull." F.D.R. said Moley has done a number of stupid things.[14]

Since Roosevelt did not want to convey so uncomplimentary a suggestion to one who had been so close to him and performed such important services, he left the unpleasant task to Howe. Moley did not take it well from Howe and insisted upon airing the question with Roosevelt. As Roosevelt first developed it, Moley was to study crime in Hawaii without resigning as assistant secretary of state, apparently in the hope that Hull's feelings would subside. Rather, after several days' deliberation, and consultation with Frankfurter, Moley accepted a temporary assignment with the attorney general to prepare a report on federal legislation to curb kidnapping and racketeering. It was as an expert on crime that Moley had first served Roosevelt. Weeks later, Moley quietly resigned at a time when he could do so without sensation, and received a warm and appreciative reply from Roosevelt.

Moley was not leaving the service of the New Deal, either as an adviser and speechwriter for Roosevelt, or as a publicist. Into 1935 he continued to slip in and out of the White House without fanfare, for a total (he has counted) of 132 days in Washington. His main thrust was, as he had been planning since April, to enter journalism. He became the editor of a new magazine, *Today*, which Vincent Astor, Averell Harriman, and Mary Harriman Rumsey financed; in 1937 it absorbed another magazine and took over its name, *Newsweek*. Moley continued to be of service, but was never again so close or so essential. Gradually he felt less and less sympathetic toward the New Deal, and by the second term was a conservative opponent.[15]

Secretary Hull never broke with the New Deal or even resigned. Upon Hull Roosevelt continued to ladle what the cynical Howe liked to call soothing syrup, and dropped extravagant political compliments where they would get back to the brooding secretary. Thus Secretary Roper reported to Hull that Roosevelt had told him "you had done a perfectly marvelous job in London." Roosevelt went so far as to write

Ambassador Bingham that Hull was the finest person he knew. Bingham, a master of political rhetoric, easily topped the President by replying: [16] "He did a really magnificent job here and emerged as the great figure of the Conference, with the respect and confidence of the delegates of all the nations represented here. I know of no finer incident in American diplomatic history than his achievements here." [17]

Secretary Hull returned to the State Department his morale much higher than when he sailed for London. "The general belief is," Moffat commented, "that henceforth he will be master in his own house and that the discordant elements will little by little disappear." During the final weeks of the Economic Conference, Roosevelt enlisted none other than Norman Davis to handle the dispatches to the delegates.[18]

Hull responded to Roosevelt's concessions with the conventional protestations of loyalty and admiration. His rancor continued to smolder, and before the end of 1933 he had added new grievances when he failed to receive as strong backing as he wished at the Inter-American Conference. Claude Bowers, returning from Spain in 1935, found Hull could talk of nothing else until he had aired thoroughly the topics of Moley, Roosevelt, London, and Montevideo. Ten years later Leith-Ross called on the secretary and heard the same bitter complaints. For years and years the relationship between Roosevelt and Hull continued much the same — the encomiums, bypassing, and resentment.[19]

The President continued his personal pursuit of foreign affairs even as the Economic Conference was slowly collapsing. Norman Davis's incredibly optimistic report on the Disarmament Conference left him still moderately hopeful for arms control.* Davis actually thought he would have achieved agreement by mid-July if the Economic Conference had not interfered. Roosevelt cheerfully informed Davis at the end of the summer, "If you pull off disarmament they will bury you in Arlington when you die if that is any comfort to you now!" By mid-October, Hitler had extinguished all but the faintest chance of disarmament, but somehow, like many men of goodwill in Europe, Davis and Roosevelt retained their hopes.[21]

Already in the summer, Roosevelt was moving toward substitutes for his grand plan in foreign policy. There was the Good Neighbor policy toward Latin America, which he had mentioned in his inaugural

* Davis had asserted at a meeting at the French Foreign Office before Daladier, Eden, and others, on June 8, 1933, "that in his opinion Hitler had decided already that it was in Germany's interest to limit armaments and that in point of fact he is less militaristic than Neurath, Von Papen and others. He thought that if we showed a willingness to discuss and good faith in drafting a disarmament program we could test German willingness to go along with us. That if they complied well and good, but that if they did not comply then public opinion of the world would come into play." [20]

At the Civilian Conservation Corps camp at Big Meadows in th
Shenandoah Valley, Virginia, August 12, 1933. From left t

right, General Paul Malone, Louis McHenry Howe, Harold Ickes,
Robert Fechner, FDR, Henry Wallace, and Rexford Tugwell.

address and used as the topic of an April address. Acute difficulties in Cuba helped turn his attention southward. In years ahead, within the framework of the Monroe Doctrine (protecting him from congressional censure), he could first work out in the Americas the security system that in the spring of 1933 he could not yet persuade the world to accept. For Secretary Hull, Latin America gave an opportunity for the development of reciprocal trade agreements. Already too, Roosevelt, without Hull being in the least involved, was well along in feelers to develop trade with the Soviet Union, and before the end of 1933 extended recognition.

These modest undertakings marked a substantial veering away from the world leadership of the spring. At the end of the summer, when Vansittart queried D'Arcy Osborne, the British *chargé d'affaires* in Washington, as to the state of affairs, Osborne confessed himself uncertain, and suggested that it all depended upon the President and the influences his advisers exerted upon him:

> His first much advertised entry into the field of foreign politics was somewhat of a fiasco and his natural reaction was to seek an excuse and an alibi, which involved establishing a grievance at home and finding a scapegoat abroad. . . . From President downwards immediate interest and sentiment of the country is concentrated on recovery programme and its domestic results, and this implies a nationalistic inspiration and orientation of foreign policy. It seems clear that, largely in conjunction with advancement of this programme, administration and state department have turned their eyes away from Europe towards South America. . . . Situation here seems to render isolation and nationalism inevitable and I think that we should do well to accept it realistically. As implications of his domestic policy become apparent and if conditions here improve, Europe will come into the perspective again. . . . But generally speaking situation here is so incalculable and President himself so mercurial and his policies so admittedly empirical that all estimates and forecasts are dangerous.

One Foreign Office expert summed up the turn of events in a sentence: "Mr. Roosevelt is giving up hope in the old world and is turning his attention to the new." [22]

Pressures from both Congress and the public were forcing Roosevelt to shift, giving validity to the British estimate of June 1933. The President's actions of the spring, it was the Foreign Office consensus, "induce in the public of the United States a feeling that their champion is playing the leading part in world affairs; and there are many indications that only so long as he can continue to play the leading part will he be allowed to participate in world affairs at all." [23]

Perhaps it would have been too much under the most favorable of circumstances for Roosevelt to initiate and implement simultaneously both national and world programs. There were compelling and vital tasks at home to challenge him in the summer of 1933. The many fledgling agencies must be put into full and successful operation, especially the great engines of recovery, the AAA and the NRA. Yet the NRA was showing signs of collapse before it could even establish its elaborate code machinery. Speculative stockpiling of industrial goods within the United States, and equally speculative driving down of the dollar on the European exchanges, created a fresh crisis within the nation before the end of July. When the dollar dropped to a ratio of 4.86 to the pound, Roosevelt became fearful of a fresh British devaluation, and resorted to the unilateral stabilization he had kept in reserve as a weapon. He laughed rather sheepishly as he informed Moley and Lewis Douglas of his secret authorization to the Federal Reserve to export as much as $30 million in gold over a two-week period in order to bolster the dollar. The news spread in several days. Stock and commodity prices fell drastically, and the spring boomlet was over. Then the rebuilding had to resume.[24]

Although Roosevelt had yet to put to test seriously his skills as a federal administrator, through the months of the interregnum and the "hundred days" he had given clear indications of what manner of President he was. Already in that short period, through restoring public morale and marshaling an unprecedented program through Congress, he had established himself as a spectacular figure, far out of the usual run of Presidents. He was creating a Roosevelt mystique, generating passionate loyalty, equally heartfelt hatred, and much puzzled support — but little indifference.

In both national and foreign affairs, Roosevelt was proclaiming a high idealism as the approach to a grand design. He was a national planner in the Theodore Roosevelt tradition, launching programs both in agricultural and industrial rehabilitation, and in areas of his keen personal interest, conservation, reforestation, and regional development. Simultaneously he was a regulator in the Wilsonian tradition of which Brandeis was high priest, a believer in the balanced budget, expressing repugnance for economic and financial oligarchy. And he was an experimenter in the unmapped regions of controlled inflation and managed currency. He had even been nudged slightly in the Keynesian direction toward the expenditure of several billions of public works money with the assurance that if the government met interest charges on this extraordinary commitment it would not threaten the nation's credit rating. Add to this in foreign affairs his faith in international economic cooperation and disarmament, undimmed despite the setbacks in London and Geneva, and his expectation that he could develop reciprocal trade agreements yet protect domestic producers. In total, he intended to develop great programs of economic nationalism and international cooperation to bring security and a better life both at home and throughout the world. Somehow he had the faith that he could undertake all these without serious contradiction.

Within his great scheme, Roosevelt kept open his option to experiment. *Fortune* commented in December 1933, "Where Wilson would sacrifice any fact to a theory, Mr. Roosevelt will sacrifice any theory to a fact." *Fortune* was unfair to both men. Wilson at least until 1919 had frequently accepted political realities; Roosevelt seldom abandoned his visions, only his means of trying to attain them. In his Fireside Chat of May 7, 1933, he asserted:

> I do not deny that we may make mistakes of procedure as we carry out the policy. I have no expectation of making a hit every time I come to bat. What I seek is the highest possible batting average, not only for myself but for the team. Theodore Roosevelt once said to me: "If I can be right 75 percent of the time I shall come up to the fullest measure of my hopes." [25]

Roosevelt was gifted in maintaining an ambience between his noble objectives and the tactics of the feasible. He had yet to demonstrate whether he could bridge the gulf between his aspirations and reality. As President he was exercising a hard-headed day-by-day realism, maintaining the initiative, keeping potential adversaries off balance, trimming, modifying, compromising, and occasionally waiting for a more propitious time. To Eleanor Roosevelt, who shared his ideals, he once early in the New Deal tried to explain his methods. "You'll never be a good politician," he admonished. "You are too impatient." He explained that one must wait until the electorate was ready to support a change, since if it were rammed through too soon the voters would revolt. His practical operations were those of the skilled politician and they were also in keeping with American democratic traditions.[26]

Critics complained that he would compromise away the essence of reforms in order to obtain the passage of a bill, and that he created unworkable complications. Some of the compromises of the spring of 1933 did lead to future problems, as witness the selection in advance of George Peek to run an AAA program quite contrary to Peek's deepest views. Again, postponement of what was not immediately essential in order to avoid congressional complications or filibuster turned out to be feasible in the instance of the reciprocal trade program but led to future impasse over the arms embargo question.

There were enigmas in Roosevelt's mode of operations. Both his reserve and his political sense of the dramatic caused him to be inscrutable or oblique at times, and to enjoy the surprise that came with some of his announcements. Nonetheless, newspapermen during the first few months of his presidency obtained in their off-the-record sessions a clear advance exposition of the way in which his thoughts were developing on major domestic policies. These sessions, leading to newspaper background articles, prepared the public for administrative actions. They mirrored discussions taking place the same day or on a previous evening with advisers, cabinet officers, or congressional leaders. For those that listened carefully at any of these sessions there was nothing misleading in Roosevelt's remarks. Unfortunately, others often interpreted his pleasant generalities, which indicated no more than his desire to be accommodating, into an acceptance of their own objectives. He frequently created a false impression through being too affable, as witness his conversations with President Hoover and the German envoy Schacht. Or he did change his mind and wriggle out of what others had thought were firm commitments.

Roosevelt's only significant rival in the spring of 1933, Huey Long, the Louisiana Kingfish, himself a politician of rare ability, knew exactly the purport of these Roosevelt conversations: "Say, listen, I went there to tell the President some very hard things — that he wasn't doing what he should for the people of the country. And then when I got there I couldn't tell him. I didn't get what I wanted and I didn't say what I wanted to say — he was so damned nice to me." [27]

Those like Moley who worked closely with Roosevelt over a period of time came to understand that warm affirmative approach and to judge his intent accordingly. They also knew what to make of the strange, sometimes weird, new schemes that he liked to bandy about in conversations. Neither his easy "fine, fine," nor these exciting ideas were to be confused with policies upon which he had firmly determined.

Roosevelt's habitual decision-making process was indeed that which Feis had fathomed early in 1933, to discuss numerous innovative approaches, ultimately settling upon a fairly conservative course, and once he had set that course standing by it quite stubbornly. To which could be added the observation that ultimately reality might force him to set a new course, at least for the time being.

There was constant speculation over the respective influence of Roosevelt's many advisers, which as a British Foreign Office expert noted, gave "a curiously Byzantine Court atmosphere" to the White House. The speculation was not very useful. Even an adviser as close to him as Moley knew only part of his overall operations. Others like Pittman and Berle found themselves consulted in depth, but only intermittently. Roosevelt did not seem to want to share power, or to become too dependent upon any one man or group of men. At a time when he was most closely following Moley's economic nationalist views he let Moley down; Warburg, who had emphatically opposed these views, was back again in the fall of 1933 giving Roosevelt more firm advice which the President again did not follow. Among these advisers, who were brilliant men working under acute pressure, there could develop unpleasant rivalries and the flash of verbal stilettos. Yet on the whole they presented vigorously their alternative views from which the President could choose, more often than not complemented each other in their thinking, and their competitiveness to achieve was of benefit to Roosevelt.[28]

Some criticisms of Roosevelt have been not over his methods — whether he was asking for a half loaf when he could have obtained the entirety — but over his objectives. Often he did not want the whole loaf, whether it were a larger public works appropriation or the establishment of Federal Deposit Insurance. The quarrel of these critics with Roosevelt would be that in the spring of 1933 he chose to restore the nation's financial and economic system to running order with relatively trivial modification. It never occurred to him to go further; one or two of his advisers talked occasionally about nationalization, but never Roosevelt. Nor was there any support for nationalization, even of banks, in Congress nor among more than a handful of proponents throughout the nation. Socialists and Communists had totally failed during the campaign of 1932 to convince the American electorate that the time had come to scrap the existing economic system.

Roosevelt and Congress had permanently and significantly modified it in the spring of 1933, introducing the element of government intervention in the economy on behalf of the general welfare to a degree never before known in peacetime. The great debate which was to wrack America through Roosevelt's remaining years in the White House and for almost a decade thereafter would not focus upon whether he had gone far enough but upon whether he had gone too far. What pained businessmen was what *Fortune* pointed out to them before the end of 1933, that Roosevelt "does not propose to restore the world of 1929 and would not restore it if he could." [29]

Into July 1933, Roosevelt through his inclusiveness had thus far avoided serious divisiveness. Through his warm, outgoing approach and his setting forth of generalities, he had kept a heavy majority in Congress and among the public behind him. They read into his promises their own wishes. No doubt Roosevelt meant to give them what they wanted. In the twentieth-century tradition, he was trying very hard to be President to all the American people. But in that time of depression deprivation he was reversing the progressive inclusiveness of Theodore Roosevelt and Wilson, who wished to serve all the people through giving favors to none. To the desperate Americans of 1933, Roosevelt wished to dispense aid to all groups — but, and here was where much trouble began, to require concessions and responsibilities from each in return. Businessmen of 1929 had enjoyed privileges and were delighted to receive them in 1933, but did not like being told by Roosevelt that they must shoulder responsibilities, especially toward their workers. As Roosevelt had to make choices and move from generalities to specifics, misunderstandings developed and disappointments burgeoned. These came later. In that first summer the New Deal seemed to encompass businessmen, farmers, workers; men and women; the white-collared and the blue-collared — all in the alliance for recovery.

There was some acute disappointment and sharp opposition. Early in the summer, as the press was heralding substantial reemployment, it was also recording the suicides of several who had lost their jobs or pensions through New Deal economy measures, one of them a woman who had been discharged because she was married. Even in the euphoric days of March, H. V. Kaltenborn, a popular radio commentator, received protests because he and Lowell Thomas were so enthusiastic about Roosevelt. "Every President is entitled to a honeymoon," Kaltenborn admonished a disgruntled Montclair, New Jersey, man. The listener retorted, "Perhaps you are right, but I do not want to be the bride." [30]

By late June 1933, a few critics had become encyclopedic in their bitterness. The Republican senator from West Virginia, Henry D. Hatfield, declared:

> [T]he destiny of a great nation is committed to the caprice of a single individual: . . . the President of the United States clothed in absolute power to control industry . . . inflate the currency. . . . [We have seen] the creation of an American monarch who may license trade . . . [and so on through a lengthy litany of powers, including that to legislate] as a result of the abdication of the Congress itself.
>
> This is despotism. This is tyranny. This is the annihilation of liberty. The ordinary American is thus reduced to the status of a robot. . . . In arrogating to himself these measures, the President, in my opinion, has not merely signed the death warrant of capitalism, but has ordained the mutilation of the Constitution unless the friends of liberty, regardless of party, band themselves together to regain their lost freedom.[31]

More foreboding for the future than this bombast were the quiet qualms that some old progressives like Justice Brandeis were expressing in private. Brandeis in mid-May wrote Frankfurter he shared his apprehensions over the National Industrial Recovery Bill. Furthermore:

> FD's readiness to Experiment is fair. But I am at times reminded of the Uncle-from India's answer in the Private Secretary. When asked by the Housekeeper "do you believe in spirits?" "Yes" — said he — "in moderation." I guess his inflation program, the refusal to pay interest

in gold on our bonds held abroad — and his Economy Control projects will do much harm — I wish he would experiment instead with banishing the banker, through opening P. O. Savings . . . & putting heavier Estate taxes.[32]

Some who had not yet made up their minds, like Roy Roberts of the *Kansas City Star*, were enjoying the spectacle: "We have gone through little short of a social revolution and the country doesn't know it. The old timers are sitting around rubbing their eyes and wondering what is happening, talking about Franklin wandering in Wonderland and all the while we are making major social moves from which there will be no turning back." [33]

The conservative editor of the *Charleston News and Courier*, William W. Ball, also regarded it as a revolution in which the business leaders had abdicated to Roosevelt, and for the moment he was amused at their plight:

One of the explanations of the serenity with which the American people receive these things and submit to them is that Roosevelt is a mild and serene gentleman — his personality is soothing and does not excite alarm. If he were a counterpart of his distant cousin, the former "Theodore," . . . half the country would be jumping out of its skin and the other half wearing cockades and mustering. . . . The great men in business, especially in the great towns, are oppressed with the sense of incapacity, or guilt, or both. . . . The "captains" of finance and industry have been exposed as empty-pates, and the "umble"-ness and filthy veneration with which millions of petty Americans have hitherto looked upon them has vanished. The "captains" are bare in their nakedness as greater fools even than knaves.[34]

Even Theodore Roosevelt's daughter, Alice Roosevelt Longworth, seemed forgiving that a Roosevelt not from Oyster Bay was in the White House. In the summer of 1932, at the ceremonies to notify Hoover of his renomination, she had remarked, "Do you know, we have spent all our lives trying to live up to father, and now we must spend all the rest of our lives trying to live down to Franklin." In April 1933, at a bridge party in Washington, she entertained the ladies by doing imitations of a society woman in her box acting adoringly when Roosevelt appeared. Moffat wrote in his diary: "Curiously enough, she was far less bitter than I have ever seen her; in fact she admitted to being quite surprised at herself in her attitude toward the President. If he can make a conquest there, then he must have the whole country at his feet." [35]

The President was still at a peak of his popularity. Former Senator Chilton of West Virginia, a Democrat, was engaging in the common hyperbole of the "hundred days" when he asserted privately, "Roosevelt has more people today who trust him and like him and would act upon his word than probably any other man in the world, unless it would be Gandhi." [36]

There was a great surge of this feeling from the ordinary people, and their opinions meant much to the President. One of Mrs. Roosevelt's woman correspondents wrote her of a conversation she had overheard among a crippled operator of a newsstand, an iceman, and a taxi driver:

> The taxicab driver was tinged with "Red" and had just said, "To hell with all your politics. What we need is a Stalin." The iceman said, "Oh yeah? We got what we want. We want Roosevelt. Look what he done with the banks. . . ." The cripple said, "Leave him be. He's got beans in Washington." The taxicab driver said, "Sez you. All the beans he's got is being fed to his forest army." Said the cripple, "I don't mean them kind of beans. I mean all the professor guys he's got down there helpin' him. All we can do is pray for him, buddy, and let him have his hand." [37]

Eleanor Roosevelt showed this passage to the President. It summed up the groping hopes of countless Americans, and it was the great challenge to Roosevelt. He accepted it with gusto. There was to be no quick or comfortable route to recovery and reform, but he had charted a possible course. In early 1934 he published a book outlining the New Deal beginnings and appropriately entitled it *On Our Way*.

Acknowledgments

The generosity of many people and institutions has helped me in writing this volume. Numerous fellow historians have aided me, most notably Barton J. Bernstein, John M. Blum, George Green, Charles C. Griffin, Barry Karl, Gabriel Kolko, William E. Leuchtenburg, Richard Lowitt, Elliot A. Rosen, Arthur M. Schlesinger, Jr., and Stephen Schuker. Several participants in the events covered in these pages were most generous with their reminiscences, manuscripts, and evaluations, especially Herbert Feis, Raymond Moley, Frances Perkins, Eleanor Roosevelt, Rexford G. Tugwell, and Charles E. Wyzanski, Jr. Thomas Griffin provided research assistance.

Without the expert advice and assistance of more librarians and archivists than I can here enumerate, I would have overlooked important materials; their hospitality did much to make research pleasant. I am especially indebted to the directors of the Roosevelt Library, Herman Kahn, Elizabeth Drewry, and Joseph C. James, and to William J. Stewart, Edgar Nixon, Jerry Deyo, Joseph Marshall, and Raymond Corry; to David C. Mearns, chief of the Manuscript Division of the Library of Congress and his staff; and to James B. Rhoads, the archivist of the United States, and his staff. Douglas W. Bryant, Harvard University librarian, and especially F. Nathaniel Bunker, Warren Bibliographer; William H. Bond, librarian of Houghton Library, and Judith A. Harding, circulation librarian, have been extraordinarily helpful. Louis M. Starr, director, and Elizabeth Mason have opened to me treasures of the Columbia University Oral History Collection.

Quotations from Crown-copyright records in the Public Record Office appear by permission of the controller of H. M. Stationery Office. I have quoted from the papers of Hiram Johnson by permission of James D. Hart, director, The Bancroft Library, University of California, Berkeley, California; from the papers and books of Raymond Moley with his permission; from the Rexford Guy Tugwell diary and manuscripts with his permission; from the James P. Warburg papers, diary, and Columbia Oral History Collection interview with the permission of Mrs. Joan Warburg; from the Henry L. Stimson diary with the permission of the Yale University Library; and from the Jay Pierrepont Moffat diary and manuscripts and the Joseph Grew diary by permission of the Harvard College Library.

Time and funds for research and writing have come through fellowships from the Center for Advanced Study in the Behavioral Sciences and the Guggenheim Foundation, and grants from the Rockefeller Foundation and the Charles Warren Center for Studies in American History.

From my wife, Madeleine Freidel, have come both perceptive criticism and unflagging encouragement.

Bibliographical Note

There are voluminous manuscript and contemporary printed materials together with numerous memoirs and scholarly studies concerning Roosevelt's interests and actions during the interregnum and the first months of the New Deal. Among manuscript and archival collections bearing upon this period, those at the Franklin D. Roosevelt Library, Hyde Park, New York, are foremost. They include the Governor's Personal File and the Democratic National Committee mss., important on the interregnum, and for the Presidency, the President's Personal File, Secretary's File, and Official File. There are finding aids for these files. Other valuable collections at the Roosevelt Library are the Eleanor Roosevelt mss., Roosevelt family letters, Franklin D. Roosevelt Memorial Foundation files; Rexford G. Tugwell mss., including a perceptive diary and "A New Deal Memoir: Early Days, 1932–1933"; Henry Morgenthau, Jr., mss., including the "Farm Credit Administration Diary," cited in the Notes as "Morgenthau diary"; Louis McHenry Howe mss.; and Mary W. Dewson mss. The Raymond Moley mss. at the Hoover Institute, Stanford University, are indispensable. They include an office diary, which Celeste Jedel kept into May 1933, and Annette Pomerantz briefly in June 1933, together with a journal Moley himself wrote covering his trip to the London Economic Conference, all cited as Moley diary. Among the manuscript collections at the Library of Congress are those of Josephus Daniels, Norman Davis, Raymond Clapper, Herbert Feis, Felix Frankfurter, Emanuel A. Goldenweiser, Cordell Hull, Robert M. La Follette, Jr., James M. Landis, Charles L. McNary, Ogden

Mills, Henrietta Nesbitt, George W. Norris, Key Pittman, Huston Thompson, Thomas J. Walsh, and William Allen White. Other collections, several of them of great importance to an understanding of Roosevelt and the period, are: Lewis W. Douglas mss., University of Arizona; Adolf A. Berle, Jr., mss., in the possession of Mrs. Beatrice B. Berle; Hiram Johnson mss. and J. F. T. O'Connor diary, Bancroft Library, University of California, Berkeley, Calif.; James F. Byrnes mss., Clemson University; Edward P. Costigan mss., University of Colorado; George L. Harrison mss. and Frances Perkins mss., Columbia University; George F. Warren diary, Cornell University; Josiah Bailey and William W. Ball mss., Duke University; Margaret Dreier Robins mss., University of Florida; Thomas W. Lamont mss., Baker Library, Harvard Business School; Joseph Grew diary, Jay Pierrepont Moffat diary and mss., and Oswald Garrison Villard mss., Houghton Library, Harvard University; Herbert Hoover mss., Herbert Hoover Library, West Branch, Iowa; James P. Warburg mss., John F. Kennedy Library; George Peek mss., University of Missouri; Norman Thomas mss. and Frank P. Walsh mss., New York Public Library; Robert L. Doughton mss. and John J. McSwain mss., University of North Carolina; John A. Simpson and Elmer Thomas mss., University of Oklahoma; Bernard Baruch mss., Princeton University; Carter Glass mss., University of Virginia; William E. Chilton mss., University of West Virginia; H. V. Kaltenborn mss., University of Wisconsin; Charles E. Wyzanski, Jr., mss., in private possession; Edward M. House and Henry L. Stimson mss., Yale University. There are a few documents not in print in the State Department records, National Archives, Washington, D.C., and a richness of material in the Foreign Office records, Public Record Office, England.

Oral history and personal interviews and correspondence have contributed significant information and interpretations. I have profited from conversations and correspondence with Thomas Corcoran, James A. Farley, Herbert Feis, James M. Landis, Raymond Moley, Frances Perkins, Eleanor Roosevelt, Lela Stiles, Rexford G. Tugwell, Henry A. Wallace, Louis Wehle, Burton K. Wheeler, and others. From the extensive holdings of the Columbia University Oral History Collection (some of which are available on microfiche), I have made considerable use of the diary entries with subsequent memoir commentary by James P. Warburg, and some use of the interviews with Roy S. Durstine, Arthur Krock, Frances Perkins, William Phillips, and M. L. Wilson. I have also quoted from Rexford G. Tugwell's interview with Henry A. Wallace in the collection of the Franklin D. Roosevelt Warm Springs Memorial Commission.

Source material available in print includes *F.D.R.: His Personal Letters, 1928–1945*, Elliott Roosevelt, editor (2 vols., 1950); *The Public Papers and Addresses of Franklin D. Roosevelt*, Samuel I. Rosenman, editor, 1928–1932 and 1933 volumes; *The Complete Presidential Press Conferences of Franklin D. Roosevelt* (12 vols., 1972), also available on microfilm. Two publications of the Roosevelt Library are outstanding in their accuracy and annotations, *Franklin D. Roosevelt and Conservation, 1911–1945*, Edgar B. Nixon, editor (2 vols., 1957), and *Franklin D. Roosevelt and Foreign Affairs*, Edgar B. Nixon, editor (3 vols. thus far, 1969–). On foreign affairs, see also numerous documents in the 1932 and 1933 volumes of *Foreign Relations of the United States*, not duplicated in the Roosevelt Library publications; Cordell Hull, *Memoirs* (2 vols., 1948); E. L. Woodward and Rohan Butler, eds., *Documents on British Foreign Policy, 1919–1939*, Second Series, Volume 5, 1933 (1956); *Documents on German Foreign Policy, 1918–1945*, Series C, Volume 1, 1933 (1957); and *Documents Diplomatiques Français, 1932–1939*, Series 1, vols. 2–3 (1967).

Basic to an understanding of Roosevelt and the early New Deal are Arthur M. Schlesinger, Jr.'s monumental study, *The Age of Roosevelt*, especially the second volume, *The Coming of the New Deal* (1959); William E. Leuchtenburg, *Franklin D. Roosevelt and the New Deal, 1932–1940* (1963), a clear, thoughtful survey; and James MacGregor Burns, *Roosevelt, the Lion and the Fox* (1956), challenging in its interpretations. Joseph P. Lash, *Eleanor and Franklin* (1971), sets the personal dimension of the Roosevelts. One memoir and two books, part memoir and part monograph, illuminate the beginnings of the New Deal. Raymond Moley's *After Seven Years* (1939), earliest of the memoirs, is still essential, although Moley (with the assistance of Elliot A. Rosen), *The First New Deal* (1966), through much research and further quotation from his papers has gone more deeply into several questions, especially on finances, money, and the London Economic Conference. Herbert Feis, *1933: Characters in Crisis* (1966), combines extensive research with personal observation focusing upon economic problems in foreign policy.

This work has benefited greatly from the diligent researches and careful interpretations that the writers of a number of monographs have contributed to specific aspects of the interregnum and early New Deal. I have cited their books and articles along with numerous memoirs and published diaries in the Notes. An extensive bibliography, unfortunately not covering books, is William J. Stewart, compiler, *The Era of Franklin D. Roosevelt, A Selected Bibliography of Periodical and Dissertation Literature, 1945–1966* (1967).

Notes

COHC: Oral History Collection, Columbia University
DNC: Democratic National Committee manuscripts, Roosevelt Library
ER: Eleanor Roosevelt
FDR: Franklin D. Roosevelt
FDRMF: Franklin D. Roosevelt Memorial Foundation mss., Roosevelt Library
FL: Family Letters, on loan to the Roosevelt Library, Hyde Park, N.Y.
FR: *Foreign Relations of the United States*
GO: Governor's Official File, Roosevelt Library
GP: Governor's Personal File, Roosevelt Library
NA: National Archives, Washington, D.C.
OF: President's Official File, Roosevelt Library
PC: Press Conference transcripts, Roosevelt Library, also available in published form
PL: *F.D.R., His Personal Letters*, Elliott Roosevelt, editor, (3 vols., New York, 1947–1950)
PPA: *The Public Papers and Addresses of Franklin D. Roosevelt*, Samuel I. Rosenman, editor (13 vols., New York, 1938–1950). These are cited by year covered by volume; i.e., PPA, 1933, etc.
PPF: President's Personal File, Roosevelt Library
PRO: Public Record Office, London

PSF: President's Secretary's File, Roosevelt Library
WSMC: Franklin D. Roosevelt Warm Springs Memorial Commission

CHAPTER I

Victory — and Responsibility

1. PPA, 1933, 10; *New York Times*, November 9, 1932; *Time*, November 14, 1932, 26.
2. James Roosevelt and Sidney Shalett, *Affectionately, F.D.R.* (1959), 232.
3. Frances Perkins to FDR, December 25, 1932, GP.
4. PL, 3:315.
5. *New York Times Magazine*, March 26, 1933, reprinted in Anne O'Hare McCormick (M. T. Sheehan, ed.,), *The World at Home* (1956), 189.
6. Raymond Moley, *After Seven Years* (1939), 65; *New York Times*, November 10, 1932; PL, 3:306.
7. McCormick, *World at Home*, 132.
8. FDR, "The Roosevelt Family in New Amsterdam . . . ," December 1901, ms.; FDR, statement, PSF, 1945, Box 154.
9. *New York Times*, December 27, 1932; PL, 3:784-785; Frank Freidel, *Franklin D. Roosevelt* (1952–   ), 1:23.
10. PL, 3:304.
11. Sherard Billings to FDR, July 4, 1932, GP; *Time*, November 14, 1932, 14; Freidel, *Roosevelt*, 1:37.
12. Langdon P. Marvin interview, April, 1949, COHC; *New York Times*, January 19, 1933.
13. Freidel, *Roosevelt*, 1:3-84; Alfred Steinberg, *Mrs. R: The Life of Eleanor Roosevelt* (1958), 47.
14. PL, 3:305-306. Daniel R. Fusfeld, *The Economic Thought of Franklin D. Roosevelt* (1956), emphasizes the influence of FDR's Harvard professors.
15. Freidel, *Roosevelt*, 2:92-121, 185.
16. *New York Times*, November 25, 1932. On Warm Springs, see Turnley Walker, *Roosevelt and the Warm Springs Story* (1953).
17. Don Wharton, ed., *The Roosevelt Omnibus* (1934), 107; *New York Times*, December 16, 1932. On FDR as governor, see Freidel, *Roosevelt*, vol. 3, and Bernard Bellush, *Roosevelt as Governor of New York* (1955).
18. FDR, address, June 2, 1931, cited in Freidel, *Roosevelt*, 3:198.
19. *Investigation of Economic Problems*, Hearings before the Committee on Finance, Senate, U.S. 72nd Cong., 2nd Sess. (1933), 856.
20. *Time*, February 13, 1933, March 13, 1933, 14; F. Z. Glick, *The Illinois Emergency Relief Commission* (1940), 14.
21. Edmund Wilson, "Hull House in 1932: III," *New Republic*, February 1, 1933, 320.
22. Huntington Park, Calif., *Signal*, September 6, 1932.
23. *Literary Digest*, November 12, 1932, 6.
24. See, for example, Herbert Hoover, *Memoirs* (1952), 3:351 et passim; Theodore Joslin, *Hoover off the Record* (1934), 330.
25. Herbert Hoover (W. S. Myers, ed.), *The State Papers and Other Public Writings* (1934), 2:408-424.

26. Hoover, *State Papers*, 2:452–453.
27. Hoover, *State Papers*, 2:454, 456.
28. Hoover, *State Papers*, 2:396.
29. Felix Frankfurter to FDR, September 14, 1931, November 10, 1932, GP.
30. Charles L. McNary to Mrs. W. T. Stolz, November 10, 1932, McNary mss.; *Literary Digest*, November 19, 1932, 7.
31. William Allen White to H. J. Allen, November 9, 1932; White to Theodore Roosevelt, Jr., February 1, 1933, White mss.
32. *Literary Digest*, November 19, 1932, 7.
33. *Time*, November 14, 1932, 26; *New York Times*, November 11, 1932.

CHAPTER II

A Fresh Challenge from Hoover

1. PPA, 1928–1932, 876; Adolf A. Berle, Jr., memorandum, November 7, 1932, Berle mss.
2. Henry L. Stimson diary, June 27, 1932, Stimson mss.
3. Herbert Hoover, *Memoirs* (1952), 3:176–177.
4. FDR to Hoover, November 9, 1932, Hoover mss. The draft is in the FDR mss. See also Raymond Moley, *After Seven Years* (1939) 67, and Edgar Eugene Robinson, *The Roosevelt Leadership, 1933–1945* (1955), 67.
5. Stimson diary, November 10, 11, 1932; see also original draft of Hoover telegram in 3F-1252, Stimson mss.
6. Hoover (W. S. Myers, ed.), *The State Papers and Other Public Writings* (1934), 2:483–486; PPA: 1928–1932, 873–881.
7. There are good surveys of the problem in Robert H. Ferrell, *American Diplomacy in the Great Depression: Hoover-Stimson Foreign Policy, 1929–1933* (1957), and L. Ethan Ellis, *Republican Foreign Policy, 1921–1933* (1968).
8. Rexford G. Tugwell diary, December 20, 1932; Moley, *After Seven Years*, 68.
9. Thomas W. Lamont to Walter Lippmann, September 16, 1932, Lamont mss.
10. FDR, speech draft, 1926, cited in Frank Freidel, *Franklin D. Roosevelt* (1952–   ), 2:235.
11. Moley, *After Seven Years*, 69.
12. PPA, 1928–1932, 802.
13. Lewis Douglas to J. D. Douglas, December 18, 1932, Douglas mss.; Stimson diary, July 12, 1932; Howe notation to FDR on Frank H. Simonds to Howe, [November] 1932, Moley mss.; E. M. House in *Foreign Affairs*, January 1933, 11:211–219.
14. Sir Ronald Lindsay, November 14, 17, 1932, FO 371/15914, C 9437, 9547.
15. Tugwell diary, December 20, 1932.
16. PPA, 1928–1932, 876–877; Moley, *After Seven Years*, 70.
17. Stimson diary, November 14, 16, 1932; see also J. Pierrepont Moffat diary, November 16, 1932.
18. Transcript in Container No. 1-G/981, Hoover mss.
19. FDR to Hoover, November 17, 1932; Hoover press statement, November 17, 1932, Hoover mss.
20. Tugwell diary, December 20, 1932.
21. Moley, *After Seven Years*, 71–72.
22. Stimson diary, November 16, 1932.

23. Stimson diary, November 19, 1932.
24. Key Pittman to Breckinridge Long, November 18, 1932, Pittman mss.
25. *New York Times*, November 16, 1932.
26. *New York Times*, November 18, 19, 1932.

CHAPTER III

The Meeting at the White House

1. PPA, 1928–1932, 868; *New York Times*, November 22, 23, 1932; Stimson diary, November 22, 1932; Herbert Hoover, *Memoirs* (1952), 3:179.
2. Hoover memorandum, November 22, 1932, Container, 1-G/981, Hoover mss.; Raymond Moley, *After Seven Years* (1939), 72–77; Hoover, *Memoirs*, 3:179–180; Stimson diary, November 22, 1932.
3. Hoover, memorandum, November 22, 1932.
4. Moley, *After Seven Years*, 72; *New York Times*, November 23, 1932; *Time*, December 5, 1932, 20:9.
5. Hoover memorandum, November 22, 1932, Hoover mss.; Moley, *After Seven Years*, 73–76.
6. Hoover memorandum, November 22, 1932.
7. Stimson diary, November 22, 23, 1932. Moffat in the State Department took the calmer view that FDR did not want to break with congressional leaders. Moffat diary, November 23, 1932.
8. *New York Times*, November 23, 1932.
9. Stimson diary, November 23, 1932.
10. Hoover, *Memoirs*, 3:182; Stimson, diary, November 27, 1932; Moley, *After Seven Years*, 77–78.
11. Stimson diary, November 27, 1932; press release, November 23, 1932, PSF, 1933–1935, Hoover; *New York Times*, November 24, 25, 1932; Hoover, *Memoirs*, 3:184; *Literary Digest*, December 3, 1932, 114:6.
12. Hoover, *Memoirs*, 3:183.
13. Stimson diary, November 30, 1932.
14. Herbert Hoover (W. S. Myers, ed.), *The State Papers and Other Public Writings* (1934), 2:554–556.
15. Moley, *After Seven Years*, 86; Herbert Feis, *1933: Characters in Crisis* (1966), 26–27.
16. Tugwell diary, December 20, 1932.
17. *New York Times*, December 20, 1932; PL, 3:311–312.
18. Stimson diary, December 19, 1932.
19. Hoover, *State Papers*, 2:547–554.
20. Tugwell diary, December 23, 1932.
21. PPA, 1928–1932, 879–881; for a somewhat different draft, see Tugwell diary, December 20, 1932.
22. Stimson diary, December 20, 1932.
23. Hoover, *State Papers*, 2:557–558.
24. Stimson diary, December 20, 1932.
25. PPA, 1928–1932, 883–884.
26. Hoover, *State Papers*, 2:554.
27. The copy in FDR's hand is "press statement," December 22, 1932, PSF, 1933–35, Hoover.

28. Stimson diary, December 13, 1932.
29. Henry F. Misselwitz to Raymond Clapper [December 1932], Clapper mss.
30. FDR to Key Pittman, December 29, 1932, DNC '32, Special; Stimson diary, December 22, 1932.
31. Grey to House, January 1, 1933, copy in Moley mss.
32. C 9437/269 PRO.
33. Lamont to FDR, January 4, 1933; Lamont to Parker Gilbert, December 29, 1932, with Gilbert notation, arranging luncheon for December 31, 1932; Lamont, notes on conversation with FDR, January, 1933, Lamont mss.
34. Tugwell diary, December 23, 1932; Stimson diary, December 21, 1932.

CHAPTER IV

The Heir Apparent and the Congressional Barons

1. *Liberty*, December 10, 1932, 7.
2. On the functioning of Congress through the Hoover administration, including the lame duck session of 1932-1933, Jordan A. Schwarz, *The Interregnum of Despair* (1970), is indispensable.
3. On assurances, see for example, Robert M. La Follette to Philip La Follette, January 24, 1933, La Follette mss.; on the role of two other progressive senators, see J. Joseph Huthmacher, *Senator Robert Wagner and the Rise of Urban Liberalism* (1968); Richard Lowitt, *George W. Norris*, vol. 2 (1971); and on La Guardia, Arthur Mann, *La Guardia: A Fighter Against His Times: 1882-1933* (1959) and Howard Zinn, *La Guardia in Congress* (1958).
4. McAdoo to Walsh, November 17, 1932, Walsh mss.
5. Walsh to McAdoo, November 28, 1932, Walsh mss.
6. Raymond Moley, *After Seven Years* (1939), 83-84; Ernest K. Lindley, *The Roosevelt Revolution* (1933), 47.
7. *New York Times*, November 23, 24, 1932; Hoover memorandum, November 22, 1932, Hoover mss.
8. Hull to House, January 2, 1933, DNC '32 special file.
9. *New Republic*, December 14, 1932, 73:126; *New York Times*, December 18, 1932; Thomas Connally as told to Alfred Steinberg, *My Name Is Tom Connally* (1954), 147; Hull to House, January 2, 1933, DNC '32 special file; Cordell Hull, *Memoirs* (1948), 1:161-162.
10. See, for example, *New York Times*, November 28, 1932.
11. *New York Times*, November 29, 1932; January 3, 1933.
12. *New York Times*, November 20, 1932.
13. Herbert Hoover, *Memoirs* (1952) 3:192; Bascom Timmons, *Garner of Texas* (1948), 171.
14. Hoover, *State Papers*, 2:508.
15. PPA, 1928-1932, 808; *New York Times*, December 30, 31, 1932.
16. *New York Times*, December 25, 29, 1932.
17. *New York Times*, December 5, 1932.
18. *New York Times*, December 28, 1932.
19. FDR to Edmund Platt, December 29, 1932, DNC '32 special file.
20. Timmons, *Garner*, 171-172, cited in Hoover, *Memoirs*, 3:192-193.
21. *New York Times*, December 28, 1932; Timmons, *Garner*, 171-172.
22. *New York Times*, December 29, 1932.

23. FDR to Pittman, December 29, 1932, DNC '32, special file.
24. *New York Times*, January 1, 1933.
25. *New York Times*, January 5, 6, 7, 19, 1933; Hoover, (W. S. Myers, ed.), *The State Papers and Other Public Writings* (1934), 2:576–581; Moley diary, January 5, 1933, Moley mss.
26. Hiram Johnson to C. K. McClatchy, January 16, 1933, Johnson mss.; Thomas Lamont, notes on conversation with FDR, Lamont mss. 127–21.
27. *New York Times*, January 17, 19, 21, 1933.
28. *New York Times*, January 20, 22, 1933; Johnson to McClatchy, January 29, 1933, Johnson mss.
29. *New York Times*, January 22, 1933.
30. On the speakership question, see *New York Times*, December 1, 31, 1932, January 1, 1933.
31. Johnson to McClatchy, January 29, 1933, Johnson mss.
32. For an analysis of the lame duck session and the progressive bills, see Schwarz, *Interregnum of Despair*, 205–229.
33. 72 Cong., 2 Sess., Senate Finance Committee, *Investigation of Economic Problems* (1933); for the economists' letter, see *New York Times*, January 3, 1933.
34. For a contemporary critical view, see George B. Brason to Moley, March 6, 1933, Moley mss.
35. Robert L. Doughton to A. A. Blackwelder, January 4, 1933, Doughton mss.

CHAPTER V

Planning the New Deal

1. *New York Times*, January 12, 1933.
2. FDR to Howe, December 14, 1932, GO.
3. Gabrielle E. Forbush to Margaret A. Durand, March 6, 1933, and enclosed memo, DNC '32 special files.
4. Guernsey Cross [dictated by FDR] to Henry Holt, November 26, 1932; Holt to FDR, November 10, 1932, GP.
5. On use of FDR's signature, which he had similarly stopped after the 1928 campaign, interview with Lela Stiles, August 11, 1951. FDR to Earle Looker, November 17, 1932, GP.
6. Hearst to FDR, February 7, 1933, PPF 62; Hearst to Joseph Kennedy, telegram, December 28, 1932, copy in Moley mss.
7. Brandeis to Frankfurter, November 24, 1932; see also Brandeis to Frankfurter, October 20, 1932, Frankfurter mss.; Frankfurter to Marguerite LeHand, November 10, 1932, GP; *New York Times*, November 24, 1932.
8. Robert M. La Follette to Philip La Follette, January 23, 1933; see also FDR to R. M. La Follette, November 19, 1932, La Follette mss.
9. Alfred B. Rollins, Jr., *Roosevelt and Howe* (1962), 369–371; Raymond Moley, *After Seven Years* (1939), 79–80.
10. R. J. Bender to Raymond Clapper and Frederick A. Stern, December 1, 1932, Clapper mss.; see also Roy S. Durstine interview, COHC.
11. Frederic C. Howe to Louis McH. Howe, [d. December 1, 1932], Moley mss.
12. Moley, *After Seven Years*, 81.
13. Moley, *After Seven Years*, 80.

14. Hiram Johnson to C. K. McClatchy, February 12, 1933; see also Johnson to his sons, February 12, 1933, Johnson mss.
15. Moley to George Creel, February 25, 1933, Moley mss.
16. Rexford G. Tugwell, *The Brains Trust* (1968), 59. In an appendix (pp. 525–528) Tugwell reprints his recommendation to FDR after the election for the creation of an economic council.
17. Tugwell diary, January 5, 1933; Dean Acheson, *Morning and Noon* (1965), 165.
18. Lewis Douglas to James S. Douglas, January 21, 1933, Douglass mss.
19. Moley to Richard Crane, December 12, 1932; Moley to Charles A. Beard, February 11, 1933; Moley to John W. Love, December 5, 1932, Moley mss.
20. Roosevelt, "The New Deal — an Interpretation," *Liberty*, December 10, 1932, 7–8.
21. Berle to Moley, November 10, 1932, Moley mss.
22. FDR to Gabrielle Forbush, November 27, 1932, GP; Berle to FDR, January 26, 1933. These files are in the Moley mss.
23. Margaret L. Coit, *Mr. Baruch* (1957), 431; Jacob S. Coxey to Moley, February 28, 1933, with enclosures, Moley mss.
24. Moley, *After Seven Years*, 386.
25. *New York Times*, December 2, 1932.
26. Moley, *After Seven Years*, 386–387.
27. Rexford G. Tugwell interview with Henry A. Wallace, June 23, 1957, FDRMC.
28. Pittman to FDR, November 17, 1932, GP.
29. Moffat diary, January 25, 1933.
30. Barry D. Karl, "Presidential Planning and Social Science Research: Mr. Hoover's Experts," *Perspectives in American History* (1969), 3:347–409.
31. Roosevelt, "Growing Up by Plan," *Survey*, February 1, 1932, 483.
32. PPA, 1928–1932, 669–701.
33. Interview with Wilson, COHC, cited in William D. Rowley, *M. L. Wilson and the Campaign for the Domestic Allotment* (1970), 151–152.
34. Gertrude A. Slichter, "Franklin D. Roosevelt's Farm Policy as Governor of New York State, 1928–1932," *Agricultural History* (October 1959), 33:167–176; Frank Freidel, *Franklin D. Roosevelt* (1952–   ), 3:224–226.
35. *Survey*, February 1, 1932, 484; Mrs. M. R. McCormack to FDR, December 31, 1931; FDR to Mrs. McCormack, December 8, 1931, GP; see also FDR to Albert Shaw, September 7, 15, 1931, Shaw mss.
36. Brandeis to Frankfurter, November 24, 1932, Frankfurter mss.; *Survey*, February 1, 1932, 67:483–485; for similar remarks at Warm Springs, see *New York Times*, November 30, 1932.
37. *New York Times*, January 17, 1933.
38. Note in Harold L. Ickes to Robert Fechner, November 8, 1933, Interior files, NA; see also FDR to William A. Welch, November 8, 1933, in Edgar B. Nixon, ed., *Franklin D. Roosevelt and Conservation* (1957), 1:183.
39. Van L. Perkins, *Crisis in Agriculture: The Agricultural Adjustment Administration and the New Deal, 1933* (1969), 13.
40. Tugwell to Moley, November 26, 1932, Moley mss.

CHAPTER VI

A First Attempt to Aid Farmers

1. For background, see especially, Van L. Perkins, *Crisis in Agriculture: The Agricultural Adjustment Administration and the New Deal, 1933* (1969), 10–35. See also Theodore Saloutos and John D. Hicks, *Agricultural Discontent in the Middle West, 1900–1939* (1951), and Gilbert C. Fite, *George N. Peek and the Fight for Farm Parity* (1954).
2. Raymond Moley, assisted by Elliott A. Rosen, *The First New Deal* (1966), 251; Perkins, *Crisis in Agriculture*, 11–12.
3. Aubrey William memoir, FDRMF mss.
4. For the statistics, see *New York Times*, January 17, 1933 and John M. Blum, *From the Morgenthau Diaries* (1959) 1:36.
5. Henry A. Wallace to FDR, January 26, 1933, and enclosed letter, DNC '32, Iowa.
6. John A. Simpson to FDR, January 11, 1933, Moley mss. On agrarian militancy, see John L. Shover, *Cornbelt Rebellion: The Farmers' Holiday Association* (1965).
7. George N. Peek and Samuel Crowther, *Why Quit Our Own* (1936), 67.
8. Perkins, *Crisis in Agriculture*, 11–12, 19.
9. Perkins, *Crisis in Agriculture*, 60–61.
10. PPA, 1928–1932, 696–697.
11. On FDR's agricultural program as Governor, see Frank Freidel, *Franklin D. Roosevelt* (1952–   ), 3:13–15, 35–41, 229–230; Gertrude Almy Slichter, "Franklin D. Roosevelt and the Farm Problem, 1929–1932," *Mississippi Valley Historical Review* (September 1956), 43:238–258.
12. Freidel, *Roosevelt*, 2:173.
13. Freidel, *Roosevelt*, 3:273–274, 342–344, 348–349; Gilbert Fite, "John A. Simpson: The Southwest's Militant Farm Leader," *Mississippi Valley Historical Review* (December 1948), 35:563–584; William D. Rowley, *M. L. Wilson and the Campaign for the Domestic Allotment* (1970).
14. M. L. Wilson, interview, COHC, cited in Rowley, *Wilson*, 151.
15. On the Atlanta speech, see *New York Times*, October 25, 1932.
16. Tugwell to Moley, November 26, 1932, Moley mss.; *New York Times*, November 27, 1932.
17. *New York Times*, November 29, 1932; on FDR's ignorance, see Tugwell diary, January 21, 1933, Tugwell mss.
18. Tugwell diary, December 31, 1932, Tugwell mss.
19. Christiana McFadyen Campbell, *The Farm Bureau and the New Deal* (1962), 51.
20. Campbell, *Farm Bureau*, 28.
21. Richard S. Kirkendall, *Social Scientists and Farm Politics in the Age of Roosevelt* (1966), 59; Peek, *Why Quit Our Own*, 65; Rexford G. Tugwell, *The Light of Other Days* (1962), 138–142; Mordecai Ezekiel to Tugwell, October 20, 1939, Tugwell mss.; Wilson interview, COHC.
22. *New York Times*, November 27, 1932.
23. *New York Times*, November 28, 1932.
24. Tugwell interview with Wallace, WSMC; Rowley, *Wilson*, 184; on Bankhead's involvement in cotton matters, see John H. Bankhead mss.
25. Tugwell interview with Wallace, WSMC.
26. Tugwell diary, January 12, 13, 1933, Tugwell mss.; see also Moley diary, January 4, 12, 1933, Moley mss.
27. On Morgenthau's achievements, see Blum, *Morgenthau Diaries*, 1:39–42.
28. Moley to Tugwell, November 30, 1932, Moley mss.; Blum, *Morgenthau Diaries*, 1:39; *New York Times*, December 13, 1932; Wilson interview, COHC.

29. Tugwell diary, December 31, 1932, Tugwell mss.
30. Tugwell diary, December 25, 31, 1932; Ezekiel to Tugwell, October 20, 1939, Tugwell mss.
31. Peek, *Why Quit Our Own*, 66–69; Bernard M. Baruch to FDR, December 6, 1932, DNC '32 Special; Hugh Johnson to Moley, November 29, 1932, Moley mss.
32. James F. Bell to Hugh Johnson, January 12, 1933, Peek mss.
33. Perkins, *Crisis in Agriculture*, 32; Adolf A. Berle, Jr., to FDR, December 2, 1932, Berle mss.
34. Perkins, *Crisis in Agriculture*, 32–33.
35. Tugwell diary, January 17 [should be 19], 21, 1933, Tugwell mss., *New York Times*, January 18, 21, 1933.
36. James F. Byrnes to Moley, February 24, 1933, Moley mss.; Perkins, *Crisis in Agriculture*, 33.
37. Peek, *Why Quit Our Own*, 73.
38. Herbert Hoover (W. S. Myers. ed.), *The State Papers and Other Public Writings* (1934), 2:598; Hoover, *Memoirs*, 3:303.
39. Rowley, *Wilson*, 190.
40. Tugwell diary, January 17 [should be 19], 1933, Tugwell mss.
41. Tugwell diary, January 16, 24, 1933, Tugwell mss.
42. Ezekiel to Tugwell, January 15, 1933, October 20, 1939, Tugwell mss.; Perkins, *Crisis in Agriculture*, 33.

CHAPTER VII

Toward a Roosevelt Foreign Policy

1. Raymond Moley, assisted by Elliot A. Rosen, *The First New Deal* (1966), 22; Berle memorandum, November 7, 1932, Berle mss.
2. For the clipping and comments, see C 9727/29/62 PRO.
3. Sir Ronald Lindsay to Sir John Simon, January 30, 1933, C 853/1/62 PRO, also in E. L. Woodward and Rohan Butler, eds., *Documents on British Foreign Policy, 1919–1939* (London 1956), 2nd series, 5:748–751.
4. London *News Chronicle*, November 10, 1932; on the interview in *Le Matin*, Norman Davis to FDR, October 15, 1932, Davis mss.
5. Norman Davis to FDR, October 15, November [c. 11], 18, 1932; FDR to Davis, November 26, 1932, Davis mss.; Brandeis to Frankfurter, November 11, 1932, Frankfurter mss.; Louis B. Wehle, *Hidden Threads of History* (1953), 120; transcript telephone conversation between Hoover and FDR, January 6, 1933, Hoover mss.; Lindsay to Simon, December 5, 1932, reporting a conversation relayed from FDR indirectly, C 10123/29/62 PRO.
6. For fuller accounts of Bullitt's missions, see Robert E. Bowers, "Senator Arthur Robinson of Indiana Vindicated: William Bullitt's Secret Mission to Europe," *Indiana Magazine of History* (September, 1965), 61:189–204; Wehle, *Hidden Threads of History*, 110–123; Orville H. Bullitt, ed., *For the President Personal and Secret: Correspondence between Franklin D. Roosevelt and William C. Bullitt* (1972), 18–32.
7. R. C. Craigie notation on Simon to Lindsay, January 22, 1933, C 660/1/62; Lindsay to Simon, January 23, 1933, C 661/1/62, PRO; Moley diary, January 21, 1933, Moley mss.
8. Bullitt to FDR, January 24, 1933, Moley mss.
9. Simon cabled Lindsay, January 22, 1933 that Bullitt had visited Chequers the

day before and declared Roosevelt contemplated reducing the British debt the equivalent of 80 percent, to put Britain on a level with Italy. See also Simon to Lindsay, January 24, 1933, C 661/1/62, PRO. On Senator Robinson's protest, see Bowers, "Senator Arthur Robinson," 189–196.

10. Lamont to FDR, January 4, 1933; Lamont to Parker Gilbert, December 29, 1932, with Gilbert notation, arranging luncheon for December 31, 1932, Lamont mss.; Moley diary, January 1, 1933; Mrs. Caspar Whitney to FDR, December 31, 1932, DNC '32, NYC; Ministère des Affaires Étrangères, *Documents Diplomatiques Français, 1932–1939* (Paris 1966), Series 1, 2:253–254, 307, 341–342, 384.

11. Claudel to Paul-Boncour, January 11, 1933, *Documents Diplomatiques,* 1st Series, 2:414–417. See also FDR statement, [January 10, 1933], FDR longhand box.

12. Tugwell diary, December 23, 1932.

13. Moley, *After Seven Years* (1939), 83; Osborne to Sargent, February 7, 1933, enclosing Gerald Campbell to Osborne, February 2, 1933, C 1610/1/62 PRO.

14. FDR to S. R. Bertron, July 8, 1931, GP, Box 1.

15. Stimson diary, December 21, 22, 1932; Notes of talk with Frankfurter, Stimson mss., 1F-2788. For a detailed account of events leading to the Stimson-FDR conversation, see Herbert Feis, *1933: Characters in Crisis* 1966), 48–55; for a briefer account, Elting E. Morison, *Turmoil and Tradition: A Study of the Life and Times of Henry L. Stimson* (1960), 437–439.

16. Stimson diary, November 13, 1932, Stimson mss.

17. Stimson diary, November 22, 1932, Stimson mss.

18. Stimson to FDR, December 10, 1932, PPF 20.

19. Stimson diary, December 23, 1932, Stimson mss.

20. Hoover to Stimson, [December 23, 1933], Hoover mss.

21. FDR to Stimson, December 24, 1932, PPF 20.

22. Stimson diary, December 24, 1932, Stimson mss.

23. FDR to Stimson via Feis, December 23, 1932, Stimson mss., 1F-2779.

24. Tugwell diary, December 24, 25, 26, 1932.

25. Norman Davis to Hull, December 20, 1932, Davis mss.; Tugwell diary, December 27, 1932.

26. *New York Times,* December 27, 1932. For a fuller account of the entire episode, see Moley, *After Seven Years,* 90–93.

27. Norman Davis to Stimson, December 28, 1932, Stimson mss., 1F-2786.

28. Stimson diary, December 28, 1932, Stimson mss.

29. Stimson diary, January 3, 4, 1933, Stimson mss.; FDR to Hoover, January 4, 1933; Hoover to FDR, January 5, 1933, Hoover mss.

30. Transcript of telephone conversation between Hoover and FDR, January 6, 1933, 4:15 P.M., Hoover mss.

31. Stimson diary, January 5, 1933; FDR to Stimson, January 4, 1933; Stimson to FDR, January 5, 1933, Stimson mss.

CHAPTER VIII

Roosevelt Takes Command of Foreign Affairs

1. Stimson diary, January 19, 1933, Stimson mss.

2. Stimson diary, January 9, 1933, Stimson mss.

3. Hoover to Stimson, February 14, 1932, Stimson mss.

4. Henry L. Stimson and McGeorge Bundy, *On Active Service in Peace and War*

(1948), 255. On Stimson's policies toward Japan, see also Elting E. Morison, *Turmoil and Tradition* (1960), Richard N. Current, *Secretary Stimson, A Study in Statecraft* (1954), and Armin Rappaport, *Henry L. Stimson and Japan* (1963). For a perceptive overview of Japanese-American relations, see Akira Iriye, *Across the Pacific* (1967), 111–137, 171–187.

5. *New York Times*, January 17, 1933; *Literary Digest*, January 28, 1933, 7.

6. FDR longhand statement; *New York Times*, January 18, 1933.

7. *New York Times*, January 18, 1933; *Literary Digest*, January 28, 1933, 7.

8. Raymond Moley, *After Seven Years* (1939), 95.

9. Tugwell diary, January 17 [should be 19], 1933.

10. Thomas Kearney to FDR, December 14, 1932, GP.

11. Moley, *After Seven Years*, 95.

12. Frank Freidel, *Franklin D. Roosevelt* (1952–   ), 1:13, 25.

13. On the discussion of the Orange plan, see Herbert Feis, *1933: Characters in Crisis*, (1966), 57–58.

14. Copy in FDRL.

15. Interview with Tugwell, May 29, 1951.

16. FDR to Ross A. Collins, May 6, 1932, GO; FDR to Francis R. Bellamy, August 10, 1929, GO; FDR to Nicholas Roosevelt, May 19, 1930, GP.

17. *New York Times*, November 30, 1932.

18. *New York Times*, December 1, 1932.

19. Bradley A. Fiske, radio address over WOR under auspices of the National Security League, December 1, 1932, mimeographed copy.

20. William V. Pratt to FDR, December 27, 1932, DNC '32, Box 820.

21. FDR to Pratt, December 29, 1932, DNC '32 Special; William Howard Gardiner to FDR, January 18, 1933, DNC '32 Special; *New York Times*, January 12, 1933.

22. *New York Times*, January 13, 1933; Lester P. Barlow to FDR, December 5, 1932, DNC '32, Box 820; Stimson diary, November 9, 1932.

23. Interview with Tugwell, May 29, 1951.

24. Tugwell, *Democratic Roosevelt*, 349–350; Hugh S. Johnson to FDR, December 1, 1932, GP.

25. See Sumner Welles's suggestion for inaugural address in PSF, Box 10, "Cuba," and commentary in Charles C. Griffin, ed., "Welles to Roosevelt: A Memorandum on Inter-American Relations, 1933," *Hispanic American Historical Review* (May 1954), 34:190–192; Stimson diary, January 10, 16, 1933.

26. See Hoover's longhand heading on Stimson memorandum, January 15, 1933, Hoover mss.

27. Hoover to Stimson, [January 15, 1933], Stimson mss.

28. Tugwell diary, January 17 [should be 19], 1933.

29. *New York Times*, January 20, 1933; Tugwell diary, January 17 [should be 19], 21, 22, 1933; Stimson diary, January 19, 1933; Moley, *After Seven Years*, 97.

30. Tugwell diary, January 30, 1933.

31. Moley diary, January 21, 1933.

32. Stimson diary, January 20, 1933.

33. Hoover memorandum on conference on January 20, 1933, between Hoover and FDR, with Hoover longhand emendations, Hoover mss.

34. Stimson diary, January 20, 1933; the original of the communiqué is in the Hoover mss.

35. Moley, *After Seven Years*, 98; Tugwell diary, January 22, 1933.

36. Tugwell diary, January 22, 1933; Moley, *After Seven Years*, 99–100; Feis, *1933*, 74.

37. *New York Times*, January 21, 1933.

38. Lindsay to Simon, January 30, 1933, FO 371/16668–417; Lindsay to Simon, January 31, 1933, FO 371/16666–426; Osborne to Simon, February 1, 1933, FO 371/16666–426, PRO.

39. Stimson diary, January 30, 1933.

40. Moley, *After Seven Years*, 102.
41. Feis, *1933*, 77–79.
42. Conversation between Stimson and FDR, January 24, 1933, Stimson mss.; Stimson to FDR, January 22, 1933, enclosing draft message to French government, PSF, 2; Stimson to FDR, January 24, 1933, enclosing copies of four *aides-mémoire;* Stimson to FDR, January 30, 1933, Stimson mss. Stimson did keep Hoover fully informed. See also Hoover memoranda, January 21, 22, 1933; Edge to Stimson, Paris, January 25, 1933, on French reaction; FDR to Stimson, January 27, 1933; and Hoover to Stimson, January 27, 1933 (copy sent to FDR), and related materials in the Hoover mss.

CHAPTER IX

Building an Administration

1. PL 1:326.
2. The lists are in the FDR longhand box; the copy of the *Official Register* in GP '32.
3. Raymond Moley, *After Seven Years* (1939), 109–137, contains a firsthand, revealing account.
4. For a list of 180 possible cabinet officers, see *New York Times*, November 13, 1932.
5. John W. Davis to Norman Davis, [November 24], 1932, Norman Davis mss.; Bernard Flexner, minutes of luncheon meeting, February 8, 1933, Moley mss.; Moley, *After Seven Years*, 112–113; Berle memorandum, November 7, 1932, Berle mss.; *New York Times*, January 30, 1933. See also Young's friendly note to FDR, November 1, 1932, GP.
6. Berle memorandum, November 7, 1932, Berle mss.; Newton D. Baker to FDR, April 21, 1933, PSF.
7. *New York Times*, January 29, 1933; Gerald Campbell to Osborne, February 2, 1933, enclosed in Osborne to Sargent, February 7, 1933, C 1610/1/62, PRO.
8. McAdoo to Baruch, February 4, 1933; Baruch to McAdoo, February 9, 1933, Baruch mss.; Bernard M. Baruch, *Baruch: The Public Years* (1960), 248; Margaret L. Coit, *Mr. Baruch* (1957), 431–432; Moley, *After Seven Years*, 111.
9. Moley, *After Seven Years*, 110–111.
10. James A. Farley, *Behind the Ballots* (1938), 183; Farley, *Jim Farley's Story* (1948), 30. On Saturday, November 5, three days before the election, he discussed the problem of selecting a cabinet with Berle. Berle memorandum, November 7, 1932, Berle mss.
11. FDR to Dern, February 2, 1933, in PL 1:326; Farley, *Behind the Ballots*, 189–190.
12. Farley, *Behind the Ballots*, 188, 201.
13. Burton K. Wheeler, *Yankee from the West* (1962), 298; interview with Wheeler, July 8, 1954; FDR to Wheeler, December 20, 1932, GP.
14. Moley, *After Seven Years*, 111–113; on Young, see Moley diary, January 22, 1933; on Davis, Stimson diary, January 19, 1933, and Max Freedman, ed., *Roosevelt and Frankfurter: Their Correspondence, 1928–1945* (1967), 103–104.
15. Moley, *After Seven Years*, 112–113; Moley diary, January 11, 1933.
16. Moley diary, January 11, 1933.
17. Presidential appointment diaries, PPF 1-0 (1) Box 185. On Hull and Davis, see, for example, Moffat diary, March 1, 1933.

18. Cordell Hull, *Memoirs* (1948), 1:156.
19. On Hull's pique, see the not entirely accurate account in Louis B. Wehle, *Hidden Threads of History* (1953), 129–131; Hull to House, January 2, 1933, DNC '32 Special. On Hull's reaction to the invitation, Hull to Norman Davis, February 10, 1933, Davis mss.; Moley diary, January 31, 1933; Moley, *After Seven Years*, 114.
20. Moley diary, February 8, 1933. On Phillips's appointment, which Moley and Howe had urged, see Phillips to FDR, February 10, 1933, PPF; Phillips interview, July 1951, COHC.
21. Hull to H. B. McGinness, February 20, 1933, Hull mss.
22. Moley diary, January 31, 1933; Moffat diary, January 28–29, 1933. On Glass's career and views, see Rixey Smith and Norman Beasley, *Carter Glass* (1939).
23. Smith and Beasley, *Glass*, 333–334.
24. Glass to Harry F. Byrd, February 4, 1933, Glass mss.; Smith and Beasley, *Glass*, 335.
25. Moley diary, January 25, 31, February 8, 11, 1933; Glass to Moley, February 8, 1933, enclosing Glass to FDR, February 7, 1933, and A. W. Terrell to Glass, February 2, 1933, Glass mss. and PPF, 687.
26. Moley, *After Seven Years*, 121–122; Moley diary, January 25, February 14, 1933. Regarding Hoover, confidential source.
27. *New York Times*, February 21, 1933; Smith and Beasley, *Glass*, 336–337.
28. Arthur Krock interview, April 1950, COHC; *New York Times*, February 22, 1933; Farley, *Behind the Ballots*, 206.
29. Josephus Daniels to FDR, March 5, 1936, Daniels mss.; Henry Latrobe Roosevelt to Howe, February 3, 1933; Howe to Henry Latrobe Roosevelt, February 9, 1933, DNC '32 Special.
30. *Washington Post*, March 5, 1933.
31. Thomas J. Walsh to J. Bruce Kremer, December 16, 1932, Walsh mss.; Robert M. La Follette to Philip F. La Follette, January 24, 1933, La Follette mss.
32. Walsh to J. E. Erickson, January 21, 1933; Walsh to H. J. Friedman, January 25, 1933; George Creel, "The Kitchen Cabinet," *Collier's*, June 17, 1933.
33. R. M. La Follette to P. F. La Follette, January 24, 1933, La Follette mss.
34. Moley diary, February 9, 1933; Wallace to FDR, February 19, 1933, PPF 41; on preference for Wallace, see *New York Times*, November 23, 1932; on Beck's poll, Sidney Hyman interview with Thomas Beck, March 13, 1949, FDRMF mss.
35. On the Strauss polls, see Frank Freidel, *Franklin D. Roosevelt* (1952–   ), 3:204–206; Daniel C. Roper, *Fifty Years of Public Life* (1941), 265–266; Moley, *After Seven Years*, 125; Hull to House, January 2, 1933, DNC '32 Special; Daniels to Hull, February 4, 1933, Hull mss.
36. Moley diary, February 24, 1933; Moley, *After Seven Years*, 125.
37. On Dern's background, see Marshall N. Dana to FDR, January 23, 1933, PPF 180.
38. Hiram Johnson to his sons, January 22, 1933, Johnson mss.
39. Johnson to C. K. McClatchy, February 26. 1933.
40. On Ickes's background, see Ickes to Key Pittman, October 11, 1933, Pittman mss.; Ickes to Hiram Johnson, August 11, 1920, April 30, 1932, Johnson mss.
41. On the Interior appointment, see Moley, *After Seven Years*, 125–127; Hiram Johnson to C. K. McClatchy, February 26, 1933; Ickes to Johnson, January 30, February 14, 1933; Johnson to Ickes, February 12, 15, 1933, Johnson mss.; Ickes to Costigan, January 23, 1933; Costigan to Ickes, January 25, 31, 1933, Costigan mss.; Harold L. Ickes, "Confessions of a Sourpuss," *Collier's*, March 27, 1943, 52; on Cutting, R. M. La Follette to P. F. La Follette, January 24, 1933, La Follette mss.; George Foster Peabody to FDR, undated, forwarding Gifford Pinchot to Peabody, December 22, 1932, DNC '32, Box 820; on Warburg's recollection, James P. Warburg, *The Long Road Home* (1964), 107.
42. William Allen White to Mary W. Dewson, January 13, 1933, White mss.;

Dewson memoirs; Clara L. Beyer to Dewson, November 14, 23, 1932; Dewson to Josephine McGowan, November 2, 1932, and numerous similar letters; Dewson to Sophonisba P. Breckinridge, January 9, 1933, Dewson mss.; Costigan to John R. Commons, December 19, 1932; Commons to Costigan, December 23, 1932, Costigan mss.

43. Frances Perkins interview, COHC.
44. Frances Perkins to FDR, February 1, 1933, FL; see also PL 1928–1945, 1:316.
45. Perkins interview, COHC.
46. Frances Perkins, *The Roosevelt I Knew* (1946), 150–152.
47. Anna Mellen to Margaret Dreier Robins, March 19, 1933, Robins mss.; Frankfurter to Perkins, February 25, 1933, Perkins mss.
48. Hull to House, January 2, 1933, DNC '32 Special; see also Breckinridge Long to FDR, March 2, 1933, DNC '32, Box 815; Wheeler, *Yankee from the West*, 300; *New York Times*, March 3, 1933.
49. James A. Haggerty published the full, accurate list in the *New York Times*, February 23, 1933; Johnson to McClatchy, February 26, 28, 1933, Johnson mss.
50. *New York Times*, March 3, 1933.
51. *New York Times*, February 26, 1933.

CHAPTER X

An Assassin's Target

1. *New York Times*, February 17, 1933.
2. *New York Times*, January 22, 1933.
3. Herman Finer, *The T.V.A.: Lessons for International Application* (1944), 1–2; "The Project is Important," *Fortune*, October 1933, 88.
4. [James Agee], "TVA," *Fortune*, May 1935, 93–98.
5. Herbert Hoover (W. S. Myers, ed.), *The State Papers and Other Public Writings* (1934), 1:526–527. On the Muscle Shoals controversy, see Richard Lowitt, *George W. Norris*, vol. 2 (1971); P. J. Hubbard, *Origins of the TVA: The Muscle Shoals Controversy, 1920–1932* (1961); C. H. Pritchett, *The Tennessee Valley Authority* (1943), 3–27.
6. *New York Times*, January 22, 1933.
7. FDR to George W. Norris, December 14, 1932, GP; Norris to FDR, December 23, 1932, DNC '32 special. See also FDR to John J. McSwain, December 29, 1932, McSwain mss.
8. Richard L. Neuberger and S. B. Kahn, *Integrity, The Life of George W. Norris* (1937), 305; Edgar B. Nixon, ed., *Franklin D. Roosevelt and Conservation* (1957), 1:133; *New York Times*, January 22, 1933.
9. *Fortune*, 8:84.
10. *New York Times*, January 22, 1933.
11. This version of his remarks is the original stenographic report, Nixon, ed., *Roosevelt and Conservation*, 1:133. Cf. PPA, 1928–1932, 888–889.
12. *New York Times*, February 3, 1933.
13. *Nation*, February 1, 1933, 105, 112–115; *Literary Digest*, February 4, 1933.
14. Costigan to Frank P. Walsh, February 12, 1933, Costigan mss.
15. *New York Times*, January 23, 1933; R. M. La Follette to P. F. La Follette, January 24, 1933, La Follette mss.; Costigan to FDR, February 3, 1933; FDR to Costigan, February 4, 1933, Costigan mss.
16. *New York Times*, January 25, 27, 1933; Baruch to McAdoo, February 9, 1933, Baruch mss.

17. Roosevelt to O'Connor, February 1, 1933, GP.
18. FDR to O'Connor, December 10, 1932, February 6, 1933; FDR to Ben E. Smith, December 10, 1932, February 21, 1933; Ben E. Smith to FDR, January 3, 30, 1933; Tom Bragg to FDR, December 5, 1932; FDR to Stuart Chevalier, February 21, 1933, GP.
19. *New York Times*, January 31, 1933.
20. Eleanor Butler Roosevelt, *Day Before Yesterday* (1959), 301.
21. Henry Pringle, "The President" (Don Wharton ed.), *The Roosevelt Omnibus* (1934), 78; *New York Times*, February 5, 1933; Vincent Astor to Grace Tully, June 28, 1949, FDRMF mss.
22. FDR to SDR, February 6, 1933, in PL, 1928–1945, 1:328.
23. *New York Times*, February 16, 1933.
24. *New York Times*, February 16, 17, 1933; FDR to Garner, December 21, 1932; Garner to FDR, December 16, 1932, GP.
25. FDR remarks, Miami, Florida, February 15, 1933, stenographic transcript, PPF 1-K.; cf. PPA, 1928–1932, 889–890.
26. *New York Times*, February 17, 1933.
27. Moley to Fred Charles, February 24, 1933, Moley mss.
28. *New York Times*, February 17, 1933; interview with Moley, October 22, 1958.
29. *New York Times*, January 21, 1933. Moley remembers that Zangara talked incessantly of how his stomach hurt; after his execution an autopsy showed that he had stomach adhesions. Interview with Moley, October 22, 1958.
30. "The Story of Harry Dial" as told to Franklin S. Driggs, Part II, *Jazz Journal* (January 1959), 12:27. I am grateful to Larry Gara for calling my attention to this account. I am grateful also to Kendell F. Crossen and Valentin H. Rabe for this slightly varying account. Crossen to Rabe, April 25, 1965, letter in possession of Rabe. On the Chicago rumors, see dispatch of the British Vice Consul Henderson, Chicago, December 20, 1932, A 583/17/43, PRO. Ickes to Editor, *Washington Post*, December 25, 1950. *Washington Post*, January 23, 1951; *New York Times*, January 21, March 7, 1933.
31. Raymond Moley, *After Seven Years* (1939), 139.
32. Interview with Moley, October 22, 1958; *New York Times*, February 17, 1933; Pringle, "The President," 60.
33. *New York Times*, February 16, 1933.
34. Thomas Minehan, *Boy and Girl Tramps of America* (1934), 170.
35. Arthur M. Schlesinger, Jr., *The Crisis of the Old Order* (1957), 466.
36. *New York Times*, February 20, 1933; cf. FDR press release, February 20, 1933, PPF 1-K; FDR to Hoover, Feb. 16, 1933, Hoover mss.
37. *New York Times*, February 18, 1933; FDR to Chief W. H. Moran, May 27, 1933, PPF 1-I Box 50.
38. W. E. Chilton to James Bledsoe, February 16, 1933, Chilton mss.
39. *Time*, February 27, 1933, 7.

CHAPTER XI

The Run on the Banks

1. PPA: 1928–1933, 871.
2. Lamont to Lady Sybil Colefax, April 14, 1933, Lamont mss.; For an authoritative overall account of the banking crisis, based upon both personal memories and materials in a number of manuscript collections, see Raymond Moley assisted by Elliot A. Rosen, *The First New Deal* (1966), 127–153.

3. The envelope is in the FDR mss.; John S. West, Operative, to W. H. Moran, chief, Secret Service Division, February 27, 1933, Mills mss.
4. Moley, *After Seven Years* (1939), 140–141.
5. Hoover to FDR, February 18, 1933, PSF, also in William S. Myers and Walter H. Newton, *The Hoover Administration* (1936), 338–340.
6. Hoover to David A. Reed, February 20, 1933, Myers and Newton, *Hoover Administration*, 341.
7. The pun was reported in Lindsay to Simon, March 15, 1933, A 2336/17/45 PRO.
8. Moley diary, February 18, 1933; Moley, *After Seven Years*, 140–142.
9. American exports had dropped from $5.3 billion of merchandise in 1929 to $1.6 billion in 1932. World depression, cutting off of American overseas investments, and the high American tariff were among other factors contributing to the drop. For a summary of British economic policy in the depression, see A. J. Youngson, *The British Economy, 1920–1957* (1960), 80–93; for an example of the Foreign Office view of Hoover's schemes, see C 9437/269 PRO.
10. On the gold crisis of 1932, see Mills in *New York Times*, May 15, 1935; Herbert Hoover, *Memoirs* (1952), 3:115–118.
11. *New York Times*, May 14, 1935.
12. *New York Times*, May 15, 1935.
13. Nigel Law to Sargent, February 24, 1933, A 1673/112 PRO; *Wall Street Journal*, March 2, 1933.
14. A 1673/112 PRO.
15. When Lamont was pressuring FDR to take action during the banking crisis, he did not suggest a guarantee of the gold standard; when FDR as President took the nation off gold, Morgan & Co. issued a press statement expressing approval. Lamont to FDR, February 27, 1933, PPF 70; Lamont to FDR, April 19, 1933, quoting Morgan statement. Lamont mss. 127–122.
16. See, for example, *Wall Street Journal*, February 24, 25, 1933; *New York Times*, February 11, 14, 22, 1933, and the other issues of both papers during the period. Noyes did mildly propose that FDR make a statement in the *New York Times*, February 13, 1933.
17. One of Hoover's requests in his letter to FDR, February 18, 1933, was that FDR stop the publicizing of RFC loans. See also Hoover, *Memoirs*, 3:198; Myers and Newton, *Hoover Administration*, 324–326; Arthur A. Ballantine, "When All the Banks Closed," *Harvard Business Review*, March 1948, 26:134; *New York Times*, February 18, 1933.
18. On postal savings, Bernard Sternsher, *Rexford Tugwell and the New Deal* (1964), 64; on bank failures, *New York Times*, February 19, 1933.
19. Louise V. Armstrong, *We Too Are the People* (1938), 49–50.
20. Ballantine, "When All the Banks Closed," 135–136, places blame upon Ford, and Hoover, *Memoirs*, 3:206–207, upon Couzens. Ford appears more favorably in Allan Nevins and F. E. Hill, *Ford: Decline and Rebirth, 1933–1962* (1963), 12–15; Couzens's role is described in detail in Harry Barnard, *Independent Man: The Life of James Couzens* (1958), 213–248. *New York Times*, February 15–19, 1933. On FDR's and Howe's reaction to Detroit events, see Moley, *After Seven Years*, 142.
21. *New York Times*, February 25, 1933.
22. Moley, *After Seven Years*, 143; on FDR's experiences as governor, Frank Freidel, *Franklin D. Roosevelt* (1952–   ), 3:186–192.
23. Tugwell diary, February 18, 1933; memorandum, February 17 *et seq.*, binder 60, George Harrison mss.; Moley diary, February 19, 1933.
24. Quoted back to Rand in a letter of confirmation, Hoover to Rand, February 28, 1933, Hoover mss., also in Myers and Newton, *Hoover Administration*, 356.
25. Sternsher, *Tugwell*, 75.
26. Hoover to Rand, February 28, 1933, Hoover mss.; Myers to Mills, December 23, 1935; Mills to Myers, December 24, 1935, Mills mss.
27. *New York Times*, February 20–27, 1933; on the "money changers," Moley diary, February 28, 1933.

28. FDR draft with attached note, FDR mss.; Samuel I. Rosenman, *Working with Roosevelt* (1952), 89–90; Moley diary, February 28, 1933; Sumner Welles memorandum, undated, in Box 10, Cuba folder, PSF 1.

29. The most detailed account of the speech drafting process is in Moley, *First New Deal*, 96–119, with reproductions of relevant documents, including the draft in FDR's hand.

30. Moffat diary, February 27, 1933. See also Feis's recollection of the dinner, Herbert Feis, *1933: Characters in Crisis* (1966), 12.

31. *New York Times*, February 27, 1933. On Hoover's efforts indirectly to pressure FDR, see Hoover memorandum, February 21, 1933; Henry M. Robinson memorandum, February 23, 1933; Robinson to Shanke, February 24, 1933; Mark Sullivan to Hoover, February 21, 1933, Hoover mss.

32. Thomas W. Lamont to FDR, letter and enclosed memorandum, February 27, 1933, PPF 70.

33. Moley, *After Seven Years*, 143.

34. Hoover to FDR, February 28, 1933, with notation in FDR's hand on envelope, PSF; John S. West to W. H. Moran, March 2, 1933, Hoover mss. West carried back FDR's reply.

35. FDR to Hoover, February 20, 28, 1933, with stenographic notes, PSF. The texts are in Myers and Newton, *Hoover Administration*, 344–345.

36. Armstrong, *We Too Are the People*, 50.

37. *New York Times*, March 1–5, 1933.

38. Moley, *After Seven Years*, 143.

39. Tugwell diary, February 27, 1933; Roland L. Redmond to FDR, March 3, 1933, DNC special; Myers and Newton, *Hoover Administration*, 363.

40. Myers and Newton, *Hoover Administration*, 362–364; Rixey Smith and Norman Beasley, *Carter Glass* (1939), 339–342; *New York Times*, March 3, 1933.

41. Minutes, Federal Reserve Board meeting, March 2, 1933, 10:00 p.m., Goldenweiser mss.; Moley, *After Seven Years*, 144; Moley, *First New Deal*, 145–148.

42. Irwin H. Hoover, *Forty-Two Years in the White House* (1934), 227; Myers and Newton, *Hoover Administration*, 365–366; Moley, *First New Deal*, 148–149.

43. Grace Tully, *F.D.R., My Boss* (1949), 64. See also the colorful account in James Roosevelt and Sidney Shalett, *Affectionately F.D.R.* (1959), 252, and Moley's comments upon it in Moley, *First New Deal*, 148.

44. Myers and Newton, *Hoover Administration*, 366; Theodore G. Joslin, *Hoover off the Record* (1934), 366; Moley, *First New Deal*, 149–151; Minutes, Federal Reserve Board meeting, March 3, 1933, 10:00 P.M. to March 4, 4:00 A.M., Goldenweiser mss.; Eugene Meyer to Hoover, March 3, 1933, Hoover mss.

45. Smith and Beasley, *Glass*, 341.

46. Minutes, Federal Reserve Board meeting, March 3–4, 1933, Goldenweiser mss.; Moley, *First New Deal*, 151–153; Allan Nevins, *Herbert H. Lehman and His Era* (1963), 136–137.

47. Joslin, *Hoover off the Record*, 364–365; Hoover, *Memoirs*, 3:215.

48. Lamont to Lady Sybil Colefax, April 14, 1933, Lamont mss.

49. Mills to Young, December 16, 1932, Mills mss.

50. *Wall Street Journal*, March 4, 1933.

CHAPTER XII

The Inauguration

1. Jane Addams to Mrs. Raymond Robins, February 20, 1933, Robins mss.; Edmund Wilson in *New Republic*, February 1, 1933, 322; March 22, 1933, 154. For descrip-

tions of the inauguration I have depended especially upon Edmund Wilson; Oliver McKee, Jr., writing in the *Boston Transcript;* the *New York Times;* and Arthur M. Schlesinger, Jr., *The Crisis of the Old Order* (1957), 1–8.

2. James A. Farley, *Jim Farley's Story* (1948), 36.
3. Farley, *Behind the Ballots* (1938), 208.
4. *Washington Post*, March 4, 1933.
5. Bishop Freeman to FDR, November 14, 1932; FDR to Freeman, December 23, 1932; *Washington Post*, March 5, 1933; *Time*, March 13, 1933, 11; Frances Perkins interview, COHC; Margaret Norris, "The President Goes to Church," *Saturday Evening Post*, September 16, 1933, 92.
6. Charles Hurd, *When the New Deal Was Young and Gay* (1965), 32.
7. Eleanor Roosevelt *This I Remember* (1949), 77; Grace Tully, *F.D.R., My Boss* (1949), 68; *Time*, June 19, 1933, 15.
8. FDR to Charles E. Cropley, February 25, 1933; Charles Evans Hughes to FDR, February 28, 1933; cf., Cropley to FDR, February 20, 1933; FDR to Hughes, February 25, 1933, PSF (Inauguration 1933).
9. Raymond Moley, assisted by Elliot A. Rosen, *The First New Deal* (1966), 117–118; Samuel I. Rosenman, *Working with Roosevelt* (1952), 91; Keith Lorenz, letter in *New York Times*, June 11, 1952.
10. Interview with ER, July 13, 1954.
11. PPA, 1933, 11–16, contains the first inaugural address without the opening sentence. On its addition, see Rosenman, *Working with Roosevelt*, 90–91.
12. Feis, *1933: Characters in Crisis* (1966), 96–97.
13. *New York Times*, March 5, 1933; Frances Perkins interview, COHC.
14. *New York Times*, March 5, 1933; *Literary Digest*, March 11, 1933, 5–6.
15. *New Republic*, March 22, 1933, 154.
16. John R. Tunis, *A Measure of Independence* (1964), 208.
17. Arthur M. Schlesinger, Jr., *The Coming of the New Deal* (1959), 1.
18. *New Yorker*, May 25, 1933, 9; Mark Sherwin and Charles Lam Markmann, *One Week in March* (1961), 67.
19. *New York Times*, March 6, 1933; Andrew Mellon to Sec. State, London, March 6, 1933, H-TH 811,001-Roosevelt, F.D./67; Robert Woods Bliss to Sec. State, Buenos Aires, March 10, 1933, H/DP 811.001 Roosevelt, F. D./150, NA S.
20. Joseph Grew, Tokyo, to Sec. State, March 10, 1933, F/HS 711.94/794; Irwin Laughlin, Madrid, to Sec. State, March 6, 1933, H/DIP 811,001 Roosevelt, F.D./197; M. L. Stafford, Kaunas, to Sec. State, March 10, 1933, H/DP 811,001 Roosevelt, F.D./214; Jefferson Caffery, Bogotá, to Sec. State, March 16, 1933, H/DP 811.001 Roosevelt, F.D./219, NA S.
21. *New York Times*, January 19, 1933.
22. ER, *This I Remember*, 78; Irwin H. Hoover, *Forty-Two Years in the White House* (1934), 226; FDR to Cary T. Grayson, November 25, 1932. PPF 10; FDR to Grayson, undated, PSF (Inauguration 1933); FDR to John J. Pershing, January 13, 1933; Pershing to FDR, January 19, 1933, PSF.
23. Charles Hurd, *When the New Deal Was Young and Gay*, 35; Ernest K. Lindley, *The Roosevelt Revolution* (1933), 81.
24. *New Republic*, March 22, 1933, 154; *New York Times*, March 5, 1933.
25. *New York Times*, March 5, 1933; Hurd, *op. cit.*, 31; Sherwin and Markmann, *op. cit.*, 70; Mary Dewson, "An Aid to the End."
26. MacVeagh to ER, March 6, 1933, ER PL.
27. Frances Perkins interview, COHC.
28. Farley, *Behind the Ballots*, 209; Farley, *Jim Farley's Story*, 37.

CHAPTER XIII

Reopening the Banks

1. PPA, 1933: 64.
2. Rexford G. Tugwell, *The Democratic Roosevelt* (1957), 270–271. Tugwell points out the error in FDR's recollection.
3. On FDR's activities that Sunday, see FDR diary, March 5, 1933, PSF 1, in PL, 1928–1945, 1:335; Margaret Norris, "The President Goes to Church," *Saturday Evening Post*, September 16, 1933, 32, 92.
4. Raymond Moley, assisted by Elliot A. Rosen, *The First New Deal* (1966), 160; for a careful, detailed account of this phase of the banking crisis, see their study, pp. 154–199.
5. Moley, *After Seven Years* (1939), 148; FDR diary, PL, 1928–1945, 1:335.
6. Frances Perkins memoir, COHC.
7. FDR diary, PL, 1928–1945, 1:335; Hiram Johnson to his sons, March 12, 1933, Johnson mss.
8. Raymond Clapper diary, March 5, 1933, Clapper mss.; Clapper in *Washington Daily News*, March 6, 1933.
9. PPA, 1933: 17, 24–29; Franklin D. Roosevelt, *On Our Way* (1934), 8.
10. *Wall Street Journal*, March 13, 1933.
11. Moley, *First New Deal*, 161.
12. Eleanor Roosevelt, *This I Remember* (1949), 79.
13. Mark Sherwin and Charles L. Markmann, *One Week in March* (1961), 107–112.
14. PPA, 1933: 19.
15. Paul Warburg diary, March 4, 1933, COHC; Ernest Gruening to Norman Thomas, March 9, 1933, Thomas mss.
16. Moley, *After Seven Years*, 150.
17. Moley, *After Seven Years*, 151.
18. Moley, *After Seven Years*, 151–152.
19. Mills memoranda, enclosed in Mills to Hoover, March 13, 1933, Mills mss.; Moley, *First New Deal*, 174–175.
20. *New York Times*, March 8, 1933.
21. Press Conference #1, March 8, 1933; see also PPA, 1933: 30–31; Clapper to Robert J. Bender, March 1, 1933; Clapper diary, March 8, 1933, Clapper mss.; *New York Times*, March 9, 1933.
22. Hiram Johnson to his sons, March 12, 1933, Johnson mss.
23. La Follette to Johnson, March 8, 1933; La Follette and Costigan to FDR, March 8, 1933, La Follette mss.
24. Marquis W. Childs, *I Write from Washington* (1942), 21. La Follette's recollection was wrong in placing the site of his conversation with FDR at Warm Springs.
25. PPA, 1933: 45–46.
26. *New York Times*, March 10, 1933; Clapper diary, March 9, 1933, Clapper mss.; Childs, *I Write from Washington*, 21.
27. PPA, 1933: 54, 56, 60.
28. Park to FDR, March 12, 1933; Pinchot to FDR, March 12, 1933; Pollard to FDR, March 12, 1933, PPF 200-B; PPA, 1933: 63.
29. M. H. Aylesworth to FDR, Dec. 9, 1932; FDR to Aylesworth, December 15, 1932, GP; on FDR's use of the radio in New York, see Frank Freidel, *Franklin D. Roosevelt* (1952–   ), 3:60–61.
30. PPA, 1933: 61–65; Moley, *First New Deal*, 194–196.

31. Columbia National Bank to FDR, March 13, 1933; George Washington Norris to FDR, March 16, 1933, PPF 200-B; Moley, *First New Deal*, 196–197.

32. Moley, *First New Deal*, 192–193; Thomas Storke, *California Editor* (1958), 344–345, says Calkins used outdated figures against the bank; Moley diary, March 12, 1933; Hiram Johnson to Hiram Johnson, Jr., March 14, 1933, Johnson mss.

33. J. F. T. O'Connor diary, May 29, 1933, O'Connor mss.; O'Connor to Roosevelt, June 1, 1933; A. P. Giannini to O'Connor, September 7, 1933, OF 21B; Jesse H. Jones and Edward Angly, *Fifty Billion Dollars* (1951), 19–20.

34. Jones and Angly, *Fifty Billion Dollars*, 25.

35. Moley, *First New Deal*, 196–197.

36. *New York Times*, June 17, 1933.

37. Jones and Angly, *Fifty Billion Dollars*, 27.

38. Bascom Timmons, *Jesse H. Jones* (1956), 198–200.

39. Jones and Angly, *Fifty Billion Dollars*, 31–32; Timmons, *Jones*, 201–205; PPA, 1933: 436–438.

40. Ballantine, "When All the Banks Closed," *Harvard Business Review* (March 1948), 26:41; *Wall Street Journal*, March 13, 1933.

CHAPTER XIV

Economy, Reorganization — and the Veterans

1. PPA, 1933: 49–50.

2. Tugwell diary, December 1932.

3. Raymond Moley, assisted by Elliot A. Rosen, *The First New Deal* (1966), 200; PPA, 1933:49.

4. Charles A. Beard, *The Myth of Rugged American Individualism* (1932).

5. PPA, 1928–1932: 807–808.

6. William S. Myers and Walter H. Newton, *The Hoover Administration* (1936), 532; Moley, *After Seven Years* (1939), 153; Harold L. Ickes, *The Secret Diary of Harold L. Ickes* (1953), 1:40.

7. Herbert Hoover, *Memoirs* (1952), 3:275; Sir Ronald Lindsay to Sir John Simon, March 15, 1933, A 2336/17/45 PRO.

8. Hoover, *Memoirs*, 3: 275; *Time*, March 20, 1933; Morris Market, "He's Got His Hand in Your Pocket," *American Magazine*, June 1933, 77.

9. See Frank Freidel, *Franklin D. Roosevelt* (1952–   ), especially 2:31–32, 160, 3:36–37, 47–59, 85–96; PL, 1928–1945: 311–312.

10. PPA, 1928–1932: 810.

11. Tugwell diary, December 25, 1932, January 13, 1933.

12. Lewis Douglas to J. S. Douglas, March 12, 1933, Douglas mss.; *American Magazine*, June 1933, 77.

13. Tugwell diary, December 25, 1932; Douglas to J. S. Douglas, April 5, 1933, Douglas mss.

14. Tugwell diary, December 25, 1932.

15. Barry D. Karl, *Executive Reorganization and Reform in the New Deal* (1963), 189–191; Hoover, *Memoirs*, 3:194; *New York Times*, March 4, 1933.

16. Ernest K. Lindley, *The Roosevelt Revolution* (1933), 87–88.

17. Moley, *First New Deal*, 200–207; *New York Times*, March 11, 1933; *Time*, March 20, 1933.

18. PPA, 1933: 49–51.
19. *New York Times*, March 11, 13, 1933; Lawrence Sullivan, "The Veteran Racket," *Atlantic Monthly*, April 1933, 400–401; Roger Burlingame, "The Counter Attack," *Atlantic Monthly*, November 1933, 527–538.
20. *New York Times*, March 13, 1933.
21. Lindley, *Roosevelt Revolution*, 91; Howard L. McBain to Moley, November 14, 1932, Moley mss.
22. PPA, 1933: 66–67.
23. *New York Times*, March 14, 1933.
24. Burlingame, "The Counter Attack," 527–538.
25. Robert L. Doughton to C. A. Millsaps, March 14, 1933, Doughton mss.; Jordan Schwarz, *The Interregnum of Despair* (1970), 160; William E. Leuchtenburg, "The New Deal and the Analogue of War," in John Braeman et al., eds., *Change and Continuity in Twentieth-Century America* (1964), 81–143.
26. FDR press conference, June 2, 1933, 1:338; Vincent Astor to FDR, January 7, 1933, PPF, 40.
27. PPA, 1933: 224, 226; *Fortune*, July 1933, 22; June 1939, 102, 104, 106; Freidel, *America in the Twentieth Century*, 3rd ed. (1970), 307.
28. Tugwell diary, December 25, 1932, January 13, February 27, 1933; Freidel, *America in the Twentieth Century*, 307.
29. Ickes, *Diary*, 1:11, 14, 16.
30. Hoover, *Memoirs*, 3:468–469.
31. FDR press conference, March 22, 1933, 1:62; June 2, 1933, 1:337–338.
32. PPA, 1933: 222–223.
33. PPA, 1933: 223–225.
34. *Time*, June 19, 1933.
35. FDR to Douglas, October 20, 1933; Douglas to FDR, November 3, 1933, and accompanying documents in OF 6-Y; PPA, 1933: 227.
36. T.W.B. to Frances Perkins, June 9, 1933, Perkins mss.
37. Douglas to J. S. Douglas, March 19, 1933, Douglas mss.; Moley, *27 Masters of Politics* (1949), 41.
38. FDR to Josephus Daniels, March 27, 1933, Daniels mss.
39. Lindsay to Simon, March 15, 1933, A 2336/17/45 PRO.

CHAPTER XV

Employing an Army of Youths in the Woods

1. For FDR's denial, see press conference, March 17, 1933, 1:56.
2. Frank Freidel, *Franklin D. Roosevelt* (1952–   ), 3:139; Raymond Moley, *After Seven Years* (1939), 173, 175.
3. Moley diary, March 24, 1933.
4. Harold L. Ickes, *The Secret Diary of Harold L. Ickes* (1953), 1:4, 5; Frances Perkins, *The Roosevelt I Knew* (1946), 184.
5. John A. Salmond, *The Civilian Conservation Corps, 1933–1942* (1967), 4–5. Throughout this chapter I have made extensive use of Salmond's fine study. Raymond Moley, *After Seven Years* (1939), 173–174; Moley, assisted by Elliot A. Rosen, *The First New Deal* (1966), 5.
6. Edgar B. Nixon, ed., *Franklin D. Roosevelt and Conservation* (1957), 1:123, 126–134; Nixon's work is valuable on this subject both for its documents and the

careful, illuminating notes. Salmond, *The C.C.C.*, 5, 8; Howe to L. W. Robert, Jr., October 13, 1933, PPF 2265, regarding origin of CCC — Robert was inquiring for a friend. Tugwell, introduction to diary. Nelson C. Brown to FDR, December 28, 1932; Brooks Hays to FDR, January 28, 1933, DNC '32.

7. FDR to Nelson C. Brown, March 8, 1933, in Nixon, ed., *Roosevelt and Conservation*, 1:137.
8. The secretaries of war, interior, and agriculture, together with the director of the Budget, were present. *Aide-mémoire* by Colonel Kyle Rucker, March 11, 1933; Interior Department Solicitor Edward C. Finney to Helen L. Moore, February 12, 1953; *Happy Days*, September 30, 1933, all in Nixon, ed., *Roosevelt and Conservation*, 138–139.
9. Moley diary, March 14, 1933.
10. Moley, *After Seven Years*, 173; Perkins, *The Roosevelt I Knew*, 184–185.
11. Moley, *After Seven Years*, 174; FDR to secretaries of war, interior, agriculture, labor, March 14, 1933, OF 6; Dern et al. to FDR, March 15, 1933, OF 268, in Nixon, ed., *Roosevelt and Conservation*, 1:138, 141–142.
12. Press conference, March 15, 1933, 1:36–40 also in Nixon, ed., *Roosevelt and Conservation*, 140; Ickes, *Diary*, 1:7.
13. Press conference, March 15, 1933, 1:39.
14. FDR draft in "Unemployment" folder, Moley mss.
15. PPA, 1933: 80, also in Nixon, ed., *Roosevelt and Conservation*, 143.
16. Moley, *After Seven Years*, 174; Nixon, ed., *Roosevelt and Conservation*, 144.
17. PPA, 1933: 80–81; also in Nixon, ed., *Roosevelt and Conservation*, 143–144.
18. Press conference, March 24, 1933, 1:82–84.
19. *Time*, April 3, 1933, 10–11; Salmond, *The C.C.C.*, 14–15.
20. Press conference, March 22, 1933, 1:64–66.
21. Salmond, *The C.C.C.*, 16–17, 20–24.
22. Salmond, *The C.C.C.*, 28–29.
23. For the change in the director's title, see draft of Executive Order of April 5. 1933, creating the CCC, PPF 1F, Box 35; for the final version, see PPA, 1933: 107–108. Horace Albright, director of the National Park Service, apparently received the original of the chart; it was enclosed in Newton B. Drury to Grace G. Tully, June 16, 1948, and is now in the FDRMF mss.
24. Hines to FDR, March 29, 1933, with FDR notation; Douglas to FDR, April 2, 1933, OF 8. FDR notation on Duncan K. Major to Fechner, April 5, 1933, cited in Salmond, *The C.C.C.*, 43; Alfred B. Rollins, Jr., *Roosevelt and Howe* (1962), 404–405.
25. *Time*, April 17, 1933, 12.
26. Salmond, *The C.C.C.*, 44–45; Rollins, *Roosevelt and Howe*, 405–406.
27. Major to FDR, July 1, 1933, in Salmond, *The C.C.C.*, 40–45.
28. Salmond, *The C.C.C.*, 33–35.
29. *Literary Digest*, June 3, 1933, 9; *Time*, May 22, 1933, 17–18; Salmond, *The C.C.C.*, 35–36.
30. Press conference, May 19, 1933, 1:282; Arthur M. Schlesinger, Jr., *The Coming of the New Deal* (1959), 15; Joseph P. Lash, *Eleanor and Franklin* (1971), 367; Eleanor Roosevelt, *This I Remember* (1949), 112–113; Rollins, *Roosevelt and Howe*, 386–388. A third of the veterans left the C.C.C. within three months.
31. Salmond, *The C.C.C.*, 46–47; *Literary Digest*, September 9, 1933, 6.
32. Green to FDR, September 18, 1933, in Salmond, *The C.C.C.*, 47.
33. PPA, 1933: 322. See also Ickes, *Diary*, 78–80.
34. Perkins, *The Roosevelt I Knew*, 180–181.

CHAPTER XVI

Roosevelts in the White House

1. PPA, 1933:116; Edmund W. Starling, as told to Thomas Sugrue, *Starling of the White House* (1946), 306–307; Russell Owen in *New York Times*, March 19, 1933.
2. *New York Times*, April 2, 1933.
3. Henry Pringle in Don Wharton, ed., *The Roosevelt Omnibus* (1934), 72. Throughout this chapter I have depended upon Pringle's essay, reprinted from the *New Yorker*, June 16, 23, 30, 1934; Charles Hurd, *When the New Deal Was Young and Gay* (1965); and the dispatches of Russell Owen and Anne O'Hare McCormick in the *New York Times*.
4. *New York Times*, April 1, 1933.
5. Claude Bowers, *My Life* (1962), 259–260; Mildred Hall to ER, January 19, 1933, ER PL; Irwin H. Hoover, *Forty-Two Years in the White House* (1934), 225.
6. ER in *New York Times*, April 2, 1933; Henrietta Nesbitt diary, 1933; Henrietta Nesbitt, *White House Diary* (1948), 77–79.
7. ER to Elizabeth Banks, April 20, 1933, ER PL.
8. ER in *New York Times*, April 2, 1933.
9. Owen, *New York Times*, March 19, 1933; Pringle, in *Roosevelt Omnibus*, 64–65.
10. Nesbitt diary, November 15, 1933.
11. Alonzo Fields, *My 21 Years in the White House* (1960), 18; Pringle, in *Roosevelt Omnibus*, 70.
12. Clapper diary, March 29, 1933.
13. Pringle, in *Roosevelt Omnibus*, 70–71; Frank Kent to Baruch, May 3, 1933, Baruch mss.
14. "FDR As We Remember Him," *Saturday Evening Post*, April 10, 1965, 40; Warburg memoir, COHC.
15. Feis to Frankfurter, February 11, 1933, Feis mss.
16. Holmes to FDR, March 16, 1933, PPF 2280.
17. Harlan B. Phillips, ed., *Felix Frankfurter Reminisces* (1960), 241–243, 247; Arthur M. Schlesinger, Jr., *The Coming of The New Deal* (1959), 14.
18. *New York Times*, March 25, 1957.
19. Marvin McIntyre, "The White House Day," radio script, February 10, 1934, PPF 1-F; Pringle, in *Roosevelt Omnibus*, 66–67; Alfred B. Rollins, Jr., *Roosevelt and Howe* (1962), 415–416; Nesbitt diary, September 9, 1933.
20. ER to Mrs. R. L. Compton, [1933], ER PL.
21. Philip Hamburger, "Dean Acheson," *New Yorker*, November 19, 1949, 46–47.
22. McIntyre, "The White House Day."
23. Moffat diary, March 28, 1933.
24. Grace Tully, *F.D.R., My Boss* (1949), 78–82.
25. Press conference, March 22, 1933, 1:68.
26. Early to L. H. Robbins, October 20, 1933, PPF 1A.
27. PL, 1928–1945, 1:351–352.
28. William Phillips interview, COHC; FDR to Bingham, November 13, 1933; FDR to George V, November 5, 1933, PPF 716, also in PL, 1928–1945, 1:369–371; Schlesinger, *Coming of the New Deal*, 232.
29. Pringle, in *Roosevelt Omnibus*, 62.
30. Hurd, *When the New Deal Was Young and Gay*, 11.
31. Press conference, March 16, 1933, 1:264; Clapper diary, May 15, 1933; *Time*, May 29, 1933, 7.

32. *Time*, June 19, 1933, 11.
33. *New York Times*, June 3, 1933.
34. Hurd, *When the New Deal Was Young and Gay*, 121–122; *Saturday Evening Post*, April 10, 1965, 44.
35. *Fortune*, December 1933, 30.
36. On FDR's warning, Tully, 73–74; on the law partnership, FDR to O'Connor, March 8, July 28, 1933; O'Connor to FDR, July 7, 1933; R. H. Skinner to Marvin McIntyre, June 23, 1933; FDR memorandum, June 15, 1934, PPF 96.
37. *Forum*, August 1933, 126; FDR to Henry Goddard Leach, July 21, 1933, PPF 324.
38. *New York Sun*, March 8, 1933.
39. *Saturday Evening Post*, April 10, 1965, 40.
40. Isabella Greenway to ER, June 1, 1933; ER to Greenway, June 2, 1933, ER PL; Warburg memoir, COHC; confidential source.
41. Joseph P. Lash, *Eleanor and Franklin* (1971), 344.
42. Wharton, ed., *Roosevelt Omnibus*, 93.
43. FDR to Aymar Johnson, March 20, 1933, PPF 157; *New York Times*, May 29, 1933.
44. *New York Times*, April 18, 1933.
45. *New York Times*, May 26, 1933.
46. Moffat diary, April 7, 1933.
47. Moffat diary, April 24, 26, 1933.
48. Hiram Johnson to Hiram Johnson, Jr., April 1, 1933, Johnson mss.
49. Hurd, *When the New Deal Was Young and Gay*, 211; Clapper diary, June 3, 1933.
50. FDR to Vincent Astor, May 17, 1933; Astor to FDR, May 9, 1933, PPF 40; Pringle, in *Roosevelt Omnibus*, 59.
51. Tully, *F.D.R., My Boss*, 7; Harold L. Ickes, *The Secret Diary of Harold L. Ickes* (1953), 1:16; FDR to Farley, April 21, 1933, OF 19; Carr diary, March 5, 1933, in Katharine Crane, *Mr. Carr of State* (1960), 308.
52. FDR to Farley, August 17, 1933, OF 19, in PL, 3:358.
53. FDR, memo for third postmaster general, April 18, 1933; E. H. Suydam to FDR, March 16, 1933; FDR to Suydam, April 18, 1933, OF 19.
54. Reminiscences enclosed in Gerard Swope to Grace Tully, March 30, 1949, FDRMF mss.
55. *New York Times*, March 26, 1933.

CHAPTER XVII

A Most Extraordinary First Lady

1. Press conference, March 24, 1933, 1:85.
2. ER to Emerson Brooks, May 11, 1933, ER PL.
3. *New York Herald Tribune Books*, November 5, 1933; ER to Mary Beard, November 14, 1933, ER PL.
4. Claude Bowers, *My Life* (1962), 260.
5. FDR to Sumner Welles, February 1, 1933, and hotel bill in PSF (Inauguration); *New York Times*, February 11, 25, 1933; Joseph P. Lash, *Eleanor and Franklin* (1971), 365–366.
6. Moley, telephone conversation, August 12, 1966; *New York Times*, February 25, 1933.

7. Henry Pringle in Don Wharton, ed., *Roosevelt Omnibus* (1934), 73; Clapper diary, July 13, 1933.
8. PL, 3:339.
9. FDR to ER, undated, attached to Minnie Livingston Radcliffe to ER, November 14, 1933, ER PL.
10. ER to Miss Jennie M. Griswold, November 15, 1933.
11. *New York Times,* May 25, 1933.
12. J. R. McCarl to ER, September 14, 1933; Mrs. John Nance Garner to ER, September 8, 1933; ER to Mrs. Garner, October 7, 1933; FDR to ER, attached to Edith Eustis to FDR, April 16, 1933, ER PL.
13. ER to Mrs. A. T. Ewing, May 22, 1933, ER PL.
14. *New York Times,* April 4, 1933; on corn liquor, Clapper diary, December 10, 1935.
15. *New York Times,* April 7, 1933; Nesbitt diary, September 5, 1933, for example.
16. ER to Mrs. Carmichael, May 22, 1933, ER PL.
17. *New York Times,* March 7, 1933; Eleanor Roosevelt, *This I Remember* (1949), 102–103.
18. *New York Times,* February 25, 1933; Hurd, *When the New Deal Was Young and Gay* (1965), 213. There are several interchanges in the ER mss. with an antagonistic newspaperwoman.
19. Lash, *Eleanor and Franklin,* 363.
20. Richard E. Byrd to ER, April 19, 1933, enclosing Byrd to FDR, April 19, 1933, PPF 201.
21. ER to Mrs. Francis T. Gilling, May 22, 1933; on the volume of mail, ER to Mrs. John A. Russell, November 4, 1933, ER PL.
22. Mrs. Archibald Hopkins to ER, May 17, 1933; ER to Mrs. Hopkins, May 19, 1933, ER PL.
23. ER to Mary E. Calhoun, August 8, 1933; Grosvenor Clarkson to ER, June 1, 1933, ER PL.
24. On the Arthurdale experiment, see Paul Conkin, *Tomorrow a New World* (1960).
25. ER to Miss Alice David, November 7, 1933, ER PL.
26. ER, *This I Remember,* 127; ER to Aaron M. Mathieu, May 9, 1933; Gertrude B. Lane to ER, May 8, 1934; Helen Feris to ER, November 6, 1933; on criticisms see Mathieu to ER, April 13, 1933; Clapper diary, July 31, September 7, 1933.
27. ER to Mathieu, May 9, 1933.
28. Frances Perkins interview, 3:250, COHC.
29. *New York Times,* March 25, 1933; Mary Dewson to ER, April 27, 1933; Harriet Allen to ER, June 29, 1933; ER to Mrs. A. P. Flynn, [1933].
30. *New York Times,* April 11, 1933.
31. *New Yorker,* April 29, 1933, 9.
32. Carrie Chapman Catt to ER, August 15, 1933, ER PL.
33. Florence E. Allen to ER, May 5, 1933, ER PL.

CHAPTER XVIII

Launching a Recovery Program

1. FDR to John S. Lawrence, March 13, 1933, PPF 101.
2. John Simpson to FDR, April 3, 1933, Simpson mss.
3. *New York Times,* March 11, 1933; *Christian Science Monitor,* March 18, 1933.

4. Press conference, March 15, 1933, 1:32–34.
5. *New York Times*, March 17, 1933.
6. *New York Times*, March 10, 14, 15, 1933.
7. Raymond Moley, *After Seven Years* (1939), 165.
8. Press conference, March 17, 1933, 1:51–52.
9. Simpson log, March 6, 1933; Simpson to FDR, May 6, 1933, Simpson mss.; FDR to Simpson, May 20, 1933, PPF 471.
10. PL, 1928–1945: 466–467.
11. *New York Times*, March 17, 1933; Anne O'Hare McCormick (M. T. Sheehan, ed.), *The World at Home* (1956), 191; William Allen White to Dan Casement, January 9, 1933, White mss.
12. White to Ickes, March 11, 1933, White mss.
13. Josiah Bailey to Clarence Poe, January 10, 1933, Bailey mss.
14. E. Pendleton Herring, "First Session of the Seventy-third Congress," *American Political Science Review* (February 1934), 28:71; on patronage, *New York Times*, January 3, 11, 1933.
15. Jordan A. Schwarz, *The Interregnum of Despair* (1970), 73, 205.
16. John R. Moore, *Senator Josiah William Bailey of North Carolina* (1968).
17. Herbert Hoover, *Memoirs* (1952), 3:234; PPA, 1936:432.
18. Charles Forcey, *Crossroads of Liberalism: Croly, Weyl, Lippmann* (1961); Otis Graham, *Encore for Reform: Old Progressives and the New Deal* (1967).
19. George Norris to Ellery Sedgwick, May 1, 1933; Norris to Leon Vanderlyn, September 11, 1933, Norris mss.
20. Jouett Shouse to James M. Cox, November 16, 1932, Shouse mss.; John J. O'Connor to Basil O'Connor, undated, enclosed in Basil O'Connor memo, "The Speakership," January 3, 1933, given to Marguerite LeHand for FDR, GP; Robert Doughton to John G. Dason, January 3, 1933, Doughton mss.
21. *New York Times*, March 3, 1933; Herring, "First Session," 68–71.
22. Herring, "First Session," 67.
23. James M. Byrnes to Edward M. Gwathmey, March 25, 1933, Byrnes mss.
24. Moley diary, March 21, 1933.
25. Tugwell diary, March 31, 1933; Gregory cited in Van L. Perkins, *Crisis in Agriculture: The Agricultural Adjustment Administration and the New Deal* (1969), 38.
26. On the drafting and enactment of the farm bill, Perkins, *Crisis in Agriculture*, 36–78 is clear, succinct, and authoritative. George N. Peek and Samuel Crowther, *Why Quit Our Own* (1936), 80; Gilbert C. Fite, *George N. Peek and the Fight for Farm Parity* (1954), 248–249.
27. Cited in Christiana M. Campbell, *The Farm Bureau and the New Deal* (1962), 65; John Kenneth Galbraith to Freidel, May 10, 1972.
28. Henry A. Wallace, *New Frontiers* (1934), 162–163.
29. Peek, *Why Quit Our Own*, 82.
30. Peek, *Why Quit Our Own*, 38–39, emphasizes the significance of the debate; memorandum, March 15, 1933, OF 1.
31. Press conference, March 15, 1933, 1:34, 44.
32. Russell Lord, *The Wallaces of Iowa* (1947), 330.
33. Peek, *Why Quit Our Own*, 82; M. L. Wilson interview, COHC; Tugwell diary, March 31, 1933; PPA, 1933: 74.
34. *New York Times*, March 19, 1933.
35. *New York Times*, March 23, 1933.
36. Feis to Stimson, March 15, 1933, Feis mss. On the postal card poll and its flaws, see *New York Times*, March 17, 26, 1933 and Perkins, *Crisis in Agriculture*, 66–67.
37. *New York Times*, March 22, 23, 1933; Perkins, *Crisis in Agriculture*, 52.
38. Perkins, *Crisis in Agriculture*, 54; Campbell, *Farm Bureau and the New Deal*, 66.
39. *New York Times*, March 17, 1933.
40. Tugwell diary, March 31, 1933.

41. *New York Times*, March 18, 1933.
42. Elmer Thomas to Frank Hudson, March 29, 1933, Thomas mss.
43. *New York Times*, March 23, 1933.
44. *New York Times*, March 28, 1933; Perkins, *op. cit.*, 62.
45. Fite, "Farmer Opinion and the Agricultural Adjustment Act, 1933," *Mississippi Valley Historical Review* (March 1962), 48:656–673, cited and corroborated in Perkins, *Crisis in Agriculture*, 65–67.
46. *New York Times*, March 20, 1933.
47. PPA, 1933: 84–90.
48. Press conference, March 22, 1933, 1:59; March 24, 1933, 1:72–73.
49. PPA, 1933: 101.
50. Hugh Johnson to FDR, March 30, 1933, Peek mss.; Johnson to Moley, March 30, 1933, Moley mss. See also Moley to Johnson, April 1, 1933, Moley mss.
51. Peek, *Why Quit Our Own*, 14–19; Perkins, *Crisis in Agriculture*, 69; *New York Times*, March 28, 1933.
52. E. Francis Brown, "Presidential Planning," *Current History* (June 1933), 38: 334.
53. Perkins, *Crisis in Agriculture*, 64–65, 72.

CHAPTER XIX

Going Off Gold

1. FDR to Louis Wiley, PPF 675.
2. *Christian Science Monitor*, May 8, 1933; Ernest K. Lindley, *The Roosevelt Revolution* (1933), 116.
3. Franklin D. Roosevelt, *On Our Way* (1934), 62.
4. FDR to House, April 5, 1933, PPF 222, also in PL 1925–1945: 342.
5. Press conference, April 7, 1933, 1:125–129.
6. Rene Léon to Arthur M. Schlesinger, Jr., January 5, [1959]; Moley, *First New Deal*, 157; Lindley, *Roosevelt Revolution*, 78; Tugwell diary, March 31, 1933.
7. John M. Blum, *From the Diaries of Henry Morgenthau, Jr.* (1959), 1:62; Tugwell diary, April 21, 1933; Herbert Hoover, *Memoirs* (1952), 3:214.
8. Irving Fisher to FDR, May 13, 1933, PPF 431.
9. Will Rogers to FDR, March 7, 1933, PSF, Drawer 1.
10. Raymond Moley, assisted by Elliot A. Rosen, *The First New Deal* (1966), 299.
11. Clarence D. Dill to FDR, March 24, 1933, PPF 243.
12. FDR to Dill, April 7, 1933, PPF 243; Robert J. Bender to Raymond Clapper, January 10, 1933, Clapper mss. FDR was referring at this time not to gold and silver but to the potentialities in the Glass bill.
13. Moley, "There Are Three Brains Trusts," *Today*, April 11, 1934, 4.
14. See, for instance, Tugwell diary, April 21, 1933.
15. Warren diary, February 16, 1933; James P. Warburg interview, COHC, 164–165.
16. Warren diary, March 5, 1933.
17. Press conference, March 8, 1933, 1:8–10; FDR to Ralph Robey, December 12, 1932, GP; Ralph Robey, *Roosevelt versus Recovery* (1934), 56–57; PPA, 1933: 111–116.
18. Warburg diary, March 15, 1933, COHC, 149–153.
19. Warburg diary, March 15, 1933, COHC, 154.

20. The proposals appear in full in the Warburg diary, and in summary in Herbert Feis, *1933: Characters in Crisis* (1966), 121–122 and Moley, *First New Deal*, 397.

21. Warburg diary, April 4, 1933, COHC, 366–367.

22. Warburg diary, loc. cit., Moley, *First New Deal*, 397.

23. Lindsay to Simon, March 30, 1933, W 4009/5/50. See also Moley diary, March 27, 1933.

24. Warren diary, April 6–12, 1933.

25. Warren diary, April 12, 1933.

26. PPA, 1933: 110–116.

27. Warburg diary, April 13, 1933, COHC, 455–456.

28. Lindley, *Roosevelt Revolution*, 117–118; Robey, *Roosevelt versus Recovery*, 58–60, blames the continued drop in the dollar on delays in issuing licenses. See also Harold L. Ickes, *The Secret Diary of Harold L. Ickes* (1953), 1:23.

29. Ickes, *Diary*, 21.

30. Moley diary, April 18–19, 1933; Moley, *First New Deal*, 300; Lindley, *Roosevelt Revolution*, 119.

31. Press conference, April 19, 1933, 1:153; Lippmann cited in Lindley, *Roosevelt Revolution*, 120–121.

32. FDR to Hiram Johnson, November 5, 1933, Johnson mss.; "A Statesman's Eyes," *Collier's*, June 24, 1933, 21; on T.R.'s maneuver, see Blum, *The Republican Roosevelt* (1954), 73–105.

33. Elmer Thomas, "40 Years a Legislator," (1951), Thomas mss., 233.

34. Thomas, "40 Years," 230; Moley diary, April 18, 1933; James F. Byrnes, *All in One Lifetime* (1958), 76–77.

35. Warburg diary, April 18, 1933, COHC, 496.

36. Van L. Perkins, *Crisis in Agriculture: The Agricultural Adjustment Administration and the New Deal* (1969), 73.

37. Moley diary, April 18–19, 1933; Warburg diary, April 18, 1933, COHC, 497; Moley, *After Seven Years* (1939), 159. There is a Pikeville in Tennessee, but its population is only about 800 inhabitants.

38. Lewis Douglas to J. S. Douglas, April 23, 1933, Douglas mss.; Moley, *After Seven Years*, 160, Warburg diary, April 18, 1933, COHC, 497; Warburg interview, COHC, 504.

39. Press conference, April 19, 1933, 155.

40. Ickes, *Diary*, 1:23.

41. Baruch to Byrnes, April 22, 1933 (unsent), Baruch mss.

42. Brendan Bracken to Baruch, April 19, 1933, Baruch mss.

43. Lamont telegram to FDR, April 19, 1933, quoting Morgan statement; Lamont to Leffingwell [January 1934], Lamont mss.; see also extensive Leffingwell correspondence with FDR in PPF 866.

44. Warburg diary, April 19, 1933, COHC, 513.

45. Burton K. Wheeler, *Yankee from the West* (1962), 302–304; interview with Wheeler, July 8, 1954.

46. T. Harry Williams, *Huey Long* (1969), 63.

47. Emergency Farm Mortgage Act of 1933, Title III, in Henry Steele Commager, *Documents of American History* (1968 ed.), 2:245–246. Pittman had proposed accepting silver in payment of war debts. See Pittman to FDR, February 13, 1933, Moley mss.

48. Simpson to FDR, May 6, 1933; Simpson to Thomas E. Cashman, May 13, 1933, Simpson mss.; Perkins, *Crisis in Agriculture*, 74–75; PPA, 1933: 175–176.

49. Perkins, *Crisis in Agriculture*, 75–78.

50. Wallace to FDR, April 22, 1933, OF 1; Press conference, April 21, 1933, 1:164.

51. *Christian Science Monitor*, May 8, 1933; Moley diary, April 18–19, 1933; Lindley, *Roosevelt Revolution*, 123.

CHAPTER XX

A Thrust of Reform: The Securities Act and TVA

1. PPA, 1933: 93–94.
2. Frank Freidel, *Franklin Roosevelt* (1952–   ), 2:138–159; 3:86–87, 162.
3. PPA, 1928–1932: 107, 114.
4. Ralph F. de Bedts, *The New Deal's SEC: The Formative Years* (1964), 24–27, 30–32.
5. On Untermyer and the Pujo Committee, see Vincent P. Carosso, *Investment Banking in America: A History* (1970), 137–155; on state "blue sky" laws, see Michael E. Parrish, *Securities Regulation and the New Deal* (1970), 5–7, 37–38. Both de Bedts's and Parrish's monographs are valuable on the background and legislative history of the Securities Act of 1933; Parrish's is especially detailed, making use of numerous manuscript collections.
6. Raymond Moley, *After Seven Years* (1939), 177–178; Huston Thompson diary, March 13, 1933.
7. Huston Thompson diary, March 19, 1933. Throughout this passage I have corrected Thompson's spelling of Untermyer's name.
8. Moley, *After Seven Years*, 178.
9. PPA, 1933: 93; cf. pp. 94, 96, and draft with FDR's revisions in PPF 1F Box 35.
10. Press conference, March 29, 1933, 1:87–88.
11. Parrish, *Securities Regulation*, 48–56.
12. Moley, *After Seven Years*, 179.
13. Parrish, *Securities Regulation*, 59–60.
14. Frankfurter diary, May 8, 1933; James M. Landis, "The Legislative History of the Securities Act of 1933," *George Washington Law Review* (October 1959), 28:33–35.
15. Thompson diary, April 7, 1933; Harold L. Ickes, *The Secret Diary of Harold L. Ickes* (1953), 1:17–18.
16. Thompson diary, April 13, 21, 23, 24, 1933.
17. Thompson diary, April 10, 11, 1933; FDR to Rayburn, April 12 [1933], handwritten note in Thompson mss.
18. Thompson diary, April 21, May 5, 1933; Frankfurter diary, May 8, 1933.
19. Landis, "Legislative History," 40–41.
20. Carosso, *Investment Banking*, 340–342.
21. Carosso, *Investment Banking*, 330–335, on National City Bank; Landis, "Legislative History," 39.
22. Parrish, *Securities Regulation*, 69–70, 73–74; Landis, "Legislative History," 42–43.
23. Parrish, *Securities Regulation*, 74–75; Landis, "Legislative History," 42–43.
24. Landis, "Legislative History," 48–49; Parrish, *Securities Legislation*, 69–70; on the involved development of the private bondholders' association, see Parrish, *Securities Regulation*, 83–107.
25. PPA, 1933: 214.
26. FDR to John S. Lawrence, May 18, 1933, PPF 101; Carosso, *Investment Banking*, 358–361; William O. Douglas, "Foreword," *George Washington Law Review* (October 1959), 28:1.
27. For evaluations, see de Bedts, *The New Deal's SEC*, 48–55; Carosso, *Investment Banking*, 357–367.
28. Eric F. Goldman, *Rendezvous with Destiny* (1952), 263.
29. Arthur M. Schlesinger, Jr., *The Coming of the New Deal* (1959), 323; on Morgan, see *New York Times*, May 20, 1933.
30. Arthur E. Morgan, *Bench-Marks in the Tennessee Valley* (1934), 8.
31. On the message and legislative history of the bill, see Edgar B. Nixon, ed.,

Franklin D. Roosevelt and Conservation (1957), 1:152; Ickes, *Diary*, 1:15; Frank P. Walsh to McSwain, January 16, 1935, McSwain mss.

32. Frank Freidel, *Franklin D. Roosevelt* (1952–   ), 3:353.

33. Norris had expected FDR's support on transmission lines; Norris to M. S. Roberts, February 17, 1933, Norris mss.; Moley, assisted by Elliot A. Rosen, *The First New Deal* (1966), 328–330.

34. PPA, 1933: 122–123. The final draft, containing FDR's handwritten changes, is in PPF 1F, Box 35, and printed in Nixon, ed., *Roosevelt and Conservation*, 1:151–152.

35. FDR memorandum, "President Roosevelt on Muscles Shoals Conference," May 9, 1933, McSwain mss.

36. Moley, assisted by Elliot A. Rosen, *The First New Deal* (1966), 331; Ickes, *Diary*, 1:32–33; on House debate, focussing on fertilizer production, *New York Times*, April 22, 1933; John Robertson to John G. Maher, June 3, 1933, Norris mss.

37. John Robertson to John G. Maher, June 3, 1933, Norris mss.

CHAPTER XXI

Two Roads in World Policy

1. PPA, 1933: 167.

2. *New York Times*, May 7, 1933, also in Anne O'Hare McCormick (M. T. Sheehan, ed.), *The World at Home* (1956), 202.

3. PPA, 1933: 167.

4. Edgar B. Nixon, ed., *Franklin D. Roosevelt and Foreign Affairs* (1969), 1:21–24.

5. FDR to Mary Dewson, February 25, 1932, GP Box 3. The fable was for a friend of Miss Dewson.

6. FDR to Key Pittman, December 29, 1932, DNC '32 special; Hiram Johnson to Hiram Johnson, Jr., April 1, 1933, Johnson mss.

7. Moffat diary, March 28, 1933.

8. On croquet playing, see Hull, *Memoirs*, 1:179.

9. Moffat diary, May 12, 1933; Herbert Feis, *1933: Characters in Crisis* (1966), 99–100.

10. Moffat diary, April 18, 1933. Norman Davis had tried hard to keep Gibson in Europe, but "highest authority" had ruled otherwise.

11. Lamont, notes on conversation with FDR, January 1933, Lamont mss.

12. FDR penciled note, [1933], Hull mss.

13. Grenville T. Emmet to FDR, April 14, 1933, PPF 372; Raymond Moley, *After Seven Years* (1939), 132–133.

14. FDR to Hull and Moley, April 6, 1933, Hull mss.

15. Walter F. George to FDR, May 3, 1933, Hull mss.; Clark Howell to FDR, May 10, 1933, PPF 604. For Long's letters, see Nixon, ed., *Roosevelt and Foreign Affairs*.

16. Warburg diary, March 17, 1933; Moley diary, May 15, 1933; Nixon, ed., *Roosevelt and Foreign Affairs*, 58. Robert Dallek, *Democrat & Diplomat, The Life of William E. Dodd* (1968), 184–190, details the offer to several persons.

17. Moley, *After Seven Years*, 132; FDR to Hull, March 9, 1933, OF 20, in Nixon, ed., *Roosevelt and Foreign Affairs*, 21; Claude Bowers, *My Life* (1962); E. David Cronon, *Josephus Daniels in Mexico* (1960).

18. FDR longhand note, [1933], Hull mss.
19. Moffat to Hugh R. Wilson, January 31, 1933, Moffat diary, January 23, 1933; Earle to Moffat, October 24, 1933, Moffat mss.
20. Grew to Norman Armour, September 11, 1933, Grew mss.; Hull, *Memoirs*, 1:181.
21. Moley, *After Seven Years*, 131–132; Feis, *1933*, 100–101.
22. Lindsay to Vansittart, March 30, 1933, Private. A 2839/17/45, PRO.
23. Moffat diary, May 16, 1933.
24. Moffat to Hugh R. Wilson, April 22, 1933, Moffat mss.
25. James A. Farley, *Jim Farley's Story* (1948), 39; MacDonald in CAB 23/76, p. 55, PRO.
26. Dorothy Borg, *United States and the Far Eastern Crisis of 1933–1938* (1964), 20–21; Waldo Heinrichs, *American Ambassador: Grew* (1966).
27. FR, 1933, 3:195–196.
28. FR, 1933, 3:232.
29. FR, 1933, 1:367; for both background and details on the arms embargo, emphasizing Hornbeck's cautionary role, see Robert A. Divine, "Franklin D. Roosevelt and Collective Security, 1933," *Mississippi Valley Historical Review* (June 1961), 48:42–59.
30. Moley, *After Seven Years*, 163–164; draft statement with changes in Moley's and FDR's hand, together with attached notes, and Hornbeck to Hull, March 12, 1933, Moley mss.
31. FR, 1933, 1:260–261; Robert J. Bender to [U.P. correspondents overseas], January 17, 1933, Clapper mss.; Borg, *United States*, 25.

CHAPTER XXII

Assuming Leadership toward World Order

1. FR, 1933, 1:504.
2. Moffat to Hugh R. Wilson, April 22, 1933, Moffat mss. Moffat was referring to some proposals of Wilson's, not FDR's, when he wrote this letter.
3. Walter Lippmann, ed., *United States in World Affairs, 1933* (1934), 53–63.
4. *Literary Digest*, August 26, 1933, 3–4.
5. Douglas MacArthur, *Reminiscences* (1964), 101.
6. Moffat diary, April 4, 1932, March 16, 1933, in Hooker, ed., *Moffat Papers*, 63–64, 91–92.
7. Stimson diary, November, 1932. On French armament, see Judith Hughes, *To the Maginot Line* (1972), 71.
8. FDR to Hull, undated [before April 22, 1933], S 550. S 1/678 1/2, NA.
9. *Time*, March 13, 1933, 16–18; March 15, 1933, 15.
10. Minutes of meeting at French Ministry of War, March 10, 1933, W 2782/2792/17, PRO; *Documents Diplomatiques Français, 1932–1939* (Paris 1966), Series 1, 2:777–785. On the staffing of the American section of the French Foreign Office, Theodore Marriner to Moffat, October 3, 1932, Moffat mss.
11. Lippmann, *United States*, 62–63.
12. Lindsay to Simon, March 16, 1933, C/2571/1/62. See also FDR to Lillian D. Wald, March 16, 1933; W.D.B. to FDR, February 24, 1933, enclosing MacDonald to Wald, February 7, 1933, PPF, 114.
13. Frederick W. Leith-Ross to Chancellor of the Exchequer, April 4, 1933,

C 3157/335; Lindsay to Vansittart, March 24, 1933, C 2750/1/62, PRO, and latter in *Documents on British Foreign Policy*, 2nd Ser., 5:781–782.

14. Orme Sargent, Minute, March 29, 1933, C 2853/272, PRO.

15. FR, 1933, 1:474–486; Edgar B. Nixon, ed., *Franklin D. Roosevelt and Foreign Affairs* (1969), 31–32, 44–48. See comments of Herbert Feis, *1933: Characters in Crisis* (1966) 102–103.

16. Ernest K. Lindley, *The Roosevelt Revolution* (1933), 180.

17. Moffat diary, April 6, 1933; Vansittart, *aide-mémoire* of conversation with Ambassador de Fleuria, W 3764/5/50, PRO.

18. Moffat diary, April 6, 1933.

19. Moffat diary, April 7, 1933; FR, 1933, 1:489–490; Lindley, *Roosevelt Revolution*, 180–182.

20. Claudel to Paul-Boncour, April 5, 1933, *Documents Diplomatiques*, Series 1, 3:148–149.

21. Moley, *After Seven Years*, 207.

22. Nixon, ed., *Roosevelt and Foreign Affairs*, 15; Frederick W. Leith-Ross, *Money Talks* (1968), 160–161; Laboulaye to Paul-Boncour, April 19, 1933, *Documents Diplomatiques*, Series 1, 3:245–246; Moffat diary, April 17, 20, 1933.

23. Warburg memoir and diary on events of April 24, 1933, COHC; James P. Warburg, *The Long Road Home* (1964), 122; Moffat diary, April 24, 1933.

24. Warburg diary, April 24, 1933.

25. Concerning Davis's and State Department views, see Moffat diary, April 19, 20, 24, 25, 1933.

26. *Time*, May 1, 1933, 9.

27. FR, 1933, 1:102–104. For the French report on FDR's proposal, see Herriot to Paul-Boncour, #179 [April 24?, 1933], *Documents Diplomatiques*, Series 1, 3:314.

28. Moffat diary, April 24, 1933; FR, 1933, 1:102–104.

29. Moffat diary, April 25, 1933.

30. FR, 1933, 1:107–108.

31. Phillips, memorandum, April 26, 1933, FR, 1933, 1:109–111; Herriot to Paul-Boncour, April 25, 26, 1933, *Documents Diplomatiques*, Series 1, 3:316–317, 326–327. For additional French dispatches on the meetings, see *Documents Diplomatiques*, Series 1, 3:320–325, 328, 332–333, 334, 366.

32. Moley assisted by Elliot A. Rosen, *The First New Deal* (1966), 393–402, 411–419; Warburg, *Long Road Home*, 121–126; Feis, *1933*, 132–152; Leith-Ross, *Money Talks*, 160–177.

33. Warburg diary, April 24, 1933.

34. Warburg memoir, April 25, 1933, COHC.

35. Warburg memoir, April 24, 1933; Warburg diary, April 28, 1933, COHC; Moley, *First New Deal*, 396–397. On French attitudes, see, for example, FR, 1933, 1:606–607, 609; *Documents Diplomatiques*, Series 1, 3:457, 482–483. On Bullitt, see Jeannette P. Nichols, "Roosevelt's Monetary Diplomacy in 1933," *American Historical Review*, January 1951. For a clear analysis of the problem, see Feis, *1933*, 144–146.

36. Warburg, *Long Road Home*, 123.

37. Robert Lincoln O'Brien to Grace G. Tully, December 28, 1948, FDRMF mss.

38. See especially Warburg memoir and diary, May 7, 1933, COHC; Moley, *First New Deal*, 400–403.

39. Moley, *First New Deal*, 402; FR, 1933, 1:605.

40. On FDR's decision, before the meetings, see FDR to Hull, [prior to April 22, 1933], Hull mss.; Moley, *First New Deal*, 399.

41. Statement of April 26, 1933, FR, 1933, 1:492.

42. FR, 1933, 1:492, 500.

CHAPTER XXIII

The Initial Skirmish with Hitler

1. Morgenthau diary, May 15, 1933; PPA, 1933: 185.
2. Oswald Garrison Villard to Edwin M. Borchard, April 5, 1933, Villard mss.; *Time*, April 3, 1933, 15–17.
3. *Time*, April 3, 1933, 17.
4. Moffat diary, March 29, 30, 1933.
5. Moffat diary, March 30, 1933; Moffat to Gordon, April 4, 1933, Moffat mss.
6. *Time*, April 10, 1933, 23–24; Moffat diary, March 31, 1933; Gordon memorandum, "Record of Events in Connection with the Situation of Jews in Germany beginning March 30, 1933," April 1, 1933, copy in Moffat mss.
7. FDR to Governor I. C. Blackwood, April 12, 1933, in Edgar B. Nixon, ed., *Franklin D. Roosevelt and Foreign Affairs* (1969), 1:51.
8. FDR to Philip Slomovitz, March 7, 1935.
9. *Time*, April 17, 1933, p. 17.
10. Brandeis to Frankfurter, April 13, 18, 26, 29, 1933, Frankfurter mss.
11. Max Freedman, ed., *Roosevelt and Frankfurter: Their Correspondence, 1928–1945* (1967), 109–138.
12. Moffat diary, April 20, 1933.
13. Messersmith to Moffat, May 20, 1933, Moffat mss.
14. Frankfurter to Perkins, December 21, 1933, Perkins mss.; Moffat diary, April 20, 21, 1933; Moffat to Gordon, May 9, 1933, Moffat mss. On May 10, 1933, Brandeis sold Hull on a stronger policy, and once again his subordinates objected and restrained him. Moffat diary, May 11, 1933; Brandeis to Frankfurter, May 14, 1933, Frankfurter mss.
15. Schacht told Warburg he was not an anti-Semite and that the trouble in Germany was past its crest. Warburg diary, May 8, 1933. On Schacht's background, see Hjalmar H. G. Schacht, *Confessions of the "Old Wizard"* (1956).
16. *Documents on German Foreign Policy, 1918–1945* (1957), Series C, 1:392–393.
17. FDR to Hull, May 6, 1933, in Nixon, ed., *Roosevelt and Foreign Affairs*, 95.
18. Moffat diary, May 6, 1933.
19. *Documents on German Foreign Policy*, Ser. C 1:283, 394.
20. Warburg diary and memoir, May 8, 1933, COHC; Herbert Feis, *1933: Characters in Crisis* (1966), 138–139.
21. Cordell Hull, *Memoirs* (1948), 1:237–238; Warburg diary, May 9, 1933.
22. Schacht, *Confessions*, 283–284; *Documents on German Foreign Policy*, Ser. C, 1:396, 423.
23. FDR to Irving Lehman, May 18, 1933, PPF 436.
24. Nixon, ed., *Roosevelt and Foreign Affairs*, 174–175.
25. Moley diary, May 8, 9, 1933; on overall effect, Gerhard L. Weinberg, "Schacht's Besuch in den USA im Jahre 1933," *Viertel jahrshefte für Zeitsgeschichte* (1963), 11:166–180, especially 179.
26. FDR to Hull, handwritten memorandum, April 4, 1933, N 550. S 1/612, NA; also in FR, 1933, 1:81.
27. Moffat diary, May 2, 11, 1933; Nixon, ed., *Roosevelt and Foreign Affairs*, 1:173–174; *Christian Science Monitor*, May 12, 1933.
28. James G. McDonald to ER, April 27, 1933, ER PL.
29. Moffat diary, May 2, 1933.
30. Morgenthau diary, May 9, 1933.
31. Frankfurter to FDR, May 9, 1933, in Nixon, ed., *Roosevelt and Foreign Affairs*, 1:101–102, and Freedman, ed., *Roosevelt and Frankfurter*, 130–131.
32. *Christian Science Monitor*, May 12, 13, 15, 1933; *Time*, May 22, 1933, 19–21;

for Hitler's private plans, see *Documents on German Foreign Policy*, Ser. C,
1:410–412.

33. Moffat diary, May 15, 1933.
34. Moffat to Hugh Wilson, May 16, 1933; Huston Thompson diary, May 16, 1933.
35. PPA, 1933: 185–188.
36. PPA, 1933:192.
37. Warburg diary, May 16, 1933.
38. *Time*, May 29, 1933, 7, 12; *Christian Science Monitor*, May 17, 1933; *New York Times*, May 18, 1933. Hitler's text is in the *Times* and *Documents on German Foreign Policy*, Ser. C, 1:451–455; see also 447, 451.
39. *New York Times*, May 17, 1933; *Christian Science Monitor*, May 17, 1933.
40. PPA, 1933: 193–201.
41. Morgenthau diary, May 22, 1933. No indication of a message appears in *Documents on German Foreign Policy*.
42. FR, 1933, 1:146–151; Press conference, May 16, 1933, 1:266; *Documents Diplomatiques Français, 1932–1939* (Paris 1966), Series 1, 3:496–497.
43. FR, 1933, 1:156.
44. *New York Times*, May 17, 1933; *Christian Science Monitor*, May 17, 1933.
45. Moffat diary, May 17, 1933; FR, 1933, 1:160.
46. See Gordon's reports on these units, especially in FR, 1933, 1:161–162.
47. *Time*, April 3, 16; June 5, 14; Press conference, May 24, 1933, 1:295.
48. John Campbell White to Moffat, November 27, 1933.
49. *New York Times*, May 18, 1933.

CHAPTER XXIV

Toward Planned Industrial Recovery

1. PPA, 1933: 6.
2. PPA, 1933: 246; Raymond Moley, *After Seven Years* (1939), 185–186; James P. Warburg, *The Long Road Home* (1964), 112.
3. [FDR], confidential memorandum for the Vice President, April 19, 1933, OF 12.
4. Press conference, April 26, 1933, 1:192–193.
5. Moley, *After Seven Years*, 24, 184; Tugwell, preface to diary.
6. Tugwell, *Industrial Discipline and Governmental Arts* (1933); *New York Times*, May 4, 1933.
7. Tugwell diary, April 21, 1933.
8. Earl Latham, *The Politics of Railroad Coordination, 1933–1936* (1959), 8. Latham's study is full and definitive. Claude M. Fuess, *Joseph B. Eastman, Servant of the People* (1952), 185.
9. Fuess, *Eastman*, 105–106.
10. Latham, *Railroad Coordination*, 23. By 1935, Eastman no longer thought federal ownership or operation feasible. Latham, *Railroad Coordination*, 19.
11. Latham, *Railroad Coordination*, 26–34.
12. Latham, *Railroad Coordination*, 11–15; Fuess, *Eastman*, 187; Berle to Baruch, January 11, 1933; Churchill to Baruch [received February 16, 1933], Baruch mss. With FDR's approval, Baruch had brought Berle into the work of the National Transportation Committee, and in effect he acted as FDR's representative in its work and that of financial aid and reorganization of railroads. Berle to FDR, December 16, 30, 1932, DNC '32 Special; Berle to FDR, December 22, 1932, DNC '32, NYC.

13. Berle to FDR, March 11, 1933, enclosing memorandum; Le Hand to Moley, March 16, 1933, conveying FDR's query to Moley whether Berle should be attached to the RFC; Berle to Moley, March 13, 1933, Moley mss.
14. *Time*, April 24, 1933; Lindley, *Roosevelt Revolution*, 134; Berle to Moley, March 13, 1933, Moley mss.
15. Latham, *Railroad Coordination*, 35–48, 292.
16. Latham, *Railroad Coordination*, 36.
17. Fuess, *Eastman*, 196, cf. 345–346; Latham, *Railroad Coordination*, 51.
18. Latham, *Railroad Coordination*, 49, 53.
19. PPA, 1933: 153.
20. Latham, *Railroad Coordination*, 66, 85; *Time*, May 15, 1933.
21. Fuess, *Eastman*, 203.
22. Latham, *Railroad Coordination*, 73.
23. Ernest K. Lindley, *Roosevelt Revolution* (1933), 134.
24. Warburg diary, March 25, 1933; Moley, *After Seven Years*, 185–186; Raymond Moley assisted by Eliot A. Rosen, *The First New Deal* (1966), 286; on the RFC proposal see O. Max Gardner to FDR, May 5, 1933; FDR to Gardner, May 8, 1933, PPF 392.
25. On the background of the NRA concept and enactment of the legislation, the two indispensable studies are Ellis W. Hawley, *The New Deal and the Problem of Monopoly* (1966), 3–34, and Charles F. Roos, *NRA Economic Planning* (1937), 1–54; also essential on the labor aspects is Irving Bernstein, *New Deal Collective Bargaining Policy* (1950), 29–33.
26. Frank Freidel, *Franklin D. Roosevelt* (1952–   ), 2:151–158.
27. Herbert Hoover, *Memoirs* (1952), 3:334, 420; Swope to Grace Tully, March 30, 1949, FDRMF.
28. Frederic A. Delano to Howe, April 7, 1933, enclosing memorandum of March 31, 1933; Le Hand to Howe, April 13, 1933, PPF 72; see also Delano to FDR, memorandum, March 9, 1933, Moley mss.
29. William H. Jarvis to R. L. Doughton, [spring 1933], Doughton mss.
30. Doughton to George Gantt, May 16, 1933, Doughton mss.
31. Frances Perkins, *The Roosevelt I Knew* (1946), 193–194.
32. *New Republic*, August 9, 1933.
33. Charles E. Wyzanski, Jr., to his parents, May 12, 1933, Wyzanski mss.; Hawley, *New Deal*, 22; Perkins, *The Roosevelt I Knew*, 195–196; PPA, 1933: 133; *Time*, April 24, 1933.

CHAPTER XXV

"Twin Efforts — Public Works and Industrial Reemployment"

1. PPA, 1933: 246.
2. Irving Bernstein, *New Deal Collective Bargaining Policy* (1950), 31–32; J. Joseph Huthmacher, *Senator Robert F. Wagner and the Rise of Urban Liberalism* (1971), 146.
3. Tugwell diary, May 30, 1933; Huthmacher, *Wagner*, 147. For details on each participant's views in both groups, see Charles F. Roos, *NRA Economic Planning* (1937), 37–39.
4. Raymond Moley, *After Seven Years* (1939), 188; Hugh Johnson, *The Blue Eagle from Egg to Earth* (1935), 193, 196.
5. Tugwell diary, May 30, 1933; *New York Times*, May 11, 1933.

6. Senator Wagner statement, June 13, 1933, cited in Roos, *NRA Economic Planning*, 277–279.
7. Press conference, April 12, 1933, 1:133–135.
8. Harold L. Ickes, *The Secret Diary of Harold L. Ickes* (1953), 1:10, 24, 30, 33; Press conference, May 3, 1933, 1:220.
9. Ickes, *Diary*, 1:6; Donald R. McCoy, *Landon of Kansas* (1966), 67–90, 137. McCoy's biography contains the best account of this problem.
10. McCoy, *Landon*, 131.
11. J. Edward Jones, *"And So — They Indicted Me!"* (1938), 59–61.
12. Press conference, March 31, 1933, 1:101. FDR formally expressed the same view in a letter he sent governors of oil producing states on April 3, 1933. PPA, 1933: 103–104.
13. Ickes, *Diary*, 1:31–32; PPA, 1933: 208–209; for Section 9 of the Act, see Roos, *NRA Economic Planning*, 487.
14. Address of May 4, 1933, PPA, 1933: 156–157.
15. *Time*, May 15, 1933; William H. Wilson, "How the Chamber of Commerce Viewed the NRA: A Re-examination," *Mid-America* (April 1962), 44:96–97.
16. *New York Times*, May 6, 1933; *Time*, May 15, 1933; Ickes, *Diary*, 1:32.
17. Bernstein, *New Deal Collective Bargaining Policy*, 32–33; Ronald R. Richberg, *The Rainbow* (1936), 109.
18. Alexander Sachs to Moley, April 15, 1933, Moley mss.; for lengthy memoranda by Sachs, see Roos, *NRA Economic Planning*, 520–536.
19. Johnson, *Blue Eagle*, 163–164.
20. Wyzanski to parents, April 29, 1933, Wyzanski mss.
21. Ickes, *Diary*, 1:28.
22. Ickes, *Diary*, 1:34. On the allocation of public works funds to the navy and its background, the fullest account is Robert H. Levine, "The Politics of American Naval Rearmament, 1930–1938," (Ph.D. thesis, Harvard University, 1972).
23. Levine, "Politics of American Naval Rearmament"; *New York Times*, May 2, 1933.
24. *New York Times*, May 10, 12, 14, 15, 1933.
25. *New York Times*, May 16, 1933.
26. PPA, 1933: 202–204; see also explanatory note giving the rationale of the bill, 204–206.
27. PPA, 1933: 164–165.
28. Moley, *After Seven Years*, 189.

CHAPTER XXVI

Enacting the Final Measures

1. PPA, 1933: 256–257.
2. Hiram Johnson to his sons, April 16, 1933, Johnson mss.
3. Henry Morgenthau, Jr., Farm Security Administration diary, May 15, 1933, Morgenthau mss.
4. *New York Times*, May 6, 1933.
5. *New York Times*, May 7, 1933.
6. *New York Times*, May 8, 1933.
7. Press conference, May 10, 1933, 1:241–242.

8. Press conference, May 31, 1933, 1:323-324.
9. PPA, 1933: 101; on the conflict within the administration over the tariff, see Moley diary, April 17, 24, May 6, 1933; *New York Times*, May 22, 23, 1933.
10. Press conference, May 31, 1933, 1:324-325.
11. Press conference, June 9, 1933, 1:365-369.
12. Press conference, May 24, 1933, 1:300.
13. FDR to La Follette, June 8, 1933, published in *New York Times*, June 9, 1933.
14. Ernest K. Lindley, *The Roosevelt Revolution* (1933), 135-137.
15. Press conference, April 12, 1933, 1:131.
16. Raymond Moley, assisted by Elliot A. Rosen, *The First New Deal* (1966), 316-320.
17. Harold L. Ickes, *The Secret Diary of Harold L. Ickes* (1953), 1:41; *New York Times*, May 26, 30, June 6, 1933.
18. J. F. T. O'Connor diary, June 1, 7, 1933. O'Connor wrote "borrower," when what FDR said must have been "depositor." FDR to Arthur Iselin, June 6, 1933, PPF 566; Lindley, *Roosevelt Revolution*, 136.
19. O'Connor diary, June 6, 7, 1933.
20. Lindley, *Roosevelt Revolution*, 143; *New York Times*, June 14, 1933.
21. Vincent P. Carosso, *Investment Banking in America: A History* (1970), 371-375.
22. *New York Times*, May 16, 18, 21, 1933.
23. Lindley, *Roosevelt Revolution*, 162; Charles F. Roos, *NRA Economic Planning* (1937), 43-44; *New York Times*, May 7, 21, 1933.
24. Morgenthau diary, May 22, 29, 1933; *New York Times*, May 7, 21, June 6, 1933.
25. Morgenthau diary, April 28, 1933; *New York Times*, May 18, 1933.
26. *New York Times*, May 20, 1933; see also May 15, 1933.
27. *New York Times*, May 19, 23, 1933.
28. *New York Times*, May 26, 1933; *Time*, June 5, 1933.
29. *New York Times*, May 26, 27, 1933.
30. Johnson to sons, June 4, 1933, Johnson mss.
31. *New York Times*, June 1, 1933.
32. Roger Burlingame, "The Counter Attack," *Atlantic Monthly*, November 1933, 527-538.
33. PPA, 1933: 99-100.
34. Roy Roberts to Stephen Early, May 9, 1933, with enclosure, Reed to Roberts, May 9, 1933; Early to Hines, May 13, 1933, OF 95.
35. PPA, 1933: 168.
36. Burlingame, "The Counter Attack," 527-538; *Literary Digest*, June 17, 1933; Norman Thomas to George Gegner, Jr., September 28, 1933, Thomas mss.
37. *New York Times*, June 3, 1933.
38. Roos, *NRA Economic Planning*, 49.
39. *New York Times*, June 6, 7, 8, 14, 1933.
40. *New York Times*, June 9, 10, 1933; E. Pendleton Herring, "First Session of the Seventy-third Congress," *American Political Science Review*, February 1934, 28:80.
41. PPA, 1933: 222; *New York Times*, June 11, 1933; Clapper diary, June 11, 1933.
42. James F. Byrnes to F. H. Griffin, June 27, 1933, Byrnes mss.; Burlingame, "The Counter Attack," 527-538.
43. Morgenthau diary, June 12, 1933; *New York Times*, June 14, 1933.
44. Burlingame, "The Counter Attack," 527-538; Herring, "First Session," 81-82; Press conference, June 14, 1933, 1:391-392. The statistics are from the *Annual Reports* of the Veterans' Administration, cited in Herbert Hoover, *Memoirs* (1952), 3:468-469.
45. Hiram Johnson to his sons, June 16, 1933, Johnson mss.
46. PPA, 1933: 246.
47. *New York Times*, June 17, 1933.

CHAPTER XXVII

A Tack toward Nationalism

1. FR, 1933, 1:634.
2. Hiram Johnson to his sons, June 14, 1933, Johnson mss.; *New York Times*, May 26, 1933.
3. *New York Times*, May 26, 30, 1933; Press conference, May 26, 1933, 1:303–312.
4. FR, 1933, 1:365–366.
5. Memorandum read by Joseph D. Green, executive 'session, Senate Foreign Relations Committee, May 17, 1933, FR, 1933, 1:375–377.
6. Hull to FDR, May 27, 1933, Hull mss.; Cordell Hull, *Memoirs* (1948), 1:229–230.
7. FR, 1933, 1:378; Press conference, June 2, 1933, 1:343. For an estimate of this episode quite critical of FDR, see Divine, "Franklin D. Roosevelt and Collective Security, 1933," *Mississippi Valley Historical Review* (June 1961), 48:54–59.
8. Dorothy Borg, *United States and Far Eastern Crisis of 1933–1938* (1964), 33–39; Phillips to FDR, May 9, 1933, enclosing Hornbeck memorandum, May 9, 1933, in Edgar B. Nixon, ed., *Franklin D. Roosevelt and Foreign Affairs* (1969), 1:103–107.
9. Morgenthau diary, May 17, 1933; FR, 1933, 3:366, 488–489, 503–504.
10. Borg, *United States*, 33–39.
11. Press conference, March 17, 1933, 1:54; May 12, 1933, 1:255; June 16, 1933, 1:399; *Time*, June 12, 1933, 15.
12. FDR to Capt. Thomas G. Frothingham, May 21, 1930, GP.
13. FR, 1933, 1:380.
14. Morgenthau diary, May 9, 1933; FDR to MacDonald [May 22, 1933], Nixon, ed., *Roosevelt and Foreign Affairs*, 1:154.
15. Moley diary, May 6, 18, 19, 1933.
16. James P. Warburg, *The Long Road Home* (1964), 226; Warburg diary, May 29, 1933; Moley diary, May 16, 1933; Tugwell diary, May 31, 1933.
17. State Department press releases, May 6, 20, 1933, both cited in Walter Lippmann, ed., *United States in World Affairs, 1933*, 83–84.
18. Raymond Moley, assisted by Elliot A. Rosen, *The First New Deal* (1966), 405.
19. *Documents on British Foreign Policy*, 2nd Ser., 5:803.
20. Lindsay to Simon, May 14, 1933, C 4293/61/1G PRO.
21. Moley diary, May 16, 1933; Moley, *After Seven Years*, 219.
22. Moley, *After Seven Years* (1939), 217–218; FDR to Hull, March 20, 1933, OF 206, Nixon, ed., *Roosevelt and Foreign Affairs*, 27; Hiram Johnson to sons, June 4, 1933, Johnson mss.
23. Bullitt to Moley, March 19, 1933, Moley mss.; Warburg diary, May 26, 1933; Moley, *After Seven Years*, 217–218.
24. Press conference, May 26, 1933, 1:307–309.
25. Warburg diary, May 26, 1933.
26. Warburg diary, May 29, 1933; Moley, *After Seven Years*, 219.
27. Herbert Hoover, *Memoirs* (1952), 1:250–251; FR, 1933, 1:923–924.
28. FR, 1933, 1:631–633. For the clause in the National Industrial Recovery Act, see C. F. Roos, *NRA Economic Planning* (1937), 480–481; see also Phillips to Hull, June 26, 1933, FR, 1933, 1:657.
29. FDR to Hull, June 11, 1933, FR, 1933, 1:634.
30. Memo in Moley mss., Moley, *First New Deal*, 424.
31. Moley, *First New Deal*, 421; Moley diary [kept by Annette Pomerantz], June 10, 12, 1933.
32. Moley, journal of London Economic Conference; Hull, *Memoirs*, 1:256–257.

33. Press conference, June 7, 1933, 1:352–355, Nixon, ed., *Roosevelt and Foreign Affairs*, 1:208–209.
34. Warburg, *Long Road Home*, 132; Moley, *First New Deal*, 426; Warburg diary, July 22, 1933; FR, 1933, 1:627–629.
35. FR, 1933, 1:641.
36. Moley, *First New Deal*, 428–429; FR, 1933, 1:644–646; Moley diary, June 16, 17, 1933.
37. Nixon, ed., *Roosevelt and Foreign Affairs*, 1:237; Moley, *First New Deal*, 431.

CHAPTER XXVIII

The Bombshell

1. PPA, 1933: 264, which cites the date of release, July 3, 1933, rather than the date of FDR's transmission of the message; *New York Times*, June 17, 18, 1933.
2. *New York Times*, June 19, 20. See also the detailed reminiscences of this trip by Charles Hurd, the *New York Times* correspondent, in *When the New Deal Was Young and Gay* (1965), 146–161.
3. FDR to Phillips, June 19, 1933, FR, 1933, 1:647–649.
4. FDR to Hull, June 20, 1933, Moley mss., cited in Raymond Moley, assisted by Elliot A. Rosen, *The First New Deal* (1966), 440; FR, 1933, 1:650.
5. Press conference, June 7, 1933, 1:354.
6. Raymond Moley, *After Seven Years* (1939), 236; Swope memorandum [June 1933], Edgar B. Nixon, ed., *Franklin D. Roosevelt and Foreign Affairs* (1969), 248–250.
7. *New York Times*, June 24, 26, 1933; Alfred B. Rollins, Jr., *Roosevelt and Howe* (1962), 398.
8. FDR to Phillips, June 26, 1933, FR, 1933, 1:657.
9. Moley, assisted by Elliot A. Rosen, *The First New Deal* (1966), 446–447.
10. *New York Times*, June 28, 1933.
11. *New York Times*, June 29, 1933; Moley, *First New Deal*, 449.
12. Cordell Hull, *Memoirs* (1948), 1:260; Moley, *First New Deal*, 454–455.
13. Warburg to FDR, June 22, 1933; Cox to FDR, June 22, 1933, FR, 1933, 1:653–654.
14. FR, 1933, 1:655.
15. FR, 1933, 1:658, 660–661, 663.
16. Moley, *First New Deal*, 454; Moley diary, June 29, 1933.
17. FR, 1933, 1:665–671.
18. FR, 1933, 1:626.
19. FR, 1933, 1:670–671.
20. Nixon, ed., *Roosevelt and Foreign Affairs*, 1:244–248; Arthur M. Schlesinger, Jr., *The Coming of the New Deal* (1959), 219; Moley diary, June 29, 1933; *New York Times*, June 22, 1933.
21. Morgenthau diary, June 29, 1933.
22. Nixon, ed., *Roosevelt and Foreign Affairs*, 1:236f.; *New York Times*, July 1, 1933.
23. Hurd, *When the New Deal Was Young and Gay*, 166–171. Hurd's memory slipped on several minor points, which can be corrected by consulting his *New York Times* dispatches, June 29–July 1, 1933. On the major point there can be no doubt: FDR informed the press of his opposition to stabilization before he had read Moley's proposal.

24. *New York Times*, July 1, 1933.
25. Morgenthau diary, June 30, 1933. On difficulties in receiving the message, see Nixon, ed., *Roosevelt and Foreign Affairs*, 1:263–264.
26. Morgenthau diary, June 30, 1933.
27. Nixon, ed., *Roosevelt and Foreign Affairs*, 248–250, also copy in Moley mss.
28. FDR to Phillips, June 30, 1933, 11:55 P.M., Nixon, ed., *Roosevelt and Foreign Affairs*, 264–266; FR, 1933, 1:669–670.
29. Moffat to James Grafton Rogers, August 21, 1933, Moffat mss.
30. Moley, *First New Deal*, 460; Herbert Feis, *1933: Characters in Crisis* (1966), 228; Moley diary, July 2, 1933.
31. FR, 1933, 1:672; Moley, *First New Deal*, 461.
32. *New York Times*, July 3, 1933.
33. Morgenthau diary, July 2, 1933.
34. FDR to Phillips, July 2, 1933, 6 P.M., Nixon, ed., *Roosevelt and Foreign Affairs*, 1:268–270.
35. Moley diary, July 3, 1933.
36. FDR, telephone conversation with Hull and Moley, July 5, 1933, FR, 1933, 1:691.
37. Warburg diary, July 3, 1933; Moley, *First New Deal*, 468.
38. Warburg memorandum, July 4, 1933, copy in diary.
39. Feis, *1933*, 224–225.
40. British envoy in Berne to Simon, July 7, 1933, W 8352 PRO; Feis, *1933*, 238–240; Schlesinger, *Coming of the New Deal*, 223–224; *New York Times*, July 4, 1933.
41. Krock interview, COHC; FDR to William Wickham Hoffman, August 10, 1933, PPF 705.

CHAPTER XXIX

The End of the Beginning

1. FR, 1933, 1:686–687; Press conference, July 7, 1933, 2:25–26.
2. FR, 1933, 1:688.
3. Memo of telephone conversation, FDR and Hull, July 5, 1933, FR, 1933, 1:691. Apparently this conversation followed the cable by only about an hour.
4. Herbert Feis, *1933: Characters in Crisis* (1966), 255.
5. Clapper diary, September 14, 1933.
6. FR, 1933, 1:705.
7. Hugh Cumming, memo of conversation with Secretary Moley, July 1, 1933, Hull mss.
8. Moley to FDR, July 4, 1933, FR, 1933, 1:680; Bullitt to Hull, July 2, 1933; R. W. Morrison to Hull, July 31, 1933, Hull mss.
9. Warburg memoir, p. 1060.
10. Feis, *1933*, 247–248.
11. Hull to FDR, July 11, 1933, Edgar B. Nixon, ed., *Franklin D. Roosevelt and Foreign Affairs* (1969), 1:298–300.
12. Krock to Baruch, [July 11, 1933], Baruch mss.
13. Moley diary (Celeste Jedel), July 14, 1933; Swope to Baruch, Baruch mss.; FDR to Hull, July 26, 1933, Hull mss.
14. Morgenthau diary, July 30, 1933.

15. Moley diary, July 24, 29, 1933; Raymond Moley, assisted by Elliot A. Rosen, *The First New Deal* (1966), 502–513.
16. Roper to Hull, July 11, 1933, Hull mss.
17. FDR to Robert Bingham, August 11, 1933; Bingham to FDR, September 8, 1933, PPF 716.
18. Moffat to James Grafton Rogers, August 21, 1922, Moffat mss.; Phillips to Hull, July 7, 1933, Hull mss.; Feis, *1933*, 251–252.
19. Claude Bowers, *My Life* (1962), 286–287; Frederick W. Leith-Ross, *Money Talks* (1968), 168–169.
20. Memo of meeting at French Foreign Office, June 8, 1933, Davis mss.; cf. Davis to Phillips, June 8, 1933, FR, 1933, 1:190–192.
21. FDR to Davis, August 31, 1933, Davis mss. On Davis's views, see Davis to Herbert Hoover, July 13, 1933, Davis mss.
22. Osborne to Vansittart, August 27, 1933, with comments, A 6330/252/45, PRO.
23. Memorandum on the powers and policy of President Roosevelt's administration at the opening of the World Economic Conference, [revised memorandum], June 16, 1933, FO 371/16606/9074 PRO.
24. FDR to Fred I. Kent, July 11, 1933; Moley diary, July 14, 1933; Harrison telephone call to Montagu Norman, July 14, 1933, Harrison mss.; Feis, *1933*, 255.
25. PPA, 1933:165; *Fortune*, cited in Don Wharton, ed., *Roosevelt Omnibus* (1934), 104.
26. Interview with Eleanor Roosevelt, July 13, 1954.
27. *Today*, December 30, 1933, 15.
28. Osborne to Vansittart, August 27, 1933, with comments, A 6330/252/45, PRO.
29. *Fortune*, loc. cit.
30. H. V. Kaltenborn to G. E. Stringfellow, March 13, 1933; Stringfellow to Kaltenborn, March 23, 1933. See also a number of similar letters in the Kaltenborn mss.
31. Statement enclosed in Hatfield to W. E. Chilton, June 23, 1933, Chilton mss.
32. Brandeis to Frankfurter, May 14, 1933, Frankfurter mss.
33. Roberts to William Allen White, May 3, 1933, White mss.
34. William W. Ball to Hoyt, May 14, 1933, Ball mss.
35. Moffat diary, April 2, 1933; Theodore G. Joslin, *Hoover off the Record* (1934), 284.
36. W. E. Chilton to John Kee, May 29, 1933, Chilton mss.
37. Beatrice B. Beecher to ER, May 24, 1933, ER mss.

Index

128n, 371–372; and dissident leaders, 128; and Mills, 132; and selection of administration officials, 137–160, 185; and Morgan, 148; appearance of, 154; attempted assassination of, 161, 169–174; and public power, 163–165, 350–354; and conservation, 165; and back-to-the-farm movement, 165; and unemployment, 165, 255–261, 300, 389; and Warm Springs, 166–168; and cruise on *Nourmahal*, 168–169; and crowds, 169; and "little people," 183, 184; and bankers, 183, 184, 186, 186n, 188, 195, 203, 214–215, 219, 226, 233–234, 238, 340, 397; speeches of, 186; inaugural address of, 186, 186n, 187, 201, 202–207, 212; inauguration of, 196–212; and dictatorial power, 205, 247–249, 447–448, 503; and President Jackson, 210, 289; and reopening of banks, 213, 214–236; first day in office, 213–214; diary of, 216, 218; and Governors' Conference, 218–219; and Banking Bill of 1933, 220, 226–229, 441–444; and Fireside Chats, 230–232, 287, 287n, 356, 433, 437, 438, 500; and deflation, 237–238; and business, 238–239, 250, 254, 409, 428–429, 504; and veterans' pensions, 238, 239–240, 243–244, 448–449, 451–452, 452n; and proposed book on government, 241; and CCC, 255, 256–266; and correspondence, 261–263, 277–278; at White House, 267–288; informality of, 272–273, 275; favorite newspapers of, 274–275; and cigarette holders, 274n; daily routine of, 274–281, 285–288; "colds" of, 275; eating habits of, 276–277; and royalty, 278–279; sense of humor, 278, 279–280, 281; and cabinet, 279; and swimming, 280–281; and investment, 281, 341; and Campobello Island, 283–284, 478–480; recreations of, 284, 287; stamp collection of, 287; and Eleanor Roosevelt, 290–292, 400; and Lucy Mercer, 291; and legalization of beer, 293–294; and Washington's black slums, 296; and patronage, 303, 445; and communism, 313; and silver, 324, 328, 336–337; and Brandeis, 340; and reform, 340; and 1929 crash, 341; and securities' regulation, 341, 342–345, 346, 349; and foreign service appointments, 359–362; and anti-Semitism, 393–394; popularity of, 400, 504–505; and railroads, 408, 409, 410–415; and industrial recovery, 408–435,

459; and National Industrial Recovery Act, 408, 418, 422, 424, 428–434, 444–447; and novelty, 413; and American Construction Council, 417–418; and thirty-hour-week bill, 418, 419–420; and minimum wage laws, 420; and price-fixing, 425; and monopoly, 425, 434; and coal industry, 425–426; and oil production, 426–428; and competition, 428, 434; and public works, 430, 431–433; and Hiram Johnson, 437; and St. Lawrence Waterway, 440–441; and tax deductions, 446–447; and Hull, 457, 459, 467, 467n, 493–495; seamanship of, 470–471; June vacation of, 470–482; and dinard, 472, 472n; and Moley, 472, 487, 493–494, 501–502; compared to other Presidents, 499; and Keynes, 499; and compromise, 500; and experimentation, 500; and politics, 500

AND HOOVER, 13–14, 18–45, 54, 103, 109, 116–117, 434, 467n, 501; November meeting with, 26–27, 28, 29, 31–36, 49; telegram to, 40–41; and foreign policy, 103, 110–111, 116, 123, 129; January meeting with, 129–133; and banking panic, 176, 178, 181–185, 188–194, 194n, 214–215, 216n; and economy measures, 237, 238–239; and public works, 255

FARM POLICIES OF, 56–57, 64, 72, 79–80, 308–312, 316–319; creation of, 83, 86, 87, 88, 89, 90, 93, 96–97, 99, 100–101; and farmers' problems, 83–89; and farmers' support, 86–90, 300–301; failure to understand, 90; farm shortages, 316–317, 318; and silver amendment, 330–331; and Thomas amendment, 332–338; and cost of production, 337

AND PLANNING, 78–79, 351, 352, 433–445, 499; regional, 164–166, 409; industrial, 408, 409, 410, 416, 417–421, 422, 433–434

FOREIGN POLICY OF, 102–124, 128–136, 355–358, 365–370, 372, 374–389, 454–489, 495–500; and war debts, 22–29, 33–34, 35–36, 38–45, 66, 103, 105, 108–110, 130–136, 168, 365, 374, 377, 384–385, 438–439, 458, 479, 487; and World Economic Conference, 38–42, 110, 114–115, 369–370, 375–379, 384, 385, 388–389, 395, 402, 450, 454, 458–479, 490–491; and disarmament, 104, 105, 124, 301, 371–375, 377, 379, 380–383, 389, 390, 396–398, 400, 402–

Frank Freidel is Charles Warren Professor of American History at Harvard. In addition to the three volumes of the Roosevelt biography already published — *The Apprenticeship, The Ordeal* and *The Triumph* — Professor Freidel is the author of two pictorial histories, *The Splendid Little War* and *Over There*. He has also published articles in the *Historical Review*, the *Missouri Journal*, *American Heritage* and other historical journals.